IF FOUND, please notify and arrange return to owner. This handbook is important for the owner's/pilot's responsibilities as a private pilot. Thank you.

Pilot's Name: _____

Address: _____

_____

City   State   Zip Code

Telephone: (_____) _____

Additional copies of *Private Pilot FAA Practical Test Prep* are available from

Gleim Publications, Inc.
P.O. Box 12848, University Station
Gainesville, Florida 32604
(904) 375-0772 or (800) 87-GLEIM

> If you have not yet passed your FAA written test, you should order Gleim's *Private Pilot FAA Written Exam* immediately.

The price is $16.95. Orders must be prepaid. Use the order form in the back of this book. Shipping and handling charges will be added to telephone orders. Add applicable sales tax to shipments within Florida.

Gleim Publications, Inc. guarantees the immediate refund of all resalable materials returned within 30 days. Shipping and handling charges are nonrefundable.

ALSO AVAILABLE FROM GLEIM PUBLICATIONS, INC.

ORDER FORM IN THE BACK OF THIS BOOK

PRIVATE PILOT/RECREATIONAL PILOT FAA WRITTEN EXAM
PRIVATE PILOT HANDBOOK
RECREATIONAL PILOT FLIGHT MANEUVERS

Advanced Pilot Training Books

INSTRUMENT PILOT FAA WRITTEN EXAM
INSTRUMENT PILOT FAA PRACTICAL TEST PREP

COMMERCIAL PILOT FAA WRITTEN EXAM
COMMERCIAL PILOT FAA PRACTICAL TEST PREP

FLIGHT/GROUND INSTRUCTOR FAA WRITTEN EXAM
FUNDAMENTALS OF INSTRUCTING FAA WRITTEN EXAM
FLIGHT INSTRUCTOR FAA PRACTICAL TEST PREP

AIRLINE TRANSPORT PILOT FAA WRITTEN EXAM

> **AVAILABLE JUNE 1993**
>
> *Aviation Weather and Aviation Weather Services* is a rewrite in outline format of *Aviation Weather* AC 00-6A and *Aviation Weather Services* AC 00-45D. Use this easy-to-understand book to save you time and effort.

This book contains a systematic discussion and explanation of the FAA's Private Pilot Practical Test Standards (Airplane), which will assist you in (1) preparing for and (2) successfully completing your Private Pilot FAA Practical Test!

REVIEWERS AND CONTRIBUTORS

Maria M. Bolanos, B.A., University of Florida, has 9 years of production experience in scientific and technical publications. Ms. Bolanos coordinated the production of the text and reviewed the final manuscript.

Gillian Hillis, B.A., University of Florida, is our production assistant. Ms. Hillis reviewed the entire manuscript and revised it for readability.

Barry A. Jones, CFII, B.S. in Air Commerce/Flight Technology, Florida Institute of Technology, is a charter pilot and flight instructor with Gulf Atlantic Airways in Gainesville, FL. Mr. Jones organized and assembled the text, added new material, incorporated extensive revisions, and provided technical and production assistance throughout the project.

Heiko E. Kallenbach, ATP, CFII, MEI, MFA, Carnegie Mellon University, is a flight instructor in single and multiengine airplanes, and is a ShandsCair pilot with Kenn-Air Corporation. Mr. Kallenbach reviewed the manuscript and provided technical assistance.

John F. Rebstock, B.S., School of Accounting, University of Florida, reviewed the entire edition and composed the page layout.

The many FAA employees who helped, in person or by telephone, primarily in Gainesville, Florida; Orlando, Florida; Oklahoma City, Oklahoma; and Washington, DC.

A PERSONAL THANKS

This manual would not have been possible without the extraordinary efforts and dedication of Jim Collis, Ann Finnicum, and Connie Steen, who typed the entire manuscript and all revisions, as well as prepared the camera-ready pages.

The author also appreciates the proofreading assistance of Alison Barrett, Wendy Brenner, Patty Justice, and Gregory Mullins, and the art work and illustration production by Bob Barrett and Barry Jones.

Finally, I appreciate the encouragement, support, and tolerance of my family throughout this project.

PRIVATE PILOT

FAA PRACTICAL TEST PREP

FIRST EDITION

by Irvin N. Gleim, Ph.D., CFII

ABOUT THE AUTHOR

Irvin N. Gleim earned his private pilot certificate in 1965 at the Institute of Aviation at the University of Illinois, where he subsequently received his Ph.D. He is a commercial pilot and flight instructor (instrument) with multiengine and seaplane ratings, and is a member of the Aircraft Owners and Pilots Association, American Bonanza Society, Civil Air Patrol, Experimental Aircraft Association, and Seaplane Pilots Association. He is author of "practical test standard" prep books for the private, instrument, multiengine, commercial, and flight instructor certificates/ratings, and study guides for the private/recreational, instrument, commercial, flight/ground instructor, fundamentals of instructing, and airline transport pilot FAA written tests.

Dr. Gleim has also written articles for professional accounting and business law journals, and is the author of the most widely used review manuals for the CIA exam (Certified Internal Auditor), the CMA exam (Certified Management Accountant), and the CPA exam (Certified Public Accountant). He is Professor Emeritus, Fisher School of Accounting, University of Florida, and is a CIA, CMA, and CPA.

iv

Gleim Publications, Inc.
P.O. Box 12848 • University Station
Gainesville, Florida 32604
(904) 375-0772
(800) 87-GLEIM

Library of Congress Catalog Card No. 92-90641

ISBN 0-917539-37-0

Second Printing: April 1993

> **CAUTION:** This book is an academic presentation for training purposes only. Under **NO** circumstances can it be used as a substitute for your *Pilot's Operating Handbook* or *FAA-Approved Airplane Flight Manual*. **You must fly and operate your airplane in accordance with your *Pilot's Operating Handbook* or *FAA-Approved Airplane Flight Manual*.**

The author is indebted to Beech Aircraft Corporation for permission to reprint various checklists, diagrams, and charts from the Beechcraft Skipper Pilot Operating Handbook, © 1980. These are reprinted **for academic illustration/training purposes only.** FOR FLIGHT, use your *Pilot's Operating Handbook* or *FAA-Approved Airplane Flight Manual*.

The author is indebted to Cessna Aircraft Corporation for permission to reprint various checklists, diagrams, and charts from the Cessna-152 Pilot Operating Handbook, © 1980. These are reprinted **for academic illustration/training purposes only.** FOR FLIGHT, use your *Pilot's Operating Handbook* or *FAA-Approved Airplane Flight Manual*.

The author is indebted to Piper Aircraft Corporation for permission to reprint various checklists, diagrams, and charts from the Piper Tomahawk Pilot Operating Handbook, © 1978. These are reprinted **for academic illustration/training purposes only.** FOR FLIGHT, use your *Pilot's Operating Handbook* or *FAA-Approved Airplane Flight Manual*.

HELP !!

Please send any corrections and suggestions for subsequent editions to me, Irvin N. Gleim, c/o Gleim Publications, Inc. • P.O. Box 12848 • University Station • Gainesville, Florida • 32604. The last page in this book has been reserved for you to make your comments and suggestions. It should be torn out and mailed to me.

Also, please bring this book to the attention of flight instructors, fixed base operators, and others interested in flying. Wide distribution of our books and increased interest in flying depend on your assistance and good word. Thank you.

TABLE OF CONTENTS

Page

PREFACE vi

PART I -- GENERAL INFORMATION

Chapter 1:   The Private Certificate 2

Chapter 2:   Your *Pilot's Operating Handbook* 9

Chapter 3:   Private Certificate Related FARs 21

Chapter 4:   Optimizing Your Ground and Flight Training 59

Chapter 5:   Your FAA Practical (Flight) Test 69

PART II -- FAA PRACTICAL TEST STANDARDS: DISCUSSED AND EXPLAINED

Chapter I: Preflight Preparation 82

Chapter II: Ground Operations 177

Chapter III: Airport and Traffic Pattern Operations 215

Chapter IV: Takeoffs and Climbs 251

Chapter V: Cross-Country Flying 275

Chapter VI: Flight by Reference to Instruments 301

Chapter VII: Flight at Critically Slow Airspeeds 329

Chapter VIII: Flight Maneuvering by Reference to Ground Objects 363

Chapter IX: Night Flight Operations 381

Chapter X: Emergency Operations 397

Chapter XI: Approaches and Landings 415

APPENDIX A   FAA Private Pilot Practical Test Standards 459

APPENDIX B   FAR Part 141 -- Private Pilot Certification Course (Airplanes) 471

APPENDIX C   FAA Suggested Part 61 Flight Syllabus 473

APPENDIX D   Aviation Weather Reports and Forecasts 487

INDEX   529

PREFACE

This book will assist you in passing your PRIVATE PILOT FAA PRACTICAL TEST!

The private pilot practical test is a rigorous test of both concept knowledge and motor skills. This book explains all of the knowledge that your FAA examiner will expect you to demonstrate and discuss with him/her. Previously, private pilot candidates had only the FAA PTS "reprints" to study. Now you have PTSs followed by a thorough explanation of each task. Thus, through careful organization and presentation, we will decrease your preparation time, effort, and frustration, **and** increase your knowledge and understanding.

To save you time, money, and frustration, we have listed the common errors made by pilots in executing each flight maneuver or operation. You will be aware of *what not to do*. We all learn by our mistakes, but our *common error* list provides you with an opportunity to learn from the mistakes of others.

Most books create additional work for the user. In contrast, *Private Pilot FAA Practical Test Prep* facilitates your effort; i.e., it is easy to use. The outline format, numerous illustrations and diagrams, type styles, and spacing are designed to improve readability. Concepts are often presented as phrases rather than complete sentences.

Relatedly, our outline format frequently has an "a" without a "b" or a "1" without a "2." While this violates some journalistic *rules of style*, it is consistent with your cognitive processes. This book was designed, written, and formatted to facilitate your learning and understanding. Another similar counterproductive "rule" is *not to write in your books*. I urge you to mark up this book to facilitate your learning and understanding.

I am confident this book will facilitate speedy completion of your practical (flight) test. I also wish you the very best in subsequent flying, and in obtaining additional ratings and certificates. If you have *not* passed your private pilot FAA written test and do *not* have *Private Pilot and Recreational Pilot FAA Written Exam* (another book with a red cover), order today -- see the order form in the back of this book.

I encourage your suggestions, comments, and corrections for future editions. The last page of this book has been designed to help you note corrections and suggestions throughout your preparation process. Please use it, tear it out, and mail it to me. Thank you.

Enjoy Flying -- Safely!

Irvin N. Gleim
June 1992

PART I
GENERAL INFORMATION

Part I (Chapters 1 through 5) of this book provides general information to assist you in obtaining your Private Pilot Certificate:

		Pages
Chapter 1:	The Private Certificate	2-8
Chapter 2:	Your *Pilot's Operating Handbook*	9-20
Chapter 3:	Private Certificate Related FARs	21-58
Chapter 4:	Optimizing Your Ground and Flight Training	59-68
Chapter 5:	Your FAA Practical (Flight) Test	69-80

Part II consists of Chapters I through XI, which provide an extensive explanation of each of the 44 tasks required of those taking the private pilot FAA practical test in a single-engine airplane (land). Part II is followed by four appendices:

		Pages
Appendix A:	FAA Private Pilot Practical Test Standards	459-470
Appendix B:	FAR Part 141 -- Private Pilot Certification Course (Airplanes)	471-472
Appendix C:	FAA Suggested Part 61 Flight Syllabus	473-486
Appendix D:	Aviation Weather Reports and Forecasts	487-520

This book should be used in conjunction with *Private Pilot FAA Written Exam* and *Private Pilot Handbook*, both by Irvin N. Gleim (additional discussion and an order form are provided at the back of this book). These two books provide the information necessary to understand and successfully complete both the private pilot airplane written and practical tests.

CHAPTER ONE
THE PRIVATE CERTIFICATE

What is a Private Pilot Certificate? 2
Requirements to Obtain a Private Pilot Certificate 3
How to Get Started 7

In order to fly (pilot) an airplane the U.S. Federal Aviation Administration (FAA) requires a formal training program, i.e., flight lessons. Learning to fly and obtaining your private pilot certificate are fun. Begin today! The purpose of this chapter is to acquaint you with the requirements and procedures to obtain your private pilot certificate.

WHAT IS A PRIVATE PILOT CERTIFICATE?

A private pilot certificate is much like an ordinary driver's license. A private pilot certificate will allow you to fly an airplane and carry passengers and baggage, although not for compensation or hire. However, operating expenses may be shared with other travelers in the airplane. The certificate will be sent to you by the FAA upon satisfactory completion of your training program, a written examination, and a practical test comprised of an oral exam and a flight test.

Front   Back

REQUIREMENTS TO OBTAIN A PRIVATE PILOT CERTIFICATE

A. **Obtain a third-class FAA medical certificate.**

1. You must undergo a routine medical examination which may only be administered by FAA-designated doctors called aviation medical examiners.

2. To obtain this medical certificate, you must be at least 16 years of age and be able to read, speak, and understand the English language.

3. The medical certificate necessary for a private pilot certificate is called a third-class medical. It is valid for 2 years and expires on the last day of the month issued (then another medical examination is required).

4. Even if you have a physical handicap, medical certificates can be issued in many cases. Operating limitations may be imposed depending upon the nature of the disability.

5. Your flight instructor or FBO (Fixed Base Operator) will be able to recommend an aviation medical examiner.

   a. An FBO is an airport business that gives flight lessons, sells aviation fuel, and repairs and rents airplanes, etc.

   b. Also, the FAA publishes a directory that lists all authorized aviation medical examiners by name, with address. Copies of this directory are kept at all FAA District Offices, Air Traffic Control facilities, and Flight Service Stations.

6. One of the major obstacles in obtaining medicals is the vision requirement. The following table gives a breakdown of the vision requirement for each class of medical. The vision requirements for first-class to third-class medical certificates are considerably different. **NOTE: Waivers are granted by the FAA.** Ask your medical examiner.

Type of Vision	1st-Class Medical	2nd-Class Medical	3rd-Class Medical
Distance	20/20 each eye uncorrected; or at least 20/100 correctable to 20/20.	Same as 1st-class	20/50 each eye uncorrected. If poorer than 20/50, must be correctable to 20/30.
Near	At least 20/40 each eye corrected/uncorrected	Ability to read aeronautical maps	At least 20/60 each eye corrected/uncorrected
Color Vision	Normal	Normal	Ability to distinguish red, green, and white
Field of Vision	Normal	Normal	Normal

7. Although you may begin your flight lessons with an instructor before obtaining your medical certificate, your author recommends that you see an aviation medical examiner and obtain a medical certificate before spending money on flight lessons.

8. The medical certificate will function as your student pilot certificate once it is signed by you and the medical examiner.

   a. Note that the back of your student pilot certificate must be signed by your certified flight instructor (CFI) prior to solo flight (flying by yourself).

   b. The only substantive difference between a regular medical certificate and a medical/student pilot certificate is that the back of the medical/student pilot certificate provides for CFI signatures.

   c. Also, the combined medical/student pilot certificate is on slightly heavier paper.

d.   The front and back of a sample FAA medical/student pilot certificate are reproduced below.

Front   Back

Front of certificate:

UNITED STATES OF AMERICA
DEPARTMENT OF TRANSPORTATION
FEDERAL AVIATION ADMINISTRATION

BB-5342031

MEDICAL CERTIFICATE _3rd_ CLASS
AND STUDENT PILOT CERTIFICATE

THIS CERTIFIES THAT (Full name and address)

Richmond, Kane Everett
1771 Coral Way
N. Ft. Myers, Fl. 33903

DATE OF BIRTH	HEIGHT	WEIGHT	HAIR	EYES	SEX
1/30/67	5'9"	140	Brn	Brn	M

has met the medical standards prescribed in Part 67, Federal Aviation Regulations for this class of Medical Certificate, and the standards prescribed in Part 61 for a Student Pilot Certificate.

LIMITATIONS

STUDENT PILOTS ARE PROHIBITED FROM CARRYING PASSENGERS

None

DATE OF EXAMINATION	EXAMINER'S SERIAL NO.
10-25-85	11967-1

EXAMINER SIGNATURE

TYPED NAME E.W. Williams II, D.O.

AIRMAN'S SIGNATURE

FAA FORM 8420-2 (10-73) SUPERSEDES PREVIOUS EDITION

Back of certificate:

CONDITIONS OF ISSUE: This certificate shall be in the personal possession of the airman at all times while exercising the privileges of his airman certificate. As a medical certificate, it is temporary for a period of 60 days; if no notice to the contrary is received within such periods, it will remain in effect until the expiration dates as provided in Sections 61.19 and 61.23 of the Federal Aviation Regulations, unless modified or recalled by proper authority. The holder of this certificate is governed by the provisions of FAR Secs. 61.53, 63.19, and 65.49(d) relating to physical deficiency.

CERTIFICATED INSTRUCTOR'S ENDORSEMENTS FOR STUDENT PILOTS

I certify that the holder of this certificate has met the requirements of the regulations and is competent for the following:

	DATE	MAKE AND MODEL OF AIRCRAFT	INSTRUCTOR'S SIGNATURE	INSTRUCTOR'S CERTIFICATE NO.	EXP DATE
A. TO SOLO THE FOLLOWING AIRCRAFT	1-29-86	C-152	*Tracy Linkin*	267-15891	9/87
		AIRCRAFT CATEGORY			
		AIRPLANE			
		GLIDER			
		ROTOCRAFT			
B. TO MAKE SOLO CROSS-COUNTRY FLIGHTS					

NOTICE: Any alteration of this certificate is punishable by a fine not exceeding $1,000, or imprisonment not exceeding 3 years, or both.

B. Pass a written test with a score of 70% or better.

1.   Most FAA written tests are administered by FAA-designated written test examiners. This test is administered at some Flight Standards District Offices (FSDOs) and certain airport FBOs. After you take your written test at one of these facilities, your answer sheet is sent to the FAA's Aeronautical Center in Oklahoma City. It takes about 4-6 weeks for the FAA to process your answer sheet and return an FAA written test report (Form 8080-2) to you. Thus, you should take your written test about 2 months before you schedule your practical test.

   a.   The FAA has contracted with several computer testing services to administer FAA written tests. The advantage is that you get an immediate test report (FAA Form 8080-2) on completion of the computer test. Thus, you do not have to wait to have your written test sent to the FAA in Oklahoma City for grading and then have the results mailed to you.

      1)   Each of these computer testing services has testing centers throughout the country. You register by calling an 800 number. Call the following testing services for information regarding

         a)   The location of their testing center most convenient to you,
         b)   The time allowed, and
         c)   The cost to take their private pilot (airplane) written test.

DRAKE	(800) 359-3278
PLATO	(800) 869-1100
SYLVAN	(800) 967-1100

      2)   Note that the FAA corrects (redoes) defective questions on the computer tests, which it cannot do in the written test books. Thus, it is important to carefully study questions that are noted to have no correct answer in test prep books such as Gleim's *Private Pilot and Recreational Pilot FAA Written Exam*. On the pencil and paper test, you will get credit for these defective questions, but on the computer tests, the questions will probably have been rephrased.

    b.   The FAA permits FAR Part 141 schools to develop, administer, and grade their own written tests as long as they use the FAA written test books, i.e., those with the same questions as in Gleim's FAA Written Exam books. The FAA does not provide the correct answers to the 141 schools and the FAA only reviews the 141 school test question selection sheets. Thus, some of the answers used by 141 test examiners may not agree with the FAA or those in Gleim's FAA Written Exam books. This may explain why you miss a question in a 141 written test using an answer presented in Gleim's FAA Written Exam books.

      1)   Also, about 20 Part 141 schools use the AVTEST computer testing system, which is very similar to the computer testing services described above.

2.   The written or computerized test consists of 60 multiple-choice questions selected from the 708 airplane-related questions in the *FAA Private Pilot Written Test Book*.

    a.   Each of the FAA's airplane questions is reproduced in *Private Pilot and Recreational Pilot FAA Written Exam* by Irvin N. Gleim with complete explanations to the right of each question. The questions test the following topics:

        Introduction to Airplanes and Aerodynamics
        Airplane Performance
        Airplane Instruments, Engines, and Systems
        Airports and Air Traffic Control
        Weight and Balance
        Weather
        Federal Aviation Regulations
        Navigation Charts
        Other Navigational Publications
        Navigation
        Flight Computers
        Flight Physiology
        Cross-Country Flying

3.   You are required to satisfactorily complete a ground instruction or home-study course prior to taking the written test. See page 523 for a standard authorization form which can be completed, signed by a flight instructor or ground instructor, torn out, and taken to the examination site.

4.   FAR 61.105 provides the following description of private pilot ground school topics:

    (1)   The accident reporting requirements of the National Transportation Safety Board and the Federal Aviation Regulations applicable to private pilot privileges, limitations, and flight operations for airplanes, the use of the "Airman's Information Manual," and FAA advisory circulars;

    (2)   VFR navigation using pilotage, dead reckoning, and radio aids;

    (3)   The recognition of critical weather situations from the ground and in flight, the procurement and use of aeronautical weather reports and forecasts.

    (4)   The safe and efficient operation of airplanes including high-density airport operations, collision avoidance precautions, and radio communication procedures;

    (5)   Basic aerodynamics and the principles of flight which apply to airplanes; and

    (6)   Stall awareness, spin entry, spins, and spin recovery techniques.

5.   You must be at least 15 years of age to take the Private Pilot written test.

C. **Obtain required flight experience (FAR 61.109).**

   1. A total of at least 40 hr. of flight instruction and solo flight time. The requirements include

      a. 20 hr. of flight instruction from an authorized flight instructor, including at least

         1) 3 hr. of cross-country, i.e., to other airports.

         2) 3 hr. at night, including 10 takeoffs and landings for applicants seeking night flying privileges.

         3) 3 hr. in airplanes in preparation for the private pilot flight test within 60 days prior to that test.

      b. 20 hr. of solo flight time, including at least

         1) 10 hr. in airplanes (some could be in a glider, etc.).

         2) 10 hr. of cross-country flights

            a) Each flight with a landing more than 50 NM from the point of departure.

            b) One flight of 300 NM, with landings at three points, one of which is more than 100 NM from the point of departure.

         3) Three solo takeoffs and landings to a full stop at an airport with an operating control tower.

   2. FAA-certificated pilot schools (Part 141) may obtain approval of a private pilot (airplane) training course providing for a total of 35 hr. of flight and other special instruction time.

      a. These programs are known as Part 141 programs because they are authorized by Part 141 of the Federal Aviation Regulations (FARs) issued by the FAA.

      b. All other regulations concerning certification of pilots are found in Part 61 of the FARs.

D. **Obtain required flight instruction.**

   1. FAR 61.107 specifies instruction in the following 10 areas:

      (1) Preflight operations, including weight and balance determination, line inspection, and airplane servicing;

      (2) Airport and traffic pattern operations, including operations at controlled airports, radio communications, and collision avoidance precautions;

      (3) Flight maneuvering by reference to ground objects;

      (4) Flight at slow airspeeds with realistic distractions, and the recognition of and recovery from stalls entered from straight flight and from turns;

      (5) Normal and crosswind takeoffs and landings;

      (6) Control and maneuvering an airplane solely by reference to instruments, including descents and climbs using radio aids or radar directives;

      (7) Cross-country flying, using pilotage, dead reckoning, and radio aids, including one 2-hour flight;

      (8) Maximum performance takeoffs and landings;

      (9) Night flying, including takeoffs, landings, and VFR navigation; and

      (10) Emergency operations, including simulated aircraft and equipment malfunctions.

E. **Successfully complete a practical (flight) test.**

    1.   Both an oral exam and a flight test will be given by an FAA inspector or a designated examiner. The test is prescribed by the FAA's Private Pilot Practical Test Standards, which are reprinted and discussed throughout Chapters I through XI and also reprinted verbatim in Appendix A of this book.

    2.   FAA inspectors are FAA employees and do not charge for their services. They administer very few private practical tests. They administer primarily flight instructor practical tests.

    3.   FAA-designated examiners are proficient, experienced flight instructors who are authorized by the FAA to conduct flight tests. They do charge a fee.

    4.   Prepare for your practical test throughout your ground and flight training. Begin by studying (not reading) Chapters 2 through 5 in this book as soon as possible. Next, study Chapters I through XI as appropriate. Each chapter describes one of the Areas of Operation contained in the Practical Test Standards. Study Chapters I through III immediately or before beginning your flight training.

            Chapter I: Preflight Preparation
            Chapter II: Ground Operations
            Chapter III: Airport and Traffic Pattern Operations

    Areas of Operation I through III contain 15 tasks. The 29 tasks in Areas of Operation IV through XI relate to airplane maneuvers. Study *thoroughly* the tasks relevant to each flight lesson. Discuss the relevant task(s) with your CFI before and after each flight lesson. See Chapter 4, Optimizing Your Ground and Flight Training.

HOW TO GET STARTED

A. **Talk to several people who have recently completed their private certificate.** Visit your local airport and ask for the names of several people who have just completed their private certificate. When you locate one person, (s)he can usually refer you to another. How did they do it?

    1.   *Flight training:* Airplane? CFI? What period of time? Cost? How structured was the program?

    2.   *Ask for their advice.* How would they do it differently? What do they suggest to you?

    3.   *What difficulties did they encounter?*

B. **Talk to several CFIs.** Tell them you are considering a private certificate. Evaluate each as a prospective instructor.

    1.   *What do they recommend?*

    2.   *Ask to see their flight syllabus. How structured is it?*

    3.   *What are their projected costs?*

    4.   *What is the rental cost for their training aircraft, solo and dual?*

    5.   *Ask for the names and phone numbers of several persons who recently completed the private certificate under their direction.*

    6.   *Does the flight instructor's schedule and the schedule of available aircraft fit your schedule?*

    7.   *Where will they recommend you take your flight test? What is its estimated cost?*

C. Once you have made a preliminary choice of flight instructor and/or FBO, **sit down with your CFI and plan a schedule of flight instruction.**

1. When and how often you will fly.
2. When you will take the FAA written test.
3. When you should plan to take your practical (flight) test.
4. When and how payments will be made for your instruction.
5. Review, revise, and update the total cost to obtain your private certificate (see below).

D. **Prepare a tentative written time budget and a written expenditure budget.**

Hours Solo: ____ hours x $_____	$_____
Hours Dual with CFI: ____ hours x $_____	$_____
Written or Computerized Test Cost	$_____
Flight Test (Examiner)	$_____
Flight Test (Airplane)	$_____
This book	$ 16.95
Gleim's *Private Pilot and Recreational Pilot FAA Written Exam*	$ 12.95
Gleim's *Private Pilot Handbook*	$ 11.95
Other books:	
Airman's Information Manual	$_____
Flight Training Handbook	$_____
One or more Sectional Chart(s)	$_____
FAR Book	$_____
Information Manual for your training airplane	$_____
TOTAL	$_____

E. **Consider purchasing an airplane (yourself, or through joint ownership) or joining a flying club.** Frequently, shared expenses through joint ownership can significantly reduce the cost of flying.

1. Inquire about local flying clubs.
2. Call a member and learn about the club's services, costs, etc.

END OF CHAPTER

CHAPTER TWO
YOUR *PILOT'S OPERATING HANDBOOK*

Pilot's Operating Handbook 9
Learning Your Airplane 10
Performance Data 13
Minimum Equipment List 14
Cockpit Familiarity 15
Weight and Balance 16
Checklists 19
Electronic Checklists 20

PILOT'S OPERATING HANDBOOK

The FAA requires a *Pilot's Operating Handbook* (also called an *FAA-Approved Airplane Flight Manual*) (FAR 23.1581). These usually are 6" x 8" ring notebooks, so pages can be updated, deleted, added, etc. They typically have nine sections:

1. General .... Description of the airplane
2. Limitations .... Description of operating limits
3. Emergency Procedures .... What to do in each situation
4. Normal Procedures .... Checklists
5. Performance .... Graphs and tables of airplane capabilities
6. Weight and Balance .... Equipment list, airplane empty weight
7. Description of Operating Systems .... As discussed in this chapter
8. Servicing and Maintenance .... Explanation of what and when
9. Supplements .... Usually describes available optional equipment

You must rely completely on your airplane's *Pilot's Operating Handbook (POH)*, or *FAA-Approved Airplane Flight Manual*, for your airplane's specific operating procedures and limitations. Your *POH* is also critical for emergency operations. Your *POH* must be easily accessible to you during flight.

In this chapter and throughout Part II of this book, we reproduce numerous excerpts from Beech Skipper (BE-77), Cessna 152, and Piper Tomahawk (PA-38) *POHs*. **They are for illustration purposes only.** These three are recently manufactured and widely used representative single-engine training airplanes. By providing you with differing checklists, you are better able to understand the nature of each type of checklist rather than memorize a single checklist. **FOR FLIGHT, only use your airplane's *POH*, or *FAA-Approved Airplane Flight Manual*.**

Also be aware that some *POHs* have two parts to each section: abbreviated procedures (which are checklists) and amplified procedures (which consist of discussion of the checklists). In this book, we generally reproduce only the checklists. In your airplane's *POH*, use **both** the abbreviated and the amplified procedures!

As a practical matter, after you study your *POH* and gain some experience in your airplane, you may wish to retype some of the standard checklists on heavy manila paper. This is more convenient than finding checklists in your *POH* while engaged in other cockpit activities. Also, electronic checklists are available (see page 20) which provide checklist items one at a time.

Most late-model popular airplanes have *POH*s reprinted as perfect-bound books (called Information Manuals) available at FBOs and aviation bookstores. If possible, purchase a *POH* for your training airplane before you begin your flight lessons. Read it cover-to-cover and study (committing to memory) the normal operating checklists, standard airspeeds, and emergency procedures.

Call or visit your flight school in advance of your private pilot training. If a *POH* (information manual) is not available, borrow one overnight and photocopy the entire *POH* at a local copy center (estimated cost: 200 pages @ $.05 = $10.00). Even if you are told this is unnecessary, do it anyway. It will be very helpful. If your flight school is out of town, call the school and insist on help in locating a *POH* for your advance study. Alternatively, locate the owner of the same model airplane locally and borrow a *POH* to photocopy. While you meet with the owner, take several photographs of the control panel and cockpit from the back seat of the airplane (do this also if your flight school is local).

LEARNING YOUR AIRPLANE

You must become an expert on the airplane in which you are going to train and take your practical test.

Step One: Obtain a *POH*
Step Two: Read it cover-to-cover
Step Three: Memorize important data (see below)

Begin with weights and airspeeds (below and on page 11). Some figures may not be given in your *POH*. Talk to your instructor when you begin your training.

The following weight definitions are taken from the Piper Tomahawk's *Pilot's Operating Handbook*. Learn them and the relationship between the weights.

Maximum Ramp Weight	Maximum weight approved for ground maneuvers (includes weight of start, taxi, and run-up fuel).
Maximum Takeoff Weight	Maximum weight approved for the start of the takeoff run.
Maximum Landing Weight	Maximum weight approved for the landing touchdown.
Maximum Zero Fuel Weight	Maximum weight exclusive of usable fuel.
Standard Empty Weight	Weight of a standard airplane including unusable fuel, full operating fluids, and full oil.
Basic Empty Weight	Standard empty weight plus optional equipment.
Payload	Weight of occupants, cargo, and baggage.
Useful Load	Difference between takeoff weight, or ramp weight if applicable, and basic empty weight.

List your airplane's weights below based on your *POH*. For each flight: your basic empty weight, plus fuel weight, plus payload, must **not exceed** maximum ramp weight.

Weights for (Make/Model) (_____/_____)

Max. Ramp	_____	Basic Empty Weight	_____
Max. T/O	_____	Max. Payload	_____
Max. Landing	_____	Max. Fuel Weight	_____
Max. Zero Fuel	_____	Max. Baggage	_____

List your airplane's speeds below based on your *POH* and discussion with your CFI. *V* is used as an abbreviation of *velocity*.

These are standard airspeeds, with which you should be conversant regarding any airplane: V_{S0}, V_{S1}, V_R, V_X, V_Y, V_A, V_{NO}, V_{NE}, V_{FE}, and $V_{Max\ Glide}$.

Airspeeds   **KT or MPH***

V_{S0} .... (bottom of white arc) _____

V_{S1} .... (bottom of green arc) _____

V_R .... (rotation) _____

V_X .... (best angle-of-climb) _____

V_Y .... (best rate-of-climb) _____

V_{FE} .... (flap extension) _____

V_A .... (maneuvering speed) _____

V_{NO} .... (top of green, bottom of yellow) _____

V_{NE} .... (red line, never exceed) _____

$V_{Max\ Glide}$ .... (obtain from Section 3, *POH*) _____

*Circle one

Next, see the systems description in Section 7 of your *POH*. Note these usually are systems containing multiple and often numerous components and dimensions. Understand each system and its components. The following is a list of systems typically found in training airplanes and discussed in your *POH*.

Airframe	Avionics
Instrument Panel	Engine
Flight Controls System	Propeller
Nosewheel Steering System	Heating, Ventilating, and Defrosting System
Wing Flaps System	Baggage Compartment
Landing Gear System	Airplane Tiedown Provisions and Jack
Fuel System	Points
Brake System	Seats, Seat Belts, and Shoulder Harnesses
Electrical System	Doors, Windows, and Exits
Lighting System	Control Locks
Pitot Pressure System	
Static Pressure System	**For Academic Illustration/Training Purposes Only!**
Vacuum System	***For Flight:*** **Use your Pilot's Operating Handbook**
Flight Instruments	**or FAA-Approved Airplane Flight Manual.**
Stall Warning System	

Related to *POH* Section 7 is Section 9, Supplements, which discusses and illustrates optional equipment and systems. Study it as suggested above.

Also related is Section 8 of the *POH*, Servicing and Maintenance. Study it and, in conjunction with Section 1, General, list the following data for your airplane:

Fuel
Type/Grade Used _____
Capacity of Each Tank: Left   Right
    Mains   _____   _____
    Auxiliary   _____   _____
    Other   _____   _____

Oil   **Brake Fluid Reservoirs**
    Type/Weight   _____   Location   _____
    Capacity   _____   Type of Fluid _____
    Minimum Level _____   Capacity   _____
    Suggested Level _____

Tire Pressure
    Mains   _____
    Nose   _____

PERFORMANCE DATA

A. **Normal power settings and airspeeds.** These are for normal operations and must be memorized. Obtain them from your CFI and confirm them in your *POH*.

	Airspeed	Power (RPM)
Rotation (V_R)	_____	_____
Climbout	_____	_____
Cruise climb	_____	_____
Cruise level	_____	_____
Cruise descent	_____	_____
Slow cruise level	_____	_____
Traffic pattern	_____	_____
Approach	_____	_____
Landing (flare)	_____	_____

B. **Takeoff data.** Prior to **each** flight, you should work through each of the following. Consult your *POH* and the next few pages in this chapter.

1. Weight and balance. (See discussion on Weight and Balance beginning on page 16.)
   Airplane weight, takeoff . . . . _____
   Airplane weight, landing . . . . _____
2. Runway length (at all airports of intended use) . . . . _____
3. Headwind component . . . . _____
4. Temperature . . . . _____
5. Field altitude MSL . . . . _____
6. Pressure altitude . . . . _____
7. End-of-runway conditions, obstructions, etc.
   _____
8. Normal takeoff distance
   Ground roll . . . . _____
   50-ft. obstacle . . . . _____
9. Maximum performance takeoff
   Ground roll . . . . _____
   50-ft. obstacle . . . . _____
10. Rotation (liftoff) airspeed . . . . _____
11. Normal landing distance . . . . _____
12. Ground roll over 50-ft. obstacle . . . . _____

These are the *numbers* you will use to fly various portions of your flight. Learn them and be comfortable with them. Assume two people are on board: you and your CFI or examiner. Note the effects that varying weights have on these numbers.

1. As soon as you schedule your practical test (or if you now know who will be your designated examiner and which airplane you will be flying) complete the worksheet above (estimate your examiner's weight and assume full fuel) and remember to take a copy to your practical test.

C. **POH performance data.** Refer to Section 5 in your *POH* and study topic by topic. For illustration, the table of contents of Section 5 for the Beech Skipper is shown below.

Beech Skipper -- Pilot's Operating Handbook
PERFORMANCE -- TABLE OF CONTENTS

Introduction to Performance and Flight Planning

Comments Pertinent to the Use of Performance Graphs

Airspeed Calibration - Normal System

Airspeed Calibration - Alternate System

Altimeter Correction - Normal System

Altimeter Correction - Alternate System

Fahrenheit to Celsius Temperature Conversion

ISA Conversion

Stall Speeds

Wind Components

Take-Off Distance - Hard Surface

Take-Off Distance - Grass Surface

Climb

Time, Fuel, and Distance to Climb

Cruise Speeds

Cruise Performance

Range Profile - 29 Gallons

Endurance Profile - 29 Gallons

Landing Distance - Hard Surface - Flaps Down (30°)

Landing Distance - Grass Surface - Flaps Down (30°)

> **For Academic Illustration/Training Purposes Only!**
> *For Flight:* Use your Pilot's Operating Handbook or FAA-Approved Airplane Flight Manual.

MINIMUM EQUIPMENT LIST

FAR 91.213 prohibits takeoff in an airplane with inoperative instruments or installed equipment unless a Minimum Equipment List (MEL) exists for the airplane. The MEL does **not** specify required equipment! The MEL specifies equipment that does not have to be operating and provides an explanation of how the airplane can be safely flown without the equipment and/or instruments being operational. Turn to page 51 in Chapter 3 of this book for the outline of FAR 91.213.

A. Thus, the FAA permits the publication of an MEL designed to provide owners/operators with the authority to operate an aircraft with certain items or components inoperative, provided the FAA finds an acceptable level of safety maintained by

1. Appropriate operations limitations,
2. A transfer of the function to another operating component, and
3. Reference to other instruments or components providing the required information.

B. The MEL does not include obviously required items such as wings, rudders, flaps, engines, landing gear, etc.

1. The list may not include items that do not affect the airworthiness of the aircraft, such as galley equipment, entertainment systems, convenience items, etc.

2. ALL ITEMS RELATED TO THE AIRWORTHINESS OF THE AIRCRAFT AND NOT INCLUDED IN THE LIST ARE AUTOMATICALLY REQUIRED TO BE OPERATIVE.

COCKPIT FAMILIARITY

Before getting ready to start the engine on your first flights and whenever you get ready to fly an unfamiliar airplane, take a few minutes to acquaint yourself with the cockpit, i.e., the flight controls, radios, and instruments. Your *POH* should have a control panel diagram similar to those of the Piper Tomahawk illustrated below.

As you begin your orientation flight, ask your instructor for a complete explanation of the control panel, flight instruments, and radios, including location of each and how they operate. Your first and subsequent flights will be much more productive (and safer).

After your first flights and debriefing with your flight instructor, return to the airplane and sit in the pilot's seat and study the location of all instruments, radios, and control devices. Mentally review their location, operation, and use. Then mentally review your flight and how it could have been improved. After subsequent flight lessons you may find this procedure continues to be constructive if the airplane is available.

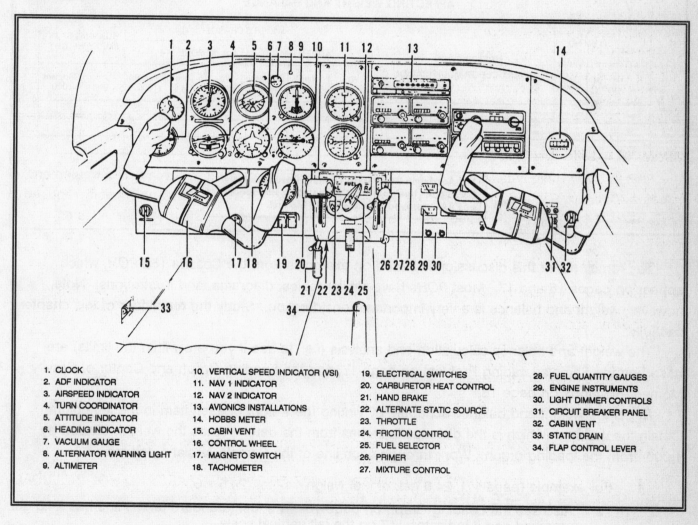

1. CLOCK
2. ADF INDICATOR
3. AIRSPEED INDICATOR
4. TURN COORDINATOR
5. ATTITUDE INDICATOR
6. HEADING INDICATOR
7. VACUUM GAUGE
8. ALTERNATOR WARNING LIGHT
9. ALTIMETER
10. VERTICAL SPEED INDICATOR (VSI)
11. NAV 1 INDICATOR
12. NAV 2 INDICATOR
13. AVIONICS INSTALLATIONS
14. HOBBS METER
15. CABIN VENT
16. CONTROL WHEEL
17. MAGNETO SWITCH
18. TACHOMETER
19. ELECTRICAL SWITCHES
20. CARBURETOR HEAT CONTROL
21. HAND BRAKE
22. ALTERNATE STATIC SOURCE
23. THROTTLE
24. FRICTION CONTROL
25. FUEL SELECTOR
26. PRIMER
27. MIXTURE CONTROL
28. FUEL QUANTITY GAUGES
29. ENGINE INSTRUMENTS
30. LIGHT DIMMER CONTROLS
31. CIRCUIT BREAKER PANEL
32. CABIN VENT
33. STATIC DRAIN
34. FLAP CONTROL LEVER

Next, take a blank sheet of paper and, without the aid of a diagram or photo, sketch your control panel and review normal control positions and normal gauge indications.

WEIGHT AND BALANCE

The Weight and Balance is a very important section of your *POH*. The equipment list in this section lists all of the equipment required in your airplane as well as optional equipment available from the factory. The equipment installed in your airplane at the factory is clearly marked. The weight and C.G. moment of each piece of equipment is given.

More important is your Weight and Balance Record, which consists of an ongoing record of weight and balance changes in your airplane. Every time a component is added or deleted that changes the weight and/or balance, this Weight and Balance Record is updated. Thus, this is the source of your standard empty weight and its moment. See the illustration below. The last entries at the right would be your airplane's basic empty weight and moment/1,000.

WEIGHT AND BALANCE RECORD
CONTINUOUS HISTORY OF CHANGES IN STRUCTURE OR EQUIPMENT AFFECTING WEIGHT AND BALANCE

DATE	ITEM NO.		DESCRIPTION OF ARTICLE OR MODIFICATION	WEIGHT CHANGE						RUNNING BASIC EMPTY WEIGHT	
	In	Out		ADDED (+)			REMOVED (-)				
				Wt. (lb.)	Arm (In.)	Moment /1000	Wt. (lb.)	Arm (In.)	Moment /1000	Wt. (lb.)	Moment /1000

> **For Academic Illustration/Training Purposes Only!**
> *For Flight:* **Use your Pilot's Operating Handbook or FAA-Approved Airplane Flight Manual.**

The remainder of this discussion is based on examples from the Cessna 152 *POH*, which appear on pages 16 and 17. Most *POHs* have similar tables, diagrams, and illustrations. Note, however, weight and balance is a very important consideration. Study the remainder of this chapter carefully.

The weight and balance calculation and analysis (i.e., to see if you are within the limits) are based on the Sample Loading Problem on page 17, and the Loading Graph and Center of Gravity Moment Envelope on page 18.

Begin the weight and balance schedule by writing the weight of each item in the left column. Obtain the moment (which is the distance in inches from the datum, times the weight, divided by 1,000) from the loading graph. Work through each line of the Sample Airplane column.

1. For example (page 17), 24.5 gal. of fuel weigh 147 lb. (24.5 x 6).

   a. Also see the Loading Graph on page 18. The fuel (standard tanks) line has 24.5 gal. marked and it indicates 147 on the left vertical scale.

   b. For 24.5 gal., the moment is 6.2 on the bottom horizontal scale.

   c. Continue with the pilot and passenger (340 lb.), and baggage in Area 1 (52 lb.).

   d. Note the total moment of 56.6 for 1,670 lb.

SAMPLE LOADING PROBLEM	SAMPLE AIRPLANE		YOUR AIRPLANE	
	Weight (lbs.)	Moment (lb.-ins. /1000)	Weight (lbs.)	Moment (lb.-ins. /1000)
1. Basic Empty Weight (Use the data pertaining to your airplane as it is presently equipped. Includes unusable fuel and full oil)	1136	34.0		
2. Usable Fuel (At 6 Lbs./Gal.) Standard Tanks (24.5 Gal. Maximum)	147	6.2		
Long Range Tanks (37.5 Gal. Maximum)				
Reduced Fuel (As limited by maximum weight)				
3. Pilot and Passenger (Station 33 to 41)	340	13.3		
4. *Baggage - Area 1 (Or passenger on child's seat) (Station 50 to 76, 120 Lbs. Max.)	52	3.3		
5. *Baggage - Area 2 (Station 76 to 94, 40 Lbs. Max.)				
6. RAMP WEIGHT AND MOMENT	1675	56.8		
7. Fuel allowance for engine start, taxi, and runup	-5	-.2		
8. TAKEOFF WEIGHT AND MOMENT (Subtract Step 7 from Step 6)	1670	56.6		

9. Locate this point (1670 at 56.6) on the Center of Gravity Moment Envelope, and since this point falls within the envelope, the loading is acceptable.

* The maximum allowable combined weight capacity for baggage areas 1 and 2 is 120 pounds.

> **For Academic Illustration/Training Purposes Only!**
> *For Flight:* Use your Pilot's Operating Handbook or FAA-Approved Airplane Flight Manual.

2. Consult the Center of Gravity Moment Envelope, also on page 18.

    a. Find the weight and moment intersection to determine if the Weight/C.G. relationship is within acceptable limits.

    b. Note that the intersection of 56.6 moments for 1,670 lb. appears at the top of the envelope and within limits.

    c. While within limits, the C.G. is somewhat aft and the airplane is at maximum weight which will affect the airplane's performance. This is useful information for the pilot.

Note the C.G. moment envelope takes the place of dividing the total weight into the total moment to determine the C.G. in inches and comparing the C.G. in inches to the acceptable C.G. range. You must be within the enclosed moment envelope or you must reload the airplane to get it within the enclosed area -- add or remove weight and move weight forward or backward.

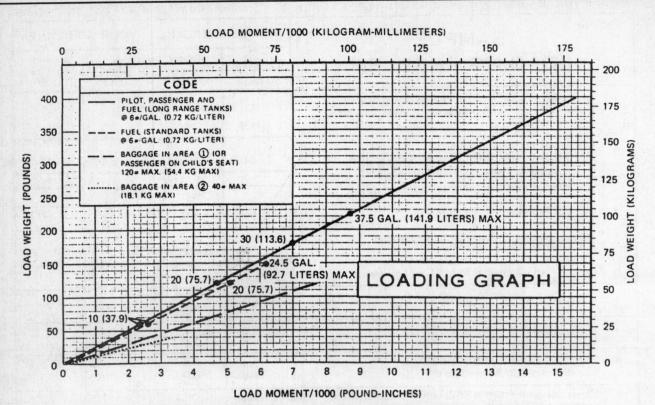

NOTES: Line representing adjustable seats shows the pilot or passenger center of gravity on adjustable
          seats positioned for an average occupant. Refer to the Loading Arrangements Diagram for
          forward and aft limits of occupant C.G. range.

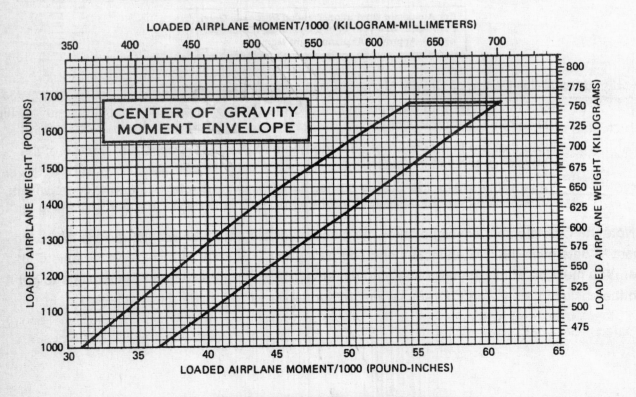

For Academic Illustration/Training Purposes Only!
For Flight: Use your Pilot's Operating Handbook
or FAA-Approved Airplane Flight Manual.

Also, if you are near any edge of the shaded area, you should consider the effect on airplane performance.

Bottom .... Light, good performance
Top .... Heavy, sluggish performance
Right .... Aft C.G.
Left .... Forward C.G.

The C.G. position influences the lift and angle of attack of the wing, the amount and direction of force on the tail, and the degree of deflection of the stabilizer needed to supply the proper tail force for equilibrium. The latter is very important because of its relationship to elevator control force.

1. The airplane will stall at a higher speed with a forward C.G. location because the critical angle of attack is reached at a higher speed due to increased wing loading.

2. Higher elevator control forces usually exist with a forward C.G. location due to the increased stabilizer deflection required to balance the airplane.

3. The airplane will cruise faster with an aft C.G. location because of reduced drag. The drag is reduced because a smaller angle of attack and less downward deflection of the stabilizer are required to balance the airplane and overcome the nose-down pitching tendency.

4. The airplane becomes less and less stable as the C.G. is moved rearward. Recovery from stalls and spins also becomes more difficult.

5. A forward C.G. location increases the need for greater back elevator pressure. If forward of acceptable limits, the elevator may no longer be able to oppose any increase in nose-down pitching as airspeed is reduced for landing. Remember, adequate elevator control is needed to control the airplane throughout the airspeed range down to the stall.

CHECKLISTS

A. The use of checklists is vital to the safety of each flight. Airplanes have many controls, switches, instruments, and indicators. Failure to correctly position or check any of these could have serious results.

B. Each item on the checklist requires evaluation and possible action:

1. Is the situation safe?

2. It not, what action is required?

3. Is the overall airplane/environment safe when you take all factors into account?

C. There are different types of checklists:

1. "Read and do" -- e.g., pretakeoff checklist.

2. "Do and read" -- e.g., in reacting to emergencies, you do everything that comes to mind and then confirm on research in the *POH*.

D. In other words, checklists are not an end in and of themselves. Checklists are a means of flying safely. Generally, they are to be used as specified in your *POH* to accomplish safe flight.

E.   Most *Pilot's Operating Handbooks* provide checklists for:

1.   Preflight
2.   Before starting
3.   Taxi
4.   Before takeoff
5.   Takeoff
6.   Climb
7.   Cruise
8.   Descent
9.   Before landing
10.   After landing
11.   Before shutdown
12.   Shutdown
13.   Emergencies

F.   These checklists from the Tomahawk, Skipper, and Cessna 152 are reproduced as appropriate in later chapters.

ELECTRONIC CHECKLISTS

A.   A recent aid to reduce pilot workload is the electronic checklist. Mounted in the control panel, the unit is about the size of a radio. The unit provides either an aural or visual listing of the checklists for each stage of flight (start, taxi, takeoff, descent, landing, and shutdown) and possible emergencies.

B.   The pilot, instead of reading off a traditional printed card, selects the appropriate checklist and presses a start button. The box will then proceed through the specified checklist, stopping after each item. Depending on the model, the pilot will either verbally command it to go onto the next item, or will press a button moving it to the next item.

C.   The checklist is standardized as well as complete, so no items are forgotten, as is the case when pilots do it from memory or glancing over a printed checklist. By forcing the pilot to respond to each item, there is less chance an item will be overlooked, as can happen with written checklists during busy periods in the cockpit. Also, by being mounted high in the panel, the pilot can focus his/her attention outside the cockpit where it should be, instead of buried while reading from a printed checklist.

D.   Depending on the sophistication of the model, the checklist will be either of a generic variety or one especially tailored to the make and model of aircraft flown. Ones that are programmed for a particular aircraft will also usually have an emergency checklist that will call out the exact items needed to cope with a particular emergency.

1.   Although originally developed for high-performance turboprop and jet aircraft, models are reaching the market designed for and in the price range of single-engine airplanes.

END OF CHAPTER

CHAPTER THREE
PRIVATE CERTIFICATE RELATED FARs

Federal Aviation Regulations 23

Part 1 -- Definitions and Abbreviations 24
    1.1   *General Definitions* 24
    1.2   *Abbreviations and Symbols* 24

Part 61 -- Certification: Pilots and Flight Instructors 25
    61.1   *Applicability* 25
    61.3   *Requirement for Certificates, Rating, and Authorizations* 25
    61.5   *Certificates and Ratings Issued under This Part* 26
    61.13   *Application and Qualification* 26
    61.15   *Offenses Involving Alcohol or Drugs* 26
    61.16   *Refusal to Submit to an Alcohol Test or to Furnish Test Results* 26
    61.17   *Temporary Certificate* 26
    61.19   *Duration of Pilot and Flight Instructor Certificates* 26
    61.23   *Duration of Medical Certificates* 27
    61.25   *Change of Name* 27
    61.29   *Replacement of Lost or Destroyed Certificate* 27
    61.31   *General Limitations* 27
    61.35   *Written Test: Prerequisites and Passing Grades* 27
    61.37   *Written Test: Cheating or other Unauthorized Conduct* 28
    61.39   *Prerequisites for Flight Tests* 28
    61.43   *Flight Tests: General Procedures* 28
    61.45   *Flight Tests: Required Aircraft and Equipment* 28
    61.47   *Flight Tests: Status of FAA Inspectors and Other Authorized
             Flight Examiners* 29
    61.49   *Retesting after Failure* 29
    61.51   *Pilot Logbooks* 29
    61.53   *Operations during Medical Deficiency* 30
    61.55   *Second-in-Command Qualifications* 30
    61.56   *Flight Review* 30
    61.57   *Recent Flight Experience: Pilot in Command* 30
    61.59   *Falsification, Reproduction, or Alteration of Applications,
             Certificates, Logbooks, Reports, or Records* 30
    61.60   *Change of Address* 31
    61.81   *Applicability* 31
    61.83   *Eligibility Requirements: Student Pilots* 31
    61.85   *Application* 31
    61.87   *Solo Flight Requirements for Student Pilots* 31
    61.89   *General Limitations* 32
    61.93   *Cross-Country Flight Requirements (For Student and Recreational
             Pilots Seeking Private Pilot Certification)* 32
    61.95   *Operations in a Terminal Control Area and at Airports Located
             within a Terminal Control Area* 33
    61.102 *Applicability* 33
    61.103 *Eligibility Requirements: General* 33
    61.105 *Aeronautical Knowledge* 34
    61.107 *Flight Proficiency* 34
    61.109 *Airplane Rating: Aeronautical Experience* 34
    61.111 *Cross-Country Flights: Pilots Based on Small Islands* 35

(Continued next page)

61.118   Private Pilot Privileges and Limitations: Pilot in Command 35
61.120   Private Pilot Privileges and Limitations: Second in Command
         of Aircraft Requiring More Than One Required Pilot 36

Part 67 -- Medical Standards and Certification 37
67.1   Applicability 37
67.17   Third-Class Medical Certificate 37
67.19   Special Issuance of Medical Certificates 38

Part 91 -- General Operating and Flight Rules 39
91.1   Applicability 39
91.3   Responsibility and Authority of the Pilot in Command 39
91.7   Civil Aircraft Airworthiness 39
91.9   Civil Aircraft Flight Manual, Marking, and Placard Requirements 39
91.11   Prohibition against Interference with Crewmembers 39
91.13   Careless or Reckless Operation 40
91.15   Dropping Objects 40
91.17   Alcohol or Drugs 40
91.19   Carriage of Narcotic Drugs; Marijuana, and
         Depressant or Stimulant Drugs or Substances 40
91.25   Aviation Safety Reporting Program: Prohibition against Use
         of Reports for Enforcement Purposes 40
91.101   Applicability 42
91.103   Preflight Action 42
91.105   Flight Crewmembers at Stations 42
91.107   Use of Safety Belts 42
91.111   Operating near Other Aircraft 42
91.113   Right-of-Way Rules: Except Water Operations 43
91.117   Aircraft Speed 43
91.119   Minimum Safe Altitudes: General 43
91.121   Altimeter Settings 43
91.123   Compliance with ATC Clearances and Instructions 44
91.125   ATC Light Signals 44
91.127   Operating on or in the Vicinity of an Airport: General Rules 44
91.129   Operation at Airports with Operating Control Towers 44
91.130   Airport Radar Service Areas 45
91.131   Terminal Control Areas 45
91.133   Restricted and Prohibited Areas 46
91.137   Temporary Flight Restrictions 46
91.139   Emergency Air Traffic Rules 47
91.141   Flight Restrictions in the Proximity of the Presidential and
         Other Parties 47
91.143   Flight Limitations in the Proximity of Space Flight Operations 47
91.151   Fuel Requirements for Flight in VFR Conditions 47
91.153   VFR Flight Plan; Information Required 47
91.155   Basic VFR Weather Minimums 48
91.157   Special VFR Weather Minimums 49
91.159   VFR Cruising Altitude or Flight Level 49
91.203   Civil Aircraft: Certifications Required 49
91.205   Powered Civil Aircraft with Standard Category U.S. Airworthiness
         Certificates: Instrument and Equipment Requirements 49
91.207   Emergency Locator Transmitters 50
91.209   Aircraft Lights 50
91.211   Supplemental Oxygen 50
91.213   Inoperative Instruments and Equipment 51
91.215   ATC Transponder and Altitude Reporting Equipment and Use 52

(Continued next page)

91.217	Data Correspondence between Automatically Reported Pressure Altitude Data and the Pilot's Altitude Reference	52
91.303	Aerobatic Flight	52
91.305	Flight Test Areas	52
91.307	Parachutes and Parachuting	52
91.401	Applicability	53
91.403	General	53
91.405	Maintenance Required	53
91.407	Operation after Maintenance, Preventive Maintenance, Rebuilding, or Alteration	53
91.409	Inspections	53
91.413	ATC Transponder Tests and Inspections	53
91.415	Changes to Aircraft Inspection Programs	54
91.417	Maintenance Records	54
91.419	Transfer of Maintenance Records	54
91.421	Rebuilt Engine Maintenance Records	54

NTSB Part 830 -- Notification and Reporting of Aircraft Accidents or Incidents and Overdue Aircraft, and Preservation of Aircraft Wreckage, Mail, Cargo, and Records ... 56

830.1	Applicability	56
830.2	Definitions	56
830.5	Immediate Notification	57
830.6	Information to Be Given in Notification	57
830.10	Preservation of Aircraft Wreckage, Mail, Cargo, and Records	58
830.15	Reports and Statements to Be Filed	58

FEDERAL AVIATION REGULATIONS

The Federal Aviation Regulations (FARs) are organized by part, i.e., the FARs are grouped into chapters that are called parts. Many parts are not relevant to private pilots, e.g., Part 103, Ultralight Vehicles.

The parts covered in this chapter are

Part 1 -- Definitions and Abbreviations

Part 61 -- Certification: Pilots and Flight Instructors

Part 67 -- Medical Standards and Certification

Part 91 -- General Operating and Flight Rules

NTSB Part 830 -- Notification and Reporting of Aircraft Accidents or Incidents and Overdue Aircraft, and Preservation of Aircraft Wreckage, Mail, Cargo, and Records.

This chapter outlines (paraphrases) only the FARs we feel are particularly relevant to private pilots. These paragraph numbers and titles are listed beginning on the next page. Only selected sections of FAR Parts 61, 67, and 91 are outlined. Those sections not outlined are listed at the end of the discussion for your information. This is to acquaint you with the FARs. You can refer to your copy of a reprint of the FARs for any definition or FAR paragraph in which you have an interest. Reprints by aviation publishers are available at most FBOs and/or aviation bookstores for $5 to $10.

Part 1 -- DEFINITIONS AND ABBREVIATIONS

A.   This Part contains several pages of definitions of terms and abbreviations used throughout the FARs.

B.   You should use Part 1 anytime you do not understand the meaning of a word and/or abbreviation.

1.1 General Definitions

Only selected terms most relevant to the private certificate are included here.

1.   **Administrator** means the FAA administrator or any person to whom (s)he has delegated his authority in the matter concerned.

2.   **Airplane** means an engine-driven fixed-wing aircraft heavier than air, that is supported in flight by the dynamic reaction of the air against its wings.

3.   **Airport** means an area of land or water that is used or intended to be used for the landing and takeoff of aircraft, and includes its buildings and facilities, if any.

4.   **Air traffic control** means a service operated by appropriate authority to promote the safe, orderly, and expeditious flow of air traffic.

5.   **Controlled airspace** means airspace designated as a continental control area, control area, control zone, terminal control area, or transition area, within which some or all aircraft may be subject to air traffic control.

6.   **Flight time** means the time from the moment the aircraft first moves under its own power for the purpose of flight until the moment it comes to rest at the next point of landing ("Block-to-block" time).

7.   **Instrument** means a device using an internal mechanism to show visually or aurally the attitude, altitude, or operation of an aircraft or aircraft part.

8.   **Medical Certificate** means an acceptable evidence of physical fitness on a form prescribed by the Administrator.

9.   **Operator** is a person who uses or authorizes use of an aircraft.

10. **Pilot in Command (PIC)** means the pilot responsible for the operation and safety of an aircraft during flight time.

11. **Rating** means a statement that, as part of a certificate, sets forth special conditions, privileges, and limitations.

12. **Traffic pattern** means the traffic flow that is prescribed for aircraft landing at, taxiing on, or taking off from, an airport.

1.2 Abbreviations and Symbols

"AGL" means above ground level.
"ASR" means airport surveillance radar.
"ATC" means air traffic control.
"CAS" means calibrated airspeed.
"DME" means distance measuring equipment compatible with TACAN.
"EAS" means equivalent airspeed.
"FAA" means Federal Aviation Administration.
"HIRL" means high-intensity runway light system.
"IAS" means indicated airspeed.

"ICAO" means International Civil Aviation Organization.
"IFR" means instrument flight rules.
"ILS" means instrument landing system.
"MALS" means medium intensity approach light system.
"MALSR" means medium intensity approach light system with runway alignment indicator lights.
"MSL" means mean sea level.

"NDB(ADF)" means nondirectional beacon (automatic direction finder).

"PAR" means precision approach radar.

"RAIL" means runway alignment indicator light system.

"RBN" means radio beacon.

"RCLM" means runway centerline marking.

"RCLS" means runway centerline light system.

"REIL" means runway end identification lights.

"RR" means low or medium frequency radio range station.

"SALS" means short approach light system.

"SSALS" means simplified short approach light system.

"SSALSR" means simplified short approach light system with runway alignment indicator lights.

"TACAN" means ultra-high frequency tactical air navigational aid.

"TAS" means true airspeed.

"TDZL" means touchdown zone lights.

"TVOR" means very high frequency terminal omnirange station.

V_A means design maneuvering speed.

V_B means design speed for maximum gust intensity.

V_{FE} means maximum flap extended speed.

V_{LE} means maximum landing gear extended speed.

V_{LO} means maximum landing gear operating speed.

V_{NE} means never-exceed speed.

V_{NO} means maximum structural cruising speed.

V_R means rotation speed.

V_{SO} means the stalling speed or the minimum steady flight speed in the landing configuration.

V_{S1} means the stalling speed or the minimum steady flight speed obtained in a specific configuration.

V_X means speed for best angle of climb.

V_Y means speed for best rate of climb.

"VFR" means visual flight rules.

"VHF" means very high frequency.

"VOR" means very high frequency omnirange station.

"VORTAC" means collocated VOR and TACAN.

Part 61 -- CERTIFICATION: PILOTS AND FLIGHT INSTRUCTORS

Part 61 contains seven subparts, labeled A through G. Parts E, F, and G are not immediately related to private pilots.

Subpart A -- General
Subpart B -- Aircraft Ratings and Special Certificates
Subpart C -- Student and Recreational Pilots
Subpart D -- Private Pilots

Subpart E -- Commercial Pilots
Subpart F -- Airline Transport Pilots
Subpart G -- Flight Instructors

Subpart E is thoroughly covered in Gleim's *Commercial Pilot FAA Practical Test Prep*. Subpart G is thoroughly covered in Gleim's *Flight Instructor FAA Practical Test Prep*. **Note:** Only selected sections are outlined in the following 11 pages. Pages 36 and 37 contain the section titles of Part 61 that are not outlined.

Subpart A -- General

61.1 Applicability

1. Part 61 prescribes the requirements for issuing pilot and flight instructor certificates and ratings, the conditions under which these certificates and ratings are necessary, and the privileges and limitations of these certificates and ratings.

2. For a certificate or rating, you must meet the requirements in Part 61, unless you are enrolled in a Part 141 flight school.

   a. Part 141 schools have different requirements (e.g., flight time).

61.3 Requirement for Certificates, Rating, and Authorizations

1. Both appropriate pilot certificate and current and appropriate medical certificate are required to be in your personal possession when acting as pilot in command or as a required flight crewmember.

61.5 Certificates and Ratings Issued under This Part

1. Category with respect to airman certification is:

   a. Lighter-Than-Air
   b. Airplane
   c. Rotorcraft
   d. Glider

2. Airplane Class Ratings refer to pilot certificates, and are:

   a. Single-Engine Land
   b. Multiengine Land
   c. Single-Engine Sea
   d. Multiengine Sea

61.13 Application and Qualification

1. If you want to apply for a certificate or rating, or to add a rating to an existing certificate, you must do so in the manner and on the form designated by the FAA.

2. If you are not a citizen or resident alien, you must also show proof that you have paid the fee prescribed by Part 187 (fee for processing services provided by the FAA in Oklahoma City).

3. If you meet all the requirements of Part 61, you are entitled to the certificate or rating sought.

4. If you cannot comply with all the requirements, except for flight proficiency, you may apply for the certificate or rating with limitations placed on it.

61.15 Offenses Involving Alcohol or Drugs

1. Conviction for a violation of any law relating to drugs or alcohol is the basis for:

   a. The denial of an application for a certificate or rating for up to 1 year after the final conviction.

   b. The suspension or revocation of any existing certificates or ratings.

61.16 Refusal to Submit to an Alcohol Test or to Furnish Test Results

1. If you refuse to submit test results for drugs or alcohol when requested by the FAA, you may not receive a certificate or rating for a period of 1 year.

2. This is also grounds to suspend or revoke existing certificates or ratings.

61.17 Temporary Certificate

1. A temporary certificate is issued to you after successful completion of your practical test. It is valid for a maximum of 120 days or until

   a. You receive your permanent certificate.
   b. Notice is given that the certificate or rating sought is denied.

61.19 Duration of Pilot and Flight Instructor Certificates

1. All pilot certificates (except a student pilot certificate) issued under Part 61 are issued without an expiration date.

2. Flight instructor certificates expire at the end of the 24th month after it was last issued or renewed.

3. Any pilot or flight instructor certificate is no longer valid if it is surrendered, suspended, or revoked.

   a. The FAA may request that a suspended or revoked certificate be returned to them.

61.23 Duration of Medical Certificates

1. A third-class medical certificate expires for private pilot purposes at the end of the last day of the 24th month after the month of the date of examination shown on the certificate.

61.25 Change of Name

1. To change your name on your pilot certificate, you must submit your current certificate and a copy of the marriage license, court order, or other document verifying the change.

    a. The documents will be returned after inspection.

61.29 Replacement of Lost or Destroyed Certificate

1. An application for a replacement certificate must be made by letter to the Department of Transportation • FAA Airman Certification Branch • P.O. Box 25082 • Oklahoma City, Oklahoma 73125.

2. It must include your name, social security number, date and place of birth, and $2.00.

3. A telegram from the FAA showing that the certificate was issued may be used for a period not to exceed 60 days, pending the arrival of the replacement certificate.

61.31 General Limitations

1. Type ratings are required when operating any turbojet-powered airplane or airplane having a gross weight of 12,500 lb.

2. To act as pilot in command of a high-performance airplane (retractable landing gear, flaps, a controllable propeller, and/or more than 200 horsepower), you must receive flight instruction in such an airplane and obtain a logbook endorsement of competence.

3. To act as pilot in command of a pressurized airplane that has a service ceiling or maximum operating altitude, whichever is lower, above 25,000 ft. MSL, you must have both ground and flight instruction in such an airplane and obtain a logbook endorsement.

4. To act as pilot in command of a tailwheel airplane you must receive flight instruction in such an airplane and obtain a logbook endorsement of competence. Training must include:

    a. Normal and crosswind takeoffs and landings,
    b. Wheel landings, unless manufacturer does not recommend them, and
    c. Go-around procedures.

61.35 Written Test: Prerequisites and Passing Grades

1. To take a written test you must:

    a. Show that you have satisfactorily completed the ground or home-study course required by Part 61.

    b. Present personal identification such as an Airman Certificate, driver license, or other official document.

        1) The identification presented must include a photograph, signature, and your actual residential address, if different from the mailing address.

    c. Present a birth certificate showing that the age requirements of Part 61 are met or will be met within 2 years of taking the test. A driver license will suffice.

2. The minimum passing grade for the test specified by the FAA is printed on the test booklets (usually 70%).

3. This section does not pertain to the written test for an ATP certificate. The ATP written test requires an authorization from the FAA.

61.37 Written Tests: Cheating or Other Unauthorized Conduct

1.   You may not:

    a.   Copy or intentionally remove a written test from the testing site.

    b.   Give to another or receive from another a copy of the test.

    c.   Give help to another or receive help from another while taking the test.

    d.   Take the test on behalf of another.

    e.   Use any material as an aid during the test.

        1)   Note: You are permitted to take and use a flight computer, plotter, and calculator (you must erase all memory before you start your test).

    f.   Intentionally cause, assist, or participate in any act contrary to this part.

2.   If caught in any of these acts you will be ineligible to take the test or receive any certificates or ratings for a period of 1 year.

3.   This is also grounds to suspend or revoke any certificate or ratings you already possess.

61.39 Prerequisites for Flight Tests

1.   To be eligible for a flight test, you must have:

    a.   Passed any required written tests within the preceding 24 months.

    b.   Have the required instruction and aeronautical experience as prescribed in Part 61.

    c.   Have a current and appropriate medical certificate for the rating sought.

    d.   Meet the minimum age requirements as given in Part 61.

    e.   Have a written statement from a CFII certifying that (s)he has given you flight instruction in preparation for the flight test within the preceding 60 days and finds you competent to pass the test and have satisfactory knowledge of the areas shown to be deficient on the written test.

61.43 Flight Tests: General Procedures

1.   The ability to pass the flight test for a new certificate or rating is judged by the ability to:

    a.   Execute procedures and maneuvers within the aircraft's performance capabilities and limitations.

    b.   Execute emergency procedures and maneuvers appropriate to the aircraft.

    c.   Pilot the aircraft with smoothness and accuracy.

    d.   Exercise judgment.

    e.   Apply aeronautical knowledge.

    f.   Show that you are the master of your aircraft and the outcome of any maneuver is never seriously in doubt.

2.   If you fail any of the required pilot operations, the entire checkride is failed.

3.   Either you or the examiner may discontinue the flight test at any time when the failure of a pilot operation has caused the failure of the checkride.

61.45 Flight Tests: Required Aircraft and Equipment

1.   For your practical (flight) test you must furnish an appropriate U.S. registered aircraft that has a current airworthiness certificate.

2.   Aircraft furnished for the flight test must have:

    a.   The equipment for each pilot operation required by the flight test.

    b.   No operating limitations precluding the performance of a required pilot operation.

    c.   Pilot seats with adequate outside visibility for each pilot to operate the aircraft safely.

d.   All flight and power controls accessible and easily controlled by both pilots.

e.   For testing of flight by reference to instruments only, you must provide a satisfactory view-limiting device.

61.47 Flight Tests: Status of FAA Inspectors and Other Authorized Flight Examiners

1.   An FAA inspector or a designated examiner conducts the flight test for certificates and ratings for the purpose of observing your ability to perform the required maneuvers.

2.   The FAA inspector/examiner is not the pilot in command unless (s)he acts in that capacity in order to perform the flight test, e.g., your practical test is for a second in command for an airplane that requires more than one pilot. This determination must be made prior to starting the checkride.

   a.   For most practical tests (e.g., instrument, commercial, etc.) you are the pilot in command.

3.   Neither you nor your examiner are considered a passenger of one another and are thereby not responsible for the passenger-carrying provisions of the FARs.

61.49 Retesting after Failure

1.   If you fail a written or flight test you may not apply for retesting until 30 days have passed since the failure.

2.   In the case of a first-time failure, you may apply within the 30-day period if a written statement is presented from a CFII stating that the CFII has given additional instruction and finds you competent to pass the test.

61.51 Pilot Logbooks

1.   All the aeronautical training and experience used to meet the requirements for a certificate or rating must be shown by a reliable record, e.g., a logbook.

2.   All flight time used to meet the recent flight requirements must also be logged in a reliable record (e.g., three takeoffs and landings within the preceding 90 days).

3.   All other time need only be logged at your discretion.

4.   Each logbook entry shall include:

   a.   Date.
   b.   Total time of flight.
   c.   Points of departure and arrival.
   d.   Type and identification of aircraft.
   e.   Type of pilot time (e.g., PIC, SIC, solo, dual, etc.).
   f.   Conditions of flight (e.g., day or night).

5.   Types of flight time:

   a.   Solo is logged when you are the sole occupant of an aircraft you are training in before obtaining your private pilot certificate.

   b.   PIC is logged when you are the sole manipulator of the controls in an aircraft you are rated in, or you are the PIC during a flight in which an SIC is required.

   c.   SIC time is logged when you are acting as a second in command on an aircraft requiring more than one pilot by the type certificate or FARs.

   d.   Instrument time is logged when you operate the aircraft solely by reference to instruments under actual or simulated conditions.

   e.   All time logged as instruction must be certified by an appropriately rated and certificated instructor giving the instruction.

6.   You must present your logbook upon reasonable request by the FAA, or a member of the NTSB, or a local or state law enforcement officer.

61.53 Operations during Medical Deficiency

1.   You may not act as a pilot in command or required crewmember while you have a known medical problem which would make you unable to meet the requirements of your current medical certificate (i.e., Class I, II, or III).

61.55 Second-in-Command Qualifications

1.   To serve as second in command of an airplane certified for operation by more than one required pilot flight crewmember, you must hold at least a private pilot certificate with appropriate category and class ratings.

61.56 Flight Review

1.   To fly solo or act as pilot in command of an aircraft, you must have:

   a.   Satisfactorily accomplished a biennial flight review or completed a proficiency check or a practical test for a new certificate/rating within the preceding 24 calendar months, or

   b.   Satisfactorily completed one or more phases of an FAA-sponsored pilot proficiency award program.

      1)   This is commonly known as the "Wings" program.

         a)   There are nine levels and satisfactory completion of a level will qualify as a flight review.

         b)   Requires 3 hr. of dual flight instruction and attendance of one FAA-sponsored safety seminar, such as Operation Raincheck.

      2)   For more information visit your nearest FSDO or your local accident prevention counselor.

2.   The FAA is currently deciding if an annual flight review will be required for all recreational pilots and non-instrument-rated private pilots with fewer than 400 hr. of flight time.

   a.   As of now the annual flight review requirement will be effective on August 31, 1993.

61.57 Recent Flight Experience: Pilot in Command

1.   You may not act as pilot in command of an airplane carrying passengers, or of an airplane certificated for more than one required pilot flight crewmember, unless you have:

   a.   Made three takeoffs and landings within the preceding 90 days in an aircraft of the same category and class of the aircraft to be flown, and if a type rating is required, in the same type.

      1)   In a tailwheel airplane, the landings must have been made to a full stop.

   b.   For night experience -- made three takeoffs and landings to a full stop within the preceding 90 days in the category and class of aircraft to be used.

61.59 Falsification, Reproduction, or Alteration of Applications, Certificates, Logbooks, Reports, or Records

1.   You may not make a false or fraudulent statement on any:

   a.   Application for a certificate or rating
   b.   Required record
   c.   Required logbook
   d.   Existing certificate or rating.

2.   Any commission of one of the above acts is grounds to suspend or revoke any existing certificate or rating, and can be used to deny any application for a certificate or rating.

61.60 Change of Address

1. If you make a change in your permanent address, you may not exercise the privileges of your pilot certificate after 30 days (from the day you move) unless you notify the FAA in writing to

   a. Department of Transportation • Federal Aviation Administration • Airman Certification Branch • Box 25082 • Oklahoma City, OK 73125.

Subpart C -- Student and Recreational Pilots

61.81 Applicability

1. This Subpart prescribes the requirements for the issuance of student pilot certificates, the conditions under which those certificates are necessary, and the general rules for holders of those certificates.

61.83 Eligibility Requirements: Student Pilots

1. To be eligible for a student pilot's certificate, you must:

   a. Be at least 16 yr. old.

   b. Be able to read, speak, and understand the English language or you will have limitations placed on the certificate as necessary for safety.

   c. Hold at least a current third-class medical certificate issued under FAR Part 67.

61.85 Application

1. An application for a student pilot certificate is made on a form and in a manner approved by the FAA.

2. It is submitted to a designated aviation medical examiner when applying for an FAA medical certificate, or to an FAA inspector or designated examiner when it is accompanied by a current FAA medical certificate.

61.87 Solo Flight Requirements for Student Pilots

1. You must have demonstrated to a CFI that you are knowledgeable about FAR Parts 61 and 91 and the flight and operational characteristics of the make and model of the airplane to be soloed in.

   a. This will be confirmed by a written test administered by the CFI.

2. Before you are allowed to solo, you must receive flight instruction in the following 15 flight maneuvers:

(1) Flight preparation procedures, including preflight inspections, powerplant operation, and aircraft systems;	(7) Descents with and without turns using high and low drag configurations;	(13) Go-arounds from final approach and from the landing flare in various flight configurations including turns;
(2) Taxiing or surface operations, including runups;	(8) Flight at various airspeeds from cruising to minimum controllable airspeed;	(14) Forced landing procedures initiated on takeoff, during initial climb, cruise, descent, and in the landing pattern; and
(3) Takeoffs and landings, including normal and crosswind;	(9) Emergency procedures and equipment malfunctions;	(15) Stall entries from various flight attitudes and power combinations with recovery initiated at the first indication of a stall, and recovery from a full stall.
(4) Straight-and-level flight, shallow, medium, and steep banked turns in both directions;	(10) Ground reference maneuvers;	
(5) Climbs and climbing turns;	(11) Approaches to the landing area with engine power at idle and with partial power;	
(6) Airport traffic patterns including entry and departure procedures, and collision and wake turbulence avoidance;	(12) Slips to a landing;	

3. You may not fly solo without your logbook and student pilot certificate endorsed by your CFI indicating:

    a. Flight instruction in the make and model of the plane to be used for solo flight.
    b. Proficiency in the above maneuvers.
    c. Competency for safe solo flight in that make and model.

61.89 General Limitations

1. As a student pilot you may **not** act as a pilot in command of an aircraft:

    a. Carrying passengers.
    b. Carrying property for compensation or hire.
    c. In return for compensation or hire.
    d. In furtherance of a business.
    e. On an international flight.
    f. If visibility is below 3 SM during daylight hours or below 5 SM at night.
    g. Above overcast, i.e., without visual reference to the surface.
    h. In violation of any CFI-imposed limitations in your logbook.

2. You may not act as a crewmember on an aircraft requiring more than one pilot unless you are receiving dual instruction on board the aircraft and no passengers are carried.

61.93 Cross-Country Flight Requirements (For Student and Recreational Pilots Seeking Private Pilot Certification)

1. You may not operate an aircraft in solo cross-country unless properly authorized by an instructor.

2. You may not make a solo landing (except in an emergency) other than the one from which you are authorized to depart.

    a. Your CFI may, however, authorize you to practice solo takeoffs and landings at an airport within 25 NM of the base airport after

        1) (S)he determines that you are competent and proficient to make those takeoffs and landings.

        2) (S)he has flown with you prior to authorizing those takeoffs and landings.

        3) (S)he endorses your logbook with an authorization to make those takeoffs and landings.

3. You must receive training from a CFI in the following areas before being authorized to conduct solo cross-country flights:

    a. The use of aeronautical charts for VFR navigation using pilotage and dead reckoning with the aid of a magnetic compass.

    b. Aircraft cross-country performance, and procurement and analysis of aeronautical weather reports and forecasts, including

        1) Recognition of critical weather situations, and
        2) Estimating visibility while in flight.

    c. Cross-country emergency procedures including

        1) Lost procedures,
        2) Adverse weather conditions, and
        3) Simulated precautionary off-airport approaches and landing procedures.

    d. Traffic pattern procedures including

        1) Normal area arrival and departure,
        2) Collision avoidance, and
        3) Wake turbulence precautions.

    e. Recognition of problems caused by peculiar terrain features, if applicable.

      f.   Proper operation of instruments and equipment.

      g.   Short- and soft-field procedures as well as crosswind takeoffs and landings.

      h.   Takeoffs at best rate and best angle of climb.

      i.   Control and maneuvering solely by reference to flight instruments.

          1)   Straight-and-level flight, turns, descents, and climbs.
          2)   Use of radio aids and radar directives.

      j.   The use of radio VFR navigation and two-way communication.

      k.   For night privileges: takeoffs, landings, go-arounds, and VFR night navigation.

4.   Your student pilot certificate must be endorsed by your CFI attesting that you have received the above instruction and have demonstrated an acceptable level of competency and proficiency.

5.   A CFI must endorse your logbook for each solo cross-country flight after

      a.   Reviewing your preflight planning and preparation,

      b.   Certifying that you are prepared to make a safe flight under the known circumstances and any CFI imposed limitations listed in the endorsement.

6.   An endorsement can be made for repeated solo cross-country flight to an airport less than 50 NM after dual cross-country flight in both directions with landings and takeoffs at the airports to be used, with any given conditions set by your CFI.

61.95 Operations in a Terminal Control Area and at Airports Located within a Terminal Control Area

1.   In order for you to solo in a Terminal Control Area (TCA) or at a specific airport within a TCA, you must have:

      a.   Received both ground and flight instruction concerning TCA operations. The flight instruction must have been given in the TCA or at the specific airport in the TCA where you will be operating.

      b.   A current 90-day logbook endorsement from the CFI who gave the training which says that you have received the required training and have been found competent to operate in that specific TCA or at that specific airport within the TCA.

      c.   At least a private pilot certificate is required for operation at the primary airports of certain TCAs.

Subpart D -- Private Pilots

61.102 Applicability

1.   This subpart gives the requirements for the issuance of private pilot certificates and ratings issued on a private pilot certificate.

61.103 Eligibility Requirements: General

1.   To be eligible to be a private pilot, you must:

      a.   Be at least 17 yr. of age.

      b.   Be able to read, speak, and understand the English language or you will have limitations placed on the certificate as necessary for safety.

      c.   Hold at least a valid third-class medical certificate issued under Part 67.

      d.   Pass a written examination (covered by Gleim's *Private Pilot FAA Written Exam* book).

      e.   Pass a practical test appropriate to the rating sought (e.g., Airplane Single-Engine Land).

61.105 Aeronautical Knowledge

1. As an applicant for a private pilot certificate you must have logged ground instruction from an authorized instructor, or

2. Must present evidence showing you have satisfactorily completed a course of instruction for home study in the following areas of aeronautical knowledge for airplanes:

    a. The accident reporting requirements of the National Transportation Safety Board and the Federal Aviation Regulations applicable to private pilot privileges, limitations, and flight operations for airplanes or rotorcraft, as appropriate, the use of the *Airman's Information Manual*, and FAA advisory circulars.

    b. VFR navigation using pilotage, dead reckoning, and radio aids.

    c. The recognition of critical weather situations from the ground and in flight, the procurement and use of aeronautical weather reports and forecasts.

    d. The safe and efficient operation of airplanes, including high-density airport operations, collision avoidance precautions, and radio communication procedures.

    e. Basic aerodynamics and the principles of flight.

    f. Stall awareness, spin entry, spins, and spin recovery techniques for airplanes. (Actual spin training for private pilot applicants is not required.)

61.107 Flight Proficiency

1. As an applicant for a private pilot certificate you must have logged instruction from an authorized flight instructor in at least the following pilot operations:

    a. Preflight operations, including weight and balance determination, line inspection, and airplane servicing.

    b. Airport and traffic pattern operations, including operations at controlled airports, radio communications, and collision avoidance precautions.

    c. Flight maneuvering by reference to ground objects.

    d. Flight at slow airspeeds with realistic distractions, and the recognition of and recovery from stalls entered from straight flight and from turns.

    e. Normal and crosswind takeoffs and landings.

    f. Control and maneuvering an airplane solely by reference to instruments, including descents and climbs using radio aids or radar directives.

    g. Cross-country flying, using pilotage, dead reckoning, and radio aids, including one 2-hour flight.

    h. Maximum performance takeoffs and landings.

    i. Night flying, including takeoffs, landings, and VFR navigation.

    j. Emergency operations, including simulated aircraft and equipment malfunctions.

61.109 Airplane Rating: Aeronautical Experience

1. As an applicant for a private pilot certificate with an airplane rating you must have a total of at least 40 hr. of total flight time.

    a. 20 hr. of flight instruction given by an authorized flight instructor, including at least:

        1) 3 hr. of cross-country.

        2) 3 hr. at night, including 10 takeoffs and landings if you are seeking night flying privileges.

        3) 3 hr. in airplanes in preparation for the private pilot flight test within 60 days prior to your practical test.

    b.   20 hr. of solo flight time, including at least:

        1)   10 hr. in an airplane.

        2)   10 hr. of cross-country flights.

            a)   Each flight with a landing more than 50 NM from the point of departure.

            b)   One flight of 300 NM, with landings at a minimum of three points, one of which is more than 100 NM from the original departure point.

        3)   Three takeoffs and landings to a full stop at an airport with an operating control tower.

61.111 Cross-Country Flights: Pilots Based on Small Islands

1.   If you are located on an island from which the required cross-country flights cannot be made without flying over water more than 10 NM from the nearest shoreline you need not comply with 61.109(b)(2).

    a.   If airports are available without flying over water more than 10 NM from the nearest shoreline, you must complete two round trip solo flights between those two airports that are farthest apart.

        1)   Do a landing at each airport on both flights.

    b.   A certificate issued under these conditions will contain the following endorsement:

    Passenger carrying prohibited on flights more than 10 NM from (name of island).

2.   If you do not have 3 hr. of solo cross-country flight time, including a round trip flight to an airport at least 50 NM from the place of departure with at least two full stop landings at different points along the route, the certificate will be endorsed as follows:

    Holder does not meet the cross-country flight requirements of ICAO.

61.118 Private Pilot Privileges and Limitations: Pilot in Command

1.   As a private pilot you may not act as pilot in command of an aircraft that is carrying passengers or property for compensation or hire, nor may you be paid to act as pilot in command, **except**

    a.   You may act as pilot in command, for compensation or hire, of an aircraft in connection with any business or employment if the flight is only incidental to that business or employment and the aircraft does not carry passengers or property for compensation or hire.

    b.   You may share the operating expenses of a flight with your passengers.

    c.   If you are an aircraft salesman and have at least 200 hr. of logged flight time you may demonstrate an aircraft to a prospective buyer.

    d.   You may act as pilot in command of an aircraft used in a passenger-carrying airlift sponsored by a charitable organization for which passengers make a donation if

        1)   The sponsor of the airlift notifies the appropriate FAA FSDO at least 7 days before the flight,

        2)   The flight is conducted from a public airport, or an airport approved by an FAA inspector,

        3)   You have logged at least 200 hr. of flight time,

        4)   No acrobatic or formation flights are conducted,

        5)   Each aircraft used is certificated in the standard category and complies with the 100-hr. inspection requirement, and

        6)   The flight is made under VFR during the day.

61.120 Private Pilot Privileges and Limitations: Second in Command of Aircraft Requiring More Than One Required Pilot

1. You may not be paid to act as second in command of an aircraft type certificated for more than one required pilot, except under 61.118(a) through (d).

    a. Nor may you act in such capacity if the aircraft is operated for compensation or hire.

Part 61 sections not outlined above and on pages 25 through 35:

Subpart A -- General

61.2   Certification of foreign pilots and flight instructors
61.7   Obsolete certificates and ratings
61.9   Exchange of obsolete certificates and ratings for current certificates and ratings
61.11   Expired pilot certificates and reissuance
61.14   Refusal to submit to a drug test
61.21   Duration of Category II pilot authorization
61.27   Voluntary surrender or exchange of certificate
61.33   Tests: General procedure
61.41   Flight instruction received from flight instructors not certificated by FAA
61.58   Pilot-in-command proficiency check: Operation of aircraft requiring more than one required pilot

Subpart B -- Aircraft Ratings and Special Certificates

61.61   Applicability
61.63   Additional aircraft ratings (other than airline transport pilot)
61.65   Instrument rating requirements
61.67   Category II pilot authorization requirements
61.69   Glider towing: Experience and instruction requirements
61.71   Graduates of certificated flying schools: Special rules
61.73   Military pilots or former military pilots: Special rules
61.75   Pilot certificate issued on basis of a foreign pilot license
61.77   Special purpose pilot certificate: Operation of U.S.-registered civil airplanes leased by a person not a U.S. citizen

Subpart C -- Student and Recreational Pilots

61.91   Aircraft limitations: Pilot in command
61.96   Eligibility requirements: Recreational pilots
61.97   Aeronautical knowledge
61.98   Flight proficiency
61.99   Airplane rating: Aeronautical experience
61.100 Rotorcraft rating: Aeronautical experience
61.101 Recreational pilot privileges and limitations

Subpart D -- Private Pilots

61.113 Rotorcraft rating: Aeronautical experience
61.115 Glider rating: Aeronautical experience
61.117 Lighter-than-air rating: Aeronautical experience
61.119 Free balloon rating: Limitations

Subpart E -- Commercial Pilots

61.121 Applicability
61.123 Eligibility requirements: General
61.125 Aeronautical knowledge
61.127 Flight proficiency
61.129 Airplane rating: Aeronautical experience
61.131 Rotorcraft ratings: Aeronautical experience
61.133 Glider rating: Aeronautical experience

Part 61 sections not outlined on pages 25 through 36:

    61.135 Airship rating: Aeronautical experience
    61.137 Free balloon rating: Aeronautical experience
    61.139 Commercial pilot privileges and limitations: General
    61.141 Airship and free balloon ratings: Limitations

Subpart F -- Airline Transport Pilots

    61.151 Eligibility requirements: General
    61.153 Airplane rating: Aeronautical knowledge
    61.155 Airplane rating: Aeronautical experience
    61.157 Airplane rating: Aeronautical skill
    61.159 Rotorcraft rating: Aeronautical knowledge
    61.161 Rotorcraft rating: Aeronautical experience
    61.163 Rotorcraft rating: Aeronautical skill
    61.165 Additional category ratings
    61.167 Tests
    61.169 Instruction in air transportation service
    61.171 General privileges and limitations

Subpart G -- Flight Instructors

    61.181 Applicability
    61.183 Eligibility requirements: General
    61.185 Aeronautical knowledge
    61.187 Flight proficiency
    61.189 Flight instructor records
    61.191 Additional flight instructor ratings
    61.193 Flight instructor authorizations
    61.195 Flight instructor limitations
    61.197 Renewal of flight instructor certificates
    61.199 Expired flight instructor certificates and ratings
    61.201 Conversion to new system of instructor ratings

Part 67 -- MEDICAL STANDARDS AND CERTIFICATION

Note: Only knowledge of Parts 1, 61, and 91 are specifically required for your private pilot certificate. The following summary of selected paragraphs from Part 67 is presented for your information. Page 39 contains the section titles of Part 67 that have not been outlined.

67.1 Applicability

    1.   This subpart prescribes the medical standards for issuing medical certificates for airmen.

67.17 Third-Class Medical Certificate

    1.   To be eligible for a third-class medical certificate, you must meet the following requirements:

        a.   Eyes

            1)   Distant Vision: 20/50 or better in each eye separately or corrected to 20/30 or better in each eye with corrective lenses (glasses or contacts).

            2)   No serious pathology of the eye.

            3)   Ability to distinguish aviation signal red, aviation signal green, and white.

        b.   Ear, Nose, Throat, and Equilibrium

            1)   Ability to hear the whispered voice at 3 ft.

            2)   No acute or chronic disease of the internal ear.

    3) No disease or malformation of the nose or throat that might interfere with, or be aggravated by, flying.

    4) No disturbance in equilibrium.

  c. Mental and Neurologic

    1) Mental -- No established medical history or clinical diagnosis of any of the following:

      a) A personality disorder.

      b) A psychosis.

      c) Alcoholism, unless there is established clinical evidence of recovery, including sustained total abstinence from alcohol of at least 2 yr.

      d) Drug dependence.

    2) Neurologic -- No established medical history or clinical diagnosis of the following:

      a) Epilepsy.

      b) A disturbance of consciousness without satisfactory medical explanation of the cause.

  d. Cardiovascular

    1) No established medical history or clinical diagnosis of:

      a) Myocardial infarction.

      b) Angina pectoris.

      c) Coronary heart disease that has required treatment or, if untreated, that has been symptomatic or clinically significant.

  e. General medical condition

    1) No established medical history or clinical diagnosis of diabetes mellitus that requires insulin or any other hypoglycemic drug for control.

    2) No other organic, functional, or structural disease, defect, or limitation that the Federal Air Surgeon finds would cause you to be unable to perform your pilot duties safely.

  f. If you do not meet the conditions for a medical certificate you may apply for a discretionary issuance of a certificate under 67.19.

67.19 Special Issuance of Medical Certificates

1. The Federal Air Surgeon may issue a medical certificate to you (if you do not meet the standards) if you show that you can perform the duties authorized by the certificate without endangering air commerce during that period (e.g., two years for a third-class medical certificate).

  a. The Federal Air Surgeon may authorize a special medical flight test, practical test, or medical evaluation for this purpose.

2. In issuing a medical certificate under this section, the Federal Air Surgeon may do any or all of the following:

  a. Limit the duration of the certificate.

  b. Condition the continued effect of the certificate on the result of subsequent medical tests, examinations, or evaluations.

    c. Impose any operational limitation on the certificate needed for safety.

    d. Condition the continued effect of a third-class medical certificate on compliance with a statement of functional limitations issued to you in coordination with the Director, Flight Standards Service.

Part 67 sections not outlined above and on pages 37 and 38:

Subpart A -- General

67.3   Access to the National Driver Register
67.11 Issue
67.12 Certification of foreign airmen
67.13 First-class medical certificate
67.15 Second-class medical certificate
67.20 Applications, certificates, logbooks, reports, and records: Falsification, reproduction or alteration.

Subpart B -- Certification Procedures

67.21 Applicability
67.23 Medical examinations: Who may give
67.25 Delegation of authority
67.27 Denial of medical certificate
67.29 Medical certificates by senior flight surgeons of armed forces
67.31 Medical records

Part 91 -- GENERAL OPERATING AND FLIGHT RULES

Subpart A -- General

91.1 Applicability

1. This part prescribes rules governing the operation of aircraft within the U.S., including the waters within 3 NM of the U.S. coast.

91.3 Responsibility and Authority of the Pilot in Command

1. As the pilot in command of an aircraft you are directly responsible for, and are the final authority as to, the operation of that aircraft.

2. Thus, in emergencies, you may deviate from the FARs to the extent needed to maintain the safety of the airplane and passengers.

3. A written report shall be filed with the FAA upon request.

91.7 Civil Aircraft Airworthiness

1. You may not operate an aircraft that is not in an airworthy condition.

2. You, as the pilot in command, are responsible for determining whether the aircraft is fit for safe flight.

91.9 Civil Aircraft Flight Manual, Marking, and Placard Requirements

1. You may not operate an aircraft that has an approved flight manual unless that manual is aboard the aircraft.

2. You may not operate contrary to any limitations specified in that manual.

91.11 Prohibition against Interference with Crewmembers

1. No person may intimidate, assault, threaten, or interfere with a crewmember while (s)he is performing his/her duties aboard an aircraft.

91.13 Careless or Reckless Operation

1.   You may not operate an aircraft in a careless or reckless manner so as to endanger the life or property of another.

91.15 Dropping Objects

1.   Dropping objects from an airplane is not prohibited provided you take reasonable precautions to avoid injury or damage to persons or property.

91.17 Alcohol or Drugs

1.   You may not act, or attempt to act, as a crewmember of a civil aircraft:

   a.   While under the influence of drugs or alcohol.
   b.   Within 8 hr. after the consumption of any alcoholic beverage.
   c.   While having .04% by weight or more alcohol in your blood.
   d.   While using any drug that affects your faculties in any way contrary to safety.

2.   Except in an emergency, no person who appears to be under the influence of drugs or alcohol (except those under medical care) may be carried aboard an aircraft.

91.19 Carriage of Narcotic Drugs; Marijuana, and Depressant or Stimulant Drugs or Substances

1.   You may not operate an aircraft within the United States with knowledge that any of these substances are aboard. This does not apply to flights that are authorized by the Federal government or a state government or agency.

91.25 Aviation Safety Reporting Program: Prohibition against Use of Reports for Enforcement Purposes

1.   The FAA will not use reports submitted to the National Aeronautics and Space Administration (NASA) under the Aviation Safety Reporting Program (ASRP) in any enforcement action except those concerning criminal offenses and/or accidents.

   a.   ASRP is a voluntary program designed to encourage a flow of information concerning deficiencies and discrepancies in the aviation system. It is explained in AC 00-46 Aviation Safety Reporting Program.

   b.   The primary objective is to obtain information to evaluate and enhance the safety and efficiency of the present system. Operations covered include:

      1)   Departure, en route, approach, and landing operations and procedures.
      2)   ATC procedures.
      3)   Pilot/controller communications.
      4)   Aircraft movement on the airport.
      5)   Near midair collisions.

   c.   NASA acts as an independent third party to receive and analyze these reports.

      1)   NASA ensures that no information which might reveal the identity of any party involved in an occurrence or incident reported under the ASRP is released to the FAA, except:

         a)   Information concerning criminal offenses, and

         b)   Information concerning accidents.

         c)   Reports concerning criminal activities or accidents are not de-identified prior to their referral to the appropriate agency.

      2)   Each report (see page 41) has a tear-off portion which contains your name and address. This portion is returned to you with a date indicating NASA's receipt of the report.

Form Approved. OMB No. 04–R0206

IDENTIFICATION STRIP: *Please fill in all blanks. This section will be returned to you promptly; no record will be kept.*

TELEPHONE NUMBERS where we may reach you
for further details of this occurrence:

AREA_____ NO._____ HOURS_____

AREA_____ NO._____ HOURS_____

TYPE OF OCCURRENCE/INCIDENT:_____

_____

DATE OF OCCURRENCE_____

TIME *(local, 24-hr. clock)*_____

NAME_____

ADDRESS_____

_____

_____

_____

(This space reserved for NASA receipt stamp)

Please fill in appropriate spaces and circle or check all terms which apply to this occurrence or incident.

1. **Location:** *(Geographic (including State), airport, runway, ATC facility and sector, navigation aid reference, etc.)*

2. **Type of operation:**

SCHEDULED AIR CARRIER	SUPPLEMENTAL CARRIER	CORPORATE AVIATION	MILITARY: ARMY
DOMESTIC OPERATION	CHARTER OPERATION	PERSONAL BUSINESS	NAVY/CG/MC
INTERNATIONAL OPN.	UTILITY OPERATION	PLEASURE FLIGHT	AIR FORCE
AIR TAXI	AGRICULTURAL OPN.	TRAINING FLIGHT	GOVERNMENT

3. **Type of aircraft:**

FIXED WING, LOW	RETRACTABLE GEAR	RECIPROCATING	GROSS WT.: <2500	25,000-50,000
HIGH WING	CONST. SPEED PROP	TURBOPROP	2500-5000	50,000-100,000
ROTARY WING	FLAPS	TURBOJET	5000-12,500	100,000-300,000
NO. OF SEATS:	NO. OF ENGINES:	WIDE BODY JET	12,500-25,000	OVER 300,000

4. **Second aircraft TYPE:** *(if two aircraft involved)*

5. **Reported by:** PILOT   CREWMEMBER   CONTROLLER   OTHER *(specify)*
   If pilot: TOTAL HOURS: HRS. LAST 90 DAYS:

6. **Light conditions:** DAWN   DAYLIGHT   DUSK   NIGHT   7. **Altitude:**   FEET MSL.

8. **Flight plan:** IFR   VFR   DVFR   SVFR   NONE   9. **Flight conditions:**   VFR   IFR

10. **Flight phase:** PREFLIGHT   TAXI   TAKEOFF   CLIMB   CRUISE   DESCENT
    HOLDING   TRAFFIC PATTERN   APPROACH   LANDING   MISSED APPROACH

11. **Airspace:** POSITIVE CONTROL AREA (PCA)   TERMINAL CONTROL AREA (TCA)   ON AIRWAYS
    AIRPORT TRAFFIC AREA   UNCONTROLLED AIRSPACE

12. **Air Traffic Control:** GROUND   TOWER   DEPARTURE   CENTER   APPROACH   FSS   NONE

13. **Weather factors:** RESTRICTED VISIBILITY   TURBULENCE   THUNDERSTORM   AIRCRAFT ICING
    CROSSWIND   PRECIPITATION   NONE   OTHER *(specify)*

14. *(Circle all which you believe apply to this occurrence)*
    AIRPORT   AIR TRAFFIC CONTROL   AIR NAVIGATION FACILITY   AIRCRAFT
    FLIGHT CREW   AERONAUTICAL PUBLICATIONS/CHARTS   OTHER *(specify below)*

15. **NARRATIVE DESCRIPTION:** *(Please describe the occurrence as clearly and precisely as possible. Include information on: what happened . . . how was the problem discovered . . . what actions were taken . . . was evasive action required . . . what factors contributed to the situation . . . why do you believe the situation occurred . . . your suggestions as to how to prevent a recurrence.*
    USE BOTH SIDES OF THE FORM, AS REQUIRED.)

FIRST FOLD HERE   FIRST FOLD HERE

Continue on other side.

NASA ARC Form 277 (March 1976)

d. The filing of a report concerning an incident or occurrence involving a violation of the FARs is considered by the FAA to be an indication of a constructive attitude. Such an attitude will help prevent future violations. Accordingly, although a finding of a violation may be made, neither a civil penalty nor certificate suspension will be imposed if:

1) The violation was inadvertent and not deliberate.

2) The violation did not involve a criminal offense or action which shows a lack of qualification or competency.

3) The person has not been found in any prior FAA enforcement action to have committed a violation of the FARs for a period of 5 years prior to the date of the occurrence.

4) The person proves (by the returned identification portion) that, within 10 days after the violation, (s)he completed and delivered or mailed a written report of the incident to NASA under the ASRP.

2. If you believe you have violated an FAR and may be subject to an enforcement action, you can complete and mail a NASA ARC Form 277 (available from FSS and FSDO offices) within 10 days and avoid possible enforcement action.

a. You should also use the form to report any deficiencies and discrepancies in our aviation system.

b. NASA ARC Form 277 is reproduced on page 41.

Subpart B -- Flight Rules

91.101 Applicability

1. This subpart prescribes flight rules governing the operation of aircraft within the U.S. and within 12 NM from the coast of the U.S.

91.103 Preflight Action

1. You are required to familiarize yourself with all available information concerning the flight prior to every flight, and specifically to determine:

a. For any flight, runway lengths at airports of intended use and your airplane's takeoff and landing requirements.

b. For a cross-country flight, weather reports and forecasts, fuel requirements, alternatives available if the flight cannot be completed as planned, and any known traffic delays.

91.105 Flight Crewmembers at Stations

1. Required flight crewmembers' seatbelts must be fastened while the crewmembers are at their stations.

2. Required flight crewmembers must keep their shoulder harnesses fastened, if available, during takeoff and landing.

91.107 Use of Safety Belts

1. You may not take off without first briefing your passengers on how to use the seatbelts and shoulder harnesses, if available.

2. You must also notify them and they must use their seatbelts during taxi, takeoff, and landing.

91.111 Operating near Other Aircraft

1. You may not operate your airplane so close to another aircraft as to create a collision hazard.

2. You may not operate your airplane in formation flight except by arrangement with the pilot in command of each aircraft in the formation.

91.113 Right-of-Way Rules: Except Water Operations

1. *Converging.* When aircraft of the same category are converging at approximately the same altitude (except head-on), the aircraft to the right has the right-of-way.

    a. Balloons, gliders, and airships have the right-of-way over an airplane.

    b. Aircraft towing or refueling other aircraft have the right-of-way over all other engine-driven aircraft.

2. *Approaching head-on.* The pilot of each aircraft shall alter course to the right.

3. *Overtaking.* An aircraft that is being overtaken has the right-of-way.

    a. The overtaking aircraft shall alter course to the right.

4. *Landing.* Aircraft while on final approach to land or while landing have the right-of-way over other aircraft in flight or on the ground.

    a. When two or more aircraft are approaching the airport for landing, the lower aircraft has the right-of-way.

        1) You may not take advantage of this rule to cut in front of another aircraft which is on final approach or to overtake that aircraft.

91.117 Aircraft Speed

1. You may not operate an airplane at an indicated airspeed greater than 250 kt. if you are under 10,000 ft. MSL or operating within a TCA.

2. When operating in an Airport Traffic Area, you are limited to 200 kt. (This does not apply to any operations within a TCA.)

3. You may not operate under a TCA or in a VFR corridor through a TCA at an indicated airspeed greater than 200 kt.

4. If your minimum safe speed in your airplane is faster than the speed normally allowed, you may operate at that minimum safe speed.

91.119 Minimum Safe Altitudes: General

1. Except for takeoff and landing, the following altitudes are required:

    a. You must have sufficient altitude for an emergency landing without undue hazard to persons or property on the surface if your engine fails.

    b. Over congested areas of a city, town, or settlement, or over an open-air assembly of persons, you must have 1,000 ft. of clearance over the highest obstacle within 2,000-ft. radius of your airplane.

    c. Over other than congested areas, an altitude of 500 ft. above the surface.

    d. Over open water or sparsely populated areas, you must remain at least 500 ft. from any person, vessel, vehicle, or structure.

91.121 Altimeter Settings

1. At all times you must maintain a cruising altitude or flight level by reference to an altimeter that has been set to

    a. The current reported altimeter setting of a station along the route and within 100 NM of your aircraft,

    b. An appropriate available station, or

    c. The elevation of your departure airport or an appropriate altimeter setting available before departure.

91.123 Compliance with ATC Clearances and Instructions

1.   Once an ATC clearance has been obtained, you may not deviate from that clearance unless you obtain an amended clearance, except in an emergency.

    a.   If you deviate from a clearance in an emergency, you must notify ATC as soon as possible.

    b.   If you are given priority by ATC in an emergency, you must submit a detailed report of the emergency within 48 hr. to the manager of that ATC facility, if requested.

        1)   This may be requested even if you do not deviate from any rule of Part 91.

2.   If you are uncertain about the meaning of an ATC clearance, you should immediately ask for clarification from ATC.

91.125 ATC Light Signals

1.   ATC light signals have the meaning shown in the following table:

Light Signal	On the Ground	In the Air
Steady Green	Cleared for takeoff	Cleared to land
Flashing Green	Cleared to taxi	Return for landing *(to be followed by steady green at proper time)*
Steady Red	Stop	Give way to other aircraft and continue circling
Flashing Red	Taxi clear of runway in use	Airport unsafe -- Do not land
Flashing White	Return to starting point on airport	Not applicable
Alternating Red and Green	General warning signal -- Exercise extreme caution	General warning signal -- Exercise extreme caution

91.127 Operating on or in the Vicinity of an Airport: General Rules

1.   When operating to or from an airport without an operating control tower, you should make all turns in the traffic pattern to the left unless the airport displays light signals or markings indicating right turns.

    a.   When departing, you must comply with the established traffic pattern for that airport.

2.   You may not operate your airplane within an airport traffic area except for the purpose of landing at, or taking off from, an airport within that area.

    a.   ATC may authorize exceptions.

91.129 Operation at Airports with Operating Control Towers

1.   Communications with control towers operated by the U.S.

    a.   You may not, within an airport traffic area, operate your airplane to, from, or on an airport having a control tower operated by the U.S. unless two-way radio communication is maintained with the control tower.

        1)   If your radio fails in flight, you may operate your airplane and land if weather conditions are at or above basic VFR weather minimums, visual contact with the tower is maintained, and a clearance to land is received (e.g., light signal).

2. Communications with other control towers.

    a. If your airplane's radio equipment allows, you should maintain two-way radio communications with the tower.

    b. If your airplane's radio only allows reception from the tower, you should monitor the tower's frequency.

3. When operating to an airport with an operating control tower, and you are approaching to land on a runway served by a visual approach slope indicator, you must remain at or above the glide slope until a lower altitude is necessary for a safe landing.

    a. This does not prohibit you from making normal bracketing maneuvers above or below the glide slope for the purpose of remaining on the glide slope.

4. When approaching to land you should make left turns in the traffic pattern unless directed otherwise by the tower.

5. When departing you must comply with any departure procedures established for that airport by the FAA.

6. You may not operate your airplane on a runway or taxiway, or take off or land, unless an appropriate clearance is received by ATC.

91.130 Airport Radar Service Areas

1. You must establish two-way radio communication with the appropriate ATC facility before entering an airport radar service area (ARSA), and maintain communication while you are within the ARSA.

2. If you depart from the primary airport (the airport for which the ARSA is designated) or satellite airport (any other airport within the ARSA) with an operating control tower, two-way radio communication must be established and maintained with the tower and as instructed by ATC while in the ARSA.

    a. From a satellite airport without an operating control tower, you must establish two-way radio communication with ATC as soon as practicable.

3. Unless otherwise authorized by the ATC facility having jurisdiction over the ARSA, you must have a transponder with altitude encoding while operating in the ARSA, and the airspace above the ceiling and within the lateral boundaries of the ARSA.

91.131 Terminal Control Areas

1. You must have an ATC clearance to operate in a TCA.

2. If it is necessary to conduct training operations within the TCA, procedures established for these flights within the TCA will be followed.

3. In order to land at an airport within the TCA or even operate within the TCA, you must:

    a. Be at least a private pilot; or

    b. Be a student pilot who has been instructed and authorized to operate in that specific TCA by a flight instructor (a specific CFI logbook signoff is required).

4. However, there are certain TCA primary airports that require the pilot to hold at least a private pilot certificate to land or take off. These are the busiest airports such as Atlanta Hartsfield and Chicago O'Hare.

5. The equipment aboard your aircraft must include operative two-way radio communications, and radar transponder with altitude encoding.

91.133 Restricted and Prohibited Areas

1. You may not operate your airplane within a restricted area contrary to the restrictions imposed, or within a prohibited area, unless you have the permission of the using or controlling agency, as appropriate.

91.137 Temporary Flight Restrictions

1. The FAA may issue a Notice to Airmen (NOTAM) to establish temporary flight restrictions

    a. To protect persons and property from a hazard associated with an incident on the surface.

    b. To provide a safe environment for the operation of disaster relief aircraft.

    c. In airspace above events generating a high degree of public interest.

2. When a NOTAM is issued under 1.a., you may not operate your airplane in the area unless it is directed by an official in charge of on-scene emergency activities.

3. When a NOTAM is issued under 1.b., you may not operate your airplane in that area unless one of the following conditions is met:

    a. Your airplane is involved in relief activity and directed by an official in charge on the scene.

    b. Your airplane is carrying law enforcement officials.

    c. The operation is conducted directly to or from an airport in the area or is necessitated because VFR flight is impracticable; notice is given to the proper authority for receiving disaster relief advisories; relief activities are not hampered; and the flight is not solely for observation of the disaster.

    d. Your airplane is carrying properly accredited news representatives; a proper flight plan is filed; and the flight is above the altitude used by relief aircraft.

4. When a NOTAM is issued under 1.c., you may not operate your airplane in the area unless one of the following conditions is met:

    a. See 3.c., except for the notice requirement.
    b. Your airplane is carrying incident or event personnel or law enforcement officials.
    c. See relevant portions of 3.d.

5. Flight plans filed and notice given must include the following:

    a. Aircraft identification, type, and color.
    b. Radio frequencies to be used.
    c. Times of entry and exit from the area.
    d. Name of news organization and purpose of flight.
    e. Any other information requested by ATC.

91.139 Emergency Air Traffic Rules

1. When the Administrator determines that an emergency condition exists, or will exist, relating to the FAA's ability to operate the ATC system and during which normal flight operations conducted under Part 91 cannot be done at the required level of safety and efficiency, the following will be done.

    a. The Administrator immediately issues an air traffic rule or regulation in response to the emergency.

    b. The Administrator or Associate Administrator for Air Traffic may utilize the NOTAM system to provide notification of the issuance of the rule or regulation.

        1) The NOTAMs will have information concerning the rules and regulations that govern flight operations, navigational facilities, and the designation of that airspace in which the rules and regulations apply.

2. When a NOTAM has been issued under this section, you may not operate your airplane within the designated airspace, except in accordance with the authorizations, terms, and conditions prescribed in the regulation covered by the NOTAM.

91.141 Flight Restrictions in the Proximity of the Presidential and Other Parties

1. You may not operate your airplane over or in the vicinity of any area to be visited or travelled by the President, the Vice President, or other public figures contrary to the restrictions established by the FAA in a NOTAM.

91.143 Flight Limitations in the Proximity of Space Flight Operations

1. You may not operate your airplane within the areas designated by NOTAM for space flight operation except when authorized by ATC.

91.151 Fuel Requirements for Flight in VFR Conditions

1. You may not fly VFR during the day unless there is enough fuel to fly to the destination and then at least 30 min. beyond that.

2. You may not fly VFR at night unless there is enough fuel to fly to the destination and at least 45 min. beyond that.

91.153 VFR Flight Plan; Information Required

1. Unless authorized by ATC, when filing a VFR flight plan you will include the following information:

    a. Aircraft identification number and, if necessary, radio call sign.
    b. Type aircraft.
    c. Full name and address of pilot in command.
    d. Point and proposed time of departure.
    e. Proposed route, cruising altitude, and true airspeed.
    f. Point of first intended landing and the estimated time en route.
    g. Amount of fuel on board (in hours).
    h. Number of persons in the airplane.
    i. Any other information you or ATC believes is necessary.

2. If a flight plan has been activated, the pilot in command should notify the appropriate authority (i.e., Flight Service Station) upon canceling or completing the flight.

91.155 Basic VFR Weather Minimums

1. Except as provided in this section and 91.157, you may not operate your airplane under VFR when the flight visibility is less, or at a distance from clouds that is less, than prescribed for the corresponding altitude in the following table:

BASIC VFR WEATHER MINIMUMS

Altitude	Flight Visibility	Distance From Clouds
1,200 feet or less above the surface— Within controlled airspace:	3 statute miles	500 feet below. 1,000 feet above. 2,000 feet horizontal.
Outside controlled airspace: Day: (except as provided in section 91.155(b))	1 statute mile	Clear of clouds.
Night: (except as provided in section 91.155(b))	3 statute miles	500 feet below. 1,000 feet above. 2,000 feet horizontal.
More than 1,200 feet above the surface but less than 10,000 feet MSL— Within controlled airspace:	3 statute miles	500 feet below. 1,000 feet above. 2,000 feet horizontal.
Outside controlled airspace: Day:	1 statute mile	500 feet below. 1,000 feet above. 2,000 feet horizontal.
Night:	3 statute miles	500 feet below. 1,000 feet above. 2,000 feet horizontal.
More than 1,200 feet above the surface and at or above 10,000 feet MSL—.	5 statute miles	1,000 feet below. 1,000 feet above. 1 mile horizontal.

2. You may operate your airplane outside of controlled airspace below 1,200 ft. AGL when the visibility is less than 3 SM but not less than 1 SM at night if you are operating in an airport traffic pattern within ½ mi. of the runway.

3. Except as provided in 91.157, you may not operate your airplane under VFR within a control zone beneath the ceiling when the ceiling is less than 1,000 ft.

   a. You may not take off, land, or enter the traffic pattern of an airport unless ground visibility is at least 3 SM. If ground visibility is not reported, flight visibility must be at least 3 SM.

91.157 Special VFR Weather Minimums

1. These special minimums apply to VFR traffic operating in a control zone with a special ATC clearance.

2. You must be clear of clouds.

3. Flight visibility must be at least 1 SM.

4. To take off or land under VFR, ground visibility must be at least 1 SM. If that is not reported, flight visibility during landing or takeoff must be at least 1 SM.

5. Operation under special VFR at night is prohibited unless both the pilot and aircraft are IFR capable.

91.159 VFR Cruising Altitude or Flight Level

1. All VFR aircraft above 3,000 ft. AGL and below 18,000 ft. MSL in level cruising flight must maintain specified altitudes.

2. The altitude prescribed is based upon the magnetic course (not magnetic heading).

3. For magnetic courses of 0° to 179°, use odd thousand foot MSL altitudes plus 500 ft., e.g., 3,500, 5,500, or 7,500.

4. For magnetic courses of 180° to 359°, use even thousand foot MSL altitudes plus 500 ft., e.g., 4,500, 6,500, or 8,500.

Subpart C -- Equipment, Instrument, and Certificate Requirements

91.203 Civil Aircraft: Certifications Required

1. You may not operate a civil aircraft unless it has in it:

    a. An appropriate and current airworthiness certificate which is posted near the aircraft entrance for passengers and crew to see.

    b. A registration certificate issued to the aircraft owner.

91.205 Powered Civil Aircraft with Standard Category U.S. Airworthiness Certificates: Instrument and Equipment Requirements

1. You may not operate a powered civil aircraft with a standard category U.S. airworthiness certificate without the specified operable instruments and equipment.

2. Required Equipment: VFR - day

    a. Airspeed indicator.

    b. Altimeter.

    c. Magnetic direction indicator (compass).

    d. Tachometer for each engine.

    e. Oil pressure gauge for each engine using a pressure system.

    f. Temperature gauge for each liquid-cooled engine.

    g. Oil temperature gauge for each air-cooled engine.

    h. Manifold pressure gauge for each altitude engine.

    i. Fuel gauge indicating the quantity of fuel in each tank.

    j. Landing gear position indicator if the aircraft has a retractable landing gear.

    k.   Approved flotation gear for each occupant and one pyrotechnic signaling device if the aircraft is operated for hire over water beyond power-off gliding distance from shore.

    l.   Safety belt with approved metal to metal latching device for each occupant.

    m. For small civil airplanes manufactured after July 18, 1978, an approved shoulder harness for each front seat.

3.   Required Equipment: VFR - night.

    a.   All equipment listed in 2. above.

    b.   Approved position (navigation) lights.

    c.   Approved aviation red or white anticollision light system on all U.S.-registered civil aircraft.

    d.   If the aircraft is operated for hire, one electric landing light.

    e.   An adequate source of electricity for all electrical and radio equipment.

    f.   A set of spare fuses or three spare fuses for each kind required which are accessible to the pilot in flight.

91.207 Emergency Locator Transmitters

1.   ELT batteries must be replaced after 1 cumulative hr. of use or after 50% of their useful life expires.

2.   Airplanes may be operated for training purposes within 50 mi. of the originating airport without an ELT.

3.   The expiration date for batteries used in an ELT must be legibly marked on the outside of the transmitter.

91.209 Aircraft Lights

1.   During the period from sunset to sunrise, you may not operate an aircraft unless it has lighted position lights.

2.   You may not park or move an aircraft in, or in dangerous proximity to, a night flight operations area of an airport unless the aircraft:

    a.   Is clearly illuminated,
    b.   Has lighted position lights, or
    c.   Is in an area which is marked by obstruction lights.

3.   During the period of sunset to sunrise you must use anticollision lights (i.e., rotating beacon and/or strobe lights) if your airplane is so equipped.

    a.   The anticollision light may be turned off if you (the pilot in command) determine that it would be in the interest of safety, given the operating conditions, to turn it off.

91.211 Supplemental Oxygen

1.   At cabin altitudes above 12,500 ft. MSL up to and including 14,000 ft. MSL, the required minimum crew must use oxygen after 30 min. at those altitudes.

2.   At cabin altitudes above 14,000 ft. MSL, the required minimum flight crew must continuously use oxygen.

3.   At cabin altitudes above 15,000 ft. MSL, each passenger must be provided supplemental oxygen.

91.213 Inoperative Instruments and Equipment (also see page 14 in Chapter 2)

1. You may not take off in an aircraft with inoperable instruments or equipment installed unless:

   a. An approved minimum equipment list (MEL) exists for that specific aircraft. Note that the MEL is a list of equipment that does NOT have to be operable.

      1) This includes the different flight limitations placed upon the aircraft when that equipment is inoperative, e.g., you cannot fly at night if the landing light is out.

   b. The aircraft has within it a letter of authorization, issued by the FAA FSDO in the area where the operator is based, authorizing operation of the aircraft under the minimum equipment list. The MEL and authorization letter constitute an STC (supplemental type certificate) for the aircraft.

   c. The approved MEL must:

      1) Be prepared in accordance with specified limitations.

      2) Provide how the aircraft is to be operated with the instruments and equipment in an inoperable condition.

   d. The aircraft records available to you must include an entry describing the inoperable instruments and equipment.

   e. The aircraft must be operated under all applicable conditions and limitations contained in the MEL.

2. The following instruments and equipment may NOT be included in an MEL:

   a. Instruments and equipment that are specifically or otherwise required by the airworthiness requirements under which the aircraft is type-certificated and which are essential to the safe operation of the aircraft.

   b. Instruments and equipment required by an Airworthiness Directive.

   c. Instruments and equipment required for operations by the FARs.

3. Except as described above, you may take off with inoperative equipment and NO MEL if:

   a. An FAA Master MEL has not been developed by the FAA and the inoperative equipment is not required by the aircraft manufacturer's equipment list, any other FARs, ADs, etc.

   b. If an FAA Master MEL (MMEL) exists, and the inoperative equipment is not required by the MMEL, the aircraft manufacturer's equipment list, any other FARs, ADs, etc.

   c. The inoperative equipment is removed, or deactivated and placarded "inoperative."

   d. You or an appropriate maintenance person determines that the inoperative equipment does not constitute a hazard.

   e. Then the aircraft is deemed to be in a "properly altered condition" by the FAA.

4. Special flight permits (from the FAA) are possible under FAR 21 when the above requirements cannot be met.

5. Author's note: 91.213 applies the MEL concept to all aircraft but provides an "out" for Part 91 operations if an FAA Master MEL has not been developed for a particular type of aircraft **or** the equipment is not required by the Master MEL, the aircraft manufacturer's equipment list, FARs, ADs, etc.

91.215 ATC Transponder and Altitude Reporting Equipment and Use

1. Mode C is required in all TCAs, ARSAs, and in the positive control area (above 18,000 ft. MSL).

2. All aircraft certified with an engine-driven electrical system must have the appropriate transponder equipment (Mode C)

   a. Within 30 NM of the primary airport of a TCA from the surface up to 10,000 ft. MSL.

   b. Above 10,000 ft. MSL and below the floor of the positive control area, excluding airspace at or below 2,500 ft. AGL.

3. All aircraft must have Mode C transponder equipment

   a. Within ARSAs and when above the ceiling and within the lateral limits of the ARSA.

   b. Within 10 NM of specified airports (except below 1,200 ft. AGL outside of the airport traffic area).

91.217 Data Correspondence between Automatically Reported Pressure Altitude Data and the Pilot's Altitude Reference

1. You may not operate your transponder on Mode C (automatic pressure altitude reporting equipment):

   a. When ATC directs you to turn off Mode C, or

   b. Unless, as installed, the equipment was tested and calibrated to transmit altitude data within 125 ft. of the altimeter used to maintain flight altitude for altitudes ranging from sea level to maximum operating altitude of the airplane, or

   c. Unless the altimeters and digitizers in that equipment meet certain specified standards.

Subpart D -- Special Flight Operations

91.303 Aerobatic Flight

1. Aerobatic flight is not permitted

   a. Over any congested area of a city, town, or settlement.
   b. Over an open air assembly of persons.
   c. Within a control zone or Federal airway.
   d. Below an altitude of 1,500 ft. AGL.
   e. When flight visibility is less than 3 SM.

2. Aerobatic flight means an intentional maneuver involving an abrupt change in an aircraft's attitude, an abnormal attitude, or abnormal acceleration, not necessary for normal flight.

91.305 Flight Test Areas

1. Flight tests may only be conducted over open water or sparsely populated areas, having light air traffic.

91.307 Parachutes and Parachuting

1. Emergency parachutes cannot be carried aboard an airplane unless they meet FAA specifications.

2. Except in emergencies, persons may not make parachute jumps from airplanes unless in accordance with FAR 105.

3. Unless each occupant of the aircraft is wearing an approved parachute, no pilot of a civil aircraft carrying any person (other than a crewmember) may execute any intentional maneuver that exceeds

   a. A bank of 60° relative to the horizon, or
   b. A nose-up or nose-down attitude of 30° relative to the horizon.

4. Paragraph 3. does not apply to flight tests for pilot certifications or ratings, or to spins and other flight maneuvers required for any certificate or rating if given by a CFI.

Subpart E -- Maintenance, Preventive Maintenance, and Alterations

91.401 Applicability

1. This subpart gives the rules governing maintenance, preventive maintenance, and the alteration of U.S. registered aircraft.

91.403 General

1. The owner or operator of an aircraft is primarily responsible for maintaining the aircraft in an airworthy condition.

2. You may not perform work on aircraft in a manner contrary to this subpart.

3. You may not operate an aircraft contrary to any airworthiness limitations specified by the manufacturer. This includes following the required replacement time, inspection intervals, and related procedures.

91.405 Maintenance Required

1. Each owner or operator shall have the aircraft inspected as prescribed in 91.409, 91.411, and 91.413.

2. Between inspections, any discrepancies shall be dealt with in accordance with FAR Part 43.

91.407 Operation after Maintenance, Preventive Maintenance, Rebuilding, or Alteration

1. You may not operate an aircraft that has undergone any maintenance, preventive maintenance, rebuilding, or alteration unless:

    a. It has been approved for return to service by a person authorized by FAR 43.7.
    b. The logbook entry required by FARs 43.9 and 43.11 has been made.

2. You may not operate an aircraft that has significantly been altered or rebuilt, to the extent that it changes its flight characteristics, until it has been test-flown by an appropriately rated pilot with at least a Private Pilot certificate.

91.409 Inspections

1. Annual inspections are good through the last day of the 12th calendar month after the previous annual inspection.

2. For commercial operations, an inspection is required every 100 hr.

    a. The 100 hr. may not be exceeded by more than 10 hr. if necessary to reach a place at which an inspection can be performed.

    b. The next inspection, however, is due 200 hr. from the prior inspection; e.g., if the inspection is done at 105 hr., the next inspection is due in 95 hr.

    c. If you have an inspection done prior to 100 hr., you cannot add the time remaining to 100 hr. to the next inspection.

91.413 ATC Transponder Tests and Inspections

1. You may not use an ATC Transponder unless it has been tested within the last 24 calendar months and found to comply with Appendix F of FAR Part 43.

2. The test must be done by a certified repair shop.

91.415 Changes to Aircraft Inspection Programs

1. Whenever the FAA determines that a change is required in the approved aircraft inspection program is necessary to maintain safety, the owner or operator shall, after notification, make the required changes.

2. The owner or operator may petition against this change within 30 days of receiving the notice of the change.

91.417 Maintenance Records

1. Each owner or operator shall keep the following records:

   a. Alteration or rebuilding records
   b. 100-hr. inspections
   c. Annual inspections
   d. Progressive and other required inspections.

2. The records must be kept for each aircraft (airframe), engine, propeller, and appliance.

3. Each record shall include a description of the work performed, the date of completion, and the signature and certificate number of the person performing the work.

91.419 Transfer of Maintenance Records

1. Any owner or operator who sells as U.S. registered aircraft must, at the time of the sale, transfer to the new owner the following records:

   a. Records of maintenance, preventive maintenance, and alteration.
   b. Records of all 100-hr., annual, progressive, and other required inspections.

91.421 Rebuilt Engine Maintenance Records

1. The owner or operator may use a new maintenance record for an aircraft engine rebuilt by the manufacturer or a shop approved by the manufacturer.

2. Each shop that grants zero time to an engine shall enter in the new record:

   a. A signed statement of the date it was rebuilt.
   b. Each change made as required by an Airworthiness Directive.
   c. Each change made in compliance with a Manufacturer's Service Bulletin.

3. A rebuilt engine is one that is completely disassembled, inspected, repaired, reassembled, tested, and approved to the same tolerances as new.

Part 91 sections not outlined above and on pages 39 through 53:

Subpart A -- General

91.5   Pilot in command of aircraft requiring more than one required pilot
91.21   Portable electronic devices
91.23   Truth-in-leasing clause requirement in leases and conditional sales contracts

Subpart B -- Flight Rules

General
91.109 Flight instruction; Simulated instrument flight and certain flight tests
91.115 Right-of-way rules: Water operations
91.135 Positive control areas and route segments

Instrument Flight Rules
91.167 Fuel requirements for flight in IFR conditions
91.169 IFR flight plan: Information required
91.171 VOR equipment check for IFR operations
91.173 ATC clearance and flight plan required
91.175 Takeoff and landing under IFR

Part 91 sections not outlined on pages 39 through 54:

91.177 Minimum altitudes for IFR operations
91.179 IFR cruising altitude or flight level
91.181 Course to be flown
91.183 IFR radio communications
91.185 IFR operations: Two-way radio communications failure
91.187 Operation under IFR in controlled airspace: Malfunction reports
91.189 Category II and III operations: General operating rules
91.191 Category II manual
91.193 Certificate of authorization for certain Category II operations

Subpart C -- Equipment, Instrument, and Certificate Requirements

91.219 Altitude alerting system or device: Turbojet-powered civil airplanes
91.221 Traffic alert and collision avoidance system equipment and use

Subpart D -- Special Flight Operations

91.309 Towing: Gliders
91.311 Towing: Other than under § 91.309
91.313 Restricted category civil aircraft: Operating limitations
91.315 Limited category civil aircraft: Operating limitations
91.317 Provisionally certificated civil aircraft: Operating limitations
91.319 Aircraft having experimental certificates: Operating limitations
91.321 Carriage of candidates in Federal elections
91.323 Increased maximum certificated weights for certain airplanes operated in Alaska

Subpart E -- Maintenance, Preventive Maintenance, and Alterations

91.411 Altimeter system and altitude reporting equipment tests and inspections

Subpart F -- Large and Turbine-Powered Multiengine Airplanes

91.501 Applicability
91.503 Flying equipment and operating information
91.505 Familiarity with operating limitations and emergency equipment
91.507 Equipment requirements: Over-the-top or night VFR operations
91.509 Survival equipment for overwater operations
91.511 Radio equipment for overwater operations
91.513 Emergency equipment
91.515 Flight altitude rules
91.517 Smoking and safety belt signs
91.519 Passenger briefing
91.521 Shoulder harness
91.523 Carry-on baggage
91.525 Carriage of cargo
91.527 Operating in icing conditions
91.529 Flight engineer requirements
91.531 Second-in-command requirements
91.533 Flight attendant requirements

Subpart G -- Additional Equipment and Operating Requirements for Large and Transport Category Aircraft

91.601 Applicability
91.603 Aural speed warning device
91.605 Transport category civil airplane weight limitations
91.607 Emergency exits for airplanes carrying passengers for hire
91.609 Flight recorders and cockpit voice recorders
91.611 Authorization for ferry flight with one engine inoperative
91.613 Materials for compartment interiors

Part 91 sections not outlined on pages 39 through 54:

Subpart H -- Foreign Aircraft Operations and Operations of U.S.-Registered Civil Aircraft Outside of the United States

91.701 Applicability
91.703 Operations of civil aircraft of U.S. registry outside of the United States
91.705 Operations within the North Atlantic Minimum Navigation Performance Specifications Airspace
91.707 Flights between Mexico or Canada and the United States
91.709 Operations to Cuba
91.711 Special rules for foreign civil aircraft
91.713 Operation of civil aircraft of Cuban registry
91.715 Special flight authorizations for foreign civil aircraft

Subpart I -- Operating Noise Limits

91.801 Applicability: Relation to Part 36
91.803 Part 125 operators: Designation of applicable regulations
91.805 Final compliance: Subsonic airplanes
91.807 Phased compliance under Parts 121, 125, and 135: Subsonic airplanes
91.809 Replacement airplanes
91.811 Service to small communities exemption: Two-engine, subsonic airplanes
91.813 Compliance plans and status: U.S. operations of subsonic airplanes
91.815 Agricultural and fire fighting airplanes: Noise operating limitations
91.817 Civil aircraft sonic boom
91.819 Civil supersonic airplanes that do not comply with Part 36
91.821 Civil supersonic airplanes: Noise limits

Subpart J -- Waivers

91.903 Policy and procedures
91.905 List of rules subject to waivers

NTSB Part 830 -- NOTIFICATION AND REPORTING OF AIRCRAFT ACCIDENTS OR INCIDENTS AND OVERDUE AIRCRAFT, AND PRESERVATION OF AIRCRAFT WRECKAGE, MAIL, CARGO, AND RECORDS

830.1 Applicability

1. This part concerns reporting accidents, incidents, and certain other occurrences involving U.S. civil aircraft and preservation of the wreckage, mail, cargo, and records.

830.2 Definitions

1. Aircraft Accident -- An occurrence that takes place between the time any person boards an aircraft with the intention of flight until such time as all such persons have disembarked, and in which

    a. Any person suffers death or serious injury as a result of being in or upon the aircraft or by direct contact with the aircraft or anything attached thereto, or

    b. The aircraft receives substantial damage.

2. Fatal injury -- An injury resulting in death within 30 days of the accident.

3. Incident -- An occurrence other than an accident, associated with the operation of an aircraft, that affects or could affect the safety of operations.

4. Operator -- means any person who causes or authorizes the operation of an aircraft, such as the owner, lessee, or bailee of an aircraft.

5. Serious injury -- means any injury that

    a. Requires hospitalization for more than 48 hr., commencing within 7 days from the date the injury was received.

    b. Results in a fracture of any bone (except simple fractures of fingers, toes, or nose).

    c. Causes severe hemorrhages, nerve, muscle, or tendon damage.

    d. Involves injury to any internal organ.

    e. Involves second- or third-degree burns, or any burns affecting more than 5% of the body surface.

6. Substantial damage -- Damage or failure that adversely affects the structural strength, performance, or flight characteristics of the aircraft, and that would normally require major repair or replacement of the affected component.

    a. Engine failure, damage limited to an engine, bent fairings or cowling, dented skin, small punctured holes in the skin or fabric, ground damage to rotor or propeller blades, damage to landing gear, wheels, tires, flaps, engine accessories, brakes, or wingtips are not considered "substantial damage."

830.5 Immediate Notification

1. The nearest NTSB office must be notified immediately when an aircraft is overdue and believed to be involved in an accident, when an accident occurs, or when any of the following incidents occurs:

    a. Flight control system malfunction or failure.

    b. Inability of any required flight crewmember to perform normal flight duties as a result of injury or illness.

    c. Failure of structural components of a turbine engine excluding compressor and turbine blades and vanes.

    d. Inflight fire.

    e. Aircraft collision in flight.

830.6 Information to Be Given in Notification

1. The operator shall file a report on the prescribed form within 10 days after an accident (7 days if an overdue aircraft is missing). A report on an incident for which notification is required shall be filed only upon request.

2. Name of owner, and operator of the aircraft.

3. Name of the pilot in command.

4. Date and time of the accident.

5. Last point of departure and point of intended landing of the aircraft.

6. Position of the aircraft with reference to some easily defined geographical point.

7. Number of persons aboard, number killed, and number seriously injured.

8. Nature of the accident, the weather and the extent of damage to the aircraft, so far as is known.

9. A description of any explosives, radioactive materials, or other dangerous articles carried.

830.10 Preservation of Aircraft Wreckage, Mail, Cargo, and Records

1. The operator of an aircraft is responsible for preserving any aircraft wreckage, cargo, mail, and all records until the Board takes custody.

2. The wreckage may only be disturbed to

    a. Remove persons injured or trapped.
    b. Protect the wreckage from further damage.
    c. Protect the public from injury.

3. When it is necessary to disturb or move aircraft wreckage or mail or cargo, sketches, descriptive notes, and photographs shall be made if possible of the accident locale, including original position and condition of the wreckage and any significant impact marks.

4. The operator of an aircraft involved in an accident or incident shall retain all records and reports, including all internal documents and memoranda dealing with the event, until authorized by the NTSB to the contrary.

830.15 Reports and Statements to Be Filed

1. See 830.6(a) on the previous page.

2. Each crewmember shall, as soon as physically able, attach a statement concerning the facts, conditions, and circumstances relating to the accident or incident.

3. The report shall be filed at the nearest NTSB office.

NTSB DISTRICT OFFICES

ANCHORAGE
222 West 7th Avenue
Room 142, Box 11
Anchorage, AK 99513
(907) 271-5001

ARLINGTON
1200 Copeland Road, Suite 300
Arlington, TX 76011
(817) 885-6800

ATLANTA
1720 Peachtree Street, NW
Atlanta, GA 30309
(404) 347-7385

CHICAGO
31 West 775 N. Avenue
West Chicago, IL 60185
(708) 377-8177

DENVER
4760 Oakland Street
Suite 500
Denver, CO 80239
(303) 361-0611

LOS ANGELES
Federal Building
1515 W. 109th Street
Suite 555
Gardena, CA 90248
(213) 297-1041

MIAMI
8405 N.W. 53rd Street
Miami, FL 33166
(305) 597-4610

NEW YORK
Federal Building, Room 102
JFK International Airport
Parsippany, NJ 11430
(212) 995-3716

SEATTLE
19415 Pacific Highway South
Room 201
Seattle, WA 98188
(206) 764-3782

WASHINGTON (Home Office)
490 L'Enfant Plaza East, S.W.
Washington, D.C. 20594
(202) 382-6714

END OF CHAPTER

CHAPTER FOUR
OPTIMIZING YOUR GROUND AND FLIGHT TRAINING

Working to Be a Private Pilot 59
FAA Written Test vs. FAA Practical Test 60
How Pilots Learn 60
Part 61 vs. Part 141 Flight Training Programs 63
Ground Instruction 63
Flight Instruction 64
Flight Maneuver Analysis Sheets (FMAS) 65

The purpose of this chapter is to help you get the most out of your ground training and your flight training. They should support each other: ground training should facilitate your flight training and vice versa. While your immediate objective is to pass your practical test, your long-range goal is to become a very proficient pilot and enjoy a successful aviation career. Thus, you have to work hard to be able to **do your best**. No one can ask for more!

This is not a filler chapter that can be passed over. The more you get out of each study session, whether in the air or on the ground, the quicker you will become a more proficient pilot. Conscientious study and consideration of the recommendations in this chapter will increase your ability to learn and understand the concepts and motor skills required of private pilots.

WORKING TO BE A PRIVATE PILOT

Training, study, experience, and determination will make you a safe and proficient pilot.

1. **Training:** You are spending 40+ flight hr. as well as much ground time preparing for your private certificate. See pages 34 and 35 (FAR 61.109) in Chapter 3 for a listing of flight experience requirements for the private certificate.

2. **Study:** You have prepared for the FAA written test for your private certificate. Additionally, you should read aviation magazines, newsletters, *AIM*, etc.

   a. Preparation for the private practical test requires study of aeronautical concepts underlying each and every FAA practical test task. Thus, you will build upon your aviation knowledge as you prepare for your private pilot practical test.

3. **Experience:** You are in the process of obtaining 40+ hr. of flight experience.

4. **Determination:** You are committed to always be in control of your airplane in compliance with ATC, FARs, your *POH*, and common sense, as our system really works if you fly by the book.

Therefore, as you work toward your private certification, your goal is to apply your assets of training, study, experience, and determination. Remember that this process does NOT stop once you obtain your certificate.

FAA WRITTEN TEST vs. FAA PRACTICAL TEST

You must pass both! And through careful and systematic planning, you should learn a lot in the process.

The written test, unfortunately, does not determine whether you will be and/or are a safe and proficient pilot. The private pilot written test consists of 50 multiple choice questions taken from a test bank of 708 questions, all of which are available to you in Gleim's *Private Pilot and Recreational Pilot FAA Written Exam*. With a little study and a lot of memorization, it is possible to pass the written test even if you do not understand the underlying concepts.

Conversely, the FAA practical test requires you to demonstrate the knowledge and skill required of private pilots. During your practical test, you are required to explain aviation concepts to your examiner as well as demonstrate maneuvers. In order to explain aviation concepts to your examiner, you must understand the aviation concepts. Thus, the FAA practical test is a good system to motivate private pilot applicants to learn and understand the concepts, skills, and abilities required of private pilots.

HOW PILOTS LEARN

Learning in the broad sense is the change in behavior, knowledge, or sensorimotor skill as a result of experience, practice, effort, etc. We are interested in the narrower (and aviation-related) definitions of knowledge and the sensorimotor skills of flying an airplane, in contrast to other behaviors.

In other words, psychologists have defined many categories of learning, such as classical conditioning, trial-and-error learning, sensorimotor learning, verbal learning, concept learning, and rule learning (Wingfield, p. 8)[1]. We are interested in concept and rule learning (ground school) and sensorimotor learning (flight maneuvers).

Wingfield (p. 25) sets forth a learning model consisting of three major stages: input, storage, and retrieval. Furthermore, he distinguishes between short-term and long-term memory, as diagrammed below.

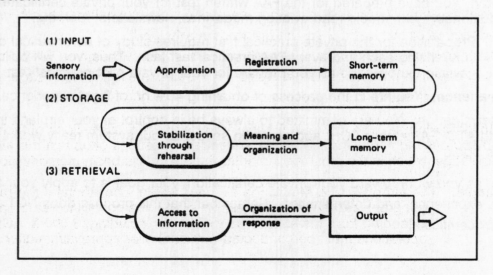

---

[1] Arthur Wingfield, *Human Learning and Memory: An Introduction*, copyright © 1979 by Harper & Row.

While this illustration is very useful, it is an oversimplification because it does not focus on the multidimensionality of knowledge. The multidimensionality of knowledge is how meaning and organization are added to information.

Most aviation concepts are multidimensional. Much more can be learned about an airplane by walking around it and looking at it from all sides (and getting in it, opening the cowling, etc.) than merely viewing a picture of the airplane, which is two-dimensional. Aviation concepts can be better understood by examining their multiple aspects. For example, a flight maneuver may be viewed in light of the

- Objective of the maneuver
- Flight path of the airplane through the maneuver
- Related FARs
- Airplane -- make and model
- Aerodynamic theory
- Weather, e.g., wind

- Airspeeds/power settings
- Visual cues -- horizon
- Flight instrument cues
- Airplane configuration -- flaps and gear
- Altitudes
- Other traffic

This multidimensionality describes understanding, i.e., relating many concepts, rules, relationships. The list of multiple aspects of flight maneuvers is incomplete; take a few minutes to pencil in a few additional dimensions in the margin. As you study, try to interrelate data. Ask and answer the question *WHY?* to all rules, conclusions, and observations.

Levels of Cognitive Ability

In ascending order of complexity, one categorization (Bloom)[2] of the levels of knowledge is

1. Recall knowledge.
2. Understanding to interpret.
3. Application of knowledge to solve problems.
4. Analytical skills.
5. Synthesis.
6. Ability to evaluate.

Each of Bloom's levels of knowledge is discussed briefly. An example of each is presented based on knowledge of airport traffic areas and related knowledge.

Multiple levels of knowledge exist above recall and tend to be cumulative. They constitute building blocks of cognitive processes. To interpret, you need some recall knowledge; to solve problems, you must understand to interpret, etc.

1. **Recall knowledge.** The first level is recall knowledge, e.g., definitions of technical terms and sources of information. The FAA written test questions often test this kind of knowledge, which is the most fundamental since it entails basic memorization.

    Example: The Airport Traffic Area is the airspace within a horizontal 5 SM radius from the geographical center of any airport at which a control tower is operating, extending from the surface up to, but not including, 3,000 ft. AGL. All aircraft operations must be conducted with controller approval/direction.

---

[2]Bloom's *Taxonomy of Educational Objectives*, copyright © 1956 by David McKay Company, Inc.

2. **Understanding to interpret.** The second level of knowledge is the understanding and interpretation of written and quantitative data. Questions at this level test understanding of concepts, including interrelationships within data. This level of knowledge is also called comprehension.

   Example: If there is a blue airport symbol on the VFR Sectional Chart and the letters CT (meaning *control tower*) followed by a frequency, a pilot must use this communications frequency to talk with the controller in the control tower.

3. **Application of knowledge to solve problems.** The third level of knowledge is problem solving. Questions at this level examine practical applications of concepts to solve a problem. Unfortunately, some problem solving is based only on recall knowledge.

   Example: Application of this knowledge occurs when the pilot is actually operating the airplane and about to enter an Airport Traffic Area, determines the control tower frequency and enters it on the radio, lifts the microphone to verbalize a call to the controller, and identifies his/her position to the controller.

4. **Analytical skills.** The fourth level of knowledge is analytical ability, including identification of cause-and-effect relationships, internal inconsistencies or consistencies, relevant and irrelevant items, and underlying assumptions.

   Example: The pilot is given a pattern entry and a traffic report regarding an airplane that is 3 mi. ahead. (S)he must enter the assigned pattern with the underlying assumption that (s)he will be able to adjust his/her glideslope properly for landing. (S)he must also disregard the traffic report as unimportant, since the other airplane will be on the ground well ahead of him/her.

5. **Synthesis.** The fifth level is the ability to put parts together to form a new whole.

   Example: All of the elements of analysis of the controller's clearance -- watching for other traffic and operating the airplane within its stated limitations in existing weather conditions -- must be synthesized to produce a successful approach to the airport.

6. **Ability to evaluate.** The sixth level is evaluative ability. What is the best (most effective) method (alternative)? Evaluation has in common with analysis and synthesis the consideration of qualitative as well as quantitative variables. Qualitative variables are usually multidimensional and thus cannot be meaningfully quantified or measured on a single dimension.

   Example: In evaluating the approach to the airport, the pilot may determine that another type of pattern entry may better facilitate safety. (S)he may ask for an amended clearance, or his/her evaluation may indicate that the currently assigned entry is acceptable.

PART 61 vs. PART 141 FLIGHT TRAINING PROGRAMS

The general requirement for attaining the private pilot certificate is a minimum of 40 hr. of flight. The 40-hr. program laid out in FAR Part 61 is available to anyone in conjunction with a flight program taught by any Certificated Flight Instructor (CFI).

An alternative is to enter a FAR Part 141 training program, which is a program conducted by an FAA approved flight school. Part 141 flight schools are more highly regulated by the FAA and require physical facility inspection, approval of ground school and flight training syllabi, etc. Part 141 flight school will include a minimum of 35 hr. of ground training and a minimum of 35 hr. of flight training. Thus, with 35 hr. of formal ground training, you can save 5 hr. of flight time. (Ground training is required even under Part 61, but Gleim's *Private Pilot Handbook*, *Private Pilot FAA Practical Test Prep*, and *Private Pilot and Recreational Pilot FAA Written Exam* will suffice.) Also, your flight test in a Part 141 program can be conducted by the chief instructor of the school rather than by an FAA-designated examiner or FAA inspector. Most Part 141 programs use audio tapes, programmed learning, etc., which are made available by an airplane manufacturer, e.g., Beech, Cessna, Piper, etc. However, our texts (*Private Pilot Handbook*, *Private Pilot and Recreational Pilot FAA Written Exam*, and *Private Pilot FAA Practical Test Prep*) are a valuable supplement to all Part 141 ground schools.

Do not confuse Part 61 and Part 141 training programs. Part 61 is the standard program. Part 141 is a special program that may or may not be advantageous to a particular student pilot. Also note that it may be complicated to transfer from one Part 141 flight school to another.

Appendix B, FAR Part 141 -- Private Pilot Certification Course (Airplanes), on page 471, contains an excerpt from Appendix A to FAR Part 141 which outlines Part 141 flight training programs. Note the required flight and written tests.

GROUND INSTRUCTION

First and foremost: ground instruction is extremely important to facilitate flight training. Each preflight and postflight discussion *is as important as* the actual flight instruction of each flight training lesson!

Unfortunately, most students and some CFIs incorrectly overemphasize the in-airplane portion of a flight lesson. The airplane, all of its operating systems, ATC, other traffic, etc., are major distractions from the actual flight maneuver and the aerodynamic theory/factors underlying the maneuver. This is not to diminish the importance of dealing with operating systems, ATC, other traffic, etc.

Note: The effort and results are those of the student. Instructors are responsible to direct student effort so that the results are maximized.

Pilots often minimize their effort and are used to instructors (teachers) who are babysitters and/or entertainers. Be honest: to become a proficient pilot is a lot of work, in addition to being costly. You must develop and commit to a mindset that it is worthwhile (rewarding) to become a safe and proficient pilot.

Formal ground school to support flight training generally does **not** exist except at aeronautical universities and Part 141 programs. Most community college, adult education, and FBO ground schools are directed toward FAA written tests.

Again, **the effort and results are those of the student.** Instructors are responsible for directing student effort for maximum results. Prepare for each flight lesson so you know, before the fact, exactly what is going to happen and why. The more you prepare, the better you will do, both in execution of maneuvers and acquisition of knowledge.

1. At the end of each flight lesson, find out exactly what is planned for the next flight lesson.

2. At home, begin by reviewing everything that occurred during the last flight lesson -- preflight briefing, flight, and postflight briefing. Make notes on follow-up questions and discussion with your CFI to occur at the beginning of the next preflight briefing.

3. Study all new flight maneuvers scheduled for the next flight lesson and review flight maneuvers that warrant additional practice (refer to the appropriate chapters in Part II of this book). Make notes on follow-up questions and discussion with your CFI to occur at the beginning of the next preflight briefing.

4. Before each flight sit down with your CFI for a preflight briefing. Begin with a review of the last flight lesson. Then focus on the current flight lesson. Go over each maneuver to be executed, including maneuvers to be reviewed from previous flight lessons.

5. During each flight lesson be diligent about safety (continuously check traffic and say so as you do it). Always use clearing turns. During maneuvers, compare your actual experience with your expectations (based on your prior knowledge from completing your Flight Maneuver Analysis Sheet).

6. Your postflight briefing should begin with a self-critique by you, followed by evaluation by your CFI. Ask questions until you are satisfied that you have expert knowledge.

FLIGHT INSTRUCTION

Once in the airplane, the FAA recommends that your CFI use the *telling and doing* technique:

1. Instructor tells, instructor does.
2. Student tells, instructor does.
3. Student tells, student does.
4. Student does, instructor evaluates.

Each attribute of the maneuver should be discussed before, during, and after execution of the maneuver.

Integrated flight instruction: the FAA pushes instrument flight training in conjunction with initial flight instruction, i.e., "from the first time each maneuver is introduced." The intent is to teach students to perform flight maneuvers both by outside visual references and by reference to flight instruments. This approach was instituted by the FAA in reaction to private pilot accidents after encountering IFR weather conditions.

Integrated flight instruction should be redefined! Additional student home study of flight maneuvers needs to be **integrated** with in-airplane training to make in-airplane training both more effective and more efficient. Effectiveness refers to learning as much as possible (i.e., getting pilot skills *down pat* so as to be a safe and proficient pilot). Efficiency refers to learning as much as possible in a reasonable amount of time.

FLIGHT MANEUVER ANALYSIS SHEET (FMAS)

We have developed a method of analyzing and studying flight maneuvers that incorporates 10 variables. You can remember the items by the vertical listing of letters.

M	Maneuver title
O	Objectives/Purpose
F	Flight path
PS	Power Setting
AL	ALtitude(s)
A	Airspeed(s)
CF	Control Forces
T	Time(s)
TR	TRaffic considerations
CS	Completion Standards

A copy of an FMAS (front and back) appears on pages 66 and 67 for your convenience. When you reproduce the form for your own use, photocopy on the front and back of a single sheet of paper to make the form more convenient. The front side contains space for analysis of the above variables. The back side contains space for

1. Make- and model-specific information:

   a. Weight
   b. Airspeeds
   c. Fuel
   d. Center of gravity
   e. Performance data

2. Flight instrument review of maneuver.

   a. Attitude Indicator .... AI
   b. Airspeed Indicator .... ASI
   c. Turn Coordinator .... TC
   d. Heading Indicator .... HI
   e. Vertical Speed Indicator ..... VSI
   f. Altimeter .... ALT

3. Common errors.

You should prepare/study/review FMAS for each maneuver you intend to perform before each flight lesson. Photocopy the form (front and back) on single sheets of paper. Changes, amplifications, and other notes should be added subsequently. Blank sheets of paper should be attached (stapled) to the FMAS including self-evaluations, *to do* items, questions for your CFI, etc., for your home study during your flight instruction program. FMAS are also very useful to prepare for the practical test.

A major benefit of the FMAS is preflight lesson preparation. It serves as a means to discuss maneuvers with your CFI before and after flight. It emphasizes preflight planning, make and model knowledge, and flight instruments.

Also, the FMAS helps you, in general, to focus on the operating characteristics of your airplane, including weight and balance. Weight and balance, which includes fuel, should be carefully reviewed prior to each flight.

GLEIM'S
FLIGHT MANEUVER ANALYSIS SHEET

CFI _____
Student _____
Date _____

1.   **MANEUVER** _____

2.   **OBJECTIVES/PURPOSE** _____
_____

3.   **FLIGHT PATH (visual maneuvers)**

4.   **POWER SETTINGS**   **5. ALT   6. A/S**

MP	RPM	SEGMENT OF MANEUVER		
_____	_____	a. _____	___	___
_____	_____	b. _____	___	___
_____	_____	c. _____	___	___

Pencil in expected indication on each of 6 flight instruments on reverse side.

7.   **CONTROL FORCES**

a.   _____
_____

b.   _____
_____

c.   _____
_____

8.   **TIME(S), TIMING** _____
_____

9.   **TRAFFIC CONSIDERATIONS**   **CLEARING TURNS REQUIRED** _____
_____

10.   **COMPLETION STANDARDS/ATC CONSIDERATIONS** _____
_____
_____

AIRPLANE MAKE/MODEL _____

WEIGHT

Gross _____
Empty _____
Pilot/Pasngrs _____
Baggage _____
Fuel (gal x 6) _____

AIRSPEEDS

V_{SO} _____
V_{S1} _____
V_X _____
V_Y _____
V_A _____
V_{NO} _____
V_{NE} _____
V_{FE} _____
V_{LO} _____

CENTER OF GRAVITY

Fore Limit _____
Aft Limit _____
Current C.G. _____

ASI	AI	ALT
TC	HI	VSI

PRIMARY vs. SECONDARY INSTRUMENTS

(IFR maneuvers) -- instruments: AI, ASI, ALT, TC, HI, VSI, RPM and/or MP
(most relevant to instrument instruction)

	PITCH	BANK	POWER
ENTRY			
primary	_____	_____	_____
secondary	_____	_____	_____
ESTABLISHED			
primary	_____	_____	_____
secondary	_____	_____	_____

FUEL

Capacity L _____ gal R _____ gal
Current Estimate L _____ gal R _____ gal
Endurance (Hr.) _____
Fuel Flow -- Cruise (GPH) _____

PERFORMANCE DATA

	Airspeed	Power* MP	RPM
Takeoff Rotation	_____	_____	_____
Climbout	_____	_____	_____
Cruise Climb	_____	_____	_____
Cruise Level	_____	_____	_____
Cruise Descent	_____	_____	_____
Approach**	_____	_____	_____
Approach to Land (Visual)	_____	_____	_____
Landing Flare	_____	_____	_____

* If you do not have a constant-speed propeller, ignore manifold pressure (MP).
** Approach speed is for holding and performing instrument approaches.

COMMON ERRORS

_____

_____

_____

_____

END OF CHAPTER

CHAPTER FIVE
YOUR FAA PRACTICAL (FLIGHT) TEST

FAA Practical Test Standard Tasks 70
Format of PTS Tasks 71
Oral Portion of the Practical Test 72
Flight Portion of the Practical Test 72
Airplane and Equipment Requirements 72
What to Take to Your Practical Test 73
Practical Test Application Form 73
Flight Instructor Logbook Endorsement 77
Your Temporary Pilot Certificate 78
Failure on the Flight Test 79

After all the training, studying, and preparation, the final step to receive your private pilot certificate is the FAA practical test. It requires you to demonstrate to your examiner your previously gained knowledge and that you are a proficient and safe private pilot.

Your practical test is merely repeating to an examiner flight maneuvers that are familiar and well practiced. Conscientious flight instructors do not send applicants to an examiner until the applicant can pass the flight test on an average day, i.e., an exceptional flight will not be needed. Theoretically, the only way to fail would be to commit an error beyond the scope of what your CFI expects.

Most applicants pass the private pilot practical test on the first attempt. The vast majority of those having trouble will succeed on the second attempt. This high pass rate is due to the high quality of flight instruction and the fact that most examiners test on a human level, not a NASA shuttle pilot level. The FAA Practical Test Standards (PTSs) required to pass the test are reprinted in Chapters I through XI and again in their entirety in Appendix A (pages 459 to 470). Study Chapters I through XI carefully so you know exactly what will be expected of you. Your goal is to exceed each requirement. This will ensure even a slight mistake will fall within the limits, especially if you recognize it and explain your error to your examiner.

As you proceed with your flight training, you and your instructor should plan ahead and schedule your practical test. Several weeks before your flight test is scheduled, contact one or two individuals who took the private pilot practical test with your FAA-designated examiner. Ask each person to explain the routine, length, emphasis, maneuvers, and any peculiarities (i.e., surprises). This is a very important step because, like all people, examiners are unique. One particular facet of the flight exam may be tremendously important to one examiner, while another examiner may emphasize an entirely different area. By gaining this information beforehand, you can focus on the areas of apparent concern to the examiner. Also, knowing what to expect will relieve some of the apprehension and tension about your flight test.

FAA PRACTICAL TEST STANDARD TASKS

The intent of the FAA is to structure and standardize flight tests by specifying required tasks and acceptable error rates to FAA inspectors and FAA-designated examiners. These tasks (procedures and maneuvers) listed in the PTSs are mandatory on each flight test unless specified otherwise.

The 44 tasks for the private pilot certificate (single-engine airplane) are listed below in 11 areas of operation as organized by the FAA. The six tasks that can be completed away from the airplane are indicated below as "Oral" and are termed "Knowledge Only" tasks by the FAA. The 38 tasks that are usually completed in the airplane are indicated "Flight" and are termed "Knowledge and Skill" tasks by the FAA.

Page*

I. PREFLIGHT PREPARATION
A. Certificates and Documents - Oral 83
B. Obtaining Weather Information - Oral 89
C. Determining Performance and
   Limitations - Oral 98
D. Cross-Country Flight Planning - Oral 114
E. Airplane Systems - Oral 132
F. Aeromedical Factors - Oral 171

II. GROUND OPERATIONS
A. Visual Inspection - Flight 178
B. Cockpit Management - Flight 185
C. Starting Engine - Flight 189
D. Taxiing - Flight 195
E. Pretakeoff Check - Flight 205
F. Postflight Procedures - Flight 211

**III. AIRPORT AND TRAFFIC PATTERN
OPERATIONS**
A. Radio Communications and ATC
   Light Signals - Flight 216
B. Traffic Pattern Operations - Flight 228
C. Airport and Runway Marking and
   Lighting - Flight 239

IV. TAKEOFFS AND CLIMBS
A. Normal and Crosswind Takeoffs
   and Climbs - Flight 252
B. Short-Field Takeoff and Climb - Flight 261
C. Soft-Field Takeoff and Climb - Flight 268

V. CROSS-COUNTRY FLYING
A. Pilotage and Dead Reckoning - Flight 276
B. Radio Navigation - Flight 282
C. Diversion - Flight 294
D. Lost Procedures - Flight 297

Page*

VI. FLIGHT BY REFERENCE TO INSTRUMENTS
A. Straight-and-Level Flight - Flight 306
B. Straight, Constant Airspeed Climbs - Flight .. 309
C. Straight, Constant Airspeed
   Descents - Flight 313
D. Turns to Headings - Flight 317
E. Unusual Flight Attitudes - Flight 321
F. Radio Aids and Radar Services - Flight 326

VII. FLIGHT AT CRITICALLY SLOW AIRSPEEDS
A. Full Stalls -- Power Off - Flight 334
B. Full Stalls -- Power On - Flight 340
C. Imminent Stalls -- Power On and Power
   Off - Flight 346
D. Maneuvering at Critically Slow
   Airspeed - Flight 351
E. Constant Altitude Turns - Flight 356

**VIII. FLIGHT MANEUVERING BY REFERENCE TO
GROUND OBJECTS**
A. Rectangular Course - Flight 364
B. S-Turns across a Road - Flight 371
C. Turns around a Point - Flight 376

IX. NIGHT FLIGHT OPERATIONS
A. Night Flight - Flight 382

X. EMERGENCY OPERATIONS
A. Emergency Approach and Landing
   (Simulated) - Flight 399
B. System and Equipment
   Malfunctions - Flight 408

XI. APPROACHES AND LANDINGS
A. Normal and Crosswind Approaches and
   Landings - Flight 416
B. Forward Slips to Landing - Flight 436
C. Go-Around - Flight 441
D. Short-Field Approach and Landing - Flight .. 446
E. Soft-Field Approach and Landing - Flight ... 452

*Page number on which discussion begins in Chapters I through XI.

In the PTS format, the FAA has done away with reference to "oral tests" and "flight tests." Now the emphasis is that all tasks require oral examining about the applicant's knowledge. Nonetheless, we feel it is useful to separate the "Knowledge Only" tasks from the "Knowledge and Skill" tasks.

This chapter is based on PTSs from FAA-S-8081-1A, dated November 1987 by the FAA. Call your local Flight Standards District Office (FSDO) to determine the most current version of the PTSs. We will revise this First Edition into a Second Edition to reflect the new PTSs when they become available.

FORMAT OF PTS TASKS

Each of the FAA's 44 private pilot tasks listed on the opposite page is presented in a shaded box in Chapters I through XI, similar to Task I.A. reproduced below.

I.A. TASK: CERTIFICATES AND DOCUMENTS

PILOT OPERATION - 1

REFERENCES: FAR Parts 61 and 91; AC 61-21, AC 61-23; Pilot's Handbook and Flight Manual.

Objective. To determine that the applicant:

1. Exhibits knowledge by explaining the appropriate --

   a. pilot certificate, privileges and limitations.

   b. medical certificate, class and duration.

   c. personal pilot logbook or flight record.

   d. FCC station license and operator's permit, as required.

2. Exhibits knowledge by locating and explaining the significance and importance of the --

   a. airworthiness and registration certificates.

   b. operating limitations, handbooks, or manuals.

   c. equipment list.

   d. weight and balance data.

   e. maintenance requirements and appropriate records.

The task number is followed by the title. "Pilot Operation" refers to FAR 61.107(a), which lists 10 pilot operations required of private pilots.

    1. Preflight operations
    2. Airport and traffic pattern operations
    3. Flight maneuvering by reference to ground objects
    4. Flight at slow airspeeds and stall recovery
    5. Normal and crosswind takeoffs and landings
    6. Flight solely by reference to instruments
    7. Cross-country flying
    8. Maximum performance takeoffs and landings
    9. Night flying operations
   10. Emergency operations

Each task will refer to one of the above numbers which provide little, if any, information to you. The references are important, however, and this is where we obtained our discussion and analysis of each task for you. Our discussion and analysis follows each task in Chapters I through XI.

Next the task has "**Objective.** To determine that the applicant . . ." followed by a number of "Exhibits adequate knowledge of . . ." about aviation concepts and "Demonstrates . . ." various maneuvers.

Each task is followed by

A. General information

    1. A sentence explaining how this task relates to other tasks
    2. Explanation of the "pilot operation"
    3. The titles of the FAA's references
    4. The FAA's objective and/or rationale for this task
    5. Any general discussion relevant to the task

B. Comprehensive discussion of each concept or item listed in the FAA's task.

C. Common errors for each of the flight maneuvers, i.e., tasks appearing in Chapters II through XI, relative to knowledge and skill tasks. Chapter I contains "Knowledge Only" tasks.

ORAL PORTION OF THE PRACTICAL TEST

Your practical test will probably begin in your examiner's office. You should have with you this book, your *Pilot's Operating Handbook (POH)* for your airplane, your FARs and AIM, and all of the items listed on page 73 (this is the FAA's list and they omitted the FARs and your *POH*). You also need your FAA Form 8710-1, your Airman Written Test Report (AC Form 8080-2), and a logbook signoff by your CFI.

Your examiner will probably begin by reviewing your paperwork (Form 8710-1, Form 8080-2, logbook signoff, etc.) and receiving payment for his/her services. Typically you will plan a VFR cross-country flight for your examiner with discussion of weather, charts, FARs, etc.

As your examiner asks you questions, attempt to position yourself in a discussion mode with him/her rather than being interrogated by the examiner. Be respectful, but do not be intimidated. Both you and your examiner are professionals. Draw on your knowledge from this book and other books, your CFI, and your prior experience. Ask for amplification of any points your CFI may have appeared uncertain about. If you do not know an answer, try to explain how you would research the answer.

You will do well. You are a good pilot. You have adequately prepared for this discussion by studying the subsequent pages and have worked diligently with your CFI. After you discuss various aspects of the six "Knowledge Only" tasks which we explain thoroughly in Chapter I, Preflight Preparation, you will move out to your airplane to begin your flight test, which consists of 38 "Knowledge and Skill" tasks (explained in Chapters II through XI).

If possible and appropriate in the circumstances, thoroughly preflight your airplane just before you go to your examiner's office. As you and your designated examiner approach your airplane, explain that you have already preflighted the airplane (explain any possible problems and how you resolved them) and volunteer to answer any questions. Also, make sure you walk around the airplane to observe any possible damage by ramp vehicles or other aircraft while you were in your examiner's office.

FLIGHT PORTION OF THE PRACTICAL TEST

As your begin the flight portion of your practical test, your examiner will expect you to depart on the VFR cross-country flight you previously planned. You will taxi out, depart, and proceed on course to your destination.

Your departure procedures usually permit demonstration/testing of many of the tasks in Areas of Operation III, IV, V, and VI. After completing these tasks your examiner will probably have you discontinue your cross-country flight so you can demonstrate additional flight maneuvers. Note that you are required to perform all 44 tasks during your practical test.

Remember that at all times you are the pilot in command of this flight. Take polite, but firm, charge of your airplane and instill in your examiner a confidence in you as a safe and competent pilot.

AIRPLANE AND EQUIPMENT REQUIREMENTS

You are required to provide an appropriate and airworthy aircraft for the practical test. The aircraft must be equipped for, and its operating limitations must not prohibit, the pilot operations required on the test.

WHAT TO TAKE TO YOUR PRACTICAL TEST

The following checklist from the FAA's Practical Test Standards should be reviewed with your instructor both 1 week before and 1 day before your scheduled flight test:

1. Acceptable Airplane with Dual Controls

    a. View-Limiting Device (extended visor cap, foggles, hood)
    b. Aircraft Documents

        1) Airworthiness Certificate
        2) Registration Certificate
        3) Operating Limitations

    c. Aircraft Maintenance Records

        1) Airworthiness Inspections

    d. FCC Station License

2. Personal Equipment

    a. Current Aeronautical Charts
    b. Computer and Plotter
    c. Flight Plan Form
    d. Flight Logs
    e. Current AIM

3. Personal Records

    a. Pilot Certificate
    b. Medical Certificate
    c. Completed Application for an Airman Certificate and/or Rating (FAA Form 8710-1)
    d. Airman Written Test Report (AC Form 8080-2)
    e. Logbook with Instructor's Endorsement for your Private Pilot Practical Test
    f. Notice of Disapproval (only if you previously failed your flight test)
    g. Approved School Graduation Certificate (if applicable)
    h. FCC Radiotelephone Operator Permit (if applicable)
    i. Examiner's Fee (if applicable)

PRACTICAL TEST APPLICATION FORM

Prior to your practical test, you and your instructor will complete FAA Form 8710-1 (which appears on pages 75 and 76), and your instructor will sign the top of the back side of the form and will assist in completing it. An explanation on how to complete the form is attached to the original and we have reproduced it on page 74. The form is not largely self-explanatory. For example, the FAA wants dates shown as 02-14-92, **not** 02/14/92. Also social security and pilot certificate numbers should be written 418721474, not 418-72-1474. Do not go to your practical test without FAA Form 8710-1 properly filled out; remind your CFI about it as you schedule your practical test.

If you are enrolled in a Part 141 flight school, the Air Agency Recommendation block of information on the back side may be completed by the chief instructor of your Part 141 flight school. (S)he, rather than a designated examiner or FAA inspector, will administer the flight test if flight test examining authority has been granted to your flight school.

If your private pilot flight test is with a designated examiner or a Part 141 flight school chief instructor, (s)he will forward this and other required forms (listed on the bottom of the back side) to the nearest FAA Flight Standards District Office (FSDO) for review and approval before they are sent to Oklahoma City, where your new pilot certificate will be issued and mailed to you.

AIRMAN CERTIFICATE AND/OR RATING APPLICATION
INSTRUCTIONS FOR COMPLETING FAA FORM 8710-1

I. APPLICATION INFORMATION *Check appropriate block(s).*

Block A. Name. Enter legal name but no more than one middle name for record purposes and do not change the name on subsequent applications unless it is done in accordance with FAR Section 61.25. If you have no middle name, enter "NMN." If you have a middle initial only, indicate "Initial only." If you are a Jr., or a 2nd or 3rd, so indicate. If you have an FAA pilot certificate, the name on the application should be the same as the name on the certificate unless you have had it changed in accordance with FAR Section 61.25.

Block B. Social Security Number. Optional: See supplemental Information Privacy Act. Do not leave blank: Enter either SSN or the words "Do not use" or "None."

Block C. Date of Birth. Check for accuracy. Enter six digits: Use numeric characters, i.e.; 07-09-25 instead of July 9, 1925. Check to see that DOB is the same as it is on the medical certificate.

Block D. Place of Birth. If you were born in the USA, enter the city and state where you were born. If the city is unknown, enter the county and state. If you were born outside the USA, enter the name of the city and country where you were born.

Block E. Permanent Mailing Address. The residence number and street, or when applicable, P.O. Box or rural route number goes in the top part of the block above the line. The City, State, and ZIP code go in the bottom part of the block below the line. Check for accuracy. Make sure the numbers are not transposed. FAA policy requires that you use your permanent mailing address. **Justification must be provided on a separate sheet of paper and submitted with the application when a P.O. Box or rural route number is used in place of your permanent address.**

Block F. Nationality. Check USA if applicable. If not, enter the country where you are a citizen.

Block G. Do You Read, Speak, and Understand English? Check yes or no.

Block H. Height. Enter your height in inches. Example: 5'9" should be entered as 69 in. No fractions. Whole inches only.

Block I. Weight. Enter your weight in pounds. No fractions. Whole pounds only.

Block J. Hair. Spell out the color of your hair. If bald, enter "Bald." Color should be listed as black, red, brown, blond, or gray. If you wear a wig or toupee, enter the color of your hair under the wig or toupee.

Block K. Eyes. Spell out the color of your eyes. The color should be listed as blue, brown, black, hazel, green, or gray.

Block L. Sex. Check male or female.

Block M. Do You Now Hold or Have You Ever Held An FAA Pilot Certificate? Check yes or no. (NOTE: A student pilot certificate *is* a "Pilot Certificate.")

Block N. Grade Pilot Certificate. Enter the grade of pilot certificate (i.e., Student, Recreational, Private, Commercial, or ATP). Do *NOT* enter flight instructor certificate information.

Block O. Certificate Number. Enter the number as it appears on your pilot certificate.

Block P. Date Issued. Date your pilot certificate was issued.

Block Q. Do You Now Hold A Medical Certificate? Check yes or no. If yes, complete Blocks R, S, and T.

Block R. Class of Certificate. Enter the class as shown on the medical certificate, i.e., 1st, 2nd, or 3rd class.

Block S. Date Issued. Date your medical certificate was issued.

Block T. Name of Examiner. As shown on the medical certificate.

Block U. Narcotics, Drugs, Alcohol. Check appropriate block. This should be checked "Yes" only if you have been actually convicted. If you have been charged with a violation which has not been adjudicated, check "No."

Block V. If block "U" was checked "Yes" give the date of final conviction.

Block W. Glider or free balloon pilots should sign the medical certification in this block, if you do not hold a medical certificate. If you hold a medical certificate, be sure Blocks Q, R, S, and T are completed.

Block X. Date. Date you sign this self-certification statement.

II. CERTIFICATE OR RATING APPLIED FOR ON BASIS OF
Block A. Completion of Required Test.
1. AIRCRAFT TO BE USED (If flight test required) —Make and model. If more than one aircraft is to be used, indicate such.
2. TOTAL TIME IN THIS AIRCRAFT TYPE (Hrs.) —(a) Total Flight Time - In each make and model. (b) Pilot-In-Command Flight Time - In each make and model.

Block B. Military Competence Obtained In. Enter your branch of service, date rated as a military pilot, your rank or grade and service number, and the military aircraft in which you have flown 10 hours as pilot in command in the last 12 months in the boxes indicated.

Block C. Graduate of Approved Course.
1. NAME AND LOCATION OF TRAINING AGENCY / CENTER. As shown on the graduation certificate. Be sure the location is entered.
2. AGENCY SCHOOL/CENTER CERTIFICATION NUMBER. As shown on the graduation certificate.
3. CURRICULUM FROM WHICH GRADUATED. As shown on the graduation certificate.
4. DATE. Date of graduation from indicated course. Approved course graduate must also complete Block "A" *COMPLETION OF REQUIRED TEST.*

Block D. Holder of Foreign License Issued By.
1. COUNTRY. Country which issued the license.
2. GRADE OF LICENSE. Grade of license issued, i.e., private, commercial, etc.
3. NUMBER. Number which appears on the license.
4. RATINGS. All ratings that appear on the license.

Block E. Completion of Air Carrier's Approved Training Program
1. Name of Air Carrier
2. Date program was completed.
3. Identify the Training Cirriculum

III. Record of Pilot Time. The minimum pilot experience required by the appropriate regulation must be entered. It is recommended, however, that *ALL* pilot time be entered. If decimal points are used, be sure they are legible. Night flying must be entered when required. You should fill in the blocks that apply, and ignore the blocks that do not. Training Device/Simulator, Total, instruction received, and Instrument Time should be entered in the top or bottom half of the boxes provided as appropriate.

IV. Have You Failed A Test For This Certificate or Rating Within The Past 30 Days? Check appropriate blocks.

V. Applicant's Certification.
    A. SIGNATURE. The way you normally sign your name.
    B. DATE. The date you sign the application.

TYPE OR PRINT ALL ENTRIES IN INK

Form Approved OMB No: 2120-0021

Airman Certificate and/or Rating Application

U.S. Department of Transportation
Federal Aviation Administration

I Application Information ☐ Student   ☐ Recreational   ☐ Private   ☐ Commercial   ☐ Airline Transport   ☐ Instrument
☐ Additional Aircraft Rating   ☐ Airplane Single-Engine   ☐ Airplane Multiengine   ☐ Rotorcraft   ☐ Glider   ☐ Lighter-Than-Air
☐ Flight Instructor _____ Initial _____ Renewal _____ Reinstatement   ☐ Additional Instructor Rating   ☐ Ground Instructor
☐ Medical Flight Test   ☐ Reexamination   ☐ Reissuance of _____ Certificate   ☐ Other _____

A. Name (Last, First, Middle)	B. SSN (US Only)	C. Date of Birth Mo. Day Year	D. Place of Birth

E. Address (Please See Instructions Before Completing)	F. Nationality (Citizenship) Specify ☐ USA ☐ Other_____	G. Do you read, speak and understand English? ☐ Yes ☐ No
City, State, Zip Code	H. Height ___ in. I. Weight ___ Lbs. J. Hair K. Eyes L. Sex ☐ Male ☐ Female	

M. Do you now hold, or have you ever held an FAA Pilot Certificate? ☐ Yes ☐ No	N. Grade Pilot Certificate	O. Certificate Number	P. Date Issued

Q. Do you hold a Medical Certificate? ☐ Yes ☐ No	R. Class of Certificate	S. Date Issued	T. Name of Examiner

U. Have you been convicted for violation of Federal or State statutes relating to narcotic drugs, marijuana, or depressant or stimulant drugs or substances ☐ Yes ☐ No	V. Date of Final Conviction

W. Glider or Free Balloon Pilots only:	Medical Statement: I have no known physical defect which makes me unable to pilot a glider or free balloon. Signature	X. Date

II Certificate or Rating Applied For on Basis of:

☐ A. Completion of Required Test	1. Aircraft to be used (if flight test required)		2a. Total time in this aircraft hours	2b. Pilot in command hours
☐ B. Military Competence Obtained in	1. Service	2. Date Rated	3. Rank or Grade and Service Number	
	4. Has flown at least 10 hours as pilot in command during the past 12 months in the following military aircraft.			
☐ C. Graduate of Approved Course	1. Name and Location of Training Agency or Training Center			1a Certification Number
	2. Curriculum From Which Graduated			3. Date
☐ D. Holder of Foreign License Issued By	1. Country	2. Grade of License	3. Number	
	4. Ratings			
☐ E. Completion of Air Carrier's Approved Training Program	1. Name of Air Carrier	2. Date	3. Which Curriculum ☐ Initial ☐ Upgrade ☐ Transition	

III Record of Pilot time (Do not write in the shaded areas.)

	Total	Instruction Received	Solo	Pilot in Command	Second in Command	Cross Country Instruction Received	Cross Country Solo	Cross Country Pilot in Command	Instrument	Night Instruction Received	Night Take-off/ Landing	Night Pilot in Command	Night Take-off/ Landing Pilot in Command	Number of Flights	Number of Aero-Tows	Number of Ground Launches	Number of Powered Launches	Number of Free Flights
Airplanes																		
Rotor-craft																		
Gliders																		
Lighter than Air																		
Training Device Simulator																		

IV Have you failed a test for this certificate or rating?   ☐ Yes   ☐ No   **Within the Past 30 days?**   ☐ Yes   ☐ No

V Applicant's Certification — I certify that all statements and answers provided by me on this application form are complete and true to the best of my knowledge, and I agree that they are to be considered as part of the basis for issuance of any FAA certificate to me. I have also read and understand the Privacy Act statement that accompanies this form.

Signature of Applicant   Date

FAA Use Only

EMP	REG	D.O.	SEAL	CON	ISS	ACT	LEV	TR	S.H.	SRCH	#RTE	RATING (1)

FAA Form 8710-1 (7-92) Supersedes Previous Edition

Instructor's Recommendation

I have personally instructed the applicant and consider this person ready to take the test.

Date	Instructor's Signature	Certificate No:	Certificate Expires

Air Agency's Recommendation

The applicant has successfully completed our _____ course, and is recommended for certification or rating without further _____ test.

Date	Agency Name and Number	Official's Signature
		Title

Designated Examiner's Report

☐ Student Pilot Certificate Issued *(Copy attached)*

☐ I have personally reviewed this applicant's pilot logbook, and certify that the individual meets the pertinent requirements of FAR 61 for the pilot certificate or rating sought.

☐ I have personally reviewed this applicant's graduation certificate, and found it to be appropriate and in order, and have returned the certificate.

☐ I have personally tested and/or verified this applicant in accordance with pertinent procedures and standards with the result indicated below.

  ☐ Approved—Temporary Certificate Issued *(Copy Attached)*

  ☐ Disapproved—Disapproval Notice Issued *(Copy Attached)*

Location of Test *(Facility, City, State)*	Duration of Test		
	Ground	Simulator	Flight

Certificate or Rating for Which Tested	Type(s) of Aircraft Used	Registration No.(s)

Date	Examiner's Signature	Certificate No.	Designation No.	Designation Expires

Evaluator's Record For Airline Transport Certificate/Rating Only

	Inspector	Examiner	Signature	Date
Oral	☐	☐		
Approved Simulator/Training Device Check	☐	☐		
Aircraft Flight Check	☐	☐		
Advanced Qualification Program	☐	☐		

Inspector's Report

I have personally tested this applicant in accordance with or have otherwise verified that this applicant complies with pertinent procedures, standards, policies, and or necessary requirements with the result indicated below.

  ☐ **Approved**—Temporary Certificate Issued   ☐ **Disapproved**—Disapproval Notice Issued

Location of Test *(Facility, City, State)*	Duration of Test		
	Ground	Simulator	Flight

Certificate or Rating for Which Tested	Type(s) of Aircraft Used	Registration No.(s)

☐ Student Pilot Certificate issued
☐ Examiner's Recommendation
  ☐ ACCEPTED ☐ REJECTED
☐ Reissue or Exchange of Pilot Certificate
☐ Special medical test conducted—report forwarded to Aeromedical Certification Branch, AAM-130

☐ Certificate or Rating Based on
  ☐ Military Competence
  ☐ Foreign License
  ☐ Approved Course Graduate
  ☐ Other Approved FAA Qualification Criteria
  ☐ Certificate Issued
  ☐ Certificate Denied

☐ Instructor ☐ Flight ☐ Ground
☐ Renewal ☐ Approved
☐ Reinstatement ☐ Disapproved
Instructor Renewal Based on
☐ Activity ☐ Training Course
☐ Acquaintance ☐ Test

Training Course (FIRC) Name	Graduation Certificate No.	Date

Date	Inspector's Signature	FAA District Office

Attachments:

☐ Student Pilot Certificate (copy)
☐ Report of Written Examination
☐ Temporary Pilot Certificate (copy)

☐ Airmans Identification (ID)

Form of ID _____

Number _____

Expiration Date _____

☐ Notice of Disapproval
☐ Superseded Pilot Certificate
☐ Answer Sheet Graded
☐ Answer Sheet Graded (Foreign Instrument)

★U.S.GPO:1992-0-343-105/73558

FLIGHT INSTRUCTOR LOGBOOK ENDORSEMENT

Your flight instructor will write the following endorsement in your logbook.

Endorsement for flight proficiency: FAR § 61.107(a)

I certify that I have given _____ the flight instruction required by FAR 61.107(a)(1) through (10) and find him/her competent to perform each pilot operation safely as a private pilot.

_____   _____   _____   _____
Date   Signature   CFI No.   Expiration Date

When you pass your private pilot written test you will receive AC Form 8080-2 which indicates your test score. It will also list the subject matter code for each question you missed. Make a list of the subject matter codes and the topic associated with each subject matter code (see Gleim's *Private Pilot and Recreational Pilot FAA Written Exam*).

DO NOT DESTROY THIS TEST REPORT This Test Report must be presented for retesting or certification.	DEPARTMENT OF TRANSPORTATION · FEDERAL AVIATION ADMINISTRATION **AIRMAN WRITTEN TEST REPORT (RIS: AC 8080-2)**								1466 41 SSN 434-80-6677		
TEST		**GRADES BY SECTION**							**FAA OFFICE NO.**	**TEST DATE**	**EXPIRATION DATE**
TAKE NO.	TITLE •	1	2	3	4	5	6	7			
01	PA	77							SO 07	02-18-92	02-28-94
EXPIRATION DATE (Last day of month)											

*See codes on reverse side:

MECHANICS ONLY · EXPIRATION DATE CODES
The first character designates the month; the second and third characters, the year. January through September as shown by numbers 1 through 9; October as "O"; November as "N"; December as "D".

LAST NAME, FIRST MIDDLE

FLANAGAN WILLIAM PATRICK JR
4720 NW 39TH ST
GAINESVILLE FL   32601

EXAMPLES:
Month (June) _____ 6   75   D 75
Year (1975) _____
Month (December) _____
Year (1975) _____

1   B05 C01 C10 D06 D26 D27 H03 J10 J11 K18 K25 Q02 Q12 R11

When applicable, an authorized instructor may complete and sign this statement:

I HAVE GIVEN THIS APPLICANT ADDITIONAL INSTRUCTION IN EACH OF THE SUBJECT AREAS FAILED AND CONSIDER THE APPLICANT COMPETENT TO PASS THE TEST.

LAST_____ INITIAL_____ CERTIFICATE NO._____ TYPE_____ INSTRUCTOR'S SIGNATURE_____
    INSTRUCTOR'S NAME (Print)

FRAUDULENT ALTERATION OF THIS FORM BY ANY PERSON IS A BASIS FOR SUSPENSION OR REVOCATION OF ANY CERTIFICATES OR RATINGS HELD BY THAT PERSON.

AC Form 8080-2 (10-83)

ISSUED BY: ADMINISTRATOR
                      FEDERAL AVIATION ADMINISTRATION

Present this subject matter code and title listing to your CFI and discuss the topics missed. Also have your CFI endorse the bottom of your 8080-2. Keep the subject matter code and title listing and paper clip it to your 8080-2 to bring to your practical test. If your examiner wishes to discuss it with you, you are/will be prepared.

YOUR TEMPORARY PILOT CERTIFICATE

When you successfully complete your practical test, your examiner will prepare a temporary pilot certificate similar to the one illustrated below. Your permanent certificate will be sent to you directly from the FAA Aeronautical Center in Oklahoma City in about 60 to 90 days. The temporary certificate is valid for 120 days. If you do not receive your permanent certificate within that time, your FAA inspector or designated flight test examiner can arrange an extension of your temporary certificate.

I. UNITED STATES OF AMERICA DEPARTMENT OF TRANSPORTATION—FEDERAL AVIATION ADMINISTRATION	III. CERTIFICATE NO.
II. **TEMPORARY AIRMAN CERTIFICATE**	

THIS CERTIFIES THAT   IV.
                        V.

DATE OF BIRTH	HEIGHT	WEIGHT	HAIR	EYES	SEX	NATIONALITY	VI.
	IN.						

IX.   has been found to be properly qualified and is hereby authorized in accordance with the conditions of issuance on the reverse of this certificate to exercise the privileges of

RATINGS AND LIMITATIONS

XII.

XIII.

THIS IS ☐ AN ORIGINAL ISSUANCE ☐ A REISSUANCE OF THIS GRADE OF CERTIFICATE   DATE OF SUPERSEDED AIRMAN CERTIFICATE

VII. AIRMAN'S SIGNATURE

BY DIRECTION OF THE ADMINISTRATOR	EXAMINER'S DESIGNATION NO. OR INSPECTOR'S REG. NO.
X. DATE OF ISSUANCE X. SIGNATURE OF EXAMINER OR INSPECTOR	DATE DESIGNATION EXPIRES

FAA Form 8060-4 (4-69) Supersedes Previous Edition

FAILURE ON THE FLIGHT TEST

About 90% of applicants pass their private pilot practical test the first time, and virtually all who experienced difficulty on their first attempt pass the second time. If you have a severe problem with a maneuver or have so much trouble that the examiner has to take control of the airplane to avoid a dangerous situation, your examiner or inspector will fail you. If so, the test will be terminated at that point.

When on the ground, your examiner will complete the Notice of Disapproval of Application, FAA Form 8060-5, which appears below, and will indicate the areas necessary for reexamination.

Your examiner will give you credit for the flight maneuvers you successfully completed. You should indicate your intent to work with your instructor on your deficiencies. Inquire about rescheduling the next flight test and having your flight instructor discuss your proficiencies and deficiencies with the examiner. Many examiners have a reduced fee for a retake (FAA inspectors do not charge for their services).

UNITED STATES OF AMERICA
DEPARTMENT OF TRANSPORTATION–FEDERAL AVIATION ADMINISTRATION

NOTICE OF DISAPPROVAL OF APPLICATION

NOTE
PRESENT THIS FORM UPON APPLICATION FOR REEXAMINTION

NAME AND ADDRESS OF APPLICANT

CERTIFICATE OR RATING SOUGHT

On the date shown, you failed the examination indicated below:

☐ FLIGHT   ☐ ORAL   ☐ PRACTICAL

AIRCRAFT USED *(Make and Model)*

FLT. TIME RECORDED IN LOGBOOK

PILOT-IN-COMM. OR SOLO	INSTRUMENT	DUAL

UPON REAPPLICATION YOU WILL BE REEXAMINED ON THE FOLLOWING:

I have personally tested this applicant and deem his performance unsatisfactory for the issuance of the certificate or rating sought.

DATE OF EXAMINATION	SIGNATURE OF EXAMINER OR INSPECTOR	DESIGNATION OR OFFICE NO.

FAA Form 8060—5 (5-80)

END OF CHAPTER

This is the end of Part I. Part II consists of Chapters I through XI. Each chapter covers one Area of Operation in the Private Pilot Practical Test Standards.

80   *Blank Page*

PART II
FAA PRACTICAL TEST STANDARDS:
DISCUSSED AND EXPLAINED

Part II of this book (Chapters I through XI) provides an in-depth discussion of the Private Pilot Practical Test Standards (PTS). Each of the 11 Areas of Operation is presented in a separate chapter. Within each chapter the tasks of that Area of Operation are reprinted followed by thorough discussion of each Objective within each PTS. Additionally, each flight maneuver is explained and illustrated.

    I. Preflight Preparation -- 6 tasks
   II. Ground Operations -- 6 tasks
  III. Airport and Traffic Pattern Operations -- 3 tasks
   IV. Takeoffs and Climbs -- 3 tasks
    V. Cross-Country Flying -- 4 tasks
   VI. Flight by Reference to Instruments -- 6 tasks
  VII. Flight at Critically Slow Airspeeds -- 5 tasks
 VIII. Flight Maneuvering by Reference to Ground Objects -- 3 tasks
   IX. Night Flight Operations -- 1 task
    X. Emergency Operations -- 2 tasks
   XI. Approaches and Landings -- 5 tasks

CHAPTER I
PREFLIGHT PREPARATION

I.A. Certificates and Documents 83
I.B. Obtaining Weather Information 89
I.C. Determining Performance and Limitations 98
I.D. Cross-Country Flight Planning 114
I.E. Airplane Systems 132
I.F. Aeromedical Factors 171

This chapter explains the six tasks (A-F) of the Preflight Preparation. These tasks are "knowledge only."

Each objective of a task lists, in sequence, the important elements that must be satisfactorily performed. The object includes:

1. Specifically what you should be able to do.
2. The conditions under which the task is to be performed.
3. The minimum acceptable standards of performance.

Be confident. You have prepared diligently and are better prepared and more skilled than the average private pilot applicant. Your examiner will base your ability to perform these tasks on the following.

1. Executing the task within your airplane's capabilities and limitations, including use of the airplane's systems.

2. Piloting your airplane with smoothness and accuracy.

3. Exercising good judgment.

4. Applying your aeronautical knowledge.

5. Showing mastery of your airplane within the standards outlined in this area of operation, with the successful outcome of a task never seriously in doubt.

This chapter will help you become thoroughly prepared for discussion of the preflight preparation tasks with your examiner. Plan to get your practical test off to a great start by understanding and explaining to your examiner the concepts underlying each of the objectives listed under these six tasks.

Your examiner is required to test you on all six of these tasks. Each task is reproduced verbatim from the FAA Practical Test Standards in a shaded box. General discussion is presented under "A. General Information." This is followed by "B. Task Objectives," which is a detailed discussion of each element of the FAA's task.

CERTIFICATES AND DOCUMENTS

I.A. TASK: CERTIFICATES AND DOCUMENTS

PILOT OPERATION - 1

REFERENCES: FAR Parts 61 and 91; AC 61-21, AC 61-23; Pilot's Handbook and Flight Manual.

Objective. To determine that the applicant:

1. Exhibits knowledge by explaining the appropriate --

   a. Pilot certificate, privileges and limitations.

   b. Medical certificate, class and duration.

   c. Personal pilot logbook or flight record.

   d. FCC station license and operator's permit, as required.

2. Exhibits knowledge by locating and explaining the significance and importance of the --

   a. Airworthiness and registration certificates.

   b. Operating limitations, handbooks, or manuals.

   c. Equipment list.

   d. Weight and balance data.

   e. Maintenance requirements and appropriate records.

A. General Information

1. This is one of six tasks (A-F) in this area of operation. Your examiner is required to test you on this task.

2. *Pilot Operation - 1* refers to FAR 61.107(a)(1): Preflight operations, including weight and balance determination, line inspection, and airplane servicing.

3. FAA References

    FAR 61: Certification: Pilots and Flight Instructors
    FAR 91: General Operating and Flight Rules
    AC 61-21: Flight Training Handbook
    AC 61-23: Pilot's Handbook of Aeronautical Knowledge
    Pilot's Operating Handbook (FAA-Approved Airplane Flight Manual)

4. The objective of this task is to determine your knowledge of various pilot and airplane certificates and documents.

B.   **Task Objectives**

1.   **You must be able to exhibit your knowledge of the following certificates and documents by explaining them to your examiner.**

a.   **Pilot certificates** are issued without an expiration date (except student certificates, which expire after 24 calendar months). Your new pilot certificate will say "Private Pilot." You will receive a temporary certificate at the successful completion of your practical test.

Recall your currency requirements to carry passengers and the fact that you cannot receive compensation for airplane operations as a private pilot.

1)   *Flight Review:* A private pilot may not act as pilot in command unless, within the preceding 24 months, you have

a)   Accomplished a flight review, in an aircraft for which you are rated, given by an appropriate CFI or FAA-designated person, and had your logbook endorsed by the reviewer certifying that (s)he has satisfactorily accomplished the review, OR

b)   Satisfactorily completed a pilot proficiency check (flight test) conducted by the FAA or the equivalent. Thus, new ratings and certificates substitute for the biennial review, OR

c)   Satisfactorily completed one or more phases of an FAA-sponsored pilot proficiency award program. This will substitute for a flight review.

i)   This is the Pilot Proficiency Award Program, commonly known as the "Wings" program.

ii)   For more information and/or to enroll contact your nearest FSDO or your local FAA accident prevention counselor.

d)   The effective date of the annual flight review requirement for noninstrument-rated private pilots with less than 400 hr. of flight time has been delayed until August 31, 1993.

e)   *Scope of Flight Review*:

i)   A review of the general operating and flight rules of FAR Part 91, and

ii)   A review of those flight maneuvers and procedures that are deemed necessary by the reviewer for you to demonstrate that you can safely exercise the privileges of your pilot certificate.

2)   *General Experience:* To act as pilot in command of an aircraft carrying passengers, you must have completed three takeoffs and landings within the preceding 90 days as sole manipulator of the flight controls in an aircraft of the same category and class and, if a type rating is required, of the same type of aircraft. If made in a tailwheel aircraft, the landings must be to a full stop. *(Category means airplane, rotorcraft, glider, or lighter than air. Class means single-engine land, multiengine land, single-engine sea, multiengine sea.)*

3)   *Night Experience:* Night officially begins (for the logging of night experience under FAR 61.57) 1 hr. after sunset and ends 1 hr. before sunrise. To carry passengers legally at night, you must have made, within the preceding 90 days, three takeoffs and landings to a full stop during night flight in an aircraft of the same category and class.

4)   For a complete listing of privileges and limitations, refer to FARs 61.118 and 61.120 on pages 35 and 36 of Chapter 3, Private Certificate Related FARs.

b.   **Medical Certificate.** To obtain and exercise the privileges of a private pilot certificate you must have a current third-class medical certificate. It is good through the last day of the 24th month after issuance.

c. **Personal Pilot Logbook.** FAR 61.51 requires you to log aeronautical training and experience to meet the requirements for a certificate rating or recent flight experience. You have been maintaining a logbook that indicates the

1) Date,

2) Length of flight,

3) Place, or points of departure and arrival,

4) Type and identification of aircraft used,

5) Type of experience or training (e.g., solo/pilot in command, flight instruction from a CFI), and

6) Conditions of flight (e.g., day or night VFR).

While you are required to carry your medical and pilot certificates, you are not required to have your logbooks with you at all times (as you did as a student pilot) while exercising your private pilot privileges.

d. **FCC station license and operators permit.**

1) The Federal Communications Commission (FCC) is responsible for regulating the types of aircraft radios.

2) When any type of radio (e.g., communication, transponder) is used aboard an aircraft for transmitting, that aircraft is a radio station.

   a) The FCC requires a *radio station license* for radio transmitters used for aviation purposes.

   b) This is an FCC requirement, not an FAA requirement.

SHIP/AIRCRAFT RADIO STATION LICENSE FEDERAL COMMUNICATIONS COMMISSION WASHINGTON, D.C. 20554

[x] **AIRCRAFT**	FAA NUMBER OR FCC CONTROL NUMBER N66421	NUMBER AIRCRAFT IN FLEET	EFFECTIVE DATE 03-08-82	EXPIRATION DATE 03-08-87
[ ] **SHIP**	NAME OF SHIP		OFFICIAL NUMBER	RADIO CALL SIGN	SELECTIVE CALLING NO.
EFFECTIVE DATE	EXPIRATION DATE	ENDORSEMENT DATES		

FREQUENCIES AND CONDITIONS

```
PRIVATE AIRCRAFT (SECTION 87.201)
TRANSMITTERS:  VHF COMM. (118-136 MHZ)  EMERGENCY LOCATOR (121.5 & 243 MHZ)
DISTANCE MEASURING EQUIPMENT (DME) (960-1215 MHZ)
TRANSPONDER (1090 MHZ)
```

THIS LICENSE SUBJECT TO FURTHER
CONDITIONS SET FORTH ON THE REVERSE SIDE

NOT TRANSFERABLE

(Must be posted aboard aircraft or ship)

FCC Form 559
March 1980

IRVIN N GLEIM
POB 12848 UNIVERSITY STATION
GAINESVILLE   FLA
32604

---

3) A *restricted radiotelephone operator permit* is required by the FCC for pilots who use high frequency (HF) radios or those who fly internationally.

   a) Permit is obtained by filling out an FCC application form.

   b) This is normally not required for most pilots.

2.   **You must be able to demonstrate your knowledge of the following certificates and documents by locating and explaining the significance and importance of each to your examiner.**

    a.   **Airworthiness and Registration Certificates.** Your airplane must have both an airworthiness certificate and a certificate of aircraft registration. An illustration of each certificate is shown below.

        1)   An airworthiness certificate is issued to an aircraft by the FAA at the time of manufacture. It remains in force as long as all maintenance, airworthiness directives, and equipment FARs are complied with.

        2)   A registration certificate is issued to the current owner of an aircraft as registered with the FAA.

UNITED STATES OF AMERICA
DEPARTMENT OF TRANSPORTATION FEDERAL AVIATION ADMINISTRATION
STANDARD AIRWORTHINESS CERTIFICATE

1 NATIONALITY AND REGISTRATION MARKS	2 MANUFACTURER AND MODEL	3 AIRCRAFT SERIAL NUMBER	4 CATEGORY
N66421	BEECH AIRCRAFT CORP. - V35B	D-10267	UTILITY

5. AUTHORITY AND BASIS FOR ISSUANCE
This airworthiness certificate is issued pursuant to the Federal Aviation Act of 1958 and certifies that, as of the date of issuance, the aircraft to which issued has been inspected and found to conform to the type certificate therefor, to be in condition for safe operation, and has been shown to meet the requirements of the applicable comprehensive and detailed airworthiness code as provided by Annex 8 to the Convention on International Civil Aviation, except as noted herein.
Exceptions:

NONE

6. TERMS AND CONDITIONS
Unless sooner surrendered, suspended, revoked, or a termination date is otherwise established by the Administrator, this airworthiness certificate is effective as long as the maintenance, preventative maintenance, and alterations are performed in accordance with Parts 21, 43, and 91 of the Federal Aviation Regulations, as appropriate, and the aircraft is registered in the United States.

DATE OF ISSUANCE	FAA REPRESENTATIVE D. M. Porteous	DESIGNATION NUMBER
June 22, 1989		DOA, PC#8

Any alteration, reproduction, or misuse of this certificate may be punishable by a fine not exceeding $1,000, or imprisonment not exceeding 3 years, or both. THIS CERTIFICATE MUST BE DISPLAYED IN THE AIRCRAFT IN ACCORDANCE WITH APPLICABLE FEDERAL AVIATION REGULATIONS.

FAA Form 8100-2 (7-67) FORMERLY FAA FORM 1362

UNITED STATES OF AMERICA
DEPARTMENT OF TRANSPORTATION — FEDERAL AVIATION ADMINISTRATION
CERTIFICATE OF AIRCRAFT REGISTRATION

This certificate must be in the aircraft when operated.

NATIONALITY AND REGISTRATION MARKS N 66421	AIRCRAFT SERIAL NO D-10267

MANUFACTURER AND MANUFACTURER'S DESIGNATION OF AIRCRAFT
BEECH   V35B

ISSUED TO
GLEIM IRVIN N
UNIVERSITY STATION PO BOX 12848
GAINSVILLE FL 32604

INDIVIDUAL

This certificate is issued for registration purposes only and is not a certificate of title. The Federal Aviation Administraton does not determine rights of ownership as between private persons.

It is certified that the above described aircraft has been entered on the register of the Federal Aviation Administration, United States of America, in accordance with the Convention on International Civil Aviation dated December 7, 1944, and with the Federal Aviation Act of 1958, and regulations issued thereunder

DATE OF ISSUE
JUNE 04, 1980   Administrator

AC Form 8050-3 (5-77)

b. The **operating limitations** of your airplane will be found in your airplane's *POH*. This is also referred to as the *FAA-Approved Airplane Flight Manual.* Your airplane *POH* must be accessible to you during flight. This includes instruction books for all added equipment, e.g., autopilots. You need to obtain your *POH*, manual, or other reprints or materials prior to beginning your private pilot flight instruction.

c. The **equipment list** is part of your *POH*. See Section 6, "Weight and Balance/ Equipment List." It shows the weight and moment of each accessory added to the basic airframe. After each modification or equipment addition, the repair facility will recompute the airplane's empty weight and center of gravity. These figures are used in your weight and balance computations.

d. **Weight and balance data** are very important, and are presented and explained in the *POH* or included with that type of information. It is important that you understand the weight and balance calculations for the airplane you will be training in, and work through several examples to verify that you will be in the proper weight and balance given one or two persons aboard the airplane and various fuel loads.

   1) Obtain a Weight and Balance form for your airplane from your *POH* or CFI.

   2) For additional assistance, see Task I.C., Determining Performance and Limitations, beginning on page 98.

e. The **maintenance requirements** on aircraft that are used in commercial operations (i.e., flight training, charter, etc.) are more stringent than on non-commercial Part 91, which requires maintenance only on an annual basis.

   1) All aircraft must undergo an annual inspection by a Certified Airframe and Powerplant (A&P) mechanic who also possesses an Inspection Authorization (IA).

   2) Aircraft used for compensation or hire must also undergo an inspection every 100 hr. of flight time. The 100-hr. interval may be exceeded by no more than 10 hr. to facilitate transport of the aircraft to a maintenance location where the inspection can be performed.

      a) However, if the 100-hr. inspection is overflown, the next inspection will be due after 100 hr. of flight time **less** the amount overflown.

      b) EXAMPLE: If the check is performed at the 105-hr. point, the next 100-hr. check is due at the end of 95 hr., not 100 hr.; thus, it would be due at the 200-hr. point.

   3) Based on the specific make and model aircraft, further checks beyond the 100-hr. check may be necessary to comply with the FARs. This additional maintenance may be required at the 50-, 150-, or 250-hr. point.

   4) You may not use an ATC transponder unless it has been tested and inspected within the preceding 24 calendar months.

   5) The emergency locator transmitter (ELT) battery must be replaced after half its useful life has expired, or after 1 hr. of cumulative use.

   6) Examine the engine logbooks and the airframe logbook of your training airplane (presumably the one you will use for your practical test) and ask your instructor for assistance as appropriate.

      Locate and paperclip the most recent signoff for

      a) 100-hr. inspection.
      b) Transponder test.
      c) ELT battery (the expiration date is on the battery and in the logbook).

7) Maintenance that may be performed by pilots:

    a) You may perform *preventive maintenance* on any aircraft owned or operated by you which is not used under FAR Part 121, 127, 129, or 135.

    b) Preventive maintenance includes (Appendix A, FAR 43):

- Removal, installation, and repair of landing gear tires.
- Replacing elastic shock absorber cords on landing gear.
- Servicing landing gear shock struts by adding oil, air, or both.
- Servicing landing gear wheel bearings, such as cleaning and greasing.
- Replacing defective safety wiring or cotter keys.
- Lubrication not requiring disassembly other than removal of nonstructural items such as cover plates, cowlings, and fairings.
- Making simple fabric patches not requiring rib stitching or the removal of structural parts or control surfaces.
- Replenishing hydraulic fluid in the hydraulic reservoir.
- Refinishing decorative coating when removal or disassembly of any primary structure or operating system is not required.
- Applying preservative or protective material to components where no disassembly of any primary structure or operating system is involved.
- Repairing upholstery and decorative furnishings.
- Making small simple repairs to fairings, nonstructural cover plates, cowlings, and small patches and reinforcements not changing the contour so as to interfere with proper air flow.
- Replacing side windows where that work does not interfere with the structure or any operating system such as controls, electrical equipment, etc.
- Replacing safety belts.
- Replacing seats or seat parts with replacement parts approved for the aircraft, not involving disassembly of any primary structure or operating system.
- Trouble shooting and repairing broken circuits in landing light wiring circuits.
- Replacing bulbs, reflectors, and lenses of position and landing lights.
- Replacing wheels and skis where no weight and balance computation is involved.
- Replacing any cowling not requiring removal of the propeller or disconnection of flight controls.
- Replacing or cleaning spark plugs and setting of spark plug gap clearance.
- Replacing any hose connection except hydraulic connections.
- Replacing prefabricated fuel lines.
- Cleaning or replacing fuel and oil strainers or filter elements.
- Replacing and servicing batteries.
- Replacement or adjustment of nonstructural standard fasteners incidental to operations.
- The installations of anti-misfueling devices to reduce the diameter of fuel tank filler openings.
- Removing, checking, and replacing magnetic chip detectors.

END OF TASK

OBTAINING WEATHER INFORMATION

I.B. TASK: OBTAINING WEATHER INFORMATION

PILOT OPERATION - 1

REFERENCES: AC 00-6, AC 00-45, AC 61-21, AC 61-23, AC 61-84.

Objective. To determine that the applicant:

1. Exhibits knowledge of aviation weather information by obtaining, reading, and analyzing --

    a. Weather reports and forecasts.
    b. Weather charts.
    c. Pilot weather reports.

    d. SIGMET's and AIRMET's.
    e. Notices to Airmen.
    f. Wind-shear reports.

2. Makes a competent go/no-go decision based on the available weather information.

A. General Information

    1. This is one of six tasks (A-F) in this area of operation. Your examiner is required to test you on this task.

    2. *Pilot Operation - 1* refers to FAR 61.107(a)(1): Preflight operations, including weight and balance determination, line inspection, and aircraft servicing.

    3. FAA References

        AC 00-6:   Aviation Weather
        AC 00-45: Aviation Weather Services
        AC 61-21: Flight Training Handbook
        AC 61-23: Pilot's Handbook of Aeronautical Knowledge
        AC 61-84: Role of Preflight Preparation

    4. The objective of this task is to determine your knowledge of obtaining, reading, and analyzing aviation weather information and making a competent go/no-go decision based on that information.

    5. Review Appendix D, Aviation Weather Reports and Forecasts, pages 487 to 520, which provides more detailed discussion and illustration of the following weather reports and forecasts.

        1. Surface Aviation Weather Report (SA)
        2. Satellite Weather Pictures
        3. Area Forecast (FA)
        4. Terminal Forecast (FT)
        5. Inflight Advisories (WST, WS, WA, CWA)
        6. Pilot Weather Report (PIREP)
        7. Radar Weather Report (RAREP)
        8. Surface Analysis Chart

        9. Weather Depiction Chart
        10. Radar Summary Chart
        11. Low-Level Prognostic Charts
        12. Winds and Temperatures Aloft Forecast (FD)
        13. Composite Moisture Stability Charts
        14. Severe Weather Outlook Chart
        15. Constant Pressure Analysis Charts

    6. The National Weather Service made the following changes in the summer of 1991:

        a. Area Forecast (FA)

            1) No longer in the following five-section format.

                a) Hazards/flight precautions,
                b) Synopsis,
                c) Icing,
                d) Turbulence/low-level wind shear, and
                e) Significant clouds and weather.

2) The area forecast is now in a three-section format.

a) The first is "Hazards/Flight Precautions" and is identified by the letter "H."

i) Area identifier followed by "H."

ii) Heading (FA) with effective date/time group.

iii) Hazards explained with valid time.

iv) FLT PRCTN ("flight precautions") summarizes expected hazardous weather.

b) The second section is "Synopsis, VFR Clouds/Weather" and is identified by the letter "C."

i) Area identifier followed by "C."

ii) Heading (FA) with effective date/time group.

iii) Synopsis.

iv) Clouds and weather.

v) SIG CLDS AND WX ("significant clouds and weather") provides a summary of cloudiness and weather significant to flight operations, broken down by state or other geographical areas.

c) The third section is a state by state summary of the forecast.

b. AIRMETs

1) Issued every 6 hr. with amendment issued as necessary.
2) Will have fixed designators.

a) Zulu for icing and freezing level.
b) Tango for turbulence, strong winds/low-level wind shear.
c) Sierra for IFR conditions and mountain obscuration.

i) IFR conditions are only in the AIRMET and no longer in the Hazards/Flight Precautions section of the FA.

c. SIGMETs

1) Identifiers have changed.

a) November through Yankee are used.
b) Excluding Sierra, Tango, and Zulu which are AIRMET identifiers.

7. Flight Service Stations (FSSs) are the primary source for obtaining preflight briefings and inflight weather information.

a. Prior to your flight, and before you meet with your examiner, you should visit or call the nearest FSS for a complete briefing.

b. Available aviation weather reports and forecasts are displayed at each FSS.

c. There are four basic types of preflight briefings to meet your needs.

1) Standard briefing:

a) Should be requested any time you are planning a flight and have not received a previous briefing.

b) The briefer will provide the following information in sequence.

i) Adverse Conditions -- significant weather and aeronautical information that might influence you to alter the proposed flight; e.g., hazardous weather conditions, runway closures, NAVAID outages, etc.

ii) VFR Flight Not Recommended. When VFR flight is proposed and conditions are present or forecast, surface or aloft, that in the briefer's judgment would make flight under VFR doubtful, the briefer will describe the conditions, affected locations, and announce, "VFR flight is not recommended."

- This is advisory in nature.

- You are responsible to make a final decision as to whether the flight can be conducted safely.

iii) Synopsis. A brief statement describing the type, location, and movement of weather systems and/or air masses which may affect the proposed flight.

iv) Current Conditions. Reported weather conditions applicable to the flight will be summarized from all available sources.

- This is omitted if the proposed time of departure is over 2 hr., unless requested by you.

v) En Route Forecast. Conditions for the proposed route are summarized in logical order; i.e., departure/climbout, en route, and descent.

vi) Destination Forecast. At the planned ETA, any significant changes within 1 hr. before and after the planned arrival are included.

vii) Winds Aloft. Forecast winds aloft will be summarized for the proposed route and altitude.

viii) NOTAMs. Information from any NOTAM (D) or NOTAM (L) pertinent to the proposed flight, and pertinent FDC NOTAMs within approximately 400 mi. of the FSS providing the briefing.

- NOTAM (D) and FDC NOTAMs which have been published in the Notices to Airmen publication are not included, unless requested by you.

ix) ATC Delays. Any known ATC delays and flow control advisories which might affect the proposed flight.

x) The following may be obtained on your request.

- Information on military training routes (MTR) and military operations area (MOA) activity within the flight plan area and a 100 NM extension around the flight plan area.

- Approximate density altitude data.

- Information regarding such items as air traffic services and rules, customs/immigration procedures, ADIZ rules, etc.

- LORAN-C NOTAMs.

- Other assistance as required.

2) Abbreviated Briefing:

a) Request when you need information to supplement mass disseminated data (e.g., TWEB, PATWAS, etc.), update a previous briefing, or when you only need one or two specific items.

b) Provide the briefer information regarding the:

i) Appropriate background information,
ii) Time you received the previous information, and/or
iii) The specific items needed.

        c)   Sequence will be the same as in the Standard Briefing, to the extent possible.

        d)   If you requested one or two specific items, the briefer will advise you if adverse conditions are present or forecast.

             i)   Details will be provided only at your request.

    3)   Outlook Briefing:

        a)   Request whenever your proposed time of departure is 6 hr. or more from the time of the briefing.

        b)   You will be provided available forecast data applicable to the proposed flight.

        c)   This type of briefing is for planning purposes only.

             i)   Obtain a Standard or Abbreviated Briefing prior to departure.

    4)   Inflight Briefing:

        a)   In situations where you need to obtain a preflight briefing or an update by radio, you should contact the nearest FSS to obtain this information.

        b)   After communications have been established, advise the FSS of the type of briefing you require.

        c)   You may be advised to shift to the flight watch frequency (122.0) when conditions indicate that it would be advantageous.

  d.   Ask for any information that you or the briefer may have missed.

    1)   Save your questions until the briefing is complete.

  e.   You may want to obtain an Abbreviated Briefing as an update before your flight portion of the practical test.

B.   Task Objectives

  1.   Exhibit your knowledge of aviation weather information by obtaining, reading, and analyzing the following items.

    a.   Weather Reports and Forecasts

      1)   Surface Aviation Weather Reports

        a)   These are actual weather observations made at least once each hour at each reporting station.

        b)   These are coded by the letters "SA," and are also referred to as sequence reports.

      2)   Radar Weather Report (RAREP)

        a)   RAREPs help you plan ahead to avoid thunderstorm areas.

        b)   Remember -- weather radar can only detect drops or ice particles of precipitation size or greater. It will not detect fog, low stratus, etc., unless precipitation-size particles are also present.

      3)   Satellite Weather Pictures

        a)   The visible pictures are primarily used to determine the presence of clouds and the type of cloud from shape and texture.

        b)   Infrared pictures are used to determine cloud top temperatures and thus the approximate height of the cloud.

4) **Area Forecasts**

   a) Area forecasts (FA) are a forecast for a portion of a state and/or several states.

   b) Issued every 8 hr. and valid for a period of 18 hr., they are

      i) Expected weather for 12 hr.
      ii) An additional 6-hr. categorical outlook.

5) **Terminal Forecasts**

   a) A terminal forecast (FT) is a description of the surface weather expected to occur at an airport.

   b) The forecast cloud heights and amounts, visibility, weather, and wind relate to flight operations within 5 NM of the center of the runway complex.

6) **Inflight Advisories (AWW, WST, WS, CWA, WA)**

   a) Inflight weather advisories are unscheduled forecasts to advise en route aircraft of the development of potentially hazardous weather.

7) **Winds and Temperatures Aloft Forecast**

   a) Prepared for 6,000; 9,000; 12,000; 18,000; 24,000; 30,000; 34,000; and 39,000 ft. MSL.

   b) Use the winds aloft charts to determine winds at a proposed flight altitude or to select the best altitude for a proposed flight. Temperatures can also be determined from the forecast charts.

8) **TWEB Route Forecast and Synopsis**

   a) The TWEB route forecast is similar to the FA except information is contained in a route format.

   b) Forecast conditions are described for a corridor of 25 NM on either side of the route.

   c) The synopsis is a brief statement of frontal and pressure systems affecting the route.

9) **Special Flight Forecast**

   a) When planning a special category flight and scheduled forecasts are insufficient to meet your needs, you may request a special flight forecast through any FSS.

   b) Special category flights are hospital or rescue flights; experimental, photographic, or test flights; record attempts; and mass flights such as air tours, air races, and fly-aways from special events.

10) **Hurricane Advisory**

    a) When a hurricane threatens a coast line, but is located at least 300 NM offshore, an abbreviated hurricane advisory (WH) is issued to alert aviation interests.

    b) The WH gives location of the storm center, its expected movement, and maximum winds in and near the storm center.

11) **Convective Outlook**

    a) A convective outlook (AC) describes the prospects for general thunderstorm activity during the next 24 hr.

b. Weather Charts

1) Surface Analysis Chart

a) The surface analysis chart provides you with a ready means of locating pressure systems and fronts. It also gives you an overview of winds, temperatures, and dew point temperatures as of chart time.

b) When using the chart, keep in mind that weather moves and conditions change.

2) Weather Depiction Chart

a) The weather depiction chart is a choice place to begin your weather briefing and flight planning.

b) This chart gives you a bird's eye view at chart time of areas of favorable and adverse weather and frontal systems associated with weather.

c) This chart is prepared from surface aviation (SA) reports.

3) Radar Summary Chart

a) The radar summary chart aids in preflight planning by identifying general areas and movement of precipitation and/or thunderstorms. Radar detects only drops or ice particles of precipitation size, not clouds or fog.

i) The absence of echoes does not guarantee clear weather and cloud tops may be higher than precipitation tops detected by radar.

b) The chart must be used in conjunction with other charts, reports, and forecasts.

4) Low-Level Significant Weather Prognostic

a) Significant weather prognostic charts, called "progs" for short, show forecast weather which may influence your flight planning.

5) Freezing Level Charts

a) The freezing level chart is the lower left panel of the Composite Moisture Stability Chart. It is an analysis of observed freezing level data from upper air observations.

b) Always plan for possible icing in clouds or precipitation at altitudes above the freezing level, especially between 0°C and −10°C.

6) Stability Charts

a) The stability chart is the upper left panel of the Composite Moisture Stability Chart. It outlines areas of stable and unstable air.

b) When clouds and precipitation are forecast or are occurring, the stability chart can be used to determine the types of clouds and precipitation.

7) Severe Weather Outlook Chart

a) A 24-hr. outlook for thunderstorm activity.

b) The severe weather outlook chart is for advanced planning. It alerts all interests to the possibility of future storm development.

8) Constant Pressure Charts

a) A constant pressure analysis chart is an upper air weather map where all the information depicted is at the specified pressure level of the chart.

Information includes the observed temperature, temperature-dew point spread, wind, height of the pressure surface, as well as height changes over the previous 12-hr. period.

    i)   Remember this is observed data, not a forecast.

  b) Constant pressure charts often show the cause of weather and its movement more clearly than does the surface map.

c. Pilot Weather Reports (PIREPs)

  1) No more timely or helpful weather observation fills the gaps between reporting stations than observations and reports made by fellow pilots during flight. Aircraft in flight are the only source of directly observed cloud tops, icing, and turbulence.

  2) PIREPs are also reported in the remarks section of the hourly weather reports (SAs).

d. SIGMETs and AIRMETs

  1) Convective SIGMET

    a) A Convective SIGMET (WST) is a weather advisory concerning convective weather significant to the safety of all aircraft.

  2) SIGMET (WS)

    a) A SIGMET (WS) is a weather advisory issued concerning weather significant to the safety of all aircraft.

  3) AIRMET (WA)

    a) An AIRMET (WA) is a weather advisory issued concerning weather which is of operational interest to all aircraft and potentially hazardous to aircraft having limited capability because of lack of equipment, instrumentation, or pilot qualifications.

    b) AIRMETs concern weather of less severity than that covered by SIGMETs or Convective SIGMETs.

  4) Center Weather Advisory

    a) A Center Weather Advisory (CWA) is used by ATC to alert pilots of existing or anticipated adverse weather conditions within the next 2 hr.

    b) A CWA may modify or redefine a SIGMET.

e. Notices to Airmen (NOTAMs) are notices containing information (not known sufficiently in advance to publicize by other means) concerning the establishment, condition, or change in any component in the National Airspace System (e.g., facility, service, hazard, etc.) that the timely knowledge of which is essential for flight planning.

  1) NOTAM (D) gives distant, as well as local, dissemination beyond the area of responsibility of the originating FSS.

    a) Provide information such as the status of navigation aids, airport closures, and radar services available.

  2) NOTAM (L) is given local dissemination in the FSS area of responsibility.

    a) Provides information such as runway/taxiway closures and construction near runways.

  3) FDC (Flight Data Center) NOTAMs are regulatory in nature such as amendments to aeronautical charts.

    a) May be used to issue temporary flight restrictions.

f.   Wind-Shear Reports

    1)   PIREPs. Because unexpected change in wind speed and direction can be hazardous to aircraft operations at low altitudes (i.e., takeoff and landing) near an airport, pilots are urged to promptly volunteer reports to controllers of wind shear encounters.

        a)   The recommended method of reporting is to state the loss or gain of airspeed and the altitudes at which it was encountered.

            i)   If you cannot be this specific just report the effects it had on your airplane.

    2)   Low Level Wind Shear Alert System (LLWAS) is a computerized system that detects the presence of possible low-level wind shear by continuously comparing the winds measured by sensors installed around the periphery of an airport with the wind measured at the center field location.

        a)   When conditions exists, the tower controller will provide arriving and departing aircraft with an advisory of the situation which includes the wind at the center field plus the remote site location and wind.

            i)   Remote site locations will be given based on an eight-point compass system.

2.   Make a competent go/no-go decision based on the available weather information.

    a.   In a well-equipped plane with a proficient pilot flying, any ceiling and visibility within legal minimums should be flyable. In a poorly equipped plane or with a new or rusty pilot, marginal VFR (MVFR) should be avoided.

    b.   Another factor to consider in your Go/No-Go decision is the weather. MVFR in smooth air caused by a stalled front is considerably different from heavy turbulence ahead of a strong front or in a squall line. The following forecast conditions may lead to a No-Go decision:

        1)   Thunderstorms.

        2)   Embedded thunderstorms.

        3)   Lines of thunderstorms.

        4)   Fast-moving fronts or squall lines.

        5)   Flights that require you to cross strong or fast-moving fronts.

        6)   Reported turbulence that is moderate or greater. (Remember, moderate turbulence in a Boeing 727 is usually severe in a Cessna 152.)

        7)   Icing.

        8)   Fog. Unlike when in a ceiling, you usually cannot maintain visual references with ground fog. This is especially important if sufficient fuel may be a concern.

    c.   These factors must be considered in relation to the equipment to be flown. Thunderstorms are less of a problem in a radar-equipped airplane. The only way to fly safely is to be able to weigh each factor against the other. This is done only by using common sense and gaining experience.

    d.   Flying MVFR is a continuing process of decision-making throughout the whole flight. You must use your certificate to gain experience, but you must also temper it so you do not get in beyond your capabilities or the capabilities of your airplane.

e. A final factor which must be considered in the Go/No-Go decision is your physical and mental condition. Are you sick, tired, upset, depressed, etc.? See Task I.F., Aeromedical Factors, beginning on page 171. These factors greatly affect your ability to handle normal and abnormal problems.

1) A good method to ensure safety is the "I'm Safe" checklist.

I	Illness
M	Medication
S	Stress
A	Alcohol
F	Fatigue
E	Emotion

END OF TASK

DETERMINING PERFORMANCE AND LIMITATIONS

I.C. TASK: DETERMINING PERFORMANCE AND LIMITATIONS

PILOT OPERATION - 1

REFERENCES: AC 61-21, AC 61-23, AC 61-84; Airplane Handbook and Flight Manual.

Objective. To determine that the applicant:

1. Exhibits knowledge by explaining airplane weight and balance, performance, and limitations, including adverse aerodynamic effects of exceeding the limits.

2. Uses available and appropriate performance charts, tables, and data.

3. Computes weight and balance, and determines that weight and center of gravity will be within limits during all phases of the flight.

4. Calculates airplane performance, considering density altitude, wind, terrain, and other pertinent conditions.

5. Describes the effects of atmospheric conditions on airplane performance.

6. Makes a competent decision on whether the required performance is within the operating limitations of the airplane.

A. General Information.

1. This is one of six tasks (A-F) in this area of operation. Your examiner is required to test you on this task.

2. *Pilot Operation - 1* refers to FAR 61.107(a)(1): Preflight operations, including weight and balance determination, line inspection, and airplane servicing.

3. FAA References

      AC 61-21: Flight Training Handbook
      AC 61-23: Pilot's Handbook of Aeronautical Knowledge
      AC 61-84: Role of Preflight Preparation
      Pilot's Operating Handbook (FAA-Approved Airplane Flight Manual)

4. The objective of this task is for you to demonstrate your knowledge of determining your airplane's performance and limitations.

5. This task is also make and model specific, and applies to the airplane used on your practical test. This task covers Sections 2, 5, and 6 of your *POH.*

   a. Section 2: Limitations
   b. Section 5: Performance
   c. Section 6: Weight and Balance/Equipment List

6. The charts used in this discussion are for **illustrative purposes only.** You must use the performance charts in your airplane's *POH.*

B. Task Objectives

1. **Exhibit your knowledge by explaining weight and balance, performance, and limitations, including adverse aerodynamic effects of exceeding the limits.**

    a. The subject of weight and balance means that you are concerned not only with the weight of the airplane but also the location of its center of gravity (CG). You should not attempt a flight until you are satisfied with the weight and balance condition.

        1) Effects of weight on flight performance.

            a) Excessive weight reduces the flight performance of your airplane in almost every respect. The most important performance deficiencies of the overloaded airplane are:

                i)   Higher takeoff speed required.
                ii)   Longer takeoff run required.
                iii)   Reduced rate and angle of climb.
                iv)   Shorter range.
                v)   Reduced cruising speed.
                vi)   Reduced maneuverability.
                vii)   Higher stalling speed.
                viii) Higher landing speed required.
                ix)   Longer landing roll required.

            b) Excessive weight in itself reduces the safety margins available to you, and becomes even more hazardous when other performance-reducing factors (e.g., high density altitude, low engine power) are combined with overweight conditions.

        2) Effects of adverse balance.

            a) There are two essential airplane characteristics which may be seriously affected by improper balance; these are stability and control.

                i)   Loading in a nose-heavy direction causes problems in controlling and raising the nose, especially during takeoff and landing.

                ii) Loading in a tail-heavy direction has the most serious effect upon longitudinal stability, even to the extent of reducing your airplane's ability to recover from stalls and spins.

        3) The CG position influences the lift and angle of attack of the wing, the amount and direction of force on the tail, and the degree of deflection of the stabilizer needed to supply the proper tail force for equilibrium. The latter is very important because of its relationship to elevator control force.

            a) Your airplane will stall at a higher airspeed with a forward CG location. This is because the stalling angle of attack is reached at a higher speed due to increased wing loading.

            b) High elevator control forces normally exist with a forward CG location due to the increased stabilizer deflection required to balance your airplane.

                i)   The elevator may no longer be able to oppose any increase in nose-down pitching.

                ii) Adequate elevator control is needed to control your airplane throughout the airspeed range down to the stall.

            c) Your airplane will cruise faster with an aft CG location because of reduced drag. The drag is reduced because a smaller angle of attack and less downward deflection of the stabilizer are required to support the airplane and overcome the nose-down pitching tendency.

      d) Your airplane will become less and less stable as the CG is moved rearward. The horizontal stabilizer is closer to the CG as the CG moves rearward, resulting in an increasingly shorter moment, which decreases its ability to stabilize the airplane.

         i) At the point when the wing and tail contributions balance, neutral stability exists and any CG movement further aft will result in an unstable airplane.

    b. Airplane performance can be defined as the ability to operate or function; i.e., the ability of an airplane to accomplish certain things that make it useful for certain purposes.

      1) The chief elements of performance are:

         a) Takeoff and landing distance.
         b) Rate of climb and ceiling.
         c) Fuel economy and speed.
         d) Range and payload.
         e) Stability and maneuverability.

    c. You should be able to explain the adverse effects of exceeding your airplane's limitations. These may include

      1) Attempting a takeoff or landing without a long enough runway.

      2) Not enough fuel to make your airport of intended landing, while cruising at a high speed/power setting.

      3) Exceeding your airplane's structural limits by being over gross weight and/or outside center of gravity limits.

2. Uses available and appropriate performance charts, tables, and data.

    a. Performance charts, tables, and data are found in Section 5, Performance, of your *POH*. From that information, you will be able to determine your airplane's performance in various phases of flight.

    b. Two commonly used methods of depicting performance data are by tables and graphs.

      1) Tables are compact arrangements of conditions and performance values placed in an orderly sequence and are usually arranged in rows and columns.

      2) Graphs are pictorial presentations consisting of straight lines, curves, broken lines, or a series of bars representing the successive changes in the value of a variable quantity or quantities.

    c. Because not all values are listed on the tables or graphs, interpolation is often required to determine intermediate values for a particular flight condition or performance situation.

3. Compute weight and balance, and determine that weight and center of gravity will be within limits during all phases of the flight.

    a. You will need to use Section 6, Weight and Balance/Equipment List, in your airplane's *POH* to accomplish this element. You should calculate the weight and balance for takeoff, cruise, and landing.

      1) You must assume a large part of the weight and balance management (i.e., control over the loading and fuel management).

b.　The center of gravity is determined by the total moments divided by the total weight.

　　1)　Total moments are the sum of the weights of individual items multiplied by their arm.

　　　　a)　The arm is the number of inches from the reference point (also called the datum).

　　　　b)　The moment is a measure of the gravitational force which causes a tendency of the weight to rotate about a point or axis. It is usually expressed in pound-inches.

c.　The loading graph is frequently used to determine the load moment.

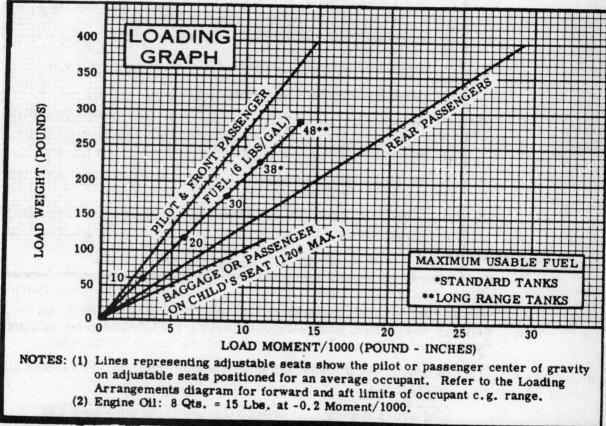

NOTES: (1) Lines representing adjustable seats show the pilot or passenger center of gravity on adjustable seats positioned for an average occupant. Refer to the Loading Arrangements diagram for forward and aft limits of occupant c.g. range.
(2) Engine Oil: 8 Qts. = 15 Lbs. at -0.2 Moment/1000.

NOTE:　The empty weight of this airplane *does not include* the weight of the oil.

　1)　On most graphs, the load weight in pounds is listed on the left (vertical) axis. Diagonal lines usually indicate fuel, baggage, pilot and front seat passengers, and back seat passengers. Move horizontally to the right across the chart from the amount of weight to intersect the line indicating where the weight is located.

　2)　From the point of intersection of the weight with the appropriate diagonal line, drop straight down to the bottom of the chart to the moments displayed on the horizontal axis.

　3)　The last step is to total the weights and moments for all items being loaded.

d.   The center of gravity moment envelope chart is a graph showing CG limits for various gross weights. Acceptable limits are established as an area on the graph. This area is called the envelope. Weight is on the vertical axis and moments on the horizontal axis.

    1)   Identify the center of gravity point on the center of gravity moment envelope graph by plotting the total loaded aircraft weight across to the right.

    2)   Plot the moment upward from the bottom.

    3)   The intersection is either within or outside the CG moment envelope.

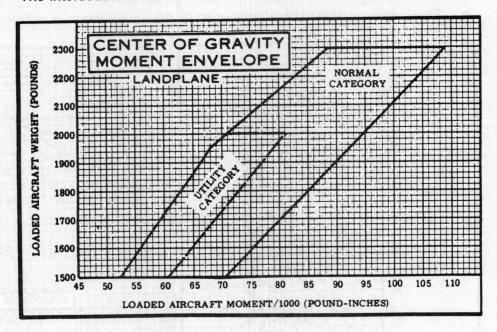

e.   There are two formulas for determining the amount of weight that can be added or removed at a specific point without exceeding the CG limit. The bold areas in Formula I and Formula II emphasize the differences in the formulas.

    1)   Formula I: Old gross weight and new CG.

$$\frac{\textit{Weight Change}}{\textbf{\textit{Old Gross Weight}}} = \frac{\textit{CG Change}}{\textit{Weight Change Location} - \textbf{\textit{New CG}}}$$

    2)   Formula II: New gross weight and old CG.

$$\frac{\textit{Weight Change}}{\textbf{\textit{New Gross Weight}}} = \frac{\textit{CG Change}}{\textit{Weight Change Location} - \textbf{\textit{Old CG}}}$$

f.   Use the following formula for determining the effect of a **weight shift** on the CG change:

$$\frac{\textit{Weight Shifted}}{\textit{Total Weight}} = \frac{\textit{CG Change}}{\textit{Weight Shift Distance}}$$

g.   On the above CG and weight change problems, remember that if you move weight forward (datum assumed at front of airplane), you move the CG forward; i.e., use common sense to envision which way the CG moves.

h. *Author's Note: The following is an effective, intuitively appealing handout used by Dr. Melville R. Byington at Embry-Riddle Aeronautical University (used with permission).*

Alternative Weight Change and Weight Shift Computations

1) **Basic theory** -- The foregoing "methods" obscure what can and should be a logical, straightforward approach. The standard question is **If the CG started out there, and certain changes occurred, where is it now?** It can be answered directly using a SINGLE, UNIVERSAL, UNCOMPLICATED FORMULA.

a) At **any** time, the CG is simply the sum of all moments divided by the sum of all weights.

$$CG = \frac{\Sigma M}{\Sigma W}$$

b) Since CG was known at some previous (#1) loading condition (with moment = M_1 and weight = W_1), it is logical that this become the point of departure. Due to weight addition, removal, or shift, the moment has changed by some amount, ΔM. The total weight has also changed, if and only if, weight has been added or removed. Therefore, the current CG is merely the current total moment divided by the current total weight. In equation format,

$$CG = Current\ Moment/Current\ Weight\ becomes\ CG = \frac{M_1 \pm \Delta M}{W_1 \pm \Delta W}$$

2) Application -- This UNIVERSAL FORMULA will accommodate ANY CG SHIFT PROBLEM! Before proceeding, certain conventions deserve review:

a) Any weight added causes a + moment change (Weight removed is −).
b) Weight shifted rearward causes a + moment change (Forward is −).
c) A weight shift changes only the moment ($\Delta W = 0$).

4. **Calculate airplane performance, considering density altitude, wind, terrain, and other pertinent conditions.**

a. Density altitude chart.

1) Adjust the airport elevation to pressure altitude based upon the actual altimeter setting in relation to the standard altimeter setting of 29.92.

a) On the chart, the correction in feet is provided for different altimeter settings.

2) Plot the intersection of the actual air temperature (listed on the horizontal axis of the chart) with the pressure altitude (indicated by the diagonal lines).

3) Move straight across to the vertical column. This is the density altitude.

4) EXAMPLE: Outside air temperature   90°F
            Altimeter setting   30.20" Hg
            Airport elevation   4,725 ft.

a) Note that the altimeter setting of 30.20 requires a −257 correction factor.

b) Subtract 257 from field elevation of 4,725 ft. to obtain pressure altitude of 4,468 ft.

c) Locate 90°F on the bottom axis of the chart and move up to intersect the diagonal pressure altitude line of 4,468 ft.

d) Move horizontally to the left axis of the chart to obtain the density altitude of 7,400 ft.

DENSITY ALTITUDE CHART

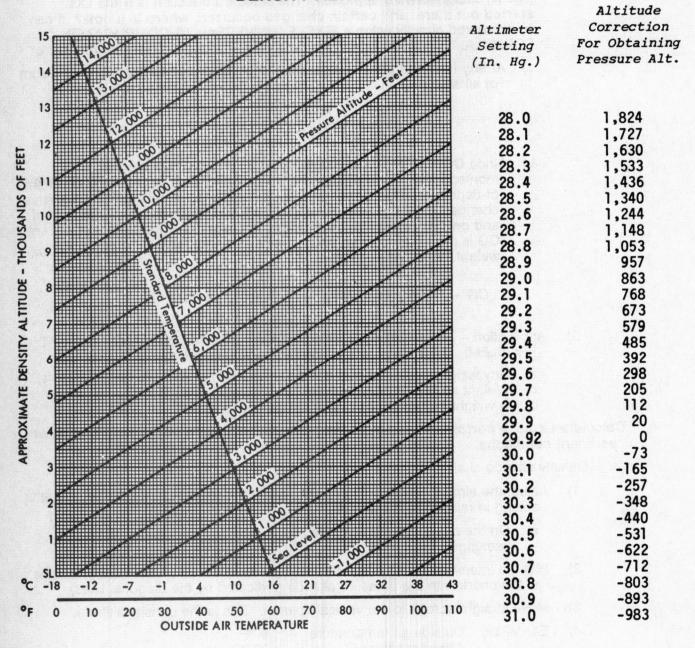

Altimeter Setting (In. Hg.)	Altitude Correction For Obtaining Pressure Alt.
28.0	1,824
28.1	1,727
28.2	1,630
28.3	1,533
28.4	1,436
28.5	1,340
28.6	1,244
28.7	1,148
28.8	1,053
28.9	957
29.0	863
29.1	768
29.2	673
29.3	579
29.4	485
29.5	392
29.6	298
29.7	205
29.8	112
29.9	20
29.92	0
30.0	-73
30.1	-165
30.2	-257
30.3	-348
30.4	-440
30.5	-531
30.6	-622
30.7	-712
30.8	-803
30.9	-893
31.0	-983

5) Your *POH* may contain performance charts that only require pressure altitude and temperature, thus you will not use a density altitude chart.

b. Takeoff performance chart.

    1) Takeoff performance graphs are either presented in terms of density altitude (as in the following example) or in terms of pressure altitude and temperature.

        a) Refer to the example takeoff distance graph below.

        b) First, compute the density altitude.

        c) Second, find the density altitude on the left-hand side of the graph. Move horizontally to the right until you intersect the ground run line or the 50-ft. barrier line as appropriate.

        d) From either point of intersection, drop vertically to the bottom of the graph to determine the takeoff distance in feet for your airplane.

        e) EXAMPLE: At 1,000-ft. density altitude the ground run would be just over 750 ft. and it would require just over 1,750 ft. to clear a 50-ft. obstacle with flaps at 25° and a paved, level, and dry runway.

    2) Obstacles other than 50 ft. in height: trees, power lines, etc., are not all 50 ft. in height. To determine the distance over a 100-ft. high obstacle, add the distance from ground roll to double the distance from liftoff to the 50-ft. obstacle.

        a) EXAMPLE: On the "Take-off Distance vs. Density Altitude" graph below, at 0 density altitude the ground roll is about 700 ft. and the distance over a 50-ft. obstacle is 1,600 ft. Thus, from liftoff to 50 ft. is 900 ft. (1,600 − 700); and distance over

            i) a 100-ft. obstacle would be 2,500 ft. (700 + 900 + 900).
            ii) a 75-ft. obstacle would be 2,050 ft. (700 + 900 + 450).

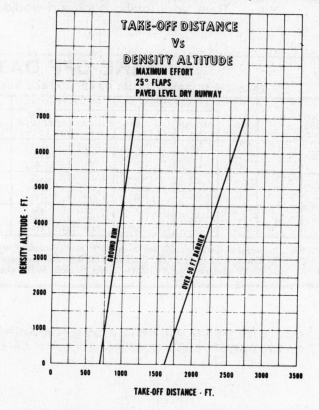

3)   Takeoff performance charts can often incorporate more variables, including headwind, gross weight, altitude, and temperature.

a)   Takeoff performance is affected by your airplane's gross weight. The chart below gives the data for gross weight of 1,700, 2,000, and 2,300 lb. If you are carrying a gross weight between these figures, you must interpolate.

b)   Headwind alternatives are 0, 10, and 20 kt. If actual headwind is between these figures, you must interpolate.

c)   The altitudes given are sea level, 2,500, 5,000, and 7,500 ft. MSL. You must interpolate for altitudes between these numbers.

d)   Separate distances are given for ground runs and to clear a 50-ft. obstacle.

e)   The notes to the chart indicate that you must

i)   Increase the distance 10% for each 25°F above standard temperature at any altitude. Temperatures given on the chart are standard.

ii)   Increase distance (for either a ground run or to clear an obstacle) by 7% of the "50-ft. obstacle" distance if using a dry grass runway rather than a paved runway.

f)   EXAMPLE: If your gross weight is 2,150 lb. with no headwind at 5,000 ft. and 41°F, your ground run on a paved runway with no flaps would be 1,080 ft. This is halfway between the 905 ft. at 2,000 lb. and 1,255 ft. at 2,300 lb.

i)   If the temperature was 66°F, you would have to add 10%, or 108 ft. Thus, your total ground run would be 1,188 ft.

TAKE-OFF DATA
TAKE-OFF DISTANCE FROM HARD SURFACE RUNWAY WITH FLAPS UP

GROSS WEIGHT POUNDS	IAS AT 50' MPH	HEAD WIND KNOTS	AT SEA LEVEL & 59°		AT 2500 FT. & 50°F		AT 5000 FT. & 41°F		AT 7500 FT. & 32°F	
			GROUND RUN	TOTAL TO CLEAR 50 FT OBS	GROUND RUN	TOTAL TO CLEAR 50 FT OBS	GROUND RUN	TOTAL TO CLEAR 50 FT OBS	GROUND RUN	TOTAL TO CLEAR 50 FT OBS
2300	68	0	865	1525	1040	1910	1255	2480	1565	3855
		10	615	1170	750	1485	920	1955	1160	3110
		20	405	850	505	1100	630	1480	810	2425
2000	63	0	630	1095	755	1325	905	1625	1120	2155
		10	435	820	530	1005	645	1250	810	1685
		20	275	580	340	720	425	910	595	1255
1700	58	0	435	780	520	920	625	1095	765	1370
		10	290	570	355	680	430	820	535	1040
		20	175	385	215	470	270	575	345	745

NOTES: 1.   Increase distance 10% for each 25°F above standard temperature for particular altitude.
2.   For operation on a dry, grass runway, increase distances (both "ground run" and "total to clear 50 ft. obstacle") by 7% of the "total to clear 50 ft. obstacle" figure.

c. Rate of climb performance.

1) This chart provides information at various gross weights, altitudes, and temperatures. It states the indicated airspeed, the rate of climb (ft./min.), and gallons of fuel used.

2) In the example chart below, the gross weights of 1,700, 2,000, or 2,300 lb. are given on the left.

3) Altitudes of sea level, 5,000, 10,000, or 15,000 ft. are given. Interpolate as necessary.

4) The notes give important information. In the example chart, Note 3 says to decrease rate of climb by 20 fpm for each 10°F above the standard temperatures.

5) EXAMPLE: With a gross weight of 2,000 lb. and field elevation of 5,000 ft. with a temperature of 61°F, the rate of climb would be 570 fpm. Note that the 610-fpm rate of climb must be reduced by 40 fpm since the temperature of 61°F is 20° above the standard temperature of 41°F.

MAXIMUM RATE-OF-CLIMB DATA

GROSS WEIGHT POUNDS	AT SEA LEVEL & 59°F			AT 5000 FT. & 41°F			AT 10,000 FT. & 23°F			AT 15,000 FT. & 5°F		
	IAS MPH	RATE OF CLIMB FT/MIN	GAL. OF FUEL USED	IAS MPH	RATE OF CLIMB FT MIN	FROM S.L. FUEL USED	IAS MPH	RATE OF CLIMB FT MIN	FROM S.L. FUEL USED	IAS MPH	RATE OF CLIMB FT MIN	FROM S.L. FUEL USED
2300	82	645	1.0	81	435	2.6	79	230	4.8	78	22	11.5
2000	79	840	1.0	79	610	2.2	76	380	3.6	75	155	6.3
1700	77	1085	1.0	76	825	1.9	73	570	2.9	72	315	4.4

NOTES:
1. Flaps up, full throttle, mixture leaned for smooth operation above 3000 ft.
2. Fuel used includes warm up and take-off allowance.
3. For hot weather, decrease rate of climb 20 ft./min. for each 10°F above standard day temperature for particular altitude.

d.   Cruise and range performance.

1)   The cruise and range performance of your airplane is based upon the density altitude, the engine RPM setting, and fuel capacity.

2)   Charts in your *POH* will provide the following information:

a)   The percentage of brake horsepower (% of power)
b)   True airspeed
c)   Range in miles
d)   Endurance in time (hours)

3)   Example of one type of cruise performance chart (see below).

a)   Given the first two columns (altitude and RPM), the last five columns are the result.

b)   EXAMPLE: Given an altitude of 6,000 ft. and 2,500 RPM, you are using 66% power, will achieve a true airspeed of 126 mph, use 7.5 gal./hr., have an endurance of 4.7 hr., and have a range of 587 SM assuming no wind.

i)   As in all performance charts, you must read the conditions and notes that apply (e.g., Note 4 refers to nonstandard temperature conditions).

CRUISE & RANGE PERFORMANCE

GROSS WEIGHT-2200 LBS.
STANDARD CONDITIONS
ZERO WIND
LEAN MIXTURE

ALTITUDE	RPM	PERCENT POWER	TRUE AIR SPEED—MPH	GALLONS/ HOUR	ENDURANCE HOURS	RANGE MILES
2500	2600	81	136	9.3	3.9	524
	2500	73	129	8.3	4.3	555
	2400	65	122	7.5	4.8	586
	2300	58	115	6.6	5.4	617
	2200	52	108	6.0	6.0	645
4500	2600	77	135	8.8	4.0	539
	2500	69	129	7.9	4.5	572
	2400	62	121	7.1	5.0	601
	2300	56	113	6.4	5.5	628
	2200	51	106	5.7	6.1	646
6500	2700	81	140	9.3	3.8	530
	2600	73	134	8.3	4.2	559
	2500	66	126	7.5	4.7	587
	2400	60	119	6.8	5.2	611
	2300	54	112	6.1	5.7	632
8500	2700	77	139	8.8	4.0	547
	2600	70	132	7.9	4.4	575
	2500	63	125	7.2	4.9	599
	2400	57	118	6.5	5.3	620
	2300	52	109	5.9	5.8	635
10500	2700	73	138	8.3	4.2	569
	2600	66	130	7.6	4.6	590
	2500	60	122	6.9	5.0	610
	2400	55	115	6.3	5.4	625
	2300	50	106	5.7	5.9	631

NOTES:

1. Range and endurance data include allowance for take-off and climb.
2. Fuel consumption is for level flight with mixture leaned. See Section III for proper leaning technique. Continuous operations at powers above 75% should be with full rich mixture.
3. Speed performance is without wheel fairings. Add 2 MPH for wheel fairings.
4. For temperatures other than standard, add or subtract 1%power for each 10° F. below or above standard temperature respectively.

e. Glide performance.

1) Glide performance is based on engine-out glide angle.

a) EXAMPLE: A 10 to 1 glide angle permits 10,000 ft. of forward movement (in no wind) for every 1,000 ft. of descent.

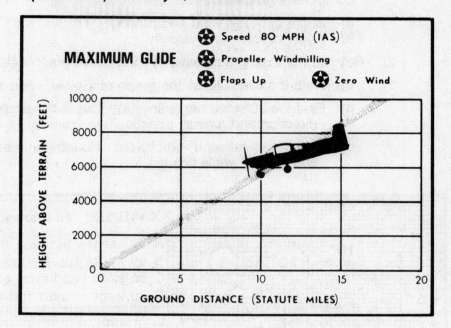

2) The chart above illustrates a glide ratio of 52,800/6,000 = 8.8 to 1.0 because the airplane will glide 10 SM from 6,000 ft. (in no wind, flaps up, etc.). Said differently, when the airplane is at 6,000 ft., the airplane can glide for 10 SM (5,280 ft. in a SM times 10 SM is 52,800 ft.).

f.   Crosswind performance.

1)   Many airplanes have an upper limit to the amount of direct crosswind in which they can land (usually about 20% of stall speed). Crosswinds of less than 90° are converted into a 90° component on graphs. Variables on crosswind component graphs are

a)   Angle between wind and runway
b)   Knots of total wind velocity

2)   Refer to the example crosswind component graph below.

a)   Note the example on the graph of a 40-kt. wind at a 30° angle.

b)   Find the 30° wind angle line (A). This is the angle between the wind direction and runway direction, e.g., runway 16 and wind from 190°.

c)   Find the 40-kt. wind velocity arc. Note the intersection of the wind arc and the 30° angle line (B).

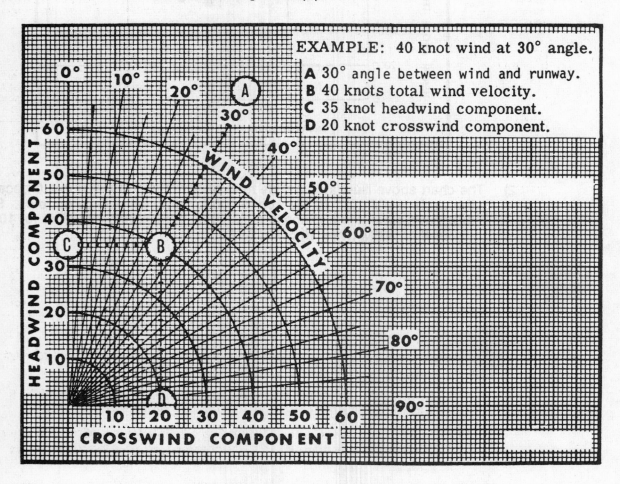

d)   Drop straight down from B to determine the crosswind component of 20 kt. Landing in this situation is like having a direct crosswind of 20 kt.

e)   Back at B, move horizontally to the left to determine the headwind component of 35 kt. Landing in this situation is like having a headwind of 35 kt.

g.   Landing performance.

1)   The data on the chart are based on the listed associated conditions, i.e., power, flaps, gear, runway, weight, and approach speed.

2)   You need to distinguish between distances for clearing a 50-ft. obstacle and no 50-ft. obstacle at the end of the runway.

a)   Ground roll is the term for landing distance given **no** 50-ft. obstacle.

3)   Example landing distances chart.

NORMAL LANDING DISTANCES

ASSOCIATED CONDITIONS

POWER	OFF
FLAPS	35°
GEAR	DOWN
RUNWAY	PAVED, LEVEL, DRY SURFACE
WEIGHT	2750 POUNDS
APPROACH SPEED	85 MPH/74 KTS IAS

NOTES:

1. GROUND ROLL IS APPROXIMATELY 45% OF TOTAL DISTANCE OVER 50 FT. OBSTACLE
2. FOR EACH 100 LBS. BELOW 2750 LBS. REDUCE TABULATED DISTANCE BY 3% AND APPROACH SPEED BY 1 MPH.

WIND COMPONENT DOWN RUNWAY KNOTS	SEA LEVEL OAT °F	TOTAL OVER 50 FT OBSTACLE FEET	2000 FT OAT °F	TOTAL OVER 50 FT OBSTACLE FEET	4000 FT OAT °F	TOTAL OVER 50 FT OBSTACLE FEET	6000 FT OAT °F	TOTAL OVER 50 FT OBSTACLE FEET	8000 FT OAT °F	TOTAL OVER 50 FT OBSTACLE FEET
0	23	1578	16	1651	9	1732	2	1820	-6	1916
	41	1624	34	1701	27	1787	20	1880	13	1983
	59	1670	52	1752	45	1842	38	1942	31	2050
	77	1717	70	1804	63	1899	56	2004	49	2118
	95	1764	88	1856	81	1956	74	2066	66	2187
15	23	1329	16	1397	9	1472	2	1555	-6	1644
	41	1372	34	1444	27	1524	20	1611	13	1707
	59	1414	52	1491	45	1575	38	1668	31	1770
	77	1458	70	1540	63	1626	56	1727	49	1833
	95	1502	88	1588	81	1682	74	1784	66	1898
30	23	1079	16	1142	9	1212	2	1289	-6	1372
	41	1119	34	1186	27	1260	20	1341	13	1430
	59	1158	52	1230	45	1308	38	1395	31	1489
	77	1199	70	1275	63	1357	56	1449	49	1548
	95	1240	88	1320	81	1407	74	1502	66	1608

a)   Headwind alternatives are 0, 15, and 30 kt. If the actual headwind is between these figures, you must interpolate.

b)   The altitudes given are sea level, 2,000, 4,000, 6,000, and 8,000 ft. MSL. If your altitude is between these figures, you must interpolate.

c)   For each headwind and altitude, five outside air temperatures are given. You must interpolate if the current temperature is between these figures.

d)   Ground roll is approximately 45% of the total distance over a 50-ft. obstacle (see Note 1 on the Normal Landing Distances chart).

e)   EXAMPLE: Given a weight of 2,750 lb., a 15-kt. headwind at 2,000 ft., and 52°F, the landing distance over a 50-ft. obstacle would be 1,491 ft. Ground roll would be 671 ft. (45% x 1,491 ft.).

5. **Describe the effects of atmospheric conditions on your airplane's performance.**

   a. Air density is perhaps the single most important factor affecting airplane performance. The general rule is as air density decreases, so does airplane performance.

      1) Temperature, altitude, barometric pressure, and humidity all affect air density. The density of the air DECREASES

         a) As air temperature INCREASES.
         b) As altitude INCREASES.
         c) As barometric pressure DECREASES.
         d) As humidity INCREASES.

      2) The engine produces power in proportion to the weight or density of the air.

         a) As air density decreases, the power output of the engine decreases.

            i) This is true of all engines not equipped with a supercharger or turbocharger.

      3) The propeller produces thrust in proportion to the mass of air being accelerated through the rotating blades.

         a) As air density decreases, propeller efficiency decreases.

      4) The wings produce lift as a result of the air passing over and under them.

         a) As air density decreases, the lift efficiency of the wing decreases.

   b. Conditions which affect your airplane's takeoff performance are

      1) As density altitude increases, takeoff performance decreases.

      2) A headwind will shorten the takeoff run and increase the angle of climb.

      3) A tailwind will increase the takeoff run and decrease the angle of climb.

      4) A runway which is muddy, wet, soft, rough, or covered with snow or tall grass has a retarding force and increases the takeoff distance.

      5) On takeoff, an upslope runway provides a retarding force which impedes acceleration, resulting in a longer ground run. Downhill will usually shorten the distance.

   c. A headwind during flight has an effect on performance. It decreases groundspeed and consequently increases the total amount of fuel consumed for that flight.

      1) A tailwind during flight increases the groundspeed and conserves fuel.

   d. Required landing distances differ due to changes in air density and other factors.

      1) However, indicated airspeed for landing is the same for your airplane at all altitudes.

      2) A headwind will steepen the approach angle and shorten the landing roll.

      3) A tailwind will decrease the approach angle and increase the landing roll.
         NOTE: Downwind operations should be considered very carefully before you attempt one.

      4) A runway which is muddy, wet, soft, rough, or covered with snow or tall grass may decrease the landing roll.

         a) However, ice or snow covering the surface will affect braking action and increase the landing roll considerably.

      5) Landing uphill usually results in a shorter landing roll.

         a) Downhill operations will usually increase the landing roll.

6.   **Make a competent decision on whether the required performance is within the operating limitations of the airplane.**

   a.   As a private pilot you must display sound judgment when determining whether the required performance is within your airplane's and your own capabilities and operating limitations.

      1)   Remember the performance charts in your *POH* do not make allowance for pilot proficiency or mechanical deterioration of the aircraft.

      2)   You can determine your airplane's performance in all phases of flight if you follow and use the performance charts in your *POH*.

END OF TASK

CROSS-COUNTRY FLIGHT PLANNING

I.D. TASK: CROSS-COUNTRY FLIGHT PLANNING

PILOT OPERATION - 7

REFERENCES: AC 61-21, AC 61-23, AC 61-84.

Objective. To determine that the applicant:

1. Exhibits knowledge by planning, within 30 min., a VFR cross-country flight of a duration near the range of the airplane, considering fuel and loading.

2. Selects and uses current and appropriate aeronautical charts.

3. Plots a course for the intended route of flight with fuel stops, if necessary.

4. Selects prominent en route checkpoints.

5. Computes the flight time, headings, and fuel requirements.

6. Selects appropriate radio navigation aids and communication facilities.

7. Identifies airspace, obstructions, and alternate airports.

8. Extracts pertinent information from the Airport/Facility Directory and other flight publications, including NOTAM's.

9. Completes a navigation log.

10. Completes and files a VFR flight plan.

A. General Information

1. This is one of six tasks (A-F) in this area of operation. Your examiner is required to test you on this task.

2. *Pilot Operation - 7* refers to FAR 61.107(a)(1): Cross-country flying, using pilotage, dead reckoning, and radio aids, including one 2-hr. flight.

3. FAA References

    AC 61-21: Flight Training Handbook
    AC 61-23: Pilot's Handbook of Aeronautical Knowledge
    AC 61-84: Role of Preflight Preparation

4. The objective of this task is for you to demonstrate your ability to properly plan a cross-country flight.

5. Review all your VFR cross-country flight planning skills in Gleim's *Private Pilot Handbook*, referring to Chapters 9, 10, 11, 12, and 14. Flipping through these chapters will be a good review. Stop and study topics as appropriate.

    a.   Chapter 9. Navigation Charts and Airspace
    b.   Chapter 10. Other Navigation Publications
    c.   Chapter 11. Navigation Made Easy
    d.   Chapter 12. Flight Computers
    e.   Chapter 14. Cross-Country Flying

B.   Task Objectives

1.   **Exhibit your knowledge by planning, within 30 min., a VFR cross-country flight of a duration near the range of your airplane, considering fuel and loading.**

   a.   Your examiner will inform you what airport will be your destination.

   b.   You will normally do your cross-country planning before the oral portion of your practical test. At that time, you will obtain your weather and determine your airplane's performance. Your examiner will then discuss your planning with you.

2.   **Select and use current and appropriate aeronautical charts.**

   a.   You must bring current VFR navigational charts (e.g., a sectional chart) to your practical test.

   b.   Obsolete charts must be discarded and replaced by new editions. This is important because revisions in aeronautical information occur constantly.

      1)   These revisions may include changes in radio frequencies, new obstructions, temporary or permanent closing of certain runways and airports, and other temporary or permanent hazards to flight.

   c.   The National Oceanographic Survey (NOS) publishes and sells aeronautical charts of the United States and foreign areas. The type of charts most commonly used by pilots flying VFR include

      1)   Sectional Charts. The scale is 1:500,000 (1 in. = 6.86 NM).

         a)   This chart is normally used for VFR navigation, and we will refer to this chart in this task.

      2)   VFR Terminal Area Charts. The scale is 1:250,000 (1 in. = 3.43 NM).

         a)   VFR Terminal Area Charts depict the airspace designated as a "Terminal Control Area." The information found on these charts is similar to that found on sectional charts. They exist for large metropolitan areas such as Atlanta and New York.

      3)   Both the sectional and VFR Terminal Area charts are revised semiannually.

   d.   VFR aeronautical charts are also available from the Aircraft Owners and Pilots Association (AOPA) on an individual or subscription basis. Call 1-800-872-2672 for information or to order.

      1)   Sectional and VFR Terminal Area Charts are also available at most FBOs.

   e.   The Sectional and VFR Terminal Area charts are designed for visual navigation by slow and medium speed aircraft.

      1)   The topographical information featured on these charts portrays surface elevation levels and a great number of visual checkpoints used for VFR flight.

      2)   Checkpoints include populated places, drainage, roads, railroads, and other distinctive landmarks.

      3)   The aeronautical information on sectional charts includes visual and radio aids to navigation, airports, controlled airspace, restricted areas, obstructions, and related data.

f.   The following information appears on the front of every sectional chart. Study it here! Few pilots take time to study the whole legend as they are in a hurry to look at the map itself. Your examiner will ask you to identify and explain some of these items while you are discussing your flight planning.

1)   Airports.

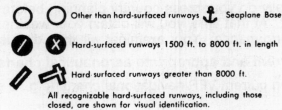

a)   Additional airport information.

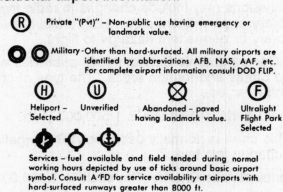

b)   Airports having control towers (airport traffic areas) are shown in blue, all others in magenta.

2)   Airport data.

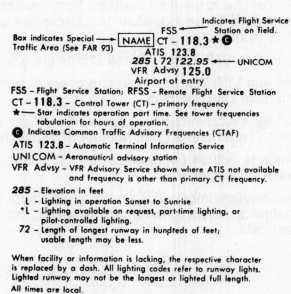

3)   Radio aids to navigation and communication boxes.

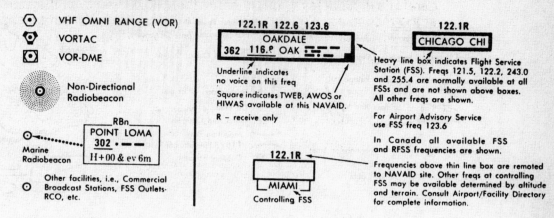

⊙   VHF OMNI RANGE (VOR)

⬡   VORTAC

▣   VOR-DME

Non-Directional Radiobeacon

Marine Radiobeacon

RBn
POINT LOMA
302 • ▬ ▬
H+00 & ev 6m

⊙   Other facilities, i.e., Commercial Broadcast Stations, FSS Outlets-RCO, etc.

122.1R 122.6 123.6
OAKDALE
362 116.? OAK

Underline indicates no voice on this freq

Square indicates TWEB, AWOS or HIWAS available at this NAVAID.

R – receive only

122.1R
MIAMI
Controlling FSS

122.1R
CHICAGO CHI

Heavy line box indicates Flight Service Station (FSS). Freqs 121.5, 122.2, 243.0 and 255.4 are normally available at all FSSs and are not shown above boxes. All other freqs are shown.

For Airport Advisory Service use FSS freq 123.6

In Canada all available FSS and RFSS frequencies are shown.

Frequencies above thin line box are remoted to NAVAID site. Other freqs at controlling FSS may be available determined by altitude and terrain. Consult Airport/Facility Directory for complete information.

4)   Airspace information. (NOTE: The 700-ft. floor, MOA and TRSA are magenta, while the similar-looking diagram near each is blue.)

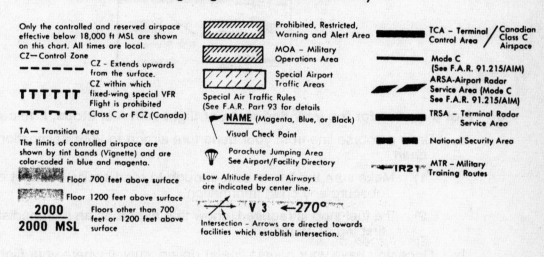

Only the controlled and reserved airspace effective below 18,000 ft MSL are shown on this chart. All times are local.

CZ—Control Zone

▬ ▬ ▬ ▬ ▬   CZ - Extends upwards from the surface.

ꞱꞱꞱꞱꞱꞱ   CZ within which fixed-wing special VFR Flight is prohibited

▪ ▪ ▪ ▪   Class C or F CZ (Canada)

TA— Transition Area

The limits of controlled airspace are shown by tint bands (Vignette) and are color-coded in blue and magenta.

Floor 700 feet above surface

Floor 1200 feet above surface

2000
2000 MSL   Floors other than 700 feet or 1200 feet above surface

Prohibited, Restricted, Warning and Alert Area

MOA – Military Operations Area

Special Airport Traffic Areas

Special Air Traffic Rules (See F.A.R. Part 93 for details

NAME (Magenta, Blue, or Black)
Visual Check Point

Parachute Jumping Area
See Airport/Facility Directory

Low Altitude Federal Airways are indicated by center line.

V 3 ←270°

Intersection - Arrows are directed towards facilities which establish intersection.

TCA – Terminal Control Area   /   Canadian Class C Airspace

Mode C
(See F.A.R. 91.215/AIM)

ARSA-Airport Radar Service Area (Mode C See F.A.R. 91.215/AIM)

TRSA – Terminal Radar Service Area

National Security Area

←IR21   MTR – Military Training Routes

5)   Obstructions.

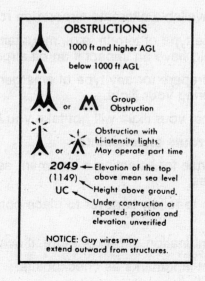

OBSTRUCTIONS

1000 ft and higher AGL

below 1000 ft AGL

or   Group Obstruction

or   Obstruction with hi-intensity lights. May operate part time

2049 ← Elevation of the top above mean sea level
(1149) ← Height above ground.
UC ← Under construction or reported: position and elevation unverified

NOTICE: Guy wires may extend outward from structures.

6)   Topographical information.

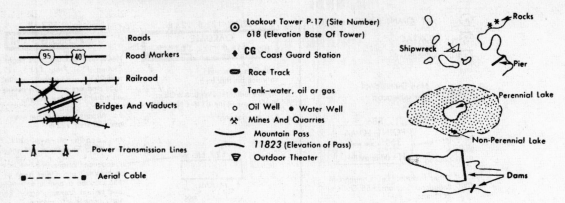

7)   Miscellaneous.

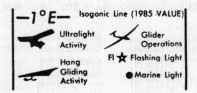

3.   **Plot a course for the intended route of flight with fuel stops, if necessary.**

   a.   Draw a course line from your departure airport to your destination on your sectional chart.

      1)   Make sure the line is dark enough to read easily, but light enough not to obscure any chart information.

      2)   If a fuel stop is required, show that airport as an intermediate stop, or as the first leg of your flight.

   b.   Once you have your course line(s) drawn, survey where your flight will be taking you.

      1)   Look for available alternate airports en route.

      2)   Look at the type of terrain, e.g., mountains, swamps, large bodies of water, that would have an impact if an off-airport landing became necessary.

      3)   Mentally prepare for any type of emergency situation and the action to be taken during your flight.

      4)   Be sure that your flight will not take you into restricted or prohibited airspace.

4. **Select prominent en route checkpoints.**

   a.   There is no set rule for selecting a landmark as a checkpoint. Every locality has its own peculiarities.

   b.   The general rule to follow is never to place complete reliance on any single landmark.

      1)   Use a combination of two or more, if available.

   c.   Select prominent landmarks as checkpoints.

5. Compute the flight time, headings, and fuel requirements.

    a. After obtaining your weather information (including winds aloft), as discussed in Task I.B., Obtaining Weather Information, beginning on page 89, you can select the most favorable altitude for your flight.

        1) You must maintain basic VFR weather minimums.

            a) When flying below 10,000 ft. MSL in controlled airspace, you must remain at least 500 ft. below, 1,000 ft. above, and 2,000 ft. horizontally from the clouds, with at least 3 SM flight visibility.

                i) This also applies in uncontrolled airspace above 1,200 ft. AGL and below 10,000 ft. MSL, at night (only 1 SM visibility required during the day).

        2) When operating your airplane under VFR in level cruising flight more than 3,000 ft. AGL, you must maintain the appropriate altitude, unless otherwise authorized by ATC.

VFR CRUISING ALTITUDES AND FLIGHT LEVELS			
If your magnetic course (ground track) is:	*And you are more than 3,000 feet above the surface but below 18,000 feet MSL, fly:*	*And you are above 18,000 feet MSL to FL 290 (except within Positive Control Area, FAR 71.193), fly:*	*And you are above FL 290 (except within Positive Control Area, FAR 71.193), fly 4,000 foot intervals:*
0° to 179°	Odd thousands MSL, plus 500 feet (3,500, 5,500, 7,500, etc.).	Odd Flight Levels plus 500 feet (FL 195, FL 215, FL 235, etc.).	Beginning at FL 300 (FL 300, 340, 380, etc.).
180° to 359°	Even thousands MSL, plus 500 feet (4,500, 6,500, 8,500, etc.).	Even Flight Levels plus 500 feet (FL 185, FL 205, FL 225, etc.).	Beginning at FL 320 (FL 320, 360, 400, etc.).

        3) Ensure that you maintain an altitude appropriate to obstacle or terrain clearance.

        4) Ensure that you maintain an altitude to maintain reception of any radio navigation facilities that you will be using.

        5) Once you determine your cruising altitude, you can complete this element.

    b. Your flight computer assists you in solving navigational problems. It is essentially a circular slide rule and operates on the same principles. Or you may have an electronic flight computer which solves navigational problems and is used like a pocket calculator. Some (not all) of the possible calculations are

        1) Time and fuel required to reach a destination
        2) True airspeed and/or groundspeed
        3) Effect of wind on each of the above
        4) Changing nautical miles into statute miles and vice versa
        5) True altitude
        6) True/magnetic heading and/or course.

   c.   Speed, distance, and time are three interrelated elements. With any two of these elements, you can compute the third (missing) element.

      1)   The computations are:

          a)   Speed = distance + time
          b)   Distance = speed x time
          c)   Time = distance + speed

      2)   You can use your flight computer to make the above computations.

          a)   Note that if you solve for a distance problem in NM, the airspeed must be given in kt., i.e., in any problem both the speed and distance must be in either SM or NM.

   d.   You need to be able to compute either fuel burned, fuel consumption rate, or time remaining when you only know two of these three elements.

      1)   The computations are:

          a)   Fuel burned = fuel consumption rate x time
          b)   Time (available) = fuel to burn + fuel consumption rate
          c)   Fuel consumption rate = fuel burned + time

   e.   The wind side of your flight computer is used to compute the effect of wind on your heading, i.e., direction of flight, and your groundspeed.

      1)   In order to compute your true heading (the direction in which the airplane should be pointed to maintain the true course) and the groundspeed, you will need the following information:

          a)   True course. Plotted on your sectional chart based on your planned flight.

          b)   True airspeed. Estimated from normal cruise speeds for your airplane.

          c)   Wind direction. From winds aloft forecast for your planned flight level.

          d)   Wind speed. From winds aloft forecast for your planned flight level.

      2)   Before turning to the wind side of your flight computer, make sure your wind speed and groundspeed are both in either MPH or kt. If not, convert one to the other on the calculator side of your flight computer.

6.   Select appropriate radio navigation aids and communication facilities.

   a.   From studying your course on your sectional chart, you can determine which radio navigation aids (e.g., VOR and NDB) you may use for navigation and communication requirements for entering TCAs, ARSAs, and/or airport traffic areas.

      1)   These frequencies can be found on either your sectional chart and/or the Airport/Facility Directory.

   b.   See Task V.B., Radio Navigation, beginning on page 282 for a detailed discussion of radio navigation equipment, procedures, and limitations.

7.   Identify airspace, obstructions, and alternate airports.

   a.   You must be prepared to identify and explain the various types of airspace and the operational requirement that may affect your VFR flight.

      1)   Controlled airspace

          a)   *Continental Control Area* -- consists of the airspace at and above 14,500 ft. MSL over the continental United States and eastern Alaska except

             i)   The airspace less than 1,500 ft. AGL.
             ii)   Prohibited and some restricted areas.

General Dimensions of Airspace Segments

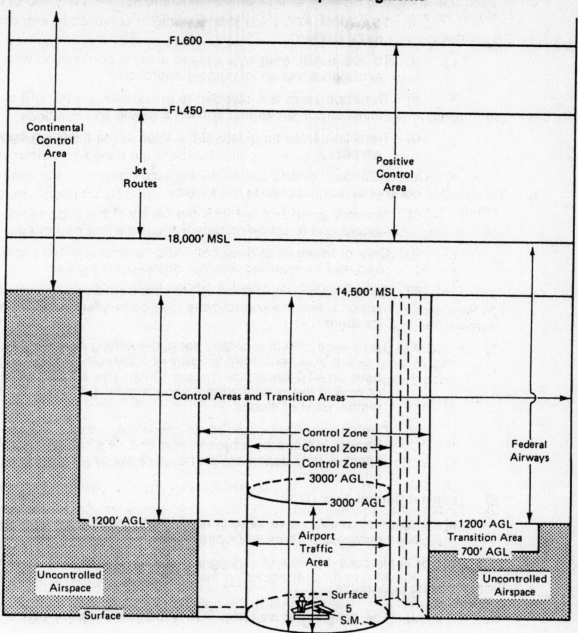

b) *Control Areas* -- a general term for Federal Airways and other controlled airspace.

c) *Positive Control Area* -- most of the airspace within the continental U.S. from 18,000 ft. MSL to and including FL 600.

    i) Within the Positive Control Area (PCA), all pilots must be instrument rated and all aircraft must operate under instrument flight rules.

d) *Transition Areas* -- extend controlled airspace closer to the ground.

    i)   To 1,200 ft. AGL (blue shaded area) in conjunction with airway route system.

    ii)   To 700 ft. AGL (magenta shaded area) in conjunction with an airport that has an instrument approach.

    iii) Transition areas are intended to provide for stricter VFR weather minimums in areas that contain IFR activity.

    iv) Transition areas terminate at the base of the overlying controlled airspace.

e) *Control Zones* -- extend controlled airspace down from the base of the continental control area to the surface.

    i)   Normally extends 5 SM from the center of the airport and may have extensions to accommodate IFR arrivals and departures.

    ii)   Control zones must have both ATC communications capabilities and an FAA-qualified weather observer on the field.

    iii) Control zones are located at both controlled and uncontrolled airports, and the control zone may be in effect part-time at some locations.

    iv) To operate VFR in a control zone, the ceiling must be 1,000 ft. AGL, and flight visibility of 3 SM; otherwise, you must have an ATC clearance (special VFR). This allows you to take off or land in the control zone if you maintain 1 SM visibility and remain clear of clouds.

    v)   Control zones are depicted on charts (e.g., on the Sectional Charts) outlined by a broken blue line. If a control zone is effective only during certain hours of the day, it will be so noted on the charts.

2) Terminal Control Area (TCA)

  a)   Major metropolitan area airports, such as Atlanta or New York, have been designated Terminal Control Areas.

  b)   TCA airspace consists of varying lateral and vertical limits, as well as a 30-NM ring (or veil) encircling the primary TCA airport and are depicted on sectional charts.

    i)   The geographic area of a TCA is marked by heavy blue lines.

    ii)   The 30-NM veil is marked by a lighter blue circle.

  c)   Operation within a TCA.

    i)   Two-way communication capability is required.

        • An ATC clearance to enter the TCA is mandatory.

    ii)   Mode C (altitude encoding) transponder is required within the TCA and also within the 30-NM veil.

3) Airport Radar Service Area (ARSA)

  a)   Certain busy airports and clusters of airports have been designated Airport Radar Service Areas.

  b)   ARSA airspace consists of two circles, both centered on the primary/ARSA airport, plus an outer area.

i) ARSAs are depicted by heavy dashed magenta lines on a sectional chart.

ii) The inner circle has a radius of 5 NM.

- The airspace of the inner circle extends from the surface of the ARSA airport up to 4,000 ft. above that airport.

iii) The outer circle has a radius of 10 NM.

- The airspace area between the 5-NM and 10-NM rings begins at a height of 1,200 ft. AGL and extends to the same altitude cap as the inner circle.

iv) The normal radius of the outer area will be 20 NM, with some variations based on site requirements.

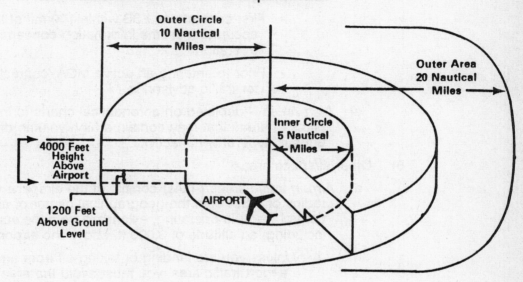

c) Operation within an ARSA:

i) Two-way radio communication must be maintained with ATC while within the ARSA.

- Aircraft departing satellite airports or heliports within the ARSA surface area must establish two-way communication with ATC as soon as possible.

- Pilots must comply with approved FAA traffic patterns when departing these airports.

ii) Mode C transponder is required within and above ARSAs.

4) Special use airspace

a) *Prohibited Areas* -- airspace of defined dimensions identified by an area on the surface within which flight is prohibited. Such areas are established for security or other reasons of national welfare.

b) *Restricted Areas* -- airspace identified by an area on the surface within which flight, while not wholly prohibited, is subject to restrictions.

i) Restricted Areas denote the existence of unusual, often invisible hazards to aircraft such as artillery firing, aerial gunnery, or guided missiles.

ii) Entering Restricted Areas without authorization from the using or controlling agency may be extremely hazardous.

c) *Warning Areas* -- airspace which may contain hazards to nonparticipating aircraft in international airspace. Warning Areas are established beyond the 3-mi. limit.

    i) Warning Areas cannot be legally designated as Restricted Areas because they are over international waters, but the activities conducted within Warning Areas may be as hazardous as those in Restricted Areas.

d) *Military Operations Areas (MOA)* -- airspace of defined vertical, lateral, and time limits established to separate certain military training activities from IFR traffic.

    i) Pilots operating under VFR should exercise extreme caution while flying within an MOA when military activity is being conducted.

- First contact any FSS within 100 mi. of the area to obtain accurate real-time information concerning the MOA hours of operation.

- Prior to entering an active MOA, contact the controlling agency for traffic advisories.

e) *Alert Areas* -- depicted on aeronautical charts to inform nonparticipating pilots of areas that may contain a high volume of pilot training or an unusual type of aerial activity.

5) Other airspace areas

a) *Airport traffic areas (ATAs)* consist of the airspace within a horizontal radius of 5 SM from the geographical center of any airport at which a control tower is operating, extending from the surface up to, but not including, an altitude of 3,000 ft. above the airport.

    i) Unless you are landing or taking off from an airport within the airport traffic area, you must avoid the area unless specifically authorized by ATC.

    ii) When operating to or from an airport served by a control tower, you must

- Establish and maintain radio communications with the tower prior to and while operating in the airport traffic area.

- Maintain radio communications with the tower while taxiing on the airport.

    iii) Remember, ATAs are not control zones. Controlled airspace requires ATC authorization when IFR conditions exist. ATAs require ATC authorization for VFR as well as IFR conditions.

b) The *airport advisory area* is the area within 10 SM of an airport that has no operating control tower but where an FSS is located. At such locations, the FSS provides advisory service to arriving and departing aircraft. Participation is recommended but not required.

c) *Military training routes (MTR)* are developed for use by the military for the purpose of conducting low-altitude, high-speed training.

    i) The routes above 1,500 ft. AGL are flown, to the maximum extent possible, under IFR.

- The routes at 1,500 ft. AGL and below are flown under VFR.

     ii)   MTRs are identified on aeronautical charts as follows:

- IR for IFR or VR for VFR.

- Routes below 1,500 ft. AGL use 4-digit identifiers, e.g., IR 1006, VR 1007.

- Routes above 1,500 AGL use 3-digit identifiers, e.g., IR 008, VR 009.

     iii)   Extreme vigilance should be exercised when flying through or near these routes.

- You should contact the FSS within 100 NM of a particular MTR to obtain current information on route use in the vicinity.

- Available information includes times of scheduled activity, altitudes in use on each route segment, and actual route width.

    d)   Temporary flight restrictions may be put into effect in the vicinity of any incident or event which by its nature may generate such a high degree of public interest that hazardous congestion of air traffic is likely.

     i)   NOTAMs implementing temporary flight restrictions will contain a description of the area in which the restrictions apply.

     ii)   Normally the area will include the airspace below 2,000 ft. above the surface within 5 mi. of the site of the incident. The exact dimensions will be included in the NOTAM.

  b.   Effective September 16, 1993, the current airspace designations will be changed to simplify airspace designation.

    1)   Beginning on approximately October 15, 1992, the first sectional charts, WACs, and Terminal Area Charts will have both the existing and the new airspace classifications.

    2)   The chart below summarizes the new airspace classifications.

AIRSPACE CLASSIFICATIONS

Airspace features	Class A airspace	Class B airspace	Class C airspace	Class D airspace	Class E airspace	Class G airspace
Current Airspace Equivalent...	Positive Control Areas.	Terminal Control Areas.	Airport Radar Service Areas.	Airport Traffic Areas and Control Zones.	General Controlled Airspace.	Uncontrolled Airspace
Operations Permitted	IFR	IFR and VFR	IFR and VFR	IFR and VFR	IFR and VFR	IFR and VFR
Entry Prerequisites	ATC clearance	ATC clearance	ATC clearance for IFR Radio contact for all.	ATC clearance for IFR Radio contact for all.	ATC clearance for IFR Radio contact for all IFR.	None
Minimum Pilot Qualifications	Instrument rating	Private or student certificate.	Student certificate	Student certificate	Student certificate	Student certificate
Two-way radio communications.	Yes	Yes	Yes	Yes	Yes for IFR operations.	No
VFR Minimum Visibility	Not applicable	3 statute miles	3 statute miles	3 statute miles	* 3 statute miles	** 1 statute mile
VFR Minimum Distance from Clouds.	Not applicable	Clear of clouds	500 feet below, 1,000 feet above, and 2,000 feet horizontal.	500 feet below, 1,000 feet above, and 2,000 feet horizontal.	* 500 feet below, 1,000 feet above, and 2,000 feet horizontal.	** 500 feet below, 1,000 feet above, and 2,000 feet horizontal
Aircraft Separation	All	All	IFR, SVFR, and runway operations.	IFR, SVFR, and runway operations.	IFR, SVFR.	None
Conflict Resolution	Not applicable	Not applicable	Between IFR and VFR operations.	No	No	No
Traffic Advisories	Not applicable	Not applicable	Yes	Workload permitting	Workload permitting	Workload permitting
Safety Advisories	Yes	Yes	Yes	Yes	Yes	Yes

* Different visibility minima and distance from cloud requirements exist for operations above 10,000 feet MSL.
** Different visibility minima and distance from cloud requirements exist for night operations, operations above 10,000 feet MSL, and operations below 1,200 feet AGL

c.   Obstructions can be man-made or natural. Check your route for changes in terrain elevation (indicated by shading on the sectional chart) and marked man-made obstructions and their height.

d.   Review your route to check the possible alternate airports available to you during your flight. This will prepare you should you encounter problems (e.g., weather, mechanical, etc.) and need to change your destination.

   1)   Once again review the terrain you will be flying over and plan for an emergency off-airport landing.

8.   **Extract pertinent information from the Airport/Facility Directory and other flight publications, including NOTAMs.**

a.   Airport/Facility Directory

   1)   The Airport/Facility Directory is a Civil Flight Information Publication published and distributed every 8 weeks by the NOS.

      a)   It contains a listing of all airports, seaplane bases, and heliports open to the public; communications data; navigational facilities; and certain special notices and procedures.

      b)   If you have any problem understanding an entry, refer to the "Legend for the Airport/Facility Directory" for a detailed explanation.

   2)   The Directory also contains National Weather Service telephone numbers listed alphabetically by state. Special services available at some locations are noted by the following symbols to the right of the phone numbers:

> ★ Indicates Pilots Automatic Telephone Weather Answering Service (PATWAS)
> ■ Indicates Telephone connected to the Transcribed Weather Broadcast (TWEB) providing transcribed aviation weather information.
> ◆ Indicates a restricted number, used for aviation weather information.
> ▼ Call FSS for "one call" FSS—Weather Service (WS) Briefing Service.
> §§ Indicates Fast File telephone number for pre-recorded and transcribed flight plan filing only.

      a)   Tabulations of parachute jump areas are contained in the Airport/Facility Directory.

b.   Notices to Airmen (NOTAMs)

   1)   NOTAMs offer time-critical aeronautical information which is of a temporary nature not sufficiently known in advance to permit publication on aeronautical charts or on other operational publications. These notices are disseminated immediately via telecommunications. They are published biweekly or held for local use depending on their urgency and applicability.

   2)   The biweekly publication of NOTAMs consists of two parts.

      a)   NOTAM (D) -- those expected to remain in effect for an extended period, and

      b)   All FDC NOTAMs.

      c)   The second section contains NOTAMs that are too long or affect a large area.

   3)   Note that NOTAMs of a temporary nature and those not yet published (in the biweekly booklet) are part of the hourly SA (weather) reports.

      a)   Only the NOTAMs (D) and FDC NOTAMs are included in the SA reports.

    4)   Sample NOTAMs.

        a)   !TLH Ø4/ØØ9 TLH 9-27 CLSD TIL Ø7182359.

        b)   !TLH Ø4/Ø11 TLH 27 ALS OTS TIL Ø7182359.

        c)   !TLH Ø4/Ø12 TLH 27 ILS GS OTS TIL Ø7182359.

    5)   If you do not have access to published NOTAMs, always ask the FSS briefer for any NOTAMs that are pertinent to your flight.

  c.   The AIM provides you with basic information and Air Traffic Control (ATC) procedures in the United States.

9.   Complete a navigation log.

  a.   Always use a flight log to assist you in planning and conducting a cross-country flight. The following discussion explains the flight log presented below. (Feel free to photocopy it to use on your cross-country flights.)

    1)   Note that the top half is the actual "flight log." The bottom should be used for notes about weather, winds, NOTAMs, and radio frequencies.

        a)   Write down all the radio frequencies you will need at each airport and for each VOR you will use for navigation. Thus, you will not be frantically fumbling for them during flight. This will give you added confidence.

    2)   The left two-thirds of the top is completed prior to your flight (once you have your winds aloft data), and the right third of the top is completed while you are en route.

FLIGHT LOG

			PREFLIGHT									ENROUTE				
From	To	True Course	Wind Corr.	True Head.	Var.	Mag. Head.	Dist. Log/Total	Est. GS	Time Log/Total	Est. Fuel	Act'l. Time	Act'l. GS	Dist. Next Pt.	Est. Arrv'l.	Fuel Used	Fuel Remain

Weather Reports	Winds Aloft	Radio and Navigation Frequencies
Terminal Forecasts	**NOTAMS**	

3)   The "From" and "To" columns are the origin and destination points (or checkpoints) between which you are navigating.

4)   The true course is measured relative to true north, as measured by your protractor on your sectional chart.

5)   Wind correction (plus or minus) is computed on the wind side of your flight computer.

6)   Your true heading is your true course adjusted for wind correction.

7)   The magnetic heading is the true heading adjusted for magnetic variation.

   a)   Magnetic variation is the difference between true north and magnetic north. The amount of variation is identified in your geographic area by red dashed isogonic lines on the sectional charts.

   b)   Remember, subtract easterly variation and add westerly variation.

      i)   Memory aid: East is least, West is best.

   c)   Remember that compass heading is the magnetic heading adjusted for compass error using the compass correction card, which is found on the front of your compass. It tells you what compass heading to hold to obtain a magnetic heading.

8)   The distance is measured between the two points on your sectional chart with a navigational plotter. Remember to use the side with the 1:500,000 scale for sectional charts.

9)   Remember that, if you are using VORs to navigate from and to, the directions of the airways are magnetic; i.e., they are adjusted for local magnetic variation.

   a)   The same is true for the compass rose encircling each VOR.

   b)   Thus, when using VORs, you should start with the magnetic course (unadjusted for wind) directly from the sectional chart. Then compute the wind correction angle (after you convert wind from true to magnetic) and adjust the magnetic course to the adjusted magnetic heading.

10) When you compute the wind correction on your flight computer, also note your estimated groundspeed.

11) Based on the distance and groundspeed, you can determine your estimated time for each leg and the cumulative estimated time for the flight.

12) Given the estimated time en route and your planned fuel consumption, determine the fuel to be used on each leg.

13) Once en route, you should mark down the time over every checkpoint. Then you can compare your estimated groundspeed to actual groundspeed and revise your estimated fuel (used and remaining).

b.   Note that the preceding procedures are not mandatory. There are many possible shortcuts. On very routine flights, you may not even use a flight log.

1)   For your Private Pilot Practical Test, however, you should work up a complete flight log.

2)   Normally, you may want to use an abbreviated flight log. A sample is reproduced on the opposite page. It is the reverse side of the FAA flight plan (Form 7233-1) which is reproduced on page 130. Feel free to photocopy it for your own use.

FLIGHT LOG

DEPARTURE POINT	VOR		RADIAL		DISTANCE		TIME			GROUND SPEED
	IDENT.		TO		LEG		POINT-POINT		TAKEOFF	
	FREQ.			FROM	REMAINING		CUMULATIVE			
CHECK POINT									ETA	
									ATA	
DESTINATION										
					TOTAL					

PREFLIGHT CHECK LIST

DATE

EN ROUTE WEATHER/WEATHER ADVISORIES

DESTINATION WEATHER   **WINDS ALOFT**

ALTERNATE WEATHER

FORECASTS

NOTAMS/AIRSPACE RESTRICTIONS

10. **Complete and file a VFR flight plan.**

a. The final step in your cross-country flight planning is to complete and file a VFR flight plan.

b. VFR flight plans are not mandatory but they are highly recommended as a safety precaution. In the event you do not reach your destination as planned, the FAA will institute a search for you. This process begins 30 min. after you were scheduled to reach your destination.

c. Flight plans can be filed in person at FSSs, in which case you give them a completed flight plan form.

1) Flight plans may also be called in by telephone or radioed in when in flight.

2) The flight plan form below may be photocopied for your own use. It is also available at FSSs and other FAA offices. The abbreviated flight log (page 129) is printed on the back of this FAA flight plan.

Form Approved: OMB No. 2120-0026

U.S. DEPARTMENT OF TRANSPORTATION FEDERAL AVIATION ADMINISTRATION **FLIGHT PLAN**	(FAA USE ONLY) ☐ PILOT BRIEFING ☐ VNR ☐ STOPOVER		TIME STARTED	SPECIALIST INITIALS

1. TYPE VFR / IFR / DVFR	2. AIRCRAFT IDENTIFICATION	3. AIRCRAFT TYPE/ SPECIAL EQUIPMENT	4. TRUE AIRSPEED KTS	5. DEPARTURE POINT	6. DEPARTURE TIME PROPOSED (Z) ACTUAL (Z)	7. CRUISING ALTITUDE

8. ROUTE OF FLIGHT

9. DESTINATION (Name of airport and city)	10. EST. TIME ENROUTE HOURS MINUTES	11. REMARKS

12. FUEL ON BOARD HOURS MINUTES	13. ALTERNATE AIRPORT(S)	14. PILOT'S NAME, ADDRESS & TELEPHONE NUMBER & AIRCRAFT HOME BASE 17. DESTINATION CONTACT/TELEPHONE (OPTIONAL)	15. NUMBER ABOARD

16. COLOR OF AIRCRAFT	CIVIL AIRCRAFT PILOTS. FAR Part 91 requires you file an IFR flight plan to operate under instrument flight rules in controlled airspace. Failure to file could result in a civil penalty not to exceed $1,000 for each violation (Section 901 of the Federal Aviation Act of 1958, as amended). Filing of a VFR flight plan is recommended as a good operating practice. See also Part 99 for requirements concerning DVFR flight plans.

FAA Form 7233-1 (8-82)   CLOSE VFR FLIGHT PLAN WITH_____ FSS ON ARRIVAL

d.   As illustrated on page 130, a flight plan requires the following 16 points of information:

1)   Type -- VFR, IFR, DVFR (DVFR refers to defense VFR flights. They are VFR flights into air defense identification zones which require a VFR flight plan to be filed)

2)   Airplane identification

3)   Airplane type/special equipment

4)   True airspeed (kt.)

5)   Departure point

6)   Departure time -- proposed (Z) and actual (Z)

7)   Cruising altitude

8)   Route of flight

9)   Destination (name of airport and city)

10)   Estimated time en route -- hours and minutes

11)   Remarks

12)   Fuel on board -- hours and minutes

13)   Alternate airport(s)

14)   Pilot's name, address, and telephone number, and airplane home base

15)   Number of people aboard

16)   Color of aircraft

e.   Your FSS specialist will be glad to assist you and answer any questions. Occasionally you may have to file a flight plan without an FAA form in front of you. Ask the briefer to prompt you for the required information.

f.   CLOSE YOUR FLIGHT PLAN: REMEMBER! REMEMBER!

1)   Add "Close your flight plan" to your after-landing checklist.

2)   If you do not close your flight plan, the FAA will have to devote its limited and valuable resources attempting to determine if you did in fact arrive safely.

a)   If they cannot locate you or your airplane, they will contact a Rescue Coordination Center which will institute a "Search and Rescue" mission, the cost of which you may be responsible for.

3)   Thus, it is particularly important to notify any FAA facility when you are late (over 30 min.) or have diverted to an alternate route or destination.

4)   While en route, you can identify yourself and your location to FSSs along your route (especially convenient if you are obtaining weather information), which will assist the FAA if they have to look for you.

5)   If you cannot reach the FSS to close your flight plan, call any ATC (Air Traffic Control) facility, which will relay the message.

6)   A memory jogger: When you open your flight plan put your watch on your right wrist if you normally wear it on your left wrist (or vice versa). Do not put it back until the flight plan is closed.

END OF TASK

AIRPLANE SYSTEMS

> **I.E. TASK: AIRPLANE SYSTEMS**
>
> *PILOT OPERATION - 1*
>
> REFERENCES: AC 61-21; Airplane Handbook and Flight Manual.
>
> **Objective.** To determine that the applicant exhibits knowledge by explaining the airplane systems and operation including, as appropriate:
>
> | | | | |
> |---|---|---|---|
> | 1. | Primary flight controls and trim. | 8. | Hydraulic system. |
> | 2. | Wing flaps, leading edge devices, and spoilers. | 9. | Electrical system. |
> | 3. | Flight instruments. | 10. | Environmental system. |
> | 4. | Landing gear. | 11. | Oil system. |
> | 5. | Engine. | 12. | Deice and anti-ice systems. |
> | 6. | Propeller. | 13. | Avionics. |
> | 7. | Fuel system. | 14. | Vacuum system. |

A. General Information

1. This is one of six tasks (A-F) in this area of operation. Your examiner is required to test you on this task.

2. *Pilot Operation - 1* refers to FAR 61.107(a)(1): Preflight operations, including weight and balance determination, line inspection, and aircraft servicing.

3. FAA References

    AC 61-21: Flight Training Handbook
    Pilot's Operating Handbook (FAA-Approved Airplane Flight Manual)

4. The objective of this task is for you to demonstrate your knowledge of your airplane's systems and their operation.

    a. This task is make and model specific, and applies to the airplane used on your practical test.

5. To prepare for this task, systematically study, not just read, Sections 1, 7, 8, and 9 of your *POH*:

    a. Section 1. General.
    b. Section 7. Airplane and Systems Descriptions.
    c. Section 8. Airplane Handling, Service and Maintenance.
    d. Section 9. Supplement (Optional Systems Description and Operating Procedures).

6. Finally, make a list of the make and model of all avionics equipment in your training airplane. Make yourself conversant with the purpose, operation, and capability of each unit. You should be constantly discussing your airplane's systems with your CFI.

7. As an example of what you should study, the table of contents of Sections 1, 7, 8, and 9 of the *Beech Skipper POH* are reproduced on the following pages.

Beechcraft Skipper 77

SECTION I - GENERAL

- Important Notice
- Use of the Handbook
- Revising the Handbook
- Airplane Flight Manual
- Supplements Revision Record
- Vendor-Issued STC Supplements
- Airplane Three View
- Ground Turning Clearance

> **For Academic Illustration/Training Purposes Only!**
> *For Flight:* **Use your Pilot's Operating Handbook and FAA-Approved Airplane Flight Manual.**

- Descriptive Data
  Engine
  Propeller
  Fuel
    Approved Fuel Types
  Oil
    Oil Capacity
    Approved Oil Types
  Maximum Certificated Weights
  Standard Airplane Weights
  Cabin and Entry Dimensions
  Baggage Space Dimensions
  Specific Loadings
- Symbols, Abbreviations, and Terminology
  Airspeed Terminology
  Meteorological Terminology
  Power Terminology
  Engine Controls and Instruments Terminology
  Airplane Performance and Flight Planning
    Terminology
  Weight and Balance Terminology

Beechcraft Skipper 77

SECTION VII - SYSTEMS DESCRIPTION

- Airframe
    - Seating Arrangements
- Flight Controls
    - Control Surfaces
    - Operating Mechanisms
    - Trim Control
        - Elevator Trim
        - Rudder Trim
- Instrument Panel
    - Illustration
    - Flight Instruments
- Ground Control
- Wing Flaps
- Landing Gear
    - Brakes
- Baggage Compartment
- Seats, Seat Belts, and Shoulder Harnesses
    - Seats
    - Seat Belts
    - Shoulder Harnesses
- Doors and Exits
    - Cabin Doors
    - Emergency Exit
- Control Locks
- Engine
    - Engine Controls
    - Engine Instruments
- Engine Break-in Information

- Lubrication System
- Engine Ice Protection
    - Carburetor Heat
- Induction Air
- Starter
- Propeller
- Fuel System
    - Fuel Tanks
    - Fuel Quantity Indicators
    - Low Fuel Quantity Warning Light
    - Fuel System Schematic
    - Fuel Drains
    - Fuel Boost Pump
    - Fuel Required for Flight
- Electrical System
    - Battery
    - Electrical Schematic
    - Alternator
    - Starter
    - Starter Engaged Warning Light
    - External Power
- Lighting System
    - Interior Lighting
    - Exterior Lighting
- Environmental Systems
    - Cabin Heating
    - Heater and Defroster Operation
    - Environmental Schematic
    - Cabin Ventilation
    - Exhaust Vent
- Pitot and Static Systems
    - Pitot System
        - Pitot Heat
    - Static Air System
    - Alternate Static Air System
- Pressure System
- Stall Warning
- Emergency Locator Transmitter (ELT)
- Fire Extinguisher

Beechcraft Skipper 77

SECTION VIII - HANDLING, SERVICING, AND MAINTENANCE

- Introduction
- Publications
- Airplane Inspection Periods
- Preventative Maintenance That May Be Accomplished By a Certificated Pilot
- Alterations or Repairs to Airplane
- Ground Handling
    - Towing
    - Parking
    - Tie-Down
    - Jacking
- Prolonged Out-of-Service Care
    - Flyable Storage - 7 to 30 Days
        - Mooring
        - Engine Preparation for Storage
        - Fuel Tanks
        - Flight Control Surfaces
        - Grounding
        - Pitot Tube
            - During Flyable Storage
            - Preparation for Service
- External Power

- Servicing
    - Fuel System
    - Oil System
    - Recommended Oil Grades
    - Battery
    - Tires
    - Shock Strut
    - Shimmy Damper
    - Brakes
    - Induction Air Filter
    - Instrument Air Filter
    - Propeller Blades
- Minor Maintenance
    - Rubber Seals
    - Alternators
    - Magnetos
- Cleaning
    - Exterior Painted Surfaces
    - Lacquer Paint Finishes
    - Urethane Paint Finishes
    - Windshields and Windows
    - Engine
    - Interior
- Lubrication Points
- Recommended Servicing Schedule
- Consumable Materials
- Approved Engine Oils
- Lamp Replacement Guide
- Overhaul and Replacement Schedule
- Inspections

For Academic Illustration/Training Purposes Only!
For Flight: **Use your Pilot's Operating Handbook and FAA-Approved Airplane Flight Manual.**

SECTION IX - SUPPLEMENTS

Pilot's Operating Handbook
and
FAA-Approved Airplane Flight Manual
Log of Supplements

For Academic Illustration/Training Purposes Only!
For Flight: **Use your Pilot's Operating Handbook and FAA-Approved Airplane Flight Manual.**

FAA Supplements must be in the airplane for flight operation when subject equipment is installed:

Supp No.	Part Number	Subject	Rev. No.	Date

B.   Task Objectives

1.   **Primary flight controls and trim.**

a.   The airplane's attitude is controlled by deflection of the primary flight controls. These are hinged, movable surfaces attached to the trailing edges of the wings and vertical and horizontal stabilizers. When deflected, these surfaces change the camber (curvature) and angle of attack of the wing or stabilizer, and thus, its lift and drag characteristics.

1)   The pilot operates the flight controls through connecting linkage to the rudder pedals and the control yoke.

a)   The control yoke may be either a wheel or a stick.

2)   The rudder is attached to the vertical stabilizer. Controlled by the rudder pedals, the rudder is used to control the direction (left or right) of yaw about the airplane's vertical axis. The rudder is not used to make the airplane turn, as is often erroneously believed. Remember, banking the airplane makes it turn.

a)   When the rudder is deflected to one side (left or right), it protrudes into the airflow, causing a horizontal force to be exerted in the opposite direction.

b)   This pushes the tail of the airplane in that direction and yaws the nose in the desired direction.

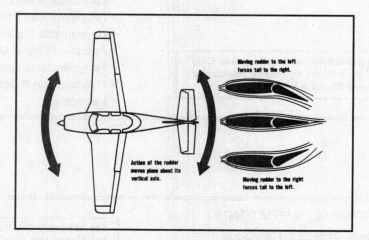

c)   Remember, the primary purpose of the rudder in flight is to counteract the effect of adverse yaw and to help provide directional control of the airplane.

i)   It does not turn the airplane.

d)   When only the rudder is used for steering during ground taxiing, the propeller slipstream provides the force to yaw or turn the airplane in the desired direction.

3)   The elevators are attached to the horizontal stabilizer. The elevators provide you with control of the pitch attitude about the airplane's lateral axis. The elevators are controlled by pushing or pulling the control yoke.

a)   You adjust the angle of attack of the entire horizontal stabilizer by raising or lowering the elevators. The horizontal stabilizer normally has a negative angle of attack to provide a downward force (rather than a lifting force) in the rear of the plane to offset the heaviness of the airplane's nose.

b)   Applying back pressure on the control yoke (i.e., pulling the yoke toward you) raises the elevators. The raised elevators increase the horizontal stabilizer's negative angle of attack and consequently increase the downward tail force. This forces the tail down, increasing the angle of attack of the wings.

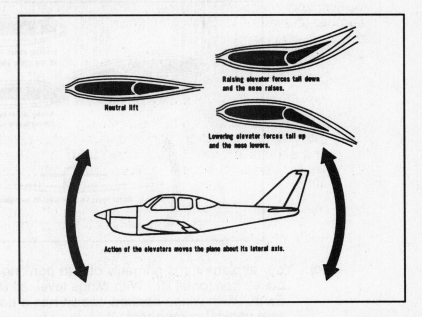

c)   Applying forward pressure to the control yoke (i.e., pushing it away) lowers the elevators. The lowered elevators decrease the horizontal stabilizer's negative angle of attack and consequently decrease the downward force on the tail. The tail rises, decreasing the angle of attack of the wings.

d)   Some airplanes have a movable horizontal surface called a stabilator, which combines the horizontal stabilizer and elevators. When the control yoke is moved the stabilator is moved to raise or lower its leading edge, thus changing its angle of attack and amount of lift.

4)   The ailerons (the French term for "little wing") are located on the trailing (rear) edge of each wing near the outer wingtips. The ailerons are used to rotate (bank) the airplane about the longitudinal axis to control roll.

a)   The ailerons are interconnected in the control system to operate simultaneously in opposite directions from each other. As the aileron on one wing is deflected downward, the aileron on the opposite wing is deflected upward.

i)   Turning the control wheel or pushing the control stick to the right raises the aileron on the right wing and lowers the aileron on the left wing.

ii) Turning the control wheel or pushing the control stick to the left raises the aileron on the left wing and lowers the aileron on the right wing.

b) When an aileron is lowered, the angle of attack on that wing will increase, which increases the lift. When an aileron is raised, the angle of attack will decrease, which decreases the lift. This permits rolling (banking) the airplane laterally around the longitudinal axis.

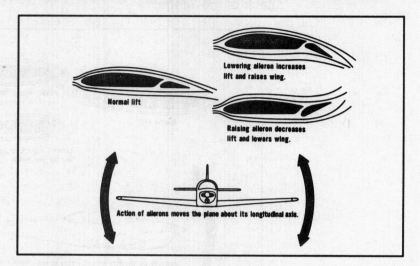

c) Your airplane turns primarily due to banking of the wings, which produces horizontal lift. With wings level, all lift is perpendicular to the Earth. With wings banked, the lift has a horizontal component as well as a vertical component.

i) The horizonal component (i.e., when the wings are lifting sideways as well as up) counteracts the centrifugal force pulling the airplane straight ahead.

ii) The rudder is required to coordinate the turn.

b. Trim devices are commonly used to relieve you of the need of maintaining continuous pressure on the primary controls. Thus, you can "retrim" at each power setting, airspeed, and/or flight attitude to neutralize control pressure.

1) These devices are small airfoils attached to, or recessed into, the trailing edge of the primary control surfaces (i.e., elevator, aileron, and/or rudder).

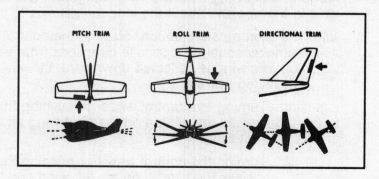

2)   Trim tabs are moved in a direction opposite to the direction that pressure is being applied on the control yoke.

    a)   If the elevator requires a constant up deflection, the back pressure on the control yoke can be relieved by deflecting the trim tab down.

3)   Anti-servo tabs also look similar to trim tabs. The anti-servo tab is coupled to the control surface by a rod, so that when the control surface is moved in any direction, the tab is automatically deflected in the same direction. These are commonly found on aircraft with stabilators. Anti-servo tabs are designed to prevent a control surface from moving to full deflection due to aerodynamic forces.

4)   Balancing tabs look like trim tabs and are hinged in approximately the same places as trim tabs. The essential difference between the two is that the balancing tab is coupled to the control surface by a rod, so that when the primary control surface is moved in any direction, the tab automatically is moved in the opposite direction. In this manner, the airflow striking the tab counterbalances some of the air pressure against the primary control surface and enables the pilot to more readily move and hold it in position.

5)   Servo tabs, sometimes referred to as flight tabs, are used primarily on large airplanes. They aid the pilot in moving the control surface and in holding it in the desired position. Only the servo tab moves in response to movement of the pilot's flight control, and the force of the airflow on the servo tab then moves the primary control surface.

6)   The trim tab should not be used to position the primary control. Rather, control pressure should be used on the control yoke or rudder pedals to position the primary control, then the trim tab should be adjusted to relieve the control pressure.

    a)   Most airplanes provide a trim control wheel or electric switch for adjustment of the trim devices. To apply a trim force, the trim wheel or switch must be moved in the desired direction.

    b)   The position in which the trim device is set can usually be determined by reference to a trim indicator in the cockpit.

2.   **Wing flaps, leading edge devices, and spoilers.**

   a.   Wing flaps are used on most airplanes. Flaps increase both lift and drag and have three important functions:

    1)   First, they permit a slower landing speed which decreases the required landing distance.

    2)   Second, they permit a comparatively steep angle of descent without an increase in speed. This makes it possible to safely clear obstacles when making a landing approach to a small field.

    3)   Third, they may also be used to shorten the takeoff distance and provide a steeper climb path.

4)   Types of wing flaps

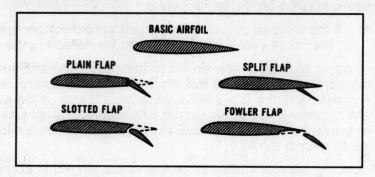

a)   Plain flap

   i)   Is a portion of the trailing edge of the wing on a hinged pivot which allows the flap to be moved downward.

   ii) This changes the chord line, angle of attack, and camber of the wing.

b)   Split flap

   i)   A hinged portion of only the bottom surface of the wing.

   ii) Increases the angle of attack by changing the chord line.

   iii) Split flap creates the least change in pitching moment.

c)   Slotted flap

   i)   Similar to a plain flap but provides a gap between the trailing edge of the wing and the leading edge of the flap.

   ii) Permits air to pass through and delays the airflow separation along the top of the wing.

d)   Fowler flap

   i)   Not only tilts downward but also slides rearward on tracks.

   ii) Increases the angle of attack, wing camber, and wing area.

   iii) Provides additional lift without significantly increasing drag.

   iv) Fowler flap provides the greatest amount of lift with the least amount of drag, which creates the greatest change in pitching moment.

5)   Most wing flaps are hinged near the trailing edges of the wings, inboard of the ailerons.

a)   They are controllable by the pilot either manually, electrically, or hydraulically.

b)   When they are in the up (retracted) position, they fit flush with the wings and serve as part of the wing's trailing edge.

c)   When in the down (extended) position, the flaps pivot downward from the hinge points to various angles ranging up to 40° to 50° from the wing.

6)   Flaps should be used in accordance with your airplane's *POH*. They should be engaged and disengaged slowly and deliberately.

    a)   When the flaps are extended, the airspeed should be at or below your airplane's maximum flap extended speed (V_{FE}).

        i)   If extended above this speed, the force exerted by the airflow may result in damage to the flaps.

        ii)   If the airspeed limitations are exceeded unintentionally with the flaps extended, you should retract them immediately regardless of airspeed.

    b)   It is extremely important that you form a habit of positively identifying the flap control before attempting to use it to raise or lower the flaps.

        i)   This is to prevent inadvertent landing gear operation in an airplane with the two controls in relative proximity.

b.   Leading edge devices are used on many larger airplanes.

1)   High-lift leading edge devices are applied to the leading edge of the airfoil.
2)   Fixed slots direct airflow to the upper wing surface.

    a)   This allows for smooth airflow over the wing at increasing angles-of-attack, and delays the airflow separation.

    b)   Does not increase the wing camber.

    c)   Stalls are delayed to a higher angle of attack.

3)   A slat consists of a leading edge segment which is free to move on tracks.

    a)   At low angles of attack the slat is held flush against the leading edge.

    b)   At high angles of attack, either a low pressure area at the wing's leading edge or pilot operated controls force the slat to move forward.

        i)   This opens a slot and allows the air to flow smoothly over the wing's upper surface, delaying the airflow separation.

c.   Spoilers, found only on certain airplane designs and most gliders, are mounted on the upper surface of each wing. Their purpose is to "spoil" or disrupt the smooth flow of air over the wing to reduce the wing's lifting force. It is a means of increasing the rate of descent without increasing the airplane's speed.

3.   Flight Instruments.

a.   Pitot-static system provides the source of air pressure for the operation of the altimeter, vertical speed indicator, and the airspeed indicator.

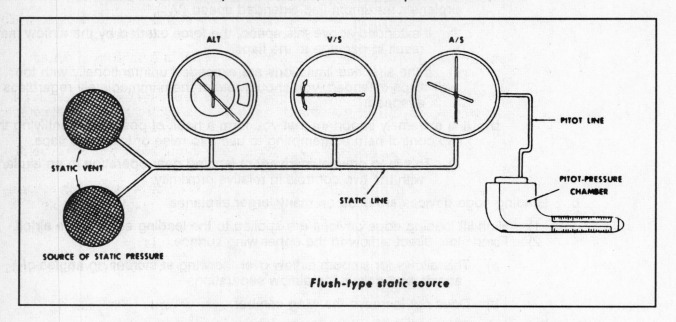

Flush-type static source

1)   The two major parts of the pitot-static system are the impact and static pressure and chamber lines.

a)   The impact air pressure (air striking the airplane because of its forward motion) is taken from a pitot tube. It is mounted either on the leading edge of the wing or on the nose and is aligned to the relative wind.

i)   The pitot tube provides impact air pressure only to the airspeed indicator.

b)   The static pressure (pressure of the still air) is usually taken from the static line attached to a vent or vents mounted flush with the side of the fuselage. Most airplanes using a flush-type static source have one vent on each side of the fuselage. This compensates for any possible variation in static pressure due to erratic changes in airplane attitude.

i)   The static pressure lines provide static air pressure to the altimeter, vertical speed indicator, and airspeed indicator.

c)   An alternate source for static pressure is provided in most airplanes in the event the static ports become clogged. This source usually is vented to the inside of the cockpit.

i)   Because of the venturi effect of the flow of air around the cockpit, this alternate static pressure is usually lower than the pressure provided by the normal static air source.

•   Since the air flowing around the cockpit is accelerated, there is a lower pressure around the cockpit (similar to air flowing over a wing). The air pressure in the cockpit is then lower as well.

      ii)   When the alternate static source is used, the following differences in the instrument indications usually occur:

- The altimeter may indicate a higher than actual altitude.
- The vertical speed indicator will initially indicate a climb while in level flight then return to a level indication.
- The airspeed indicator will indicate a greater than actual airspeed.

2)   The altimeter (ALT) measures the height of the airplane above a given level. Since it is the only instrument that gives altitude information, the altimeter is one of the most important instruments in the airplane.

    a)   Knowing your airplane's altitude is vitally important to you for several reasons:

      i)   You must be sure that the airplane is flying high enough to clear the highest terrain or obstruction along the intended route.

      ii)   To reduce the possibility of a midair collision, you must maintain altitudes in accordance with air traffic rules.

      iii)   Altitudes are often selected to take advantage of favorable winds and weather conditions.

      iv)   You must know the altitude to calculate true airspeed.

    b)   Principle of Operation. The pressure altimeter is an aneroid (mechanical) barometer that measures the pressure of the atmosphere at the altimeter's location to display an altitude indication in feet.

      i)   The altimeter uses static pressure as its source of operation.

      ii)   Altitude is thus determined in terms of air pressure.

      iii)   As altitude increases, atmospheric pressure decreases. This difference causes the altimeter to indicate changes in altitude.

    c)   Effect of Nonstandard Pressure and Temperature

      i)   Pressure and temperature affect air density, and thus altimeter indications.

- You adjust for nonstandard pressure by correctly entering the altimeter setting.
- If terrain or obstacle clearance is a factor in selecting a cruising altitude, particularly at higher altitudes, remember to anticipate that COLDER-THAN-STANDARD TEMPERATURE will place the aircraft LOWER than the altimeter indicates. Therefore, a higher indicated altitude should be used to provide adequate terrain clearance.

    d)   Setting the Altimeter. To adjust the altimeter for variation in atmospheric pressure, the pressure scale in the altimeter setting window (calibrated in inches of mercury) is adjusted to correspond with the given altimeter setting.

      i)   Flight service stations reporting the altimeter setting take a measurement of the station's atmospheric pressure hourly and correct it to sea level pressure. These altimeter settings are applicable only in the vicinity of the reporting station. Therefore, it is necessary to readjust the altimeter setting as the flight progresses.

ii)   FAA regulations (91.121) concerning altimeter settings:

- The cruising altitude of an airplane below 18,000 ft. MSL shall be maintained by reference to an altimeter that is set to the current reported altimeter setting of a station located along the route of flight and within 100 NM of the airplane.

- If there is no such station, the current reported altimeter setting of an appropriate available station shall be used.

iii)   Over high mountainous terrain, certain atmospheric conditions can cause the altimeter to indicate an altitude of 1,000 ft., or more, HIGHER than the actual altitude.

- For this reason a generous margin of altitude should be allowed.

e)   **Types of Altitude**

i)   **Absolute Altitude** -- The vertical distance of an airplane above the terrain. It is expressed as a number of ft. AGL.

ii)   **True Altitude** -- The vertical distance of the aircraft above sea level -- the actual altitude. It is expressed as a number of ft. MSL.

- Airport, terrain, and obstacle elevations found on aeronautical charts are true altitudes.

iii)   **Indicated Altitude** -- The altitude read directly from the altimeter after it is set to the current altimeter setting.

iv)   **Pressure Altitude** -- The altitude indicated when the altimeter setting window is adjusted to 29.92" Hg.

v)   **Density Altitude** -- This is pressure altitude corrected for nonstandard temperature variations.

3)   **The vertical speed indicator (VSI) indicates whether the airplane is climbing, descending, or in level flight. The rate of climb or descent is indicated in ft. per min. (fpm). If properly calibrated, the indicator will register zero in level flight.**

a)   **Principle of Operation.** Although the vertical speed indicator operates solely from static pressure, it is a differential pressure instrument.

i)   The case of the instrument is airtight except for a restricted passage (also known as a calibrated leak) to the static line of the pitot-static system. The sealed case contains a diaphragm with connecting linkage and gearing to the indicator pointer. The diaphragm also receives air from the static line but this is not a restricted passage.

ii)   When the airplane is on the ground or in level flight, the pressures inside the diaphragm and the instrument case remain the same and the pointer indicates zero.

iii)   When the airplane climbs or descends, the pressure inside the diaphragm changes immediately. But the restricted passage causes the pressure of the rest of the case to remain higher or lower for a short time. This differential pressure causes the diaphragm to contract or expand. The movement of the diaphragm is indicated on the instrument needle as a climb or descent.

b)   **While on the ground, the VSI should read "0" fpm. Some VSIs are adjustable by a set-screw on the face of the dial.**

4)   The airspeed indicator (ASI) is a sensitive differential-pressure gauge which measures the difference between (1) pitot or impact pressure and (2) static pressure.

   a)   These two pressures will be equal when the airplane is parked on the ground in calm air.

   b)   As the airplane moves, air strikes the pitot tube (hence, impact pressure). The impact pressure on the pitot line exceeds the pressure in the static lines. This difference in pressure is registered by the airspeed pointer on the face of the instrument, which is calibrated in miles per hour, knots, or both.

   c)   The three kinds of airspeed useful for pilots:

      i)   Indicated Airspeed (IAS) -- the direct instrument reading obtained from the airspeed indicator.

      ii)   Calibrated Airspeed (CAS) -- indicated airspeed corrected for installation error and instrument error.

         •   At varying angles of attack, the pitot tube does not always point directly into the relative wind.

         •   At certain airspeeds and with certain flap settings, this error may be several knots. This error is generally greatest at low airspeeds.

         •   In the cruising and higher airspeed ranges, IAS and CAS are approximately the same.

      iii)   True Airspeed (TAS) -- Calibrated airspeed corrected for density altitude.

         •   Because air density decreases with an increase in altitude, the airplane must be flown faster at higher altitudes to cause the same pressure difference between the pitot impact and static pressures.

            --   Therefore, for a given TAS, IAS decreases as altitude increases.

            --   For a given IAS, TAS increases with an altitude increase.

         •   You can find TAS by two methods. The first and more accurate method uses the flight computer. The CAS is corrected for temperature and pressure altitude on the airspeed correction scale.

            --   Some airspeed indicators have a rotating scale built in.

         •   A second method, which is a "rule of thumb," computes the approximate TAS. Add to IAS 2% for each 1,000 ft. of altitude.

            --   EXAMPLE: Given IAS is 140 kt. and altitude is 6,000 ft., find TAS.

                  Solution:
                     2% x 6 = 12% (.12)
                     140 x .12 = 16.8
                     140 + 16.8 = 156.8 kt. (TAS)

d) Single-engine light airplanes use a standard color code on airspeed indicators.

    i) Flap operating range (the white arc).

    ii) Power-off stalling speed with the wing flaps and landing gear in the landing position (the lower limit of the white arc).

    iii) Maximum flaps extended speed (the upper limit of the white arc). This is the highest airspeed at which you should extend full flaps. Flap extension at higher airspeeds could result in severe strain or structural failure.

    iv) Normal operating range (the green arc).

    v) Power-off stalling speed with the wing flaps and landing gear retracted (the lower limit of the green arc).

    vi) Maximum structural cruising speed (the upper limit of the green arc). This is the maximum speed for normal operation.

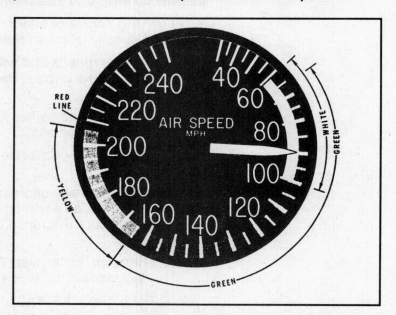

    vii) Caution range (the yellow arc). You should avoid this area unless in smooth air.

    viii) Never-exceed speed (the red line). This is the maximum speed at which the airplane can be operated safely. This speed should never be exceeded.

e) Other Airspeed Limitations. Some other important airspeed limitations are not marked on the face of the airspeed indicator. These speeds are generally found on placards in your view in the cockpit and/or in your *POH*.

    i) Design maneuvering speed (V_A) is the maximum speed at which full, abrupt deflection of the controls may be made without overstressing the airplane before a stall occurs.

      • Your airplane should be flown at or below this airspeed when turbulence is expected.

ii) Landing gear operating speed (V_{LO}) is the maximum speed for extending or retracting the landing gear.

iii) Best glide airspeed is that airspeed that provides the best lift/drag ratio angle of attack.

f) The following are abbreviations for performance speeds. These need to be memorized.

V_A -- design maneuvering speed.

V_{FE} -- maximum flap extended speed.

V_{LE} -- maximum landing gear extended speed.

V_{LO} -- maximum landing gear operating speed.

V_{NE} -- never-exceed speed.

V_{NO} -- maximum structural cruising speed.

V_R -- rotation speed.

V_{S0} -- the stalling speed or the minimum steady flight speed in the landing configuration.

V_{S1} -- the stalling speed or the minimum steady flight speed obtained in a specified configuration.

V_X -- speed for best angle of climb.

V_Y -- speed for best rate of climb.

Best glide speed.

b. Several flight instruments contain gyroscopes which are used for their operation. These instruments are the attitude indicator, the heading indicator, the turn and slip indicator, and the turn coordinator.

1) Gyroscopic instruments are operated either by a vacuum or an electrical system. In some airplanes, all the gyros are either vacuum or electrically operated. In others, vacuum systems power heading and attitude indicators and the electrical system provides the power to drive the gyroscope of the turn needle or the turn coordinator.

a) The vacuum system will be discussed on page 170 in Element 14 of this task.

b) Gyroscopic Principles. Any spinning object exhibits gyroscopic properties. A wheel designed and mounted to utilize these properties is called a gyroscope. The two fundamental properties of gyroscopic action are illustrated below: rigidity in space and precession.

i) Rigidity in space can best be explained by applying Newton's First Law of Motion, which states: "A body at rest will remain at rest; or if in motion in a straight line, it will continue in a straight line unless acted upon by an outside force."

• An example of this law is the rotor of a universally (freely) mounted gyro. When the wheel is spinning, it exhibits the ability to remain in its original plane of rotation regardless of how the base is moved.

• The attitude indicator and the heading indicator use the gyroscopic property of rigidity for their operation. Therefore, their rotors must be freely or universally mounted.

ii)   Precession is the deflection of a spinning wheel when a deflective force is applied to its rim. The deflection is 90° ahead in the direction of rotation and in the direction of the applied force, as illustrated below.

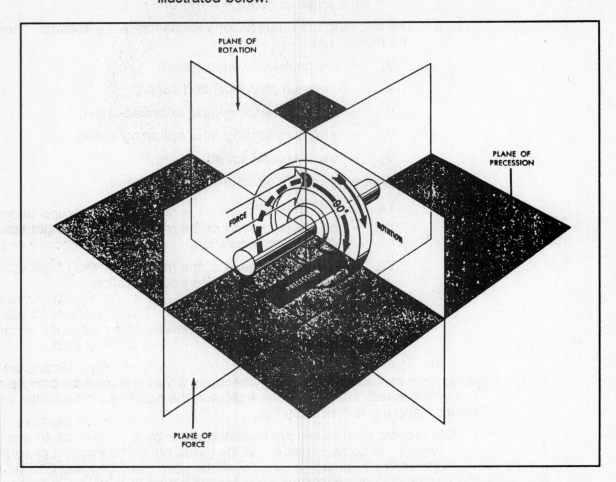

iii)   Two important design characteristics of an instrument gyro are

- Great weight or high density for size.
- Rotation at high speeds with low friction bearings.

iv)   The mountings of the gyro wheels are called "gimbals." They may be circular rings, rectangular frames, or a part of the instrument case itself (as in flight instruments).

2)   The attitude indicator (AI), with its miniature aircraft and horizon bar, depicts the pitch and bank attitude of the airplane.

a)   The relationship of the miniature airplane to the horizon bar is the same as the relationship of the real airplane to the actual horizon.

b)   The instrument gives an instantaneous indication of even the smallest changes in attitude.

    c)   The gyro in the AI is mounted on a horizontal plane and depends upon rigidity in space for its operation. The horizon bar is fixed to the gyro. It remains in a horizontal plane as the airplane is pitched or banked about its lateral or longitudinal axis. The dial (banking scale) indicates the bank angle.

    d)   An adjustment knob is provided with which the pilot may move the miniature airplane up or down to align it with the horizon bar to suit the pilot's line of vision. Normally, it is adjusted so that the wings overlap the horizon bar during straight-and-level cruising flight.

    e)   The AI is highly reliable and the most realistic flight instrument on the instrument panel. Its indications are very close approximations of the actual attitude of your airplane.

3)   The heading indicator (HI) is fundamentally a mechanical instrument designed to facilitate use of the magnetic compass.

    a)   Errors in the magnetic compass are numerous. This makes straight flight and precision turns to headings difficult, particularly in turbulent air.

    b)   The HI is not affected by the forces that make the magnetic compass difficult to interpret.

    c)   Operation of the HI also depends upon the principle of rigidity in space.

        i)   The rotor turns in a vertical plane. Fixed to the rotor is a compass card.

        ii)   Since the rotor remains rigid in space, the points on the card hold the same position in space relative to the vertical plane.

        iii)   As both the instrument case and the airplane revolve around the vertical axis, the card provides clear and accurate heading information.

    d)   Because of precession, caused chiefly by bearing friction or improper vacuum pressure, the heading indicator may creep or drift from a heading to which it is set.

        i)   Among other factors, the amount of drift depends largely upon the condition of the instrument. If the bearings are worn, dirty, or improperly lubricated, drift may be excessive.

e) The bank and pitch limits of the HI vary with the particular design and make of instrument.

    i) Some HIs found in light airplanes have limits of approximately 55° of pitch and 55° of bank.

- When either of these attitude limits is exceeded, the instrument "tumbles" or "spills" and no longer gives the correct indication until reset.

- After spilling, it may be reset with the adjustment knob at the edge of the indicator.

    ii) Some HIs are designed not to tumble.

4) The turn-and-slip indicator (T&SI) is used in some airplanes to indicate rate and quality of turn and to serve as an emergency source of bank information if the attitude indicator fails.

a) The turn-and-slip indicator is actually a combination of two instruments: the turn needle and the ball or inclinometer (like a carpenter's level).

    i) The turn needle is gyro-operated to show rate of turn.

    ii) The ball reacts to gravity and/or centrifugal force to indicate the need for directional trim.

b) The turn needle is operated by a gyro (normally driven by electricity). Semirigid mounting of the gyro permits it to rotate freely about the lateral and longitudinal axes of the airplane but restricts its rotation about the vertical axis.

    i) When the airplane is turned or rotated around the vertical axis, a deflective force is set up causing the gyro to precess (i.e., to tilt). The amount of this tilting is transmitted to the turn needle through linkage.

    ii) As the rate of turn increases, the precession of the gyro increases, resulting in an indicated increased rate of turn.

    iii) The turn needle indicates the rate (in number of degrees per second) at which the airplane is turning about its vertical axis. Unlike the attitude indicator, the turn indicator does not give a direct indication of the banked attitude of the airplane.

    iv) For any given airspeed, a specific angle of bank is necessary to maintain a coordinated turn at a given rate. The faster the airspeed, the greater the angle of bank required to obtain a given rate of turn. This is why the turn needle gives only an indirect indication of the airplane's banking attitude or angle of bank.

    v) Types of turn needles: the "2-min." and the "4-min."

- When using a 2-min. turn needle, it would take 2 min. to make a 360° turn at a rate indicated by the needle pointing to one of the small side marks (doghouses) as shown on the opposite page.

  - The airplane would be turning at a rate of 3° per sec., which is considered a standard rate of turn.

- When using a 4-min. turn needle, it would take 4 mins. to make a 360° turn at a rate indicated by the needle pointing to one of the small side marks (doghouses) as shown on the opposite page.

  - The airplane would be turning at a rate of 1.5° per sec.

c) The ball part of the turn and slip indicator is a simple inclinometer consisting of a sealed, curved glass tube containing kerosene and a black agate or steel ball bearing which is free to move inside the tube. The fluid provides a dampening action which ensures smooth and easy movement of the ball.

   i) The tube is curved so that when the airplane is horizontal (i.e., during coordinated straight-and-level flight), the ball tends to seek the lowest point (gravity). Two reference markers aid in determining when the ball is in the center of the tube.

   ii) During a coordinated turn, turning forces are balanced, causing the ball to remain centered in the tube. See the turn-and-slip indi-cator on the left of the diagram below.

   iii) If turning forces are unbalanced, i.e., a slip or skid, the ball moves away from the center of the tube in the direction of the excessive force.

     • In a skid, the rate of turn is too great for the angle of bank, and excessive centrifugal force moves the ball to the outside of the turn. See the middle turn-and-slip indicator in the diagram below.

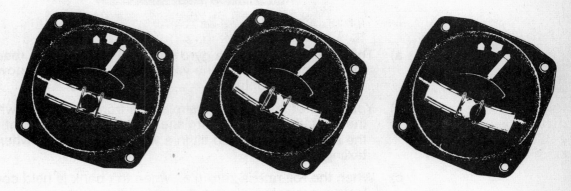

     • In a slip, the rate of turn is too slow for the angle of bank, and the lack of centrifugal force moves the ball to the inside of the turn. See the turn-and-slip indicator on the right of the diagram above.

     • Remember: In slips you have used too little rudder (or opposite rudder). In skids you have used too much rudder.

   iv) The ball then is a visual aid to determine coordinated use of the aileron and rudder control. During a turn it indicates the "quality" of the turn or whether the airplane has the correct angle of bank for the rate of turn.

d) A note on *centrifugal force*: It does not exist. It describes inertia, i.e., the tendency to continue in a direction rather than "curve." We use the term only because it is commonly used.

   i) The correct term is *centripetal force* which is a force that is necessary to keep an object moving in a circular path.

5)   The turn coordinator (TC) is another type of turn indicator that is used extensively. It replaces the turn needle of the turn and slip indicator with a miniature airplane to show the movement of the airplane about both the longitudinal axis and vertical axis.

a)   This design realigns the gyro so that it precesses in reaction to movement about both the yaw and roll axes, thus showing rate of roll as well as rate of turn.

b)   Your view of the miniature airplane is from the tail, so when you roll to the right, the miniature airplane also banks to the right proportionally to the roll rate. It will also tilt in a wings level skid or when turning while taxiing.

c)   When the roll rate is zero (i.e., when the bank is held constant), the instrument only indicates the rate of turn.

d)   The conventional inclinometer (ball) is also incorporated in this instrument.

4. The **landing gear system** supports the airplane during the takeoff run, landing, taxiing, and when parked. The landing gear can be fixed or retractable and must be capable of steering, braking, and absorbing shock.

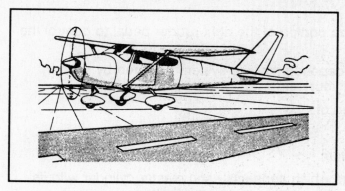

Fixed Gear   *Retractable Gear*

 a. Most single-engine training airplanes are equipped with fixed landing gear.

  1) Retractable gear are found in the so-called complex airplanes.

 b. The main landing gear assembly consists of two main wheels and struts. Each main strut is attached to the primary structure of the fuselage or the wing.

  1) Airplanes with a nosewheel (tricycle gear) have the struts attached aft of the airplane's CG.

  2) Airplanes with a tailwheel (conventional) have the struts attached slightly forward of the airplane's CG.

  3) The landing gear shock-struts may be either self-contained hydraulic units or flexible spring-like structures.

   a) These support the airplane on the ground and protect the airplane's structure by absorbing and dissipating the shock loads of landing and taxiing over rough surfaces.

   b) Many airplanes are equipped with oleo or oleo-pneumatic struts, the basic parts of which are a piston and a cylinder.

    i) The lower part of the cylinder is filled with hydraulic fluid and the piston operates in this fluid.

    ii) The upper part is filled with air.

    iii) Several holes in the piston permit fluid to pass from one side of the piston to the other as the strut compresses and expands and forces the piston back and forth.

 c. The brakes and tires on your airplane are very important for safe operations. Check your *POH* for operation and recommended maintenance.

  1) Brakes are used for slowing, stopping, or steering (at very slow speeds) the airplane. They must develop sufficient force to stop the airplane in a reasonable distance.

   a) They must hold the airplane stationary during engine run-ups, and
   b) Permit steering of the airplane on the ground.

2) The brakes are installed in each main landing wheel and are operated independently of each other.

    a) Apply pressure to the top portion of the left rudder pedal to control the left-hand brake.

    b) Apply pressure to the top portion of the right rudder pedal to control the right-hand brake.

3) Most small aircraft have an independent brake system powered by master cylinders, similar to those in your car.

    a) The system is composed of:

        i) Reservoir.

        ii) Two master cylinders.

        iii) Mechanical linkage which connects each master cylinder with its corresponding brake pedal.

        iv) Connecting fluid lines.

        v) A brake assembly in each main landing gear wheel.

4) Use the brakes in an efficient manner.

    a) Use a combination of power reduction and planning so as to use the least amount of braking action.

    b) Do not ride the brakes.

    c) Always taxi as though you have no brakes at all.

5) Ensure your tires are properly inflated and there is proper tread on the tires.

d. A steerable nose gear permits you to control your airplane throughout all ground operations.

1) Most light airplanes are provided with steering capabilities through a simple linkage connected to the rudder pedals.

    a) Most common is push-pull rods to connect the pedals to fittings located on the pivotal portion of the nosewheel strut.

2) Larger airplanes may utilize a separate power source for more positive control during steering operations.

3) The nosewheel can vibrate and shimmy during taxiing, takeoff, or landing, under certain situations.

    a) If shimmy becomes excessive, it can damage the nose gear or attaching structure.

    b) Most airplanes have a system with built-in features to prevent the shimmy.

4) On most tailwheel type airplanes, directional control while taxiing is facilitated by the use of a steerable tailwheel which operates along with the rudder.

    a) The steering mechanism remains engaged when the tailwheel is operated through an arc of 16° to 18° each side of neutral and becomes full swiveling when turned to a greater angle.

    b) While taxiing, the steerable tailwheel should be used for making normal turns, and your feet should be kept off the brake pedals to avoid unnecessary wear on the brakes.

5. Engine.

a.   In reciprocating aircraft engines, the induction system serves the function of taking in outside air, mixing it with fuel, and delivering this mixture to the cylinders.

    1)   The system includes the air scoops and ducts, the carburetor, and the intake manifold.

b.   In the carburetor system (see the diagram below), the outside air first flows through an air filter, usually located at an air intake in the front part of the engine cowling.

    1)   This filtered air flows into the carburetor and through a venturi (a narrow throat in the carburetor). When the air flows rapidly through the venturi, a low pressure area is created which draws the fuel from a main fuel jet located at the throat and into the airstream where it is mixed with the flowing air.

    2)   The fuel/air mixture is then drawn through the intake manifold and into the combustion chambers where it is ignited.

    3)   The "float-type carburetor" acquires its name from a float which rests on fuel within the float chamber. A needle attached to the float opens and closes an opening in the fuel lines.

        a)   This meters the correct amount of fuel into the carburetor, depending upon the position of the float, which is controlled by the level of fuel in the float chamber.

        b)   When the level of the fuel forces the float to rise, the needle closes the fuel opening and shuts off the fuel flow to the carburetor. It opens when the engine requires additional fuel.

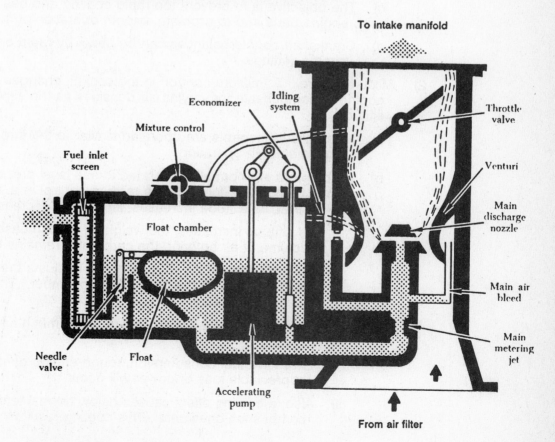

4) By using the throttle control, you can vary the airflow by adjusting the throttle valve in the throat of the carburetor.

    a) The accelerating pump is also connected to the throttle linkage.

        i) This allows an extra amount of fuel to flow into the carburetor as the throttle is opened.

        ii) If the throttle is opened quickly, the airflow initially increases at a rate greater than the fuel flow (i.e., lean mixture). The accelerator pump prevents this from occurring.

5) The idling system provides sufficient fuel to mix with the air to keep the engine idling at low RPM.

6) The economizer is connected to the mixture control linkage. Moving the mixture control back moves a small needle in the carburetor which restricts the fuel flow through the main metering jet.

c. Engine operations require gentle throttle movements and careful control of the mixture.

1) The throttle controls the amount of fuel/air mixture that goes into the engine. Generally, the more fuel, the more power is developed by the engine.

    a) The throttle is controlled by you with a hand control in the cockpit.

    b) The throttle is opened (more fuel/air mixture) by a forward movement of the control and closed (less fuel/air mixture) by a rearward movement of the control.

    c) The objective is to prevent too-rapid cooling and heating of various engine parts and to promote smooth operation of the airplane.

    d) Crankshaft counterbalances can be upset by rapid changes in engine throttle settings.

2) Mixture control. A "mixture control" in the cockpit changes the fuel flow to the engine to compensate for varying air densities as the airplane changes altitude.

    a) Most mixture controls are operated similar to the throttle control and require smooth operation.

    b) Carburetors are normally calibrated at sea level pressure to meter the correct amount of fuel with the mixture control in a "full rich" position. Recall that, as altitude increases, air density decreases.

        i) As altitude increases, the weight of air decreases, even though the volume of air entering the carburetor remains the same.

        ii) To compensate, the mixture control adjusts the ratio of fuel-to-air mixture entering the combustion chamber. This also regulates fuel consumption.

    c) If the fuel/air mixture is too rich, there is too much fuel in terms of the weight of air.

        i) Excessive fuel consumption, rough engine operation, and appreciable loss of power will occur.

        ii) Also, a cooling effect causes below normal temperatures in the combustion chambers. This cooling results in spark plug fouling.

    d)   Conversely, operation with an excessively lean mixture (too little fuel in terms of the weight of air) will result in rough engine operation, detonation, overheating, and a loss of power.

        i)   Richened settings are used to aid in engine cooling during climb.

    e)   Engines are designed to operate with maximum power at a set air/fuel ratio (e.g., 12:1). Because an airplane is constantly operating at variable altitudes that imply varying air densities, the ratio of fuel to air must be varied to produce optimum power. "Leaning" can be done in a few different ways, depending on the sophistication of the engine and instrumentation.

    f)   In engines equipped with a float-type carburetor and no instruments to help in leaning, a simplistic method is to lean until engine roughness develops, then enrich slightly until the engine runs smoothly again.

    g)   You should lean the engine of your airplane according to the procedures outlined in your *POH*.

3)   Some airplanes have additional instruments to aid you in proper leaning and operation of the engine.

    a)   The tachometer is an instrument for indicating the speed at which the engine crankshaft is rotating. The dial is calibrated in RPM.

        i)   You control the RPM by use of the throttle control.

    b)   Exhaust Gas Temperature (EGT) gauges indicate the temperature of the exhaust gas just as it exits the cylinder.

        i)   Some engines are designed to operate at peak EGT, others at 25°, 50°, 75°, etc., rich of peak.

        ii)   The EGT gauge is the most accurate method in leaning the mixture, since exhaust gas temperature is related to fuel/air ratio.

    c)   Cylinder Head Temperature (CHT) gauges measure temperature of the metal at the top of the cylinder.

        i)   This allows you to keep from running the engine too hot, which is a by-product of a too-lean situation.

        ii)   The CHT is generally not used to lean the engine because it is not immediately sensitive to slight changes in the fuel/air mixture.

    d)   Carburetor Air Temperature Gauge. Some airplanes are equipped with this gauge, useful in detecting potential icing conditions.

        i)   Usually, the face of the gauge is calibrated in degrees Celsius. A yellow arc indicates the carburetor air temperatures at which icing may occur. This yellow arc ranges between −15°C and +5°C.

    e)   Outside Air Temperature Gauge (OAT). Most airplanes are equipped with this gauge, calibrated in degrees both Celsius and Fahrenheit. It is useful for obtaining the outside or ambient air temperature for calculating true airspeed and also in detecting potential icing conditions.

d.   Cooling System.

1)   The burning fuel within the cylinders produces intense heat, most of which is expelled through the exhaust. Much of the remaining heat, however, must be removed to prevent the engine from overheating.

2)   Most light airplane engines are air cooled. Cool air is forced into the engine compartment through openings in front of the engine cowl.

        a)   This ram air is routed by baffles over fins attached to the engine cylinders and other parts of the engine. As it passes through, this outside air absorbs the engine heat.

        b)   The hot air is expelled through one or two openings at the bottom rear of the engine cowling.

    3)   Operating the engine at higher than its designed temperature can cause loss of power, excessive oil consumption, and detonation (untimed explosion of the burning fuel/air mixture). It will also lead to serious permanent damage, scoring the cylinder walls, damaging the pistons and rings, and burning and warping the valves. You should monitor the engine temperature instruments in the cockpit during flight to avoid excessive temperatures.

        a)   Oil pressure gauge -- indicates that the oil pump is working correctly to circulate the engine oil to all moving parts. Engine oil is very important both as a lubricant and for dissipating engine temperature.

        b)   Oil temperature gauge -- indicates the temperature of the oil. This gauge gives only an indirect and delayed indication of rising engine temperatures. However, it should be used to determine engine temperature if this is the only means available.

    4)   The engine temperature can be controlled under normal operating conditions by changing the airspeed or the power output of the engine.

        a)   High engine temperatures can be decreased by increasing airspeed and/or reducing power.

        b)   A richer fuel to air mixture also helps an engine run cooler.

e.   Ignition system.

    1)   The function of the ignition system is to provide an electrical spark to ignite the fuel/air mixture in the cylinders.

    2)   The ignition system of the engine is completely separate from the airplane's electrical system.

        a)   The magneto-type ignition system is used on most reciprocating airplane engines.

    3)   Magnetos are engine-driven self-contained units supplying electrical current without using an external source of current. However, before they can produce current, the magnetos must be actuated as the engine crankshaft is rotated by some other means.

        a)   This is normally done by your airplane's battery supplying power to the starter which rotates the crankshaft, thus allowing the magnetos to produce the sparks for the ignition of the fuel in each cylinder.

        b)   After the engine starts, the starter system is disengaged, and the battery no longer contributes to the actual operation of the engine.

    4)   Your airplane is equipped with a dual magneto ignition system.

        a)   Each cylinder has two spark plugs. One magneto supplies the current to one set of plugs; the second magneto supplies the current to the other set of plugs.

        b)   The ignition switch has four positions: OFF, L, R, and BOTH.

            i)   For normal operations, the switch will be on the BOTH position.

        c)   The dual system allows for more complete and even combustion of the mixture, and consequently, improved engine performance (i.e., the fuel mixture will be ignited on each side of the combustion chamber and burn toward the center).

6. Propeller.

a. The airplane propeller consists of two or more blades and a central hub to which the blades are attached. Each blade of an airplane propeller is essentially a rotating wing which produce forces that create the thrust to pull, or push, the airplane through the air.

b. The power needed to rotate the propeller blades is furnished by the engine. The engine rotates the airfoils of the blades through the air at high speeds, and the propeller transforms the rotary power of the engine into forward thrust.

c. A cross section of a typical propeller blade is shown below. This section or blade element is an airfoil comparable to a cross section of an airplane wing.

   1) One surface of the blade is cambered or curved, similar to the upper surface of an airplane wing, while the other surface is flat like the bottom surface of a wing.

   2) The chord line is an imaginary line drawn through the blade from its leading edge to its trailing edge.

   3) As in a wing, the leading edge is the thick edge of the blade that meets the air as the propeller rotates.

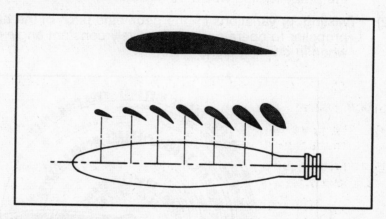

d. When specifying a fixed-pitch propeller for a new type of airplane, the manufacturer usually selects one with a pitch which will operate efficiently at the expected cruising speed of the airplane.

   1) Every fixed pitch propeller must be a compromise, because it can be efficient at only a given combination of airspeed and RPM.

   2) You do not have it within your power to change this combination in flight.

   3) Propeller efficiency varies from 50% to 87%, depending on how much the propeller "slips."

e. Propeller slip is the difference between the geometric pitch of the propeller and its effective pitch.

   1) Geometric pitch is the theoretical distance a propeller should advance in one revolution; effective pitch is the distance it actually advances.

2)   Geometric or theoretical pitch is based on no slippage, but actual or effective pitch includes propeller slippage in the air.

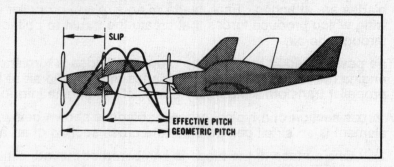

f.   A propeller is twisted because the outer parts of the propeller blades, like all things that turn about a central point, travel faster than the portions near the hub (see below).

1)   If the blades had the same geometric pitch throughout their lengths, at cruise speed the portions near the hub could have negative angles of attack while the propeller tips would be stalled.

2)   Twisting, or variations in the geometric pitch of the blades, permits the propeller to operate with a relatively constant angle of attack along its length when in cruising flight.

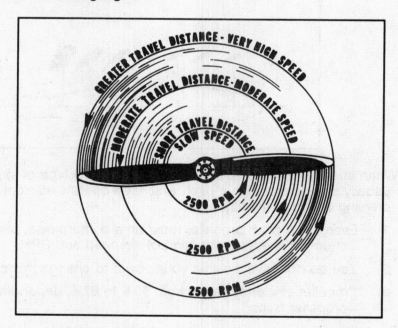

7.   Fuel System.

a.   The fuel system stores fuel and transfers it to the airplane engine. Fuel systems are classified according to the way the fuel is moved to the engine from the fuel tanks: "gravity feed" and the "fuel pump system."

1)   The gravity feed system uses the force of gravity to transfer the fuel from the tanks to the engine. It can be used on high-wing airplanes. If the fuel tanks are installed in the wings, they are above the carburetor and the fuel is gravity-fed through the system and into the carburetor.

a) An example of a gravity feed system is shown below.

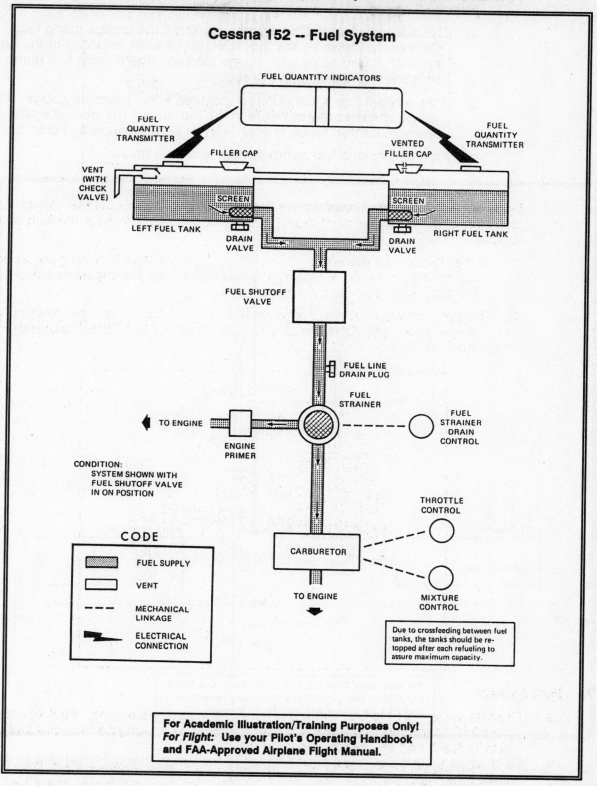

Cessna 152 -- Fuel System

FUEL QUANTITY INDICATORS

FUEL QUANTITY TRANSMITTER

FUEL QUANTITY TRANSMITTER

FILLER CAP

VENTED FILLER CAP

VENT (WITH CHECK VALVE)

SCREEN

SCREEN

LEFT FUEL TANK

RIGHT FUEL TANK

DRAIN VALVE

DRAIN VALVE

FUEL SHUTOFF VALVE

FUEL LINE DRAIN PLUG

FUEL STRAINER

TO ENGINE

ENGINE PRIMER

FUEL STRAINER DRAIN CONTROL

CONDITION: SYSTEM SHOWN WITH FUEL SHUTOFF VALVE IN ON POSITION

THROTTLE CONTROL

CARBURETOR

TO ENGINE

MIXTURE CONTROL

CODE

FUEL SUPPLY

VENT

MECHANICAL LINKAGE

ELECTRICAL CONNECTION

Due to crossfeeding between fuel tanks, the tanks should be re-topped after each refueling to assure maximum capacity.

For Academic Illustration/Training Purposes Only!
For Flight: Use your Pilot's Operating Handbook and FAA-Approved Airplane Flight Manual.

2)   Most airplanes that are equipped with the fuel pump system have two fuel pumps. The primary fuel pump is engine-driven (mechanical).

   a)   The auxiliary electric-driven pump is used if the engine pump fails. Commonly known as the "boost pump," it adds reliability to the fuel system. It also helps with engine starting. The electric fuel pump is controlled by a switch in the cockpit.

   b)   If the system has a fuel pump, it includes a fuel pressure gauge. This gauge indicates the pressure in the fuel lines. The normal operating pressure can be found in your *POH* or on the gauge by color coding.

   c)   An example of a fuel pump system is shown below.

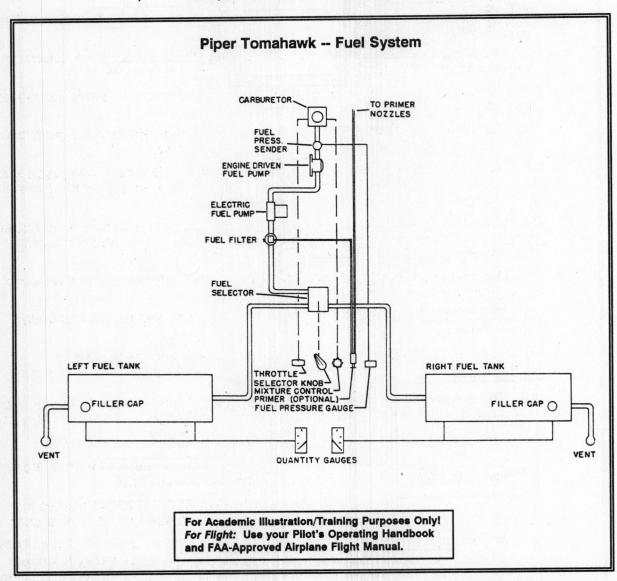

b.   Most airplanes are designed to use space in the wings to mount fuel tanks. All tanks have filler openings covered by a cap.

   1)   Fuel overflow vents are provided to discharge fuel if it expands because of high temperatures.

c. Fuel lines transfer the fuel from the tanks to the carburetor.

    1) Fuel lines pass through a selector assembly located in the cockpit.

        a) The fuel selector assembly may be a simple on/off valve or a more complex arrangement which permits the pilot to select individual tanks or use all tanks at the same time.

d. Many airplanes are equipped with fuel strainers, called sumps, located between the fuel selector and the carburetor.

    1) Similar to the fuel tank drains, these are placed at low points in the fuel lines.

    2) The sumps filter the fuel and trap water and sediment in a drainable container.

    3) This is where you will check for fuel contamination (i.e., water and/or sediment) before flight.

e. Fuel quantity gauges are available for each fuel tank and can assist in determining the amount of fuel in the tanks.

f. A manual fuel primer in some airplanes helps to start the engine, particularly in cold weather.

    1) Activating the primer draws fuel from the tanks and vaporizes it directly into one or two of the cylinders through small fuel lines.

    2) When engines are cold, they do not generate sufficient heat to vaporize the fuel. The primer helps start the engine and keep it running until sufficient engine heat is generated.

g. During refueling, the flow of fuel through the hose and nozzle creates a fire hazard. This is due to static electricity. Following some simple procedures can minimize the hazards.

    1) A ground wire should be attached to the aircraft before the cap is removed from the tank.

    2) The refueling nozzle should be grounded to the aircraft before and during refueling.

    3) The fuel truck should be grounded to the aircraft and the ground.

h. Octane/Grade

    1) The proper fuel for an engine will burn smoothly from the spark plug outward, exerting a smooth pressure downward on the piston.

        a) Using low-grade fuel or too lean a mixture can cause detonation.

        b) Detonation or knock is a sudden explosion or shock to a small area of the piston top, similar to striking it with a hammer.

            i) Detonation produces extreme heat which often progresses into preignition, causing severe structural stresses on engine parts.

    2) Anti-knock qualities of aviation fuels are designated by grades, such as 80/87, 100LL, 100/130, 108/135, and 115/145 (the latter are generally no longer available). The higher the grade, the more compression the fuel can stand without detonating. The more compression the fuel can stand without detonation, the more power can be developed from it. The first of the two numbers in a fuel designation indicates the lean-mixture rating (as during cruise), and the second the rich-mixture rating (as during takeoff and climb).

3)   No engine manufacturer recommends that you use a fuel with a lower octane/ grade rating than that specified for your engine. When you are faced with a shortage of the correct type of fuel, always use whatever alternate fuel grade is specified by the manufacturer or the next higher grade. Availability of different fuel grades at servicing facilities will be largely dependent on the classes of aircraft using the particular airport. The engine manufacturers have made information available concerning satisfactory alternate grade fuels for those which have been discontinued.

4)   DO NOT USE AUTOMOTIVE FUEL unless an appropriate supplemental type certificate (STC) has been obtained for those engines approved for auto gas use.

5)   Fuel Color

    a)   Most fuel pumps or trucks are plainly marked indicating the type and grade of fuel. However, you may determine whether you are receiving the proper grade by the color of the fuel itself.

    b)   Dyes are added by the refinery for ready identification of the various grades of aviation gasoline:

GRADE	COLOR
80/87	Red
100LL (low lead)	Blue
100/130	Green

8.   Hydraulic System.

a.   Most small aircraft have an independent hydraulic brake system powered by master cylinders, similar to those in your car.

    1)   The system is composed of:

        a)   Reservoir.

        b)   Two master cylinders.

        c)   Mechanical linkage which connects each master cylinder with its corresponding brake pedal.

        d)   Connecting fluid lines.

        e)   A brake assembly in each main landing gear wheel.

9.   Electrical System.

a.   Electrical energy is required to operate the starter, navigation and communication radios, lights, and other airplane equipment.

    1)   Most light airplanes are equipped with a 12-volt battery and a 14-volt direct-current electrical system.

    2)   A basic airplane electrical system consists of the following components:

        a)   Alternator or generator
        b)   Battery
        c)   Master switch or battery switch
        d)   Bus bar, fuses, and circuit breakers
        e)   Voltage regulator
        f)   Ammeter
        g)   Starting motor
        h)   Associated electrical wiring
        i)   Accessories

3)   Some airplanes are equipped with receptacles to which external auxiliary power units (APUs) can be connected to provide electrical energy for starting.

a)   These are very useful, especially during cold weather starting.

b)   Do NOT start an engine using an auxiliary power unit when the battery is dead. Electrical energy will be forced into the dead battery, causing the battery to overheat and possibly explode, resulting in damage to the airplane.

b.   A master switch is installed to turn the electrical system on or off. Turning the master switch on provides electrical energy to all the electrical equipment circuits except the ignition system (which receives electricity from the magnetos).

1)   In addition, an alternator switch permits you to exclude the alternator from the electrical system in the event of alternator failure. With the alternator switch off, the entire electrical load is placed on the battery.

a)   In such case, all nonessential electrical equipment should be turned off to conserve the energy stored in the battery.

2)   An ammeter is an instrument used to monitor the performance of the airplane electrical system.

a)   Not all airplanes are equipped with an ammeter. Some are equipped with a light which, when lit, indicates a discharge in the system as a generator/alternator malfunction.

b)   An ammeter shows if the generator/alternator is producing an adequate supply of electrical power by measuring the amperes of electricity.

i)   This instrument also indicates whether the battery is receiving an electrical charge.

c)   Ammeters are of either the center-zero or the left-zero type.

i)   A center-zero ammeter shows charge to or discharge from the battery.

•   If the needle indicates a positive value, it means that the battery is being charged.

•   If the needle indicates a negative value, it means that the battery is being discharged. This may occur during starting. At any other time, a negative value indicates an overload on the system or a defective alternator or generator.

ii)   A left-zero ammeter shows the amount of current coming from the alternator/generator.

•   If the needle indicates zero and electrical equipment is being used, it means the generator/alternator has failed and current is being drawn from the battery.

c.   Engine-driven generators or alternators supply electric current to the electrical system and also maintain a sufficient electrical charge in the battery.

1)   Electrical energy stored in a battery provides a source of electricity for starting the engine and a limited supply of electricity for use if the alternator or generator fails.

2)   Most airplanes are equipped with an alternator. It produces a sufficient amount of electrical current at low engine RPM by first producing alternating current which is converted to direct current.

a)   Another advantage is that the electrical output of an alternator is more constant throughout the ranges of engine speed.

        b)   Alternators are also lighter in weight, less expensive to maintain, and less prone to overloading during conditions of heavy electrical loads.

  d.   Fuses or circuit breakers protect the circuits and equipment from electrical overload.

     1)   Spare fuses of the proper amperage limit should be carried in the airplane at all times to replace defective or blown fuses.

     2)   Circuit breakers have the same function as a fuse but can be manually reset (rather than replaced) if an overload condition occurs in the electrical system.

         a)   They are usually manually reset by pushing them in when they "pop out."

         b)   If they "pop out" as soon as they are pushed in, there is probably a short in the accessory feed through that circuit breaker. Accordingly, you should not continue to push the circuit breaker in. Fire may result.

     3)   Placards at the fuse or circuit breaker location identify the circuit by name and, if fuses are used, show the amperage limit of the fuse.

     4)   During preflight you should check that all circuit breakers are in

         a)   **Safety alert:** Make sure no circuit breakers are pulled out. Some people disengage stall warning horns and other safety devices for convenience or for training purposes. Failure to put these devices back into service has caused numerous accidents. Make sure that all circuit breakers have been returned to service.

         b)   Develop "an understanding" with your CFI and examiner if the airplane is to be intentionally operated without all equipment functioning.

  e.   The electrical system operates the following lighting systems:

     1)   Position (navigation) lights
     2)   Landing lights
     3)   Taxi lights
     4)   Anticollision (strobe) lights
     5)   Interior cabin lights
     6)   Instrument lights

  f.   Although additional electrical equipment may be found in some airplanes, the following flight instruments commonly use the electrical system:

     1)   Radio equipment
     2)   Turn indicator
     3)   Fuel gauges
     4)   Stall warning system
     5)   Pitot heat

10. Environmental System.

  a.   Heating in most training airplanes is accomplished by an air intake in the nose of the airplane.

     1)   This is directed into a shroud, where the air is heated by the engine.
     2)   This is then delivered through vents into the cabin, or used for the defroster.

  b.   Cooling and ventilation are controlled by outlets.

     1)   Some airplanes are equipped with an air conditioner for cooling.

     2)   Outside air used for cooling and ventilation is normally supplied through air inlets that are located in the wings or elsewhere on the airplane.

     3)   Learn how your system works by reading your *POH*.

    c.   Controls for heat and defroster located on the instrument panel, or within easy reach.

        1)   Most aircraft are equipped with outlets that can be controlled by each occupant of the airplane.

        2)   Your *POH* will explain the operation of the controls.

    d.   Inherent in this type of heating system is the danger of carbon monoxide poisoning from exhaust gases passing into the cabin from cracked manifolds.

        1)   Airplanes equipped with this type of system should have a carbon monoxide detector installed.

        2)   See the discussion on carbon monoxide poisoning in Task I.F., Aeromedical Factors, on page 171.

11.   The **oil system** provides a means of storing and circulating oil throughout the internal components of a reciprocating engine.

    a.   Usually the oil is stored in a sump at the bottom of the engine crankcase.

        1)   This is where the oil dipstick measures the amount of oil.

        2)   Check your *POH* for the capacity and operating limits.

        3)   The four basic functions of engine oil are:

            a)   To Lubricate -- to maintain a film of lubricant on meeting surfaces between which relative motion occurs.

            b)   To Seal -- as in the case of the oil seal between the cylinder walls and the piston and rings; also to prevent the passage of combustion gases past the pistons.

            c)   To Clean -- by carrying off metal and carbon particles and other oil contaminants.

            d)   To Cool -- by carrying heat away from hot engine parts and keeping their temperatures within acceptable limits. Cooling is most important. Always remember to maintain proper oil levels on long summer cross-country flights.

        4)   Always make certain that the oil filler cap and the oil dipstick are secure after adding oil or checking the oil level. If these are left off or not properly secured, oil loss may occur. Remember, a proper oil supply and properly functioning oil system are extremely important items for safe airplane operation. You cannot be too careful.

    b.   The wrong type of oil, or an insufficient oil supply, may interfere with any or all of the basic oil functions, and cause serious engine damage. Use only oil that has been recommended by the engine manufacturer, or its equivalent. Never use any oil additive that has not been recommended by the engine manufacturer or authorized by the FAA.

    c.   Each engine is equipped with an oil pressure gauge and an oil temperature gauge which you monitor to determine that the oil system is functioning properly.

        1)   Oil pressure gauges indicate lb. of pressure per square in. (psi), and are color coded with a green arc to indicate the normal operating range.

            a)   At each end of the arc, some gauges have a red line to indicate high or low pressure.

            b)   Low oil pressure can be the result of a mechanical problem or an inadequate amount of oil.

     i) Low oil pressure necessitates an immediate landing.

   2) The oil temperature gauge indicates the temperature of the oil and is color-coded in green to indicate the normal operating range.

     a) This gauge gives only an indirect and delayed indication of rising engine temperature.

     b) Many airplanes circulate the oil through an oil radiator for cooling.

12. Deice and Anti-ice Systems.

  a. Airframe ice-protection systems.

   1) Deicer boots

     a) Deicer boots are fabric-reinforced rubber sheets containing inflation tubes within them. They are normally cemented to the leading edges of the wings, vertical stabilizer, and horizontal stabilizer.

     b) During normal operation, vacuum pressure holds the boots in the deflated position. After ice accumulation of ¼ to ½ in. is present, the system is activated by the pilot. A pneumatic pump controlled by a timer inflates segments of the boots. This inflation breaks off the accumulated ice.

   2) Weeping wing deicers

     a) The weeping wing system uses a special leading edge on the airplane's wings and stabilizers which is laser drilled with very small holes.

     b) A deicing fluid is pumped out of these holes, causing any built-up ice to fall off. The remaining fluid deters further ice buildup.

   3) Thermal anti-icing.

     a) Uses heated air flowing through passages in the leading edge of wings, stabilizers, and engine cowlings to prevent the formation of ice.

     b) Heat source normally comes from combustion heaters in reciprocating-engine-powered airplanes and from engine bleed air in turbine-powered airplanes.

  b. Propeller/intake ice-protection systems.

   1) Two primary methods used in propeller ice-protection.

     a) Electric deicing.

       i) The heating elements softens the ice.

       ii) Normally has two elements.

        • A heater element near the propeller hub, and
        • An outboard heater.

       iii) Elements are enclosed in a rubber pad which is normally cemented to the heading edge of the propeller blades, near the hub.

     b) Fluid anti-icing.

       i) Normally isopropyl alcohol is used.

       ii) Most effective if used before ice starts accumulating.

       iii) Normally the fluid is released from a slinger ring assembly to the leading edge of the blades.

        • The fluid is thrown out along the blades by centripetal force.

2)   The most common intake ice-protection is the use of heated air flowing around the engine cowling.

    a)   You should be concerned of ice/water being sucked into the induction/induction system icing system.

    b)   Prevent by use of carburetor heat or an alternate air source.

c.   Fuel system ice-protection.

1)   Fuel system icing results from the presence of water in the fuel system. This may cause freezing of screen, strainers, and filters.

    a)   When fuel enters the carburetor, the additional cooling may freeze the water.

2)   Normally, proper use of carburetor heat can warm the air sufficiently in the carburetor to prevent ice formation.

3)   Some airplanes are approved to use anti-icing additives to the fuel.

    a)   Remember that an anti-icing additive is not a substitute for carburetor heat.

d.   Pitot-static ice-protection system.

1)   Pitot heat is an electrical system.

    a)   Puts a severe drain on the electrical system on some airplanes.

    b)   Monitor your ammeter for the effect pitot heat has on your airplane's electrical system.

        i)   Pitot heat should be used prior to encountering visible moisture.

    c)   If the pitot tube ices over, only the airspeed indicator (ASI) is affected.

        i)   If both the pitot tube and drain holes are blocked, the ASI will respond like an altimeter, it indicates high as the airplane climbs, and low as the airplane descends.

        ii)   If only the pitot tube is blocked, the pressure will dissipate through the open drain holes, and the ASI will indicate zero.

2)   Blockage of the static port by ice could affect the ASI, altimeter (ALT), and the vertical speed indicator (VSI).

    a)   Many airplanes have two static ports, one on either side of the fuselage, to help reduce faulty indications due to a blocked static port.

    b)   In a climb with a blocked static port, the ALT would indicate a constant altitude, the VSI would indicate zero, and the ASI would indicate a lower-than-actual airspeed.

        i)   In a descent the indications would be the same, except the ASI would indicate a higher-than-actual airspeed.

    c)   An alternate static source may be available in case of a blockage. This normally measures the pressure in the cockpit, which is less than the external static pressure.

        i)   This would cause slight errors as the ALT and ASI would indicate slightly high, and the VSI would momentarily show a climb before settling down.

e.   Induction system (carburetor) ice protection system.

  1)   This is the basic, and probably the only ice protection system in your airplane.
  2)   Carburetor heat warms the air before it enters the carburetor.

  a)   Used to remove and/or prevent ice formation.

f.   Be emphatic with your examiner that icing conditions are to be avoided in both flight planning and in the air!

  1)   Most training airplanes have placards that prohibit flight into known icing conditions.

g.   Check your *POH* for the appropriate, if any, system in your airplane.

13.   Avionics are all your airplane's aviation electronic equipment.

a.   Be able to explain how all your communication and navigation systems operate.

b.   Make a list of the make, model, type of radio, and related equipment in your airplane.

  1)   Handwrite a list of the radios and their functions. As appropriate, consult and study their instruction manuals.

14.   Vacuum system.

a.   The vacuum or pressure system spins the gyros of the gyroscopic instruments by drawing a stream of air against the rotor vanes to spin the rotor at high speeds. This is essentially the same way a water wheel or turbine operates. Normally, a vacuum pump is used to provide the vacuum required to spin the rotors.

b.   A typical vacuum system (illustrated below) consists of an engine-driven vacuum pump, an air/oil separator, a vacuum regulator, a relief valve, an air filter, and tubing and manifolds necessary to complete the connections. A suction gauge on the airplane instrument panel indicates the amount of vacuum in the system.

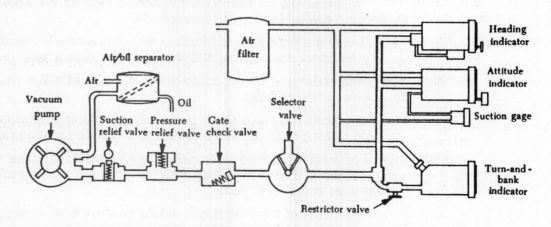

c.   Check your *POH* for the proper operational limits of the vacuum system.

END OF TASK

AEROMEDICAL FACTORS

I.F. TASK: AEROMEDICAL FACTORS

  PILOT OPERATION - 1

  REFERENCES: AC 61-21, AC 67-2; AIM.

Objective. To determine that the applicant:

1. Exhibits knowledge of the elements related to aeromedical factors, including the symptoms, effects, and corrective action of --

   a. Hypoxia.
   b. Hyperventilation.
   c. Middle ear and sinus problems.
   d. Spatial disorientation.

   e. Motion sickness.
   f. Carbon monoxide poisoning.

2. Exhibits knowledge of the effects of alcohol and drugs, and the relationship to flight safety.

3. Exhibits knowledge of nitrogen excesses during scuba dives, and how this affects a pilot or passenger during flight.

A. General Information

   1. This is one of six tasks (A-F) in this area of operation. Your examiner is required to test you on this task.

   2. *Pilot Operation - 1* refers to FAR 61.107(a)(1): Preflight operations, including weight and balance determination, line inspection, and airplane servicing.

   3. FAA References

      AC 61-21: Flight Training Handbook
      AC 67-2: Medical Handbook for Pilots
      Airman's Information Manual (AIM)

   4. The objective of this task is to determine your knowledge of aeromedical factors as they relate to safety of flight.

   5. It is your responsibility to consider the status of your health.

      a. The FARs prohibit you from performing crewmember (piloting) duties while using any medication that affects the faculties in any way contrary to safety.

   6. Pilot Personal Checklist

      a. Aircraft accident statistics show that pilots should conduct preflight checklists on themselves as well as their aircraft. Pilot impairment contributes to many more accidents than do failures of aircraft systems.

      b. I am NOT impaired by

         I llness
         M edication

         S tress
         A lcohol
         F atigue
         E motion

B. Task Objectives

   1. **Exhibit knowledge of the elements related to aeromedical factors, including the symptoms, effects, and corrective actions to be taken.**

a.   **Hypoxia** is a state of oxygen deficiency in the body sufficient to impair functions of the brain and other organs.

   1)   Although a deterioration in night vision occurs at a cabin pressure altitude as low as 5,000 ft. MSL, other significant effects of altitude hypoxia usually do not occur in the normal, healthy pilot below 12,000 ft. MSL.

   2)   From 12,000 to 15,000 ft. MSL (without supplemental oxygen), judgment, memory, alertness, coordination, and ability to make calculations are impaired.

   3)   Headache, drowsiness, dizziness, and either a sense of well-being (euphoria) or belligerence occur.

   4)   The effects appear after increasingly shorter periods of exposure to increasing altitude.

      a)   Pilot performance can seriously deteriorate within 15 min. at 15,000 ft. MSL.

      b)   At altitudes above 15,000 ft. MSL, the periphery of the visual field turns gray. Only central vision remains (tunnel vision).

      c)   A blue color (cyanosis) develops in the fingernails and lips.

      d)   You lose the ability to take corrective and protective action in 20 to 30 min. at 18,000 ft. MSL.

         i)   This happens in 5 to 12 min. at 20,000 ft. MSL, followed soon by unconsciousness.

   5)   Significant effects of hypoxia can occur at even lower altitudes given one or more of the following factors:

      a)   Carbon monoxide inhaled in smoking or from exhaust fumes.

      b)   Small amounts of alcohol and low doses of certain drugs (e.g., antihistamines, tranquilizers, sedatives, and analgesics).

      c)   Extreme heat or cold, fever, and/or anxiety.

   6)   Hypoxia is prevented by understanding the factors that reduce your tolerance to altitude and by using supplemental oxygen above 10,000 ft. during the day, and above 5,000 ft. at night.

   7)   Corrective action if hypoxia is suspected or recognized includes

      a)   Use of supplemental oxygen.
      b)   An emergency descent to a lower altitude.

b.   **Hyperventilation** usually results from an emotional reaction such as fear; the rapid deep breathing of hyperventilation causes insufficient carbon dioxide in the blood.

   1)   As more and more carbon dioxide is blown off from rapid breathing, lower carbon dioxide in the blood causes the condition known as respiratory alkalosis, which is an increase in the pH of the blood.

   2)   This chemical imbalance in the body is responsible for the symptoms of lightheadedness, tingling in the hands and feet, sensation of body heat, rapid heart rate, and blurring of vision.

      a)   A pilot may react to these symptoms with even greater hyperventilation.

      b)   Incapacitation can eventually result from incoordination, disorientation, and painful muscle spasms.

         i)   Finally, unconsciousness can occur.

    c) Remember, early symptoms of hyperventilation and hypoxia are similar and both can occur at the same time.

   3) The symptoms of hyperventilation subside within a few minutes after the rate and depth of breathing are consciously brought back under control.

    a) The buildup of the appropriate balance of carbon dioxide in the body can be hastened by controlled breathing in and out of a paper bag held over the nose and mouth.

c. Middle ear and sinus problems. During ascent and descent, air pressure in the sinuses equalizes with aircraft cabin pressure through small openings that connect the sinuses to the nasal passages. An upper respiratory infection (e.g., a cold or sinusitis) or nasal allergies can produce enough congestion around one or more of these small openings to slow equalization. Then, as the difference in pressure between the sinus and cabin mounts, the opening may become plugged.

   1) As the cabin pressure decreases during ascent, the expanding air in the middle ear pushes the eustachian tubes open and escapes down them to the nasal passages, thus equalizing ear pressure with the cabin pressure.

   2) During descent, you must periodically reopen the eustachian tubes to equalize pressure.

    a) This can be accomplished by swallowing, yawning, tensing muscles in the throat, or if these do not work, by the combination of closing the mouth, pinching the nose closed, and attempting to blow through the nostrils (Valsalva maneuver).

    b) Again, an upper respiratory infection (e.g., a cold or sore throat) or nasal allergies can produce enough congestion around the eustachian tubes to make equalization difficult.

   3) A middle ear block produces severe ear pain and loss of hearing that can last from several hours to several days.

    a) Rupture of the ear drum can occur in flight or after landing.
    b) Fluid can accumulate in the middle ear, causing infection.

   4) A sinus block can occur in the frontal sinuses, located above each eyebrow, or in the maxillary sinuses, located in each upper cheek.

    a) It usually produces severe pain over the sinus area.
    b) A maxillary sinus block can also make the upper teeth ache.
    c) Bloody mucus may discharge from the nasal passages.

   5) Middle ear and sinus problems are prevented by not flying with an upper respiratory infection or nasal allergic condition.

    a) Adequate protection is not provided by decongestant spray or drops to reduce congestion around the eustachian tubes or the sinus openings.

    b) Oral decongestants have side effects that can significantly impair pilot performance.

d. Spatial disorientation is a state of temporary confusion resulting from misleading information being sent to the brain by various sensory organs. The condition is sometimes called vertigo.

   1) Sight, supported by other senses such as the inner ear and muscle sense, is normally used to maintain spatial orientation.

    a) Normally occurring during periods of low visibility, the supporting senses sometimes conflict with what is seen. This is when you are particularly vulnerable to spatial disorientation.

      b) Spatial disorientation to you means simply the inability to tell "which way is up."

  2) The best way to overcome the effects of spatial disorientation is to rely on the airplane instruments and ignore body (kinesthetic) signals.

  e. **Motion sickness** is caused by continued stimulation of the tiny portion of the inner ear which controls your sense of balance.

    1) The symptoms are progressive.

       a) First, the desire for food is lost.

       b) Then saliva collects in the mouth and you begin to perspire freely.

       c) Eventually, you become nauseated and disoriented.

       d) The head aches and there may be a tendency to vomit.

    2) If suffering from airsickness, you should

       a) Open the air vents.
       b) Loosen clothing.
       c) Use supplemental oxygen.
       d) Keep the eyes on a point outside the airplane.
       e) Avoid unnecessary head movements.
       f) Cancel the flight and land as soon as possible.

    3) Although motion sickness is uncommon among experienced pilots, it does occur occasionally.

       a) Most important, it jeopardizes your flying efficiency, particularly in turbulent weather.

       b) Student pilots are frequently surprised by an uneasiness usually described as motion sickness.

          i) This is probably a result of combining anxiety, unfamiliarity, and the vibration or jogging received from the airplane. These sensations are usually overcome with experience.

       c) Pilots who are susceptible to airsickness should NOT take the preventive drugs which are available over the counter or by prescription.

          i) Research has shown that most motion sickness drugs cause a temporary deterioration of navigational skills or ability to perform other tasks demanding keen judgment.

  f. **Carbon monoxide** is a colorless, odorless, and tasteless gas contained in tobacco smoke and exhaust fumes. When breathed even in minute quantities over a period of time, it can significantly reduce the ability of the blood to carry oxygen. Consequently, effects of hypoxia occur.

    1) Most heaters in light aircraft work by air flowing over the manifold. Using these heaters when exhaust fumes are escaping through manifold cracks and seals is responsible every year for both nonfatal and fatal aircraft accidents from carbon monoxide poisoning.

    2) One of the more common sources of carbon monoxide intoxication in an airplane is tobacco smoke.

       a) Tests have shown that carbon monoxide in tobacco smoke can lower the pilot's tolerance to altitude by as much as 5,000 to 6,000 ft.

3) A pilot who detects the odor of exhaust or experiences symptoms of headache, drowsiness, or dizziness while using the heater should suspect carbon monoxide poisoning and immediately shut off the heater and open the air vents.

   a) If symptoms are severe, or continue after landing, medical treatment should be sought.

2. **Exhibit knowledge of the effects of alcohol and drugs, and the relationship to flight safety.**

   a. There is only one safe rule to follow with respect to combining flying and drinking -- **DON'T**.

   b. The inherent danger in drinking and flying apparently has not impressed some pilots. Possibly they labor under the deadly delusion that flying after a few drinks is no more dangerous than driving while in the same condition (which can be quite dangerous in itself).

   1) Flying an airplane is more complex than the two-dimensional demands of driving a car.

   2) Increased altitude multiplies the intoxicating effect of alcohol on the body.

   3) Alcohol also increases susceptibility to hypoxia.

   c. Any pilot who flies within 8 hr. after the consumption of alcoholic beverages or while under the influence of alcohol or drugs is not only extremely dangerous but is in violation of the FARs (91.17).

   d. Pilot performance can be seriously degraded by both prescribed and over-the-counter medication.

   1) Many have primary effects that may impair judgment, vision, memory, alertness, coordination, and the ability to make calculations.

   2) Any medication that depresses the nervous system, i.e., sedative, tranquilizer, or antihistamine, can make a pilot more susceptible to hypoxia.

   3) Safest rule is not to fly as a pilot (or crewmember) while taking medication, unless approved to do so by the FAA.

3. **Exhibit knowledge of nitrogen excesses during scuba dives, and how this affects a pilot or passenger during flight.**

   a. A pilot or passenger who intends to fly after scuba diving should allow the body sufficient time to rid itself of excess nitrogen absorbed during diving. If this is not done, decompression sickness due to evolved gas (bubbles in the bloodstream) can occur at low altitudes and create a serious in-flight emergency.

   1) The recommended waiting time before flight to altitudes of up to 8,000 ft. is at least 12 hr. after a dive which has not required controlled ascent (nondecompression diving). You should allow at least 24 hr. after diving which has required controlled ascent (decompression diving).

   2) The waiting time before flight to cabin pressure altitudes above 8,000 ft. should be at least 24 hr. after any scuba diving.

   3) These recommended altitudes are actual flight altitudes above mean sea level (MSL) and not pressurized cabin altitudes.

END OF TASK -- END OF CHAPTER

176   Blank Page

CHAPTER II
GROUND OPERATIONS

II.A. Visual Inspection 178
II.B. Cockpit Management 185
II.C. Starting Engine 189
II.D. Taxiing 195
II.E. Pretakeoff Check 205
II.F. Postflight Procedures 211

This chapter explains the six tasks (A-F) of Ground Operations. These tasks include both knowledge and skill.

Each objective of a task lists, in sequence, the important elements that must be satisfactorily performed. The object includes:

1. Specifically what you should be able to do.
2. The conditions under which the task is to be performed.
3. The minimum acceptable standards of performance.

Be confident. You have prepared diligently and are better prepared and more skilled than the average private pilot applicant. Your examiner will base your ability to perform these tasks on the following.

1. Executing the task within your airplane's capabilities and limitations, including use of the airplane's systems.

2. Piloting your airplane with smoothness and accuracy.

3. Exercises good judgment.

4. Applying your aeronautical knowledge.

5. Showing mastery of your airplane within the standards outlined in this area of operation, with the successful outcome of a task never seriously in doubt.

This chapter discusses the procedures and techniques essential to the safe operation of your airplane on the ground from the visual inspection to the completion of the pretakeoff check and at the end of your flight with the postflight procedures.

Your examiner is required to test you on all six tasks. Each task is reproduced verbatim from the FAA Practical Test Standards in a shaded box. General discussion is presented under "A. General Information." This is followed by "B. Task Objectives," which is a detailed discussion of each element of the FAA's task.

VISUAL INSPECTION

II.A. TASK: VISUAL INSPECTION

  PILOT OPERATION - 1

  REFERENCES: AC 61-21; Airplane Handbook and Flight Manual.

Objective. To determine that the applicant:

1. Exhibits knowledge of airplane visual inspection by explaining the reasons for checking all items.

2. Inspects the airplane by following a checklist.

3. Determines that the airplane is in condition for safe flight emphasizing --

  a. Fuel quantity, grade, and type.

  b. Fuel contamination safeguards.

  c. Fuel venting.

  d. Oil quantity, grade, and type.

  e. Fuel, oil, and hydraulic leaks.

  f. Flight controls.

  g. Structural damage.

  h. Exhaust system.

  i. Tiedown, control lock, and wheel chock removal.

  j. Ice and frost removal.

  k. Security of baggage, cargo, and equipment.

A. **General Information**

1. This is one of six tasks (A-F) in this area of operation. Your examiner is required to test you on this task.

2. *Pilot Operation - 1* refers to FAR 61.107(a)(1): Preflight operations, including weight and balance determination, line inspection, and airplane servicing.

3. FAA References

    AC 61-21: Flight Training Handbook
    Pilot's Operating Handbook (FAA-Approved Airplane Flight Manual)

4. The objective of this task is for you to demonstrate the proper visual inspection procedures.

5. You, as pilot in command, are responsible for determining whether your airplane is airworthy and safe to fly. FAR 91.7 states, "The pilot in command is responsible for determining whether that aircraft is in condition for safe flight."

B.   Task Objectives

   1.   **Exhibit your knowledge of an airplane visual inspection by explaining the reasons for checking all items.**

      a.   The objective of the preflight visual inspection is to ensure your airplane has no obvious problems prior to taking off. The preflight is carried out in a systematic walk around the airplane and generally consists of the following.

         1)   Make sure all necessary documents, maps, safety equipment, etc., are aboard. The word ARROW will help you to remember the required documents:

            a)   **A** irworthiness Certificate.

            b)   **R** egistration Certificate.

            c)   **R** adio station license.

            d)   **O** perating limitations, usually in the *Pilot's Operating Handbook* (*POH*).

            e)   **W** eight and balance information (also in the *POH*).

            f)   Engine and airframe logbooks (must be available, but not necessarily aboard the airplane).

            g)   Flotation gear if the flight is to be conducted over water.

         2)   You need to make sure your airplane has the required equipment for the flight you are about to take.

            a)   This includes items like Mode C transponder for an operation in a TCA or ARSA.

         3)   Operating limitations can be presented in *POH* (FAA-approved airplane flight manuals), in the form of placards (small metal or plastic plaques), or a combination of both.

            a)   Airplanes must have a *POH* (FAA-approved flight manual) in the cockpit. Most airplanes have placards which define important operational information mounted on the instrument panel or other areas in plain sight.

               i)   Weight and balance information is also in the *POH*.

            b)   In many older airplanes, manufacturers met the operating limitation requirements by mounting placards in the cockpit and putting a copy of the weight and balance information aboard.

            c)   In older airplanes without an FAA-approved flight manual, be sure the weight and balance information is aboard, and the placards have not been removed or painted over.

            d)   The airplane as loaded must be within weight and balance operating limitations per the *POH*.

   2.   **Inspect your airplane by following a checklist.**

      a.   Each airplane has a specific list of preflight procedures recommended by the airplane manufacturer, which are found in Section 4, Normal Procedures, of your *POH*.

         1)   The written checklist is a systematic set of procedures.
         2)   Always have your checklist in hand and follow it item by item.

      b.   The Piper Tomahawk preflight checklist appears on page 180 as an example of the presentation you will find in your airplane's *POH*.

Piper Tomahawk
PREFLIGHT INSPECTION

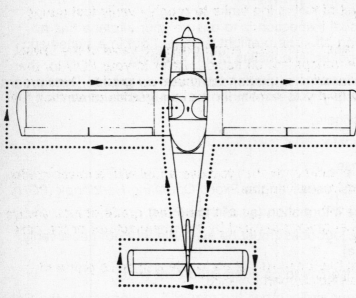

For Academic Illustration/Training Purposes Only!
For Flight: **Use your Pilot's Operating Handbook
(FAA-Approved Airplane Flight Manual).**

1. COCKPIT

    a. Control wheel - RELEASE CONSTRAINTS.

    b. Ignition - OFF.

    c. Master switch - ON.

    d. Fuel Quantity Gauges - CHECK.

    e. Alternator Warning Light - CHECK.

    f. Master Switch - OFF.

    g. Primary Flight Controls - PROPER
        OPERATION.

    h. Flaps - PROPER OPERATION.

    i. Static Drain - DRAINED.

    j. Windows - CHECK CLEAN.

    k. Baggage - STOWED PROPERLY.

    l. Required Papers - ON BOARD.

    m. Parking Brake - SET ON.

2. LEFT WING

    a. Surface Condition - CHECK.
    b. Flap and Hinges - CHECK.
    c. Aileron and Hinges - CHECK.
    d. Wing Tip - CHECK.
    e. Lights - CHECK.
    f. Fuel Cap - OPEN.
    g. Fuel Quantity and Color - CHECK.
    h. Fuel Cap - CLOSE AND SECURE.
    i. Fuel Vent - OPEN.
    j. Fuel Tank Sump - DRAIN.
    k. Pitot Head - UNOBSTRUCTED.
    l. Stall Warning - CHECK.
    m. Landing Gear and Tire - CHECK.
    n. Brake Block and Disc - CHECK.
    o. Chock and Tie-Down - REMOVED.

3. NOSE SECTION

    a. Fuel Strainer - DRAIN.

    b. General Condition - CHECK.

    c. Propeller and Spinner - CHECK.

    d. Air Inlets - CLEAR.

    e. Engine Compartment - CHECK.

    f. Oil - CHECK QUANTITY.

    g. Dipstick - PROPERLY SEATED.

    h. Alternator Belt - CHECK TENSION.

    i. Cowling - CLOSED AND SECURE.

    j. Nose Wheel Tire - CHECK.

    k. Nose Gear Strut - PROPER INFLATION (3 in.
        exposure).

    l. Windshield - CLEAN.

4. RIGHT WING - Check as left wing.

5. FUSELAGE (RIGHT SIDE)

    a. General condition - CHECK.
    b. Antennas - CHECK.
    c. Side and Rear Window - CLEAN.
    d. Static Vents - UNOBSTRUCTED.

6. EMPENNAGE

    a. General Condition - CHECK.
    b. Hinges and Attachments - CHECK.

7. FUSELAGE (LEFT SIDE) - Check as right side.

3. **Determine that your airplane is in condition for safe flight.**

   a. **Fuel quantity, grade, and type.**

      1) You should check the level of fuel in the tanks to roughly verify fuel gauge indications.

      2) A fuel sample should be taken from each sump drainage valve at the lowest point of each tank into a transparent container. Refer to your *POH* for the manufacturer's recommendation regarding the minimum grade. Dyes are added by the refinery to help you identify the various grades of aviation fuel.

         a) 80/87 is red.
         b) 100LL is blue.
         c) 100/130 is green.

      3) No engine manufacturer recommends that you use a fuel with a lower grade rating than that specified for your engine.

         a) When you are faced with a shortage of the correct grade of fuel, always use the alternate fuel grade specified by the manufacturer or the next higher grade.

         b) Every aircraft engine has been designed to use a specific grade of aviation fuel for satisfactory performance.

      4) DO NOT USE AUTOMOTIVE FUEL unless an FAA supplemental type certificate (STC) has been obtained for your airplane that approves auto gas use.

   b. **Fuel contamination safeguards.**

      1) You should always assume that the fuel in your airplane is contaminated. A generous fuel sample should be taken from each sump drainage valve at the lowest point of each tank and from other parts of the fuel system.

      2) Water will be noticeable because it will sink to the bottom of the container. Since water is heavier than the fuel, it will be located at the lowest levels in the fuel system.

         a) If water is found in the first sample, drain further samples until no water appears.

         b) Water is the most common fuel contaminant, and is usually caused by condensation inside the tank.

      3) Also check for other contaminants, e.g., dirt, sand, rust.

         a) Keep draining until no trace of the contaminant appears.

         b) A preventive measure is to avoid refueling from cans and drums, which may introduce fuel contaminants such as dirt or other impurities.

      4) Wait at least 15 min. (per ft.-depth of fuel) after your airplane has been refueled before you take a fuel sample.

         a) This will allow time for any contaminants to settle to the bottom of the tank.

c.   Fuel venting.

1)   Fuel tank vents allow air to replace the fuel consumed during flight, so the air pressure inside the tank remains the same as outside the tank. It is very important that you visually inspect these vents to ensure they are not blocked.

   a)   Any degree of blockage (partial or complete) can cause a vacuum to form in the fuel tank and prevent the flow of fuel to the engine.

2)   Some systems do not have a vent tube, but a small vent hole in the fuel cap.

   a)   Some of these vents face forward on the fuel cap and, if replaced backwards with the tube facing rearward, fuel-flow difficulty or in-flight siphoning may occur.

3)   Fuel tanks also have an overflow vent that prevents the rupture of the tank due to fuel expansion, especially on hot days.

   a)   This may be combined with the fuel tank vent or separate.

4)   Study your *POH* to learn the system on your airplane.

d.   Oil quantity, grade, and type.

1)   Usually the oil is stored in a sump at the bottom of the engine crankcase. An opening to the oil sump is provided through which oil can be added and a dipstick is provided to measure the oil level.

   a)   Your *POH* will specify the quantity of oil needed for safe operation.

   b)   Always make certain that the oil filler cap and the oil dipstick are secure after adding and/or checking the oil level. If these are not properly secured, oil loss may occur.

2)   Use only the type and grade of oil that has been recommended by the engine manufacturer, or its equivalent. Never use any oil additive that has not been recommended by the engine manufacturer or authorized by the FAA.

   a)   The type and grade of oil to use can be found in your *POH*, or on placards on or near the oil filler cap.

3)   The wrong type of oil, or an insufficient oil supply, may interfere with any or all of the basic oil functions, and can cause serious engine damage and/or an engine failure during flight.

e.   Fuel, oil, and hydraulic leaks.

1)   Check to see that there are no oil puddles or other leakages under your airplane, inside the engine cowling, or on the wheel struts.

2)   Ask someone more experienced and/or knowledgeable to look at any leakage. Know what is the cause and make the necessary repairs before flying.

f.   Flight controls.

1)   Visually inspect the flight control surfaces (ailerons, elevators, rudder) to ensure they move smoothly and freely for their entire movement span.

   a)   They also must be securely attached, with no missing, loose, or broken nuts, bolts, or rivets.

2)   Inspect any mass balance weights on control surfaces (designed to keep the control surface's center of gravity forward of the hinge so as to preclude possible shudder).

3) Check to see that the control yoke moves in the proper direction as the control surfaces move.

4) Place the flaps in the full down position to examine the attaching bolts and the entire flap surface.

    a) Ensure that the flaps operate correctly with the flap control, and lock into position.

g. Structural damage.

1) Check for dents, cracks, or tears (cloth cover) on all surfaces of the airplane. These can disrupt the smooth airflow and change your airplane's performance.

    a) These can also lead to structural weakness and/or failures due to the stress that is put on the airplane during flight.

    b) Surface deformities can also be the result of bent or broken underlying structure.

    c) One method of checking the wings on a cloth-covered airplane is to grasp the wing spars at the wing tip and gently push down and pull up.

        i) Any damage may be evident by sound and/or wrinkling of the skin.

2) Inspect the propeller for nicks and/or cracks.

    a) A small nick that is not properly repaired can become a stress point where a crack could develop and cause the blade to break.

3) If you have any doubts, get assistance from a qualified mechanic.

h. Exhaust system.

1) Check the exhaust system for visible damage and/or holes.

    a) This could lead to carbon monoxide poisoning. The effects of this are discussed in Task I.F., Aeromedical Factors, on page 171.

i. Tiedown, control lock, and wheel chock removal.

1) Tiedowns are chains or ropes used to secure the airplane to the ground from three locations on the airplane: usually, the midpoint of each wing and the tail.

    a) Tiedown hooks or eyelets are provided at these locations on most airplanes.

2) Control locks keep the control surfaces stationary so they do not move back and forth in the wind. There are three methods:

    a) A control or "gust" lock which is a pin that prevents the control yoke from turning or moving in or out.

    b) The control yoke can be secured tightly with a seatbelt.

    c) In older airplanes it is sometimes accomplished by clamping the aileron, elevator, and rudder to adjacent stationary surfaces so they cannot move.

3) Chocks are normally blocks of wood placed both in front of and behind a tire to keep the airplane from rolling.

j.   Ice and frost removal.

    1)   Frost, ice, frozen rain, or snow may accumulate on parked airplanes. All of these should be removed before takeoff.

        a)   Ice is removed by parking the airplane in a hangar or spraying deicing compounds on the airplane.

        b)   Frost should also be removed from all airfoils before flight. Even small amounts can disrupt the airflow, increase stall speed, and reduce lift.

k.   Security of baggage, cargo, and equipment.

    1)   Secure all baggage, cargo, and equipment during the preflight inspection. Make sure everything is in its place and secure.

        a)   You do not want items flying around the cockpit if you encounter turbulence.

        b)   Cargo and baggage should be secured to prevent movement which could damage the airplane and/or cause a shift in the airplane's CG.

C.   Common errors during the visual inspection

  1.   Failure to use or the improper use of the checklist.

    a.   Checklists are guides for use in ensuring that all necessary items are checked in a logical sequence.

    b.   You must not get the idea that the list is merely a crutch for poor memory.

  2.   Hazards which may result from allowing distractions to interrupt a visual inspection.

    a.   This could lead to missing items on the checklist, or

    b.   Not recognizing a discrepancy.

    c.   You must keep your thoughts on the visual inspection.

    d.   If you are distracted, either start at the beginning of the visual inspection or repeat the preceding two or three items.

  3.   Inability to recognize discrepancies.

    a.   You must understand what you are looking at during the visual inspection.

  4.   Failure to assure servicing with the proper fuel and oil.

    a.   It is easy to determine whether the correct grade of fuel has been used. Even if you are present during fueling, you should be in the habit of checking by draining a sample of fuel from the airplane to check for the proper grade and for any contamination.

    b.   Oil is not color-coded for identification. You will need to check the proper grade before you or any line personnel adds oil to the airplane.

END OF TASK

COCKPIT MANAGEMENT

II.B. TASK: COCKPIT MANAGEMENT

    PILOT OPERATION - 1

    REFERENCE: AC 61-21.

Objective. To determine that the applicant:

1. Exhibits knowledge of cockpit management by explaining related safety and efficiency factors.

2. Organizes and arranges the material and equipment in an efficient manner.

3. Ensures that the safety belts and shoulder harnesses are fastened.

4. Adjusts and locks the rudder pedals and pilot's seat to a safe position and ensures full control movement.

5. Briefs occupants on the use of safety belts and emergency procedures.

6. Exhibits adequate crew coordination.

A. General Information

    1. This is one of six tasks (A-F) in this area of operation. Your examiner is required to test you on this task.

    2. *Pilot Operation - 1* refers to FAR 61.107(a)(1): Preflight operations, including weight and balance determination, line inspection, and airplane servicing.

    3. FAA Reference

        AC 61-21: Flight Training Handbook

    4. The objective of this task is for you to explain and demonstrate efficient procedures for good cockpit management and related safety factors.

        a. This includes both maintaining an organized cockpit and understanding the aeronautical decision making process.

    5. Checklists. We emphasize the appropriate use of checklists throughout this book.

        a. A checklist provides a listing of "actions" and or "confirmations." For example, you either "turn on the fuel pump" or confirm that the fuel pump is on.

        b. If the desired condition is not available, you have to decide whether to accept the situation or take action. For example, if your engine oil temperature is indicating a higher than normal temperature while en route, you may continue your flight or attempt to divert for a landing, depending upon the level of overheating and relative changes in the temperature.

        c. Each item on the checklist requires evaluation and possible action:

           1) Is the situation safe?
           2) If not, what action is required?
           3) Is the overall airplane/environment safe when you take all factors into account?

        d. There are different types of checklists:

           1) "Read and do" -- e.g., pretakeoff checklist.

           2) "Do and read" -- e.g., in reacting to emergencies, you do everything that comes to mind and then confirm or research in your *POH*.

        e. In other words, checklists are not an end in and of themselves. Checklists are a means of flying safely. Generally, they are to be used as specified in the *POH* and to accomplish safe flight.

B. Task Objectives

1. **Exhibit your knowledge of cockpit management by explaining related safety and efficiency factors.**

   a. Cockpit management is more than just maintaining an organized and neat cockpit. Safety is a major factor and you should have an understanding of how you, your airplane, and the environment interact with each other.

      1) Cockpit management is a process that combines you, your airplane, and the environment for safer and more efficient operations.

   b. Some of the elements of cockpit management include:

      1) *Communication.* You must exchange information with ATC, FSS personnel, maintenance personnel, and other pilots.

         a) To be effective you must develop good speaking and listening skills.

      2) *Decision making and problem solving.* This is how you respond to problems that you encounter from preflight preparation to your postflight procedures.

      3) *Situational Awareness.* This is your knowledge of how you, your airplane, and the environment are interacting. This is a continuous process throughout your flight.

         a) As you increase your situational awareness you will become a safer pilot by being able to identify clues that signify a loss of situational awareness that precedes an impending accident or incident.

      4) *Standardization.* This involves your use of standardized checklists and procedures.

         a) Checklist discipline will help you because you will develop a habit of reading a checklist item, then performing the task.

         b) Procedural learning is learning a standardized procedure pattern while using the checklist as a backup

            i) As you may do in the first few steps of an emergency.

      5) *Leader/Follower.* These are the desirable characteristics of both.

         a) A leader will manage those resources that contribute to a safe flight, i.e., ensuring the proper quantity, grade, and type of fuel.

         b) A good follower will ask for help at the first indication of trouble.

      6) *Psychological factors.* These include your attitude, personality, and motivation in the decision-making process.

         a) Hazardous attitudes include: anti-authority, impulsiveness, invulnerability, macho, and resignation.

         b) Personality is the way you cope with problems.

         c) Your motivation to achieve a goal. This can be internal (you are attracted to the goal) or external (an outside force is driving you to perform).

      7) *Plan ahead.* Anticipate future situations and prepare for them.

         a) Set radio frequencies on navigation and communication radios prior to the required frequency change.

         b) Always think and stay ahead of what needs to be done at any specific time.

        c)   Always picture where you are and your heading with respect to nearby NAVAIDs, airports, and other geographical fixes.

        d)   Confirm your present position and anticipate future positions with as many NAVAIDs as possible, i.e., use them all.

    8)   *Stress management.* This is how you manage the stress in your life, which will follow you into the cockpit. Stress is your reaction to a perceived (real or not) threat to your body's equilibrium.

        a)   Learn to reduce the stress in your life or to cope with it better.

2.   **Organize and arrange the material and equipment in an efficient manner.**

    a.   On every flight you should be in the habit of organizing and neatly arranging your materials and equipment in an efficient manner that makes them readily available.

    b.   Be in the habit of "good housekeeping."

        1)   A disorganized cockpit will complicate even the simplest of flights.

    c.   Organization will contribute to safe and efficient flying.

    d.   The cockpit and/or cabin should be checked for loose articles or cargo which may be tossed about if turbulence is encountered and must be secured.

3.   **Ensure that the safety belts and shoulder harnesses are fastened.**

    a.   Once you are comfortably seated, the seatbelt and shoulder harness, if installed, should immediately be fastened and adjusted to a comfortably snug fit.

        1)   This should be accomplished even if the engine is only to be run up momentarily.

    b.   FAR 91.107 requires you to wear your seatbelt and shoulder harness, if equipped, during takeoff and landing.

    c.   While at your crewmember station, you are required to keep your seatbelt fastened as stated in FAR 91.105.

4.   **Adjust and lock the rudder pedals and your seat to a safe position and ensure full control movement.**

    a.   On each flight you should be seated in the same position.

        1)   If the seat is adjustable, it should be moved so that your knees are slightly bent with the balls of your feet placed on the rudder pedals.

            a)   This will allow full movement of the pedals.

        2)   If the seat is not adjustable, cushions should be used to provide proper seating.

            a)   This may sacrifice comfort and ease of control movements.

    b.   You must be able to see both inside and outside the cockpit without straining.

        1)   Poor vision will not only cause apprehension and confusion, but presents a hindrance to the control of the airplane.

    c.   If the seat is adjustable, it is important to ensure that your seat is locked in position.

        1)   Accidents that caused the pilot to lose control of the airplane have occurred as a result of the seat moving.

    d.   When you are positioned correctly for vision and operation of the pedals, you need to check that the control yoke has freedom of full movement.

        1)   This includes full forward, backward, and side movement.

5. **Brief occupants on the use of safety belts and emergency procedures.**

   a. FAR 91.107 requires you, as pilot in command, to ensure that each person on board is briefed on the use of safety belts and shoulder harnesses, if equipped.

      1) You are responsible to notify each person on board to fasten his/her seat belt and shoulder harness, if equipped, before takeoff or landing.

   b. At this time you need to brief the occupants on the emergency procedures of the airplane that are relevant to them.

      1) Inform them of what they should do before and after an off-airport landing is made.

      2) You can determine if an occupant is competent to assist you in reading an emergency checklist. This would allow you to perform the tasks as they are read item by item.

6. **Exhibit adequate crew coordination.**

   a. If you are flying with another pilot, you can share certain flight duties.

   b. The pilot in command will always be in charge.

   c. Duties that may be shared with another pilot include

      1) Taking care of the radios, and
      2) Reading of the checklists.

   d. An additional pilot is a resource that should be utilized as part of cockpit management.

      1) Ensure the responsibilities are thoroughly discussed and agreed upon.

      2) Each crewmember has assigned responsibilities that (s)he is responsible for while cross-checking the other crewmember.

C. Common errors in cockpit management

   1. **Failure to place and secure essential materials and equipment for easy access during flight.**

      a. Do not use the top of the instrument panel as a storage area.

      b. You need to maintain an organized cockpit and stress the safety factors of being organized.

   2. **Improper adjustment of equipment and controls.**

      a. Determine the proper seat and control adjustment and always use those positions when flying.

         1) Ensure proper control movement after the seat is adjusted for vision and operation of controls.

   3. **Failure to use the appropriate checklist.**

      a. You should always use the appropriate checklist for that specific phase of your flight while on the ground or in the air.

END OF TASK

STARTING ENGINE

II.C. TASK: STARTING ENGINE

   PILOT OPERATION - 1

   REFERENCES: AC 61-21, AC 61-23, AC 91-13, AC 91-55; Airplane Handbook and Flight Manual.

Objective. To determine that the applicant:

1. Exhibits knowledge by explaining engine starting procedures, including starting under various atmospheric conditions.

2. Performs all the items on the checklist.

3. Accomplishes correct starting procedures with emphasis on

   a. Positioning the airplane to avoid creating hazards.

   b. Determining that the area is clear.

   c. Adjusting the engine controls.

   d. Setting the brakes.

   e. Preventing airplane movement after engine start.

   f. Avoiding excessive engine RPM and temperatures.

   g. Checking the engine instruments after engine start.

A. **General Information**

   1. This is one of six tasks (A-F) in this area of operation. Your examiner is required to test you on this task.

   2. *Pilot Operation - 1* refers to FAR 61.107(a)(1): Preflight operations, including weight and balance determination, line inspection, and airplane servicing.

   3. FAA References

        AC 61-21: Flight Training Handbook
        AC 61-23: Pilot's Handbook of Aeronautical Knowledge
        AC 91-13: Cold Weather Operation of Aircraft
        AC 91-55: Reduction of Electrical System Failures Following Aircraft Engine Starting
        Pilot's Operating Handbook (FAA-Approved Airplane Flight Manual)

   4. The objective of this task is for you to explain and demonstrate correct engine starting procedures.

B. **Task Objectives**

   1. **Exhibit your knowledge by explaining engine starting procedures, including starting under various atmospheric conditions.**

      a. The correct engine starting procedure for your airplane is explained in your *POH*. You should also know how to start your engine with an external power source and hand propping procedures.

         1) Some airplanes are equipped with an external power receptacle.

            a) This allows you to connect an external power (battery) to your airplane's electrical system without accessing the battery in the airplane.

            b) You can also use an external battery and connect it to the airplane's battery to provide power to the starter.

            c) Read your *POH* for the correct procedures.

2)   Even though most airplanes are equipped with electric starters, you should know the procedures and danger involved in hand propping.

    a)   It is recommended that a competent pilot, or a qualified person thoroughly familiar with the operation of all the controls, be seated at the controls in the cockpit and that the person turning the propeller be thoroughly familiar with this technique.

    b)   The traditional approach with the person "pulling through" the propeller in front of the propeller follows.

    c)   To start the plane, the propeller is rotated in the clockwise direction (as seen from the cockpit).

    d)   Never lean into the propeller as you pull it. You must not be in a position where you would fall forward if your feet slip. You should have one foot forward and one foot back. As you pull down, you should shift your weight to your rear foot and back away.

    e)   You should not wrap your fingers around the propeller. You should have your fingers just over the trailing edge. This is to prevent injury if the engine misfires (or backfires) and turns backward.

        i)   Before pulling the propeller through slowly so the engine sucks gas into the cylinders, the person pulling the propeller should shout, "brakes on, mag (magneto, i.e., ignition) off." The pilot inside the plane should confirm by repeating, "brakes on, mag off." But always assume the mag switch is on. That is, always be in a safe position relative to the propeller and keep the area clear.

        ii)   Before moving the propeller, the pilot outside should check the brakes by pushing on the propeller spinner (center of the propeller) to see that the airplane cannot be pushed backward.

        iii)   After pulling the propeller through a few times, the propeller should be positioned with the left side (when facing the airplane from the front) at the 10 to 11 o'clock position. This will facilitate spinning the propeller by pulling down against the engine's compression.

        iv)   When the person on the propeller is ready to attempt starting and the propeller (left blade when facing the nose of the plane) is at 10 to 11 o'clock, the person on the propeller should shout, "brakes on, throttle cracked, mag on." The pilot in the plane should make the required adjustments and repeat, "brakes on, throttle cracked, mag on."

        v)   After checking to see that the brakes are on (by pushing the spinner), the person on the propeller should then spin the propeller as hard as possible by pulling down on the left blade. Be sure to stand on firm ground. Stand close enough to the propeller to be able to step away easily. As the propeller is pulled through, the person should step back away from the propeller to avoid being hit as the engine starts.

    f)   Especially if you are starting the engine yourself, you should stand behind the propeller on the right side when facing the direction the plane is facing. This will permit you to place one foot in front of the right main tire in addition to having the brakes set full on or having the airplane tied down (both if possible). Note, this is an extremely dangerous procedure. USE EXTREME CARE.

        i)   Some experts advocate that this approach should also be used when there is a pilot in the cockpit at the controls.

b. You must be able to explain engine starting procedures under various atmospheric conditions (i.e., cold or hot weather).

1) During cold weather the oil in your airplane's engine becomes very thick. There are several methods to assist in starting a cold engine. Check your *POH* for the recommended procedure.

a) One method is the propeller should be pulled through (turned) several times to loosen the oil.

i) This saves battery energy, which is already low due to the low temperature.

ii) When performing this procedure, take the same precautions as you would if you were hand propping. Ensure that the ignition/magneto switch is off, throttle is closed, mixture is lean/idle cut-off position, that nobody is standing in or near the propeller arc, the parking brake is on, and the airplane is chocked and/or tied down.

iii) A loose or broken groundwire on either magneto could cause the engine to fire or backfire.

b) Cold weather starting can be made easier by preheating the engine.

i) Many fixed based operators (FBOs) in cold weather locations offer this service.

ii) Small, portable heaters are available which can blow hot air into the engine to warm it.

iii) This is generally required when outside air temperatures are below 0°F, and is recommended by most engine manufacturers when the temperature is below 20°F.

c) To start a cold engine it should be primed with fuel first.

i) In carburetor engines, the primer is a small manual or electric pump which draws fuel from the tanks and vaporizes it directly into one or two of the cylinders through small fuel lines.

• Continuous priming may be required to keep the engine running until sufficient engine heat is generated to vaporize the fuel.

d) After a cold engine has been started, it should be idled at low RPMs for 2 to 5 min. to allow the oil to warm and begin circulating throughout the system.

2) During hot weather and/or with a hot engine, the cylinders tend to become overloaded with fuel. This could lead to a flooded engine situation.

a) Follow the appropriate checklist for either a HOT or FLOODED engine in your *POH*.

i) Flooded engine normally requires you to have the mixture in the lean position and the throttle full open.

• This helps clear the cylinders of the excess fuel and allows the engine to start.

ii) As the engine starts, ensure that you close the throttle and move the mixture to rich.

   c.   Using incorrect starting procedures could be very hazardous. It could also lead to overpriming or priming your engine when it is not necessary.

       1)   Operating your starter motor for long periods of time may cause it to overheat and/or completely drain your battery.

       2)   Follow the recommendations and procedures that are in your *POH*.

2.   Perform all the items on the checklist.

   a.   As explained in Task II.B., Cockpit Management, on page 185, it is vital that you make a habit of appropriate use of a checklist for every operation in flying.

       1)   This ensures that every item is completed and checked.

   b.   You must use the checklist in your *POH* for the before-starting and the starting procedures.

   c.   ALL CHECKLISTS should be read aloud at all times.

       1)   Especially during flight tests and even when you are by yourself.
       2)   Pretend you are working with a copilot.

   d.   Call out each item on the checklist as you undertake the action or make the necessary observation.

       1)   "Engine instruments OK" after engine start and you have examined your engine instruments **and** they indicate normal operation.

   e.   Examples of checklists for the Cessna 152 appear below. Again, we emphasize that for each item you have to be satisfied that, after your examination and evaluation, the situation is "safe" and you can proceed to the next item on your checklist.

CESSNA 152
BEFORE STARTING ENGINE

1. Preflight Inspection . . . . Complete	4. Radios, Electrical Equipment . . . . Off
2. Seats, Seat Belts, Shoulder Harnesses . . . . Adjust and Lock	5. Brakes . . . . Test and Set
3. Fuel Shutoff Valve . . . . On	6. Circuit Breakers . . . . Check In

> **For Academic Illustration/Training Purposes Only!**
> *For Flight:* **Use your Pilot's Operating Handbook and FAA-Approved Airplane Flight Manual.**

CESSNA 152
STARTING ENGINE
(Temperatures above Freezing)

1. Mixture . . . . Rich	8. Throttle . . . . Adjust for 1000 RPM or less
2. Carburetor Heat . . . . Cold	9. Oil Pressure . . . . Check
3. Prime . . . . As Required	10. Flashing Beacon and Navigation Lights -- On as required
(up to 3 strokes - none if engine is warm)	
4. Throttle . . . . Open ½ inch	11. Radios . . . . On
(closed if engine is warm)	
5. Propeller Area . . . . Clear	
6. Master Switch . . . . On	
7. Ignition Switch . . . . Start	
(release when engine starts)	

> **For Academic Illustration/Training Purposes Only!**
> *For Flight:* **Use your Pilot's Operating Handbook and FAA-Approved Airplane Flight Manual.**

3.   **Accomplish the correct starting procedures with emphasis on the following.**

    a.   **Position your airplane to avoid creating hazards.**

        1)   Always start the engine with enough room in front of the airplane so you could turn off the engine if the brakes failed.

        2)   Also, do not start the engine with the tail of the airplane pointed (i.e., think about direction of prop blast) toward an open hangar door, toward parked cars, or toward a group of bystanders.

            a)   It is a violation of FAR 91.13 to operate your airplane on any part of the surface of an airport in a careless or reckless manner that endangers the life or property of another.

        3)   Be cautious of loose debris, e.g., rocks or dirt, that can become projectiles when you start the engine.

    b.   **Determine that the area around your airplane is clear** by observing the area and shouting, "Clear Prop!" out your open window, before cranking the engine.

        1)   Allow a few seconds for a response if someone is nearby or under the airplane.

    c.   **Adjust the engine controls.**

        1)   While activating the starter, and during ground operations while the engine is running, one hand should be kept on the throttle at all times.

            a)   During starting, this allows you to advance the throttle if the engine falters or to prevent excessive RPM just after starting.

    d.   **Set the brakes.**

        1)   Some airplanes have a parking brake which should be set in the manner prescribed in your *POH*.

        2)   In airplanes without a parking brake you must ensure that your airplane's brakes are set, normally by applying appropriate pressure on the toe (or pedal) brakes.

        3)   Before starting the engine, remember to position your airplane to avoid creating a hazard.

            a)   If for some reason the brakes are not set properly and your airplane moves forward when the engine is started, you must have an area in which you can stop your airplane by engine shut-down.

    e.   **Prevent airplane movement after engine start.**

        1)   You must prevent your airplane from moving after you start the engine. This is done with your brakes.

        2)   You must look outside your airplane to ensure that you are not moving. Be aware of what is happening around you.

f. **Avoid excessive engine RPM and temperatures.**

    1) This requires that you monitor your engine instruments during your ground operations.

        a) Your *POH* will have the recommended RPM and temperature ranges for the warm-up and other ground operations.

        b) If your engine temperature begins to rise and you have adjustable cowl flaps, open them.

    2) Follow the checklist in your *POH* if the engine temperature begins to rise above the normal operating range.

g. **Check the engine instruments after engine start.**

    1) As soon as the engine is started and operating you should check the oil pressure gauge. If it does not rise to the normal operating range in about 30 sec. in summer or 60 sec. in winter, the engine may not be receiving proper lubrication and should be shut down immediately.

    2) Check all other engine instruments to ensure they are also operating within the normal limits as prescribed in your *POH*.

C. Common errors during engine start

  1. Failure to use, or the improper use of, the checklist.

    a. You must be in the habit of properly using the correct checklist for engine starting.
    b. This ensures that every item is completed and checked in a logical order.

  2. Excessively high RPM after starting.

    a. You should constantly monitor the engine instruments while the engine is operating.

  3. Improper preheat of the engine during severe cold weather conditions.

    a. Severe cold weather will cause a change in the viscosity of engine oils, batteries may lose a high percentage of their effectiveness, and instruments may stick.

    b. During preheat operations, do not leave the airplane unattended, and keep a fire extinguisher nearby.

    c. There is a tendency to overprime, which washes down cylinder walls, and scoring of the walls may result.

    d. Icing on the sparkplug electrodes can short them out. The only remedy is heat.

  4. Failure to ensure proper clearance of the propeller.

    a. During the visual inspection, the propeller path should be checked for debris or obstructions, especially on the ground.

    b. Before starting, ensure that no person or object will be struck by the propeller.

END OF TASK

TAXIING

II.D. TASK: TAXIING

     PILOT OPERATION - 2

     REFERENCES: AC 61-21.

Objective. To determine that the applicant:

1. Exhibits knowledge by explaining safe taxi procedures.

2. Adheres to signals and clearances, and follows the proper taxi route.

3. Performs a brake check immediately after the airplane begins moving.

4. Controls taxi speed without excessive use of brakes.

5. Recognizes and avoids hazards.

6. Positions the controls for the existing wind conditions.

7. Avoids careless and reckless operations.

A. General Information

    1. This is one of six tasks (A-F) in this area of operation. Your examiner is required to test you on this task.

    2. *Pilot Operation - 2* refers to FAR 61.107(a)(2): Airport and traffic pattern operations, including operations at controlled airports, radio communications, and collision avoidance precautions.

    3. FAA Reference

        AC 61-21: Flight Training Handbook

    4. The objective of this task is to determine your knowledge of safe taxiing procedures.

    5. Although not specified as an element of this task, you must use and follow the taxi checklist, if any, that is in your *POH*. It may be combined as "after-engine start/taxiing." Before you start to taxi it is a good habit to include the following in your checklist.

        a. Set your heading indicator to your magnetic compass.

            1) While taxiing you can check that it moves freely and indicates known headings.

        b. Set your attitude indicator. It may not have had enough time for the gyro to stabilize, but within 5 min. it should be stable with a level attitude.

            1) While taxiing it should not indicate a bank.

        c. Set your altimeter to the altimeter setting, if available. If not, set it to the airport elevation.

        d. If your airplane has a clock, you should set it to the correct time.

        e. By setting your flight instruments before taxiing, you have a base on which to make a determination of their proper operation.

        f. Make sure the taxi area is clear (behind you to avoid prop washing other people or aircraft, as well as in front of you) before you start to taxi.

6.   Taxiing is the controlled movement of your airplane under its own power while on the ground.

    a.   Taxiing occurs about the airport on ramps and taxiways, to move onto and off the active runway.

        1)   Ramps are the areas where airplanes are parked (tied down), fueled, etc.
        2)   Taxiways are the roadways from the ramps to the end of the runways.

    b.   Some small airports have virtually no taxiways, and taxiing is done on the runway itself.

B.   Task Objectives

    1.   Exhibit your knowledge by explaining safe taxi procedures.

        a.   The primary requirements of safe taxiing are safe positive control and the ability to stop or turn where and when desired.

        b.   Taxi speed is controlled primarily with the throttle and, only **secondarily, with the brakes.** Recommended taxi speed is about the speed of a brisk walk. Develop your skill so as to taxi as if the brakes were inoperative.

            1)   Taxi very slowly while on the ramp area near other planes and obstacles.

        c.   You steer your airplane while taxiing by means of the rudder pedals.

            1)   Ailerons and elevator should be placed in neutral position when there is no wind.

            2)   Ailerons and elevator give no control when there is no wind.

        d.   Check all wingtip clearances continuously. If there is any doubt about wingtip clearance, have someone walk along with the wingtip.

        e.   Taxiing nosewheel airplanes

            1)   Taxiing an airplane equipped with a nosewheel is relatively simple. Nosewheel airplanes generally have better ground handling characteristics (relative to tailwheel airplanes). The nosewheel is usually connected to the rudder pedals by a mechanical linkage.

            2)   When starting to taxi, the airplane should always be allowed to roll forward slowly so the nosewheel turns straight ahead in order to avoid turning into an adjacent airplane or nearby obstruction.

            3)   All turns conducted with a nosewheel airplane are started using the rudder pedals.

                a)   Power may be applied after entering the turn to counteract the increase in friction during the turn.

                b)   If it is necessary to tighten the turn after full rudder pedal deflection has been reached, the inside brake may be used as needed to aid in turning the airplane.

            4)   When stopping the airplane, it is advisable always to stop with the nosewheel straight in order to relieve any strain on the nose gear and to make it easier to start moving again.

                a)   This is particularly true when positioning yourself for the pretakeoff checklist during which you run up (operate at relatively high RPM) the airplane to check the ignition system.

f. Taxiing tailwheel airplanes

    1) Taxiing a tailwheel-type airplane is usually more difficult than taxiing nosewheel equipped airplanes, because the tailwheel provides less directional control than a nosewheel. Also, tailwheel airplanes tend to turn so the nose of the aircraft points itself into the wind (this is referred to as weathervaning).

        a) The tendency for tailwheel airplanes to weathervane is greatest in a crosswind situation.

        b) Generally, brakes play a much larger role in taxiing tailwheel equipped airplanes.

    2) Since a tailwheel-type airplane rests on its tailwheel, as well as the main landing wheels, it assumes a nose high attitude when on the ground. In most cases, this causes the engine to restrict your forward vision.

        a) It may be necessary to weave the airplane right and left while taxiing to see and avoid collision with any objects or hazardous surface conditions in front of the nose.

        b) The weave, zigzag, or short S-turns must be done slowly, smoothly, and cautiously.

g. Taxiing on other than clean pavement

    1) Operation of nosewheel equipped airplanes on other than clean pavement requires that the elevator control be held in the full back position (so the elevator is up, tail down, and nose up).

    2) High RPM settings should be avoided (except on a soft field) so that the propeller will not be damaged by sand, stones, and other debris "sucked" up from the ground by the propeller.

    3) When taxiing on soft surfaces, e.g., a muddy field, sufficient additional power should be used to keep the airplane rolling. If it stops, it would take considerable (maybe full) throttle to get the airplane moving again. Remember, full throttle will shower the airplane with debris.

2.   Adhere to signals and clearances, and follow the proper taxi route.

    a.   Markings.

        1)   Taxiway Marking -- The taxiway centerline is marked with a continuous yellow line. When the taxiway edge is marked, two continuous yellow lines spaced 6 in. apart are used.

        2)   Holding Position Markings -- There are three types of holding position markings that may be encountered on an airport.

            a)   Holding position markings for taxiway/runway intersections, taxiways located in runway approach areas, and runway/runway intersections consist of four yellow lines, two solid and two dashed, spaced 6 in. apart and extending across the width of the taxiway or runway.

                i)   The solid lines are always on the side where the aircraft is to hold.

                ii)   These markings are installed on runways only if the runway is used by ATC for "land, hold short" operations or taxiing operations and have operational significance only for those two types of operations. A sign with a white inscription on a red background (i.e., a STOP sign) is installed adjacent to these holding position markings.

                    • A land, hold short operation is one in which ATC instructions are "Cleared to land runway X, hold short of runway Y." You must either exit runway X prior to runway Y or stop prior to runway Y.

            b)   Holding position markings for ILS (instrument landing system) critical areas consist of two yellow solid lines spaced 2 ft. apart connected by pairs of solid lines spaced 10 ft. apart extended across the width of the taxiway as shown in the figure below.

                i)   A sign with an inscription "ILS" in white on a red background is installed adjacent to these holding position markings.

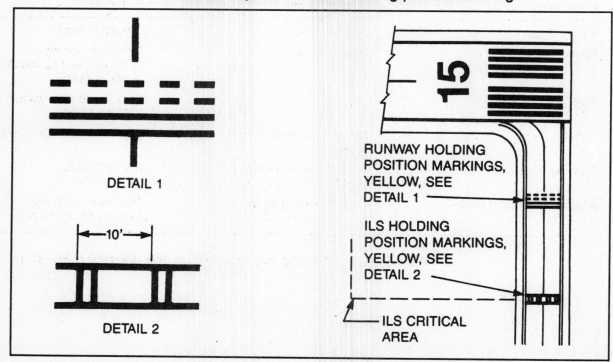

DETAIL 1

DETAIL 2

RUNWAY HOLDING POSITION MARKINGS, YELLOW, SEE DETAIL 1

ILS HOLDING POSITION MARKINGS, YELLOW, SEE DETAIL 2

ILS CRITICAL AREA

c) Holding position markings for taxiway/taxiway intersections consist of one dashed line extending across the width of the taxiway as shown below. They are installed on taxiways where ATC normally holds aircraft short of a taxiway intersection.

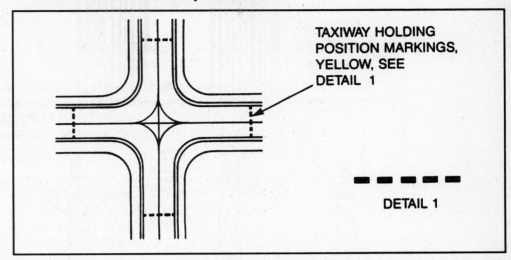

TAXIWAY HOLDING POSITION MARKINGS, YELLOW, SEE DETAIL 1

DETAIL 1

3) When instructed to hold short of a runway you need to ensure that no part of your airplane extends beyond the hold line.

4) See Task III.C., Airport and Runway Marking and Lighting, on page 239.

b. Signals.

1) An airport with an operating control tower can communicate with you by the use of various combinations of light signals. The tower can flash a green, red, or white light. While taxiing, various combinations of these signals mean different things:

Light Signal	On the Ground	In the Air
Steady Green	Cleared for takeoff	Cleared to land
Flashing Green	Cleared to taxi	Return for landing *(to be followed by steady green at proper time)*
Steady Red	Stop	Give way to other aircraft and continue circling
Flashing Red	Taxi clear of landing area (runway) in use	Airport unsafe -- Do not land
Flashing White	Return to starting point on airport	Not applicable
Alternating Red and Green	General warning signal -- Exercise extreme caution	General warning signal -- Exercise extreme caution

a) Note that, when in the air, light signals are different than on the ground.

2) You should also know the standard hand signals used by ramp personnel for the direction of pilots operating airplanes in the ramp area.

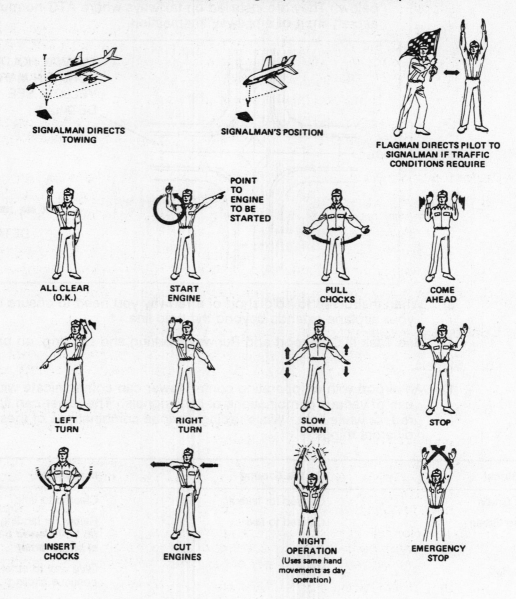

SIGNALMAN DIRECTS TOWING

SIGNALMAN'S POSITION

FLAGMAN DIRECTS PILOT TO SIGNALMAN IF TRAFFIC CONDITIONS REQUIRE

ALL CLEAR (O.K.)

POINT TO ENGINE TO BE STARTED

START ENGINE

PULL CHOCKS

COME AHEAD

LEFT TURN

RIGHT TURN

SLOW DOWN

STOP

INSERT CHOCKS

CUT ENGINES

NIGHT OPERATION (Uses same hand movements as day operation)

EMERGENCY STOP

c. Clearances.

1) When operating at an airport with an operating control tower you are required to obtain a clearance before you taxi out of the ramp area onto a taxiway.

a) Remember that ground control may not clear you all the way to the active runway, e.g., "taxi to runway 28, hold short of runway 24." This means do not cross runway 24 until given clearance. Whenever in doubt, ask!

2) At airports without operating control towers, you should use the Common Traffic Advisory Frequency (CTAF).

a) Announce your taxi intentions (especially if back taxiing on a runway).

i) EXAMPLE: "Rudy's Gliderport traffic, Piper Cub back taxiing runway 34 for departure on runway 16."

d.   You are required to follow the taxi route that is specified in your taxi clearance (at an airport with an operating control tower) or the most direct route at an uncontrolled airport.

1)   If you are at an airport with an operating control tower and you are unfamiliar with the airport taxiways, or for any reason confusion exists as to the correct taxi routing, you should request progressive taxi instructions, e.g., "Beech 66421 requests progressives." (Progressives is an FAA suggested term.)

a)   These are step-by-step routing directions.

2)   Progressive instructions may also be issued by ATC if the controller feels it is necessary due to traffic or field conditions, e.g., construction or closed taxiways.

3.   Perform a brake check immediately after your airplane begins moving.

a.   To perform a brake check on your airplane you need to begin moving your airplane forward by gradually adding power (push the throttle forward slowly) to increase the engine RPM.

1)   Reduce the power to idle as soon as your airplane begins rolling and gently apply the brakes to stop the forward motion of your airplane.

b.   If there is any question about the operation of the brakes, shut down the engine immediately and have them checked.

4.   Control taxi speed without excessive use of brakes.

a.   Your taxi speed should allow you to stop when and where you want. Do not ride the brakes. Riding the brakes means using the brakes constantly, usually while excessive power is used.

b.   Taxi speed is controlled primarily with engine speed (RPM). Develop your skill so as to taxi as if the brakes were inoperative. Use the brakes only when a reduction in engine speed (RPM) is not sufficient.

c.   Airplane brakes on newer airplanes are generally toe brakes, i.e., on the top of the rudder pedals. Thus, when you apply pressure to the top of the rudder pedals, you are also applying the brakes. Rudder pedals are usually high enough that you have to consciously move your feet up on the rudder pedals to apply the brakes.

1)   Normally (i.e., when not using the brakes) your heel rests on the floorboards and the ball (top) of your foot is on the bottom of the rudder pedal. This minimizes the possibility of having the brakes on when landing.

2)   The following diagram illustrates use of the rudder on the left and brakes on the right.

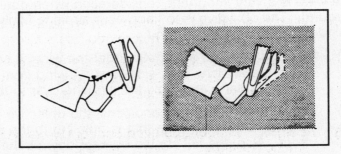

d.   Some older planes have heel brakes which are activated by separate small brakes just in front and to the inside of the rudder pedals. These, as the description implies, are activated by your heel.

e. Always use both brakes together with the same pressure. The ONLY time you use different pressure for directional purposes is for sharp turns at VERY LOW speeds, i.e., barely moving. At all other times, apply the brakes evenly and use the airplane's nosewheel or tailwheel (steerable with the rudder controls) for directional control.

5. Recognize and avoid hazards.

a. Maintaining awareness of the location and movement of all other aircraft and vehicles along the taxi path and in the traffic pattern is essential to safety.

b. Visually scan the area around you and constantly look for other traffic and/or obstructions. This is a time to be looking outside your aircraft with a minimum time looking in the cockpit to check your engine and flight instruments.

   1) Indicate your awareness of traffic and/or obstructions by pointing them out to your examiner.

c. Monitor the appropriate radio frequency for traffic and possible conflicts.

   1) At an airport with an operating control tower you will be monitoring the ground control and you will hear other aircraft requesting taxi clearance either from the ramp area or after clearing the active runway.

      a) Ground control is responsible for the movement of airplanes and other vehicles on the airport surface. Thus, you are required to remain on that frequency until you are at the hold line ready for takeoff clearance from the tower.

   2) At uncontrolled (or non-operating control tower) fields monitor the CTAF frequency for traffic, both on the ground and in the air.

d. You must apply right-of-way rules and maintain adequate spacing behind other aircraft.

   1) Generally, the right-of-way rules apply as they do while in the air, i.e., approaching head-on alter course to the right, yield to an airplane on his/her right.

      a) Ground control (at an airport with an operating control tower) may instruct one aircraft to stop or yield to another.

      b) If in doubt, always yield to other aircraft. Be safe.

   2) Avoid being too close to another airplane's prop or jet wash which could cause you to lose control of your airplane. Maintain a safe separation.

6. Position the controls for the existing wind conditions.

a. The wind is a very important consideration when operating your airplane on the ground. The objective is to keep your airplane firmly on the ground, i.e., not let the wind blow the airplane around.

   1) If a wind from the side gets under the wing, it can lift the wing up and even blow the airplane over sideways. A wind from the rear can get under the tail of the airplane and blow the airplane over to the front.

   2) When taxiing in windy conditions, the objective is to use the control surfaces to keep down the wing that is pointing to the direction the wind is coming from. Also, the tail should be kept down if the wind is blowing from the rear.

   3) Caution is recommended. Avoid sudden bursts of power and sudden braking.

b.   When taxiing in windy conditions, the control surfaces should be positioned as shown in the following diagram.

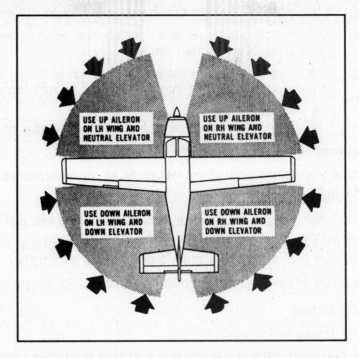

1)   When the wind is from any forward direction, the control yoke should be turned or pushed fully toward the wind.

   a)   Wind from the front makes your airplane act as it would in flight, i.e., turn the control yoke in the direction of the desired down wing.

   b)   The aileron on the side the wind is coming from will be up and the wind flowing over the wing will hold the wing down (rather than lifting the wing, which would permit the wind to get under the wing and possibly blow the airplane over on its back).

   c)   The elevators should be in a neutral position, i.e., the control yoke held neither forward nor back. This permits the nosewheel to carry its normal weight and to be used for directional control.

      i)   NOTE: On tailwheel airplanes ONLY, the elevators should be up, i.e., control yoke or stick pulled back, to keep the tail firmly down so the tailwheel can provide directional control.

2)   When the wind is from any rearwind direction, the control yoke should be turned away from the wind.

   a)   The aileron on the side the wind is coming from will be down, which will help keep the wind from getting under the wing and lifting it.

   b)   The control yoke will be full forward, causing the elevator to be pointed down. This will deter the wind from getting under the tail, raising the tail, and possibly blowing the airplane over (tail over front).

      i)   Note that on tailwheel airplanes the control yoke or stick is also held full forward to keep the tailwheel firmly on the ground for directional control.

      3)   It would be an extreme situation for an airplane to be blown (flipped) on its back.

          a)   If the wind is blowing that hard, you should not even be in the airplane.

          b)   Also, watch out for jet blast, which has been known to blow small airplanes over on their backs.

          c)   The more likely result (of a strong wind) is losing directional control of the airplane, running into something, or running off the runway due to

              i)   Panic, or
              ii)   Incorrect response which aggravates the situation.

7.   Avoid careless and reckless operations.

    a.   Be sure that your airplane's wings will clear all other airplanes or obstructions.

      1)   If in doubt, stop.

    b.   Avoid prop washing people, aircraft, or vehicles while taxiing.

      1)   FAR 91.13 prohibits you from operating your airplane in a careless or reckless manner that endangers the life or property of another.

      2)   Be polite when operating around people and/or property.

C.   Common errors during taxiing

    1.   Improper use of brakes.

      a.   The most common error is the tendency to ride the brakes while taxiing.

        1)   Correct this by using the throttle to slow the airplane down, and use the brakes to completely stop the airplane.

    2.   Improper positioning of flight controls for various wind conditions.

      a.   Always know the direction of the wind in relation to the airplane. Use all available means to determine direction, such as wind sock and/or ground control.

      b.   Picture the wind relative to your airplane at any given time by means of the heading indicator.

        1)   EXAMPLE: If the airplane is heading 090° and the wind is from 240°, you can use the heading indicator to determine that the wind is a right-quartering tailwind.

    3.   Hazards of taxiing too fast.

      a.   This occurs from the improper use of the throttle and sometimes by feeling rushed to get to the run-up area.

      b.   Taxi slowly in the ramp area and at a speed where you can stop or turn where and when you desire.

        1)   Normally it should be at such a speed that, when the throttle is closed, the airplane can be stopped promptly.

    4.   Failure to comply with markings, signals, or clearances.

      a.   Before starting to taxi at a controlled airport, ask yourself if the taxi instructions make sense and that you understand the clearance.

        1)   Contact ground control for clarification.

      b.   While taxiing, identify markings and signals to your examiner.

END OF TASK

PRETAKEOFF CHECK

II.E. TASK: PRETAKEOFF CHECK

PILOT OPERATION - 1

REFERENCES: AC 61-21; Airplane Handbook and Flight Manual.

Objective. To determine that the applicant:

1. Exhibits knowledge of the pretakeoff check by explaining the reasons for checking all items.
2. Positions the airplane to avoid creating hazards.
3. Divides attention inside and outside of the cockpit.
4. Accomplishes the checklist items.
5. Ensures that the airplane is in safe operating condition.
6. Reviews the critical takeoff performance airspeeds and distances.
7. Describes takeoff emergency procedures.
8. Obtains and interprets takeoff and departure clearances.

A. General Information

  1. This is one of six tasks (A-F) in this area of operation. Your examiner is required to test you on this task.

  2. *Pilot Operation - 1* refers to FAR 61.107(a)(1): Preflight operations, including weight and balance determination, line inspection, and airplane servicing.

  3. FAA References

     AC 61-21: Flight Training Handbook
     Pilot's Operating Handbook (FAA-Approved Airplane Flight Manual)

  4. The objective of this task is to determine your ability to perform the pretakeoff check.

B. Task Objectives

  1. **Exhibit your knowledge of the pretakeoff check by explaining the reasons for checking all items.**

     a. The pretakeoff check is the systematic procedure for making a last-minute check of the engine, controls, systems, instruments, and radio prior to flight.

        1) Normally, it is performed after taxiing to a position near the takeoff end of the runway.

        2) Taxiing to that position is usually sufficient time for the engine to have warmed up to at least minimum operating temperatures and ensures adequate lubrication of the internal moving parts of the engine before operating the engine at high power settings.

     b. Some *POH*s differentiate between a ground checklist and pretakeoff list. We have combined both, as in this Task. Both are done on a taxiway near the end of the active runway. The objective is to ascertain that all systems, instruments, etc., are working properly and are ready for flight.

     c. Your *POH* will explain the proper operating limitations while you are performing your pretakeoff check.

        1) Any deviation from these normal operating limits means that there is a possible malfunction and you should return to the ramp to determine the cause.

  2. **Position your airplane to avoid creating hazards.**

     a. As you taxi to the active runway, turn your airplane somewhat diagonal to the runway so you will not prop blast any airplanes behind you.

b.   The FAA recommends that you position your airplane into the wind, as nearly as possible, to obtain more accurate operating indications and to minimize engine overheating when the engine is run up.

1)   NOTE: In older airplanes with radial engines, the rule was to turn into the wind to provide as much cooling as possible for the engine. Generally, cooling is not a problem for today's airplane engines.

2)   If you have problems with overheating, you may wish to point the airplane into the wind to obtain the maximum cooling effect possible.

c.   You should position your airplane on a firm surface, smooth turf or paved surface that is free of debris.

1)   Otherwise, the propeller will pick up pebbles, dirt, mud, sand, or other loose particles and hurl them backward, not only damaging the tail of the airplane, but often inflicting damage to the propeller itself.

d.   Straighten your nosewheel before stopping, as your magneto check requires an engine run-up which puts considerable stress on your nosewheel (which is better absorbed with the nosewheel straight).

e.   Point your airplane in a direction so that, in the event of brake failure, you will not run into another aircraft, a ditch, a sign, etc.

3.   **Divide your attention inside and outside of the cockpit,** especially during the engine runup.

a.   If the parking brake slips, or if the application of the toe brakes is inadequate for the amount of power applied, the airplane could move forward unnoticed if your attention is fixed inside the airplane.

4.   **Accomplish the checklist items.**

a.   Follow the pretakeoff (ground check and/or before takeoff) checklists in your *POH*.

1)   You must follow the checklist item by item.

b.   You need to be critical of your airplane's performance, and determine whether your airplane meets the performance guidelines in your *POH*.

1)   Do not accept any unacceptable levels of airplane performance.

c.   The following pretakeoff checklist is from the Beech Skipper 77 *POH*.

BEECHCRAFT SKIPPER 77
BEFORE TAKEOFF

Seat Belts and Shoulder Harnesses . . . . Check	Carburetor Heat . . . . . Check and set cold for takeoff
Parking Brake . . . . Set	Throttle . . . . Idle
Avionics . . . . Check	Elevator Trim . . . . Set to take-off range
Engine Instruments . . . . Check	Rudder Trim . . . . Set to 0
Flight Instruments . . . . Check and set	Flaps . . . . Check operation, then up
Starter Engaged Warning Light (if installed) . . . . Check	Controls . . . . Check freedom of movement
(should not be illuminated). If light is not	and proper direction
installed or is inoperative, the ammeter indication	Mixture . . . . Full rich (or as required by field elevation)
should be less than 25% of full charge at 1000	Doors . . . . Secure
to 1200 RPM and should show some decrease	Parking Brake . . . . Release
from the initial indication.	Engine Instruments . . . . Check
Fuel Selector . . . . Check on	
Throttle . . . . 1800 RPM	**For Academic Illustration/Training Purposes Only!**
Magnetos . . . . Check	***For Flight:*** **Use your Pilot's Operating Handbook**
(175 RPM maximum drop, within 50 RPM of each other)	**and FAA-Approved Airplane Flight Manual.**

d. As you read your checklist out loud, touch a control to switch or adjust it to the prescribed position after identifying a checklist item.

    1) If an instrument gauge, the instrument reading should be said aloud and pointed at.

    2) Do not just perform the procedures but rather interpret them to your examiner.

5. Ensure that your airplane is in safe operating condition.

a. You, as the pilot in command, are responsible for determining whether your airplane is in condition for safe flight (FAR 91.7). You will need to emphasize the following during your preflight check, but remember everything on your checklist is very important to ensure that your airplane is safe for flight.

    1) Check flight controls for proper operation.

        a) Flight controls must move freely and properly. This means you must move your controls their entire distance and observe that the flight surfaces move correspondingly.

    2) Your flight instruments should have been checked during taxi, and they should be checked again and properly set.

        a) Clock, if equipped, should be set to the correct time.

        b) Airspeed indicator should be at 0 kt.

        c) Attitude indicator (AI) should be stabilized and the miniature airplane set on the horizon.

            i) During taxiing the AI should not have shown a bank in excess of 5°.

        d) Altimeter should be set at the current altimeter setting (which should indicate approximate field elevation). If not available, it should be set at field elevation.

        e) Turn coordinator should have the wings level and the ball centered on level ground.

            i) During taxiing the airplane should have indicated a turn in the direction of your turn and the ball should have moved opposite.

        f) Heading indicator (HI) should be checked and adjusted to the magnetic heading from the magnetic compass.

            i) During taxiing you should have checked that both the HI and magnetic compass moved freely and properly.

        g) Vertical speed indicator should be zero. If not on zero you need to make a note of where it is so when you are in level flight you should get the same indication.

        h) All communication and navigation radios set, and transponder set to proper frequencies.

    3) Ensure all your engine instruments are in normal operating range.

        a) Consult your *POH* for the normal operating ranges of all engine instruments.

4)   Engine operation checked during the engine run-up.

   a)   With the engine at the prescribed RPM setting (from your *POH*) you normally check for the following.

      i)   Check the magnetos for proper operation.

      ii)   Check the suction (vacuum) gauge for proper reading. This impacts your airplane's vacuum driven instruments, i.e., AI, HI.

      iii)   Check the oil temperature and pressure.

      iv)   Check the electrical load on the ammeter.

      v)   Check any other system that is prescribed in your *POH*.

5)   Check for carburetor ice by applying the carburetor heat.

   a)   There will be a slight drop in RPM when first applied.

      i)   No ice is present if there is no further change in RPM.
      ii)   If ice is present, there will normally be a further drop in RPM.

6)   Ensure the fuel selector and electric fuel pump (if equipped) are positioned according to your *POH*.

7)   Ensure that all seats are adjusted and locked for all occupants.

   a)   Double-check your seat to ensure it is locked in position.

8)   As pilot in command you are responsible to ensure that each occupant knows how to operate his/her seat belt and shoulder harness, if equipped.

   a)   They are required to be properly fastened and adjusted for takeoff.
   b)   Double-check your seat belt and shoulder harness.

9)   Ensure all doors and windows are closed, secured, and locked. In addition to checking the latch position, push on the door or window to make sure it is in fact secure.

b.   Stop at each discrepancy and note its effect(s). How is any problem covered by another instrument, piece of equipment, pilot workload, etc.? Relate problems to FARs.

   1)   If your suction gauge is lower than usual but is still in the green during the run-up, point this out to the examiner.

      a)   Run up to cruise power and recheck the suction gauge indication.

      b)   If it appears normal and your gyro instruments are reacting normally during taxi turns, mention this to the examiner. You may then elect to take off.

      c)   Watch your suction gauge indication more closely during the flight.

   2)   If you notice an excessive RPM drop on one mag, explain this to the examiner. Attempt to correct the problem by increasing RPM and leaning the mixture (to clear possible fouled spark plugs). If unable to correct the problem, taxi to the ramp for repairs.

   3)   You are the final authority as to the airworthiness of your airplane. Do not take chances; if in doubt, turn back and go to the ramp to get it checked out.

c.   Exercise sound judgment in determining that your airplane is safe for flight.

   1)   If you have any doubts, explain them to your examiner and return to the ramp for further investigation.

6. **Review the critical takeoff performance airspeeds and distances.**

   a. From your knowledge of the *POH* review the V_R, V_X, V_Y, and other takeoff performance factors for your airplane.

      1) As you reach these airspeeds, plan to call them out loud.

   b. From your preflight planning you have already determined the expected takeoff distance for the conditions.

   c. Review the airspeeds and the takeoff distance required before you taxi onto the active runway.

7. **Describe takeoff emergency procedures.**

   a. Takeoff emergency procedures are set forth in Section 3, Emergency Procedures, of your *POH*. Prepare ahead for all contingencies. Be prepared at all times to execute an emergency landing if you lose an engine. Remember, **maintain airspeed** so you control your situation rather than enter a stall/spin.

   b. The most common emergency you can have on takeoff is to lose engine power during the takeoff roll or during the takeoff climb.

      1) If engine power is lost during the takeoff roll, pull the throttle to idle, apply the brakes, and slow the airplane to a stop.

      2) If you are just lifting off the runway and you lose your engine power, try to land the airplane on the remaining runway. Leave it in the flair attitude which it is already in. It will settle back down to the ground, i.e., land it like a normal landing.

         a) It is very important not to lower the nose, because you do not want to come down on the nosewheel.

      3) If engine power is lost any time during the climbout, a general rule of thumb is that if the airplane is above 500 to 1,000 ft. AGL, you may have enough altitude to turn back and land on the runway you have just taken off from. This decision must be based on distance from airport, wind condition, obstacles, etc.

         a) Watch your airspeed! Avoiding a stall is the most important consideration. Remember: control yoke forward (nose down) for more airspeed.

      4) If the airplane is below 500 ft. AGL, do not try to turn back. If you turn back you will probably either stall or hit the ground before you get back to the runway.

         a) The best thing to do is land the airplane straight ahead. Land in a clear area, if possible.

         b) If you have no option but to go into trees, slow the airplane to just above the stall speed (as close to the treetops as possible) to strike the trees with the slowest forward speed possible.

   c. As in all emergencies, you must maintain your composure and remain in control. The peculiarity of engine power failures on takeoff is that you have so little time to attempt to correct the problem, i.e., you just have time to land.

      1) However, if the problem was caused by the ignition or fuel being turned off, turn them on.

      2) Here is the place to reemphasize the need for both a thorough preflight inspection and a thorough pretakeoff check (remember your checklists!).

8. **Obtain and interpret takeoff and departure clearances.**

   a. This element implies that you are operating from a controlled airport. At an uncontrolled airport, your examiner may give you instructions to simulate ATC clearances.

   b. When you have completed your pretakeoff check, hold position and contact the tower for takeoff clearance.

      1) Do not taxi to the hold line first as there may be an aircraft behind you that has already received takeoff clearance.

   c. Once you obtain your clearance(s), make sure you understand it/them.

      1) If in doubt, ask for clarification.

C. Common errors during the pretakeoff check

   1. **Failure to use or the improper use of the checklist.**

      a. You must be in the habit of properly using the prescribed checklist.
      b. This ensures that every item is completed and checked in a logical order.

   2. **Improper positioning of the airplane.**

      a. Position your airplane so you will not prop blast any airplanes behind you.

      b. The FAA recommends that the airplane be positioned into the wind as nearly as possible.

      c. The airplane should be on a surface that is firm and free of debris.

   3. **Acceptance of marginal engine performance.**

      a. You may feel that you have to complete this flight at this time, and thus accept marginal engine performance.

      b. You must determine that your airplane is in a safe operating condition.

      c. Be safe. Marginal engine performance is not acceptable and may lead to a hazardous condition.

   4. **Improper check of flight controls.**

      a. The flight controls should be visually checked for proper positioning and movement.
      b. The control yoke should move freely in the full range of positions.
      c. Call aloud the proper position and visually check it.

   5. **Hazards of failure to review takeoff and emergency procedures.**

      a. Before taxiing onto the runway a review of the critical airspeeds used for takeoff, the takeoff distance required, and takeoff emergencies must be made.

      b. You will then be thinking about this during the takeoff roll. It helps prepare you for any type of emergency that may occur.

   6. **Failure to check for hazards and other traffic.**

      a. You, the pilot in command, are responsible for collision avoidance.

         1) ATC is not responsible, but works with pilots to maintain separation.

      b. Other airplanes are not the only hazards you must look for. Vehicles, persons, and livestock could be in a hazardous position during the takeoff.

END OF TASK

POSTFLIGHT PROCEDURES

II.F. TASK: POSTFLIGHT PROCEDURES

PILOT OPERATION - 3

REFERENCES: AC 61-21; Airplane Handbook and Flight Manual.

Objective. To determine that the applicant:

1. Exhibits knowledge by explaining the postflight procedures, including taxiing, parking, shutdown, securing, and postflight inspection.

2. Selects and taxis to the designated or suitable parking area, considering wind conditions and obstructions.

3. Parks the airplane properly.

4. Follows the recommended procedure for engine shutdown, cockpit securing, and deplaning passengers.

5. Secures the airplane properly.

6. Performs a satisfactory postflight inspection.

A. General Information

   1. This is one of six tasks (A-F) in this area of operation. Your examiner is required to test you on this task.

   2. *Pilot Operation - 3* refers to FAR 61.107(a)(3): Flight maneuvering by reference to ground objects.

   3. FAA References

      AC 61-21: Flight Training Handbook
      Pilot's Operating Handbook (FAA-Approved Airplane Flight Manual)

   4. The objective of this task is for you to demonstrate your knowledge of postflight procedures.

B. Task Objectives

   1. **Exhibit your knowledge by explaining the postflight procedures, including taxiing, parking, shutdown, securing, and postflight inspection.**

      a. You postflight procedures begin after you have landed and have taxied clear of the active runway.

         1) If at a controlled airport, you will need to contact ground control for a taxi clearance to the ramp.

      b. Before taxiing, complete your after-landing checklist, which usually includes flaps up and carburetor heat off.

         1) The Cessna 152 after-landing checklist is reproduced below.

**CESSNA 152
AFTER-LANDING CHECKLIST**

1. Wing Flaps . . . . Up   2. Carburetor Heat . . . . Cold

> **For Academic Illustration/Training Purposes Only!**
> *For Flight:* Use your Pilot's Operating Handbook and FAA-Approved Airplane Flight Manual.

---

2. **Select and taxi to the designated or suitable parking area, considering wind conditions and obstructions.**

    a. You should select a spot to park your airplane based on airport custom and to be considerate of other pilots and airport personnel.

    b. Use the proper taxiing techniques to taxi to the designated or suitable parking area as described in Task II.D., Taxiing, beginning on page 195.

3. **Park your airplane properly.**

    a. Your airplane should be parked on the ramp in such a way as to facilitate taxiing and parking by other aircraft and to avoid being struck by other airplanes or their prop/jet wash.

        1) Frequently, airport ramps are marked with painted lines which indicate where and how to park. At other airports, airplane tiedown ropes (or chains) mark parking spots.

        2) Almost always, there are three ropes provided for each airplane: one rope positioned for the middle of each wing and one rope to tie the tail. If the ramp is not paved, each of the tiedown ropes (chains) is usually marked by a tire.

    b. You should "chock" and/or tie down your airplane so it cannot roll or be blown into another aircraft or other object.

        1) Chocks are usually blocks of wood placed both in front of and behind a tire to keep the plane from rolling.

        2) On an unfamiliar ramp, place the front chock an inch or so ahead of the tire. In this way it will become evident whether your airplane will roll forward later as you prepare to depart.

    c. At most transient ramps, you should **not** use your parking brake, because the FBO personnel frequently move aircraft.

        1) The normal procedure is plane locked and parking brakes off -- wheel chocks or tie-downs secure the airplane.

        2) In many airplanes, leaving the brake on is not recommended because it may cause the hydraulic lines to burst.

    d. Hand signals are used by all ground crews and are similar at all airports, i.e., this is an international language.

        1) When taxiing on a ramp, a lineman may give you hand signals to tell you how to taxi and/or how to park your airplane.

        2) Review the hand signals shown in Task II.D., Taxiing, on page 195.

4. **Follow the recommended procedure for engine shutdown, cockpit securing, and deplaning passengers.**

    a. Use the appropriate checklists for engine shutdown and cockpit securing from your *POH*.

        1) Read each item aloud, then perform that task.

            a) Ensure the magnetos are turned off by removing the ignition key after the propeller has stopped.

        2) The following Securing Airplane Checklist is from the Cessna 152 *POH*.

CESSNA 152
SECURING AIRPLANE CHECKLIST

1. Parking Brake . . . . Set		5. Master Switch . . . . Off	
2. Radios, Electrical Equipment . . . . Off		6. Control Lock . . . . Install	
3. Mixture . . . . Idle Cut-off (pull full out)			
4. Ignition Switch . . . . Off			

For Academic Illustration/Training Purposes Only!
For Flight: **Use your Pilot's Operating Handbook**
and FAA-Approved Airplane Flight Manual.

---

    b.   Once the engine has been shut down, you should secure the cockpit by gathering all personal items and ensuring that all trash is removed from the airplane.

        1)   Professionalism and courtesy dictate that the airplane should be left as it was found.

    c.   You must ensure that your passengers remain seated with seatbelts fastened until the engine is shut down. Then they should gather all personal belongings and deplane in a safe manner.

        1)   You should inform them of the safe exit from the ramp area to the terminal or have them remain next to your airplane while you finish conducting the postflight procedures.

            a)   At that time you can safely escort them off the ramp area.

5.   Secure your airplane properly.

    a.   Obviously, hangar storage is the best means of protecting aircraft from the elements, flying debris, vehicles, vandals, etc. Even in hangars, airplanes should be chocked to avoid scrapes and bumps from rolling.

    b.   Airplanes stored outside are normally tied down.

        1)   Chains or ropes are used to secure the airplane to the ground from three locations on the airplane: usually, the midpoint of each wing and the tail.

        2)   Tiedown hooks or eyelets are provided at these locations on most airplanes.

    c.   Tiedown knot for ropes.

        1)   Pull the rope through the hook or eyelet, and then use two half-hitches as illustrated below.

            a)   The first half-hitch should be tied 1 ft. away from the hook or eyelet and the second half-hitch should be about 1 ft. away from the first half-hitch.

            b)   The second half-hitch holds the first.

        c) Note that an extra loop is used on the second half-hitch to secure the knot. In the preceding diagram, the rope should be pulled tight in the direction of the arrow. This "catches" the rope between the second half-hitch knot and the rope extending from the first half-hitch and the second half-hitch.

        d) It is relatively quick and easy to tie and untie.

    2) Make sure the ropes are properly secured to the ground at appropriate intervals.

  d. When leaving the airplane tied down for an extended period of time or when expecting windy weather, you should install the control or gust locks which hold the control yoke stationary so the control surfaces cannot bang back and forth in the wind.

    1) On older planes, this is sometimes accomplished by clamping the aileron, elevator, and rudder to adjacent stationary surfaces so they cannot move.

    2) Alternatively, the control yoke (or stick) can be secured tightly with a seatbelt.

6. Perform a satisfactory postflight inspection.

  a. Finally, note any malfunctions (discrepancies) in the proper logbooks, and signal to other pilots when an unairworthy condition exists. Always take the airplane out of service if there is an airworthiness problem.

C. Common errors during postflight procedures

  1. Hazards resulting from failure to follow recommended procedures.

    a. The checklist for postflight procedures is as important as those for any other situation. You must follow recommended procedures to prevent creating unsafe situations.

  2. Poor planning, improper technique, or faulty judgment is performance of postflight procedures.

    a. Just because this is the end of a flight, do not let yourself get rushed or into bad habits in conducting postflight procedures.

    b. This task must be approached in the same professional manner as the preflight and flying procedures.

END OF TASK -- END OF CHAPTER

CHAPTER III
AIRPORT AND TRAFFIC PATTERN OPERATIONS

III.A. Radio Communications and ATC Light Signals 216
III.B. Traffic Pattern Operations 228
III.C. Airport and Runway Marking and Lighting 239

This chapter explains the three tasks (A-C) of Airport and Traffic Pattern Operations. These tasks include both knowledge and skill.

Each objective of a task lists, in sequence, the important elements that must be satisfactorily performed. The object includes:

1. Specifically what you should be able to do.
2. The conditions under which the task is to be performed.
3. The minimum acceptable standards of performance.

Be confident. You have prepared diligently and are better prepared and more skilled than the average private pilot applicant. Your examiner will base your ability to perform these tasks on the following.

1. Executing the task within your airplane's capabilities and limitations, including use of the airplane's systems.
2. Piloting your airplane with smoothness and accuracy.
3. Exercising good judgment.
4. Applying your aeronautical knowledge.
5. Showing mastery of your airplane within the standards outlined in this area of operation, with the successful outcome of a task never seriously in doubt.

This chapter explains the methods used for safely adjusting to the flow of air traffic at and near airports, and discusses communication procedures and airport markings and lighting.

Your examiner is required to test you on all three tasks. Each task is reproduced verbatim from the FAA Practical Test Standards in a shaded box. General discussion is presented under "A. General Information." This is followed by "B. Task Objectives," which is a detailed discussion of each element of the FAA's task.

RADIO COMMUNICATIONS AND ATC LIGHT SIGNALS

III.A. TASK: RADIO COMMUNICATIONS AND ATC LIGHT SIGNALS

    PILOT OPERATION - 2

    REFERENCES: AC 61-21, AC 61-23; AIM.

Objective. To determine that the applicant:

1. Exhibits knowledge by explaining radio communication, ATC light signals, procedures at controlled and uncontrolled airports, and prescribed procedures for radio failure.

2. Selects the appropriate frequencies for the facilities to be used.

3. Transmits requests and reports using the recommended standard phraseology.

4. Receives, acknowledges, and complies with radio communications.

A. General Information

  1. This is one of three tasks (A-C) in this area of operation. Your examiner is required to test you on this task.

  2. *Pilot Operation - 2* refers to FAR 61.107(a)(2): Airport and traffic pattern operations, including operations at controlled airports, radio communications, and collision avoidance precautions.

  3. FAA References

     AC 61-21: Flight Training Handbook
     AC 61-23: Pilot's Handbook of Aeronautical Knowledge
     Airman's Information Manual

  4. The objective of this task is for you to demonstrate your knowledge of radio communication, procedures at controlled and uncontrolled airports, and radio communication failure procedures including ATC light signals.

B. Task Objectives

  1. **Exhibit your knowledge by explaining radio communication, ATC light signals, procedures at controlled and uncontrolled airports, prescribed procedures for radio failure.**

    a. Airplane communication radios greatly facilitate flying. Pilots use radios to

      1) Obtain air traffic control (ATC) clearances.

        a) Ground control.
        b) Tower control, e.g., takeoffs and landings.
        c) Approach and departure control (in the vicinity of the airport).
        d) En route control (flight following) from ATC center.

      2) Obtain weather briefings, file flight plans, etc., with Flight Service Stations (FSS).

      3) Communicate with FBOs and each other on UNICOM and MULTICOM frequencies.

4) Airplane communication radios operate on frequencies between 118.0 MHz and 135.975 MHz.

    a) Most communication radios have 720 channels by having a frequency every .025 MHz.

    b) Most FAA frequencies are in multiples of .05 MHz.

    c) Some older radios only receive and transmit on every .05 MHz, which results in 360 channels of available communication.

b. ATC light signals are used to communicate with aircraft that have no radios or have experienced a radio communication equipment failure.

    1) Light signals and their meanings

Light Signal	On the Ground	In the Air
Steady Green	Cleared for takeoff	Cleared to land
Flashing Green	Cleared to taxi	Return for landing *(to be followed by steady green at proper time)*
Steady Red	Stop	Give way to other aircraft and continue circling
Flashing Red	Taxi clear of landing area (runway) in use	Airport unsafe -- Do not land
Flashing White	Return to starting point on airport	Not applicable
Alternating Red and Green	General warning signal -- Exercise extreme caution	General warning signal -- Exercise extreme caution

c. Uncontrolled airports -- see summary of recommended communication procedures on page 219.

    1) The key to communicating at an uncontrolled airport is the selection of the correct frequency. The term CTAF, which stands for Common Traffic Advisory Frequency, is synonymous with this program.

        a) CTAF is a frequency designated for the purpose of carrying out airport advisory practices at an uncontrolled airport.

        b) CTAF may be a UNICOM, MULTICOM, FSS, or tower frequency.

        c) The CTAF at an airport is indicated on the sectional chart by a © next to the appropriate frequency.

    2) An uncontrolled airport does not have a control tower; i.e., there is no traffic control over movements of aircraft on the ground or around the airport in the air. Often, FBOs operating at an uncontrolled airport will operate a radio on a UNICOM frequency (UNICOM is an acronym for Unified Communication).

        a) This frequency is most often 122.8 and is indicated on the sectional aeronautical chart as the last item in the airport information block (usually by a "U" behind the runway length).

        b) Other UNICOM frequencies are 122.7, 122.725, 122.975, and 123.0.

3) UNICOMs are used to provide advisory information for incoming aircraft, as well as provide pilot services. At controlled airports, they are only for pilot services. This includes the active runway, the wind direction and velocity, and any reported traffic in the area.

a) When you approach the airport intended for landing you call

i) Destination (name of airport).

ii) Your type of plane and your call sign.

iii) Approximate position from the airport (to advise other traffic).

iv) Request weather (generally only surface wind), active runway, and other traffic.

v) Name of airport. This should be done at the beginning and end of each self-announce transmission.

b) EXAMPLE. "Jonesville UNICOM, Cessna ONE ZERO TWO FOXTROT, TEN north, inbound, request airport advisory Jonesville."

c) Their response: "Cessna calling Jonesville, wind THREE FOUR ZERO AT ONE ZERO, runway THREE SIX is active with TWO aircraft in the pattern, over."

4) There is one MULTICOM frequency for general aviation: 122.9.

a) Use MULTICOM at airports without an assigned UNICOM frequency and for discussion with other pilots.

5) Voice announce your position and intentions on the appropriate frequency.

6) Flight service station airport advisories

a) When approaching an uncontrolled airport with a Flight Service Station (FSS) located at the airport, you should contact it for traffic and weather advisories. Additionally, they will provide information about the active runway and other helpful information.

i) This is normally on the listed CTAF frequency.

b) Their service is very similar to that provided by FBOs through UNICOM as discussed earlier in this chapter under uncontrolled airports on page 217.

i) Address them as "_____ radio," e.g., "Jonesboro radio, Piper Tomahawk 1617T, over."

ii) They respond, e.g., "Piper Tomahawk, Jonesboro flight service station, go ahead."

iii) State request and intention, e.g., "1617T is (miles out) southeast inbound, request weather and traffic advisories."

iv) They respond, e.g., "Jonesboro 3,000 scattered, 9,000 overcast, wind 170 at 8, gusting to 15, no reported traffic."

v) You should report the downwind leg of your traffic pattern, base, or final as appropriate, given other communications, traffic, etc.

• EXAMPLE: "Tomahawk 1617T entering left (right) downwind runway 16."

SUMMARY OF RECOMMENDED COMMUNICATION PROCEDURES

	FACILITY AT AIRPORT	FREQUENCY USE	COMMUNICATION/BROADCAST PROCEDURES	
			OUTBOUND	INBOUND
1.	UNICOM (No Tower or FSS)	Communicate with UNICOM station on published CTAF frequency (122.7, 122.8, 122.725, 122.975, or 123.0). If unable to contact UNICOM station, use self-announce procedures on CTAF.	Before taxiing and before taxiing on the runway for departure.	10 miles out. Entering downwind, base, and final. Leaving the runway.
2.	No Tower, FSS, or UNICOM	Self-announce on MULTICOM frequency 122.9.	Before taxiing and before taxiing on the runway for departure.	10 miles out. Entering downwind, base, and final. Leaving the runway.
3.	No Tower in operation, FSS open	Communicate with FSS on CTAF frequency.	Before taxiing and before taxiing on the runway for departure.	10 miles out. Entering downwind, base, and final. Leaving the runway.
4.	FSS closed (No Tower or Tower closed)	Self-announce on CTAF.	Before taxiing and before taxiing on the runway for departure.	10 miles out. Entering downwind, base, and final. Leaving the runway.

    d.   **Controlled airports**

        1)   Automatic Terminal Information Service (ATIS)

            a)   If available, the ATIS frequency is listed on the sectional chart just under the tower control frequency for the airport, e.g., ATIS 125.05. ATIS provides a continuous transmission that provides information for arriving and departing aircraft, including

                i)   Weather for the airport, such as time of latest weather sequence, ceiling height, and visibility information.

                ii)   Surface wind direction (magnetic) and velocity.

                iii)   Altimeter setting.

                iv)   Active runway and instrument approaches in use.

                v)   Approach and departure control frequencies.

                vi)   Other relevant airport information, e.g., closed runways.

            b)   The purpose of ATIS is to relieve the ground controllers' and approach controllers' workload. They need not repeat the same information.

            c)   The ATIS broadcast is updated whenever any official weather is received regardless of content or changes, or when a change is made in other pertinent data such as runway change. Each new broadcast is labeled with a letter of the alphabet at the beginning of the broadcast, e.g., "this is information alpha," or "information bravo."

                i)   Every aircraft arriving at or departing from an airport with ATIS should monitor ATIS before contacting approach, tower, clearance delivery, or ground control to receive that airport's weather information.

ii)   When you contact approach, tower, clearance delivery, or ground control, you should indicate you have the ATIS information by stating "with information (the letter code labeling the broadcast)."

EXAMPLES:

- "Daytona approach, Cessna 66421, TWO ZERO miles north, inbound, Daytona Regional with information alpha."

- "Daytona ground, Cessna 66421 with information bravo, Daytona Beach Aviation, request taxi for VFR southbound."

2)   Ground control

a)   At a controlled airport (an airport with an operating control tower), you will usually talk with ground control before taxiing. The ground controller coordinates the movement of aircraft on the surface of the airport. When you call ground control, you should say five things:

i)   Address the ground controller, e.g., "Gainesville ground."

ii)   Type of airplane and the airplane's number, e.g., "Beech Skipper 66421."

iii)   Where you are on the airport surface, e.g., "North ramp," and at which FBO (if more than one).

iv)   Where you want to go and that you are ready to taxi, e.g., "Taxi VFR southbound."

v)   Tell them you have ATIS (if appropriate), e.g., "with Gulf" if Gulf is the current ATIS designation.

b)   The ground controller will respond with five items:

i)   The airplane identification, e.g., "Skipper 66421."

ii)   Taxi to the active runway, e.g., "Taxi runway 10."

iii)   The wind direction and speed, e.g., "Wind 140 at 7."

iv)   The air pressure setting, or the altimeter setting, e.g., "Altimeter 29.93." At this time you should check and reset your altimeter if necessary.

v)   Wind and altimeter may not be given if ATIS is available.

c)   You should acknowledge the controller, e.g., "Beech Skipper 66421 taxi runway 10." ATC may use abbreviated call sign here, e.g., "421." Continue to monitor ground control as you taxi (you will switch to the tower frequency just before you are ready to take off).

i)   Safe ATC facilities and controllers generally require you to read back all clearances. This is a good practice.

ii)   Be careful to note if you are given a clearance other than to the active runway, e.g., "Hold short of runway 24" -- do NOT cross runway 24.

iii)   Whenever you need directions, ask ground control, e.g., "Ground, Beech Skipper 66421 unfamiliar with airport. Request progressives to active runway."

3)   Tower control

a)   The tower controller coordinates all aircraft activity on the active runway and within the airport traffic area.

b) When you are ready for takeoff, you will tell the tower three things:

   i) You will address the tower, e.g., "Gainesville tower."

   ii) Identify your airplane, e.g., "Beech Skipper 66421."

   iii) State your intention (request), e.g., "Ready to take off runway 6."

c) The tower controller may then issue a clearance for takeoff if appropriate, e.g., "Beech Skipper 66421 cleared for takeoff runway 6." However, listen carefully to the response.

   i) The controller may issue certain restrictions on your departure, such as right turn or maintain runway heading, or you may ask for your direction of flight.

   ii) Or the tower may not clear you due to traffic, e.g., "Skipper 66421, hold short, landing traffic."

   iii) Once you have received a clearance for takeoff, you should acknowledge, e.g., "Beech 66421 cleared for takeoff runway 6."

   iv) You should monitor tower control until you are 5 SM away from the airport or above 3,000 ft. AGL.

   v) If there is a departure control to contact, the tower may direct you to that frequency when appropriate, e.g., "Beech 66421 contact departure control 125.65, good day." You know the departure frequency prior to departure.

   vi) If you are going to a nearby "practice area," and it is customary to monitor the tower, you should do so.

     • Practice areas (for student pilots and instruction) are usually designated by the FAA or local airport authorities to keep instructional activities from interfering with normal traffic.

d) Tower control is also used for landing. When approaching an airport to land, you must contact the tower prior to entering the airport traffic area.

   i) Address the tower, telling them who you are, where you are, and what you want.

     • You must do so prior to entering the airport traffic area. Remember, the airport traffic area has a 5-SM radius and extends up to but does not include 3,000 ft. AGL.

     • It is good practice to contact tower control 10 SM out so they have time to route you to the active runway and coordinate you with the other traffic.

   ii) EXAMPLE. "Jacksonville Tower, Beech Skipper 66421, 10 mi. southwest, landing."

4) Approach control and departure control (for VFR aircraft)

a) The approach or departure controller coordinates arriving or departing traffic, usually to a busy airport with a control tower. These controllers coordinate traffic outside the traffic area.

   i) Use of approach and departure control is mandatory in Terminal Control Areas (TCAs) and Airport Radar Service Areas (ARSAs) for all aircraft, including VFR traffic.

     • TCAs exist around major airports (e.g., Atlanta, Georgia).

     • ARSAs exist around other busy airports (e.g., Jacksonville, Florida).

    ii)   Use of approach and departure control is highly encouraged in Terminal Radar Service Areas (TRSAs, which are being phased out by ARSAs), but is not mandatory.

  b) When approaching an area serviced by approach control, you should contact approach control for traffic advisories, sequencing for landing, and instructions for flying through a busy area.

    i)   The appropriate frequency can be found in the Airport/Facility Directory that you used during your preflight preparation.

  c) Departure control is used for leaving busy traffic areas, as well as required for use in leaving airports within TCAs and ARSAs.

    i)   If requested and/or mandatory, tower will switch you over to departure control when appropriate.

    ii)   If you request departure control from the tower without prior arrangement, you will have to give your type of airplane, call sign, location, altitude, request, etc., with departure control as you did with approach control coming in.

5)   Clearance delivery

  a) A clearance delivery frequency is used at busy airports (usually within an ARSA or TCA) to issue clearances to aircraft on the ground prior to taxiing.

    i)   Clearance delivery frequency may be found in your Airport/Facility Directory. It is also generally given in the ATIS broadcast.

  b) Call clearance delivery before contacting the ground controller, e.g., "Clearance delivery, Cessna 1152L, over."

  c) Upon response, e.g., "Cessna 1152L go ahead," tell the clearance delivery controller:

    i)   Your type of aircraft, e.g., "Cessna 172."
    ii)   You are VFR, e.g., "VFR."
    iii)   Your destination, e.g., "Jacksonville."
    iv)   The altitude at which you wish to fly, e.g., "At 3,000 ft."

  d) The controller will respond with a clearance for you consisting of

    i)   Direction to fly after departure, e.g., "Fly runway heading."

    ii)   An altitude to climb to, e.g., "Up to but not above 2,000 ft."

    iii)   A transponder code setting, e.g., "Transponder 4645."

    iv)   The frequency for departure control, e.g., "Departure frequency 125.65."

  e) You should copy the clearance, then read it back to the controller.

e.   Emergencies

1)   If your airplane is experiencing an emergency such as loss of power, or you become doubtful about a condition that could adversely affect flight safety, use the emergency frequency, which is 121.5 MHz.

  a) When you broadcast on this frequency, you will receive immediate attention at the Flight Service Stations and towers receiving 121.5.

b) All towers, Flight Service Stations, and radar facilities monitor the emergency frequency, but normally only one FAA facility at a given location monitors the frequency.

c) If you are already on an ATC control frequency, e.g., a control tower or approach control, you should declare an emergency with them, since they are already conversant with your call sign, location, etc.

d) You should immediately state your

  i)   Airplane call sign.

  ii) Location and altitude.

  iii) Problem.

  iv) Extent of the distress, e.g., requiring no delay, priority, or emergency handling.

2) If you become apprehensive about your safety for any reason, you should do the following to obtain assistance:

a) Contact the controlling agency (e.g., tower) and give nature of distress and your intentions. If unable to contact controlling agencies, use 121.5.

b) If equipped with a radar beacon transponder and if unable to establish voice communications with an air traffic control facility, set the transponder to Code 7700.

f. Radio failure procedures

1) Arriving aircraft

a) If you receive no response to your transmission inbound, you may have a radio failure.

b) If you are receiving tower transmissions, but none are directed toward you, you should suspect a transmitter failure.

  i)   Determine the direction and flow of traffic, enter the traffic pattern, and look for light gun signals.

  ii) During daylight, acknowledge tower transmissions or light signals by rocking your wings. At night, acknowledge by blinking the landing or navigation lights.

  iii) After landing, telephone the tower to advise them of the situation.

c) If you are receiving no transmissions on tower or ATIS frequency, suspect a receiver failure.

  i)   Transmit to the tower in the blind your position, situation, and intention to land.

  ii) Determine the flow of traffic, enter the pattern, and wait for light gun signals.

  iii) Acknowledge signals as described above and by transmitting in the blind.

  iv) After landing, telephone the tower to advise them of the situation.

2) Departing aircraft

a) If you experience radio failure prior to leaving the parking area, make every effort to have the equipment repaired.

      b)   If you are unable to have the malfunction repaired, call the tower by telephone and request authorization to depart without two-way radio communications.

          i)   If tower authorization is granted, you will be given departure information and requested to monitor the tower frequency or watch for light signals, as appropriate.

          ii) During daylight, acknowledge tower transmissions or light signals by promptly executing action authorized by light signals.

              • When in the air, rock your wings.

          iii) At night, acknowledge by blinking the landing or navigation lights.

      c)   If your radio malfunctions after departing the parking area (ramp), watch the tower for light signals or monitor the appropriate (ground or tower) frequency. However, you should return to the ramp.

2.   Select the appropriate frequencies for the facilities to be used.

    a.   You should always continue to work to make your radio technique as professional as possible. Selecting the appropriate frequency is obviously essential.

    b.   Your preflight planning should include looking up the frequencies of all facilities that you might use and/or need during your flight.

       1)   This information can be obtained from a current Airport/Facility Directory, sectional charts, etc.

       2)   Write this information on your navigation log or organize it so you can locate it easily in the cockpit.

    c.   You may still have to look up frequencies while you are flying.

    d.   Always plan ahead as to frequencies needed.

       1)   Listen to hand-offs by your controller to airplanes ahead of you.
       2)   Look up frequencies before you need them.

3.   Transmit requests and reports using the recommended standard phraseology.

    a.   Radio communications are a critical link in the ATC system. The link can be a strong bond between you and the controller or it can be broken with surprising speed and disastrous results.

    b.   The single most important thought in pilot-controller communications is understanding.

       1)   Good phraseology enhances safety and is a mark of a professional pilot.
       2)   Jargon, chatter, and "CB" slang have no place in ATC communications.

    c.   Phonetic alphabet

       1)   You should use the phonetic alphabet when identifying your airplane during initial contact with air traffic control facilities.

       2)   Additionally, use the phonetic equivalents for single letters and for spelling out groups of letters or difficult words during adverse communication conditions.

       3)   Work through the following listing of alphabetic phonetic equivalents, saying each out loud to learn it.

          a)   Note that the Morse code is also provided. Although it is not used as frequently as it once was, occasionally you may need it for identification, e.g., at a VOR without voice facilities. You need not learn the Morse code, just keep it handy.

A	.-	Alpha	(AL-FAH)		T	-	Tango	(TANG-GO)
B	-...	Bravo	(BRAH-VOH)		U	..-	Uniform	(YOU-NEE-FORM)
C	-.-.	Charlie	(CHAR-LEE) or (SHAR-LEE)		V	...-	Victor	(VIK-TAR)
D	-..	Delta	(DELL-TAH)		W	.--	Whiskey	(WISS-KEY)
E	.	Echo	(ECK-OH)		X	-..-	Xray	(ECKS-RAY)
F	..-.	Foxtrot	(FOKS-TROT)		Y	-.--	Yankee	(YANG-KEY)
G	--.	Golf	(GOLF)		Z	--..	Zulu	(ZOO-LOO)
H	....	Hotel	(HOH-TEL)					
I	..	India	(IN-DEE-AH)					
J	.---	Juliett	(JEW-LEE-ETT)		1	.----	One	(WUN)
K	-.-	Kilo	(KEY-LOH)		2	..---	Two	(TOO)
L	.-..	Lima	(LEE-MAH)		3	...--	Three	(TREE)
M	--	Mike	(MIKE)		4	....-	Four	(FOW-ER)
N	-.	November	(NO-VEM-BER)		5	.....	Five	(FIVE)
O	---	Oscar	(OS-CAR)		6	-....	Six	(SIX)
P	.--.	Papa	(PAH-PAH)		7	--...	Seven	(SEVEN)
Q	--.-	Quebec	(KEH-BECK)		8	---..	Eight	(AIT)
R	.-.	Romeo	(ROW-ME-OH)		9	----.	Nine	(NIN-ER)
S	...	Sierra	(SEE-AIR-RAH)		0	-----	Zero	(ZEE-RO)

d. Figures

1) Figures indicating hundreds and thousands in round numbers, as for ceiling heights, and upper wind levels up to 9,900 ft. are spoken in accordance with the following:

   a) EXAMPLES: 500 is "FIVE HUNDRED."
   4,500 is "FOUR THOUSAND FIVE HUNDRED."

2) Numbers above 9,900 shall be spoken by separating the digits preceding the word "thousand."

   a) EXAMPLES: 10,000 is "ONE ZERO THOUSAND."
   13,500 is "ONE THREE THOUSAND FIVE HUNDRED."

3) Airway numbers. Airways are routes between navigational aids, such as VORs (i.e., airways are highways in the sky).

   a) EXAMPLE: V12 is "VICTOR TWELVE."

4) All other numbers shall be transmitted by pronouncing each digit.

   a) EXAMPLE: 10 is "ONE ZERO."

5) When a radio frequency contains a decimal point, the decimal point is spoken as "POINT."

   a) EXAMPLE: 122.1 is "ONE TWO TWO POINT ONE."

e. Altitudes and flight levels

1) Up to but not including 18,000 ft. MSL, state the separate digits of the thousands, plus the hundreds, if appropriate.

   a) EXAMPLES: 12,000 is "ONE TWO THOUSAND."
   12,500 is "ONE TWO THOUSAND FIVE HUNDRED."

2) At and above 18,000 ft. MSL (FL 180), state the words "flight level" followed by the separate digits of the flight level.

   a) EXAMPLES: FL 190 is "FLIGHT LEVEL ONE NINER ZERO" (19,000 ft. MSL).

   FL 360 is "FLIGHT LEVEL THREE SIX ZERO" (36,000 ft. MSL).

f.   Directions

The three digits of bearing, course, heading, and wind direction should always be magnetic. The word "TRUE" must be added when it applies.

1)   EXAMPLES:

a)   (Magnetic course) 005 is "ZERO ZERO FIVE."
b)   (True course) 050 is "ZERO FIVE ZERO TRUE."
c)   (Magnetic bearing) 360 is "THREE SIX ZERO."
d)   (Magnetic heading) 100 is "ONE ZERO ZERO."
e)   (Wind direction) 220 is "TWO TWO ZERO."

2)   Wind velocity (speed) is always included with wind direction, e.g., "THREE FOUR ZERO AT ONE ZERO."

a)   ATC gives winds in magnetic direction.
b)   FSS gives winds in true direction, from weather reports and forecasts.

g.   Speeds

1)   Say the separate digits of the speed followed by the word "knots."

a)   EXAMPLES: 250 is "TWO FIVE ZERO KNOTS."
                 185 is "ONE EIGHT FIVE KNOTS."

2)   The controller may omit the word "knots" when using speed adjustment procedures, e.g., "INCREASE SPEED TO ONE FIVE ZERO."

h.   Time

1)   The FAA uses Coordinated Universal Time for all operations.

a)   Abbreviated as UTC, Z, or Zulu.

2)   To convert from Standard Time to Coordinated Universal Time:

a)   Eastern Standard Time, add 5 hr.
b)   Central Standard Time, add 6 hr.
c)   Mountain Standard Time, add 7 hr.
d)   Pacific Standard Time, add 8 hr.

3)   For Daylight Time, use 4-5-6-7 instead of 5-6-7-8.

4)   To convert from Zulu to local time, subtract rather than add.

5)   The 24-hr. clock system is used in radio transmissions. The hour is indicated by the first two figures and the minutes by the last two figures.

a)   EXAMPLES: 0000 is "ZERO ZERO ZERO ZERO" (midnight)
                 0920 is "ZERO NINER TWO ZERO" (9:20 a.m.)
                 1850 is "ONE EIGHT FIVE ZERO" (6:50 p.m.)

i.   Your radio broadcasts can be thought of as

1)   Who you are,
2)   Where you are, and
3)   What you want to do.
4)   This works in virtually all situations.

4.   Receive, acknowledge, and comply with radio communications.

a.   Make sure your radios, speakers, and/or headset are in good working order so you can plainly hear radio communications. Acknowledge all ATC clearances by repeating key points, e.g., *"Taxi to (or across) Runway 10," "Position and hold," "Clear for takeoff Runway 24," "Left downwind 6,"* followed by your call sign.

1)   Always repeat altitudes and headings.

2) Do not hesitate with *"Say again"* if your clearance was blocked or you did not hear or understand it.

3) As appropriate, ask for amplification or clarification, e.g., ask for "progressives" if you need taxi instructions.

b. FAR 91.123 states that once you, as pilot in command, obtain a clearance from ATC you may not deviate from that clearance, except in an emergency.

1) You have the responsibility for the safe operation of your airplane.

2) If you cannot accept a clearance from ATC (e.g., flying into clouds), inform ATC of the reason you cannot accept and obtain a new clearance.

c. FAR 91.3 states that you, the pilot in command, are directly responsible for, and the final authority as to, the operation of your airplane.

1) As a safe and competent pilot you should obtain clarification on any clearance that you do not understand or feel would put you in a bad situation.

C. Common errors with radio communications and ATC light signals

1. **Use of improper frequencies.**

a. This is caused by inadequate planning, misreading the frequency on the chart or flight log, or mistuning the frequency on the radio.

b. Double-check and read aloud the frequency numbers that are to be set in the radio.

1) Monitor the frequency before transmitting. Often you can confirm the correct frequency by listening to other transmissions.

2. **Improper procedure and phraseology when using radio voice communications.**

a. Think about what you are going to say before you transmit.

b. Be sensitive to the controller's workload and tailoring one's own broadcasts to match. Often pilots are taught correct phraseology only and never taught how to abbreviate transmissions on busy ATC frequencies.

3. **Failure to acknowledge, or properly comply with, ATC clearances and other instructions.**

a. This normally occurs because you did not hear or understand the message.

b. Developing your ability to properly divide your attention will help you not to miss ATC messages.

c. Ask ATC to repeat its message or ask for clarification. Do not assume what ATC meant or instructed.

4. **Failure to understand, or to properly comply with, ATC light signals.**

1) Periodically review the different light gun signals and their meanings.

2) If you operate where you can ask ground control to direct some practice light signals toward you, this will help you learn them.

3) Reviewing and practicing (if possible) will help you understand and comply with ATC light signals.

END OF TASK

TRAFFIC PATTERN OPERATIONS

III.B. TASK: TRAFFIC PATTERN OPERATIONS

   PILOT OPERATION - 2

   REFERENCES: AC 61-21, AC 61-23; AIM.

Objective. To determine that the applicant:

1. Exhibits knowledge by explaining traffic pattern procedures at controlled and uncontrolled airports, including collision, wind shear, and wake turbulence avoidance.

2. Follows the established traffic pattern procedures according to instructions or rules.

3. Corrects for wind drift to follow the appropriate ground track.

4. Maintains proper spacing from other traffic.

5. Maintains the traffic pattern altitude, ±100 ft.

6. Maintains the desired airspeed, ±10 kt.

7. Completes the prelanding cockpit checklist.

8. Maintains orientation with the runway in use.

A. General Information

   1. This is one of three tasks (A-C) in this area of operation. Your examiner is required to test you on this task.

   2. *Pilot Operation - 2* refers to FAR 61.107(a)(2): Airport and traffic pattern operations, including operations at controlled airports, radio communications, and collision avoidance precautions.

   3. FAA References

      AC 61-21: Flight Training Handbook
      AC 61-23: Pilot's Handbook of Aeronautical Knowledge
      Airman's Information Manual

   4. The objective of this task is for you to demonstrate your knowledge and skill in traffic pattern operations.

   5. Safety first! Commit to it and practice it. Always look for traffic and talk about it (even when you are solo). Ask your examiner to watch for traffic.

B. Task Objectives

   1. **Exhibit your knowledge by explaining traffic pattern procedures at controlled and uncontrolled airports, including collision, wind shear, and wake turbulence avoidance.**

      a. At a controlled airport (i.e., with an operating control tower), the controller will direct when and where you should enter the traffic pattern.

         1) Remember, you are required to contact the control tower (or approach control) 5 SM out from the airport or when directed by approach control. It is recommended to contact the tower 10 SM out for more efficient entrance into the traffic pattern.

         2) The controller may request that you perform some maneuvers for better traffic spacing, including

            a) Cutting the downwind leg short,
            b) Extending the downwind leg,
            c) Slowing down,
            d) A 360° turn to provide spacing ahead of you, or
            e) S-turns.

b.   To enter the traffic pattern at an airport without a control tower, inbound pilots are expected to observe other aircraft already in the pattern and to conform to the traffic pattern in use.

1)   If no other aircraft are in the pattern, traffic and wind indicators on the ground must be checked to determine which runway and traffic pattern direction should be used.

2)   Many airports have L-shaped traffic pattern indicators displayed with a segmented circle adjacent to the runway.

3)   See Task III.C., Airport and Runway Marking and Lighting, on page 239 for a detailed discussion on wind and traffic indicators.

4)   Generally, when approaching an airport for landing, you should enter the traffic pattern at a 45° angle to the downwind leg at the midpoint of the runway.

a)   Arriving airplanes should always be at the proper traffic pattern altitude before entering the pattern, and should stay clear of the traffic flow until established on the entry leg.

b)   The entry leg should be of sufficient length to provide a clear view of the entire traffic pattern.

5)   When arriving at an unfamiliar airport, or if you are uncertain of the wind direction, available runways, or traffic pattern in use, overfly the airport at least 500 to 1,000 ft. above the traffic pattern altitude.

a)   After the proper traffic pattern direction has been determined, you should proceed to a point well clear of the pattern before descending to the pattern altitude.

6)   The general procedure for departing from a traffic pattern at either a controlled or an uncontrolled airport is to make a 45° left turn (right turn for a right-hand pattern) from the upwind leg after takeoff at approximately the point one would turn crosswind if one were staying in the traffic pattern.

a)   At controlled airports, a straight-out, right turn, or downwind departure may be requested. Generally, ATC will automatically approve the most expedient turnout for the direction of flight.

i)   This request should be made when requesting takeoff clearance if not already included in your takeoff clearance.

ii)   A departure from the downwind leg should be made by a 45° turn out or by simply climbing to cruise altitude.

b)   At uncontrolled airports, straight-out departures are not uncommon.

i)   There are no FAA rules regarding departures. Check for local airport rules.

ii)   Make your intentions known by announcing your departure direction to the other traffic so there is no confusion.

c.   Scanning the sky for other aircraft is a key factor in collision avoidance. You and your copilot (or right seat passenger) should scan continuously to cover all areas of the sky visible from the cockpit.

1)   You must develop an effective scanning technique that maximizes visual capabilities.

a)   While the eyes can observe an approximate 200° arc of the horizon at one glance, only a very small center area (the fovea) can send clear, sharply focused messages to the brain. All visual information that is not processed directly through the fovea will be less detailed.

    b)   An aircraft 7 mi. away which appears in sharp focus within the foveal center of vision must be as close as 7/10 mi. to be recognized by less central vision.

2)   Because the eyes can focus only on this narrow viewing area, effective scanning is accomplished with a series of short, regularly spaced eye movements that bring successive areas of the sky into the central visual field.

    a)   Each eye movement should not exceed 10°.
    b)   Each area should be observed for at least 1 sec. to enable detection.

3)   Visual tasks inside the cabin should represent no more than 1/4 to 1/3 of the scan time outside, or no more than 4 to 5 sec. on the instrument panel for every 16 sec. outside.

    a)   You should realize that your eyes may require several seconds to refocus when switching view from items in the cockpit to distant objects.

4)   Effective scanning also helps avoid "empty-field myopia."

    a)   When flying above the clouds or in a haze layer that provides nothing specific to focus on outside the aircraft, the eyes tend to relax and seek a comfortable focal distance which may range from 10 to 30 ft.

    b)   For you, the pilot, this means looking without seeing, which is dangerous.

5)   Judgment aspects of collision avoidance

    a)   Use the horizon as a reference point. If you see another aircraft above the horizon, it is probably on a higher flight path. If it appears to be below the horizon, it is probably flying at a lower altitude.

    b)   You must be familiar with the rules of right-of-way, so that if an aircraft is on an obvious collision course, you can take the appropriate evasive action.

    c)   The decision to climb, descend, or turn is a matter of personal judgment, but you should anticipate that the other pilot may also be making a quick maneuver. Watch the other aircraft during the maneuver but begin your scanning again immediately. There may be even more aircraft in the area!

    d)   Any aircraft that appears to have no relative motion and stays in one scan quadrant is likely to be on a collision course. Also, if a target shows no lateral or vertical motion, but increases in size, take evasive action.

    e)   Airways and especially VORs and airport traffic areas are places where aircraft tend to cluster.

    f)   Remember, most collisions occur on days when the weather is good.

    g)   Study maps, checklists, and manuals BEFORE flight, with other proper preflight planning (e.g., noting necessary radio frequencies). Also, organizing cockpit materials can reduce time you need to look at them during flight, permitting more scan time.

    h)   Dirty or bug-smeared windshields can greatly reduce your ability to see other aircraft. Keep a clean windshield.

    i)   Smoke, haze, dust, rain, and flying toward the sun can also greatly reduce the ability to detect other aircraft.

j)   You may need to move your head to see around blind spots caused by fixed aircraft structures, such as door posts, wings, etc. It may even be necessary occasionally to maneuver your airplane (e.g., lift a wing) to facilitate seeing.

k)   Check that curtains and other cockpit objects (e.g., maps that glare on the windshield) are removed and stowed during flight.

l)   Day or night, exterior lights can greatly increase the visibility of any aircraft.

i)   Keep interior lights low at night so you can see out in the dark.

m)   ATC facilities often provide radar traffic advisories (e.g., flight following) on a workload-permitting basis. Use this support whenever possible or when required.

i)   But being in a "radar environment" (i.e., where traffic is separated by radar) still requires vigilance to avoid collisions.

6)   When approaching or in a traffic pattern, be especially vigilant because this is where you expect to find other aircraft.

d.   Wind shear is the unexpected change in wind direction and/or windspeed. During an approach, it can cause severe turbulence and a possible decrease to your airspeed (when a headwind changes to a tailwind) to cause your airplane to stall (and possibly crash).

1)   The best method of dealing with wind shear is avoidance. You should never conduct traffic pattern operations in close proximity to an active thunderstorm. Thunderstorms provide visible signs of possible wind-shear activity.

2)   Many large airports now have a low-level wind shear alert system (LLWAS). By measuring differences in windspeed and/or direction at various points on the airport, the controller will be able to warn arriving and departing aircraft of the possibility of wind shear.

a)   An example of an LLWAS alert:

Delta One Twenty Four - center field wind two seven zero at one zero - south boundary wind one four zero at three zero.

b)   Elsewhere, pilot reports from airplanes preceding you on the approach can be very informational.

3)   If you are conducting an approach with possible wind shear or a thunderstorm nearby, you should consider

a)   Using more power during the approach.

b)   Flying the approach at a faster airspeed (a rule of thumb is to add ½ the gust factor to your airspeed).

c)   Staying as high as feasible on the approach until it is necessary to descend for a safe landing.

d)   At the first sign of a change in airspeed or an unexpected pitch change, you should initiate a go-around. The most important factor is to go to full power and get the airplane climbing.

i)   Many accidents caused by wind shear are due to a severe downdraft (or a rapid change from headwind to tailwind) punching the aircraft into the ground. In extreme cases, even the power of an airliner is unable to counteract the descent.

e.   Wake turbulence is a phenomenon resulting from the passage of an aircraft through the atmosphere. The term includes vortices, thrust stream turbulence, jet blast, jet wash, propeller wash, and rotor wash both on the ground and in the air.

1)   Lift is generated by the pressure differential between the upper and lower wing surfaces. The lowest pressure occurs over the upper wing surface. The highest pressure occurs under the wing.

a)   This pressure differential triggers a roll-up of the airflow behind the wing.

i)   It results in swirling air masses trailing downstream of the wing tips.

b)   After the roll-up is completed, the wake consists of two counter rotating cylindrical vortices.

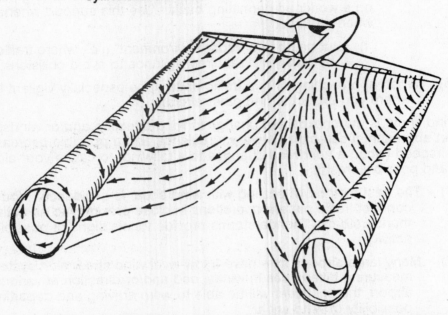

2)   The strength of the vortex is governed by the weight, speed, and wing shape of the generating aircraft.

a)   The vortex characteristics of any given aircraft can be changed by

i)   Extension of flaps or other wing-configuring devices.
ii)   Change in speed.

b)   Vortex strength increases proportionately to the airplane's weight.

c)   The greatest vortex strength occurs when the generating aircraft is HEAVY-CLEAN-SLOW, e.g., during landing and takeoff.

i)   Clean means flaps and landing gear up.

d)   An airplane encountering wake turbulence could incur major structural damage while in flight.

e)   The usual hazard is associated with induced rolling which can exceed the rolling capability of the encountering aircraft.

i)   That is, your airplane may be uncontrollable in the wake turbulence of a large transport airplane.

3)   Trailing vortices have certain behavioral characteristics which can help you visualize the wake location and avoid them:

a)   Vortices are generated from the moment the airplane rotates (nosewheel off the ground) for takeoff, since trailing vortices are a by-product of wing lift.

b) The vortex circulation is outward, upward, and around the wing tips when viewed from either ahead of or behind the aircraft. Each vortex is about two wing spans in width and one wing span in depth.

   i) The vortices remain spaced about a wing span apart, drifting with the wind, at altitudes greater than a wing span from the ground.

   ii) If you encounter persistent vortex turbulence, a slight change of altitude and lateral position (preferably upwind) will provide a flight path clear of the turbulence.

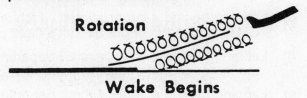

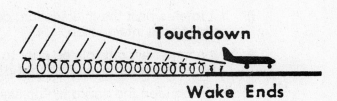

c) Vortices from large aircraft sink at a rate of about 400 to 500 fpm and level off at a distance about 900 ft. below the flight path of the generating aircraft.

   i) You should fly at or above the large aircraft's flight path, altering course as necessary to avoid the area behind and below the generating aircraft.

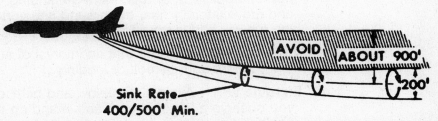

d) When the vortices of large aircraft sink close to the ground (within about 200 ft.), they tend to move laterally over the ground at a speed of about 5 kt.

   i) A crosswind will decrease the lateral movement of the upwind vortex and increase the movement of the downwind vortex.

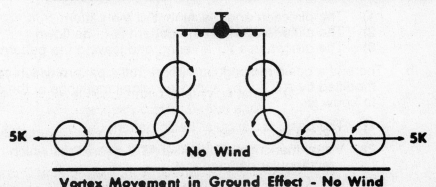

Vortex Movement in Ground Effect - No Wind

4)   The following vortex avoidance procedures are recommended:

    a)   Landing behind a larger aircraft which is landing on the same runway -- Stay at or above the larger aircraft's final approach flight path. Note the touchdown point and land beyond it.

    b)   Landing behind a larger aircraft which is landing on a parallel runway closer than 2,500 ft. to your runway -- Consider possible vortex drift to your runway. Stay at or above the larger aircraft's final approach path and note its touchdown point.

    c)   Landing behind a larger aircraft which is landing on a crossing runway -- Cross above the larger aircraft's flight path.

    d)   Landing behind a larger aircraft departing on the same runway -- Note the larger aircraft's rotation point. Land well prior to rotation point.

    e)   Landing behind a larger aircraft departing on a crossing runway -- Note the larger aircraft's rotation point.

        i)   If it rotates past the intersection, continue your approach and land prior to the intersection.

        ii)   If the larger aircraft rotates prior to the intersection, avoid flight below the larger aircraft's flight path.

            •   Abandon the approach unless your landing is assured well before reaching the intersection.

    f)   Departing behind a larger aircraft taking off -- Note the larger aircraft's rotation point. You should rotate prior to the larger aircraft's rotation point. Continue to climb above and stay upwind of the larger aircraft's climb path until turning clear of its wake.

    g)   Departing or landing after a larger aircraft has executed a low approach, missed approach, or touch-and-go landing -- Because vortices settle and move laterally near the ground, the vortex hazard may exist along the runway and in your flight path.

        i)   You should ensure that an interval of at least 2 min. has elapsed before your takeoff or landing.

    h)   En route VFR -- Avoid flight below and behind a larger aircraft's path. If you observe a larger aircraft above and on the same track as your airplane (meeting or overtaking), adjust your position laterally, preferably upwind.

2.   **Follow the established traffic pattern procedures according to instructions or rules.**

    a.   Established airport traffic patterns assure that air traffic flows into and out of an airport in an orderly manner. Airport traffic patterns establish

        1)   The direction and placement of the pattern.
        2)   The altitude at which the pattern is to be flown.
        3)   The procedures for entering and leaving the pattern.

    b.   There is a basic rectangular airport traffic pattern which you should use unless modified by ATC or by approved visual markings at the airport. Thus, all you need to know is

        1)   The basic rectangular traffic pattern,

        2)   Visual markings and typical ATC clearances which modify the basic rectangular pattern, and

        3)   Reasons for modifying the basic pattern.

c. The basic rectangular airport traffic pattern

1) The traffic pattern altitude is usually 1,000 ft. above the elevation of the airport surface (the common alternative is 800 ft. AGL). The use of a common altitude at a given airport is the key factor in minimizing the risk of collisions at uncontrolled airports.

  a) Turbine-powered and large airplanes' traffic pattern altitude is 1,500 ft. AGL and their pattern will normally be wider than those of single-engine airplanes.

2) At all airports, the direction of traffic flow (in accordance with FAR Part 91.127 and 91.129) is always to the left (counterclockwise when seen from the air), unless right turns are indicated by approved light signals, visual markings on the airport, or control tower instructions.

3) Within airport traffic areas (up to, but not including, 3,000 ft. AGL and a 5-SM radius of the airport), the maximum speed (safety permitting) is

  a) 200 kt. (230 MPH) for all aircraft.

  b) Also, speed should be adjusted when practical, so that it is compatible with the speed of other aircraft in the pattern.

  c) In terminal control areas (TCAs), the speed limit is 250 kt. because all aircraft are positively controlled and the controller can regulate airspeed.

4) **THE TRAFFIC PATTERN**

Single Runway

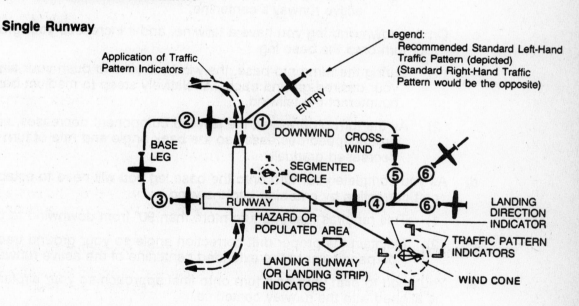

Key:

1. Enter pattern in level flight, abeam the midpoint of the runway, at pattern altitude.

2. Maintain pattern altitude until abeam approach end of the landing runway, or downwind leg.

3. Complete turn to final at least ¼ mi. from the runway.

4. Continue straight ahead until beyond departure end of runway.

5. If remaining in traffic pattern, commence turn to crosswind leg beyond the departure end of the runway, within 300 ft. of pattern altitude. Some pilots use 500 ft. AGL or similar rule of thumb.

6. If departing the traffic pattern, continue straight out, or exit with a 45° left turn beyond the departure end of the runway, after reaching pattern altitude.

3. **Correct for wind drift to follow the appropriate ground track.** This is a procedure that you have been developing since you flew your first rectangular course. See Task VIII.A., Rectangular Course, on page 364 for a detailed discussion. We will start this review on the upwind leg (i.e., after takeoff).

   a. The upwind leg should be a headwind, and you need to maintain the ground track over the extension of the centerline of the runway.

      1) The turn onto the crosswind leg should begin with a shallow bank, due to the decreased groundspeed.

      2) As the turn progresses, the bank angle must be increased because the headwind component is diminishing, resulting in an increasing groundspeed.

   b. As you roll out onto the crosswind leg you need to compensate for the wind attempting to push you inside of your desired ground track.

      1) To compensate, the amount of turn must be less than 90°.

      2) Your ground track should be perpendicular to the extended centerline of the active runway.

      3) Plan your turn to downwind and plan for turning radius and drift.

         a) It will be necessary to turn more than 90°.

         b) The turn should start with a medium bank angle gradually increasing to a steep bank as the turn progresses.

         c) The rollout should be timed to assure your ground track is parallel to the active runway's centerline.

   c. On the downwind leg you have a tailwind, and it increases your groundspeed. Plan your turn onto the base leg.

      1) During the turn onto base, the wind will tend to push your airplane away from your desired ground track. A relatively steep to medium bank is needed to counteract the tailwind.

      2) As the turn progresses, the tailwind component decreases, and the groundspeed decreases so the bank angle and rate of turn must be decreased gradually.

   d. As you complete your turn onto the base leg you will need to establish the proper drift correction by crabbing into the wind.

      1) This requires that you turn more than 90° from downwind to base.

      2) Maintain the proper drift correction angle so your ground track is perpendicular to the extended centerline of the active runway.

   e. You need to plan your next turn onto final approach so your airplane's ground track is aligned with the runway centerline.

      1) Since the crosswind will become a headwind, causing your groundspeed to decrease during this turn, the bank should be medium and must decrease as the turn proceeds.

4. **Maintain proper spacing from other traffic.**

   a. As you fly in the traffic pattern, you must observe other traffic and maintain separation, especially in the traffic pattern when smaller airplanes may have relatively slower approach speeds than your airplane.

   b. At an airport with an operating control tower, the controller may instruct you to adjust your traffic pattern to provide separation.

    c. Remember, whether you are at a controlled or uncontrolled airport, you are responsible to see and avoid other aircraft (FAR 91.113).

5. *Maintain the traffic pattern altitude, ±100 ft.*

6. *Maintain the desired airspeed, ±10 kt.*

    a. Maintain the proper airspeed for the portion of the traffic pattern prescribed in your *POH*.

    b. If ATC requests you to maintain a specified airspeed, and you determine it is safe for your operation, then maintain that airspeed.

7. Complete the prelanding cockpit checklist.

    a. Prior to or as you enter the airport traffic pattern (usually on the downwind leg), you should conduct a prelanding checklist to be sure that you and your airplane are ready to land. This should be a "do and review" (i.e., memorized) type of checklist. Generally, such a checklist includes:

        1) Seat belts fastened.

        2) Gas fullest tank (if applicable).

        3) Carburetor heat on (before power reduction, if applicable).

        4) Mixture set (usually full rich in case you have to "go around," i.e., use full power). Set according to your *POH*.

            a) Electric fuel pump on (if applicable).

        5) Speed reduced to lower flaps.

        6) Flaps partially down.

        7) Landing gear down, if retractable.

        8) Many pilots use **GUMPS**

            G Gas
            U Undercarriage
            M Mixture
            P Prop and/or Power
            S Seatbelts

    b. The Approach and Landing checklist from the Piper Tomahawk *POH* is shown below.

PIPER TOMAHAWK
APPROACH AND LANDING CHECKLIST

1. Fuel selector - proper tank	7. Trim to 70 KIAS
2. Seat backs - erect	8. Final approach speed
3. Belts/harness - fasten	Full flaps (Outboard Flow Strips Installed - 62 KIAS
4. Electric fuel pump - ON	Full flaps (Outboard and Inboard Flow Strips Installed - 67 KIAS
5. Mixture - set	
6. Flaps - set -- 89 KIAS max	**For Academic Illustration/Training Purposes Only!** *For Flight:* **Use your Pilot's Operating Handbook and FAA-Approved Airplane Flight Manual.**

8. **Maintain orientation with the runway in use.**

   a. While conducting airport traffic pattern operations you must remain oriented with the runway in use.

      1) Know which runway is in use and plan to enter properly and remain in the correct traffic pattern.

      2) When approaching an airport you should visualize your position from the airport and the relative direction of the runway. Use the airplane's heading indicator to assist you.

C. Common errors during traffic pattern operations

   1. **Failure to comply with traffic pattern instructions, procedures, and rules.**

      a. Your noncompliance with ATC instructions may be caused by not understanding or hearing radio communications.

         1) You must learn to divide your attention while in the traffic pattern between flying, collision avoidance, performing checklists, and radio communications.

   2. **Improper correction for wind drift.**

      a. Remember that a traffic pattern is no more than a rectangular course and should be performed in the same manner.

   3. **Inadequate spacing from other traffic.**

      a. This occurs when you turn onto a traffic pattern leg too soon or you are flying an airplane that is faster than the one you are following.

   4. **Poor altitude or airspeed control.**

      a. Know the airspeeds at various points in the traffic pattern.
      b. Check the airplane and engine instruments.

END OF TASK

AIRPORT AND RUNWAY MARKING AND LIGHTING

III.C. **TASK: AIRPORT AND RUNWAY MARKING AND LIGHTING**

     PILOT OPERATION - 2

     REFERENCES: AC 61-21; AIM.

Objective. To determine that the applicant:

1. Exhibits knowledge by explaining airport and runway markings and lighting aids.	2. Identifies and interprets airport, runway, taxiway marking, and lighting aids.

A. General Information

    1. This is one of three tasks (A-C) in this area of operation. Your examiner is required to test you on this task.

    2. *Pilot Operation - 2* refers to FAR 61.107(a)(2): Airport and traffic pattern operations, including operations at controlled airports, radio communications, and collision avoidance precautions.

    3. FAA References

           AC 61-21: Flight Training Handbook
           Airman's Information Manual

    4. The objective of this task is for you to demonstrate your knowledge of airport and runway marking and lighting.

B. Task Objectives

1. **Exhibit your knowledge by explaining airport and runway markings and lighting aids.**

    a. The FAA has established standard airport and runway markings. Since most airports are marked in this manner, it is important for you to know and understand these markings.

    b. This same standardization is also found in airport lighting and other airport visual aids.

2. **Identify and interpret airport, runway, taxiway marking, and lighting aids.**

    a. Airport signs are used on runways and taxiways to provide information.

        1) Mandatory instruction signs display a message which, if not obeyed, could create an unsafe condition. They have white characters on a red background. These include:

            a) Taxiway/runway intersections and instrument landing critical areas. Used to augment holding position markings.

            b) Runway/runway intersections. These signs identify intersecting runways and contain both runway numbers of the intersecting runways.

            c) Other applications. An example would be to prohibit entry into a specific area.

        2) Information signs are used to provide location or destination information and have black characters on a yellow background. These include:

            a) Taxiway identification signs. Taxiways are identified by letters, as much as possible. These signs are normally located at an intersection of taxiways or at an exit of a runway.

            b) Destination signs. These indicate the destination (e.g., a runway) and include an arrow indicating the direction to be followed.

        3) Runway distance remaining signs are located along the sides of a runway to indicate the remaining runway distance in increments of 1,000 ft. These signs have white numbers on a black background and are lighted for nighttime and/or low visibility operations.

    b. Runways are either paved or unimproved. The following runway and taxiway markings relate to improved, sophisticated airports. At smaller airports, you must learn and follow the local customs.

        1) Runway Numbers -- Runway numbers and letters are determined from the approach direction. The runway number is the whole number nearest one-tenth the magnetic direction of the runway. Letters differentiate between left (L), right (R), or center (C) parallel runways, if applicable.

            a) For two parallel runways "L" "R."
            b) For three parallel runways "L" "C" "R."

        2) Runway markings are determined by the type of operations that runway is designed to handle (i.e., VFR or IFR traffic). You should know all types of markings as you may operate on any of these runway types.

            a) Visual Runway Marking -- Used for operations under visual flight rules (VFR):

                i)   Centerline marking.

                ii) Designation (i.e., runway number) marking.

    iii) Threshold marking on runways intended to be used by international commercial air transport.

    iv) Fixed distance marking on runways 4,000 ft. or longer used by jet aircraft.

    v) Holding position markings for taxiway/runway intersections.

    vi) Holding position markings at runway/runway intersections when runways are normally used for "land, hold short operations" or taxiing.

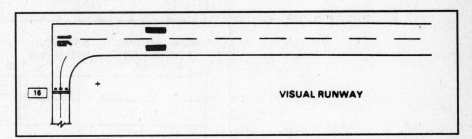

VISUAL RUNWAY

b) Nonprecision Instrument Runway Marking -- Used on runways served by an instrument approach. Includes the visual runway markings except it will always have the threshold marking.

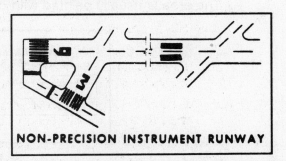

NON-PRECISION INSTRUMENT RUNWAY

c) Precision Instrument Runway Marking -- Used on runways served by an instrument approach and on runways having special operating requirements. Includes the nonprecision instrument markings except it will always have fixed distance markers, plus:

    i) Touchdown zone marking, and
    ii) Side stripes.

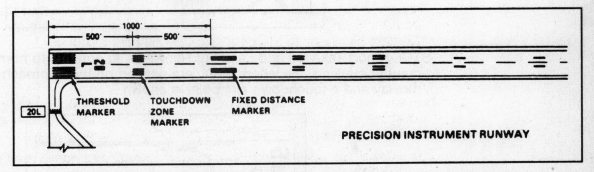

PRECISION INSTRUMENT RUNWAY

3) Threshold -- The designated beginning of the runway that is available and suitable for the landing of aircraft.

    a) Threshold marker is a set of heavy lines parallel to the runway centerline.

    b) A threshold bar is a white 10-ft. wide bar that is located across the width of the runway (see top two figures on next page).

4) Displaced Threshold -- A threshold that is not at the beginning of the paved runway. The paved area behind the displaced runway threshold is available for taxiing, the takeoff of aircraft, and the landing rollout, but not for other landing purposes. (See below).

     a) A threshold bar is located at the displaced threshold.

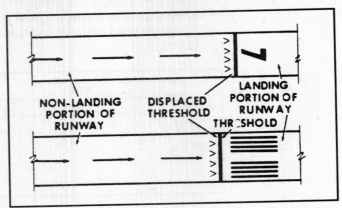

5) Stopway Areas -- Any surface or area extending beyond the runway which appears usable but which, due to the nature of its structure, is unusable. The area is usually painted with chevrons.

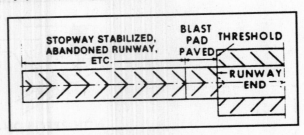

6) Closed Runway -- A runway surface which appears usable but which, due to the nature of its structure or other reasons, has become unusable. It is marked with an X.

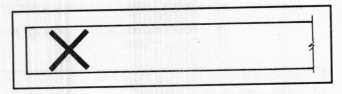

7) STOL (Short Take Off and Landing) Runway -- In addition to normal runway number marking, the letters STOL are painted on the approach end of the runway and a touchdown aim point is shown.

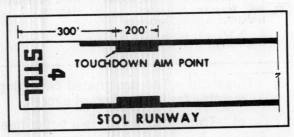

STOL RUNWAY

8) Taxiway Marking -- The taxiway centerline is marked with a continuous yellow line. When the taxiway edge is marked, two continuous yellow lines spaced 6 in. apart are used.

9) Holding Position Markings -- There are three types of holding position markings that may be encountered on an airport.

    a) Holding position markings for taxiway/runway intersections, taxiways located in runway approach areas, and runway/runway intersections consist of four yellow lines, two solid and two dashed, spaced 6 in. apart and extending across the width of the taxiway or runway.

        i) The solid lines are always on the side where the aircraft is to hold.

        ii) These markings are installed on runways only if the runway is used by ATC for "land, hold short" operations or taxiing operations and have operational significance only for those two types of operations. A sign with a white inscription on a red background is installed adjacent to these holding position markings.

           • A land, hold short operation is one in which ATC instructions are "Cleared to land runway X, hold short of runway Y." You must either exit runway X prior to runway Y or stop prior to runway Y.

    b) Holding position markings for ILS critical areas consist of two yellow solid lines spaced 2 ft. apart connected by pairs of solid lines spaced 10 ft. apart extended across the width of the taxiway as shown in the figure below.

        i) A sign with an inscription "ILS" in white on a red background is installed adjacent to these holding position markings.

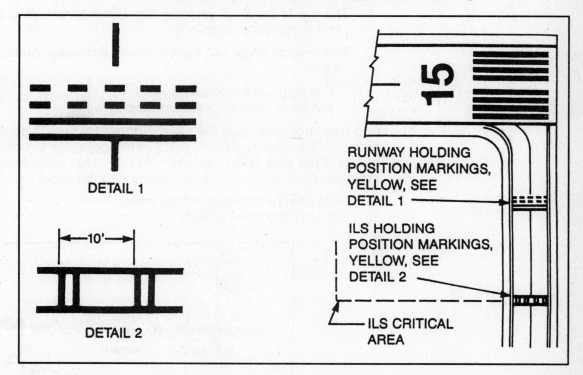

DETAIL 1

DETAIL 2

RUNWAY HOLDING POSITION MARKINGS, YELLOW, SEE DETAIL 1

ILS HOLDING POSITION MARKINGS, YELLOW, SEE DETAIL 2

ILS CRITICAL AREA

c) Holding position markings for taxiway/taxiway intersections consist of one dashed line extending across the width of the taxiway as shown below. They are installed on taxiways where ATC normally holds aircraft short of a taxiway intersection.

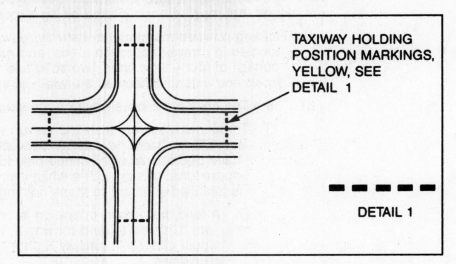

TAXIWAY HOLDING POSITION MARKINGS, YELLOW, SEE DETAIL 1

DETAIL 1

c. **Wind socks, tees, tetrahedrons, and segmented circles**

1) You need to know wind direction to select the active runway and to plan your crosswind correction technique.

2) Virtually all airports have a wind indicator of one of the following types:

a) Wind socks (or cones) are fabric "socks" through which wind blows.

   i) The toe of the sock points in the direction the wind is GOING (land in the opposite direction).

   ii) The vertical angle out from the pole indicates the strength of the wind.

   • A limp sock means no wind.
   • A horizontal sock means strong wind.

b) Wind (landing) tees have the stem (bottom) of the "T" pointing in the direction the wind is GOING (land in the opposite direction). Think of the wind tee as a small airplane with the wings represented by the crossbar (top) of the "T." It is landing into the wind.

   i) Indicates the direction of the wind,
   ii) But NOT the wind velocity.

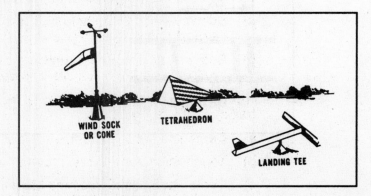

WIND SOCK OR CONE

TETRAHEDRON

LANDING TEE

      c)   Tetrahedrons point to the direction from which the wind is COMING (land in that direction).

         i)   Indicates the direction of the wind,

        ii)   But NOT the wind velocity.

3)   In no or low wind situations, airport operators will frequently adjust wind tees and tetrahedrons so that they mark the active or desired runway.

4)   Where such wind indicators do not exist, use natural indicators.

      a)   Smoke from ground fires, power plants, etc., shows wind direction.

      b)   The lee side (direction wind is coming from) of lakes and ponds tends to be smooth.

5)   The segmented circle system provides traffic pattern information at airports without operating control towers. It consists of the

      a)   Segmented circle -- Located in a position affording maximum visibility to pilots in the air and on the ground. A wind and/or landing direction indicator is usually in the center.

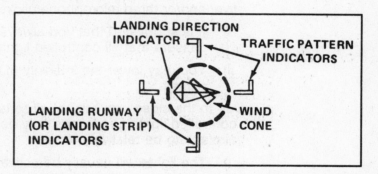

      b)   Landing strip (runway) indicators are installed in pairs as shown in the segmented circle above and are used to show the alignment of landing strips (i.e., landing runway).

      c)   Traffic pattern indicators are arranged in pairs with the landing strip indicators and are used to indicate the direction of turns when there is a variation from the normal left traffic pattern.

         i)   If the airport has no segmented circle, traffic pattern indicators may be installed on or near the runway ends.

d.   Runway lights

1)   Edge lights are white and can be low, medium, or high intensity (the latter two can be controlled by control tower personnel).

      a)   Runway edge lights help you identify runways as you approach the airport and also help you align your airplane on final approach.

      b)   Designated instrument runways have the last 2,000 ft. lighted in aviation yellow (from the opposite approach they are white).

2)   In-runway lights are found in some precision approach (designed for IFR traffic) runways.

      a)   Centerline lights at 50-ft. intervals.

      b)   Touchdown zone lights, marking the touchdown zone of the runway.

      c)   Centerline lighting systems have the last 3,000 to 1,000 ft. alternate red and white lights with the last 1,000 ft. all red (from the opposite approach these lights are white).

3) Runway threshold lights and runway end lights are straight lines of lights across each end of the runway.

    a) The threshold (beginning of runway) lights are green.

    b) The runway end lights are usually red.

4) Runway end identifier lights (REIL) are available at some airports. They are a pair of synchronized flashing strobe lights near the threshold of the runway. They indicate the runway

    a) If it is surrounded by a preponderance of other lighting.

    b) If it lacks contrast with surrounding terrain.

    c) During reduced visibility.

5) Pilot control of lighting is available at airports without specified hours for lighting and where there is no control tower or FSS (or when they are closed).

    a) All lighting systems which are radio-controlled operate on the same frequency, usually the CTAF.

    b) The control system consists of a three-step control responsive to seven, five, and/or three microphone clicks.

        i) It is suggested that you always initially key the mike seven times to assure that all controlled lights are at maximum available intensity.

        ii) You may lower the intensity (if applicable) by keying five or three times.

    c) Due to the close proximity of airports using the same frequency, radio-controlled lighting receivers may be set at a low sensitivity requiring the airplane to be relatively close.

        i) The lights will usually be activated for 15 min.

    d) The Airport/Facility Directory contains descriptions of pilot-controlled lighting at all available airports and their frequencies.

e. Taxiway lights are available at some airports.

1) They are blue and outline the usable limits of the taxiways.

2) Taxiway centerline lights are used during low visibility conditions. They emit a green light.

f. Airport rotating beacons

1) Primary purpose is to identify the location of airports at night.

2) Usually 12-30 flashes per minute.

3) White and green alternating flashes indicate a lighted land airport for civil use.

4) Two whites and a green indicate a military airport.

5) A flashing amber light near the center of an airport's segmented circle or on top of a building means that a right-hand traffic pattern is in effect.

6) Operation of the green and white rotating beacon in a control zone during the day indicates that the weather is not VFR, i.e.,

    a) Less than 3 mi. visibility, and/or

    b) Ceiling less than 1,000 ft.

    c) There is no regulatory requirement for daylight operation.

g. Approach light systems (ALS) are designed for IFR transition to the runway lights, i.e., to help pilots coming through clouds on final approach to find the runway.

   1) Approach light systems are a configuration of signal lights starting at the landing threshold and extending into the approach area (before you get to the runway) a distance of 2,400-3,000 ft. for precision instrument runways and 1,400-1,500 ft. for nonprecision instrument runways.

      a) Some systems include sequenced flashing lights which appear to the pilot as a ball of light traveling toward the runway at high speed twice a second.

h. Obstructions are marked and lighted to warn you of their presence during daytime and nighttime conditions. They may be marked/lighted in any of the following combinations:

   1) Aviation red obstruction lights -- flashing aviation red beacons and steady aviation red lights at night. Aviation orange and white paint is used for daytime marking.

   2) High-intensity white obstruction lights -- flashing high intensity white lights during daytime with reduced intensity for twilight and nighttime operation. With this type of system, the red obstruction lights and aviation orange and white paint may be omitted.

   3) Dual lighting -- a combination of flashing aviation red beacons and steady aviation red lights at night and flashing high-intensity white lights in daylight. Aviation orange and white paint may be omitted.

i. The Visual Approach Slope Indicator (VASI) provides a color-coded visual glide path using a system of lights positioned alongside the runway, near the designated touchdown point. Its visual glide path safely clears all obstructions in the final approach area.

   1) Once the principles and color code of the lighting system are understood, you simply note the colors and adjusts your airplane's rate of descent to stay on the visual glide slope.

   2) The VASI is especially effective during approaches over water or featureless terrain where other sources of visual reference are lacking or misleading, and at night.

   3) It provides optimum descent guidance for landing and minimizes the possibility of undershooting or overshooting the designated touchdown area.

   4) When you make an approach to land on a runway at a controlled airport that has an operating visual slope indicator, you are required to remain at or above the glide slope until it is necessary for a safe landing. This does not prohibit you from making normal corrections above or below the glide slope for the purpose of remaining on the glide slope (FAR 91.129).

j.   Basically, the VASI system uses color differentiation between red and white.

1)   Each light unit projects a beam of light having a white segment in the upper part of the beam and a red segment in the lower part of the beam.

2)   When on the proper glide path, you will, in effect, overshoot the downwind (near) bars and undershoot the upwind (far) bars. Thus, the downwind bars will be seen as white and the upwind bars as red.

3)   From a position below the glide path you will see all the light bars as red. From above the glide path all the light bars will appear white.

4)   Passing through the glide path from a low position, you will see a transition in color from red to white. This will occur if you maintain or gain altitude.

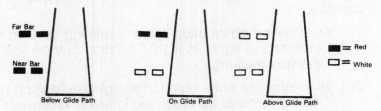

2-BAR VASI

5)   Passing through the glide path from a high position, you will see a transition in color from white to red. This will occur if you begin above the VASI glide path and your rate of descent is too great (i.e., exceeds the VASI glide path).

k.   Three-bar VASI installations provide two visual glide paths as shown below:

1)   The lower glide path is provided by the near and middle bars and is normally set at a 3° incline. The upper glide path, provided by the middle and far bars, is normally 1/4° higher. This higher glide path is intended for use only by high cockpit aircraft to provide a sufficient threshold-crossing height.

2)   When using a three-bar VASI it is not necessary to use all three bars. The near and middle bars constitute a two-bar VASI for using the lower glide path. Also, the middle and far bars constitute a two-bar VASI for using the upper glide path.

3)   Using the upper glide path just means you will come in a little steeper and land a little longer. This is not a real problem as long as the runway is long enough.

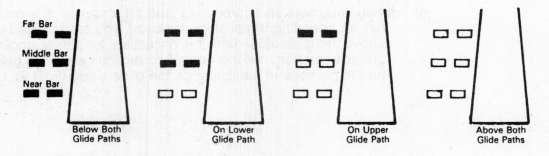

3-BAR VASI

l.   The Tri-color Approach Slope Indicator normally consists of a single light unit, projecting a three-color visual approach path into the final approach area of the runway.

    1)   In this system, the below glide path indication is red, the above glide path indication is amber, and the on-path indication is green.

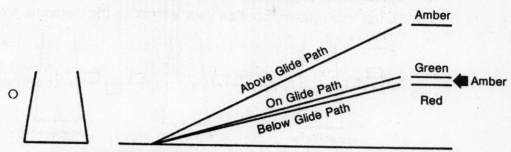

TRI-COLOR VISUAL APPROACH SLOPE INDICATOR

Caution: When the aircraft descends from green to red, the pilot may see a dark amber color during the transition from green to red.

m.   The Precision Approach Path Indicator (PAPI) uses lights similar to the VASI but in a single row of either two or four lights.

    1)   The row of light units is normally installed on the left side of the runway.
    2)   The glide path indications are depicted below.

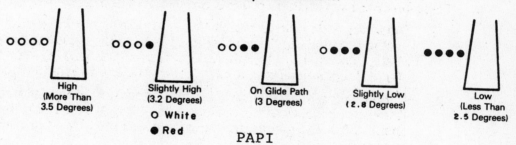

PAPI

n.   Pulsating Visual Approach Slope Indicators normally consist of a single light unit projecting a two-color visual approach path.

    1)   Below the glide slope you see a pulsating red light.
    2)   Above the glide slope you see a pulsating white light.
    3)   On the glide slope you see a steady white light.

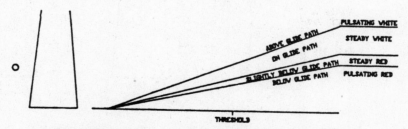

PULSATING VISUAL APPROACH SLOPE INDICATOR

Caution: When viewing the pulsating visual approach slope indicators in the pulsating white or pulsating red sectors, it is possible to mistake this lighting aid for another aircraft or a ground vehicle. Pilots should exercise caution when using this type of system.

o.   Alignment of elements system is not a lighting aid, but is included here because it is used as a visual glide slope indicator.

1)   It is a low cost system consisting of painted plywood panels, normally black and white or fluorescent orange.

2)   Some may be lighted for night operations.

3)   To use this system, position your aircraft so the elements are in alignment.

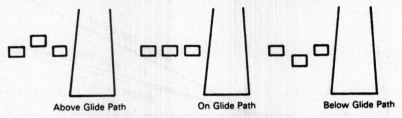

ALIGNMENT OF ELEMENTS

END OF TASK -- END OF CHAPTER

CHAPTER IV
TAKEOFFS AND CLIMBS

IV.A. *Normal and Crosswind Takeoffs and Climbs* 252
IV.B. *Short-Field Takeoff and Climb* 261
IV.C. *Soft-Field Takeoff and Climb* 268

This chapter explains the three tasks (A-C) of Takeoffs and Climbs. These tasks include both knowledge and skill.

Each objective of a task lists, in sequence, the important elements that must be satisfactorily performed. The object includes:

1. Specifically what you should be able to do.
2. The conditions under which the task is to be performed.
3. The minimum acceptable standards of performance.

Be confident. You have prepared diligently and are better prepared and more skilled than the average private pilot applicant. Your examiner will base your ability to perform these tasks on the following.

1. Executing the task within your airplane's capabilities and limitations, including use of the airplane's systems.
2. Piloting your airplane with smoothness and accuracy.
3. Exercising good judgment.
4. Applying your aeronautical knowledge.
5. Showing mastery of your airplane within the standards outlined in this area of operation, with the successful outcome of a task never seriously in doubt.

This chapter explains and describes the factors involved and the technique required for safely taking your airplane off the ground and departing the takeoff area under normal conditions, as well as in various situations where maximum performance of your airplane is essential.

Although the takeoff and climb maneuver is one continuous process, it can be divided into three basic elements.

1. The *takeoff roll* is that portion of the maneuver during which your airplane is accelerated to an airspeed that provides sufficient lift for it to become airborne.
2. The *liftoff*, or rotation, is the act of becoming airborne as a result of the wings lifting the airplane off the ground or your rotating the nose up, increasing the angle of attack to start a climb.
3. The *initial climb* begins when your airplane leaves the ground and a pitch attitude has been established to climb away from the takeoff area. Normally, it is considered complete when your airplane has reached a safe maneuvering altitude, or an en route climb has been established.

Your examiner is required to test you on all three tasks. Each task is reproduced verbatim from the FAA Practical Test Standards in a shaded box. General discussion is presented under "A. General Information." This is followed by "B. Task Objectives," which is a detailed discussion of each element of the FAA's task.

NORMAL AND CROSSWIND TAKEOFFS AND CLIMBS

IV.A. TASK: NORMAL AND CROSSWIND TAKEOFFS AND CLIMBS

> *PILOT OPERATION - 5*
>
> REFERENCES: AC 61-21; Airplane Handbook and Flight Manual.

Objective. To determine that the applicant:

1. Exhibits knowledge by explaining the elements of normal and crosswind takeoffs and climbs, including airspeeds, configurations, and emergency procedures.

2. Selects the recommended wing-flap setting.

3. Aligns the airplane on the runway centerline.

4. Applies aileron deflection properly.

5. Advances the throttle smoothly to maximum allowable power.

6. Checks engine instruments.

7. Maintains directional control on runway centerline.

8. Adjusts aileron deflection during acceleration.

9. Rotates at the recommended[1] airspeed and accelerates to V_Y, and establishes wind-drift correction.

10. Establishes the pitch attitude for V_Y and maintains V_Y, ±5 kt.

11. Retracts the wing flaps, as recommended, or at a safe altitude.

12. Retracts the landing gear, if retractable, after a positive rate of climb has been established and a safe landing can no longer be accomplished on the remaining runway.

13. Maintains takeoff power to a safe maneuvering altitude.

14. Maintains a straight track over the extended runway centerline until a turn is required.

15. Completes after-takeoff checklist.

Note: If a crosswind condition does not exist, the applicant's knowledge of the TASK will be evaluated through oral testing.

[1]The term "recommended" refers to the manufacturer's recommendation. If the manufacturer's recommendation is not available, the description contained in AC 61-21 (FAA's Flight Training Handbook) will be used.

A.   General Information

1.   This is one of three tasks (A-C) in this area of operation. Your examiner is required to test you on this task.

2.   *Pilot Operation - 5* refers to FAR 61.107(a)(5): Normal and crosswind takeoffs and landings.

3.   FAA References

   AC 61-21: Flight Training Handbook
   Pilot's Operating Handbook (FAA-Approved Airplane Flight Manual)

4.   The objective of this task is for you to demonstrate your ability to perform normal and crosswind takeoffs and climbs.

5.   Consult and complete your takeoff and climb checklist from Section 4 of your *POH*. The checklists on the next page are from the Beech Skipper *POH*.

```
┌──────────────────────────────────────────────────────────────────────────┐
│                        BEECHCRAFT SKIPPER 77                               │
│                   TAKEOFF AND CLIMB CHECKLISTS                             │
├───────────────────────────────────┬──────────────────────────────────────┤
│            TAKEOFF                 │              CLIMB                     │
│                                    │                                        │
│ Takeoff Power . . . . . Full Throttle │  1.  Power -- SET                   │
│                                    │                                        │
│ 1. Power -- SET take-off power and │  2.  Mixture -- LEAN TO MAXIMUM RPM    │
│    mixture before brake release.   │                                        │
│                                    │  3.  Engine Temperature -- MONITOR     │
│ 2. Airspeed -- ROTATE AT 56 KIAS,  │                                        │
│    ACCELERATE TO 60 KIAS.          │  4.  Fuel Boost Pump -- OFF            │
│                                    │                                        │
│ 3. ESTABLISH DESIRED CLIMB SPEED   │  ┌─────────────────────────────────┐  │
│    when clear of obstacles.        │  │ For Academic Illustration/      │  │
│                                    │  │ Training Purposes Only!         │  │
│                                    │  │ For Flight: Use your Pilot's    │  │
│                                    │  │ Operating Handbook and          │  │
│                                    │  │ FAA-Approved Airplane Flight    │  │
│                                    │  │ Manual.                         │  │
│                                    │  └─────────────────────────────────┘  │
└───────────────────────────────────┴──────────────────────────────────────┘
```

B.   Task Objectives

   1.   **Exhibit your knowledge by explaining the elements of normal and crosswind takeoffs and climbs, including airspeeds, configurations, and emergency procedures.**

   a.   Normal takeoff and climb is one in which your airplane is headed directly into the wind or the wind is very light, and the takeoff surface is firm with no obstructions along the takeoff path, and is of sufficient length to permit your airplane to gradually accelerate to normal climbing speed.

   1)   A crosswind takeoff and climb is one in which your airplane is NOT headed directly into the wind.

   b.   Section 4, Normal Procedures, in your *POH* will provide you with the proper airspeeds, e.g., V_R, V_Y, and also the proper configuration.

   1)   Best rate of climb (V_Y) is the speed which will produce the greatest gain in altitude for a given unit of time. V_Y gradually decreases (not increases) as the density altitude increases.

   c.   Section 3, Emergency Procedures, in your *POH* will provide you with specific instructions for takeoff emergencies.

   1)   The most common emergency you can have on takeoff is to lose engine power during the takeoff roll or during the takeoff climb.

   a)   If engine power is lost during the takeoff roll, pull the throttle to idle, step on the brakes, and slow the airplane to a stop.

   b)   If you are just lifting off the runway and you lose your engine power, land the airplane straight ahead. Leave it in the flair attitude which it is already in. It will settle back down to the ground, i.e., land it like a normal landing.

   i)   It is very important not to lower the nose, because you do not want to come down on the nosewheel.

   c)   If engine power is lost any time during the climbout, a general rule of thumb is that if the airplane is above 500 to 1,000 ft. AGL, you may have enough altitude to turn back and land on the runway you have just taken off from. This decision must be based on distance from airport, wind condition, obstacles, etc.

   i)   Watch your airspeed! Avoiding a stall is the most important consideration. Remember: control yoke forward (nose down) for more airspeed.

d)   If the airplane is below 500 ft. AGL, do not try to turn back. If you turn back you will probably either stall or hit the ground before you get back to the runway.

    i)   The best thing to do is land the airplane straight ahead. Land in a clear area, if possible.

    ii)   If you have no option but to go into trees, slow the airplane to just above the stall speed (as close to the treetops as possible) to strike the trees with the slowest forward speed possible.

2)   As in all emergencies, you must maintain your composure and remain in control. The peculiarity of engine power failures on takeoff is that you have so little time to attempt to correct the problem, i.e., you just have time to land.

    a)   However, if the problem was caused by the ignition or fuel being turned off, turn them on.

    b)   Here is the place to reemphasize the need for both a thorough preflight inspection and a thorough pretakeoff check (remember your checklists!).

2.   Select the recommended wing-flap setting.

    a.   Follow the procedures prescribed in your *POH*.

    b.   Normally, wing flaps are in the retracted position for normal and crosswind takeoffs and climbs.

    c.   If flaps are used, they should be extended prior to taxiing onto the active runway and always visually checked.

3.   Align your airplane with the runway centerline. Lock the tailwheel (if possible) if in a tailwheel airplane.

    a.   Before beginning your takeoff roll, study the runway and related ground reference points, such as nearby buildings, trees, runway lights (at night), etc.

        1)   This will give you a frame of reference for directional control during takeoff.
        2)   You will feel more confident about having everything under control.

4.   Apply aileron deflection properly.

    a.   Always reverify wind direction as you taxi onto the runway by observing the windsock or other wind direction indicator which may include grass or bushes.

    b.   For a crosswind takeoff, the ailerons should by FULLY deflected at the start of the takeoff roll.

        1)   The aileron should be up on the upwind side of the airplane (i.e., the control yoke turned toward the wind).

        2)   This will impose a downward force on the upwind wing to counteract the lifting force of the crosswind and prevent that wing from rising.

5.   Advance the throttle smoothly to maximum allowable power.

    a.   Recheck that the mixture is full rich (unless at high altitude).

    b.   Power should be added smoothly to allow for a controllable transition to flying airspeed.

    c.   Applying power too quickly can cause engine surging, backfiring, and a possible overboost situation (turbocharged engines). These cause unnecessary engine wear as well as possible failure.

    d.   Applying power too slowly wastes runway length.

    e.   Use the power setting that is recommended in your *POH*.

6.   Check engine instruments.

    a.   Engine instruments must be monitored during the entire maneuver.

    b.   Listen for any indication of power loss or engine roughness.

    c.   This enables you to immediately notice any malfunctions or indication of insufficient power or other potential problems. Do not commit to liftoff unless all engine indications are normal.

7.   Maintain directional control on runway centerline.

    a.   Rudder pressure must be promptly and smoothly applied to counteract yawing forces (from wind and/or torque), so your airplane continues straight down the center of the runway.

    b.   During a crosswind takeoff roll, you will normally apply downwind rudder pressure, since on the ground your airplane (especially tailwheel-type) will tend to weathervane into the wind.

    c.   When takeoff power is applied, torque, which yaws the airplane to the left, may be sufficient to counteract the weathervaning tendency caused by a right crosswind.

        1)   On the other hand, it may also aggravate the tendency to swerve left with a left crosswind.

8.   Adjust aileron deflection during acceleration.

    a.   During crosswind takeoffs the aileron deflection into the wind should be decreased as appropriate airspeed increases.

        1)   As the forward speed of your airplane increases and the crosswind becomes more of a relative headwind, the holding of full aileron into the wind should be reduced.

    b.   You will feel increasing pressure on the controls as the ailerons become more effective.

        1)   Your objective is to release enough pressure to keep the wings level.

        2)   The crosswind component does not completely vanish, so some aileron pressure will need to be maintained to prevent the upwind wing from rising.

            a)   This will hold that wing down so that your airplane will, immediately after liftoff, be slipping into the wind enough to counteract drift.

9.   Rotate at the recommended airspeed and accelerate to V_Y, and establish a wind-drift correction.

    a.   As your airplane accelerates, check your airspeed indicator to ensure the needle is moving and operating properly.

        1)   Call out your airspeed as you accelerate to V_R, e.g., "40, 60, 80."

    b.   The best takeoff attitude requires only minimal pitch adjustments just after liftoff to establish the best rate of climb airspeed, V_Y. The airplane should be allowed to fly off the ground in its normal takeoff attitude, if possible.

        1)   Rotate at V_R as recommended in your *POH*. Your airplane's V_R: _____.

c.   If your *POH* does not recommend a V_R use the following procedure from the *Flight Training Handbook* (AC 61-21).

    1)   When all the flight controls become effective during the takeoff roll in a nosewheel type airplane, back elevator pressure should be gradually applied to raise the nosewheel slightly off the runway, thus establishing the liftoff attitude.

        a)   This is referred to as rotating.

    2)   In tailwheel-type airplanes, the tail should first be allowed to rise off the ground slightly to permit the airplane to accelerate more rapidly.

    3)   At this point, the position of the nose in relation to the horizon should be noted, then elevator pressure applied as necessary to hold this attitude.

        a)   On both types of airplanes the wings must be kept level by applying aileron pressure as necessary.

d.   Forcing your airplane into the air by applying excessive back pressure would only result in an excessively high pitch attitude and may delay the takeoff.

    1)   Excessive and rapid changes in pitch attitude result in proportionate changes in the effects of torque, thus making the airplane more difficult to control.

    2)   If you force your airplane to leave the ground before adequate speed is attained, the wing's angle of attack may be excessive, causing the airplane to settle back on the runway or stall.

    3)   Also, jerking the airplane off the ground reduces passenger comfort.

e.   If not enough back pressure is held to maintain the correct takeoff attitude or the nose is allowed to lower excessively, the airplane may settle back to the runway. This occurs because the angle of attack is decreased and lift is diminished to the point where it will not support the airplane.

f.   Some airplanes and many high-performance airplanes require conscious rearward elevator pressure at V_R to establish the liftoff.

    1)   Without this conscious control pressure, the airplane may start to wheelbarrow (i.e., the main wheels break ground before the nose wheel).

    2)   Note that, in general, high-performance airplanes have heavier control pressures and require more deliberate application of control movements.

g.   During takeoffs in a strong, gusty wind, increase V_R to provide an additional margin of safety in the event of sudden changes in wind direction immediately after liftoff.

h.   In a crosswind takeoff as the nosewheel or tailwheel raises off the runway, holding the aileron control into the wind should result in the downwind wing rising and the downwind main wheel lifting off the runway first, with the remainder of the takeoff roll being made on the other main wheel (i.e., on the side the wind is coming from).

    1)   This is preferable to side skipping (which would occur if you did not turn the control yoke into the wind and use opposite rudder).

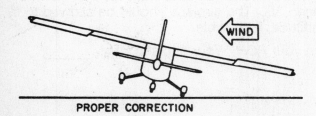

PROPER CORRECTION

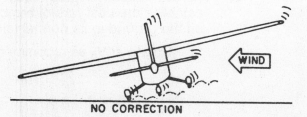

NO CORRECTION

    2) If a significant crosswind exists, the main wheels should be held on the ground slightly longer than in a normal takeoff so that a smooth but very definite liftoff can be made.

        a) Accomplish this by slightly less back pressure on the control yoke as you near V_R.

        b) This procedure will allow the airplane to leave the ground under more positive control so that it will definitely remain airborne while the proper amount of drift correction is established.

        c) More importantly, it will avoid imposing excessive side loads on the landing gear and prevent possible damage that would result from the airplane settling back to the runway while drifting (due to the crosswind).

    3) As both main wheels leave the runway and ground friction no longer resists drifting, the airplane would be slowly carried sideways with the wind unless you maintain adequate drift correction.

i. In the initial crosswind climb, the airplane will be slipping (upwind wing down to prevent drift and opposite rudder to align your flight path with the runway) into the wind sufficiently to counteract the drifting effect of the wind and to increase stability during the transition to flight.

    1) After your airplane is safely off the runway (e.g., 100 ft.) and a positive rate of climb has been established, the airplane should be headed toward the wind to establish just enough crab to counteract the wind, and then the wings should be rolled level. The climb while in this crab should be continued so as to follow a ground track aligned with the runway centerline.

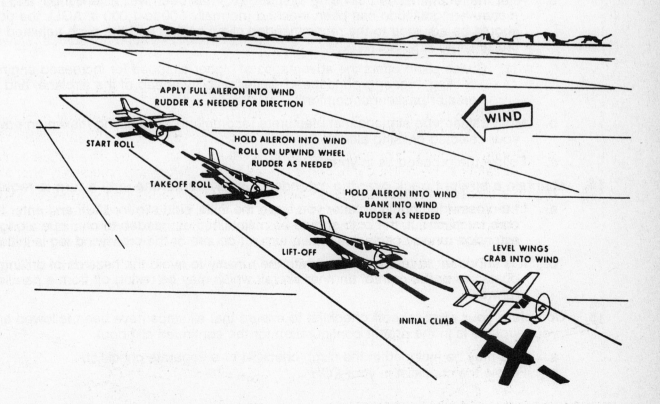

10. ***Establish the pitch attitude for V_Y and maintain V_Y, ±5 kt.***

    a.   Your airplane's V_Y _____.

11. **Retract the wing flaps, as recommended, or at a safe altitude.**

    a.   Normally after surrounding terrain and obstacles have been cleared.
    b.   Retract flaps smoothly and make the needed pitch adjustment to maintain V_Y.

12. **Retract the landing gear, if retractable, after a positive rate of climb has been established and a safe landing can no longer be accomplished on the remaining runway.**

    a.   Before retracting the landing gear, apply the brakes momentarily to stop the rotation of the wheels to avoid excessive vibration on the gear mechanism.

         1)   Centrifugal force caused by the rapidly rotating wheels expands the diameter of the tires, and if mud or other debris has accumulated in the wheel wells, the rotating wheels may rub as they enter.

    b.   Make necessary pitch adjustment to maintain the proper V_Y.

    c.   An airplane with retractable landing gear may have a V_Y for both gear up and gear down.

         1)   Your airplane's V_Y (gear down) _____

              V_Y (gear up) _____

    d.   Follow the gear retraction procedure in your *POH*.

         1)   Normally the landing gear is retracted before the flaps.

13. **Maintain takeoff power to a safe maneuvering altitude.**

    a.   After the recommended climbing airspeed (V_Y) has been well established, and a safe maneuvering altitude has been reached (normally 500 to 1,000 ft. AGL), the power should be adjusted to the recommended climb setting and the pitch adjusted for cruise climb airspeed.

         1)   Cruise climb offers the advantages of higher airspeed for increased engine cooling, higher groundspeed, better visibility ahead of the airplane, and greater passenger comfort.

    b.   Most trainer-type airplane manufacturers recommend maintaining maximum power to your selected cruising altitude.

    c.   Follow the procedures in your *POH*.

14. **Maintain a straight track over the extended runway centerline until a turn is required.**

    a.   In a crosswind condition, after you leave the initial side slip for liftoff and enter the crab for climbout, the crab should be maintained as needed to continue along the extended runway centerline until a turn on course or the crosswind leg is initiated.

    b.   It is important to remain aligned with the runway to avoid the hazards of drifting into obstacles or the path of another aircraft which may be taking off from a parallel runway.

15. **Complete your after-takeoff checklist to ensure that all steps have been followed and your airplane is in the proper configuration for the continued climbout.**

    a.   This may be included in the climb checklist or a separate checklist.
    b.   Follow the checklist in your *POH*.

C.   Common errors during a normal and crosswind takeoff and climb

   1.   Improper initial positioning of flight controls and wing flaps.

      a.   If a crosswind is present, FULL aileron should be held into the wind initially.

      b.   Flaps should be visually checked to ensure they are in the proper position recommended by your *POH*.

         1)   If used, position the flaps prior to taxiing onto the active runway.

   2.   Improper power application.

      a.   Power should be applied smoothly.

      b.   Applying power too quickly can cause engine surging, backfiring, and a possible overboost situation (turbocharged engines).

      c.   Applying power too slowly wastes runway length.

   3.   Inappropriate removal of hand from throttle.

      a.   Throughout this maneuver your hand should remain on the throttle.

      b.   Exceptions are raising the wing flaps and landing gear, and/or adjusting the trim during the climb. After completing these, your hand should return to the throttle.

   4.   Poor directional control.

      a.   Directional control is made with smooth, prompt, positive rudder corrections.

         1)   The effects of torque at the initial power application tend to pull the nose to the left.

      b.   The rudder will become more effective as airspeed increases.

      c.   A tendency to overcorrect will find you meandering back and forth across the centerline.

   5.   Improper use of ailerons.

      a.   As the forward speed of the airplane increases and the ailerons become more effective, the mechanical holding of full aileron should be reduced.

      b.   Some aileron pressure must be maintained to keep the upwind wing from rising.

         1)   This will hold that wing down so that the airplane will, immediately after liftoff, be slipping into the wind enough to counteract drift.

      c.   If the upwind wing rises, a "skipping" action may develop.

         1)   The crosswind tends to move the airplane sideways.

         2)   This side skipping imposes severe side stresses on the landing gear and could result in structural failure.

   6.   Neglecting to monitor all engine and flight instruments.

      a.   Develop a quick scan of the engine gauges to detect any abnormality.

         1)   Use it several times during your ground roll and then several times during climbout.

            a)   Engine temperatures: EGT, cylinder head, and oil.
            b)   RPM, fuel pressure.
            c)   Oil pressure.

         2)   Call out full power when you attain it on the takeoff roll, e.g., "Max RPM."

      b.   Call out your airspeed as you accelerate.

7. **Improper pitch attitude during liftoff.**

    a. Applying excessive back pressure will only result in an excessively high pitch attitude and delay the takeoff.

        1) If your airplane is forced into the air in this manner before adequate airspeed is attained, the wing's angle of attack may be too great, causing your airplane to settle back on the runway or stall.

    b. If not enough elevator pressure is held to maintain the correct attitude, your airplane may settle back on the runway and will delay climb to safe altitude.

        1) This will occur because the angle of attack is decreased and insufficient lift is being produced to support the airplane.

    c. Improper trim setting will make it harder for you to maintain the proper takeoff attitude by causing an increase in control pressure that you must hold.

        1) In a tailwheel airplane with improper trim set you may need to use forward elevator pressure to raise the tail, then lower the tail for takeoff attitude, thus leading to directional problems.

8. **Failure to establish and maintain proper climb configuration and airspeed.**

    a. Use your *POH* checklists to determine the proper climb configuration and airspeed.

    b. Maintain airspeed by making small pitch changes by outside visual references, then cross-check with the airspeed indicator.

9. **Raising the landing gear before a positive rate of climb is established** or the remaining runway is no longer sufficient to execute an emergency landing. Airplanes, especially in windy conditions, can become airborne in ground effect before sufficient airspeed is attained to sustain flight.

    a. If the landing gear is immediately raised on liftoff, the airplane may settle back down and strike the runway.

    b. Also, if an engine problem develops immediately after liftoff, the airplane should be landed immediately.

        1) If you have to wait for the landing gear to extend, there may be insufficient time and/or runway available.

10. **Drift during climb.**

    a. You must use all available outside references, to include looking behind, to maintain a track of the runway centerline extension.

    b. This will assist you in avoiding hazardous obstacles or prevent drifting into the path of another airplane which may be taking off from a parallel runway.

    c. Cross-check with the airplane's heading indicator, using enough right rudder to maintain heading with the wings level.

END OF TASK

SHORT-FIELD TAKEOFF AND CLIMB

IV.B. TASK: SHORT-FIELD TAKEOFF AND CLIMB

    PILOT OPERATION - 8

        REFERENCES: AC 61-21; Airplane Handbook and Flight Manual.

Objective. To determine that the applicant:

1. Exhibits knowledge by explaining the elements of a short-field takeoff and climb, including the significance of appropriate airspeeds and configurations, emergency procedures, and expected performance for existing operating conditions.

2. Selects the recommended wing-flap setting.

3. Positions the airplane at the beginning of the takeoff runway aligned on the runway centerline.

4. Advances the throttle smoothly to maximum allowable power.

5. Maintains directional control on the runway centerline.

6. Rotates at the recommended airspeed and accelerates to V_X.

7. Climbs at V_X or recommended airspeed, +5, –0 kt. until obstacle is cleared, or until at least 50 ft. above the surface, then accelerates to V_Y and maintains V_Y, ±5 kt.

8. Retracts the wing flaps, as recommended, or at a safe altitude.

9. Retracts the landing gear, if retractable, after a positive rate of climb has been established and a safe landing can no longer be accomplished on the remaining runway.

10. Maintains takeoff power to a safe maneuvering altitude.

11. Maintains a straight track over the extended runway centerline until a turn is required.

12. Completes after-takeoff checklist.

A. General Information

    1. This is one of three tasks (A-C) in this area of operation. Your examiner is required to test you on this task.

    2. *Pilot Operation - 8* refers to FAR 61.107(a)(8): Maximum performance takeoffs and landings.

    3. FAA References

        AC 61-21: Flight Training Handbook
        Pilot's Operating Handbook (FAA-Approved Airplane Flight Manual)

    4. The objective of this task is to determine your ability to perform a short-field takeoff and climb.

    5. When taking off from a field where the available runway is short and/or where obstacles must be cleared, you must operate your airplane to its maximum capability.

        a. Positive and accurate control of your airplane attitude and airspeed is required to obtain the shortest ground roll and the steepest angle of climb.

B. Task Objectives

    1. Exhibit your knowledge by explaining the elements of a short-field takeoff and climb, including the significance of appropriate airspeeds and configurations, emergency procedures, and expected performance for existing operating conditions.

        a. The objective is maximum takeoff and climb performance of your airplane, resulting in the shortest ground roll and the steepest angle of climb.

        b. Section 4, Normal Procedures, in your *POH* will provide you with the proper airspeeds, e.g., V_R, V_X, V_Y, and also the proper configurations.

1) Best angle of climb, V_x, is the speed which will result in the greatest gain of altitude for a given distance over the ground. This speed increases slowly as higher-density altitudes are encountered.

    a) A deviation of 5 kt. from V_x can result in a significant reduction in climb performance.

2) Always climb above the altitude of obstacles (usually powerlines or treelines) before accelerating to V_Y. This acceleration involves a reduction in pitch.

c. In Section 4, Normal Procedures, of your *POH*, find the checklist for "Short Field" or "Maximum Performance." Study it and any amplification presented at the back of Section 4, entitled "Amplified Procedures." The checklist below is from a Cessna 152 *POH*.

CESSNA MODEL C-152
SHORT FIELD TAKEOFF CHECKLIST

1. Wing Flaps -- 10°.
2. Carburetor Heat -- COLD.
3. Brakes -- APPLY.
4. Throttle -- FULL OPEN.
5. Mixture -- RICH (above 3,000 feet, LEAN to obtain maximum RPM).

6. Brakes -- RELEASE.
7. Elevator Control -- SLIGHTLY TAIL LOW.
8. Climb Speed -- 54 KIAS (until all obstacles are cleared).
9. Wing Flaps -- RETRACT slowly after reaching 60 KIAS.

> For Academic Illustration/Training Purposes Only!
> *For Flight:* Use your Pilot's Operating Handbook and FAA-Approved Airplane Flight Manual.

---

d. Section 3, Emergency Procedures, in your *POH* will provide you with specific instructions for takeoff emergencies.

1) The most common emergency you can have on takeoff is to lose engine power during the takeoff roll or during the takeoff climb.

    a) If engine power is lost during the takeoff roll and there is still enough runway to stop the airplane, pull the throttle to idle, step on the brakes, and slow the airplane to a stop.

    b) If you are just lifting off the runway and you lose your engine power, try to land the airplane on the remaining runway. Leave it in the flair attitude which it is already in. It will settle back down to the ground, i.e., land it like a normal landing.

        i) It is very important not to lower the nose, because you do not want to come down on the nosewheel.

    c) If engine power is lost anytime during the climbout, a general rule of thumb is that if the airplane is above 500 to 1,000 ft. AGL, you may have enough altitude to turn back and land on the runway you have just taken off from. This decision must be based on distance from airport, wind condition, obstacles, etc.

        i) Watch your airspeed! Avoiding a stall is the most important consideration. Remember: control yoke forward (nose down) for more airspeed.

      d) If the airplane is below 500 ft. AGL, do not try to turn back. If you turn back you will probably either stall or hit the ground before you get back to the runway.

        i) The best thing to do is land the airplane straight ahead. Land in a clear area, if possible.

        ii) If you have no option but to go into trees, slow the airplane to just above the stall speed (as close to the treetops as possible) to strike the trees with the slowest forward speed possible.

  2) As in all emergencies, you must maintain your composure and remain in control. The peculiarity of engine power failures on takeoff is that you have so little time to attempt to correct the problem, i.e., you just have time to land.

    a) However, if the problem was caused by the ignition or fuel being turned off, turn them on.

    b) Here is the place to re-emphasize the need for both a thorough preflight inspection and a thorough pre-takeoff check (remember your checklists!).

 e. Consult your *POH* before attempting a short-field takeoff, specifically taking into account the existing temperature, barometric pressure, field length, type of runway surface, and airplane operating condition.

  1) In Section 5 of your *POH*, Performance, study the Short-Field Takeoff Chart.

  2) Since the performance charts assume good pilot technique, consider your short-field takeoff proficiency.

  3) Recognize that, in some situations, you should decide NOT to attempt to take off, because the margin of safety is too small. You may have to

    a) Remove fuel, people, baggage.
    b) Wait for different wind and/or temperature conditions.
    c) Retain a more experienced pilot to make the flight.
    d) Have the airplane moved to a safer takeoff location.

2. Select the recommended wing-flap setting.

 a. If the use of flaps is recommended they should be extended prior to starting the takeoff roll.

 b. Always check your flap setting visually.

3. Position your airplane at the beginning of the takeoff runway aligned on the runway centerline.

 a. This position should be at the very beginning of the takeoff runway, thus making full use of the runway.

 b. Before beginning your takeoff roll, study the runway and related ground reference points (e.g., building, trees, obstacles).

  1) This will give you a frame of reference for directional control during takeoff.
  2) You will feel more confident about having everything under control.

 c. In a tailwheel-type airplane, you should lock the tailwheel (if applicable).

4.   Advance the throttle smoothly to maximum allowable power.

a.   Apply brakes, add takeoff power, then release the brakes smoothly. Confirm that the engine is developing takeoff power under prevailing conditions before releasing the brakes.

1)   With a fixed pitch propeller, you should confirm maximum RPM. If you are not producing full power, abort the takeoff.

b.   Engine instruments must be monitored during the entire maneuver.

1)   This enables you to immediately notice any malfunctions or indication of insufficient power or other potential problems.

2)   Listen for any indication of power loss or engine roughness.

c.   Check your airspeed indicator for movement as you accelerate.

a)   Call out your airspeed as you accelerate to V_R, e.g., "40, 60, 80."

5.   Maintain directional control on the runway centerline.

a.   Rudder pressure must be promptly and smoothly applied to counteract yawing forces (from wind and/or torque), so your airplane continues straight down the center of the runway.

b.   During a crosswind takeoff roll, you will normally apply downwind rudder pressure, since on the ground your airplane (especially tailwheel-type) will tend to weathervane into the wind.

c.   When takeoff power is applied, torque, which yaws the airplane to the left, may be sufficient to counteract the weathervaning tendency caused by a right crosswind.

1)   On the other hand, it may also aggravate the tendency to swerve left with a left crosswind.

6.   Rotate at the recommended airspeed and accelerate to V_X.

a.   At maximum performance rotation speed, you should smoothly raise the nose of your airplane to the attitude that will deliver the best angle of climb airspeed, V_X.

b.   Rotate at the recommended airspeed specified in the *POH*.

1)   If no rotation airspeed is recommended, accelerate to V_X minus 5 kt. and rotate to V_X attitude.

a)   If V_R is considerably less than V_X, accelerate to V_X minus 5 kt. before entering V_X pitch attitude for climb.

2)   DO NOT attempt to raise the nose until V_R, because this will create unnecessary drag and will prolong the takeoff roll.

a)   In a nosewheel-type airplane, you will keep the elevator in a neutral position.

i)   This will keep the airplane in a low drag attitude.

b)   In a tailwheel-type airplane, the tail should be allowed to rise off the ground slightly, then held in this tail-low flight attitude until the proper liftoff or rotation airspeed is attained.

c.   While you are practicing short-field takeoffs, you should learn the pitch attitude required to maintain V_X.

1)   Observe the position of the airplane's nose on the horizon.
2)   Note the position of the aircraft bar on the attitude indicator.

    d.   You should rotate to this predetermined pitch angle as soon as you reach V_R. As you climb out at V_X, you should maintain visual references, but occasionally glance at the attitude indicator and airspeed indicator to check the pitch angle and airspeed.

    e.   If not enough back pressure is held to maintain the correct takeoff attitude or the nose is allowed to lower excessively, your airplane may settle back to the runway. This occurs because the angle of attack is decreased and lift is diminished to the point where it will not support the airplane.

    f.   Your airplane's V_R _____ and V_X _____.

7.   *Climb at V_X or recommended airspeed, +5, −0 kt. until obstacle is cleared, or at least 50 ft. above the surface, then accelerate and maintain V_Y, ±5 kt.*

    a.   In some airplanes, a deviation of 5 kt. from V_X will result in a significant reduction of climb performance.

    b.   Maintain V_X until obstacle is cleared, or to at least 50 ft. AGL.

        1)   Your examiner will specify whether an obstacle is present when simulating a short-field environment.

    c.   Accelerate to V_Y and maintain ±5 kt.

        1)   Your airplane's V_Y _____.

8.   Retract the wing flaps, as recommended, or at a safe altitude.

    a.   Flaps are normally retracted when you are clear of any obstacle(s) and the best rate-of-climb speed, V_Y, has been established.

    b.   Raise the flaps in increments (if appropriate) to avoid sudden loss of lift and settling of the airplane.

    c.   Make needed pitch adjustment to maintain V_Y.

9.   Retract the landing gear, if retractable, after a positive rate of climb has been established and a safe landing can no longer be accomplished on the remaining runway.

    a.   Before retracting the landing gear, apply the brakes momentarily to stop the rotation of the wheels to avoid excessive vibration on the gear mechanism.

        1)   Centrifugal force caused by the rapidly rotating wheels expands the diameter of the tires, and if mud or other debris has accumulated in the wheel wells, the rotating wheels may rub as they enter.

    b.   When to retract the landing gear varies among manufacturers. Thus, it is important that you know what procedure is prescribed by that airplane's *POH*.

        1)   Some recommend gear retraction after a positive rate of climb has been established while others recommend gear retraction only after the obstacles have been cleared.

        2)   Normally, the landing gear will be retracted before the flaps.

    c.   Make necessary pitch adjustments to maintain the appropriate airspeed.

    d.   An airplane with retractable gear may have a V_X and V_Y for both gear up and gear down.

        1)   Your airplane's V_X (gear down) _____ V_X (gear up) _____

               V_Y (gear down) _____ V_Y (gear up) _____

10. **Maintain takeoff power to a safe maneuvering altitude.**

    a.   After establishing V_Y and gear and flap retraction has been completed, and a safe maneuvering altitude has been reached (normally 500 to 1,000 ft. AGL), the power should be reduced to the normal cruise climb setting and pitch adjusted for cruise climb airspeed.

    b.   Most trainer-type airplane manufacturers recommend maintaining maximum power to your selected cruising altitude.

    c.   Use the power setting recommended in your *POH*.

11. **Maintain a straight track over the extended runway centerline until a turn is required.**

    a.   After leaving the ground, a crab for any crosswind correction should be performed simultaneously with the remainder of the short-field departure, until a turn is required.

    b.   Crosswind takeoff techniques are consistent with a short-field takeoff and should be employed simultaneously, as needed.

        1)   A common error is to become preoccupied with the short-field effort at the expense of neglecting crosswind correction. The results are directional stability problems.

12. **Complete your after-takeoff checklist** to ensure that all steps have been followed and your airplane is in the proper configuration for the continued climbout.

    a.   This may be included in the climb checklist or a separate checklist.

    b.   Follow the checklist in your *POH*.

C.   Common errors during a short-field takeoff and climb

    1.   **Failure to use the maximum amount of runway available for the takeoff.**

        a.   Instead of making a wide turn onto the runway, you should begin at the end of the usable runway.

        b.   Request to use any available overrun (although not available for landing) which is structurally sound for starting the takeoff roll.

            1)   *Overrun areas* are marked with arrows pointing toward the beginning of the runway for landings and may be used for takeoff. *Chevron-marked areas* are only to be used in an emergency (which may be appropriate on a short runway).

    2.   **Improper positioning of flight controls and wing flaps.**

        a.   If a crosswind is present, FULL aileron should be held into the wind initially to prevent the crosswind from raising the upwind wing.

        b.   Flaps should be visually checked to ensure they are in the proper position recommended by the *POH*.

            1)   The short-field takeoff performance chart in your *POH* will also list the flap setting used to attain the chart performance.

            2)   Position the flaps prior to taxiing onto the active runway.

    3.   **Improper engine operation during short-field takeoff and climbout.**

        a.   In an attempt to gain the most performance, some pilots use very rapid throttle movements, overboosting of the engine, and improper power settings.

            1)   This can degrade engine performance, cause long-term engine wear, and add to the risk of engine failure.

b. The performance for short-field takeoffs should be obtained by flap settings, runway use, rotation point, climbout attitude, and climbout airspeed indicated in the *POH*, not by misusing the engine.

4. **Inappropriate removal of hand from throttle.**

a. Throughout this maneuver your hand should remain on the throttle.

b. Exceptions would be to raise the flaps, landing gear, and/or adjusting the trim during the climb. After completing these, your hand should return to the throttle.

5. **Poor directional control.**

a. Maintain the runway centerline throughout the takeoff roll by use of the rudder.

b. Poor directional control can lead to a longer takeoff roll and control problems at liftoff.

c. Positive and accurate control of your airplane is required to obtain the shortest ground roll and the steepest angle of climb (V_x).

6. **Improper use of brakes.**

a. You should not release the brakes until the engine is producing full power and you have checked that the engine instruments are operating normally.

b. When the brakes are released, ensure that your feet move to the bottom of the rudder pedal and are not on the brakes, so that no further braking can take place.

    1) Any use of brakes will increase the takeoff distance.

7. **Improper pitch attitude during liftoff.**

a. The attitude to maintain V_x will be significantly higher than that to maintain V_y, thus some pilots not completely comfortable with their airplane may find it difficult to pull the airplane into a high pitch angle.

b. Have confidence in your airplane's abilities and fly it by the numbers.

8. **Failure to establish and maintain proper climb configuration and airspeed.**

a. Follow the recommended procedures in your *POH*.
b. Maintain V_x because a 5-kt. deviation can result in a reduction of climb performance.

9. **Drift during climbout.**

a. Maintain the extended runway centerline until a turn is required.

b. Remember an airport traffic pattern can be a very busy area and collision avoidance and awareness is of extreme importance.

    1) Your fellow pilots will be expecting you to maintain the extended runway centerline during your initial climb.

END OF TASK

SOFT-FIELD TAKEOFF AND CLIMB

IV.C. TASK: SOFT-FIELD TAKEOFF AND CLIMB

PILOT OPERATION - 8

REFERENCES: AC 61-21; Airplane Handbook and Flight Manual.

Objective. To determine that the applicant:

1. Exhibits knowledge by explaining the elements of a soft-field takeoff and climb, including the significance of appropriate airspeeds and configurations, emergency procedures, and hazards associated with climbing at an airspeed less than V_x.

2. Selects the recommended wing-flap setting.

3. Taxis onto the takeoff surface at a speed consistent with safety.

4. Aligns the airplane on takeoff path, without stopping, and advances the throttle smoothly to maximum allowable power.

5. Adjusts and maintains a pitch attitude which transfers the weight from the wheels to the wings as rapidly as possible.

6. Maintains directional control on the center of the takeoff path.

7. Lifts off at the lowest possible airspeed and remains in ground effect while accelerating.

8. Accelerates to and maintains V_x, +5, −0 kt., if obstructions must be cleared, otherwise to V_Y, ±5 kt.

9. Retracts the wing flaps, as recommended, and at a safe altitude.

10. Retracts the landing gear, if retractable, after a positive rate of climb has been established and a landing can no longer be accomplished on the remaining runway.

11. Maintains takeoff power to a safe maneuvering altitude.

12. Maintains a straight track over the center of the extended takeoff path until a turn is required.

13. Completes after-takeoff checklist.

A. General Information

1. This is one of three tasks (A-C) in this area of operation. Your examiner is required to test you on this task.

2. *Pilot Operation - 8* refers to FAR 61.107(a)(8): Maximum performance takeoffs and landings.

3. FAA References

   AC 61-21: Flight Training Handbook
   Pilot's Operating Handbook (FAA-Approved Airplane Flight Manual)

4. The objective of this task is for you to demonstrate your ability to perform a soft-field takeoff and climb.

5. Before landing at a soft (unpaved) field, determine your capability to take off in your airplane from that field. Also, consider the possibility of damage and extra wear on your airplane. You may decide to wait until the takeoff surface conditions improve.

   a. If the need arises to make a soft-field departure, consult the recommendations provided by the manufacturer in your airplane's *POH*.

      1) Practice and perfect soft-field takeoffs.

6. If your airplane is parked on a soft surface, there is a possibility that other airplanes or the wind may have blown unwanted debris onto your airplane. Such materials, when trapped in the control surfaces, may jam the controls or limit their travel, which can cause disaster.

   a. Soft fields are often remote fields. Birds and animals can seek refuge or build nests (even overnight) under the cowling, in landing gear wheel wells, and elsewhere.

   b. Also, be cautious of possible vandalism of your airplane at remote airfields.

7.   Inspect your taxi route and your takeoff runway. Normally, you should walk the entire route carefully.

   a.   Note wet or soft spots and mark them as necessary (use pieces of cloth or paper tied to objects, e.g., fence posts, or anchor them to the ground at the side of the runway with stakes, sticks, etc.).

   b.   Determine and mark your takeoff abort point -- exactly where you will cut power if not airborne.

      1)   75% of V_R by the halfway point on the runway is a general rule of thumb.

8.   If the airplane wheels have settled into the ground, move the airplane forward before getting into the cockpit.

   a.   Use leverage of the wing by holding the wingtip and rocking the wingtip back and forth.

   b.   Be careful not to stress the nose wheel with side loads (have someone lift the nose or push down on the tail).

   c.   Use help as available.

B.   **Task Objectives**

   1.   **Exhibit your knowledge by explaining the elements, including the significance of appropriate airspeeds and configurations, emergency procedures, and hazards associated with climbing at an airspeed less than V_X.**

   a.   The goals of this takeoff are

      1)   To get the airplane airborne as soon as possible, and

      2)   To transfer as much weight as possible to the wings to minimize wheel friction in the soft surface.

         a)   The combination of considerable back pressure on the yoke or stick and the manufacturer's recommended flap setting is the best means of achieving a soft-field takeoff.

         b)   Weight is transferred to the wings and away from the wheels because of the high angle of attack produced by the back pressure (i.e., up elevator).

   b.   In Section 4, Normal Procedures, of your *POH*, find the soft-field takeoff checklist and study it and any amplified procedures. The checklist below is from a Piper Tomahawk *POH*.

PIPER PA-38-112, TOMAHAWK
SOFT FIELD, NO OBSTACLE TAKEOFF CHECKLIST

Flaps -- 21° (first notch).	Accelerate just above ground to best rate of climb speed, 70 KIAS.
Accelerate and lift off nose gear as soon as possible.	Flaps -- slowly retract
Lift off at lowest possible airspeed.	**For Academic Illustration/Training Purposes Only!** *For Flight:* **Use your Pilot's Operating Handbook and FAA-Approved Airplane Flight Manual.**

---

   c.   Section 3, Emergency Procedures, in your *POH* will provide you with specific instructions for takeoff emergencies.

      1)   The most common emergency you can have on takeoff is to lose engine power during the takeoff roll or during the takeoff climb.

a) If engine power is lost during the takeoff roll and there is still enough runway to stop the airplane, pull the throttle to idle, step on the brakes, and slow the airplane to a stop.

b) If you are just lifting off the runway and you lose your engine power, try to land the airplane on the remaining runway. Leave it in the flair attitude which it is already in. It will settle back down to the ground, i.e., land it like a normal landing.

   i) It is very important not to lower the nose, because you do not want to come down on the nosewheel.

c) If engine power is lost anytime during the climbout, a general rule of thumb is that if the airplane is above 500 to 1,000 ft. AGL, you may have enough altitude to turn back and land on the runway you have just taken off from. This decision must be based on distance from airport, wind condition, obstacles, etc.

   i) Watch your airspeed! Avoiding a stall is the most important consideration. Remember: control yoke forward (nose down) for more airspeed.

d) If the airplane is below 500 ft. AGL, do not try to turn back. If you turn back you will probably either stall or hit the ground before you get back to the runway.

   i) The best thing to do is land the airplane straight ahead. Land in a clear area, if possible.

   ii) If you have no option but to go into trees, slow the airplane to just above the stall speed (as close to the treetops as possible) to strike the trees with the slowest forward speed possible.

2) As in all emergencies, maintain your composure and remain in control. The peculiarity of engine power failures on takeoff is that you have so little time to attempt to correct the problem, i.e., you just have time to land.

   a) However, if the problem was caused by the ignition or fuel being turned off, turn them on.

   b) Here is the place to re-emphasize the need for both a thorough preflight inspection and a thorough pre-takeoff check (remember your checklists!).

d. Hazards of attempting to climb at airspeeds less than V_x.

   1) Reduction in climb performance.

   2) Will put the airplane near the stall speed, which could put you in a very hazardous stall (possibly a spin) situation near the ground.

2. **Select the recommended wing-flap setting.**

   a. If the use of flaps is recommended, the flaps must be extended prior to starting the takeoff roll.

   b. Always check your flap setting visually.

3. **Taxi onto the takeoff surface at a speed consistent with safety.**

   a. Keep moving once your airplane is rolling. If your airplane becomes bogged down, there may be insufficient thrust available to pull out of the mud and/or ruts, and the only choice would be to shut down and move the airplane by hand or with equipment.

   b. Use full or nearly full back pressure on the control yoke or stick while taxiing, to remove some of the stress from the nose wheel and minimize rolling resistance.

   c. Grass, sand, mud, and snow require more power than is necessary to taxi on a hard surface.

      1) Be cautious of your propeller blast and its effect on others.

      2) Also, debris may be sucked up by the propeller, causing both propeller damage and/or wear and damage to your paint job when the debris strikes the airplane.

   d. You should taxi your airplane onto the takeoff surface as fast as possible, consistent with safety.

4. Align your airplane on the takeoff path, without stopping, and advance the throttle smoothly to maximum allowable power.

   a. Stopping on a soft surface (e.g., mud or snow) might bog the airplane down; it should be kept in continuous motion with sufficient power while lining up for the takeoff roll.

      1) Line your airplane up as done on a hard-surfaced runway with a centerline.

   b. Power must be applied smoothly and as rapidly as possible.

   c. The engine instruments must be monitored during the entire maneuver.

      1) This enables you to immediately notice any malfunction or indication of insufficient power or other potential problems.

      2) Listen for any indication of power loss or engine roughness.

   d. Check your airspeed indicator for movement as you accelerate.

      1) Call out your airspeed as you accelerate to V_R, e.g., "40, 60, 80."

5. Adjust and maintain a pitch attitude which transfers the weight from the wheels to the wings as rapidly as possible.

   a. In a nose-wheel airplane, enough back elevator pressure should be applied to establish a positive angle of attack.

      1) This reduces the weight supported by the nosewheel.

      2) The nose-high attitude will allow the weight to transfer from the wheels to the wings as lift is developed.

   b. In a tailwheel airplane, the tailwheel should be raised barely off the soft runway surface.

      1) This eliminates tailwheel drag on the soft surface.

      2) The angle of attack produced in this attitude is still high enough to allow the airplane to leave the ground at the earliest opportunity and transfer weight from the main wheels to the wings.

6. Maintain directional control on the center of the takeoff path.

   a. Rudder pressure must be promptly and smoothly applied to counteract yawing forces (from wind and/or torque), so your airplane continues straight down the center of the runway.

   b. During a crosswind takeoff roll, you will normally apply downwind rudder pressure, since on the ground your airplane (especially tailwheel-type) will tend to weathervane into the wind.

   c. When takeoff power is applied, torque, which yaws the airplane to the left, may be sufficient to counteract the weathervaning tendency caused by a right crosswind.

      1) On the other hand, it may also aggravate the tendency to swerve left with a left crosswind.

7. **Lift off at the lowest possible airspeed and remain in ground effect while accelerating.**

   a. If the pitch attitude is accurately maintained during the takeoff roll, the airplane should become airborne at an airspeed slower than a safe climb speed because of the action of ground effect.

      1) Ground effect is due to the interference of the ground surface with the airflow patterns about the airplane in flight.

         a) The vertical component of the airflow around the wing is restricted which alters the wings upwash, downwash, and wingtip vortices.

         b) The reduction of the wingtip vortices alters the spanwise lift distribution and reduces the induced angle of attack and induced drag.

            i) Thus, the wing will require a lower angle of attack in ground effect to produce the same lift coefficient or, if a constant angle of attack is maintained, an increase in lift coefficient will result.

         c) Since induced drag is reduced due to ground effect, required thrust at low airspeeds is reduced.

         d) In order for ground effect to be of significant magnitude, the wing must be at a height one-half of its span or less.

         e) Due to the reduced drag in ground effect, your airplane may seem capable of takeoff well below the recommended speed.

            i) As your airplane climbs out of ground effect with a deficiency of speed, the greater induced drag may result in very marginal climb performance.

   b. After becoming airborne, the nose must be lowered very gently with the wheels just clear of the surface to allow your airplane to accelerate in ground effect.

      1) Failure to level off would mean the airplane would climb out of ground effect at too slow a speed and the increase in drag could reduce the lift sufficiently to cause the airplane to settle back onto the runway.

8. **Accelerate to and maintain V_X, +5, −0 kt. if obstructions must be cleared, otherwise to V_Y, ±5 kt.**

   a. Do not let the aircraft settle onto the soft runway.

   b. Do not attempt to climb before attaining at least V_X, or to climb too steeply.

      1) This may cause you to settle onto the surface.

   c. Accelerate to V_X, if there is an obstacle (or your examiner specifies there is an obstacle).

      1) Maintain V_X +5, −0 kt., until clear of obstruction.

         a) Then maintain V_Y.

   d. If no obstruction, accelerate to V_Y and maintain ±5 kt.

   e. Your airplane's V_X _____, V_Y _____.

9. **Retract the wing flaps, as recommended, and at a safe altitude.**

   a. Flaps are normally retracted when you are clear of any obstacle(s) and the best rate-of-climb speed, V_Y, has been established.

   b. Raise the flaps in increments (if appropriate) to avoid sudden loss of lift and settling of the airplane.

   c. Make needed pitch adjustment to maintain V_Y.

10. **Retract the landing gear, if retractable, after a positive rate of climb has been established and a landing can no longer be accomplished on the remaining runway.**

    a. Before retracting the landing gear, apply the brakes momentarily to stop the rotation of the wheels to avoid excessive vibration on the gear mechanism.

        1) Centrifugal force caused by the rapidly rotating wheels expands the diameter of the tires, and if mud or other debris has accumulated in the wheel wells, the rotating wheels may rub as they enter.

    b. When to retract the landing gear varies among manufacturers. Thus, it is important that you know what procedure is prescribed by that airplane's *POH*.

        1) Some recommend gear retraction after a positive rate of climb has been established while others recommend gear retraction only after the obstacles have been cleared.

        2) Normally, the landing gear will be retracted before the flaps.

    c. Make necessary pitch adjustments to maintain the appropriate airspeed.

    d. An airplane with retractable gear may have a V_X and V_Y for both gear up and gear down.

        1) Your airplane's V_X (gear down) _____ V_X (gear up) _____

           V_Y (gear down) _____ V_Y (gear up) _____

11. **Maintain takeoff power to a safe maneuvering altitude.**

    a. After establishing V_Y and gear and flap retraction has been completed, takeoff power should be maintained to a safe maneuvering altitude, normally 500 to 1,000 ft. AGL.

        1) Then the power should be reduced to the normal cruise climb setting and the pitch adjusted for cruise climb airspeed.

    b. Most trainer-type airplane manufacturers recommend maintaining maximum power to your selected cruising altitude.

    c. Use the power setting recommended in your *POH*.

12. **Maintain a straight track over the center of the extended takeoff path until a turn is required.**

    a. After leaving the ground, a crab for any crosswind correction should be performed simultaneously with the remainder of the soft-field departure, until a turn is required.

    b. Crosswind takeoff techniques are consistent with a soft-field takeoff and should be employed simultaneously, as needed.

        1) A common error is to become preoccupied with the soft-field effort at the expense of neglecting crosswind correction. The results are directional stability problems.

13. **Complete your after-takeoff checklist** to ensure all steps have been followed and your airplane is in the proper configuration for the continued climbout.

    a. This may be included in the climb checklist or a separate checklist.
    b. Follow the checklist in your *POH*.

C. Common errors during a soft-field takeoff and climb

    1. **Improper initial positioning of the flight controls or wing flaps.**

        a. The control yoke should be held in the full back position and turned into the crosswind (if appropriate).

        b. If wing flaps are recommended by your *POH* they should be lowered prior to the taxiing onto the takeoff path.

2. **Allowing the airplane to stop on the takeoff surface prior to initiating takeoff.**

    a.   Once stopped, your airplane may become bogged down and may not have the power to begin rolling again.

3. **Improper power application.**

    a.   Power must be used throughout the entire ground operation in a positive and safe manner.

    b.   Power must be applied smoothly and as quickly as the engine will accept (without faltering).

    c.   Remember, the goal is to get your airplane airborne as quickly as possible.

4. **Inappropriate removal of hand from throttle.**

    a.   Keep your hand on the throttle at all times except

        1)   Flap retraction.
        2)   Gear retraction.
        3)   Trim adjustment.

5. **Poor directional control.**

    a.   Maintain the center of the takeoff path by use of the rudder.
    b.   Divide your attention between the soft-field takeoff and directional control.

6. **Improper use of brakes.**

    a.   Brakes should never be used on a soft field.
    b.   Keep your feet off the brakes.

7. **Improper pitch attitude during liftoff.**

    a.   You must slowly lower the nose after liftoff to allow the airplane to accelerate in ground effect.

        1)   If done too quickly you will settle back on the runway.

    b.   Attempting to climb without the proper airspeed may cause you to settle back onto the runway due to the increase in drag.

8. **Settling back to takeoff surface after becoming airborne.**

    a.   Reduction of takeoff performance.
    b.   A wheel digging in, causing an upset of the airplane.
    c.   Side loads on the landing gear if in a crosswind crab.
    d.   A gear-up landing or a prop strike if the landing gear is retracted early.

9. **Failure to establish and maintain proper climb configuration and airspeed.**

    a.   Follow the procedures in your *POH*.

    b.   You must fly your airplane by the numbers, failure to do so means reduced performance which may be devastating on a short soft-field takeoff with an obstacle.

10. **Drift during climbout.**

    a.   Maintain the extended center of the takeoff path to avoid other obstacles.

    b.   Other pilots in the traffic pattern will be expecting this, which leads to collision avoidance.

END OF TASK -- END OF CHAPTER

CHAPTER V
CROSS-COUNTRY FLYING

V.A. Pilotage and Dead Reckoning 276
V.B. Radio Navigation 282
V.C. Diversion 294
V.D. Lost Procedures 297

This chapter explains the four tasks (A-D) of Cross-Country Flying. These tasks include both knowledge and skill.

Each objective of a task lists, in sequence, the important elements that must be satisfactorily performed. The object includes:

1. Specifically what you should be able to do.
2. The conditions under which the task is to be performed.
3. The minimum acceptable standards of performance.

Be confident. You have prepared diligently and are better prepared and more skilled than the average private pilot applicant. Your examiner will base your ability to perform these tasks on the following.

1. Executing the task within your airplane's capabilities and limitations, including use of the airplane's systems.
2. Piloting your airplane with smoothness and accuracy.
3. Exercising good judgment.
4. Applying your aeronautical knowledge.
5. Showing mastery of your airplane within the standards outlined in this area of operation, with the successful outcome of a task never seriously in doubt.

Most pilots take pride in their ability to navigate with precision. To execute a flight which follows a predetermined plan directly to the destination and arrive safely with no loss of time because of poor navigation is a source of real satisfaction. Lack of navigational skill could lead to unpleasant and sometimes dangerous situations in which adverse weather, approaching darkness, or fuel shortage may force a pilot to attempt a landing under hazardous conditions.

Your examiner is required to test you on all four tasks. Each task is reproduced verbatim from the FAA Practical Test Standards in a shaded box. General discussion is presented under "A. General Information." This is followed by "B. Task Objectives," which is a detailed discussion of each element of the FAA's task.

PILOTAGE AND DEAD RECKONING

V.A. TASK: PILOTAGE AND DEAD RECKONING

PILOT OPERATION - 7

REFERENCES: AC 61-21, AC 61-23.

Objective. To determine that the applicant:

1. Exhibits knowledge by explaining pilotage and dead reckoning techniques and procedures.

2. Follows the preplanned course solely by visual reference to landmarks.

3. Identifies landmarks by relating the surface features to chart symbols.

4. Navigates by means of precomputed headings, groundspeed, and elapsed time.

5. Combines pilotage and dead reckoning.

6. Verifies the airplane position within 3 NM of the flight planned route at all times.

7. Arrives at the en route checkpoints and destination ±5 min. of the initial or revised ETA.

8. Corrects for, and records, the differences between preflight fuel, groundspeed, and heading calculations and those determined en route.

9. Maintains the selected altitudes, within ±200 ft.

10. Maintains the desired heading, ±10°.

11. Follows the climb, cruise, and descent checklists.

A. General Information

1. This is one of four tasks (A-D) in this area of operation. Your examiner is required to test you on this task.

2. *Pilot Operation - 7* refers to FAR 61.107(a)(7): Cross-country flying using pilotage, dead reckoning, and radio aids, including one 2-hour flight.

3. FAA References

AC 61-21: Flight Training Handbook
AC 61-23: Pilot's Handbook of Aeronautical Knowledge

4. The objective of this task is for you to demonstrate your ability to navigate by use of pilotage and/or dead reckoning techniques and procedures.

5. You will not be required to fly an entire cross-country flight. Instead, your examiner will have you depart on the cross-country flight which you planned during the oral portion, and evaluate your ability to navigate by having you fly to the first several checkpoints.

B. Task Objectives

1. **Exhibit your knowledge by explaining pilotage and dead reckoning techniques and procedures.**

    a. *Pilotage* is when you fly cross-country using only your sectional chart and flying from one visible landmark to another.

        1) This may require you to fly at a comparatively low altitude so that landmarks can be seen.

            a) Pilotage cannot be used effectively in areas which lack prominent landmarks, or under conditions of low visibility.

        2) Pilotage is used when landmarks are used to identify en route checkpoints as discussed in Task I.D., Cross-Country Flight Planning, on page 114.

            a) During your flight, you will use pilotage in conjunction with dead reckoning to verify your calculations and keep track of your position.

    b. *Dead reckoning* is the navigation of your airplane solely by means of computations based on true airspeed, course, heading, wind direction and speed, groundspeed, and elapsed time.

        1) Simply, dead reckoning is a system of determining where the airplane should be on the basis of where it has been.

            a) Literally, it is deduced reckoning, which is where the term came from, i.e., ded. or "dead" reckoning.

        2) The dead reckoning procedure is done during the preflight planning, as discussed in Task I.D., Cross-Country Flight Planning, on page 114, and while en route.

            a) During the preflight, you determine the true course, wind correction angle, true heading, variation, magnetic heading, estimated groundspeed, estimated time en route, and estimate fuel consumption.

            b) During your flight, you keep track of your actual compass heading and the time.

                i)   From this you can determine the actual wind conditions, ground-speed, time en route, and fuel consumption.

                ii) Thus, you can deduce when you will arrive at your next checkpoint and the amount of fuel that will be used.

        3) A good knowledge of the principles of dead reckoning will assist you in determining your position after having become disoriented or confused.

            a) By using information from the part of the flight already completed, it is possible to restrict your search for identifiable landmarks to a limited area to verify calculations and to locate yourself.

2. **Follow the preplanned course solely by visual reference to landmarks.**

    a. As discussed above, this refers to pilotage.

    b. Pilotage is accomplished by selecting two landmarks on your desired course, and then maneuvering your airplane so that the two landmarks are kept aligned over the nose of your airplane.

        1) Before the first of the two landmarks is reached, another more distant landmark should be selected and a second course is steered.

    c. Pilotage can also be used by flying over, left/right, or between two checkpoints to fly a straight line.

3. **Identify landmarks by relating the surface features to chart symbols.**

   a. The topographical information presented on sectional charts portrays surface elevation levels (contours and elevation tinting) and a great number of visual landmarks used for VFR flight.

      1) These include airports, cities or towns, rivers and lakes, roads, railroads, and other distinctive landmarks.

      2) Throughout your training, and especially on your cross-country flights, you should have been using your chart to identify landmarks and cross-checking with other landmarks nearby.

   b. The following information appears on the legend of each sectional chart. These are landmarks that may be selected by you to use as checkpoints.

      1) Airports.

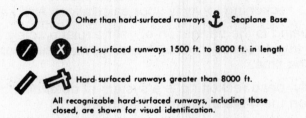

      2) Topographical information.

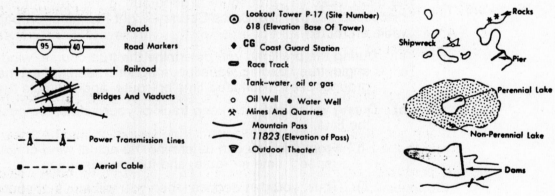

      3) Obstructions.

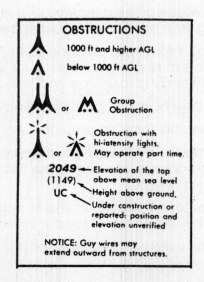

4. **Navigate by means of precomputed headings, groundspeed, and elapsed time.**

   a. As discussed earlier in this task, this refers to navigation by dead reckoning.

   b. During your cross-country preflight planning, you would have used all of the available information (e.g., winds aloft forecast, performance charts) to determine a heading, groundspeed, and elapsed time from your departure point to your destination.

   c. While en route you will maintain your heading and keep track of your time between checkpoints.

      1) During this time you will be able to compute your actual elapsed time, groundspeed, and fuel consumption.

      2) From this information you should recompute your estimated time en route (ETE) to your next checkpoint/destination and deduce when you will be there.

   d. Remember, you are determining where your airplane should be on the basis of where it has been.

5. **Combine pilotage and dead reckoning.**

   a. The most common form of VFR navigation is a combination of pilotage and dead reckoning.

   b. The course flown and the airplane's position are calculated by dead reckoning and then constantly corrected for error and variables after visually checking nearby landmarks (i.e., pilotage).

6. *Verify the airplane position within 3 NM of the flight planned route at all times.*

   a. After takeoff and initial climb are completed, you should maneuver your airplane on your desired course as soon as practicable.

      1) This is mainly done by pilotage.

      2) Once on the proper track, refine your heading by using your precomputed heading.

   b. During your flight you should know what landmarks should be ahead, to the right, and to the left of your airplane.

   c. By constantly dividing your attention between looking for other traffic, cockpit procedures, and navigating, you should have no problem in maintaining your route within 3 NM.

      1) Always be aware of where yo have been and where you are going. Use landmarks all around you to help maintain your planned route.

7. *Arrive at the en route checkpoints and destination ±5 min. of the initial or revised ETA.*

   a. Once en route, you must mark down the time over each checkpoint.

   b. Since you already know the distance between the checkpoints, you can now use your flight computer to determine your actual groundspeed.

   c. Using the new groundspeed, you now need to revise your ETA to your next checkpoint and destination.

8. **Correct for, and record, the differences between preflight fuel, groundspeed, and heading calculations and those determined en route.**

a.   Use a flight log when conducting a cross-country flight. An example of a flight log is shown below. Feel free to photocopy it to use on your cross-country flights.

FLIGHT LOG

		PREFLIGHT					Dist.		Est. GS	Time		Est. Fuel	ENROUTE					
From	To	True Course	Wind Corr.	True Head.	Var.	Mag. Head.	Log	Total		Log	Total		Act'l. Time	Act'l. GS	Dist. Next Pt.	Est. Arrv'l.	Fuel Used	Fuel Remain

Weather Reports	Winds Aloft	Radio and Navigation Frequencies
Terminal Forecasts	NOTAMS	

1)   Note that the top half is the actual "flight log."

2)   The left two-thirds of the top is completed during your preflight preparation, and the right third of the top is completed while you are en route.

a)   The distance to the next point column should also be filled in during the planning phase.

b.   Over each checkpoint write the actual time and determine the actual groundspeed.

c.   Determine the actual fuel used and revise your preflight calculations to determine that the fuel remaining will meet the fuel requirements for the flight.

d.   Complete your flight log as the flight progresses.

9. *Maintain the selected altitudes, within ±200 ft.*

a.   While conducting your cross-country flight you are required to maintain your selected cruising altitude ±200 ft.

b.   Remember to divide your attention to all of your duties, but your primary duty is to maintain control of your airplane.

1) Some pilots become too involved in looking at their charts, flight log, and flight computer that they forget to look up, and when they do, they discover that the airplane is in an unusual flight attitude.

2) Aviate first, then navigate.

10. *Maintain the desired heading, ±10°.*

a. Make the needed adjustments to the heading to maintain your selected route, and maintain that heading.

11. Follow the climb, cruise, and descent checklists.

a. You must follow the checklists found in Section 4, Normal Procedures, of your *POH*.
b. The following checklists are from the Beech Skipper *POH*.

BEECHCRAFT SKIPPER 77
CLIMB

1. Power -- SET
2. Mixture -- LEAN TO MAXIMUM RPM
3. Engine Temperature -- MONITOR
4. Fuel Boost Pump -- OFF

For Academic Illustration/Training Purposes Only!
For Flight: Use your Pilot's Operating Handbook and FAA-Approved Airplane Flight Manual.

BEECHCRAFT SKIPPER 77
CRUISE

1. Power -- SET as desired (use tables in Performance Section)
2. Mixture -- LEAN TO MAXIMUM RPM

For Academic Illustration/Training Purposes Only!
For Flight: Use your Pilot's Operating Handbook and FAA-Approved Airplane Flight Manual.

BEECHCRAFT SKIPPER 77
DESCENT

1. Altimeter -- SET
2. Power -- SET as desired (avoid prolonged idle settings)
3. Carburetor Heat -- FULL HOT or FULL COLD, AS REQUIRED
4. Mixture -- ENRICH for smooth operation
5. Windshield Defroster -- AS REQUIRED

For Academic Illustration/Training Purposes Only!
For Flight: Use your Pilot's Operating Handbook and FAA-Approved Airplane Flight Manual.

END OF TASK

RADIO NAVIGATION

V.B. TASK: RADIO NAVIGATION

    PILOT OPERATION - 7

    REFERENCES: AC 61-21, AC 61-23.

Objective. To determine that the applicant:

1. Exhibits knowledge by explaining radio navigation, equipment, procedures, and limitations.
2. Selects and identifies the desired radio facility.
3. Locates position relative to the radio navigation facility.
4. Intercepts and tracks a given radial or bearing.
5. Locates position using cross radials or bearings.
6. Recognizes or describes the indication of station passage.
7. Recognizes signal loss and takes appropriate action.
8. Maintains the appropriate altitude, ±200 ft.

A. General Information

    1. This is one of four tasks (A-D) in this area of operation. Your examiner is required to test you on this task.

    2. *Pilot Operation - 7* refers to FAR 61.107(a)(7): Cross-country flying, using pilotage, dead reckoning, and radio aids, including one 2-hour flight.

    3. FAA References

        AC 61-21: Flight Training Handbook
        AC 61-23: Pilot's Handbook of Aeronautical Knowledge

    4. The objective of this task is for you to demonstrate your ability to properly use the radio navigation equipment installed in your airplane.

    5. The most common radio navigation equipment in trainer-type airplanes are the VOR (VHF Omnidirectional Range) and the ADF (Automatic Direction Finder). Due to its decreasing cost and improved reliability, LORAN (Long Range Navigation) is gaining popularity. We will limit our discussion to the VOR and ADF.

        a. Although precision navigation is obtainable through the proper use of this equipment, you should only use this equipment to supplement navigation by pilotage and dead reckoning.

B. Task Objectives

   1. **Exhibit your knowledge by explaining radio navigation, equipment, procedures, and limitations.**

      a. Radio navigation is a means of navigation by utilizing the properties of radio waves.

         1) This is achieved by a combination of ground and airborne equipment, by means of which the ground facilities transmit signals to airborne equipment (e.g., VOR and ADF).

            a) You then determine and control ground track on the basis of the instrument indications.

      b. Ground and airborne equipment used for the VOR and ADF.

         1) VOR equipment.

            a) The ground station looks like an inverted ice cream cone about 30 ft. in height and normally white in color.

               i) It transmits within a VHF frequency band of 108.0 to 117.95 MHz.

            b) The airplane equipment includes a receiver with a tuning device and a VOR navigation instrument which consists of

               i) Omnibearing selector (OBS) sometimes referred to as the course selector,

               ii) Course deviation indicator (CDI) needle, and

               iii) A TO-FROM indicator.

         2) ADF equipment.

            a) The ground station is known as a nondirectional beacon (NDB). Standard AM broadcast stations can also be used with the ADF.

               i) NDB stations normally operate in a low or medium frequency band of 190 to 535 kHz.

            b) The airplane equipment consists of a tuner, which is used to set the desired station frequency, and the navigational display. The navigational display consists of

               i) A dial upon which the azimuth is printed, and

               ii) A needle which rotates around the dial and points to the station.

               iii) Some ADF dials can be rotated so as to align the azimuth with the airplane heading, others are fixed with the 0° to 180° points on the azimuth aligned with the airplane's longitudinal axis.

      c. Procedures are basically the same for either navigational aid.

         1) Determine the frequency of the ground station.

            a) This is normally done in your cross-country planning.

            b) Frequencies can be found in the Airport/Facility Directory or on the appropriate sectional chart.

   2) Tune and identify the station.

      a) Identification can positively be made by the VOR or NDB's Morse code identification.

      b) If you cannot identify the station, you should consider any indications as unreliable. Do NOT use unless you have positively identified the station.

   3) Determine your position relative to the station and the radial or bearing you want to be on.

   4) Intercept the appropriate radial or bearing you want and track inbound to, or outbound from, the station.

d. Limitations.

   1) VORs operate on the VHF band and are subject to line-of-sight restrictions, and the range varies proportionally to the altitude of the receiving equipment.

   2) The radio signals from NDB stations are very susceptible to electrical disturbances (lightning) and precipitation static.

      a) These disturbances create excessive static, needle deviations, and signal fades.

      b) At night these stations are vulnerable to interference from distant stations.

2. Select and identify the desired radio facility.

a. VOR and NDB frequencies are found in the Airport/Facility Directory and on sectional charts.

b. The only positive method of identifying a VOR is by its Morse code identification or by the recorded automatic voice identification, which is always indicated by the use of the word "VOR" following its name.

   1) During periods of maintenance, the facility may radiate a T-E-S-T code (– . ... –) or the code may be removed.

c. Positive identification of all radio stations used in conjunction with the ADF is extremely important, especially when using a standard broadcast station for navigation.

   1) You should continuously monitor the NDB's identification when using the ADF.

   2) Nearly all disturbances which affect the ADF bearing also affect the facility's identification. Noisy identification usually occurs when the ADF needle is erratic.

3. Locate your position relative to the radio navigation facility.

a. VOR orientation.

   1) When the OBS is rotated, the CDI needle changes to indicate the position of the radial relative to the airplane, NOT where the airplane is relative to the radial.

      a) If the course selector is rotated until the CDI needle is centered, the radial (magnetic course FROM the station) or its reciprocal (magnetic course TO the station) can be determined.

2) After centering the CDI needle with the OBS, the TO-FROM indicator will indicate either "FROM" the station or "TO" the station.

a) The TO or FROM refers to the airplane's position relative to a line through the VOR perpendicular to the omnibearing direction.

b) If a TO, the airplane is not yet to the VOR, assuming a general direction of flight similar to the omnibearing direction.

c) If a FROM, the airplane is past the VOR assuming a general direction of flight similar to the omnibearing direction.

d) If neutral (i.e., OFF or NAV), the airplane is directly over the VOR.

3) The airplane's heading DOES NOT affect the VOR receiver's indication.

a) The VOR needle does not point to the VOR.

b) The airplane's POSITION (not heading) relative to the VOR DETERMINES the CDI and TO-FROM indications.

4) The diagram below illustrates VOR indications and should be used to interpret VOR indications in flight. Remember that you must "rotate" the diagram so the omnibearing direction is "pointed" in the direction in which your OBS is set.

a) When flying, interpret the needle by envisioning your airplane being on a heading indicated by the OBS.

i) You can immediately tell which quadrant you are in -- TO or FROM, left or right.

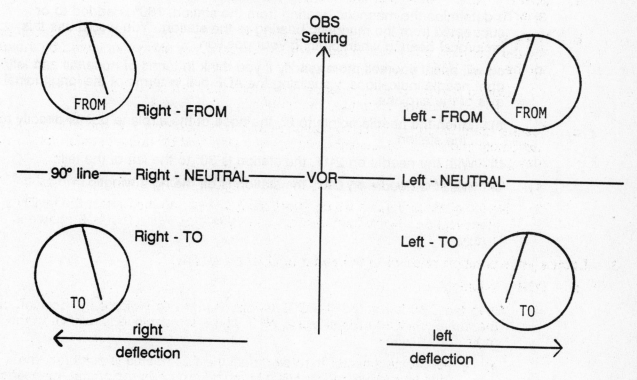

b.   ADF orientation.

1)   Relative bearing is the value to which the indicator (needle) points on the azimuth dial. This value is the angle measured clockwise from the nose of the airplane to a line drawn from the airplane to the station.

a)   In other words, the number of degrees the airplane would have to turn to the right to be pointed at the station.

2)   Magnetic bearing to the station is the angle formed by a line drawn from the airplane to the station and a line drawn from the airplane to magnetic north.

a)   In other words, the magnetic heading the airplane would be on if it were pointed at the station.

b)   The magnetic bearing (MB) to the station can be determined by adding the relative bearing (RB) to the magnetic heading (MH) of the airplane or MB (to) = RB + MH.

i)   EXAMPLE: If the relative bearing is 060° and the magnetic heading is 130°, the magnetic bearing to the station is 190° (060° + 130°). This means that in still air a magnetic heading of approximately 190° would be flown to the station.

c)   If the total is greater than 360°, subtract 360° from the total to obtain the magnetic bearing to the station.

i)   EXAMPLE: If the relative bearing is 270° and magnetic heading is 300°, 360° is subtracted from the total, or 570° − 360° = 210°, which is the magnetic bearing to the station.

3)   To determine the magnetic bearing from the station, 180° is added to or subtracted from the magnetic bearing to the station. You would use this reciprocal bearing when plotting your position.

4)   You will orient yourself more readily if you think in terms of nose/tail and left/ right needle indications, visualizing the ADF dial in terms of the longitudinal axis of the airplane.

a)   When the needle points to 0°, the nose of the airplane points directly to the station.

b)   With the needle on 210°, the station is 30° to the left of the tail.

c)   With the needle on 090°, the station is off the right wingtip.

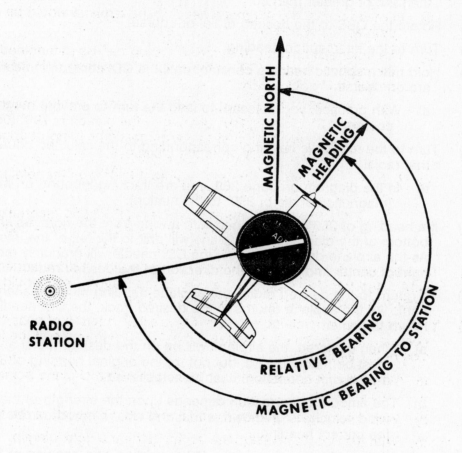

4.   Intercept and track a given radial or bearing.

    a.   VOR radial intercept and tracking, either inbound or outbound.

        1)   Turn to a heading to parallel the desire course, in the same direction as the course to be flown.

        2)   Determine the difference between the radial to be intercepted and the radial on which you are located.

        3)   Double the difference to determine the interception angle but do not use less than 20° or greater than 90°.

        4)   Rotate the OBS to the desired radial or course.

        5)   Turn to the interception heading.

        6)   Hold this magnetic heading constant until the CDI centers, indicating that you are on course.

           a)   With practice, you will learn to lead the turn to prevent overshooting the course.

        7)   Turn to the magnetic heading corresponding to the selected course and track that radial.

           a)   In the diagram on page 289, you are tracking inbound on the 170° radial (magnetic course of 350° to the station).

        8)   If a heading of 350° is maintained with a wind from the right, as shown at the bottom of the diagram, the airplane will drift to the left of the intended track. As the airplane drifts off course, the CDI needle will gradually move to the right of center and indicate the direction of the desired radial.

        9)   To return to the desired radial, the airplane heading must be altered 20° to the right. As the airplane returns to the desired track, the CDI needle will slowly return to center.

           a)   When centered, the airplane will be on the desired radial and a left turn must be made toward, but not to, the original heading of 350° because a wind drift correction must be established.

           b)   The amount of correction depends upon the strength of the wind. If the wind velocity is unknown, a trial and error method can be used to find the correct heading.

           c)   Assume, for this example, a 10° correction or a heading of 360° is maintained.

      10)   While maintaining a heading of 360°, assume that the CDI needle begins to move to the left. This means that the wind correction of 10° is too great and the airplane is flying to the right of course. A slight turn to the left should be made to permit the airplane to return to the desired radial.

      11)   When the CDI needle centers, a smaller wind drift correction of 5°, or a heading of 355°, should be flown. If this correction is adequate, the airplane will remain on the radial. If not, small heading variations should be made to keep the CDI needle centered, and consequently keep the airplane on the radial.

      12)   As the VOR station is passed, the "TO" indication will change to "FROM." If the aircraft passes to one side of the station, the CDI needle will deflect in the direction of the station as the indicator changes to "FROM."

13) Generally, the same techniques apply when tracking outbound as those used for tracking inbound.

a) If the intent is to fly over the station and track outbound on the reciprocal of the inbound radial, the course selector should not be changed. Corrections are made in the same manner to keep the CDI needle centered. The only difference is that the TO-FROM indicator will indicate "FROM."

b) If tracking outbound on a course other than the reciprocal of the inbound radial, this new course or radial must be set in the course selector and a turn made to intercept this course. After this course is reached, tracking procedures are the same as discussed above.

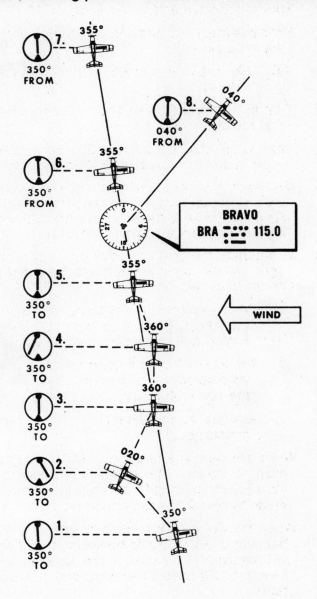

NDB Tracking -- Inbound

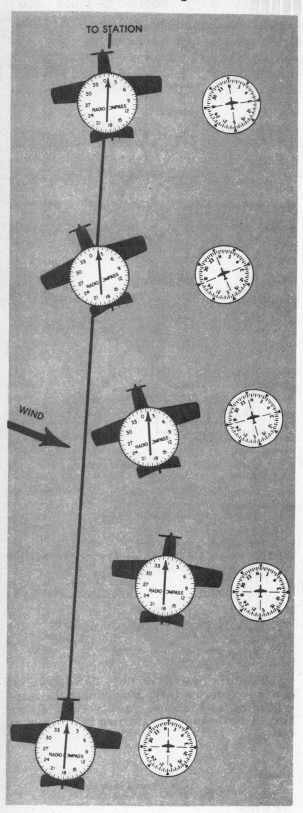

NDB Tracking -- Outbound

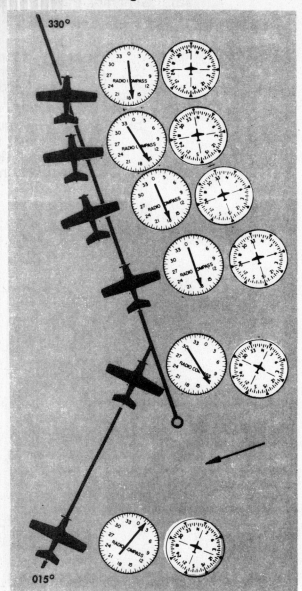

b. NDB bearing interception and tracking.

1) Determine your position in relation to the station by turning to the magnetic heading of the bearing to be intercepted.

2) Note whether the station is to the right or left of the nose to track inbound. Determine the number of degrees of needle deflection from the 0° position, and double this amount for the interception angle.

   a) Interception of an outbound bearing is accomplished in the same manner, except you substitute the 180° position for the 0° position on the ADF dial.

3) Turn your airplane toward the desired magnetic bearing the number of degrees determined for the interception angle.

4) Maintain the interception heading until the needle is deflected the same number of degrees from the zero position as the angle of interception (minus lead appropriate to the rate of bearing change).

5) Turn inbound and continue with tracking.

6) The procedures to track inbound are as follows (see figure on left-hand side of page 290):

   a) Turn airplane until the needle is on zero. Hold this heading until off-course drift is indicated by left or right needle deflection.

   b) When a 5° change in needle deflection is observed, turn 20° in the direction of needle deflection.

   c) When the needle is deflected 20° (deflection = interception angle), track has been intercepted. Turn 10° back toward the inbound course. You are now inbound with a 10° drift correction angle.

   d) If you observe off-course deflection in the original direction, turn again to the original interception heading.

   e) When the desired course has been reintercepted, turn 5° toward the inbound course, proceeding inbound with a 15° drift correction.

   f) If the initial 10° drift correction is excessive, as shown by needle deflection away from the wind, turn to parallel the desired course and let the wind drift you back on course. When the needle is again zeroed, turn into the wind with a reduced drift correction angle.

7) When tracking outbound (see figure on right-hand side of page 290), wind corrections are made similar to tracking to the station but the ADF needle points toward the tail of the airplane or the 180° position on the azimuth dial.

   a) Even though the needle points to the tail, you still turn toward the direction of the deflection.

   b) Attempting to keep the ADF needle on the 180° position during winds results in the airplane flying a curved flight leading further and further from the desired track.

5. **Locate your position using cross radials or bearings.**

   a. One of the main advantages of VOR is that you can quickly and easily locate your airplane's exact position by taking bearings from two VOR stations.

   1) The airplane's position (fix) is where the two bearings cross.

      a) The cross bearings should be as close as 90° to each other for the most accurate fix.

2) Position checks or fixes along a course are most convenient if your airplane is equipped with two VORs.

    a)   One is set to maintain course.

    b)   The second is used to take cross bearings.

3) For uniformity and to avoid confusion, a bearing to establish a fix is best made by using degrees FROM the off-course VOR rather than degrees TO.

    a)   In this manner, the radial can be drawn on your map from the station.

4) Ensure you identify the station each time you switch to a different VOR.

    a)   Always tune and identify.

b. Your ADF can also be used to locate your position.

1) While flying on a VOR radial, obtaining an ADF bearing that crosses the radial will establish a fix.

2) This is advantageous when an off-course VOR is not available for a cross bearing or when the only VOR must be used as the primary tracking system.

6. **Recognize or describe the indication of station passage.**

a. VOR station passage.

1) Approach to the station is indicated by flickering of the TO-FROM indicator and CDI needle as the airplane flies into the "cone of confusion" (no signal area).

    a)   The extent of the cone of confusion, an inverted cone, increases with altitude. Thus, flight through the cone of confusion varies from a few seconds at low levels to as much as 2 min. at high altitude.

2) Station passage is shown by complete reversal of the TO-FROM indicator.

b. NDB (ADF) station passage.

1) The closer you are to the station, the more aggravated are your errors in drift correction.

2) When you are close to the NDB, slight deviations from the desired track result in large deflections of the azimuth needle.

3) When the needle begins to rotate steadily toward a wingtip position or shows erratic left/right oscillations, you should maintain a constant heading.

4) Station passage is when the needle shows either wingtip position or settles at or near the 180° position.

    a)   The time interval from the first indication of station proximity to positive station passage varies with altitude (e.g., a few seconds at low levels to 3 min. at high altitude).

7. **Recognize signal loss and take appropriate action.**

a. VOR

1) Indications of signal loss.

    a)   A red flag or OFF indication will appear in the area of the TO-FROM indicator near the CDI.

    b)   The CDI needle may swing from side to side.

    c)   The TO-FROM indicator may settle in a neutral position and may not move from there, even though the receiver is tuned to the proper frequency.

2) These visual warnings indicate that the received signal is too weak to give reliable indications.

3) This may be caused by obstacles that interfere with the line-of-sight transmission, or the airplane is too low or too far away from the station.

4) You should tune and identify the next VOR on the course and maintain a constant heading toward that station until the flag alarm disappears and the CDI needle comes to rest.

b. ADF

1) Since ADF receivers do not have any signals to warn you when erroneous bearing information is being displayed, you should continuously monitor the NDB's identification.

2) If you can no longer hear the Morse code identifier, you should assume that the bearing information is no longer reliable.

a) Tune and identify the next NDB along your course and once you identify it, then continuously monitor that station.

8. Maintain the appropriate altitude, ±200 ft.

a. You must divide your attention between using and interpreting the radio navigation instruments and flying your airplane.

C. Common errors using radio navigation

1. Improper tuning and identification of station.

a. The only positive way to know you are receiving signals from the proper station is to verify its Morse code identifier.

2. Poor orientation.

a. This is caused by not following the proper orientation procedures and not understanding the operating principles of the radio navigation instrument.

3. Overshooting and undershooting radials/bearings during interception.

a. When using a VOR, this is due to not learning how to lead your turn to the desired heading.

b. When using an ADF, this error is often due to forgetting the course interception angle used.

4. Failure to recognize station passage.

a. Know where you are at all times and anticipate station passage.

5. Failure to recognize signal loss.

a. The VOR TO-FROM indicator will show a neutral or off position. An alarm flag may appear on some VORs.

1) All these indicate that your equipment is reading unreliable signals.

b. With the ADF, you must monitor the NDB's Morse code identification at all times.

1) If you cannot hear the identifier, you must not use that NDB station for navigation.

END OF TASK

DIVERSION

V.C. TASK: DIVERSION

PILOT OPERATION - 7

REFERENCES: AC 61-21, AC 61-23.

Objective. To determine that the applicant:

1. Exhibits knowledge by explaining the procedures for diverting, including the recognition of adverse weather conditions.

2. Selects an appropriate alternate airport and route.

3. Diverts toward the alternate airport promptly.

4. Makes a reasonable estimate of heading, groundspeed, arrival time, and fuel consumption to the alternate airport.

5. Maintains the appropriate altitude, ±200 ft.

A. General Information

1. This is one of four tasks (A-D) in this area of operation. Your examiner is required to test you on this task.

2. *Pilot Operation - 7* refers to FAR 61.107(a)(7): Cross-country flying using pilotage, dead reckoning, and radio aids, including one 2-hour flight.

3. FAA References

    AC 61-21: Flight Training Handbook
    AC 61-23: Pilot's Handbook of Aeronautical Knowledge

4. The objective of the maneuver is for you to demonstrate your knowledge of the procedures for diverting to an alternate airport.

5. Among the aeronautical skills that you must have is the ability to plot courses in flight to alternate destinations when continuation of the flight to the original destination is impracticable.

    a. Reasons include

        1) Low fuel,
        2) Bad weather,
        3) Your own or passenger fatigue, illness, etc.,
        4) Airplane system or equipment malfunction, and
        5) Any other reason that you decide to divert to an alternate airport.

    b. The diversion may be accomplished by means of pilotage, dead reckoning, and/or radio navigation aids.

B. Task Objectives

1. **Exhibit your knowledge by explaining the procedures for diverting, including the recognition of adverse weather conditions.**

    a. Procedures for diverting

        1) Confirm your present position on your sectional chart.

        2) Select your alternate airport and estimate a heading to put you on course.

        3) Write down the time and turn to your new heading.

        4) Use a straightedge to draw a new course line on your chart.

     5)   Refine your heading by using pilotage and maximum use of available radio navigation aids.

     6)   Compute new estimated groundspeed, arrival time, and fuel consumption to your alternate airport.

  b.   Recognizing adverse weather conditions.

     1)   Adverse weather conditions are those conditions that decrease visibility and/or cloud ceiling height.

     2)   Understanding your preflight weather forecasts will enable you to look for signs of adverse weather (e.g., clouds, wind changes, precipitation).

     3)   Contact the nearest FSS or en route flight advisory service (EFAS) for updated weather information.

     4)   At the first sign of deteriorating weather, you should divert to an alternate. Attempting to remain VFR while the ceiling and visibility are getting below VFR minimums is a dangerous practice.

     5)   In order to remain VFR, you may be forced to lower altitudes and possibly marginal visibility. It is here that visibility relates to time as much as distance.

        a)   At 95 kt., your airplane travels 160 ft./sec.; thus, related to 1 mi. visibility, you can see 33 sec. ahead.

           i)   This decreases as speed increases and/or visibility decreases.

        b)   It takes about 5 sec. for you to see something until you apply control pressure.

        c)   It also takes valuable distance for your airplane to turn, if you are trying to avoid an obstacle or cloud bank.

           i)   At 154 kt., your airplane will travel approximately 2,457 ft. in 90° of turn.

        d)   If you find yourself in decreasing visibility, you should slow your airplane enough to maintain full control of your airplane.

        e)   A rule of thumb for determining visibility -- when the surface is just visible over the nose of your airplane, the forward visibility is approximately 1 mi. for each 1,000 ft. of altitude (AGL).

2.   Select an appropriate alternate airport and route.

  a.   You should continuously monitor your position on your section chart and the proximity of useful alternative airports.

  b.   Check the maximum elevation figure (MEF) in each latitude-longitude quadrant of your route to determine the minimum safe altitude.

     1)   MEF is expressed in ft. MSL, which will enable you to make a quick determination by checking your altimeter.

  c.   Determine that your alternate airport will meet the needs of the situation.

     1)   If the diversion is due to weather, ensure your alternate is in an area of good weather; otherwise, you may be forced into the same situation again.

3. **Divert toward the alternate airport promptly.**

   a. Once you have decided on the best alternate airport, you should immediately estimate the magnetic course and turn to that heading.

   b. The longer you wait, the few advantages or benefits of making the diversion.

   c. In the event the diversion results from an emergency, it is vital to divert to the new course as soon as possible.

4. **Make a reasonable estimate of heading, groundspeed, arrival time, and fuel consumption to the alternate airport.**

   a. Courses to alternates can be estimated with reasonable accuracy using a straightedge and the compass roses shown at VOR stations on the sectional chart.

      1) The VOR radials and airway courses (already oriented to magnetic direction) printed on the chart can be used satisfactorily for approximation of magnetic bearings during VFR flights.

      2) Remember that the VOR radial or printed airway direction is **outbound** from the station. The course **to** the station is the reciprocal of the radial.

      3) Distances can be determined by using the measurements on a plotter, or by estimating point to point with a pencil and then measuring the approximate distance on the mileage scale at the bottom of the chart.

   b. If radio aids are used to divert to an alternate, the pilot should

      1) Select the appropriate facility.
      2) Tune to the proper frequency.
      3) Determine the course or radial to intercept or follow.

   c. Once established on your new course, use the known (or forecasted) wind conditions to determine an estimated groundspeed, ETA, and fuel consumption to your alternate airport.

      1) Update as you pass over your newly selected checkpoints.

5. *Maintain the appropriate altitude, ±200 ft.*

   a. Adjust your cruising altitude appropriately to your new magnetic course, if appropriate.

C. Common errors during a diversion

   1. **Not recognizing adverse weather conditions.**

      a. Any weather that is below the forecast has a potential to become an adverse weather condition.

      b. Any doubts of the weather, get an update from the nearest FSS or EFAS (Flight Watch).

   2. **Delaying the decision to divert to an alternate.**

      a. As soon as you suspect, or become uneasy of, a situation where you may have to divert, you should decide on an alternate airport and proceed there directly.

      b. A delay will decrease your alternatives.

END OF TASK

LOST PROCEDURES

V.D. TASK: LOST PROCEDURES

       PILOT OPERATION - 7

       REFERENCES: AC 61-21, AC 61-23.

Objective. To determine that the applicant:

1. Exhibits knowledge by explaining lost procedures, including the reasons for --

    a. Maintaining the original or an appropriate heading, identifying landmarks, and climbing, if necessary.

    b. Proceeding to and identifying the nearest concentration of prominent landmarks.

    c. Using available radio navigation aids or contacting an appropriate facility for assistance.

    d. Planning a precautionary landing if deteriorating visibility and/or fuel exhaustion is imminent.

2. Selects the best course of action when given a lost situation.

A.   General Information

    1.   This is one of four tasks (A-D) in this area of operation. Your examiner is required to test you on this task.

    2.   *Pilot Operation - 7* refers to FAR 61.107(a)(7): Cross-country flying using pilotage, dead reckoning, and radio aids, including one 2-hour flight.

    3.   FAA References

        AC 61-21: Flight Training Handbook
        AC 61-23: Pilot's Handbook of Aeronautical Knowledge

    4.   Nobody wants to get lost, especially in an airplane, but all pilots occasionally find themselves disoriented. The skill needed is to recognize disorientation quickly and then implement corrective action to become reoriented.

    5.   Steps to avoid becoming lost:

        a.   Always know where you are.

        b.   Plan ahead and know what your next landmark will be and look for it.

            1)   Similarly, anticipate the indication of your radio navigation aids.

        c.   If your radio navigation aids OR your visual observations of landmarks do not confirm your expectations, become concerned and take action.

B.   Task Objectives

1.   **Exhibit your knowledge by explaining the reasons for the following lost procedures.**

a.   **Maintain the original or an appropriate heading, identifying landmarks, and climbing, if necessary.**

1)   When unsure of your position, you should continue to fly the original heading and watch for recognizable landmarks, while rechecking the calculated position.

2)   By plotting the estimated distance and compass direction flown from your last noted checkpoint as though there was no wind, the point so determined will be the center of a circle within which your airplane's position may be located.

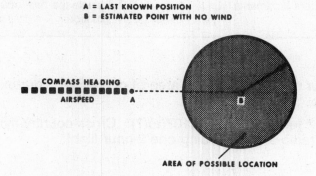

A = LAST KNOWN POSITION
B = ESTIMATED POINT WITH NO WIND

COMPASS HEADING
AIRSPEED   A

AREA OF POSSIBLE LOCATION

a)   This is often called a "circle of error."

b)   If you are certain the wind is no more than 30 kt., and it has been less than 30 min. since the last known checkpoint was crossed, the radius of the circle should be approximately 15 NM.

3)   Continue straight ahead and check the landmarks within this circle.

a)   The most likely position will be downwind from your desired course.

b.   **Proceed to and identify the nearest concentration of prominent landmarks.**

1)   If the above procedure fails to identify your position, you should change course toward the nearest concentration of prominent landmarks shown on your chart.

2)   If you have a very long known landmark, e.g., coastline, interstate highway, etc., you need to proceed toward it.

3)   Maintain the minimum safe altitudes.

4)   When a landmark is recognized, or a probable fix obtained, you should at first use the information both cautiously and profitably.

a)   No abrupt change in course should be made until a second or third landmark is positively identified to corroborate the first.

c. **Use available radio navigation aids or contact an appropriate facility for assistance.**

   1) Use all available VOR and/or NDB stations to locate your position.

      a) You must tune and properly identify each station.

      b) When using a VOR, center the CDI needle with a FROM indication and then draw a line on your chart from the VOR station outward on the shown radial.

      c) With the ADF, ensure your heading indicator is correctly set to your magnetic compass and determine the magnetic bearing to the station. The add or subtract 180° to have the magnetic bearing from the station and draw the line on your chart.

      d) Now select another station as close to 90° from the first. Repeat the process as described above and where the two lines intersect is your position.

      e) You can also fly to one of these stations if you want.

      f) Use your chart to confirm with the landmarks and proceed.

   2) If you encounter a *distress* or *urgent* condition, you can obtain assistance by contacting an ATC or FSS facility, or use the emergency frequency of 121.5 MHz.

      a) An urgent condition is when you are concerned about safety and require timely but not immediate assistance. This is a potential distress condition.

         i) Begin your transmission by announcing PAN-PAN three times.

      b) A distress condition is when you feel threatened by serious and/or imminent danger and require immediate assistance.

         i) Begin your transmission by announcing MAYDAY three times.

      c) If your airplane has a transponder and you are unable to immediately establish communications with ATC or FSS, squawk 7700 (emergency).

      d) If weather conditions permit, climb for improved communications and better radar and direction finding (DF) detection.

      e) After establishing contact, work with the person you are talking to. Remain calm, cooperate, and remain in VFR conditions.

      f) These ground stations are ready and willing to help, and there is no penalty for using them. Delay in asking for help has often caused accidents.

d. **Planning a precautionary landing if deteriorating visibility and/or fuel exhaustion is imminent.**

   1) If these conditions and others (e.g., darkness approaching) threaten, it is recommended that you make a precautionary landing while adequate visibility, fuel, and daylight are still available.

   2) It is most desirable to land at an airport, but if one cannot be found, a suitable field may be used.

      a) Prior to an off-airport landing, you should first survey the area for obstructions or other hazards.

2. **Select the best course of action when given a lost situation.**

    a.   As soon as you begin to wonder where you are, remember the point at which you last were confident of your location.

        1) Watch your heading. Know what it is and keep it constant.
        2) Do not panic. You are not "lost" yet.
        3) Recompute your expected radio navigation indications and visual landmarks.

            a) Reconfirm your heading (compass and directional gyro).
            b) Confirm correct radio frequencies and settings.
            c) Review your sectional chart, noting last confirmed landmark.

        4) Attempt to reconfirm present position.

    b.   You should use all available means to determine your present location. This includes asking for assistance.

    c.   The best course of action will depend on factors such as ceiling, visibility, hours of daylight remaining, fuel remaining, etc.

        1) Given the current circumstances, you will be the only one to decide the best course of action.
        2) Understand and respect your own and your airplane's limitations.

C. Common errors during lost procedures

    1. **Attempting to fly to where you assume your checkpoint is located.**

        a.   Maintain your current heading and use available radio navigation aids and pilotage procedures to determine your position.

        b.   Blindly searching tends to compound itself and leads to a panic situation.

    2. **Proceeding into marginal VFR weather conditions.**

        a.   Use a 180° turn to avoid marginal weather conditions.

    3. **Failure to ask for help.**

        a.   At any time you are unsure of your position, ask for help.

        b.   Do not let pride get in the way of safety.

        c.   Recognizing and seeking assistance is a sign of a mature, competent, and safe pilot.

END OF TASK -- END OF CHAPTER

CHAPTER VI
FLIGHT BY REFERENCE TO INSTRUMENTS

VI.A.   Straight-and-Level Flight 306
VI.B.   Straight, Constant Airspeed Climbs 309
VI.C.   Straight, Constant Airspeed Descents 313
VI.D.   Turns to Headings 317
VI.E.   Unusual Flight Attitudes 321
VI.F.   Radio Aids and Radar Services 326

This chapter explains the six tasks (A-F) of Flight By Reference to Instruments. These tasks include both knowledge and skill.

Each objective of a task lists, in sequence, the important elements that must be satisfactorily performed. The object includes:

1.   Specifically what you should be able to do.
2.   The conditions under which the task is to be performed.
3.   The minimum acceptable standards of performance.

Be confident. You have prepared diligently and are better prepared and more skilled than the average private pilot applicant. Your examiner will base your ability to perform these tasks on the following.

1.   Executing the task within your airplane's capabilities and limitations, including use of the airplane's systems.

2.   Piloting your airplane with smoothness and accuracy.

3.   Exercising good judgment.

4.   Applying your aeronautical knowledge.

5.   Showing mastery of your airplane within the standards outlined in this area of operation, with the successful outcome of a task never seriously in doubt.

You will be required to demonstrate your ability to maneuver your airplane for limited periods by reference solely to flight instruments, recover from unusual attitudes, and follow radar and direction finding (DF) instructions from ATC or an FSS specialist. You may also be asked to track inbound or outbound on a VOR radial or NDB bearing while flying by reference solely to flight instruments.

You must understand that this training in the use of flight instruments does not prepare you for unrestricted operations in instrument weather conditions. It is intended as an emergency measure only (although it is also excellent training in the smooth control of an airplane). Intentional flight in such conditions should be attempted only by those who have been thoroughly trained and hold their instrument rating.

Accident investigations reveal that weather continues to be cited as a factor in general aviation accidents more frequently than any other cause. The data also show that weather-involved accidents are more likely to result in fatalities than are other accidents. Low ceilings, rain, and fog continue to head the list in the fatal, weather-involved, general aviation accidents. This type of accident is usually the result of inadequate preflight preparation and/or planning, continued VFR flight into adverse weather conditions, and attempted operation beyond the pilot's experience/ability level.

Our orientation senses are not designed to cope with flight when external visual references are obscured unless visual reference is transferred to the flight instruments. The motion sensing by the inner ear in particular tends to confuse us. False sensations often are generated, leading you to believe the attitude of your airplane has changed when, in fact, it has not. These sensations result in spatial disorientation, or vertigo.

The flight instruments are divided into the following three categories.

1. Pitch instruments:

   Attitude Indicator (AI)
   Altimeter (ALT)
   Airspeed Indicator (ASI)
   Vertical-Speed Indicator (VSI)

2. Bank Instruments:

   Attitude Indicator (AI)
   Heading Indicator (HI)
   Turn Coordinator (TC) or Turn-and-Slip Indicator (T&SI)
   Magnetic Compass

3. Power Instruments:

   Tachometer (RPM)
   Airspeed Indicator (ASI)

When you are forced to fly without visual references, you must rely totally on your flight instruments. The attitude indicator (AI) should be your primary reference instrument for the control of your airplane, just as the real horizon is used in visual conditions. Your CFI will have his/her suggested approach to the instrument scan. You should write down, i.e., pencil and paper, your scan -- what you do and why. This will force you to think through "what and why" and avoid haphazard scanning of your instruments. Your author's suggestion: you always need to know:

1. Your airplane's pitch and bank (AI).
2. Your present heading (HI)

    a. And your desired heading.

3. Your present altitude

    a. And your desired altitude (ALT).

> The instruments below show straight-and-level flight.

The AI is just above the HI, both in the center of the standard flight instrument panel configuration. The ALT is over the VSI, both to the right. The ASI is over the TC (or T&SI), both to the left.

Since your AI is your primary reference instrument and provides you with a quick reference as to your pitch and bank attitude, it should be your start (or home-base) for your instrument scan. You should begin with the AI and scan one instrument (e.g., the HI) and then return to the AI before moving to a different instrument, as shown below.

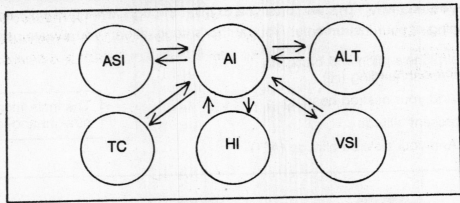

Thus, you continuously visualize your present attitude, heading, altitude in conjunction with your intended heading and altitude.

Last and certainly not least, interrupt your flight instrument scan every few minutes to review all your other instruments, including:

> Compass to HI for precession (reset HI as necessary)
> Engine RPM
> Engine temperatures (oil, cylinder head, and EGT)
> Oil pressure
> Fuel level
> Vacuum pressure
> Ammeter

There are three fundamental skills that you must develop for flight by reference to instruments.

1. Cross-checking -- The continuous and logical observation (scan) of instruments for attitude and performance information.

   a. You maintain your airplane's attitude by reference to instruments for attitude and performance information.

2. Instrument interpretation -- This is how you interpret your observation of the instruments during cross-checking.

   a. This requires you to understand each instrument's construction, operating principle, and relationship to the performance of the airplane.

3. Aircraft control -- This is how you maintain your airplane's attitude (or change it) by interpretation of the instruments. It is composed of three elements.

   a. Pitch control of your airplane about the lateral axis by movement of the elevator or stabilator.

   b. Bank control of your airplane about the longitudinal axis by movement of the ailerons.

   c. Power control of your airplane by use of the throttle when a change in thrust is required.

Keep your grip on the controls relaxed and learn to control with your eyes and your brain as well as your muscles. Keep your attitude changes smooth and small, yet with positive pressure. With the airplane properly trimmed, release all control pressure momentarily whenever you become aware of tenseness.

Your examiner is required to test you on all six tasks. Each task is reproduced verbatim from the FAA Practical Test Standards in a shaded box. General discussion is presented under "A. General Information." This is followed by "B. Task Objectives," which is a detailed discussion of each element of the FAA's task.

STRAIGHT-AND-LEVEL FLIGHT

VI.A. TASK: STRAIGHT-AND-LEVEL FLIGHT

   PILOT OPERATION - 6

   REFERENCES: AC 61-21, AC 61-23, AC 61-27.

Objective. To determine that the applicant:

1. Exhibits knowledge by explaining flight solely by reference to instruments as related to straight-and-level flight.

2. Makes smooth and coordinated control applications.

3. Maintains straight-and-level flight for at least 3 min.

4. Maintains the desired heading, ±10°.

5. Maintains the desired altitude, ±100 ft.

6. Maintains the desired airspeed, ±10 kt.

A. General Information

1. This is one of six tasks (A-F) in this area of operation. Your examiner is required to test you on this task.

2. *Pilot Operation - 6* refers to FAR 61.107(a)(6): Control and maneuvering an airplane solely by reference to instruments, including descents and climbs using radio aids or radar directives.

3. FAA References

      AC 61-21: Flight Training Handbook
      AC 61-23: Pilot's Handbook of Aeronautical Knowledge
      AC 61-27: Instrument Flying Handbook

4. The objective of this task is for you to demonstrate your ability to perform straight-and-level flight solely by reference to instruments.

B. Task Objectives

1. **Exhibit your knowledge by explaining flight solely by reference to instruments as related to straight-and-level flight.**

      a. Straight flight is maintained simply by keeping the wings level with the horizon on the attitude indicator (AI) through coordinated rudder and aileron pressure.

         1) The wings on the turn coordinator (TC) will remain level in straight flight and the ball centered.

         2) The heading indicator (HI) should be checked frequently to ensure a straight flight path (i.e., a constant heading).

      b. Level flight is maintained by reference to several instruments.

         1) The altimeter (ALT) shows whether a constant altitude is being maintained or the altitude is changing.

         2) The vertical speed indicator (VSI) indicates the rate at which altitude is changing.

         3) If level flight is not indicated, apply elevator pressure to adjust the pitch by reference to the AI.

            a) Elevator pressure should be very slight to avoid overcontrolling.

      c. Steady airspeed is maintained by holding a constant power (RPM) setting.

d.   The figure below illustrates the instrument indications for straight-and-level flight.

2.   **Make smooth and coordinated control applications.**

a.   You will need to learn to overcome a natural tendency to make a large control movement for a pitch change, and learn to apply small control pressures smoothly, cross-checking rapidly for the results of the change, and continuing with the pressures as your instruments show the desired results at a rate that you can interpret.

   1)   Small pitch changes can be easily controlled, stopped, and corrected.
   2)   Large changes are more difficult to control.

b.   Coordination of controls requires that the ball of the TC be kept centered and that the available trim control devices be used whenever a change in flight conditions disturbs the existing trim.

   1)   Trim is used to relieve all possible control pressures held after a desired attitude has been attained.

   2)   The pressure you feel on the control yoke must be that which you apply while controlling a planned change in airplane attitude, not pressure held because you are letting the airplane control you.

3.   *Maintain straight-and-level flight for at least 3 min.*

4.   *Maintain the desired heading, ±10°.*

5.   *Maintain the desired altitude, ±100 ft.*

6.   *Maintain the desired airspeed, ±10 kt.*

C. Common errors during straight-and-level flight by reference to instruments

1. **Fixation, omission, and emphasis errors during instrument cross-check.**

    a. Fixation, or staring at a single instrument, usually occurs for a good reason, but with poor results.

        1) You may stare at the ALT which indicates 200 ft. below your assigned altitude, wondering how the needle got there. During that time, perhaps with increasing tension on the controls, a heading change occurs unnoticed, and more errors may accumulate.

    b. Omission of an instrument from your cross-check may be caused by a failure to anticipate significant instrument indications following attitude changes.

    c. Emphasis on a single instrument, instead of on the combination of instruments necessary for attitude information, is normal in your initial stages of flight solely by reference to instruments.

        1) You will tend to rely on the instrument you understand the best, e.g., the AI.

2. **Improper instrument interpretation.**

    a. You can avoid this by understanding each instrument's operating principle and relationship to the performance of your airplane.

3. **Improper control applications.**

    a. This normally occurs from incorrectly interpreting the instruments and, thus, applying the improper controls.

    b. Do not disturb a flight attitude until you know what the result will be.

4. **Failure to establish proper pitch, bank, or power adjustments during altitude, heading, or airspeed corrections.**

    a. To prevent this error you must understand which instruments provide information for pitch, bank, and power.

        1) This may indicate that you do not fully understand instrument cross-check, interpretation, and/or control.

5. **Faulty trim technique.**

    a. The trim should not be used as a substitute for control with the control yoke and rudder pedals, but to relieve pressures already held to stabilize attitude.

    b. Use trim frequently and in small amounts.

    c. You cannot feel control pressures with a tight grip on the control yoke.

        1) Relax and learn to control with the eyes and the brain instead of only the muscles.

END OF TASK

STRAIGHT, CONSTANT AIRSPEED CLIMBS

VI.B. TASK: STRAIGHT, CONSTANT AIRSPEED CLIMBS

PILOT OPERATION - 6

REFERENCES: AC 61-21, AC 61-23, AC 61-27.

Objective. To determine that the applicant:

1. Exhibits knowledge by explaining flight solely by reference to instruments as related to straight, constant airspeed climbs.

2. Establishes the climb pitch attitude and power setting on an assigned heading.

3. Makes smooth and coordinated control applications.

4. Maintains the desired heading, ±10°.

5. Maintains the desired airspeed, ±10 kt.

6. Levels off at the desired altitude, ±100 ft.

A. General Information

1. This is one of six tasks (A-F) in this area of operation. Your examiner is required to test you on this task.

2. *Pilot Operation - 6* refers to FAR 61.107(a)(6): Control and maneuvering an airplane solely by reference to instruments, including descents and climbs using radio aids or radar directives.

3. FAA References

   AC 61-21: Flight Training Handbook
   AC 61-23: Pilot's Handbook of Aeronautical Knowledge
   AC 61-27: Instrument Flying Handbook

4. The objective of this task is for you to demonstrate your ability to perform straight, constant airspeed climbs solely by reference to instruments.

5. When adverse weather is encountered, a climb by reference to instruments may be required to assure clearance of obstructions or terrain, or to climb above a layer of fog, haze, or low clouds.

B. Task Objectives

1. **Exhibit your knowledge by explaining flight solely by reference to instruments as related to straight, constant airspeed climbs.**

a. To enter a constant airspeed climb, raise the nose of the representative airplane to the approximate climbing attitude on the AI. Use only a small amount of elevator back pressure to initiate and maintain the climb attitude.

1) Increase power to the desired climb power setting.

2) Give the airspeed time to stabilize, then adjust pitch as necessary to maintain the desired airspeed.

3) Trim to relieve all control pressure.

b. To maintain heading in a climb, keep the wings level on the AI and TC and the ball centered on the TC.

1) Cross-check the HI to be sure straight flight is being maintained.

c. To level off from a climb, lower the nose of the representative airplane to the horizon on the AI.

1) Lead this level-off by 10% of your vertical speed.

a) EXAMPLE: If you are climbing at 500 fpm, you will begin to level off 50 ft. (10% x 500) prior to your desired altitude.

2) Cross-check the ALT and VSI to maintain level flight as airspeed increases.
3) Adjust power as necessary to maintain desired airspeed.
4) Trim to relieve all control pressure.

d. The figure below illustrates the instrument indications for straight, constant airspeed climbs.

PRIMARY PITCH   SUPPORTING PITCH AND BANK

SUPPORTING BANK   PRIMARY BANK   SUPPORTING PITCH

2. Establish the climb pitch attitude and power setting on an assigned heading.

    a. As you establish the climb pitch attitude and power setting you must increase your rate of instrument cross-check and interpretation.

    b. As you establish the climb you will need to apply more right rudder to counteract the left-turning tendencies of the element of torque.

        1) The effect of torque increases due to the airplane's high angle-of-attack, low airspeed, and high power setting.

3. Make smooth and coordinated control applications.

    a. You will need to learn to overcome a natural tendency to make a large control movement for a pitch change, and learn to apply small control pressures smoothly, cross-checking rapidly for the results of the change, and continuing with the pressures as your instruments show the desired results at a rate that you can interpret.

        1) Small pitch changes can be easily controlled, stopped, and corrected.
        2) Large changes are more difficult to control.

    b. Coordination of controls requires that the ball of the TC be kept centered and that the available trim control devices be used whenever a change in flight conditions disturbs the existing trim.

        1) Trim is used to relieve all possible control pressures held after a desired attitude has been attained.

        2) The pressure you feel on the control yoke must be those that you apply while controlling a planned change in airplane attitude, not pressure held because you are letting the airplane control you.

4. *Maintain the desired heading, ±10°.*

5. *Maintain the desired airspeed, ±10 kt.*

6. *Level off at the desired altitude, ±100 ft.*

C. Common errors during straight, constant airspeed climbs by reference to instruments

    1. Fixation, omission, and emphasis errors during instrument cross-check.

        a. Fixation, or staring at a single instrument, usually occurs for a good reason, but with poor results.

            1) You may stare at the ASI which indicates 10 kt. above your climb airspeed, wondering how the needle got there. During that time, perhaps due to the effects of torque, a heading change occurs unnoticed, and more errors can accumulate.

        b. Omission of an instrument from your cross-check may be caused by a failure to anticipate significant instrument indications following attitude changes.

        c. Emphasis on a single instrument, instead of on the combination of instruments necessary for attitude information, is normal in your initial stages of flight solely by reference to instruments.

            1) You will tend to rely on the instrument you understand the best, e.g., the AI.

    2. Improper instrument interpretation.

        a. You can avoid this by understanding each instrument's operating principle and relationship to the performance of your airplane.

3. **Improper control applications.**

   a. This normally occurs from incorrectly interpreting the instruments and, thus, applying the improper controls.

   b. Do not disturb a flight attitude until you know what the result will be.

4. **Failure to establish proper pitch, bank, or power adjustments during heading and airspeed corrections.**

   a. You must understand which instruments provide information for pitch, bank, and power.

   b. As control pressures change with airspeed changes, your instrument cross-check must be increased and pressure readjusted.

5. **Improper entry or level-off technique.**

   a. Until you learn the pitch attitude for specific power settings used in climbs, you will tend to make larger than necessary pitch adjustments.

   b. Your rate of cross-check must be varied during speed, power, and/or attitude changes during a climb.

   c. Remember to note your rate of climb from the VSI to determine the proper lead.

      1) Failure to do this normally results in overshooting or undershooting the desired level-off altitude.

   d. Maintain an accelerated cross-check until a straight-and-level attitude is positively established, at a normal cruise speed.

6. **Faulty trim technique.**

   a. The trim should not be used as a substitute for control with the control yoke and rudder pedals, but to relieve pressures already held to stabilize attitude.

   b. Use trim frequently and in small amounts.

   c. You cannot feel control pressures with a tight grip on the control yoke.

      1) Relax and learn to control with the eyes and the brain instead of only the muscles.

END OF TASK

STRAIGHT, CONSTANT AIRSPEED DESCENTS

VI.C. TASK: STRAIGHT, CONSTANT AIRSPEED DESCENTS

> *PILOT OPERATION - 6*
>
> REFERENCES: AC 61-21, AC 61-23, AC 61-27.

Objective. To determine that the applicant:

1. Exhibits knowledge by explaining flight solely by reference to instruments as related to straight, constant airspeed descents.

2. Determines the minimum safe altitude at which the descent should be terminated.

3. Establishes the descent configuration, pitch, and power setting on the assigned heading.

4. Makes smooth and coordinated control applications.

5. Maintains the desired heading, ±10°.

6. Maintains the desired airspeed, ±10 kt.

7. Levels off at the desired altitude, ±100 ft.

A. General Information

1. This is one of six tasks (A-F) in this area of operation. Your examiner is required to test you on this task.

2. *Pilot Operation - 6* refers to FAR 61.107(a)(6): Control and maneuvering an airplane solely by reference to instruments, including descents and climbs using radio aids or radar directives.

3. FAA References

> AC 61-21: Flight Training Handbook
> AC 61-23: Pilot's Handbook of Aeronautical Knowledge
> AC 61-27: Instrument Flying Handbook

4. The objective of this task is for you to demonstrate your ability to perform straight, constant airspeed descents.

5. When unexpected adverse weather is encountered, the most likely situation is that of being trapped in or above a broken or solid layer of clouds or haze, requiring that a descent be made to an altitude where you can reestablish visual reference to the ground.

B.   Task Objectives

1.   **Exhibit your knowledge by explaining flight solely by reference to instruments as related to straight, constant descents.**

a.   To enter a constant airspeed descent, slow to your desired airspeed if necessary, by reducing power while maintaining straight-and-level flight.

  1)   Once your desired airspeed is established, reduce power further and lower the nose of the representative airplane on the AI to maintain a constant airspeed.

  2)   Correct any airspeed deviations with minor pitch adjustments.

  3)   Trim to relieve all control pressure.

b.   To maintain heading in a descent, keep the wings level on the AI and TC, and the ball centered on the TC.

  1)   Cross-check the HI to be sure straight flight is being maintained.

c.   The level-off from a descent must occur before you reach your desired altitude. Assuming a 500-fpm rate of descent, lead the altitude by 100 to 150 ft. for a level-off at an airspeed higher than the descent airspeed.

  1)   At the lead point, add power smoothly to the appropriate level flight cruise setting. Since the nose of the airplane will tend to rise as the airspeed increases, hold forward elevator pressure to maintain the descent until approximately 50 ft. above the level-off altitude, then smoothly adjust pitch to level flight attitude.

  2)   Set power for desired airspeed in level flight.

  3)   Cross-check the ALT and VSI to maintain level flight as airspeed stabilizes.

  4)   Trim to relieve all control pressure.

d.   The figure below illustrates the instrument indications for straight, constant airspeed descents.

PRIMARY POWER

SUPPORTING PITCH AND BANK

SUPPORTING BANK

PRIMARY BANK

PRIMARY PITCH

2. **Determine the minimum safe altitude at which the descent should be terminated.**

   a. As part of your preflight preparation you should have determined the height of obstructions and terrain along your route of flight.

      1) You can look on your sectional chart to locate the maximum elevation figure (MEF) for each latitude-longitude quadrant. This assumes you know your present location.

   b. You must remain 1,000 ft. above the highest obstacle, except in mountainous areas where you must remain 2,000 ft. above the highest obstacle.

   c. With this information you can determine your minimum safe altitude.

   d. If you are lost and in contact with ATC or an FSS, seek their assistance if they instruct you to descend.

3. **Establish the descent configuration, pitch, and power setting on the assigned heading.**

   a. Before beginning the descent you should first establish the descent airspeed and the desired heading while maintaining altitude.

   b. At this time the proper descent configuration should be established by positioning the flaps and/or landing gear (if retractable) up or down as desired.

   c. Establishing the desired configuration before starting the descent will permit a more stabilized descent and require less division of attention once the descent is started.

4. **Make smooth and coordinated control applications.**

   a. You will need to learn to overcome a natural tendency to make a large control movement for a pitch change, and learn to apply small control pressures smoothly, cross-checking rapidly for the results of the change, and continuing with the pressures as your instruments show the desired results at a rate that you can interpret.

      1) Small pitch changes can be easily controlled, stopped, and corrected.
      2) Large changes are more difficult to control.

   b. Coordination of controls requires that the ball of the TC be kept centered and that the available trim control devices be used whenever a change in flight conditions disturbs the existing trim.

      1) Trim is used to relieve all possible control pressures held after a desired attitude has been attained.

      2) The pressure you feel on the control yoke must be those that you apply while controlling a planned change in airplane attitude, not pressure held because you are letting the airplane control you.

5. *Maintain the desired heading, ±10°.*

6. *Maintain the desired airspeed, ±10 kt.*

7. *Level off at the desired altitude, ±100 ft.*

C. Common errors during straight, constant airspeed descents by reference to instruments

   1. **Fixation, omission, and emphasis errors during instrument cross-check.**

      a. Fixation, or staring at a single instrument, usually occurs for a good reason, but with poor results.

         1) You may stare at the HI which indicates 20° from desired heading, wondering how you came to that heading. During that time, perhaps due to increasing your grip on the control yoke, the nose of the airplane pitches down and the ASI increases unnoticed, and more errors can accumulate.

    b.   Omission of an instrument from your cross-check may be caused by a failure to anticipate significant instrument indications following attitude changes.

    c.   Emphasis on a single instrument, instead of on the combination of instruments necessary for attitude information, is normal in your initial stages of flight solely by reference to instruments.

       1)   You will tend to rely on the instrument you understand the best, e.g., the AI.

2.   **Improper instrument interpretation.**

    a.   You can avoid this by understanding each instrument's operating principle and relationship to the performance of your airplane.

3.   **Improper control applications.**

    a.   This normally occurs from incorrectly interpreting the instruments and, thus, applying the improper controls.

    b.   Do not disturb a flight attitude until you know what the result will be.

4.   **Failure to establish proper pitch, bank, or power adjustments during heading and airspeed corrections.**

    a.   You must understand which instruments provide information for pitch, bank, and power.

    b.   As control pressures change with airspeed changes, your instrument cross-check must be increased and pressure readjusted.

5.   **Improper entry or level-off technique.**

    a.   Ensure you establish the proper configuration and heading before you start your descent.

    b.   Your rate of cross-check must be varied during speed, power, and/or attitude changes during a climb.

    c.   Remember to note your rate of descent from the VSI to determine your lead for level-offs.

       1)   Failure to do so can result in overshooting or undershooting the desired altitude.

    d.   "Ballooning" (allowing the nose to pitch up) on level-off results when descent attitude with forward elevator pressure is not maintained as you increase power.

6.   **Faulty trim technique.**

    a.   The trim should not be used as a substitute for control with the control yoke and rudder pedals, but to relieve pressures already held to stabilize attitude.

    b.   Use trim frequently and in small amounts.

    c.   You cannot feel control pressures with a tight grip on the control yoke.

       1)   Relax and learn to control with the eyes and the brain instead of only the muscles.

END OF TASK

TURNS TO HEADINGS

VI.D. TASK: TURNS TO HEADINGS

PILOT OPERATION - 6

REFERENCES: AC 61-21, AC 61-23, AC 61-27.

Objective. To determine that the applicant:

1. Exhibits knowledge by explaining flight solely by reference to instruments as related to turns to headings.

2. Enters and maintains approximately a standard-rate turn with smooth and coordinated control applications.

3. Maintains the desired altitude, ±100 ft.

4. Maintains the desired airspeed, ±10 kt.

5. Maintains the desired bank angle.

6. Rolls out at the desired heading, ±10°.

A. General Information

1. This is one of six tasks (A-F) in this area of operation. Your examiner is required to test you on this task.

2. *Pilot Operation - 6* refers to FAR 61.107(a)(6): Control and maneuvering an airplane solely by reference to instruments, including descents and climbs using radio aids or radar directives.

3. FAA References

   AC 61-21: Flight Training Handbook
   AC 61-23: Pilot's Handbook of Aeronautical Knowledge
   AC 61-27: Instrument Flying Handbook

4. The objective of this task is for you to demonstrate your ability to perform turns to headings solely by reference to instruments.

5. Sometimes upon encountering adverse weather conditions, it is advisable for you to use radio navigation aids, or to obtain directional guidance from ATC facilities.

   a. This usually requires that turns be made and/or specific headings be maintained.

B.   **Task Objectives**

1.   **Exhibit your knowledge by explaining flight solely by reference to instruments as related to turns to headings.**

   a.   To enter a turn use coordinated aileron and rudder pressure to establish the desired bank angle on the AI.

      1)   Control pitch attitude and altitude throughout the turn as previously described in Task VI.A., Straight-and-Level Flight, on page 306.

   b.   To roll out on a desired heading apply coordinated aileron and rudder pressure to level the wings on the AI and stop the turn.

      1)   Begin the rollout about 10° before the desired heading (less for small heading changes).

      2)   Apply sufficient forward elevator pressure to maintain altitude.

   c.   The figure below illustrates the instrument indications while in a turn.

2.   **Enter and maintain approximately a standard rate turn with smooth and coordinated control application.**

   a.   When making turns in adverse weather conditions, there is nothing to be gained by maneuvering your airplane faster than your ability to keep up with the changes that occur in the flight instrument indications.

      1)   You should limit all turns to a standard rate, which is a turn during which the heading changes 3° per sec.

         a)   This is shown on a TC when the wing tip of the representative airplane is opposite the standard rate marker.

         b)   On most T&SIs this is shown when the needle is deflected one needle width.

         c)   Most training airplanes require 15° to 20° of bank for a standard rate turn.

    2) The rate at which a turn should be made is dictated generally by the amount of turn desired.

        a) Do not use more bank angle than the number of degrees of turn desired.

    3) Before starting the turn to a new heading you should hold the airplane straight and level and determine in which direction the turn is to be made. Then decide the rate or angle of bank required to reach the new heading.

  b. Coordination of controls requires than the ball of the TC be kept centered and that the available trim control devices be used whenever a change in flight conditions disturbs the existing trim.

    1) Trim is used to relieve all possible control pressures held after a desired attitude has been attained.

    2) The pressure you feel on the control yoke must be those that you apply while controlling a planned change in airplane attitude, not pressure held because you are letting the airplane control you.

3. *Maintain the desired altitude, ±100 ft.*

4. *Maintain the desired airspeed, ±10 kt.*

5. *Maintain the desired bank angle.*

  a. Having selected an appropriate bank angle based on the amount of turn (up to 15° to 20°), maintain that bank using the AI.

  b. Do not use more than a standard rate turn.

6. *Roll out at the desired heading, ±10°.*

C. Common errors during turns to headings by reference to instruments

  1. Fixation, omission, and emphasis errors during instrument cross-check.

    a. Fixation, or staring at a single instrument, usually occurs for a good reason, but with poor results.

      1) You may stare at the AI to maintain a desired bank angle. During this time an altitude change occurs unnoticed, and more errors accumulate.

    b. Omission of an instrument from your cross-check may be caused by a failure to anticipate significant instrument indications following attitude changes.

    c. Emphasis on a single instrument, instead of on the combination of instruments necessary for attitude information, is normal in your initial stages of flight solely by reference to instruments.

      1) You will tend to rely on the instrument you understand the best, e.g., the AI.

  2. Improper instrument interpretation.

    a. You can avoid this by understanding each instrument's operating principle and relationship to the performance of your airplane.

  3. Improper control applications.

    a. Before you start your turn, look at the HI to determine your present heading and the desired heading.

    b. Decide which direction to turn and how much bank to use, then apply control pressure to turn the airplane in that direction.

    c. Do not rush yourself.

4. **Failure to establish proper pitch, bank, and power adjustments during altitude, bank, and airspeed corrections.**

    a. You must understand which instruments provide information for pitch, bank, and power.

    b. As control pressures change with bank changes, your instrument cross-check must be increased and pressure readjusted.

5. **Improper entry or rollout technique.**

    a. This is caused by overcontrolling, resulting in overbanking on turn entry, and overshooting and undershooting headings on rollout.

        1) Enter and roll out at the rate of your ability to cross-check and interpret the instruments.

    b. Maintain coordinated flight by keeping the ball centered.

    c. Remember the heading you are turning to.

6. **Faulty trim technique.**

    a. The trim should not be used as a substitute for control with the control yoke and rudder pedals, but to relieve pressures already held to stabilize attitude.

    b. Use trim frequently and in small amounts.

    c. You cannot feel control pressures with a tight grip on the control yoke.

        1) Relax and learn to control with the eyes and the brain instead of only the muscles.

END OF TASK

UNUSUAL FLIGHT ATTITUDES

VI.E. TASK: UNUSUAL FLIGHT ATTITUDES

PILOT OPERATION - 6

REFERENCES: AC 61-21, AC 61-23, AC 61-27.

NOTE: Unusual flight attitudes, such as a start of a power-on spiral or an approach to a climbing stall, shall not exceed 45° bank or 10° pitch from level flight.

Objective. To determine that the applicant:

1. Exhibits knowledge by explaining flight solely by reference to instruments as related to unusual flight attitudes.

2. Recognizes unusual flight attitudes promptly.

3. Properly interprets the instruments.

4. Recovers to a stabilized level flight attitude by prompt, smooth, coordinated control, applied in the proper sequence.

5. Avoids excessive load factor, airspeed, and stall.

A. General Information

1. This is one of six tasks (A-F) in this area of operation. Your examiner is required to test you on this task.

2. *Pilot Operation - 6* refers to FAR 61.107(a)(6): Control and maneuvering an airplane solely by reference to instruments, including descents and climbs using radio aids or radar directives.

3. FAA References

   AC 61-21: Flight Training Handbook
   AC 61-23: Pilot's Handbook of Aeronautical Knowledge
   AC 61-27: Instrument Flying Handbook

4. The objective of this task is for you to demonstrate your ability to recover from unusual flight attitudes.

5. When visual references are inadequate or lost, you may unintentionally let your airplane enter a critical (unusual) attitude. Since such attitudes are unintentional and unexpected, the inexperienced pilot may react incorrectly and stall or overstress the airplane.

B.   Task Objectives

    1.   Exhibit your knowledge by explaining flight by reference to instruments as related to unusual flight attitudes.

        a.   The two basic unusual flight attitudes.

            1)   If the airspeed is decreasing rapidly and the altimeter indication is increasing faster than desired, and the turn coordinator (or turn needle) indicates a bank, the airplane is nose-high (climbing turn).

            2)   If the airspeed is increasing rapidly, the altimeter indication is decreasing faster than desired, and the turn coordinator (or needle) indicates a bank, the airplane is nose-low (diving spiral).

2. Recognize unusual flight attitudes promptly.

a. As a general rule, any time there is an instrument rate of movement or indication other than those associated with basic instrument flight maneuvers, you must assume an unusual attitude and increase the speed of your instrument cross-check to confirm the airplane's attitude, instrument error, or instrument malfunction.

b. When an unusual attitude is noted on the flight instruments, your immediate task is to recognize what the airplane is doing and decide how to return it to straight-and-level flight as quickly as possible.

3. Properly interpret the instruments.

a. Nose-high attitudes are shown by the rate and direction of movement of the altimeter, vertical speed, and airspeed indicator, as well as the immediately recognizable indication on the attitude indicator.

   1) Nose-low attitudes are shown by the same instruments, but needle movement is in the opposite direction.

b. Since many unusual attitudes involve a rather steep bank, it is important to determine the direction of the turn.

   1) This can be accomplished best by reference to the attitude indicator.

   2) In the absence of an attitude indicator, it will be necessary in the recovery to refer to the turn coordinator or turn needle to determine the direction of turn.

c. Your initial interpretation of the flight instruments must be accurate.

4. *Recover to a stabilized level flight attitude by prompt, smooth, coordinated control, applied in the proper sequence.*

a. Maintain coordination of the controls during recovery.

   1) Unlike the control applications in normal maneuvers, larger control movements in recoveries from critical attitudes may be necessary to bring the airplane under control.

   2) Nevertheless, such control applications must be smooth, positive, prompt, and coordinated.

   3) Once the airplane is returned to approximately straight-and-level flight, control movements should be limited to small adjustments.

   4) To avoid aggravating the critical attitude with a control application in the wrong direction, the initial interpretation of the instruments must be accurate.

b. Control sequence for recovery from a nose-high attitude.

   1) If the airspeed is decreasing rapidly and the altimeter indication is increasing faster than desired, the airplane's nose is too high.

   2) To prevent a stall from occurring, it is important to lower the nose as quickly as possible while simultaneously increasing power to prevent a further loss of airspeed.

      a) If an attitude indicator is available, the representative airplane should be lowered in relation to the artificial horizon by applying positive forward elevator pressure.

      b) If no attitude indicator is available, sufficient forward pressure should be applied to stop the movement of the pointers on the altimeter and airspeed indicators.

   3) Nose-high unusual attitude is indicated by

     a) Decreasing airspeed.
     b) Increasing altitude.
     c) Bank.

   4) Recover in the following sequence.

     a) Add power.
     b) Reduce pitch.
     c) Level wings.

c. Control sequence for recovery from a nose-low attitude.

   1) If the airspeed is increasing rapidly and the altimeter indication is decreasing faster than desired, the airplane's nose is too low.

   2) To prevent losing too much altitude or exceeding the speed limitations of the airplane, power must be reduced and the nose must be raised.

   3) With the higher-than-normal airspeed, it is vital to raise the nose very smoothly to avoid overstressing the airplane.

   4) If the airplane is in a steep bank, the wings should be leveled before attempting to raise the nose.

     a) Increasing elevator back pressure before the wings are leveled will tend to increase the bank and make the situation worse.

     b) Excessive load factors may be imposed, resulting in structural failure.

   5) Nose-low spirals are indicated by

     a) Increasing airspeed.
     b) Decreasing altitude.
     c) Bank.

   6) Recover in the following sequence:

     a) Reduce power.
     b) Level the wings (to decrease the load factor).
     c) Raise the nose (gently, if necessary to avoid excessive load factors).

5. ***Avoid excessive load factor, airspeed, and stall.***

a. Attempting to increase elevator back pressure in a nose-low unusual attitude before the wings are level will impose a significant increase in load factor.

   1) Remember to level the wings before you raise the nose of the airplane.

b. Excessive airspeed is another concern in a nose-low unusual attitude.

   1) Do not allow the airspeed to exceed your airplane's limitations. Reduce power immediately in a nose-low attitude.

c. Stall condition can be encountered in either type of unusual attitude.

   1) In a nose-high attitude the airspeed is normally decreasing rapidly to the point of stall speed.

     a) Add power and reduce pitch.

   2) In a nose-low recovery a stall may be encountered by attempting to raise the airplane's nose too rapidly.

a) Raising the pitch too quickly allows the wings to exceed their critical angle of attack. A detailed discussion is included in Chapter VII, Maneuvering at Critically Slow Airspeeds, beginning on page 351.

C. Common errors during unusual flight attitudes

1. **Failure to recognize an unusual flight attitude.**

   a. This is a sign that you are not correctly cross-checking and interpreting your instruments.

      1) You must learn to work against the impulse of stopping and staring at an instrument when you notice a discrepancy.

2. **Attempting to recover from an unusual flight attitude by "feel" rather than by instrument indications.**

   a. The most hazardous illusions that lead to spatial disorientation are created by the information received by your motion sensing system, located in each inner ear.

      1) See Task I.F., Aeromedical Factors, on page 171 for a complete explanation of various illusions.

      2) The motion sensing system is not capable of detecting a constant velocity or small changes in velocity, nor can it distinguish between centrifugal force and gravity.

      3) The system, functioning normally in flight, can produce false sensations.

   b. During unusual flight attitudes you must believe and interpret the flight instruments because spatial disorientation is normal in unusual flight attitudes.

3. **Inappropriate control applications during recovery.**

   a. This is primarily caused by not correctly interpreting the flight instruments.

      1) It is corrected by correctly cross-checking and interpreting your instruments.

   b. Follow the recovery steps in sequence.

   c. Control movements may be larger, but must be smooth, positive, prompt, and coordinated.

4. **Failure to recognize from instrument indications when the airplane is passing through level flight.**

   a. With an operative attitude indicator, level flight attitude exists when the miniature airplane is level with the horizon.

   b. Without an attitude indicator, level flight is indicated by the reversal and stabilization of the airspeed indicator and altimeter needles.

END OF TASK

RADIO AIDS AND RADAR SERVICES

VI.F. TASK: RADIO AIDS AND RADAR SERVICES

   PILOT OPERATION - 6

   REFERENCES: AC 61-21, AC 61-23, AC 61-27.

Objective. To determine that the applicant:

1. Exhibits adequate knowledge by explaining radio aids and radar services available for use during flight solely by reference to instruments.

2. Selects, tunes, and identifies the appropriate facility.

3. Follows verbal instructions or radio navigation aids for guidance.

4. Determines the minimum safe altitude.

5. Maintains the desired altitude, ±100 ft.

6. Maintains the desired heading, ±10°.

A. **General Information**

   1. This is one of six tasks (A-F) in this area of operation. Your examiner is required to test you on this task.

   2. *Pilot Operation - 6* refers to FAR 61.107(a)(6): Control and maneuvering an airplane solely by reference to instruments, including descents and climbs using radio aids or radar directives.

   3. FAA References

      AC 61-21: Flight Training Handbook
      AC 61-23: Pilot's Handbook of Aeronautical Knowledge
      AC 61-27: Instrument Flying Handbook

   4. The objective of this task is for you to demonstrate your ability to use radio aids and radar services during flight solely by reference to instruments.

   5. When a VFR flight progresses from good to deteriorating weather and you continue in the hope that conditions will improve, the need for navigational help may arise. In most cases, there will be some type of radio navigation aid available to help you return to a good weather area.

B. **Task Objectives**

   1. **Exhibit your knowledge by explaining radio aids and radar services available for use during flight solely by reference to instruments.**

      a. Any type of radio navigation equipment may be used. This may include VOR and/or ADF. These are the two most common found in trainer-type airplanes.

         1) You only have to know how to use the radio navigation equipment installed in your airplane.

      b. There are also services available to you in which all you need is a VHF radio communication system.

         1) VHF Direction Finding (DF) is a ground-based station capable of indicating the bearing from its antenna to the transmitting airplane.

            a) It is used to locate lost aircraft and to guide aircraft to areas of good (VFR) weather or to airports.

            b) The DF operator on the ground can note your airplane's bearing from the facility by looking at a scope, similar to a radar scope. Each time you transmit, it shows up on the scope as a line radiating out from the center.

2) Radar equipped ATC facilities can provide radar assistance and navigation services (vectors) provided you can talk to the controller (VHF radio), you are within radar coverage, and can be identified by the ATC radar controller.

   a) The controller will assign you a squawk code to put in your transponder to assist in positive identification.

c. Remember, the equipment that operates in the VHF radio band (i.e., VOR, communication radio, DF) are restricted to line-of-sight restrictions and you may have to climb to better utilize these tools.

2. Selects, tunes, and identifies the appropriate facility.

a. You will want to select a VOR or NDB in the direction that you just came from, since that should be an area of good weather.

   1) Use your sectional chart to find an appropriate facility to the direction you want to go and the equipment in your airplane.

b. Tune the station's frequency in your navigation equipment.

   1) The frequency can be found on your sectional chart.

c. Positively identify the station by its Morse code identifier.

   1) This is the only positive way to ensure you are receiving the signals from the station you selected.

d. For use of DF or radar services, you should contact the nearest FSS for assistance.

   1) FSS frequencies can be found on your sectional chart.

e. If you feel you are in an urgent or distress situation select the emergency frequency of 121.5 MHz on your communication radio.

3. Follow verbal instructions or radio navigation aids for guidance.

a. When using either DF or radar services you need to follow the verbal instructions you receive.

   1) If you do not understand the instructions, tell the controller and ask for clarification.

   2) Inform the controller if you regain visual reference to the ground.

      a) Once you do you must inform the controller if they give you a vector which will put you into IFR conditions.

      b) This assistance does not allow you to violate FARs.

b. When using radio navigation aids you should properly use the indications for guidance.

   1) With a VOR you should turn the OBS until the TO-FROM indicates TO and the CDI is centered.

      a) Turn to the heading indicated and proceed to the station.

   2) When using an ADF, turn your airplane until the ADF needle is pointing 0° (fixed dial).

      a) Keeping the needle in this position will result in the airplane flying to the station.

      b) Do not worry about tracking with the ADF as this increases your workload at a time when you need to concentrate more on airplane control.

   3) For more information on radio navigation see Task V.B., Radio Navigation, starting on page 282.

4. **Determine the minimum safe altitude.**

    a.   You can use the maximum elevation figures (MEF) on your sectional chart to determine the minimum safe altitude.

        1)   If you knew your location prior to losing outside references you can locate the MEF in the latitude-longitude quadrant where you are located.

        2)   Add 1,000 ft. (2,000 ft. in a mountainous area) to the MEF to determine the minimum safe altitude.

    b.   Using DF or radar services, the controller can inform you of the minimum safe altitude for your location.

5. You are required to **maintain the desired altitude, ±100 ft.**

    a.   Continue your instrument cross-check and interpretation while operating navigation equipment and/or the communication radio.

6. You are required to **maintain the desired heading, ±10°.**

    a.   Maintain your instrument cross-check and interpretation.

C. Common errors while using radio aids and radar services

    1. **Delaying the use of a radio aid or obtaining radar services.**

        a.   As soon as you encounter an urgent situation you should immediately seek assistance.

            1)   An urgent situation occurs the moment you enter weather conditions below VFR weather minimums, and/or you become doubtful about position, fuel endurance, deteriorating weather, or any other condition that may affect flight safety.

    2. **Failure to properly control the airplane.**

        a.   Your first priority is to maintain control of your airplane.

        b.   Do not increase your workload -- seek help.

    3. **Failure to properly select, tune, or identify a radio station.**

        a.   To use a radio navigation aid you must select the proper station, tune it on the receiver, and positively identify the station by its Morse code identifier.

            1)   If you do not positively identify a station, you cannot be sure you are navigating to the station that you selected.

        b.   To seek assistance from ATC, FSS, or any other facility use the appropriate frequency.

            1)   If you cannot locate a frequency, use the emergency frequency of 121.5 MHz.

            2)   Remember, if you are flying by reference to instruments and you are not instrument rated, you are in (at least) an urgent situation.

    4. **Failure to maintain minimum safe altitude.**

        a.   Maintain at least 1,000 ft. (2,000 ft. in mountainous areas) MSL above the MEF on your sectional chart.

        b.   Do not attempt to go below this altitude to regain visual references.

END OF TASK -- END OF CHAPTER

CHAPTER VII
FLIGHT AT CRITICALLY SLOW AIRSPEEDS

VII.A. Full Stalls -- Power Off 334
VII.B. Full Stalls -- Power On 340
VII.C. Imminent Stalls -- Power On and Power Off 346
VII.D. Maneuvering at Critically Slow Airspeed 351
VII.E. Constant Altitude Turns 356

This chapter explains the five tasks (A-E) of Flight at Critically Slow Airspeeds. These tasks include both knowledge and skill.

Each objective of a task lists, in sequence, the important elements that must be satisfactorily performed. The object includes:

1. Specifically what you should be able to do.
2. The conditions under which the task is to be performed.
3. The minimum acceptable standards of performance.

Be confident. You have prepared diligently and are better prepared and more skilled than the average private pilot applicant. Your examiner will base your ability to perform these tasks on the following.

1. Executing the task within your airplane's capabilities and limitations, including use of the airplane's systems.

2. Piloting your airplane with smoothness and accuracy.

3. Exercising good judgment.

4. Applying your aeronautical knowledge.

5. Showing mastery of your airplane within the standards outlined in this area of operation, with the successful outcome of a task never seriously in doubt.

A stall is a loss of lift and increase in drag when an airplane is flown at an angle of attack greater than the angle for maximum lift. The angle of attack for maximum lift is called the critical angle of attack. Thus, a stall occurs whenever the critical angle of attack is exceeded.

Your examiner is required to test you on all five tasks. Each task is reproduced verbatim from the FAA Practical Test Standards in a shaded box. General discussion is presented under "A. General Information." This is followed by "B. Task Objectives," which is a detailed discussion of each element of the FAA's task.

To understand the stall phenomenon, some basic factors affecting aerodynamics and flight should be reviewed with particular emphasis on their relation to stall speeds. The stall speed is the speed at which the critical angle of attack is exceeded. Some of these speeds are listed in your *POH*, e.g., stall speed in landing configuration, V_{SO}.

1. Angle of attack is the angle at which the wing meets the relative wind.

    a. The angle of attack must be small enough to allow smooth (attached) airflow over and under the wing to produce lift.

    b. A change in the angle of attack will affect the amount of lift that is produced. Increasing the angle of attack begins to disrupt the smooth airflow over the top of the wing, as shown in the figure below.

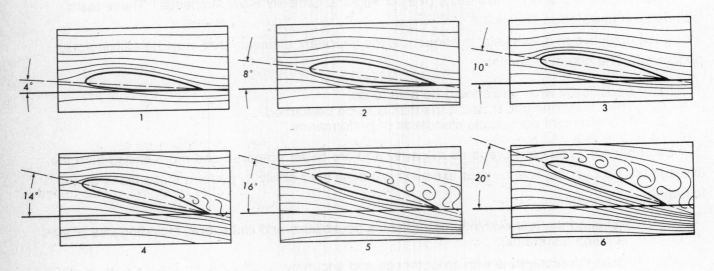

2. Most airplanes are designed so that the wings will stall progressively outward from the wing roots to the wingtips.

    a. The wings are designed so that the wingtips have less angle of incidence than the wing roots. The *angle of incidence* is the angle between the chord line of the wing and the longitudinal axis of the airplane.

    b. Thus, during flight, the tips of such wings have a smaller angle of attack than the wing roots.

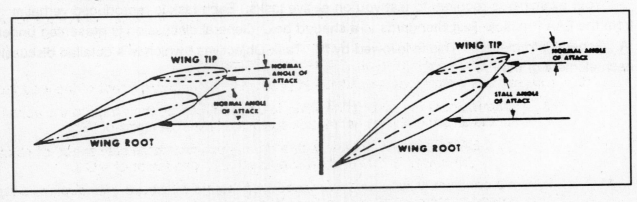

c. A stall is caused by exceeding the critical angle of attack. Since the wing roots of an airplane will exceed the critical angle before the wingtips, the roots will stall first. The wings are designed in this manner so that control of the ailerons (which are located toward the tips of the wings) will be available at high angles of attack (slow airspeed) and give the airplane more stable stalling characteristics.

3. It is vital that rudder be used properly during entry into and recovery from a stall.

   a. Rudder must be used to counteract any tendency to yaw or slip.

   b. Excessive aileron use could result in a spin unless directional control is maintained by the rudder.

4. Airspeed is controlled primarily by the elevator or longitudinal control position for a given configuration and power.

   a. If the speed is too slow, the angle of attack required for level flight will be so large that the air can no longer follow the upper curvature of the wing. The result is a separation of airflow from the wing, loss of lift, a large increase in drag, and eventually a stall if the angle of attack is not reduced.

   b. A stall can occur AT ANY AIRSPEED, IN ANY ATTITUDE, AND AT ANY POWER SETTING.

      1) Remember, a stall is the result of excessive angle of attack, not airspeed.

5. Flaps, landing gear (if retractable), and other configuring devices can affect your airplane's stall speed. Flap extension will generally increase the lifting ability of the wings, thus reducing the stall speed.

   a. The effect can be seen by markings on the airspeed indicator, where the lower airspeed limit of the white arc (V_{S0}, power-off stall speed with gear and flaps in the landing configuration) is less than the lower airspeed limit of the green arc (V_{S1}, power-off stall speed in the clean configuration).

6. Your airplane's stall speed increases in proportion to the square root of the load factor.

   a. Load factor is the ratio of the lifting force produced by the wings to the actual weight of the airplane and its contents, usually expressed in terms of "G."

      1) EXAMPLE: An airplane with a normal unaccelerated stall speed of 45 kt. can be stalled at 90 kt. when subjected to a load factor of 4 G's.

   b. In a constant altitude turn, increased load factors will cause your airplane's stall speed to increase as the angle of bank increases.

7. The center of gravity (CG) location has an indirect effect on the effective lift and angle of attack of the wing, the amount and direction of force on the tail, and the degree of stabilizer deflection needed to supply the proper tail force for equilibrium. Thus, the CG position has a significant effect on stability and stall recovery.

    a. As the CG is moved aft (rearward), the amount of elevator deflection will be reduced. An increased angle of attack will be achieved with less elevator control force.

        1) This could make entry into inadvertent stalls easier, and during recovery, it would be easier to generate higher load factors, due to the reduced forces.

    b. With an extremely aft CG, very light back elevator control forces may lead to inadvertent stall entries and if a spin is entered, the balance of forces on the airplane may result in a flat spin.

        1) Recovery from a flat spin is often impossible.

    c. A forward CG location will often cause the critical angle of attack to be reached (and the airplane to stall) at a higher airspeed.

        1) Increased back elevator control force is generally required with a forward CG location.

8. As the weight of your airplane is increased, the stall speed increases.

    a. The increased weight requires a higher angle of attack to produce additional lift to support the weight.

9. Even a small accumulation of snow, ice, or frost on your airplane can cause an increase in the stall speed.

    a. Such accumulation changes the shape of the wing, disrupting the smooth airflow over the surface and, thus, increasing drag and decreasing lift.

10. Turbulence can cause your airplane to stall at a significantly higher airspeed than in stable conditions.

    a. A vertical gust or wind shear can cause a sudden change in the relative wind and result in an abrupt increase in angle of attack.

        1) Even though a gust may not be maintained long enough for a stall to develop, the airplane may stall while you attempt to control the flight path, especially during an approach in gusty conditions.

    b. When flying in moderate to severe turbulence or strong crosswinds, a higher than normal approach speed should be maintained.

        1) In cruise flight maintain an airspeed well above the indicated stall speed and below V_A (maneuvering speed).

Improper airspeed management resulting in stalls is most likely to occur when you are distracted by one or more other tasks. Pilots at all skill levels must be aware of the increased risk of entering into an inadvertent stall/spin while performing tasks that are secondary to controlling the airplane. Some distractions include:

1. Locating a checklist,
2. Attempting a restart after an engine failure,
3. Flying a traffic pattern on a windy day,
4. Reading a chart,
5. Making fuel and/or distance calculations, or
6. Attempting to retrieve items from the floor, back seat, or glove compartment.

There are several ways to recognize that a stall is impending before it actually occurs. When one or more of these indicators is noted, initiation of a recovery should be instinctive.

1. Vision is useful in detecting a stall condition by noting the attitude of the airplane and the airspeed approaching stall speed. This sense can be fully relied on only when the stall is the result of an intentional unusual attitude of the airplane.

2. Hearing is also helpful in sensing a stall condition, since the tone level and intensity of sounds incidental to flight decrease as the airspeed decreases.

3. Kinesthesia, or the mind's sensing of changes in direction of speed of motion, is probably the most important and the best indicator to the trained and experienced pilot. If this sensitivity is properly developed, it will warn of a decrease in speed or the beginning of a settling or "mushing" of the airplane.

4. The feeling of control pressures is also very important. As speed is reduced, the "live" resistance to pressures on the controls becomes progressively less.

    a. The airplane controls become less and less effective as one approaches the critical angle of attack.

    b. In a complete stall, all controls can be moved with almost no resistance and with little immediate effect on the airplane.

5. Many airplanes are equipped with stall warning devices (e.g., a horn) to alert the pilot when the airflow over the wing(s) approaches a point that will not allow lift to be sustained.

FULL STALLS -- POWER OFF

VII.A. TASK: FULL STALLS -- POWER OFF

  PILOT OPERATION - 4

  REFERENCES: AC 61-21.

Objective. To determine that the applicant:

1. Exhibits knowledge by explaining the aerodynamic factors and flight situations that may result in full stalls -- power off, including proper recovery procedures, and hazards of stalling during uncoordinated flight.

2. Selects an entry altitude that will allow the recoveries to be completed no lower than 1,500 ft. AGL.

3. Establishes the normal approach or landing configuration and airspeed with the throttle closed or at a reduced power setting.

4. Establishes a straight glide or a gliding turn with a bank angle of 30°, ±10°, in coordinated flight.

5. Establishes and maintains a landing pitch attitude that will induce a full stall.

6. Recognizes the indications of a full stall and promptly recovers by decreasing the angle of attack, leveling the wings, and adjusting the power, as necessary, to regain normal flight attitude.

7. Retracts the wing flaps and landing gear (if retractable) and establishes straight-and-level flight or climb.

8. Avoids secondary stalls, excessive airspeed, excessive altitude loss, spins, and flight below 1,500 ft. AGL.

A. General Information

  1. This is one of five tasks (A-E) in this area of operation. Your examiner is required to test you on this task.

  2. *Pilot Operation - 4* refers to FAR 61.107(a)(4): Flight at slow airspeeds with realistic distractions, and the recognition of and recovery from stalls entered from straight flight and from turns.

  3. FAA Reference

    AC 61-21: Flight Training Handbook

  4. The objective of this task is for you to demonstrate your ability to properly recognize and recover from a full stall -- power off.

B. Task Objectives

  1. **Exhibit your knowledge by explaining the aerodynamic factors and flight situations that may result in a full stall -- power off, including proper recovery procedures, and hazards of stalling during uncoordinated flight.**

    a. Power-off stalls are practiced to simulate normal approach-to-landing conditions and configurations and are usually performed with landing gear and flaps fully extended.

      1) Many stall/spin accidents have occurred in these power-off situations, including:

        a) Cross control turns (aileron pressure in one direction, rudder pressure in the opposite direction) from base leg to final approach which results in a skidding or slipping (uncoordinated) turn,

        b) Attempting to recover from a high sink rate on final approach by only increasing pitch attitude,

        c) Improper airspeed control on final approach or in other segments of the traffic pattern, or

        d) Attempting to "stretch" a glide in a power-off approach.

b.   Recovery from power-off stalls should be practiced with and without power, although the use of power is normally expected during the practical test.

    1)   Recovery procedures are detailed on pages 336 and 337.

c.   The hazard of stalling during uncoordinated flight is that you may enter a spin.

    1)   Often a wing will drop at the beginning of a stall and the nose of your airplane will attempt to move (yaw) in the direction of the low wing.

        a)   The correct amount of opposite rudder must be applied to keep the nose from yawing toward the low wing.

    2)   By maintaining directional control (coordinated flight) the wing will not drop farther before the stall is broken, thus preventing a spin.

2.   Select an entry altitude that will allow you to complete the recovery no lower than 1,500 ft. AGL.

a.   Most training airplanes will recover from a power-off stall within 200 to 300 ft. if it is performed correctly.

b.   Your author recommends that you use an altitude that is easy to read from your altimeter.

    1)   If the terrain elevation is 300 ft. above sea level, the FAA requires a recovery no lower than 1,800 ft. MSL (1,500 ft. AGL). Round this to the nearest 500-ft. increment (2,000 ft. MSL) to make it easier to identify on your altimeter.

c.   Do not let yourself be rushed into performing this maneuver. If you do not feel that you can recover before 1,500 ft. AGL, explain this to your examiner and proceed to climb to a higher altitude.

    1)   During your training you will learn how much altitude you need to perform this maneuver.

d.   Perform clearing turns to ensure the area is clear of other traffic.

3.   Establish the normal approach or landing configuration and airspeed with the throttle closed or at a reduced power setting.

a.   Apply carburetor heat, if applicable, and retard the throttle to normal approach power while maintaining altitude.

b.   While maintaining altitude you need to lower the wing flaps.

    1)   Wing flap extension is begun when the airspeed is in the white arc of the airspeed indicator. In your airplane, V_{FE} _____.

    2)   Normally, full flaps are used.

c.   If your airplane is equipped with retractable landing gear, it should be extended.

    1)   In your airplane, V_{LE} _____.

4.   Establish a straight glide or a gliding turn with a bank angle of 30°, ±10°, in coordinated flight.

a.   As the airspeed approaches that of a normal approach, smoothly lower the nose of your airplane to the normal approach pitch attitude to maintain that airspeed.

    1)   Use the approach speed in your *POH*.

    2)   In the absence of a recommended airspeed, a speed equal to 1.3 V_{S0} should be used.

        a)   In your airplane, V_{S0} _____.

        b)   In your airplane, 1.3 V_{S0} _____.

        c)   EXAMPLE: If V_{S0} is 60 kt., approach speed is 78 kt. (1.3 x 60).

b.   You need to be proficient in performing this maneuver from straight flight and from turns.

    1)   A turn is used to simulate a stall during a turn from base leg to final approach.

        a)   Maintain a coordinated turn, i.e., keep the ball centered.

    2)   Maintain bank angle of 30°, ±10°, and use whatever control pressures are necessary to maintain the bank angle and coordination.

5.   Establish and maintain a landing pitch attitude that will induce a full stall.

a.   When the approach attitude and airspeed have stabilized, you should close the throttle and smoothly raise the airplane's nose to an attitude which will induce a stall.

    1)   In straight flight, maintain directional control with the rudder, the wings held level with the ailerons, and a constant pitch attitude maintained with the elevator.

    2)   In turning flight, maintain coordinated flight with the rudder, 30° bank angle with the ailerons, and a constant pitch attitude maintained with the elevator.

        a)   No attempt should be made to stall your airplane on a predetermined heading.

        b)   To simulate a turn from base to final, the stall normally should be made to occur within a heading change of approximately 90°.

    3)   In most training airplanes, the elevator should be smoothly brought fully back.

6.   Recognize the indications of a full stall and promptly recover by decreasing the angle of attack, leveling the wings, and adjusting the power, as necessary, to regain normal flight attitude.

a.   As discussed earlier, there are several ways to recognize that a stall is impending before it actually occurs: vision, hearing, kinesthesia, the feel of control pressures, and the stall horn.

b.   The full stall will be evidenced by such clues as full up-elevator, high sink rate, uncontrollable nose-down pitching, and possible buffeting.

c.   Stall recovery consists of the following three steps which must be taken in a coordinated manner.

    1)   The key factor in stall recovery is regaining positive control of your airplane by reducing the angle of attack.

        a)   Since the basic cause of a stall is always an excessive angle of attack, you must eliminate the cause by releasing the back elevator pressure (move the control yoke forward) that created that angle of attack.

            i)   The amount of elevator control pressure, or movement, required depends on the design of your airplane. It can range from a relaxation of the back pressure to a forcible push to the full forward position.

            ii)   Too much forward pressure can hinder recovery by imposing a negative load on the wings.

        b)   The objective is to reduce the angle of attack, but only enough to allow the wings to regain lift. Remember, you need to minimize your altitude loss.

2) Second, advance the throttle to maximum allowable power to decrease the amount of altitude loss.

    a) The throttle should be promptly but smoothly advanced to the maximum allowable power setting. In most trainer-type airplanes this would be full power.

        i) If the carburetor heat is on, you need to turn it off.

    b) Although stall recoveries should be practiced with and without use of power, in most actual stalls the application of power is an integral part of the stall recovery.

3) Finally, regain a normal flight attitude with full coordinated use of the controls.

    a) Right rudder pressure is necessary to overcome the engine torque effects as power is advanced and the nose is being lowered.

7. **Retract the wing flaps and landing gear (if retractable) and establish straight-and-level flight or climb.**

    a. Wing flaps should be adjusted immediately to provide the best lift/drag ratio (that specified for short-field takeoff) and the pitch increased to establish straight-and-level flight or climb.

        1) Check your *POH* for the correct flap position.

    b. If your airplane has retractable landing gear, you should retract the gear after a positive rate of climb has been established.

    c. Recovery can be made to straight-and-level flight or climb.

        1) Unless your examiner specifies, you should recover to your initial altitude.

        2) When recovering to a climb you should initially climb at V_X to a safe altitude, then accelerate to V_Y while incrementally retracting the wing flaps.

            a) In your airplane, V_X _____ and V_Y _____.

        3) At the appropriate altitude, level off, accelerate to cruise speed and power setting.

8. *Avoid secondary stalls, excessive airspeed, excessive altitude loss, spins, and flight below 1,500 ft. AGL.*

    a. Any of these conditions is considered unsatisfactory performance.

    b. A secondary stall is caused by attempting to hasten the completion of a stall recovery before the airplane has regained sufficient flying speed.

        1) If this stall occurs, repeat the recovery procedure discussed earlier. The key factor, again, is to release back elevator pressure.

    c. Excessive airspeed and altitude loss results from maintaining a pitch-down attitude during recovery.

        1) Relax elevator control pressure to reduce the angle of attack, then pitch to an attitude that will allow straight-and-level flight, or a climb.

    d. A spin results from an aggravated stall in either a slip or skid (i.e., uncoordinated flight).

        1) If a stall does not occur, a spin cannot occur.

    e. You must complete your recovery no lower than 1,500 ft. AGL.

C. Common errors during a full stall -- power off

1. **Failure to establish the specified flap and gear (if retractable) configuration prior to entry.**

    a. While maintaining altitude, reduce airspeed to slow flight with wing flaps and landing gear (if retractable) extended to the landing configuration.

        1) Use the landing configuration unless otherwise specified by your examiner.

    b. Remember to perform the required clearing turns.

2. **Improper pitch, heading, and bank control during straight ahead stalls.**

    a. Use your visual and instrument references as in straight descents, but with an increasing pitch attitude to induce a stall.

    b. Maintain directional control with the rudder and wings level with the ailerons.

3. **Improper pitch and bank controls during turning stalls.**

    a. Use your visual and instrument references as in turning descents, but with an increasing pitch attitude to induce a stall.

    b. Use whatever control pressure is necessary to maintain 30° angle of bank and coordinated flight.

4. **Rough or uncoordinated control technique.**

    a. As your airplane approaches the stall, the controls become increasingly sluggish, and you may assume that the controls need to be moved in a rough or jerky manner.

        1) Maintain smooth control applications at all times.

    b. Keep your airplane in coordinated flight, even if the controls feel crossed.

        1) If a power-off stall is not properly coordinated, one wing will often drop before the other and the nose will yaw in the direction of the low wing during the stall.

5. **Failure to recognize the first indications of a stall.**

    a. This is the point at which your airplane is just on the verge of a full stall.

        1) It is signaled by the first buffeting, or decay of control effectiveness.

6. **Failure to achieve a stall.**

    a. You must maintain sufficient elevator back pressure to induce a stall.
    b. A full stall is evidenced by such clues as

        1) Full back elevator pressure,
        2) High sink rate,
        3) Uncontrollable nose-down pitching, and
        4) Possible buffeting.

7. **Improper torque correction.**

    a. During recovery, right rudder pressure is necessary to overcome the engine torque effects as power is advanced and the nose is being lowered.

    b. You must cross-check outside references with the turn coordinator to ensure the ball remains centered.

8. **Poor stall recognition and delayed recovery.**

   a. Remember not to look for any one event to occur.

      1) Some pilots may attempt to hold a stall attitude because they are waiting for a particular event to occur, e.g., an abrupt pitch-down attitude.

         a) While waiting for this to occur, the airplane is losing altitude from the high sink rate of a stalled condition.

   b. Delayed recovery is aggravating the stall situation and if you do not remain in coordinated flight, the airplane is likely to enter a spin.

   c. Recognition and recovery must be immediate and prompt.

9. **Excessive altitude loss or excessive airspeed during recovery.**

   a. Do not maintain a pitch-down attitude during recovery.

      1) Move the control yoke forward to reduce the angle of attack, then smoothly adjust the pitch to the desired attitude.

10. **Secondary stall during recovery.**

   a. This happens when you hasten to complete your stall recovery (to straight-and-level flight or climb) before the airplane has realigned itself with the flight path (relative wind).

END OF TASK

FULL STALLS -- POWER ON

VII.B. TASK: FULL STALLS -- POWER ON

  PILOT OPERATION - 4

  REFERENCES: AC 61-21.

Objective. To determine that the applicant:

1. Exhibits knowledge by explaining the aerodynamic factors and flight situations that may result in full stalls -- power on, including proper recovery procedures, and hazards of stalling during uncoordinated flight.

2. Selects an entry altitude that will allow recoveries to be completed no lower than 1,500 ft. AGL.

3. Establishes takeoff or normal climb configuration.

4. Establishes takeoff or climb airspeed before applying takeoff or climb power. (Reduced power may be used to avoid excessive pitch-up during entry only.)

5. Establishes and maintains a pitch attitude straight ahead or in a turn with a bank angle of 20°, ±10°, that will induce a full stall.

6. Applies proper control to maintain coordinated flight.

7. Recognizes the indications of a full stall and promptly recovers by decreasing the angle of attack, leveling the wings, and adjusting the power, as necessary, to regain normal flight attitude.

8. Retracts the wing flaps and landing gear (if retractable) and establishes straight-and-level flight or climb.

9. Avoids secondary stalls, excessive airspeed, excessive altitude loss, spins, and flight below 1,500 ft. AGL.

A. General Information

1. This is one of five tasks (A-E) in this area of operation. Your examiner is required to test you on this task.

2. *Pilot Operation - 4* refers to FAR 61.107(a)(4): Flight at slow airspeeds with realistic distractions, and the recognition of and recovery from stalls entered from straight flight and from turns.

3. FAA Reference

   AC 61-21: Flight Training Handbook

4. The objective of this task is for you to demonstrate your ability to properly recognize and recover from a full stall -- power on.

B. Task Objectives

1. **Exhibit your knowledge by explaining the aerodynamic factors and flight situations that may result in full stalls -- power on, including proper recovery procedures, and hazards of stalling during uncoordinated flight.**

   a. Power-on stalls are practiced to simulate takeoff and climbout conditions and configurations and are usually performed in the clean configuration.

      1) Many stall/spin accidents have occurred during these phases of flight, particularly go-arounds.

         a) A causal factor in go-arounds is the pilot's failure to maintain positive control due to a nose-high trim setting or premature flap retraction.

      2) Failure to maintain positive control during short-field takeoffs has also been an accident factor.

b. Recovery from power-on stalls is generally much simpler than power-off stalls, usually requiring only a decrease in pitch.

    1) Recovery procedures are detailed on pages 342 and 343.

c. The likelihood of stalling in uncoordinated flight is increased during a power-on stall due to the greater torque from high RPM and low airspeed.

    1) A power-on stall will often result in one wing dropping.

    2) Maintaining directional control with rudder is vital to avoiding a spin.

2. Select an entry altitude that will allow you to complete the recovery no lower than 1,500 ft. AGL.

a. The increased likelihood of uncoordinated flight during a power-on stall presents the danger of excessive altitude loss.

b. Your author recommends that you use an altitude that is easy to read from your altimeter.

    1) If the terrain elevation is 300 ft. above sea level, the FAA requires a recovery no lower than 1,800 ft. MSL (1,500 ft. AGL). Round this to the nearest 500-ft. increment (2,000 ft. MSL) to make it easier to identify on your altimeter.

c. Do not let yourself be rushed into performing this maneuver. If you do not feel that you can recover before 1,500 AGL, explain this to your examiner and proceed to climb to a higher altitude.

    1) During your training you will learn how much altitude you need to perform this maneuver.

d. Perform clearing turns to ensure the area is clear of other traffic.

3. Establish takeoff or normal climb configuration.

a. Power-on stalls should be performed in a takeoff configuration (e.g., for a short-field takeoff) or in a normal climb configuration (flaps and/or gear retracted).

    1) Use the recommended takeoff or normal climb configuration in your *POH*.

b. Ensure you understand which configuration your examiner wants you to use. If you have any doubt of what (s)he wants, ask for clarification.

4. Establish takeoff or climb airspeed before applying takeoff or climb power. (Reduced power may be used to avoid excessive pitch-up during entry only.)

a. Reduce power to the normal rotation speed (V_R) while establishing the desired configuration.

    1) Maintain a constant altitude while you are slowing your airplane.
    2) In your airplane, V_R _____.

b. When the desired speed is attained, you should set the power at takeoff or recommended climb power setting, while establishing a climb attitude.

c. The purpose of reducing the speed to V_R before the throttle is advanced to the recommended setting is to avoid an excessively steep nose-up attitude for a long period before your airplane stalls.

5. **Establish and maintain a pitch attitude straight ahead or in a turn with a bank angle of 20°, ±10°, that will induce a full stall.**

   a. After the climb is established, the nose is then brought smoothly upward to an attitude which will induce a stall and is held at that attitude until the full stall occurs.

      1) This will require ever-increasing back elevator pressure.

   b. Power-on stalls should be performed either straight ahead or in a turn with a bank angle of 20°, ±10°.

6. **Apply proper control to maintain coordinated flight.**

   a. In straight flight, maintain directional control with the rudder and the wings held level with the ailerons.

   b. In turning flight, maintain coordinated flight with the rudder, and 20° bank angle with the ailerons.

   c. A power-on stall will require increasing right rudder pressure to counteract the torque effect.

7. **Recognize the indications of a full stall and promptly recover by decreasing the angle of attack, leveling the wings, and adjusting the power, as necessary, to regain normal flight attitude.**

   a. As discussed earlier, there are several ways to recognize that a stall is impending before it actually occurs: vision, hearing, kinesthesia, the feel of control pressures, and the stall horn.

   b. In most airplanes it will be found that after attaining the stalling pitch attitude, the elevator control must be moved progressively farther back as the airspeed decreases.

      1) At the full stall, it will have reached its aft limit and cannot be moved back any farther.

   c. Stall recovery consists of the following three steps which must be taken in a coordinated manner.

      1) The key factor in stall recovery is regaining positive control of your airplane by reducing the angle of attack.

         a) Since the basic cause of a stall is always an excessive angle of attack, you must eliminate the cause by releasing the back elevator pressure (move the control yoke forward) that created that angle of attack.

            i) The amount of elevator control pressure, or movement, required depends on the design of your airplane. It can range from a relaxation of the back pressure to a forcible push to the full forward position.

            ii) Too much forward pressure can hinder recovery by imposing a negative load on the wings.

         b) The objective is to reduce the angle of attack, but only enough to allow the wings to regain lift. Remember, you want to minimize your altitude loss.

      2) Next, advance the throttle to maximum allowable power to decrease the amount of altitude loss.

         a) This should be done in a smooth but positive manner.

        b)   Since the throttle is already at the takeoff or climb power setting, the addition of power will be relatively slight, if any.

           i)   Use this step to confirm you have maximum allowable power.

        c)   Although stall recoveries should be practiced with and without the use of power, in most actual stalls the application of power is an integral part of the stall recovery.

    3)   Finally, regain a normal flight attitude with full coordinated use of controls.

        a)   If in turning flight, level the wings.
        b)   Maintain directional control with the rudder to avoid uncoordinated flight.

8.   Retract the wing flaps and landing gear (if retractable) and establish straight-and-level flight or climb.

    a.   Adjust the pitch attitude to straight-and-level or climb, as desired.

    b.   Normally the wing flaps will be set at the best lift/drag ratio (that specified for a short-field takeoff) to simulate a takeoff stall, or retracted to simulate a climb-out stall.

        1)   If the flaps are extended, ensure they are at the best lift/drag ratio.

           a)   As your airplane accelerates to V_Y you should incrementally (if applicable) raise them.

        2)   Do not lower the wing flaps if they are retracted.

    c.   Normally a power-on stall is performed with the landing gear retracted (if retractable).

        1)   If you have the gear down, it should be retracted only after you have established a positive rate of climb.

    d.   Normally you will want to recover from a power-on stall in a climb to simulate reestablishing a climb-out condition.

        1)   Once you have established a climb, lower the nose and accelerate to cruise airspeed.

           a)   Then configure your airplane for cruise.

9.   *Avoid secondary stalls, excessive airspeed, excessive altitude loss, spins, and flight below 1,500 ft. AGL.*

    a.   Any of these conditions is considered unsatisfactory performance.

    b.   A secondary stall is caused by attempting to hasten the completion of a stall recovery before the airplane has regained sufficient flying speed.

        1)   If this stall occurs, repeat the stall recovery procedures. The key factor again is to release back elevator pressure.

    c.   Excessive airspeed and altitude loss results from maintaining a pitch-down attitude during recovery.

        1)   Relax elevator control pressure to reduce the angle of attack, then smoothly pitch up to an attitude that will allow straight-and-level flight, or a climb.

    d.   A spin results from an aggravated stall in either a slip or skid (i.e., uncoordinated flight).

        1)   If a stall does not occur, a spin cannot occur.

    e.   You must complete your recovery no lower than 1,500 ft. AGL.

C.   Common errors during a full stall -- power on

1.   **Failure to establish the specified landing gear and flap configuration prior to entry.**

   a.   Repeat the instructions that your examiner gave to you regarding the airplane configuration for the stall.

      1)   Your airplane will be configured for a takeoff or a normal departure climb.

   b.   Remember to perform the required clearing turns.

2.   **Improper pitch, heading, and bank control during straight ahead stalls.**

   a.   Use your visual and instrument references as in straight climbs but with an increasing pitch attitude to induce a stall.

   b.   Maintain heading and wings level during the straight ahead stall.

   c.   Use rudder pressure to counteract the torque effects.

3.   **Improper pitch and bank control during turning stalls.**

   a.   Use your visual and instrument references as in a turning climb but with an increasing pitch attitude to induce a stall.

   b.   Use whatever control pressure is necessary to maintain a bank angle of 20°, ±10°, in coordinated flight.

4.   **Rough or uncoordinated control technique.**

   a.   As your airplane approaches the stall, the controls will become increasingly sluggish, and you may assume that the controls need to be moved in a rough or jerky manner.

      1)   Maintain smooth control applications at all times.
      2)   Do not try to muscle your way through this maneuver.

   b.   Keep your airplane in coordinated flight (i.e., the ball centered), even if the controls feel crossed.

      1)   More right rudder will be needed to compensate for the torque effects.

      2)   If a power-on stall is not properly coordinated, one wing will often drop before the other wing and the nose will yaw in the direction of the low wing during the stall.

         a)   If this is not corrected a spin may develop.

5.   **Failure to recognize the first indications of a stall.**

   a.   This is the point at which your airplane is just on the verge of a full stall.

      1)   It is signaled by the first buffeting, or decay of control effectiveness.

6.   **Failure to achieve a stall.**

   a.   You must maintain sufficient elevator back pressure to induce a stall.
   b.   A full stall is evident by such clues as

      1)   Full back elevator pressure,
      2)   High sink rate,
      3)   Uncontrollable nose-down pitching, and
      4)   Possible buffeting.

7. **Improper torque correction.**

   a. Since the airspeed is decreasing with a high power setting, the effect of torque becomes more prominent.

   b. Right rudder pressure must be used to counteract torque.

8. **Poor stall recognition and delayed recovery.**

   a. Do not be waiting for any one event to happen during the stall.

      1) Some pilots may attempt to hold a stall attitude because they are waiting for a particular event to occur, e.g., an abrupt pitch-down attitude.

         a) While waiting for this to occur, the airplane is losing altitude from the high sink rate of a stalled condition.

   b. Delayed recovery aggravates the stall situation and if you do not remain in coordinated flight, the airplane is likely to enter a spin.

   c. Recognition and recovery must be immediate and prompt.

9. **Excessive altitude loss or excessive airspeed during recovery.**

   a. Do not maintain a pitch-down attitude during recovery.

      1) Move the control yoke forward to reduce the angle of attack then smoothly adjust the pitch to the desired attitude.

10. **Secondary stall during recovery.**

    a. This happens when you rush your stall recovery to straight-and-level flight or climb before the airplane has realigned itself with the flight path (relative wind).

END OF TASK

IMMINENT STALLS -- POWER ON AND POWER OFF

VII.C. TASK: IMMINENT STALLS -- POWER ON AND POWER OFF

> *PILOT OPERATION - 4*
>
> REFERENCES: AC 61-21.

Objective. To determine that the applicant:

1. Exhibits knowledge by explaining the aerodynamic factors associated with imminent stalls (power on and power off), an awareness of speed loss in different configurations, and the procedure for resuming normal flight attitude.

2. Selects an entry altitude that will allow recoveries to be completed no lower than 1,500 ft. AGL.

3. Establishes either a takeoff, a climb, or an approach configuration with the appropriate power setting.

4. Establishes a pitch attitude on a constant heading, ±10°, or 20° bank turns, ±10°, that will induce an imminent stall.

5. Applies proper control to maintain coordinated flight.

6. Recognizes and recovers from imminent stalls at the first indication of buffeting or decay of control effectiveness by reducing angle of attack and adjusting power, as necessary, to regain normal flight attitude.

7. Avoids full stall, secondary stall, excessive airspeed, excessive altitude change, spin, and flight below 1,500 ft. AGL.

A. General Information

1. This is one of five tasks (A-E) in this area of operation. Your examiner is required to test you on this task.

2. *Pilot Operation - 4* refers to FAR 61.107(a)(4): Flight at slow airspeeds with realistic distractions, and the recognition of and recovery from stalls entered from straight flight and from turns.

3. FAA Reference

    AC 61-21: Flight Training Handbook

4. The objective of this task is for you to demonstrate your ability to properly recognize and recover from imminent stalls -- power on and power off.

5. The current FAR requirement does not distinguish between full and imminent stalls.

    a. This may allow your examiner the ability to combine this task with tasks A and B of this chapter and specify whether the recovery is performed when the stall is imminent or full.

B. Task Objectives

1. **Exhibit your knowledge by explaining the aerodynamic factors associated with imminent stalls (power on and power off), an awareness of speed loss in different configurations, and the procedure for resuming normal flight attitude.**

   a. An imminent stall is one in which your airplane is approaching a stall but is not allowed to completely stall.

      1) This is for practice in retaining (or regaining) full control of your airplane immediately upon recognizing that it is almost in a full stall or that a full stall is likely to occur if timely preventive action is not taken.

   b. A stall is imminent when the *first* buffeting or decay of control is noted.

      1) Activation of the stall horn may be the first sign of an imminent stall.

   c. Unintentional speed loss can occur in several different situations, resulting in an imminent stall.

      1) Excessive pitch attitude during a short-field takeoff.
      2) Attempting to maintain altitude during severe downdrafts.
      3) Allowing the nose to pitch up during flap extension.

   d. Since you are not actually allowing the airplane to stall, recovery requires much less angle of attack reduction than in a full stall.

      1) Ideally, recovery from an imminent stall should be accomplished with no altitude loss.

      2) Recovery procedures are detailed on pages 348 and 349.

2. **Select an entry altitude that will allow you to complete the recovery no lower than 1,500 ft. AGL.**

   a. Your author recommends that you use an altitude that is easy to read from your altimeter.

      1) If the terrain elevation is 300 ft. above sea level, the FAA requires a recovery no lower than 1,800 ft. MSL (1,500 ft. AGL). Round this to the nearest 500-ft. increment (2,000 ft. MSL) to make it easier to identify on your altimeter.

   b. Do not let yourself be rushed into performing this maneuver. If you do not feel that you can recover before 1,500 AGL, explain this to your FAA inspector/examiner and proceed to climb to a higher altitude.

      1) During your training you will learn how much altitude you need to perform this maneuver.

   c. Perform clearing turns to ensure the area is clear of other traffic.

3. **Establish either a takeoff, a climb, or an approach configuration with the appropriate power setting.**

   a. Your examiner will instruct you as to which configuration you will use in the performance of this maneuver.

   b. You should slow your airplane while maintaining altitude.

      1) Slow to the following airspeeds, based on your configuration.

         a) Takeoff, use V_R. In your airplane, V_R _____.

         b) Climb, use V_Y. In your airplane, V_Y _____.

         c) Approach, use final approach speed or 1.3 V_{S0}. In your airplane, final approach _____.

    c.   As you finish your clearing turns you should have your airplane in the proper configuration and airspeed.

        1)   A takeoff configuration is normally that which your *POH* describes for a short-field takeoff.

        2)   A climb configuration is one in which your airplane is in a clean configuration, i.e., wing flaps and gear (if retractable) are retracted.

        3)   An approach configuration is one in which your airplane is in the landing (normally final) approach configuration, i.e., full flaps and gear extended.

    d.   Adjust power and pitch attitude for the proper configuration.

        1)   Takeoff and climb configurations use power on.
        2)   Approach use power off.

4.   Establish a pitch attitude on a constant heading, ±10°, or 20° bank turns, ±10°, that will induce a stall.

    a.   Once you establish a power on climb or a power off glide, you need to establish a pitch attitude that will induce a stall.

    b.   This maneuver can be entered from either straight flight or from turns.

        1)   In straight flight you must maintain a constant heading, ±10°.
        2)   In turns you must maintain 20° bank angle, ±10°.

5.   Apply proper control to maintain coordinated flight.

    a.   In straight flight, maintain directional control with the rudder and the wings held level with the ailerons.

    b.   In turning flight, maintain coordinated flight with the rudder, and 20° bank angle with the ailerons.

    c.   A power-on stall will require increasing right rudder pressure to counteract the torque effect.

6.   Recognize and recover from imminent stalls at the first indication of buffeting or decay of control effectiveness by reducing angle of attack and adjusting power, as necessary, to regain normal flight attitude.

    a.   As discussed earlier, there are several ways to recognize that a stall is impending before it actually occurs: vision, hearing, kinesthesia, the feel of control pressures, and the stall horn.

    b.   When the first buffet, decay of control effectiveness, or stall horn is noted you must initiate recovery.

        1)   This is the imminent stall.

    c.   To recover from an imminent stall (power on or power off) you use the same three steps as in a full stall recovery.

        1)   First, and the key factor, is to reduce the angle of attack to retain (or regain) full control of your airplane, by releasing the elevator back pressure.

            a)   Since the airplane will not have completely stalled, the pitch attitude needs to be decreased only to a point where minimum controllable airspeed is attained or until adequate control effectiveness is regained.

        2)   Second, advance the throttle to maximum allowable power to decrease the amount of altitude loss.

            a)   In an imminent stall -- power off this will normally be an increase to full power.

       b) In power on stalls the throttle is already at takeoff or climb power setting, thus the addition of power will be relatively slight, if any.

       c) Although stall recoveries should be practiced with and without the use of power, in most actual imminent stalls the application of power is an integral part of stall recovery.

    3) Finally, regain a normal flight attitude with full coordinated use of controls.

       a) If the flaps and/or gear are extended, they should be gradually retracted, as discussed earlier.

7. ***Avoid full stall, secondary stall, excessive airspeed, excessive altitude change, spin, and flight below 1,500 ft. AGL.***

    a. Entering into any of these conditions is considered unsatisfactory performance.

    b. Remember, an imminent stall is one in which your airplane is approaching a stall but is not allowed to completely stall.

    c. A secondary stall is caused by attempting to hasten the completion of the stall recovery before the airplane has realigned itself with the flight path (relative wind).

    d. Excessive airspeed and altitude loss occurs from maintaining a pitch-down attitude during recovery.

      1) Remember, an imminent stall occurs before the critical angle of attack is exceeded, thus only a slight release of the elevator back pressure should be enough to prevent a full stall.

    e. A spin occurs from allowing the airplane to completely stall, and maintaining this condition in either a slip or skid (i.e., uncoordinated flight).

      1) If a stall does not occur, a spin cannot occur.

    f. You must complete your recovery no lower than 1,500 ft. AGL.

C. Common errors during imminent stalls -- power on and power off

1. **Failure to establish the specified configuration prior to entry.**

    a. Repeat back to your examiner as a check of what you heard as far as the type of imminent stall (power on or power off) and the configuration.

    b. Remember to perform the required clearing turns.

2. **Improper pitch, heading, and bank control during straight ahead imminent stalls.**

    a. Use your visual and instrument references as in straight flight but with an increasing pitch attitude to approach a stall.

    b. Maintain heading and wings level during the straight ahead stall.

    c. Use rudder pressure to counteract the torque effects.

3. **Improper pitch and bank control during turning imminent stalls.**

    a. Use your visual and instrument references as in turning flight, but with an increasing pitch attitude to approach a stall.

    b. Use whatever control pressure is necessary to maintain a bank angle of 20°, ±10°, in coordinated flight.

4. **Rough or uncoordinated control technique.**

   a. As your airplane approaches the imminent stall the controls will begin to reach a point of effectiveness, and you may assume that you need to muscle the controls.

      1) Maintain smooth control applications at all times.

   b. Maintain coordinated (i.e., ball centered) flight with whatever control pressure is required, even if the controls appear crossed.

5. **Failure to recognize the imminent stall.**

   a. A stall is imminent at the first buffeting, decay of control effectiveness, or stall horn.

6. **Improper torque correction.**

   a. Apply the necessary right rudder pressure to overcome the effects of torque.

   b. Torque is prominent while climbing with maximum allowable power and during the power application during the power-off imminent stall recovery.

7. **Achieving a full stall.**

   a. Remember, an imminent stall is at the *first* buffeting or decay of control effectiveness is noted.

      1) To continue in this condition would achieve a full stall.

8. **Excessive altitude loss or excessive airspeed during recovery.**

   a. Do not maintain a pitch-down attitude during recovery.

      1) Your airplane has not exceeded the critical angle of attack, thus a slight release of back elevator pressure and adjusting power will normally allow you to recover in a normal flight attitude.

9. **Secondary stall during recovery.**

   a. This happens when you rush yourself in the recovery sequence, and the airplane does not have time to realign itself with the flight path (relative wind).

END OF TASK

MANEUVERING AT CRITICALLY SLOW AIRSPEED

VII.D. TASK: MANEUVERING AT CRITICALLY SLOW AIRSPEED

PILOT OPERATION - 4

REFERENCES: AC 61-21.

Objective. To determine that the applicant:

1. Exhibits knowledge by explaining the flight characteristics and controllability associated with maneuvering at critically slow airspeeds.

2. Selects an entry altitude that will allow the maneuver to be performed no lower than 1,500 ft. AGL.

3. Establishes and maintains a critically slow airspeed while --

    a. In coordinated straight and turning flight in various configurations and bank angles, and

    b. In coordinated departure climbs and landing approach descents in various configurations.

4. Maintains the desired altitude, ±100 ft., when a constant altitude is specified, and levels off from climbs and descents, ±100 ft.

5. Maintains the desired heading during straight flight, ±10°.

6. Maintains the specified bank angle, ±10°, in coordinated flight.

7. Maintains a critically slow airspeed, +5, −0 kt.

A. General Information

    1. This is one of five tasks (A-E) in this area of operation. Your examiner is required to test you on this task.

    2. *Pilot Operation - 4* refers to FAR 61.107(a)(4): Flight at slow airspeeds with realistic distractions, and the recognition of and recovery from stalls entered from straight flight and from turns.

    3. FAA Reference

        AC 61-21: Flight Training Handbook

    4. The objective of this task is for you to demonstrate your ability to maneuver your airplane in various configurations at airspeeds from below cruise to about 5 kt. above the stalling speed.

    5. This maneuver demonstrates the flight characteristics and degree of controllability of your airplane in slow flight.

        a. It is of great importance that you know the characteristic control responses of your airplane.

        b. You must develop this awareness in order to avoid stalls in your (or any) airplane that you may fly at the slower airspeeds which are characteristic of takeoffs, climbs, and landing approaches.

    6. Maneuvering at critically slow airspeeds may be demonstrated while simulating two distinct flight situations.

        a. Establishing and maintaining the airspeed appropriate for landing approaches and go-arounds.

        b. Turning flight at the slowest airspeed at which the airplane is capable of continued flight without stalling.

B.   Task Objectives

   1.   **Exhibit your knowledge by explaining the flight characteristics and controllability associated with maneuvering at critically slow airspeeds.**

      a.   A speed just above stall speed (about 5 kt.) is known as *Minimum Controllable Airspeed*, at which the pilot must avoid any further increase in pitch, increase in load factor, or reduction in power. If any of these three things occurs, a stall will result.

         1)   This airspeed will vary with changes in gross weight, CG location, load factors imposed by turns and pullups, and the existing density altitude.

IMPORTANT: Whenever you are at a critically slow airspeed, you will GAIN altitude by increasing power and adjusting the pitch to maintain airspeed. (In some airplanes, you may actually have to increase airspeed by pitching down to climb.) Remember to avoid the natural tendency to pull the controls back in slow flight situations where more altitude is needed. This is what contributes to most stall/spin accidents.

---

      b.   It is important to know the relationship between parasite drag, induced drag, and the power needed to maintain a given altitude (or climb angle or glide slope) at a selected airspeed.

         1)   *Parasite drag* is the drag that results from the airplane moving through the airstream. Parasite drag is increased by factors such as extended landing gear, irregularities in the skin that reduce smooth air flow, antenna mounts, dirt, etc. Parasite drag increases as the square of the airspeed and decreases with slower airspeeds.

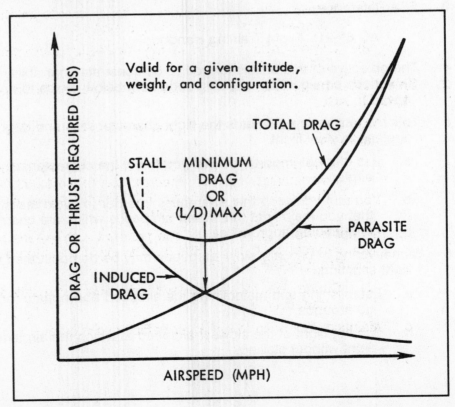

2) *Induced drag* results from the production of lift. If you fly more slowly, you have less air moving over the wings, which means you have to use a higher angle of attack to produce the lift needed to maintain your altitude (or climb angle or glide slope). Unfortunately, a greater angle of attack means more induced drag. Induced drag increases during slow flight.

   a) As gross weight increases, the amount of lift required to maintain level flight increases, as does induced drag.

   b) During turns more total lift is required to maintain a constant altitude, and the angle of attack must be increased.

3) At any particular airspeed, there is a certain amount of *total drag* (induced plus parasite) that has to be counteracted to maintain your current flight condition.

4) When your airplane is slowed down to a certain speed [*minimum drag*, which is (L/D) max], the overall drag is lower than it is at any other speed. When the airplane is slowed to less than that speed, the overall drag begins to increase again. This, in turn, means that more power is needed to fly more slowly.

   a) This is known as the region of reverse command or being behind the power curve.

   b) To gain altitude when in slow flight add power and adjust pitch to maintain or increase airspeed.

5) Gross weight, CG location, maneuvering loads, angle of bank, and power have the same effect on flight characteristics and controllability in slow flight as they do in affecting the stall speed of your airplane.

c. The flight controls in slow flight are less effective than at normal cruise due to the reduced airflow over them.

   1) Anticipate the need of right rudder to counteract the torque effect in a low airspeed, high power setting condition.

   2) Large control movements may be required, but this does not mean rough or jerky movements.

2. Select an entry altitude that will allow the maneuver to be performed no lower than 1,500 ft. AGL.

a. Your author recommends that you use an altitude that is easy to read from your altimeter.

   1) If the terrain elevation is 300 ft. above sea level, the FAA requires the maneuver to be performed no lower than 1,800 ft. MSL (1,500 ft. AGL). Round this to the nearest 500-ft. increment (2,000 ft. MSL) to make it easier to identify on your altimeter.

b. Do not let yourself be rushed into performing this maneuver. If you do not feel that you can recover before 1,500 ft. AGL, explain this to your examiner and proceed to climb to a higher altitude.

   1) During your training you will learn how much altitude you need to perform this maneuver.

c. Maintain your scan for other air traffic in your area.

3. **Establish and maintain a critically slow airspeed while --**

    a. **In coordinated straight and turning flight in various configurations and bank angles.**

        1) Begin slowing the airplane by gradually reducing power from the cruise power setting.

            a) While the airspeed is decreasing, the position of the nose in relation to the horizon should be noted and should be raised as necessary to maintain altitude.

            b) When the airspeed reaches the maximum allowable for landing gear operation (V_{LO}), the landing gear (if retractable) should be extended.

                i) Perform all gear-down checks, e.g., three in green.
                ii) In your airplane, V_{LO} _____.

            c) As the airspeed reaches the maximum allowable speed for flap operation (V_{FE}), full flaps should be incrementally lowered.

                i) This will allow you to maintain pitch control of your airplane as flaps are extended.

                ii) In your airplane, V_{FE} _____.

            d) Additional power will be required as airspeed decreases below L/D_{MAX} to maintain altitude.

                i) This assumes the airspeed will be below V_X and above the stalling speed, V_{S0} or V_{S1}.

                ii) In your airplane, V_X _____, V_{S0} _____, and V_{S1} _____.

            e) As the flight conditions change it is important to retrim your airplane as often as necessary to compensate for changes in control pressures.

            f) When the desired airspeed and pitch attitude have been established, it is important to continually cross-check the attitude indicator, altimeter, and airspeed indicator, as well as outside references to ensure that accurate control is being maintained.

        2) Once you have stabilized at a critically slow airspeed, you should maintain coordinated straight and turning flight at a constant altitude.

            a) During the turns, power and pitch attitude may need to be increased to maintain the airspeed and attitude.

                i) If you attempt an excessively steep turn, the loss of vertical lift may result in a stall.

                ii) A stall may also occur as a result of abrupt or rough control movements when flying near V_{S0} or V_{S1}.

            b) This should be practiced at various airspeeds, flap and/or gear configurations, and various angles of bank.

    b. **In coordinated departure climbs and landing approach descents in various configurations.**

        1) Once a critically slow airspeed is established for level flight, you can establish a departure climb and/or landing approach descent.

            a) Adjust the power to begin the desired climb or descent, and simultaneously adjust the pitch attitude as necessary to maintain the desired airspeed.

                i) Remember, you may need to pitch down (not up) to climb.

2) Throughout the maneuver, remain in coordinated flight by using the necessary control pressures.

3) This should be practiced at various airspeeds and flap and/or gear configurations.

4. **Maintain the desired altitude, ±100 ft., when a constant altitude is specified, and level off from climbs and descents, ±100 ft.**

5. **Maintain the desired heading during straight flight, ±10°.**

6. **Maintain the specified bank angle, ±10°, in coordinated flight.**

7. **Maintain a critically slow airspeed, +5, −0 kt.**

C. Common errors while maneuvering at critically slow airspeed

1. **Failure to establish specified configuration.**

   a. This maneuver can be performed in various configurations of landing gear and flaps.

   b. You should form a habit of repeating instructions given to you for all maneuvers. This ensures that you understand your examiner's instructions.

2. **Improper entry technique.**

   a. To begin this maneuver reduce power and gradually raise the nose. Use carburetor heat, if applicable.

   b. When the desired airspeed is attained, increase power and adjust both power and pitch to maintain airspeed and altitude.

      1) Anticipate the need of right rudder to counteract the effect of torque as power is applied.

   c. Retrim the airplane as often as necessary.

3. **Failure to establish and maintain the specified airspeed.**

   a. This is caused by the improper use of power and pitch adjustments.

4. **Excessive variations of altitude, heading, and bank when a constant altitude, heading, and bank are specified.**

   a. It is important to continually cross-check the attitude indicator, altimeter, and airspeed indicator, as well as outside references, to ensure that accurate control is being maintained.

5. **Rough or uncoordinated control technique.**

   a. A stall may occur as a result of abrupt or rough control movements.
   b. Uncoordinated control technique could risk the possibility of a crossed-control stall.

6. **Faulty trim technique.**

   a. Trim should be used to relieve control pressures.
   b. Faulty trim technique may be evidenced by poor altitude control and tiring quickly.

7. **Unintentional stall.**

   a. A stall may be caused by uneven or sudden control inputs.
   b. You must maintain your smooth control technique.

8. **Inappropriate removal of hand from throttle.**

   a. You should keep your hand on the throttle control at all times unless making an adjustment, such as trim.

END OF TASK

CONSTANT ALTITUDE TURNS

VII.E. TASK: CONSTANT ALTITUDE TURNS

　　　　PILOT OPERATION - 10

　　　　REFERENCES: AC 61-21.

Objective. To determine that the applicant:

1. Exhibits knowledge by explaining the performance factors associated with constant altitude turns, including increased load factors, power required, and overbanking tendency.

2. Selects an altitude that will allow the maneuver to be performed no lower than 1,500 ft. AGL.

3. Establishes an airspeed which does not exceed the airplane design maneuvering airspeed.

4. Enters a 360° turn maintaining a bank angle of 40° to 50° in coordinated flight.

5. Divides attention between airplane control and orientation.

6. Rolls out at the desired heading, ±10°.

7. Maintains the desired altitude, ±100 ft.

A. General Information

1. This is one of five tasks (A-E) in this area of operation. Your examiner is required to test you on this task.

2. *Pilot Operation - 10* refers to FAR 61.107(a)(10): Emergency operations, including simulated aircraft and equipment malfunctions.

3. FAA References

　　　AC 61-21: Flight Training Handbook

4. The objective of this task is for you to demonstrate your smoothness, coordination, orientation, division of attention, and control techniques in the performance of constant altitude turns.

5. This task is the same as a steep turn since you are using an angle of bank (40° to 50°) which causes an overbanking tendency.

B.   Task Objectives

    1.   **Exhibit your knowledge by explaining the performance factors associated with constant altitude turns, including increased load factors, power required, and overbanking tendency.**

       a.   Your airplane's turning performance is limited by the amount of power the engine is developing, its limit load factor (structural strength), and its aerodynamic characteristics.

       b.   A turn is made by banking the airplane so that horizontal lift from the wings pulls the airplane from its straight flight path. In a constant altitude coordinated turn, the load factor (resultant load) is the result of two forces: (1) pull of gravity and (2) centrifugal force.

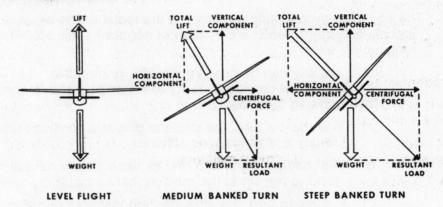

LEVEL FLIGHT   MEDIUM BANKED TURN   STEEP BANKED TURN

       1)   The load factor increases at a rapid rate after the angle of bank reaches 50°. The wing must produce lift equal to this load factor if altitude is to be maintained.

          a)   At an angle of bank of slightly more than 80° the load factor exceeds 6, which is the limit load factor for an acrobatic airplane.

          b)   The approximate maximum bank for conventional light airplanes is 60°, which produces a load factor of 2.

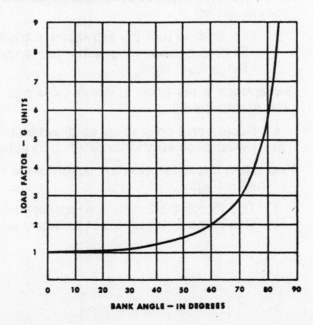

2)   At a given angle of bank in a turn during which altitude is maintained, the same load factor will always be produced.

   a)   Remember, the stalling speed increases with the square root of the load factor.

   b)   Your understanding and observance of the effects of increased load factors is an indispensable safety precaution for the performance of all turning maneuvers, particularly near the ground.

c.   In this maneuver, maintaining a constant airspeed is not required, so power is usually not adjusted.

   1)   However, some airplanes may be sufficiently underpowered as to require a slight power increase during a turn to avoid a stall.

d.   The so-called *overbanking tendency* is the result of the airplane being banked steeply enough to reach a condition of negative static stability about the longitudinal axis.

   1)   Static stability can be positive, neutral, or negative. It is the tendency of the airplane, once displaced, to try to return to a stable condition as it was before being disturbed.

      a)   In a shallow turn, the airplane displays positive static stability and tries to return to a wings-level attitude.

      b)   In a medium bank turn, the airplane shows neutral static stability and will tend to remain in the medium bank, assuming calm air.

      c)   In a steep turn, the airplane demonstrates negative static stability and tries to steepen the bank rather than remain stable. This is the overbanking tendency.

   2)   General aviation airplanes are designed with a limited amount of positive static stability around the longitudinal axis so that they will be easy to turn, but will return to straight-and-level from shallow banks.

      a)   Lateral stability about the longitudinal axis is affected by dihedral, sweepback, and keel effect.

      b)   Dihedral is the angle at which the wings are slanted upward from the root to the tip.

         i)   In a shallow turn the increased angle of attack produces increased lift on the lower wing with a tendency to return the airplane to wings-level flight.

      c)   Sweepback is the angle at which the wings are slanted rearward from the root to the tip.

         i)   Same effect on stability as dihedral, but not as pronounced.
         ii) Sweepback augments dihedral to achieve stability.

      d)   Keel effect depends upon the action of the relative wind on the side area of the fuselage.

         i)   This forces the fuselage to parallel the relative wind.
         ii) This is more noticeable in turbulent air than in turns.

3) Why overbanking occurs: As the radius of the turn becomes smaller, a significant difference develops between the speed of the inside wing and the speed of the outside wing.

    a) The wing on the outside of the turn travels a longer circuit than the inside wing, yet both complete their respective circuits in the same length of time.

    b) Therefore, the outside wing must travel faster than the inside wing; as a result, it develops more lift. This creates a slight differential between the lift of the inside and outside wings and tends to further increase the bank.

    c) When changing from a shallow bank to a medium bank, the airspeed of the wing on the outside of the turn increases in relation to the inside wing as the radius of turn decreases, but the force created exactly balances the force of the inherent lateral stability of the airplane so that, at a given speed, no aileron pressure is required to maintain that bank.

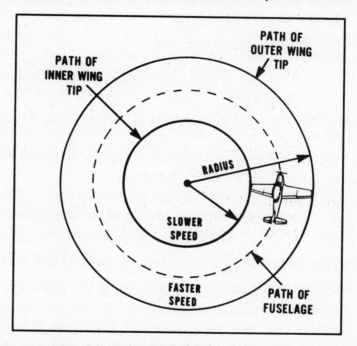

    d) As the radius decreases further when the bank progresses from a medium bank to a steep bank, the lift differential overbalances the lateral stability, and counteractive pressure on the ailerons is necessary to keep the bank from steepening.

2. **Select an altitude that will allow the maneuver to be performed no lower than 1,500 ft. AGL.**

    a. Your author recommends that you use an altitude that is easy to read from your altimeter.

        1) If the terrain elevation is 300 ft. above sea level, the FAA requires the maneuver to be performed no lower than 1,800 ft. MSL (1,500 ft. AGL). Round this to the nearest 500-ft. increment (2,000 ft. MSL) to make it easier to identify on your altimeter.

        2) The FAA allows you to maintain altitude within 100 ft. Ensure you are at least 1,600 ft. AGL.

3. **Establish an airspeed which does not exceed your airplane's design maneuvering airspeed.**

   a. Your airplane's design maneuvering airspeed (V_A) is the maximum speed at which application of full control application will not overstress the airplane.

      1) Thus, the airplane will normally stall before the load limits are exceeded, avoiding structural damage.

      2) V_A is a function of the gross weight of your airplane.

      3) See your *POH*.

         a) In your airplane, V_A _____ at _____ lb.

   b. Due to the increase in load factors during steep turns, you do not want to exceed V_A.

4. **Enter a 360° turn maintaining a bank angle of 40° to 50° in coordinated flight.**

   a. Before starting this maneuver you should perform clearing turns to ensure the area is clear of other traffic.

   b. Smoothly roll into a coordinated turn with a 40° to 50° angle of bank. If your examiner does not specify the amount of bank, use 45°.

      1) As the turn is being established, back pressure on the elevator control should be smoothly increased to increase the angle of attack.

   c. As the bank steepens beyond 30°, you may find it necessary to hold a considerable amount of back elevator control pressure to maintain a constant altitude.

      1) Additional back elevator pressure increases the angle of attack, which increases drag.

         a) Additional power may be required to maintain altitude.

      2) Retrim your airplane of excess control pressures.

         a) This will help you to maintain a constant altitude.

5. **Divide your attention between airplane control and orientation.**

   a. Do not stare at any one object during this maneuver.

   b. To maintain orientation as well as altitude requires an awareness of the relative position of the nose, the horizon, the wings, and the amount of turn.

      1) If you watch only the nose of your airplane, you will have trouble holding altitude constant and remaining oriented in the turn.

      2) By watching all available visual and instrument references you will be able to hold a constant altitude and remain oriented throughout the maneuver.

   c. Maintain control of your airplane throughout the turn.

      1) To recover from a nose-low attitude, you should first reduce the angle of bank with coordinated aileron and rudder pressure.

         a) Then back elevator pressure should be used to raise your airplane's nose to the desired pitch attitude.

         b) After completing this, reestablish the desired angle of bank.

         c) Attempting to raise the nose first will usually cause a tight descending spiral, and could lead to overstressing the airplane.

      2) If your altitude increases, the bank should be increased by coordinated use of aileron and rudder.

6. *Roll out at the desired heading, ±10°.*

    a. The roll out from the turn should be timed so that the wings reach level flight when your airplane is on the desired heading.

        1) Normally, you lead your desired heading by one-half of the number of degrees of bank, e.g., a 20° lead in a 40° bank.

            a) In a 50° bank you may want to lead by 30°, since it is easier to recognize on your heading indicator than 25°.

        2) During your training you should have developed your technique and knowledge of the lead required.

7. *Maintain the desired altitude, ±100 ft.*

    a. Maintain altitude during the constant altitude turn.

    b. The rollout from the turn should be coordinated with a gradual release of back elevator pressure and retrim so your airplane will not climb.

        1) If power was increased, decrease power during the roll out as appropriate.

C. Common errors during constant altitude turns

    1. Improper pitch, bank, and power coordination during entry and rollout.

        a. Do not overanticipate the amount of pitch change needed during entry and rollout.

            1) During entry, if the pitch is increased (nose up) before the bank is established, altitude will be gained.

            2) During recovery, if back pressure is not released, altitude will be gained.

        b. Not reaching the required amount of bank during entry and throughout the maneuver.

        c. Not using enough power during entry, or abruptly adding power.

            1) Not reducing enough power during recovery in coordination with the rollout.

    2. Uncoordinated use of flight controls.

        a. This is normally indicated by a slip, especially in right-hand turns.

        b. If the airplane's nose starts to move before the bank starts, rudder is being applied too soon.

        c. If the bank starts before the nose starts turning, or the nose moves in the opposite direction, the rudder is being used too late.

        d. If the nose moves up or down when entering a bank, excessive or insufficient back elevator pressure is being applied.

    3. Inappropriate control applications.

        a. This may be due to a lack of planning.

        b. Due to this lack of planning you may discover that a large control movement must be made to attain the desired result.

    4. Improper technique in correcting altitude deviations.

        a. When altitude is lost, you may attempt to raise the nose first by increasing back elevator pressure without shallowing the bank.

        b. This usually causes a tight descending spiral.

5. **Loss of orientation.**

   a. This can be caused by forgetting the heading or reference point from which this maneuver was started.

   b. Select a prominent checkpoint to be used in this maneuver.

6. **Excessive deviation from desired heading during rollout.**

   a. This is due to a lack of planning.
   b. The lead on the rollout should be one-half of the bank being used.

      1) If using 50° bank, 25° is needed for the rollout lead.
      2) It is easier to work with 30°, and the same result will be achieved.

END OF TASK -- END OF CHAPTER

CHAPTER VIII
FLIGHT MANEUVERING BY REFERENCE TO GROUND OBJECTS

VIII.A. Rectangular Course 364
VIII.B. S-Turns across a Road 371
VIII.C. Turns around a Point 376

This chapter explains the three tasks (A-C) of Flight Maneuvering by Reference to Ground Objects. These tasks include both knowledge and skill.

Each objective of a task lists, in sequence, the important elements that must be satisfactorily performed. The object includes:

1. Specifically what you should be able to do.
2. The conditions under which the task is to be performed.
3. The minimum acceptable standards of performance.

Be confident. You have prepared diligently and are better prepared and more skilled than the average private pilot applicant. Your examiner will base your ability to perform these tasks on the following.

1. Executing the task within your airplane's capabilities and limitations, including use of the airplane's systems.
2. Piloting your airplane with smoothness and accuracy.
3. Exercising good judgment.
4. Applying your aeronautical knowledge.
5. Showing mastery of your airplane within the standards outlined in this area of operation, with the successful outcome of a task never seriously in doubt.

These maneuvers are designed to develop your ability to control your airplane, and recognize and correct for the effect of wind while dividing attention among other matters. This requires planning ahead of your airplane, maintaining orientation in relation to ground objects, flying appropriate headings to follow a desired ground track, and being cognizant of other air traffic in the immediate vicinity.

Emphasize safety throughout your flight. Constantly check for traffic. When appropriate, say "check traffic" and point out any traffic to your FAA inspector/examiner when you see it. Also determine verbally the affect the traffic will have on your operation.

Your examiner is required to test you on all three tasks. Each task is reproduced verbatim from the FAA Practical Test Standards in a shaded box. General discussion is presented under "A. General Information." This is followed by "B. Task Objectives," which is a detailed discussion of each element of the FAA's task.

RECTANGULAR COURSE

VIII.A. TASK: RECTANGULAR COURSE

      PILOT OPERATION - 3

      REFERENCES: AC 61-21.

Objective. To determine that the applicant:

1. Exhibits knowledge by explaining wind-drift correction in straight-and-turning flight, and the relationship of the rectangular course to airport traffic patterns.

2. Selects a suitable reference area.

3. Enters a left or right pattern at a desired distance from the selected reference area and at 600 to 1,000 ft. AGL.

4. Divides attention between airplane control and ground track, and maintains coordinated flight.

5. Applies the necessary wind-drift corrections during straight-and-turning flight to maintain the desired ground track.

6. Maintains the desired altitude, ±100 ft.

7. Maintains the desired airspeed, ±10 kt.

8. Avoids bank angles in excess of 45°.

9. Reverses course, as directed by the examiner.

A. General Information

    1. This is one of three tasks (A-C) in this area of operation. Your examiner is required to test you on this task.

    2. *Pilot Operation - 3* refers to FAR 61.107(a)(3): Flight maneuvering by reference to ground objects.

    3. FAA Reference

        AC 61-21: Flight Training Handbook

    4. The objective of this task is for you to demonstrate your ability to divide your attention between airplane control and ground track while performing a rectangular course.

    5. NOTE: Your examiner will probably test you on this task while flying in the airport traffic pattern. See Task III.B., Traffic Pattern Operations, on page 228.

B. Task Objectives

    1. Exhibit your knowledge by explaining wind-drift correction in straight-and-turning flight and the relationship of the rectangular course to airport traffic patterns.

        a. As soon as your airplane becomes airborne, it is free of ground friction. Its path is then affected by the air mass (wind) and will not always track along the ground in the exact direction that it is headed.

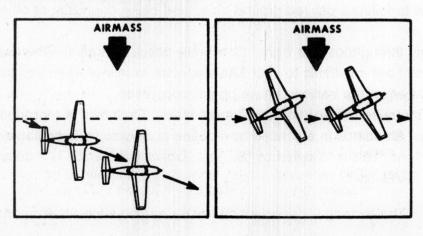

1)   In straight flight and following a selected ground track, the preferred method of correcting for wind drift is to head (crab) your airplane into the wind to cause the airplane to move forward into the wind at the same rate that the wind is moving it sideways.

    a)   Depending on the wind velocity, this may require a large crab angle or one of only a few degrees.

    b)   When the drift has been neutralized, the airplane will follow the desired ground track.

2)   In turning flight the wind will be acting on your airplane from constantly changing angles.

    a)   The time it takes for the airplane to progress through any part of a turn is governed by the relative wing angle and speed.

    b)   When your airplane is headed into the wind the groundspeed is decreased; when headed downwind the groundspeed is increased.

    c)   To fly a specific ground track, the rate of turn must be proportional to the groundspeed.

        i)   When groundspeed is higher (tailwind) the rate of turn must be greater. To get a faster rate of turn, use a steeper bank.

        ii)   Headwind results in a slower groundspeed, so use a lower rate of turn, i.e., less bank.

    d)   The diagram below shows the effect of wind during a turn. All four figures show the effect of a constant bank turn under different wind conditions.

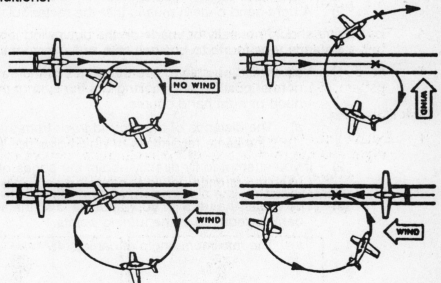

b.   The rectangular course is a practice maneuver in which the ground track of your airplane is equidistant from all sides of a rectangular area on the ground.

    1)   An objective is to develop recognition of drift toward or away from a line parallel to the intended ground track.

        a)   This will assist you in recognizing drift toward or from an airport runway during the various legs of the airport traffic pattern.

    2)   The rectangular course simulates a normal airport traffic pattern.

2.   Select a suitable reference area.

   a.   You need to select a square or rectangular field or an area bounded on four sides by section lines or roads.

   1)   The sides of the selected area should be approximately 1 mi. in length and well away from other air traffic.

   2)   The point should, however, be in an area away from communities, livestock, or groups of people on the ground to prevent possible annoyance or hazards to others.

   b.   When selecting a suitable reference area for this maneuver, you must consider possible emergency landing areas.

   1)   There is little time available to search for a suitable field for landing in the event the need arises, e.g., engine failure.

   2)   Select an area that meets the needs of the rectangular course and safe emergency landing areas.

3.   Enter a left or right pattern at a desired distance from the selected reference area and at 600 to 1,000 ft. AGL.

   a.   Your author recommends that, when given a window like this, you should always use the highest altitude, i.e., 1,000 ft. AGL.

   1)   A smart pilot is always prepared for an emergency and minimizes activity which reflects poorly on aviation.

   b.   Enter a left or right pattern as directed by your examiner.

   1)   A left-hand pattern means that the rectangular course is on your left.
   2)   A right-hand pattern means that the rectangular course is on your right.

   c.   Entry should normally be made on the downwind leg parallel to and at a uniform distance (one-fourth to one-half mile away) from the field boundaries.

   1)   You should be able to see the edges of the selected field while seated in a normal position and looking out the side of the airplane during either a left hand or right hand course.

   a)   The distance of the ground track from the edges of the field should be the same regardless of which direction the course is flown.

   2)   If you attempt to fly directly above the edges of the field, you will have no usable reference points to start and complete the turns.

   3)   The closer the track of your airplane is to the field boundaries, the steeper the bank is required at the turning points.

   a)   The maximum angle of bank is 45°.

4. **Divide attention between airplane control and ground track, and maintain coordinated flight.**

    a. As with other flight maneuvers by reference to ground objects you are required to divide your attention between maintaining control of your airplane and the desired ground track.

        1) You will also need to plan for the next leg of the course.
        2) Do not become focused on one item, e.g., watching the ground.

    b. While dividing your attention you must keep your airplane in coordinated flight.

        1) Do not use only the rudder to correct for wind drift, but turn the airplane to establish the proper ground track by coordinated use of aileron and rudder.

        2) Hold altitude by maintaining level pitch attitude.

    c. While performing this maneuver you must also divide your attention to the task of watching for other aircraft in your area, i.e., collision avoidance.

5. **Apply the necessary wind-drift corrections during straight-and-turning flight to maintain the desired ground track.**

    a. All turns should be started when your airplane is abeam the corners of the field boundaries.

    b. Although the rectangular course may be entered from any direction, this discussion begins with a downwind entry, as you would normally do in a traffic pattern.

    c. While the airplane is on the downwind leg (similar to the downwind leg in a traffic pattern), observe the next field boundary as it approaches, to plan the turn onto the crosswind leg.

        1) Maintain your desired distance (one-fourth to one-half mile) from the edge of the course.

            a) Maintain entry altitude, i.e., 1,000 ft. AGL.

        2) Since you have a tailwind on this leg, your airplane has an increased groundspeed. During the turn to the next leg, the wind will tend to move your airplane away from the field.

            a) Thus, the turn must be entered with a fairly fast rate of roll-in with a relatively steep bank.

            b) To compensate for the drift, the amount of turn must be more than 90°.

        3) As the turn progresses, the tailwind component decreases, resulting in a decreasing groundspeed.

            a) Thus, the bank angle and rate of turn must be decreased gradually to assure that, upon completion of the turn, the crosswind ground track will continue at the same distance from the field.

    d. The rollout onto this next leg (similar to the base leg in a traffic pattern), is such that as the wings become level your airplane is crabbed slightly toward the field and into the wind to correct for drift.

        1) The base leg should be continued at the same distance from the field boundary and at the entry altitude.

        2) While on the base leg the crab angle should be adjusted as necessary to maintain a uniform distance from the field.

        3) Since drift correction is being held on this leg, it is necessary to plan for a turn of less than 90° to align your airplane parallel to the upwind leg boundary.

4)   This turn should be started with a medium bank angle with a gradual reduction to a shallow bank as the turn progresses.

a)   This is due to the crosswind becoming a headwind, causing the groundspeed to decrease throughout the turn.

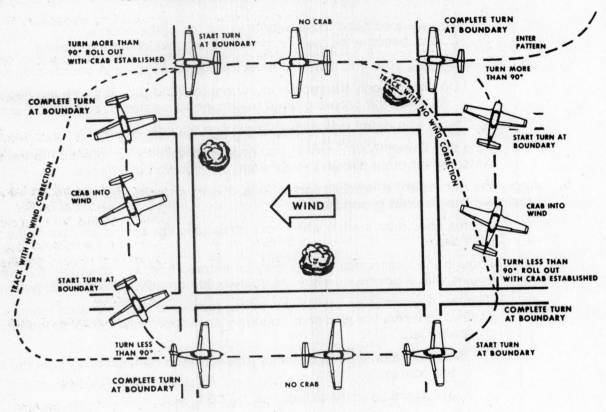

e.   The rollout onto this upwind leg (similar to the final approach and takeoff leg in a traffic pattern) should be timed to assure paralleling of the field as the wings become level.

1)   Maintain the same distance from the field boundary and maintain entry altitude.

2)   The next field boundary should be observed as it is being approached, to plan the turn onto the crosswind leg.

3)   Since the wind is a headwind on this leg, it is reducing your airplane's groundspeed and during the turn onto the crosswind leg will try to drift your airplane toward the field.

a)   Thus, the roll-in to the turn must be slow and the bank relatively shallow to counteract this effect.

b)   As the turn progresses, the headwind component decreases, allowing the groundspeed to increase.

i)   Consequently, the bank angle and rate of turn must be increased gradually to assure upon completion of the turn the crosswind ground track will continue the same distance from the edge of the field.

c)   To compensate for drift, the amount of turn will be less than 90°.

    f.   The rollout onto this crosswind leg (similar to the crosswind leg of a traffic pattern) is such that as the wings become level your airplane is crabbed slightly into the wind (i.e., away from the field) to correct for drift.

        1)   Maintain the same distance from the field boundary and at the entry altitude.

        2)   While on this leg, the crab angle should be adjusted as necessary to maintain a uniform distance from the field.

        3)   As the next field boundary is approached you should plan the turn onto the downwind leg.

            a)   Since the crab angle is being held into the wind and away from the field, this turn will be greater than 90°.

        4)   Since the crosswind will become a tailwind, causing the groundspeed to increase during this turn, the bank initially must be medium and progressively increased as the turn proceeds.

        5)   To complete the turn, the rollout must be timed so that the wings become level at a point aligned with the crosswind corner of the field just as the longitudinal axis of your airplane becomes parallel to the field boundary.

    g.   Ideally drift should not be encountered on the downwind or the upwind leg, but it may be difficult to find a situation where the wind is blowing exactly parallel to the field boundaries.

        1)   This would make it necessary to crab slightly on all legs.

        2)   It is important to anticipate the turns to correct for groundspeed, drift, and turning radius.

        3)   With a tailwind, the turn must be faster and steeper.

            a)   With a headwind, the turn must be slower and shallower.

        4)   You use these same techniques when flying an airport traffic pattern.

6. *Maintain the desired altitude, ±100 ft.*

    a.   Throughout this maneuver a constant altitude should be maintained.

    b.   As the bank increases, you will need to increase back elevator pressure to pitch the airplane's nose up to maintain altitude.

        1)   As the bank decreases, you will need to release some of the back elevator pressure to maintain altitude.

    c.   Maintain pitch awareness by visual references and use your altimeter to ensure you are maintaining altitude.

7. *Maintain the desired airspeed, ±10 kt.*

    a.   Normally, this maneuver is done at cruise airspeed in trainer-type airplanes.

    b.   Maintaining altitude will assist you in maintaining your airspeed.

        1)   Check your airspeed indicator to ensure you are maintaining your entry airspeed.

8. *Avoid bank angles in excess of 45°.*

9. **Reverse course as directed by your examiner.**

   a. To reverse course you will need to depart from the field boundaries and remain oriented with the field and wind direction.

   b. Then re-enter the course in the new direction.

   1) Remember, what was your downwind leg will now be your upwind leg.

   c. Maintain your watch for other traffic in your area.

C. Common errors while performing a rectangular course

1. **Poor planning, orientation, or division of attention.**

   a. Poor planning results in not beginning or ending the turns properly at the corners of the rectangular course. You must plan ahead and anticipate the effects of the wind.

   b. Poor orientation normally results in not being able to identify the wind direction. This will cause problems in your planning.

   c. Poor division of attention will result in your inability to maintain a proper ground track, altitude, and/or airspeed.

   1) You may not notice other aircraft that have entered the area near you.

2. **Uncoordinated flight control application.**

   a. This error normally occurs when you begin to fixate on the field boundaries and attempting to use only rudder pressure to correct for drift.

   b. Use coordinated aileron and rudder in all turns and in adjusting the crab angle when necessary.

3. **Improper wind drift correction.**

   a. This occurs from either not fully understanding the effect the wind has on the ground track or from not dividing your attention to recognize the need for wind drift correction.

   b. Once you recognize the need for a correction, take immediate steps to correct for wind drift with coordinate use of the flight controls.

4. **Failure to maintain selected altitude or airspeed.**

   a. Most student pilots will gain altitude during the initial training in this maneuver.

   b. This is due to poor division of attention and/or a lack of proper pitch awareness.

   1) You must learn the visual references to maintain altitude.

   c. By maintaining a constant altitude and not exceeding a 45° angle of bank will allow you to maintain your airspeed within the standards.

5. **Selection of a ground reference where there is no suitable emergency landing area within gliding distance.**

   a. Always be ready for any type of emergency. This is part of your planning.

   b. When you identify your course boundaries, explain to your examiner your selection of an emergency landing area.

END OF TASK

S-TURNS ACROSS A ROAD

> **VIII.B. TASK: S-TURNS ACROSS A ROAD**
>
> *PILOT OPERATION - 3*
>
> REFERENCES: AC 61-21.
>
> **Objective.** To determine that the applicant:
>
> 1. Exhibits adequate knowledge by explaining the procedures and wind-drift correction associated with S-turns.
> 2. Selects a suitable ground reference line.
> 3. Enters perpendicular to the selected reference line at 600 to 1,000 ft. AGL.
> 4. Divides attention between airplane control and ground track, and maintains coordinated flight.
> 5. Applies the necessary wind-drift correction to track a constant radius turn on each side of the selected reference line.
> 6. Reverses the direction of turn directly over the selected reference line.
> 7. Maintains the desired altitude, ±100 ft.
> 8. Maintains the desired airspeed, ±10 kt.

A. General Information

1. This is one of three tasks (A-C) in this area of operation. Your examiner is required to test you on this task.

2. *Pilot Operation - 3* refers to FAR 61.107(a)(3): Flight maneuvering by reference to ground objects.

3. FAA Reference

   AC 61-21: Flight Training Handbook

4. The objective of this task is for you to demonstrate your ability to divide your attention between airplane control and ground track while performing S-turns across a road.

B. Task Objectives

1. **Exhibit adequate knowledge by explaining the procedures and wind-drift correction associated with S-turns.**

   a. An S-turn across a road is a practice maneuver in which your airplane's ground track describes semicircles of equal radii on each side of a selected straight line on the ground.

   b. The objectives are

      1) To develop your ability to compensate for drift during turns,
      2) Orient the flight path with ground references, and
      3) Divide your attention.

   c. The maneuver consists of crossing a reference line on the ground at a 90° angle and immediately beginning a series of 180° turns of uniform radius in opposite directions, recrossing the road at 90° angle just as each 180° turn is completed.

   d. Since turns to effect a constant radius on the ground track require a changing roll rate and angle of bank to establish the crab needed to compensate for the wind, both will increase or decrease as groundspeed increases or decreases.

      1) The bank must be steepest when beginning the turn on the downwind side of the ground reference line and must be shallowed gradually as the turn progresses from a downwind heading to an upwind heading.

      2) On the upwind side, the turn should be started with a relatively shallow bank and then gradually steepen as the airplane turns from an upwind heading to a downwind heading.

2.   **Select a suitable ground reference line.**

   a.   Before starting the maneuver you must select a straight ground reference line.

      1)   This line may be a road, fence, railroad, or section line that is easily identifiable to you.

      2)   This line should be perpendicular (i.e., 90°) to the direction of the wind.

      3)   The line should be a sufficient length for making a series of turns.

      4)   The point should, however, be in an area away from communities, livestock, or groups of people on the ground to prevent possible annoyance or hazards to others.

   b.   When selecting a suitable ground reference line for this maneuver, you must also consider possible emergency landing areas.

      1)   There is little time available to search for a suitable field for landing in the event the need arises, e.g., an engine failure.

      2)   Select an area that meets the requirements of both S-turns and safe emergency landing areas.

   c.   Finally, check the area to ensure that no obstructions or other aircraft are in the immediate vicinity.

3.   **Enter perpendicular to your selected reference line at an altitude of 600 to 1,000 ft. AGL.**

   a.   Your airplane should be perpendicular to your ground reference line.

      1)   Approach the reference line from the upwind side (i.e., so the airplane is heading downwind).

      2)   You airplane should be in the normal cruise configuration.

   b.   Your author recommends that, when given an altitude window like this, you should always use the highest altitude, i.e., 1,000 ft. AGL.

      1)   A smart pilot is always prepared for an emergency and minimizes activity which reflects poorly on aviation.

   c.   When directly over the road, the first turn should be started immediately.

      1)   This normally means that when your airplane's lateral (i.e., wingtip-to-wingtip) axis is over the reference line, the first turn is started.

4.   **Divide attention between airplane control and ground track, and maintain coordinated flight.**

   a.   As with other ground reference maneuvers, you will be required to divide your attention between following the proper ground track and maintaining control of your airplane.

      1)   Your attention must be divided between watching the ground reference line, maintaining the proper ground track, watching your flight instruments, and watching for other aircraft in your area.

   b.   Since you will be changing bank constantly throughout this maneuver, you must maintain coordinated flight (i.e., keeping the ball centered).

      1)   Avoid using only the rudder to turn the airplane in order to arrive perpendicular over your reference line.

   c.   You must learn to divide your attention and not fixate on one item such as the ground reference line.

5. **Apply the necessary wind-drift correction to track a constant radius turn on each side of your selected reference line.**

   a. With your airplane headed downwind, the groundspeed is the greatest and the rate of departure from the road will be rapid.

      1) The roll into the steep bank must be fairly rapid to attain the proper crab angle.

         a) This prevents your airplane from flying too far from your selected reference line and from establishing a ground track of excessive radius.

      2) During the latter portion of the first 90° of turn when your airplane's heading is changing from a downwind heading to a crosswind heading, the groundspeed decreases and the rate of departure from the reference line decreases.

         a) The crab angle will be at the maximum when the airplane is headed directly crosswind.

   b. After turning 90°, your airplane's heading becomes more of an upwind heading.

      1) The groundspeed will decrease, and the rate of closure with the reference will become slower.

         a) Thus, it will be necessary to gradually shallow the bank during the remaining 90° of the semicircle, so that the crab angle is removed completely and the wings become level as the 180° turn is completed at the moment the reference line is reached.

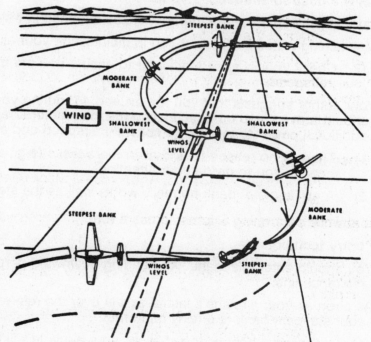

   c. Once over the reference line a turn will be started in the opposite direction. Since your airplane is still flying into the headwind, the groundspeed is relatively slow.

      1) The turn will have to be started with a shallow bank so as to avoid an excessive rate of turn which would establish the maximum crab angle too soon.

      2) The degree of bank should be that which is necessary to attain the proper crab so the ground track describes an arc the same size as the one established on the downwind side.

    d.   Since your airplane is turning from an upwind to a downwind heading, the groundspeed will increase and, after turning 90°, the rate of closure with the reference line will increase rapidly.

        1)   The angle of bank and rate of turn must be progressively increased so that your airplane will have turned 180° at the time it reaches the reference line.

    e.   Throughout this maneuver the bank angle should be changing constantly to track a constant radius turn on each side of the selected reference line.

6.   Reverse the direction of turn directly over your selected reference line.

    a.   The rollout must be timed so your airplane is in straight-and-level flight directly over and perpendicular to your reference line.

    b.   At the instant the reference line is crossed, a turn in the opposite direction should be started.

7.   *Maintain the desired altitude, ±100 ft.*

    a.   Throughout this maneuver a constant altitude should be maintained.

    b.   As the bank increases, you will need to increase back elevator pressure to pitch the airplane's nose up to maintain altitude.

        1)   As the bank decreases, you will need to release some of the back elevator pressure to maintain altitude.

    c.   Maintain pitch awareness by visual references and use your altimeter to ensure you are maintaining altitude.

8.   *Maintain the desired airspeed, ±10 kt.*

    a.   Normally this maneuver is done at cruise airspeed in trainer-type airplanes.

    b.   Maintaining altitude will assist you in maintaining your airspeed.

        1)   Check your airspeed indicator to ensure you are maintaining your entry airspeed.

    c.   Your author suggests that you not exceed 45° during your steepest banks. This should prevent you from increasing the load factor to a point that may require additional power to maintain a constant airspeed and altitude.

        1)   There is no reason to add even more tasks (e.g., addition of power) that will cause you to divide your attention.

        2)   A 45° angle of bank normally works well as the steepest bank in S-turns.

C.   Common errors while performing S-turns across a road

    1.   Faulty entry technique.

        a.   You should enter this maneuver heading downwind perpendicular to your selected reference line.

        b.   As soon as your airplane's lateral axis is over the reference line you must roll into your steepest bank at a fairly rapid rate.

            1)   If the initial bank is too shallow, your airplane will be pushed too far from the reference line and thus establishing a ground track of excessive radius.

    2.   Poor planning, orientation, or division of attention.

        a.   Poor planning is the result of not constantly changing the bank required to effect a true semicircle ground track.

            1)   This may cause your airplane to be in straight-and-level flight before the reference line, or still in a bank while crossing the reference line.

        b.   Poor orientation usually is the result of not selecting a good ground reference line and/or not identifying the wind direction.

c.   Poor division of attention will result in your inability to maintain a proper ground track, altitude, and/or airspeed.

   1)   You may not notice other aircraft that have entered the area near you.

3.   Uncoordinated flight control application.

a.   This normally occurs when you begin to fixate on the ground reference line and you then forget to use the flight controls in a coordinated manner.

b.   Do not use the rudder to yaw the nose of the airplane in an attempt to be directly over and perpendicular to the reference line.

c.   Maintain a coordinated flight condition (i.e., keep the ball centered) throughout this maneuver.

4.   Improper correction for wind drift.

a.   If a constant steep turn were maintained during the downwind side, the airplane would turn too quickly during the last 90° for the slower rate of closure, and would be headed perpendicular to the reference line prematurely (i.e., wings level before you arrive over the reference line).

   1)   To avoid this error, you must gradually shallow the bank during the last 90° of the semicircle, so that the crab angle is removed completely as the wings become level directly over the reference line.

b.   Often there is a tendency to increase the bank too rapidly during the initial part of the turn on the upwind side, which will prevent the completion of the 180° turn before recrossing the road.

   1)   To avoid this error, you must visualize the desired half circle ground track, and increase the bank during the early part of this turn.

      a)   During the latter part of the turn, when approaching the road, you must judge the closure rate properly and increase the bank accordingly, so as to cross the road perpendicular to it just as the rollout is completed.

5.   An unsymmetrical ground track.

a.   Your first semicircle will establish the radii of the semicircles.

   1)   You must be able to visualize your ground track and plan for the effect the wind will have on the ground track.

b.   The bank of your airplane must be constantly changing (except in the case of no wind) in order to effect a true semicircle ground track.

6.   Failure to maintain selected altitude or airspeed.

a.   Most student pilots will have trouble maintaining altitude or airspeed initially due to their inexperience in dividing their attention.

   1)   Learn to divide your attention between the ground reference line and airplane control (e.g., pitch awareness).

b.   By maintaining altitude, you should be able to maintain your selected airspeed, when entering at normal power setting.

7.   Selection of a ground reference line where there is no suitable emergency landing area within gliding distance.

a.   Part of your planning should be the preparation for any type of an emergency.

b.   When you identify your reference line to your examiner you should also identify your emergency landing area to him/her.

END OF TASK

TURNS AROUND A POINT

VIII.C. TASK: TURNS AROUND A POINT

   PILOT OPERATION - 3

   REFERENCES: AC 61-21.

Objective. To determine that the applicant:

1. Exhibits knowledge by explaining the procedures and wind-drift correction associated with turns around a point.

2. Selects suitable ground reference points.

3. Enters a left or right turn at a desired distance from the selected reference point at 600 to 1,000 ft. AGL.

4. Divides attention between airplane control and ground track, and maintains coordinated flight.

5. Applies the necessary wind-drift corrections to track a constant-radius turn around the selected reference point.

6. Maintains the desired altitude, ±100 ft.

7. Maintains the desired airspeed, ±10 kt.

A. General Information

   1. This is one of three tasks (A-C) in this area of operation. Your examiner is required to test you on this task.

   2. *Pilot Operation - 3* refers to FAR 61.107(a)(3): Flight maneuvering by reference to ground objects.

   3. FAA Reference

      AC 61-21: Flight Training Handbook

   4. The objective of this task is for you to demonstrate your ability to divide your attention between airplane control and ground track while performing turns around a point.

B. Task Objectives

   1. **Exhibit your knowledge by explaining the procedures and wind-drift correction associated with turns around a point.**

      a. A turn around a point is a practice maneuver in which your airplane is flown in two or more complete circles of uniform radii or distance from a prominent ground reference point.

         1) Use a maximum bank of approximately 45°.

      b. The objectives are

         1) To develop your ability to compensate for drift during turns,

         2) Orient the flight path with the ground reference point, and

         3) Divide your attention between the flight path and ground reference point, and watch for other air traffic in your area.

      c. A constant radius around a point will, if any wind exists, require a constantly changing angle of bank and angles of crab.

         1) The closer your airplane is to a direct downwind heading where the groundspeed is greatest, the steeper the bank and the faster the rate of turn required to establish the proper crab.

    2)   The closer your airplane is to a direct upwind heading where the groundspeed is least, the shallower the bank and rate of turn required to establish the proper crab.

    3)   It follows, then, that throughout the maneuver the bank and rate of turn must be gradually varied in proportion to the groundspeed.

2.   Select suitable ground reference points.

  a.   The point you select should be prominent, easily distinguished by you, and yet small enough to present a precise reference.

    1)   Isolated trees, crossroads, or other similar landmarks are usually suitable.

    2)   The point should, however, be in an area away from communities, livestock, or groups of people on the ground to prevent possible annoyance or hazards to others.

  b.   When selecting a suitable ground reference point, you must also consider possible emergency landing areas.

    1)   There is little time available to search for a safe field for landing in the event the need arises, e.g., an engine failure.

    2)   Select an area that provides a usable ground reference point and an area for the opportunity for a safe emergency landing.

3.   Enter a left or right turn at a desired distance from the selected reference point at 600 to 1,000 ft. AGL.

  a.   To enter turns around a point, your airplane should be flown on a downwind heading to one side of the selected point at a distance equal to the desired radius of turn.

    1)   To enter a left turn, the point should be to your left.

      a)   To enter a right turn, the point should be to your right.

    2)   In a high-wing airplane (e.g., C-152), the distance from the point must permit you to see the point throughout the maneuver even with the wing lowered in a bank.

      a)   If the radius is too large, the lowered wing will block your view of the point.

  b.   Your airplane should be in the normal cruise configuration.

  c.   Your author recommends that, when given an altitude window like this you should use the highest altitude, i.e., 1,000 ft. AGL.

    1)   A smart pilot is always prepared for an emergency and minimizes activity which reflects poorly on aviation.

  d.   When any significant wind exists, it will be necessary to roll your airplane into the initial bank at a rapid rate so that the steepest bank is attained abeam of the point when headed downwind.

    1)   Thus, if the maximum bank of 45° is desired, the initial bank will be 45° if your airplane is at the correct distance from the point.

4. **Divide attention between airplane control and ground track, and maintain coordinated flight.**

    a.   As with other ground reference maneuvers, you will be required to divide your attention between following the proper ground track and maintaining control of your airplane.

        1)   You must divide your attention between watching the ground reference point, maintaining the proper ground track, watching your flight instruments, and watching for other air traffic in your area.

    b.   Since you will be changing bank constantly throughout this maneuver, you must maintain coordinated flight (i.e., keeping the ball centered).

        1)   Avoid using only rudder pressure to correct for wind-drift.

           a)   Use coordinated aileron and rudder to increase or decrease bank to correct for wind-drift.

    c.   You must learn to divide your attention and not fixate on any one item such as the ground reference point.

5. **Apply the necessary wind-drift correction to track a constant radius turn around your selected reference point.**

    a.   With your airplane headed downwind, the groundspeed is the greatest. The steepest bank is used to attain the proper crab angle and to prevent your airplane from flying too far away from your reference point.

        1)   During the next 180° of turn (the downwind side), your airplane's heading is changing from a downwind to an upwind heading and the groundspeed decreases.

        2)   During the downwind half of the circle, the nose of your airplane must be progressively crabbed toward the inside of the circle.

           a)   The crab angle will be at its maximum when the airplane is headed directly crosswind (i.e., at the 90° point).

           b)   The crab is slowly taken out as your airplane progresses to a direct upwind heading.

        3)   Throughout the downwind side of the circle, your airplane's bank goes from the steepest (directly downwind) to shallowest (directly upwind).

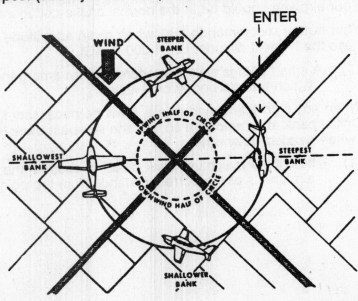

b. With your airplane headed upwind, the groundspeed is the least. This requires the shallowest bank.

   1) During the next 180° of turn (the upwind side), your airplane's heading is changing from an upwind to a downwind heading and the groundspeed increases.

   2) During the upwind half of the circle, the nose of your airplane must be progressively crabbed toward the outside of the circle.

      a) The crab angle will be at its maximum when the airplane is headed directly crosswind.

      b) The crab is slowly taken out as your airplane progresses to a direct downwind heading.

   3) Throughout the upwind side of the circle, your airplane's bank goes from shallowest (directly upwind) to steepest (directly downwind).

6. *Maintain the desired altitude, ±100 ft.*

   a. Throughout this maneuver you should maintain a constant altitude (i.e., 1,000 ft. AGL).

   b. Since your bank will constantly change, if a wind exists, you will need to adjust pitch attitude to maintain altitude.

      1) As bank increases, pitch attitude may need to be raised by back elevator pressure.

         a) As the bank decreases, release an appropriate amount of back elevator pressure to maintain altitude.

   c. Maintain pitch awareness by visual references and use your altimeter to ensure you are maintaining altitude.

7. *Maintain desired airspeed, ±10 kt.*

   a. Normally this maneuver is done at cruise airspeed in trainer-type airplanes.

   b. Maintaining altitude will assist you in maintaining your airspeed.

      1) Check your airspeed indicator to ensure you are maintaining your entry airspeed.

   c. With using 45° as your steepest angle of bank, the load factors should not be great enough to require an addition of power to maintain a constant airspeed and altitude.

C. Common errors while performing turns around a point

1. **Faulty entry technique.**

   a. Entry should be done on a downwind heading. By doing this you can establish your steepest angle of bank at the start of the maneuver.

      1) If you attempt to enter this maneuver at any other point, the radius of the turn must be carefully selected, taking into account the wind velocity and groundspeed so that an excessive angle of bank is not required later on to maintain the proper ground track.

   b. When entering downwind, if the steepest bank is not used, the wind will blow your airplane too far from your reference point to maintain a constant radius.

2. **Poor planning, orientation, or division of attention.**

   a. Poor planning is the result of not changing the bank required to counteract drift to effect a circle of equal radius about a reference point.

   b. Poor orientation is usually the result of not selecting a prominent reference point, thus losing sight of the point.

      1) It may also be not knowing the wind direction, thus becoming disoriented as to an upwind and a downwind heading.

   c. Poor division of attention will result in your inability to maintain a proper ground track, altitude, and/or airspeed.

      1) You may not notice other aircraft that have entered the area near you.

3. **Uncoordinated flight control application.**

   a. This normally occurs when you begin to fixate on your reference point and you then forget to use the flight controls in a coordinated manner.

   b. Do not attempt to crab your airplane by using only rudder pressure.

   c. Maintain a coordinated flight condition (i.e., keep the ball centered) throughout this maneuver.

4. **Improper correction for wind drift.**

   a. You should use the steepest bank (i.e., 45°) when heading directly downwind.

      1) During the downwind side, the bank will gradually decrease as you approach an upwind heading.

         a) The nose of the airplane will be crabbed toward the inside of the circle.

   b. The bank will be the shallowest when heading directly upwind.

      1) During the upwind side, the bank will gradually increase as you approach a downwind heading.

         a) The nose of the airplane will be crabbed toward the outside of the circle.

5. **Failure to maintain selected altitude or airspeed.**

   a. Most student pilots will have trouble maintaining altitude or airspeed initially due to their inexperience in dividing their attention.

      1) Learn to divide your attention between the reference point and airplane control (e.g., pitch awareness).

   b. By maintaining altitude, you should be able to maintain your selected airspeed, when entering at normal cruise power setting.

6. **Selection of a ground reference point where there is no suitable emergency landing area within gliding distance.**

   a. Part of your planning should be the preparation for any type of an emergency.

   b. When you identify your reference point to your examiner, you should also identify your emergency landing area to him/her.

END OF TASK -- END OF CHAPTER

CHAPTER IX
NIGHT FLIGHT OPERATIONS

IX.A. Night Flight 382

This chapter explains the only task of Night Flight Operations. This task includes both knowledge and skill.

Each objective of a task lists, in sequence, the important elements that must be satisfactorily performed. The object includes:

1. Specifically what you should be able to do.
2. The conditions under which the task is to be performed.
3. The minimum acceptable standards of performance.

Be confident. You have prepared diligently and are better prepared and more skilled than the average private pilot applicant. Your examiner will base your ability to perform these tasks on the following.

1. Executing the task within your airplane's capabilities and limitations, including use of the airplane's systems.
2. Piloting your airplane with smoothness and accuracy.
3. Exercising good judgment.
4. Applying your aeronautical knowledge.
5. Showing mastery of your airplane within the standards outlined in this area of operation, with the successful outcome of a task never seriously in doubt.

Night flying is considered to be an important phase in your training as a pilot. Proficiency in night flying not only increases utilization of the airplane but it provides important experience in case an extended day flight extends into darkness. Many pilots prefer night flying over day flying because the air is usually smoother and generally there is less air traffic to contend with.

If you are to be evaluated on night flying operations, your examiner must evaluate elements 1 through 3. Elements 4 through 8 may be evaluated at the option of your examiner. This task is reproduced verbatim from the FAA Practical Test Standards in the shaded box. General discussion is presented under "A. General Information." This is followed by "B. Task Objectives," which is a detailed discussion of each element of the FAA's task.

NIGHT FLIGHT

IX.A. TASK: NIGHT FLIGHT

    PILOT OPERATION - 9

    REFERENCES: AC 61-21, AC 67-2.

Objective. To determine that the applicant:

1. Explains preparation, equipment, and factors essential to night flight.

2. Determines airplane, airport, and navigation lighting.

3. Exhibits knowledge by explaining night flying procedures, including safety precautions and emergency actions.

4. Inspects the airplane by following the checklist which includes items essential for night flight operations.

5. Starts, taxies, and performs pretakeoff check adhering to good operating practices.

6. Performs takeoffs and climbs with emphasis on visual references.

7. Navigates and maintains orientation under VFR conditions.

8. Approaches and lands adhering to good operating practices for night flight operations.

A. General Information

1. This is the only task in this area of operation. Your examiner is required to test you on this task. (S)he must evaluate elements 1 through 3, while 4 through 8 may be evaluated at his/her option.

    a. You will be tested on this task only if your CFI has given you 3 hr. of instruction at night, including 10 takeoffs and landings [FAR 61.109(a)(2)].

        1) If you have not received the required night instruction, your certificate will bear the limitation, "Night Flying Prohibited."

        2) Note, however, that you must have received at least some night instruction to qualify for the private pilot certificate.

2. *Pilot Operation - 9* refers to FAR 61.107(a)(9): Night flying, including takeoffs, landings, and VFR navigation.

3. FAA References

    AC 61-21: Flight Training Handbook
    AC 67-2: Medical Handbook for Pilots

4. The objective of this task is for you to demonstrate your knowledge of the elements of night flying operations. Actual performance of these operations at night is an option to your examiner.

B. Task Objectives

1. **Explain the preparation, equipment, and factors essential to night flight.**

    a. Although careful planning of any flight is essential for maximum safety and efficiency, night flying demands more attention to all details of preflight preparation and planning.

        1) Preparation for a night flight should include a thorough study of the available weather reports and forecasts, with particular attention given to temperature/dewpoint spread because of the possibility of formation of ground fog during the night flight.

a) Upcoming clouds and areas of thunderstorms are much more difficult to see and avoid, especially on moonless or overcast nights.

b) Any haze can effectively reduce flight visibility to zero at night.

c) You also need to know the forecast wind direction and speed, since drifting cannot be detected as readily at night as during the day.

2) On night cross-country flights, as on all flights, the proper navigational (sectional) charts should be selected and available.

a) Avoid red, yellow, or orange course markings as they will tend to disappear under red map lights.

b) Checkpoints must be selected carefully to ensure being seen at night.

i) Rotating beacons at airports.
ii) Lighted obstructions.
iii) Lights of cities.
iv) Lights from major highway traffic.

c) The use of radio navigation and radar flight following is highly recommended at night.

d) Charts should be systematically folded and arranged, and a navigation log carefully filled in prior to every flight to promote cockpit organization.

e) Accurate awareness of your position and proximity to airports is vital at night.

i) Suitable emergency landing fields are almost impossible to detect in the dark.

3) All personal equipment (e.g., flashlight) should be checked prior to flight to ensure proper functioning.

b. Before beginning a night flight, you should carefully consider certain personal equipment that should be readily available during the flight.

1) This equipment may not differ greatly from that needed for a day flight, but the importance of its availability when needed at night cannot be over-emphasized.

2) At least one reliable flashlight is recommended as standard equipment on all night flights.

a) A "D" cell size flashlight with a bulb-switching mechanism that can be used to select white or red light is preferable.

i) The white light is used while performing the preflight visual inspection of the airplane, and the red light is used in performing cockpit operations.

ii) Since the red light is nonglaring, it will not impair night vision.

b) Some pilots prefer two flashlights, one with a white light for preflight, and the other a penlight type with a red light.

i) The penlight can be suspended by a string from around the neck to ensure that the light is always readily available during flight.

ii) CAUTION: If a red light is used for reading a sectional chart, the red features of the chart will not be visible to you.

3) Sectional and/or other aeronautical charts are essential for all cross-country flights.

4) To prevent losing essential items in the dark cockpit, you should have a clipboard or mapboard on which charts, navigation logs, and other essentials can be fastened.

    a) You may also want to consider a map case to store needed materials.

5) A reliable clock is needed for night flights.

c. Understanding how your eyes operate at night is an important factor in night flying. It is important for you to understand your eye's construction and how the eye is affected by darkness.

1) Two types of light-sensitive nerve endings called "cones" and "rods" are located at the back of the eye, or retina, which transmit messages to the brain via the optic nerve.

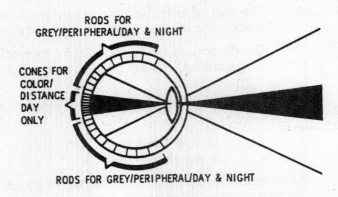

    a) The cones are located in the center of the retina, directly behind the pupil.

        i) Their function is to detect color, details, and distant objects.
        ii) They function both in daylight and in moonlight.

    b) The rods are concentrated in a ring around the cones.

        i) Their function in daylight is to detect objects, particularly those in motion, out of the corner of the eye (i.e., peripheral vision), but do not give detail or color, only shades of gray.

        ii) They function in daylight, moonlight, and in darkness.

2) The fact that the rods are distributed around the cones and do not lie directly behind the pupils, makes "off center" viewing (i.e., looking to one side of an object) important during night flight.

    a) During daylight an object can be seen best by looking directly at it.

    b) At night, you will find after some practice that you can see things more clearly and definitely at night by looking to one side of them, rather than straight at them.

        i) Remember, rods do not detect objects while your eyes are moving, only during the pauses.

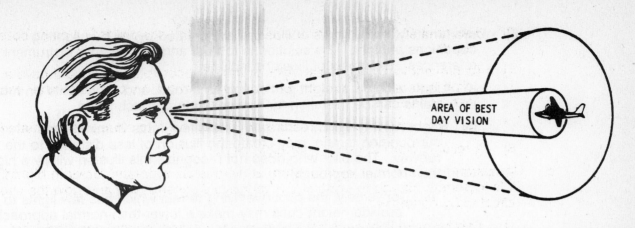

3) Adapting your eyes to darkness is an important aspect of night vision.

    a) When entering a dark area the pupils of the eyes enlarge to receive as much of the available light as possible.

    b) It will take approximately 5 to 10 min. (with enough available light) for the cones to become adjusted and your eyes become 100 times more sensitive than they were before you entered the dark area.

        i) In fact, the cones stop working altogether in semidarkness.

        ii) Since the rods can still function in light of 1/5,000 the intensity at which the cones cease to function, they are used for night vision.

    c) After about 30 min., the rods will be fully adjusted to darkness and become about 100,000 times more sensitive to light than they were in the lighted area.

    d) The rods need more time to adjust to darkness than the cones do to bright light. Your eyes become adapted to sunlight in 10 sec., whereas they need 30 min. to fully adjust to a dark night.

4) You must consider the adaptation process before and during night flight.

    a) First, your eyes must be allowed to adapt to the low level of light, and then they must be kept adapted.

    b) Next, you must avoid exposing your eyes to any bright white light which will cause temporary blindness and could result in serious consequences.

        i) This may result in illusions or "after images" during the time your eyes are recovering.

5) Unfortunately, many types of illusions are created by various lighting conditions at night. The solution is to trust and rely on your instrument references. Examples of illusions include:

   a) Lights along a straight path, such as a road, and even lights on moving trains can be mistaken for runway and approach lights.

   b) Bright runway lights, especially where few lights illuminate the surrounding terrain, may create the illusion of less distance to the runway. The pilot who does not recognize this illusion will fly a higher-than-normal approach.

   i) Conversely, the pilot overflying terrain which has few lights to provide height cues may make a lower-than-normal approach.

   c) Marine navigation lights frequently blink on and off. When taking off or on an approach over water, these blinking lights can make it appear as if the horizon and thus you are spinning.

   d) In the dark, a static light will appear to move about when stared at for a while. The disoriented pilot will lose control of his/her airplane in attempting to align it with the light. This is called autokinesis.

   i) It is prevented by keeping your eyes moving and avoid staring at a single light too long.

6) The eyes are the first part of your body to suffer from low oxygen at altitude, since the capillaries are very small and have a limited capacity to carry oxygen.

   a) Night vision may be adversely affected above 5,000 ft. MSL.

   i) Fly low and/or use oxygen at night.

   b) Good vision depends on your physical condition. Fatigue, colds, vitamin deficiency, alcohol, stimulants, smoking, or medication can seriously impair your vision.

   i) EXAMPLE: Smoking lowers the sensitivity of the eyes and reduces night vision by approximately 20%.

7) In review and in addition to the principles previously discussed, the following will aid you in increasing night vision effectiveness:

   a) Adapt your eyes to darkness prior to flight and keep them adapted.

   b) Close one eye when exposed to bright light to help avoid the blinding effect.

   c) Do not wear sunglasses after sunset.

   d) Blink your eyes if they become blurred.

   e) Concentrate on seeing objects.

   f) Force your eyes to view off center.

   g) Maintain a good physical condition.

   h) Avoid smoking, drinking, and using drugs.

2. Determine airplane, airport, and navigation lighting.

   a. Required lighting for your airplane is found in FAR 91.205(c). This requires only position lights and an anticollision light system.

     1) Airplane position lights are arranged similar to those of boats and ships.

       a) A red light is positioned on the left wingtip.
       b) A green light on the right wingtip.
       c) A white light on the tail.

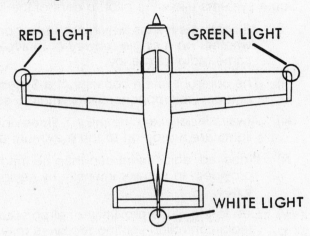

     2) This arrangement provides a means by which you can determine the general direction of movement of other airplanes.

       a) If both a red and green light are seen, the other airplane would be traveling in a general direction toward you.

       b) If only a red light is seen, the airplane is traveling from right to left.

       c) If only a green light is seen, the airplane is traveling from left to right.

       d) Note that the red and green lights cannot be seen from the rear of the airplane.

     3) An anticollision light is either a red or white light and is normally located on the vertical stabilizer of most airplanes.

     4) While not required for VFR night flight, the following lights are recommended and installed in most airplanes.

       a) Landing light, which is useful for taxi, takeoffs, landings, and a means by which your airplane can be seen by other pilots.

       b) Individual instrument lights and adequate cockpit illumination.

       c) Wingtip strobe lights.

   b. Lighted airports located away from congested areas can be identified readily at night by the lights outlining the runways. However, airports located near or within large cities are often difficult to identify in the maze of lights. Thus, it is important that you are able to identify airports by their lighting.

     1) It is recommended that prior to night flight, particularly cross-country, you should check the availability and status of lighting systems at airports along the planned route and the destination airport.

       a) This information can be found on aeronautical charts and in the Airport/Facility Directory. The status of each facility can be determined by reviewing pertinent Notices to Airmen (NOTAMs).

2) The basic runway lighting system consists of two straight parallel lines of runway-edge lights defining the lateral limits of the runway.

   a) These lights are aviation white, although aviation yellow may be substituted for the last 2,000 ft. to indicate a caution zone.

3) At some airports the intensity of the runway-edge lights can be adjusted to satisfy your individual needs.

   a) These may be controlled by a ground station (e.g., control tower, FSS).
   b) Some systems allow the pilot to control the lighting.

     i) All lighting systems which are radio controlled at an airport, whether on a single runway or multiple runways, operate on the same radio frequency.

     ii) The control system consists of a 3-step control responsive to 7, 5, and/or 3 microphone clicks within 5 sec.

     iii) Always initially key the mike 7 times; this ensures that all controlled lights are turned on to the maximum available intensity.

     iv) If desired, adjustment can then be made, where the capability is provided, to a lower intensity by keying 5 and/or 3 times within 5 sec.

     v) Due to the close proximity of airports using the same frequency, radio-controlled lighting receivers may be set at a low sensitivity requiring the aircraft to be relatively close to activate the system.

4) The ends of the runway are defined by a straight line of lights.

   a) The threshold lights are green, and the runway end lights are red.

5) At many airports the taxiways are also lighted. This consists of omnidirectional blue lights which outline the usable limits of taxiways.

6) A rotating beacon is used to indicate the location of an airport. It has a vertical light distribution to make it most effective from one to 10 degrees above the horizon. However, it can often be seen well above and below this range.

   a) The beacon rotates at a constant speed, thus producing what appears to be a series of light flashes at regular intervals.

   b) These flashes may be one or two colors alternately which are used to identify various types of landing areas.

     i) Alternating white and green indicates a lighted land airport.
     ii) A white alone indicates an unlighted airport.
     iii) A green alone is sometimes used to find a not-too-distant white and green beacon.
     iv) Dual peaked (two quick) white flashes between the green flash indicates a military airport.

7) Obstructions are marked and lighted to warn pilots of their presence during nighttime conditions. They may be lighted in any of the following combinations.

   a) Aviation red obstruction lights -- flashing aviation red beacons and steady aviation red lights at night.

      b) High-intensity white obstruction lights -- flashing, high-intensity, white lights during daytime with reduced intensity for twilight and nighttime operation.

      c) Dual lighting -- a combination of flashing aviation red beacons and steady aviation red lights at night and flashing high-intensity white lights in daylight.

    8) For discussion on other types of lighting (e.g., those used in conjunction with IFR operations) see Task III.C., Airport and Runway Marking and Lighting, on page 239.

  c. An aeronautical light beacon is a visual navigation aid displaying flashes of white and/or colored light to indicate the location of an airport, a heliport, a landmark, a certain point of a Federal airway in mountainous terrain, or an obstruction.

    1) Only a few airway beacons exist today to mark airway segments in remote mountain areas.

3. Exhibit your knowledge by explaining night flying procedures, including safety precautions and emergency actions.

  a. Night flying procedures will be discussed in detail in elements 4 through 8.

  b. Safety is important in both day and night operations. With your restricted vision at night you must place additional emphasis on safety during night flight operations.

    1) Night flying demands more attention to all details of preflight preparation and planning.

    2) Proper cockpit management will enhance safety, because you will have all of your equipment and material organized and well arranged.

    3) Understand night vision and the limitations it has on your vision.

  c. Perhaps your greatest concern about flying a single-engine airplane at night is complete engine failure, even though adverse weather and poor pilot judgment account for most serious accidents.

    1) If the engine fails at night, the first step is to maintain positive control of your airplane. DO NOT PANIC.

      a) A normal glide should be established and maintained and turn your airplane toward an airport or away from congested areas.

      b) A check should be made to determine the cause of the engine failure. This may include the position of:

        i) Magneto switches,
        ii) Fuel selectors, or the
        iii) Primer.

      c) If possible, correct the malfunction immediately and restart the engine.

    2) Maintain orientation with the wind to avoid a downwind landing.

    3) The landing light(s), if equipped, should be checked at altitude and turned on insufficient time to illuminate the terrain or obstacles along the flight path.

      a) If the landing light(s) are unusable and outside references are not available, the airplane should be held in level-landing attitude until the ground is contacted.

    4) Most important of all, positive control of your airplane must be maintained at all times.

      a) DO NOT allow a stall to occur.

4.   **Inspect your airplane by following the checklist which includes items essential for night flying operations.**

   a.   A thorough preflight check of your airplane, and a review of its systems and emergency procedures, is of particular important for night operation.

   1)   Use the checklist in your *POH* to complete these items. (See Task II.A., Visual Inspection, on page 178.)

   b.   All airplane lights should be turned on and checked (visually) for operation.

   1)   Position lights can be checked for loose connections by tapping the light fixture while the light is on.

   a)   If the lights blink while being tapped, further investigation (by a qualified mechanic) to find the cause should be initiated.

   c.   FAR 91.205(c) requires certain instruments, lights, an adequate source of electric energy, and spare fuses (if so equipped) for VFR night flight operations.

   1)   The following instruments and equipment is required.

   a)   Airspeed indicator.

   b)   Altimeter.

   c)   Magnetic direction indicator (i.e., magnetic compass).

   d)   Tachometer for each engine.

   e)   Oil pressure gauge.

   f)   Oil temperature gauge.

   g)   Manifold pressure gauge for each altitude engine.

   h)   Fuel quantity gauges.

   i)   Gear position indicator (on retractable gear airplanes).

   j)   An anticollision light system, including a flashing or rotating beacon (or strobe lights).

   k)   Position lights.

   2)   While not required for VFR night flight operations, the following instruments and equipment are recommended.

   a)   Attitude indicator, heading indicator, and a sensitive altimeter (adjustable for barometric pressure) are valuable in controlling the airplane at night.

   b)   Individual instrument lights and adequate cockpit illumination.

   c)   Landing light for all night flight operations.

   d)   At least one radio navigation receiver and a two-way radio communication capability.

   d.   All personal materials and equipment should be checked to ensure you have everything and that all equipment is functioning properly.

   1)   It is very disconcerting to find, at the time of need, that a flashlight, for example, does not work.

   e.   Finally, the parking ramp should be checked prior to entering your airplane. During the day it is easy to see stepladders, chuckholes, stray wheel chocks, and other obstructions, but at night it is more difficult and a check of the area can prevent taxiing mishaps.

5. **Start, taxi, and perform the pretakeoff check, while adhering to good operating practices.**

    a.   Follow the before engine start and engine starting procedures in your *POH*. (See Task II.C., Starting Engine, on page 189.)

        1)   Extra caution should be taken at night to ensure that the propeller area is clear.

            a)   This can be accomplished by turning on your airplane's rotating beacon (anticollision light), or flashing other airplane lights to alert any person nearby to remain clear of the propeller.

            b)   Also orally announce "clear prop" and wait a few seconds before engaging the starting.

            c)   Think safety.

        2)   To avoid excessive drain of electrical current from the battery, all unnecessary equipment should be kept off until after the engine has been started.

        3)   Once the engine has been started, turn on the airplane's position lights.

    b.   Due to your restricted vision at night, taxi speeds should be reduced. Never taxi at a speed faster than would allow you to stop within the distance your landing light is illuminating. If taxi lines are painted on the taxiway, follow them to assist in maintaining the proper task. (See Task II.D., Taxiing, on page 195.)

        1)   Continuous use of the landing light with the low power settings normally used for taxiing may place an excessive burden on your airplane's electrical system.

        2)   Overheating of the landing light bulb may become a problem because of inadequate airflow to carry away the excessive heat generated.

            a)   It is recommended generally that the landing lights be used only intermittently while taxiing, but sufficiently to ensure that the taxiway is clear.

        3)   Be sure to avoid using the wingtip strobes and landing light in the vicinity of other aircraft.

            a)   This includes being in the runup area while someone else is landing.
            b)   These lights can be distracting and potentially blinding to a pilot.
            c)   You would expect the same courtesy from others.

    c.   Use the checklist in your *POH* to perform the pretakeoff check. (See Task II.E., Pretakeoff Check, on page 205.)

        1)   Each item on the checklist should be checked carefully and the proper functioning of any of the airplane components must never be taken for granted.

        2)   During the day unintended forward movement of your airplane can be easily detected during the runup.

            a)   At night the airplane may creep forward without being noticed, unless you are alert to this possibility.

            b)   Thus, it is important to lock the brakes during the runup and be attentive to any unintentional forward movement.

6.   Perform the takeoff and climb with emphasis on visual references.

a.   At night, your visual references are limited (and sometimes nonexistent) and you will need to use the flight instruments to a greater degree in controlling the airplane, especially during night takeoffs and departure climbs.

    1)   This does not mean that you will use only the flight instruments, but that the flight instruments are used more to cross-check the visual references.

b.   The cockpit lights (if available) should be adjusted to a minimum brightness that will allow you to read the instruments and switches without hindering your outside vision.

    1)   This will also eliminate light reflections on the windshield and windows which would obstruct your outside vision.

c.   Before taxiing onto the active runway for takeoff, you should exercise extreme caution to prevent conflict with other aircraft.

    1)   At controlled airports, where ATC issues the clearance for takeoff, it is recommended that you check the final approach course for approaching aircraft.

    2)   At uncontrolled airports, it is recommended that a slow 360° turn be made in the same direction as the flow of air traffic while closely searching for other traffic.

d.   After ensuring that the final approach and runway are clear of other traffic, you should line up your airplane with the centerline of the runway.

    1)   If the runway has no painted centerline, you should use the runway lighting and align your airplane between and parallel to the two rows of runway edge lights.

    2)   Your landing light and strobe lights (if applicable) should be on as you taxi into this position.

    3)   After the airplane is aligned, the heading indicator should be set to correspond to the known runway direction.

e.   To begin the takeoff the brakes should be released and the throttle smoothly advanced to takeoff power. As your airplane accelerates, it should be kept moving parallel to the runway edge lights. This is best done by looking at the more distant runway lights rather than those close in and to the side.

    1)   At night your perception of runway length, width, airplane speed, and flight attitude will vary. You must monitor your flight instruments more closely, e.g., rotation should occur at the proper V_R based on your airspeed indicator, not your bodily senses.

    2)   As the airspeed reaches V_R, the pitch attitude should be adjusted to that which will establish a normal climb by referred to both visual and instrument references (e.g., lights and the attitude indicator).

    3)   Do not attempt to forcibly pull the airplane off the ground. It is best to let it fly off in the liftoff attitude while cross-checking the attitude indicator against any outside visual references that may be available.

f. After becoming airborne, the darkness of the night often makes it difficult to note whether the airplane is getting closer to or farther from the surface.

1) You must ensure that your airplane continues in a positive climb and does not settle back to the runway. This is accomplished by cross-checking your flight instruments.

a) A positive climb rate indicated by the vertical speed indicator,

b) A gradual but continual increase in the altimeter indication, and

c) A climb pitch attitude is indicated on the attitude indicator.

d) Check the airspeed to ensure that it is well above a stall and is stabilizing at the appropriate climb speed (e.g., V_Y).

PRIMARY POWER   SUPPORTING PITCH AND BANK

SUPPORTING BANK   PRIMARY BANK   PRIMARY PITCH

2) Use the attitude indicator as well as visual references to ensure that the wings are level and cross-check with the heading indicator to ensure you are maintaining the correct heading.

a) No turns should normally be made until reaching a safe maneuvering altitude.

3) Your landing light should be turned off after a climb is well established. This is normally completed during the climb checklist.

a) The light may become deceptive if it is reflected by haze, smoke, or fog that might exist in the takeoff climb.

7. Navigate and maintain orientation under VFR conditions.

a. Never depart at night without a thorough review of your intended flight plan. Courses, distances, and times of each leg should be computed. At night, your attention is needed for aviating, not for navigation planning.

b. In spite of fewer usable landmarks or checkpoints, night cross-country flights present no particular problem, if preplanning is adequate and you continuously monitor position, time estimates, and fuel consumed.

    1) The light pattern of towns are easily identified, especially when surrounded by dark areas.

        a) Large metropolitan areas may be of little meaning until you gain more night flying experience.

    2) Airport rotating beacons, which are installed at various military and civilian airports, are useful checkpoints.

    3) Busy highways marked by car headlights also make good checkpoints.

    4) On moonlit nights, especially in dark areas, you will be able to identify some unlit landmarks.

c. Crossing large bodies of water on night flights could be potentially hazardous, not only from the standpoint of landing (ditching) in the water should it become necessary, but also because the horizon may blend in with the water, in which case, control of your airplane may become difficult.

    1) During haze conditions over open water the horizon will become obscure, and may result in loss of spatial orientation.

    2) Even on clear nights the stars may be reflected on the water surface, which could appear as a continuous array of lights, thus making the horizon difficult to identify.

    3) Always include instrument references in your scan.

d. Lighted runways, buildings, or other objects may cause illusions to you when seen from different altitudes.

    1) At 2,000 ft. AGL a group of lights on an object may be seen individually, while at 5,000 ft. AGL or higher the same lights could appear to be one solid light mass.

    2) These illusions may become quite acute with altitude changes and if not overcome could present problems in respect to approaches to lighted runways.

e. At night it is normally difficult to see clouds and restrictions to visibility, particularly on dark nights (i.e., no moonlight) or under an overcast.

    1) You must exercise caution to avoid flying into weather conditions below VFR (i.e., clouds, fog).

    2) Normally, the first indication of flying into restricted visibility conditions is the gradual disappearance of lights on the ground.

        a) If the lights begin to take on an appearance of being surrounded by a "cotton ball" or glow, you should use extreme caution in attempting to fly further in that same direction.

3) Remember that if a descent must be made through any fog, smoke, or haze in order to land, the visibility is considerably less when looking horizontally through the restriction than it is when looking straight down through it from above.

4) You should never attempt a VFR night flight during poor or marginal weather conditions.

8. **Approach and land adhering to good operating practices for night flight operations.**

a. When arriving at the airport to enter the traffic pattern and land, it is important that the runway lights and other airport lighting be identified as early as possible.

1) If you are unfamiliar with the airport layout, sighting of the runway may be difficult until very close-in due to other lighting in the area.

2) You should fly towards the airport rotating beacon until you identify the runway lights.

3) Your landing light should be on to help other pilots and/or ATC to see you.

b. To fly a traffic pattern of the proper size and direction when there is little to see but a group of lights, the runway threshold and runway edge lights must be positively identified.

1) Once this is done, the location of the approach threshold lights should be known at all times throughout the traffic pattern.

c. Distance may be deceptive at night due to limited lighting conditions, lack of intervening references on the ground, and your inability to compare the size and location of different ground objects. This also applies to the estimation of altitude and speed.

1) Consequently, you must use your flight instruments more, especially the altimeter and the airspeed indicator.

2) Every effort should be made to execute the approach and landing in the same manner as during the day.

3) Constantly cross-check the altimeter, airspeed indicator, and vertical speed indicator against your airplane's position along the base leg and final approach.

d. After turning onto the final approach and aligning your airplane between the two rows of runway edge lights, you should note and correct for any wind-drift.

1) Throughout the final approach, power should be used with coordinated pitch changes to provide positive control of your airplane. Thus, allowing you to accurately adjust airspeed and descent angle.

2) A lighted visual approach slope indicator (i.e., VASI or PAPI) should be used if available to help maintain the proper approach angle.

a) If the runway you are using to land on has a visual approach slope indicator, you must maintain an altitude at or above the glide slope (unless you are performing normal bracketing maneuvers to remain on the glide slope) until a lower altitude is necessary for a safe landing [FAR 91.129(d)(3)].

e.   The roundout and touchdown should be made in the same manner as day landings. However, your judgment of height, speed, and sink rate may be impaired by the lack of observable objects in the landing area.

   1)   To aid you in determining the proper roundout point, it may be well to continue a constant approach descent until your airplane's landing light reflects on the runway, and the tire marks on the runway, or runway expansion joints, can be seen clearly.

      a)   At that point the roundout for touchdown should be started smoothly and the throttle gradually reduced to idle as your airplane is touching down.

   2)   During landings without the use of a landing light or where tire marks on the runway are not identifiable, the roundout may be started when the runway lights at the far end of the runway first appear to be rising higher than your airplane.

      a)   This demands a smooth and very timely roundout, and requires, in effect, that you "feel" for the runway surface, using power and pitch changes as necessary for the airplane to settle softly on the runway.

C.   Common errors during night flying

   1.   **Failure to understand the factors of night vision.**

      a.   Learn how the eye is constructed and the effects of darkness on the eye.

      b.   With your CFI, experiment how to use night vision by locating an object and concentrate to look at it directly, as you would during the day. Then view the same object by the off center technique. Practice off center viewing.

      c.   Know your night vision limitations, and possible illusions you may experience.

   2.   **Failure to properly prepare for a night flight.**

      a.   Check the weather forecasts.

      b.   Check for all materials (e.g., maps, navigation logs) and equipment (e.g., flashlight) that you will need.

         1)   Ensure all equipment is working properly.

   3.   **Failure to use checklists.**

      a.   Follow the prescribed checklist from your *POH* for the appropriate phase of flight.

END OF TASK -- END OF CHAPTER

CHAPTER X
EMERGENCY OPERATIONS

X.A. Emergency Approach and Landing (Simulated) 399
X.B. System and Equipment Malfunctions 408

This chapter explains the two tasks (A-B) of Emergency Operations. These tasks include both knowledge and skill.

Each objective of a task lists, in sequence, the important elements that must be satisfactorily performed. The object includes:

1. Specifically what you should be able to do.
2. The conditions under which the task is to be performed.
3. The minimum acceptable standards of performance.

Be confident. You have prepared diligently and are better prepared and more skilled than the average private pilot applicant. Your examiner will base your ability to perform these tasks on the following.

1. Executing the task within your airplane's capabilities and limitations, including use of the airplane's systems.

2. Piloting your airplane with smoothness and accuracy.

3. Exercising good judgment.

4. Applying your aeronautical knowledge.

5. Showing mastery of your airplane within the standards outlined in this area of operation, with the successful outcome of a task never seriously in doubt.

6. Executing emergency procedures and maneuvers appropriate to your airplane.

There are several factors that may interfere with your ability to act promptly and properly when faced with an emergency.

1. Reluctance to accept the emergency situation: Allowing your mind to become paralyzed by the emergency may lead to failure to maintain flying speed, delay in choosing a suitable landing area, and indecision in general.

2. Desire to save the aircraft: If you have been conditioned to expect to find a suitable landing area whenever your instructor simulated a failed engine, you may be apt to ignore good procedures to avoid rough terrain where the airplane may be damaged. There may be times that the airplane will have to be sacrificed so that you and your passengers can walk away.

3. Undue concern about getting hurt: Fear is a vital part of self-preservation, but it must not lead to panic. You must maintain your composure and apply the proper concepts and procedures.

Your examiner is required to test you on both of these tasks. Each task is reproduced verbatim from the FAA Practical Test Standards in a shaded box. General discussion is presented under "A. General Information." This is followed by "B. Task Objectives," which is a detailed discussion of each element of the FAA's task.

Emergency operations require that you maintain situational awareness (see Task II.B., Cockpit Management, on page 185) of what is happening. You must develop an organized process for decision making that can be used in all situations. One method is to use **DECIDE**:

D etect a change -- Recognize immediately when indications, whether visual, aural, or intuitive are different than those expected.

E stimate need to react -- Determine whether these different indications constitute an adverse situation and if so, what sort of action, if any, will be required to deal with it.

C hoose desired outcome -- Decide how, specifically, you would like the current situation altered.

I dentify actions to control change -- Formulate a definitive plan of action to remedy the situation.

D o something positive -- Even if no ideal plan of action presents itself, something can always be done to improve things at least.

E valuate the effects -- Have you solved the predicament, or is further action required?

EMERGENCY APPROACH AND LANDING (SIMULATED)

X.A. TASK: EMERGENCY APPROACH AND LANDING (SIMULATED)

PILOT OPERATION - 10

REFERENCES: AC 61-21; Airplane Handbook and Flight Manual.

Objective. To determine that the applicant:

1. Exhibits knowledge by explaining approach and landing procedures to be used in various emergencies.

2. Establishes and maintains the recommended best-glide airspeed and configuration during simulated emergencies.

3. Selects a suitable landing area within gliding distance.

4. Plans and follows a flight pattern to the selected landing area, considering altitude, wind, terrain, obstructions, and other factors.

5. Follows an appropriate emergency checklist.

6. Attempts to determine the reason for the simulated malfunction.

7. Maintains positive control of the airplane.

Note: Examiner should terminate the emergency approach at or above minimum safe altitude.

A. General Information

1. This is one of two tasks (A-B) in this area of operation. Your examiner is required to test you on this task.

2. *Pilot Operation - 10* refers to FAR 61.107(a)(10): Emergency operations, including simulated aircraft and equipment malfunctions.

3. FAA References

   AC 61-21: Flight Training Handbook
   Pilot's Operating Handbook (FAA-Approved Airplane Flight Manual)

4. The objective of this task is for you to demonstrate your ability to perform a simulated emergency approach and landing.

5. You will need to know and understand the procedures discussed in Section 3, Emergency Procedures, of your *POH*.

6. These emergency approach and landing procedures could be either with or without power.

   a. Normally, your examiner will simulate a complete power loss.

B. Task Objectives

1. **Exhibit your knowledge by explaining the approach and landing procedures to be used in various emergencies.**

   a. Emergency approaches and landings can be the result of a complete engine failure, a partial power loss, or a system and/or equipment malfunction that requires an emergency landing during which you may have engine power.

   b. During actual forced landings it is recommended that you maneuver your airplane to conform to a normal traffic pattern as closely as possible. This may necessitate a straight-in approach, a 90° approach, a 180° side approach, or a 360° overhead approach, with whatever modifications are necessary.

   1) A straight-in approach is one in which you fly your airplane straight toward your selected landing area (i.e., an extended final approach).

   a) You must constantly evaluate the situation so that you descend at an angle and airspeed that will permit your airplane to reach the desired landing area.

   2) A 90° approach is one in which you approach your selected landing area from the base leg.

   a) The approach path is varied by positioning the base leg closer to or farther away from the approach end of the desired field according to wind conditions.

   3) A 180° side approach is one in which you approach your selected landing area from the downwind leg. This is an extension of the principles of a 90° approach, but requiring more planning and judgment.

   4) A 360° overhead approach is one in which you may be circling above your selected landing area.

   a) The entire pattern is flown in a circular pattern but the turns are shallowed or steepened, or discontinued at any point to adjust the accuracy of the flight path.

   b) This approach is normally made if you are approximately 2,000 ft. AGL or more above your selected landing area.

   c. If an actual engine failure should occur immediately after takeoff and before a safe maneuvering altitude (at least 500 ft. AGL) is attained, it is usually inadvisable to attempt to turn back to the runway from which the takeoff was made.

   1) Instead, it is generally safer to immediately establish the proper glide attitude, and select a field directly ahead or slightly to either side of the takeoff path.

   2) The decision to continue straight ahead is often a difficult one to make unless you consider the problems involved in turning back.

   a) First, the takeoff was in all probability made into the wind. To get back to the runway, a downwind turn must be made which will increase your groundspeed and rush you even more in the performance of emergency procedures and in planning the approach.

   b) Next, your airplane will lose considerable altitude during the turn and might still be in a bank when the ground is contacted, thus resulting in the airplane cartwheeling.

   c) Last, but not least, after turning downwind the apparent increase in groundspeed could mislead you into attempting to prematurely slow down your airplane and cause it to stall.

3) Continuing straight ahead or making only a slight turn allows you more time to establish a safe landing attitude, and the landing can be made as slowly as possible.

    a) Importantly, the airplane can be landed while under control.

d. The following are ideas about good judgment and sound operating practice as you prepare to meet emergencies.

1) All pilots hope to be able to act properly and efficiently when the unexpected occurs. As a safe pilot, you should cultivate coolness in an emergency.

2) You must know your airplane well enough to correctly interpret the indications before you take the corrective action. This requires regular study of your airplane's *POH*.

3) While difficult, you must make a special effort to remain proficient in procedures you will seldom, if ever, have to use.

4) Do not be reluctant to accept the fact that you have an emergency. Take appropriate action immediately without overreacting. Explain your problem to ATC so they can help you plan alternatives and be in a position to grant you priority.

5) You should assume that an emergency will occur every time you take off, i.e., expect the unexpected. If it does not happen, you have a pleasant surprise. If it does, you will be in the correct mind-set to recognize the problem and handle it in a safe and efficient manner.

6) Avoid putting yourself into a situation where you have no alternatives. Be continuously alert for suitable emergency landing spots.

e. The main objective when a forced landing is imminent is to complete a safe landing (for you and your passengers) in the largest and best field available.

1) This involves getting the airplane on the ground in as near a normal landing attitude as possible without hitting obstructions.

2) Your airplane may suffer damage, but as long as you keep the airplane under control, you and your passengers should survive.

2. **Establish and maintain the recommended best-glide airspeed and configuration during simulated emergencies.**

a. Your examiner can and will normally simulate a complete power loss with the airplane in any configuration and/or altitude. This is accomplished by the reduction of power to idle and your examiner stating that you have just experienced an engine failure.

b. Your first reaction should be to immediately establish the best-glide attitude and ensure that the landing gear and flaps are retracted (if so equipped).

1) The best glide airspeed is indicated in your *POH*.

    a) In your airplane, best glide airspeed _____.

2) If the airspeed is above the proper glide speed, altitude should be maintained, and the airspeed allowed to dissipate to the best glide speed.

    a) When the proper glide speed is attained, the nose of your airplane should then be lowered to maintain that speed.

c. A constant gliding speed and pitch attitude should be maintained, because variations of gliding speed will disrupt your attempts at accuracy in judgment of gliding distance and the landing spot.

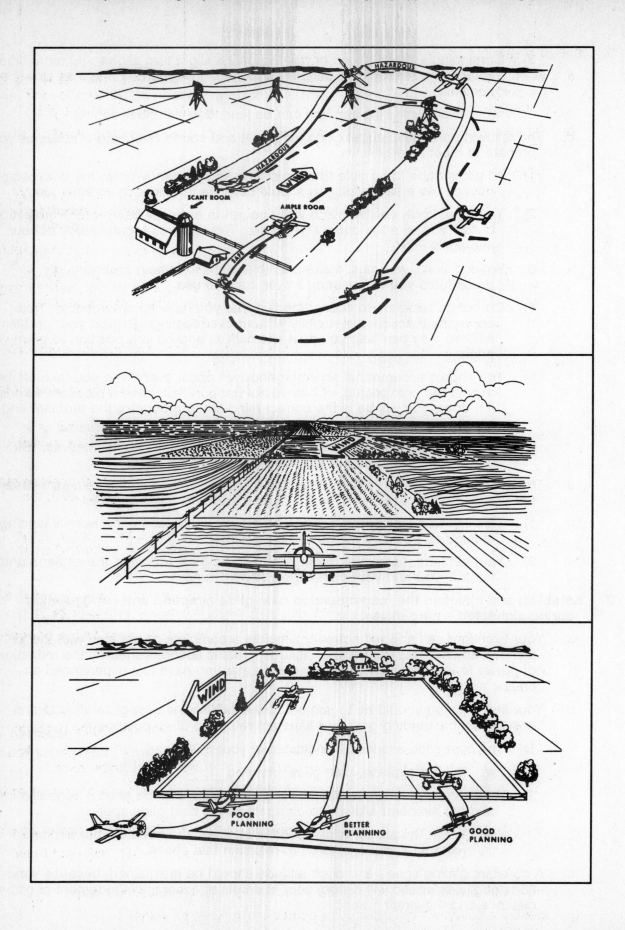

3. Select a suitable landing area within gliding distance.

    a.   Many inexperienced pilots select from locations in front of them when there may be a perfect site just behind them. You may want to perform a 180° turn to look for a suitable field if altitude permits and you do not have a suitable field in sight.

    b.   Be aware of wind direction and velocity both for the desired landing direction and for their effect on glide distance.

    c.   Check for traffic and ask your examiner to check for traffic.

        1)   Inform him/her that you would ask your passengers, especially one sitting in the right front seat, to assist you in looking for other traffic and pointing it out to you.

        2)   (S)he may instruct you to simulate that you are the only person in the airplane.

    d.   You should always be aware of suitable forced-landing fields. The perfect field would be an established airport, or a hard-packed, long, smooth field with no high obstacles on the approach end. You need to select the best field available.

        1)   A forced landing is a soft-field touchdown without power.

        2)   Attempt to land into the wind, although other factors may dictate a crosswind or downwind landing.

            a)   Insufficient altitude may make it inadvisable or impossible to attempt to maneuver into the wind.

            b)   Ground obstacles may make landing into the wind impractical or inadvisable because they shorten the effective length of the available field.

            c)   The distance from a suitable field upwind from the present position may make it impossible to reach the field from the altitude at which the engine failure occurs.

            d)   The best available field may be on a hill and at such an angle to the wind that a downwind landing uphill would be preferable and safer.

            e)   See the top diagram on the opposite page.

        3)   Choose a smooth, grassy field if possible. If you land in a cultivated field, land parallel to the furrows. See the middle diagram on the opposite page.

        4)   Plan your turn onto final approach. See the bottom diagram on the opposite page.

    e.   Your altitude at the time of engine failure will determine.

        1)   The number of alternative landing sites available.
        2)   The type of approach pattern.
        3)   The amount of time available to determine and correct the engine problem.

    f.   Roads should be used only as a last resort. They almost always have power lines crossing them which cannot be seen until you are committed to the road.

        1)   Wires often are not seen at all, and the airplane just goes out of control, to the surprise of the pilot.

        2)   The presence of wires can be assumed if you see telephone or power poles.

        3)   Also, roads must be wide (e.g., 4 lanes) because of fences, adjacent trees, and road signs.

        4)   Use roads only if clear of BOTH traffic and electric/telephone wires.

    g.   Identify a suitable landing site and point it out to your examiner.

4. **Plan and follow a flight pattern to the selected landing area, considering altitude, wind, terrain, obstructions, and other factors.**

    a. During your selection of a suitable landing area you should have taken into account your altitude, the wind speed and direction, the terrain, obstructions, and other factors.

        1) Now you must finalize your plan and follow your flight pattern to the landing area.

        2) You are now executing what you planned.

    b. You can utilize any combination of normal gliding maneuvers, from wings level to spirals.

        1) You should eventually arrive at the normal "key" position at a normal traffic pattern altitude for your selected field, i.e., abeam the touchdown point on downwind.

        2) From this point on, your approach should be similar to a soft-field power-off approach.

    c. You need to make a decision as to whether to land with the gear up or down (if retractable).

        1) When the field is smooth and firm, and long enough to bring your airplane to a stop, a gear down landing is appropriate.

            a) If the field has stumps, rocks, or other large obstacles, the gear down will better protect you and your passengers.

            b) If you suspect the field to be excessively soft, wet, short, or snow-covered, a gear-up landing will normally be safer, to eliminate the possibility of your airplane nosing over as a result of the wheels digging in.

        2) Allow time for the gear to extend, or for you to manually lower the gear.

        3) Lower the gear and any flaps only after a landing at your selected field is assured.

    d. The altitude is, in many ways, the controlling factor in the successful accomplishment of an emergency approach and landing.

        1) If you realize you have selected a poor landing area (one that would obviously result in a disaster) AND there is a more advantageous field within gliding distance, a change should be made and explained to your examiner.

            a) You must understand that this is an exception and the hazards involved in last-minute decisions (i.e., excessive maneuvering at very low altitudes) must be thoroughly understood.

        2) Slipping (i.e., forward slip if approved) the airplane, using flaps, varying the position of the base leg, and varying the turn onto final approach are ways of correcting for misjudgment of altitude and glide angle.

5. **Follow an appropriate emergency checklist.**

a. Use the appropriate checklist in your *POH*. Below are checklists for a Cessna 152.

CESSNA MODEL 152
ENGINE FAILURE and FORCED LANDING CHECKLISTS

ENGINE FAILURE DURING TAKEOFF RUN
1. Throttle -- IDLE.
2. Brakes -- APPLY.
3. Wing Flaps -- RETRACT.
4. Mixture -- IDLE CUT-OFF.
5. Ignition Switch -- OFF.
6. Master Switch -- OFF.

ENGINE FAILURE DURING FLIGHT
1. Airspeed -- 60 KIAS.
2. Carburetor Heat -- ON.
3. Primer -- IN and LOCKED.
4. Fuel Shutoff Valve -- ON.
5. Mixture -- RICH.
6. Ignition Switch -- BOTH (or START if propeller is stopped).

PRECAUTIONARY LANDING WITH ENGINE POWER
1. Airspeed -- 60 KIAS.
2. Wing Flaps -- 20°.
3. Selected Field -- FLY OVER, noting terrain and obstructions, then retract flaps upon reaching a safe altitude and airspeed.
4. Radio and Electrical Switches -- OFF.
5. Wing Flaps -- 30° (on final approach).
6. Airspeed -- 55 KIAS.
7. Master Switch -- OFF.
8. Doors -- UNLATCH PRIOR TO TOUCHDOWN.
9. Touchdown -- SLIGHTLY TAIL LOW.
10. Ignition Switch -- OFF.
11. Brakes -- APPLY HEAVILY.

ENGINE FAILURE IMMEDIATELY AFTER TAKEOFF
1. Airspeed -- 60 KIAS.
2. Mixture -- IDLE CUT-OFF.
3. Fuel Shutoff Valve -- OFF.
4. Ignition Switch -- OFF.
5. Wing Flaps -- AS REQUIRED.
6. Master Switch -- OFF.

EMERGENCY LANDING WITHOUT ENGINE POWER
1. Airspeed -- 65 KIAS (flaps UP). 60 KIAS (flaps DOWN).
2. Mixture -- IDLE CUT-OFF.
3. Fuel Shutoff Valve -- OFF.
4. Ignition Switch -- OFF.
5. Wing Flaps -- AS REQUIRED (30° recommended).
6. Master Switch -- OFF.
7. Doors -- UNLATCH PRIOR TO TOUCHDOWN.
8. Touchdown -- SLIGHTLY TAIL LOW.
9. Brakes -- APPLY HEAVILY.

> For Academic Illustration/Training Purposes Only! *For Flight:* Use your Pilot's Operating Handbook and FAA-Approved Airplane Flight Manual.

---

b. You should be in the habit of performing from memory the first few critical steps that would be necessary to get the engine operating again.

c. Depending on the situation and altitude, you will complete the checklist(s) in one of two ways.
   1) Do and review, or
   2) Review and do.
   3) These are discussed in detail in Task II.B., Cockpit Management, on page 185.

d. If you are at sufficient altitude you should use your printed checklist (review and do).
   1) Select the correct checklist and read each item out loud and comment on your action as you perform the task.

    e.   Remember to switch your communication radio to 121.5 and simulate reporting "Mayday, Mayday, Mayday."

        1)   Once contact is established identify yourself, position, problem, and intentions.

6.   Attempt to determine the reason for the simulated malfunction.

    a.   As you follow your prescribed checklist you will be attempting to determine the reason for the loss of engine power and to restart the engine.

    b.   If you regain power, level off and continue circling your selected landing area until you are assured that the problem has been corrected.

7.   Maintain positive control of the airplane.

    a.   You must maintain positive control of your airplane from the time you lose power (simulated or actual) to the minimum safe altitude (simulated) or to the end of the landing roll (actual).

    b.   Maintain your best glide airspeed. Avoid a stall/spin situation at all costs, in both simulated and actual emergencies.

    c.   During the simulation you need to ensure that the engine is kept warm and cleared by gentle bursts of power.

        1)   It must be clear between you and your examiner as to who will do this procedure.

        2)   Remember, when your examiner terminates the simulation you are in complete control of your airplane.

C.   Common errors during an emergency approach and landing (simulated)

1.   Improper airspeed control.

    a.   Eagerness to get down to the ground is one of the most common errors.

        1)   In your rush to get down, you will forget about maintaining your airspeed and arrive at the edge of the landing area with too much speed to permit a safe landing.

    b.   Once you establish the best glide airspeed you should trim off the control pressures for hands-off flying.

        1)   This will assist you in airspeed control as you perform the various tasks of the checklist(s) and planning your approach.

    c.   Monitor your airspeed indicator and pitch attitude.

2.   Poor judgment in the selection of an emergency landing area.

    a.   Always be aware of suitable fields.

    b.   Make timely decisions and stay with your decision. Even at higher altitudes this should be done in a timely manner.

3.   Failure to estimate the approximate wind speed and direction.

    a.   Use all available means to determine wind speed and direction.

        1)   Smoke, trees, windsocks, and/or wind lines on water are good indicators of surface winds.

        2)   Be aware of the crab angle you are maintaining for wind-drift correction.

    b.   Failure to know the wind speed and direction will lead to problems during the approach to your selected field.

4. **Failure to fly the most suitable pattern for existing situation.**

   a. Constantly evaluate your airplane's position relative to the intended spot for landing.

   b. Attempt to fly as much of a normal traffic pattern as possible since that is known to you and the key points will prompt you to make decisions.

   c. Do not rush to the landing spot and do not attempt to extend a glide to get to that spot.

5. **Failure to accomplish the emergency checklist.**

   a. The checklist is important from the standpoint that it takes you through all the needed procedures to regain power.

   b. If power is not restored, the checklist will prepare you and your airplane for the landing.

6. **Undershooting or overshooting selected emergency landing area.**

   a. This is due to poor planning and not constantly evaluating and making the needed corrections during the approach.

   b. Familiarity with your airplane's glide characteristics and the effects of forward slips (if permitted), flaps, and gear (if retractable) is essential.

END OF TASK

SYSTEM AND EQUIPMENT MALFUNCTIONS

X.B. TASK: SYSTEM AND EQUIPMENT MALFUNCTIONS

  PILOT OPERATION - 10

  REFERENCES: AC 61-21; Airplane Handbook and Flight Manual.

Objective. To determine that the applicant:

1. Exhibits knowledge by explaining causes of, indications of, and pilot actions for, malfunctions of various systems and equipment.

2. Analyzes the situation and takes appropriate action for simulated emergencies such as --

  a. Partial power loss.
  b. Rough running engine or overheat.
  c. Carburetor or induction icing.

  d. Loss of oil pressure.
  e. Fuel starvation.
  f. Engine compartment fire.
  g. Electrical system malfunction.
  h. Gear or flap malfunction.
  i. Door opening in flight.
  j. Trim inoperative.
  k. Loss of pressurization.
  l. Other malfunctions.

A. General Information

   1. This is one of two tasks (A-B) in this area of operation. Your examiner is required to test you on this task.

   2. *Pilot Operation - 10* refers to FAR 61.107(a)(10): Emergency operations, including simulated aircraft and equipment malfunctions.

   3. FAA References

      AC 61-21: Flight Training Handbook
      Pilot's Operating Handbook (FAA-Approved Airplane Flight Manual)

   4. The objective of this task is to determine your knowledge and handling of various system and equipment malfunctions.

B. Task Objectives

   1. **Exhibit your knowledge by explaining causes of, indications of, and pilot actions for, malfunctions of various systems and equipment.**

      a. To best prepare for this element you must have a good working knowledge of all the systems and equipment in your airplane.

      b. In the next element we will cover the general aspects of the listed items. Since this will be airplane specific, you will need to know Section 3, Emergency Procedures, of your *POH*.

         1) This will include both the checklists and the amplified procedures.
         2) Have these checklists within easy access to you in the cockpit at all times.

   2. **Analyze the situation and take appropriate action for the following simulated emergencies.**

      a. **Partial power loss.**

         1) The most common cause of partial power loss is carburetor/induction icing.

            a) The first reaction to a drop in RPM should be the application of carburetor heat.

            b) Keep the heat fully applied until you are certain all the ice has been removed.

         2) Another reason for a partial power loss is an over-lean mixture. In this case, adjust the mixture to a richer setting, then lean the mixture according to your *POH*.

b. Rough running engine or overheat.

1) Engine roughness may be caused by an excessively rich or lean mixture, a bad magneto, induction system icing, spark plug fouling, or clogged fuel injectors in a fuel-injected engine.

    a) First adjust the mixture.

        i) The engine will run rough if the mixture is too rich or too lean.

    b) Sudden roughness or misfiring is usually caused by magneto problems.

        i) Switch from BOTH to either L or R ignition switch position to identify the bad magneto.

        ii) Try different power settings and enrich the mixture to determine if you can operate on BOTH magnetos.

        iii) If not, operate on the good magneto and proceed to the nearest airport for repairs.

    c) Induction system icing could be a problem. Apply carburetor heat or use the alternate air source in fuel-injected engines. This could be the cause of an unexplained drop in RPM or MP and eventual roughness.

    d) Slight engine roughness may possibly be caused by spark plug fouling from operating with a mixture that is too rich or too lean.

        i) Adjust mixture properly in flight to prevent spark plug fouling.

    e) Consult your *POH* for more specific procedures.

2) The oil temperature gauge is the primary engine instrument for determining if the engine is starting to overheat.

    a) Remember that this will be a delayed indication.

    b) High oil temperature can be caused by:

        i) Low oil level.
        ii) Obstruction in the oil cooler.
        iii) Damaged or improper baffle seals.
        iv) Defective gauge.

    c) A rapid rise is an indication of trouble. Land at the nearest airport for repairs.

3) Monitor your airplane's cylinder head and/or exhaust temperature gauges, if equipped.

    a) If these are showing a higher temperature than normal you should increase the mixture to see if the temperature decreases.

4) Also check the fuel system if the engine is running rough. Switch tanks, fuel pump on, mixture rich to see if that solves the problem.

c. Carburetor or induction icing.

1) Carburetor icing is one cause of engine failure. The vaporization of fuel, combined with the decreasing air pressure as it flows through the carburetor, causes a sudden cooling of the mixture.

    a) The temperature of the air passing through the carburetor may drop as much as 15°C (27°F) within a fraction of a second. Water vapor in the air is "squeezed out" by this cooling.

        i) If the temperature in the carburetor reaches 0°C (32°F) or below, the moisture will be deposited as frost or ice inside the carburetor passages.

ii) Even a slight accumulation of ice will reduce power and may lead to complete engine failure, particularly when the throttle is partially or fully closed.

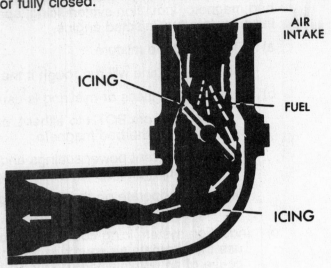

b) **Conditions Conducive to Carburetor Icing.** On dry days, or when the temperature is well below freezing, there is generally not enough moisture in the air to cause trouble. But if the temperature is between −7°C (20°F) and 21°C (70°F), with visible moisture or high humidity, the pilot should be constantly on the alert for carburetor ice.

c) **Indications of Carburetor Icing.** For airplanes with fixed-pitch propellers, the first indication of carburetor icing is a loss of RPM. For airplanes with controllable pitch (constant-speed) propellers, the first indication is usually a drop in manifold pressure (MP).

   i) In both cases, a roughness in engine operation may develop later.

   ii) There will be no reduction in RPM in airplanes with constant-speed propellers, since propeller pitch is automatically adjusted to compensate for the loss of power, thus maintaining constant RPM.

d) **Use of Carburetor Heat.** The carburetor heater is an anti-icing device that preheats the air before it reaches the carburetor. It can be used to melt any ice or snow entering the intake, to melt ice that forms in the carburetor passages (provided the accumulation is not too great), and to keep the fuel mixture above the freezing temperature to prevent formation of carburetor ice.

   i) When conditions are conducive to carburetor icing during flight, periodic checks should be made to detect its presence. If detected, FULL carburetor heat should be applied immediately, and remain in the "on" position until the pilot is certain that all the ice has been removed. If ice is present, applying partial heat or leaving heat on for an insufficient time might aggravate the condition.

   ii) When carburetor heat is first applied there will be an initial drop in RPM in airplanes equipped with fixed-pitch propellers. There will be a drop in MP in airplanes equipped with controllable-pitch propellers.

   • If there is no carburetor ice present, there will be no further change in RPM or MP until the carburetor heat is turned off. Then the RPM or manifold pressure will return to the original reading before heat was applied.

- If carburetor ice is present, there will normally be a gradual rise in RPM or MP after the initial drop (often accompanied by intermittent engine roughness). This engine roughness is due to the ingestion of the water from the melted ice. When the carburetor heat is turned off, the RPM or MP will rise to a setting greater than that before application of the heat because ice was restricting the airflow in the carburetor. The engine should also run more smoothly after the ice melts.

iii) Whenever the throttle is closed during flight, the engine cools rapidly and vaporization of the fuel is less complete than if the engine is warm. In this condition the engine is more susceptible to carburetor icing.

- If you suspect carburetor-icing conditions and anticipate closed-throttle operation, the carburetor heat should be turned to "full-on" before closing the throttle, and left on during the closed-throttle operation. The heat will aid in vaporizing the fuel and preventing carburetor ice.

- Periodically, the throttle should be opened smoothly for a few seconds to keep the engine warm, otherwise the carburetor heater may not provide enough heat to prevent icing.

iv) Use of carburetor heat tends to reduce the output of the engine and also to increase the operating temperature.

- Therefore, the heat should not be used when full power is required (as during takeoff) or during normal engine operation except to check for the presence or removal of carburetor ice.

- In extreme cases of carburetor icing, after the ice has been removed it may be necessary to apply just enough carburetor heat to prevent further ice formation. However, this must be done with caution.

- If carburetor ice still forms, apply FULL heat to remove it.

  NOTE: Partial use of carburetor heat may raise the temperature of the induction air into the range that is likely for the formation of ice, thus increasing the risk of icing.

v) Check the engine manufacturer's recommendations for the correct use of carburetor heat.

e) Carburetor Air Temperature Gauge. Some airplanes are equipped with this gauge useful in detecting potential icing conditions.

i) Usually, the face of the gauge is calibrated in degrees Celsius. A yellow arc indicates the carburetor air temperatures at which icing may occur. This yellow arc ranges between −15°C and +5°C.

ii) If the air temperature and moisture content of the air are such that carburetor icing is improbable, the engine can be operated with the indicator in the yellow range with no adverse effects.

iii) However, if the atmospheric conditions are conducive to carburetor icing, the indicator must be kept outside the yellow arc by application of carburetor heat.

f) Outside Air Temperature Gauge (OAT). Most airplanes are equipped with this gauge calibrated in degrees both Celsius and Fahrenheit. It is useful for obtaining the outside or ambient air temperature for calculating true airspeed and also in detecting potential icing conditions.

2) Induction System Icing. This kind of icing forms under a variety of conditions on both piston and turbine aircraft. As air is ingested through the engine intakes, the moisture can freeze inside the induction system, reducing or stopping the flow of combustible air into the engine. The ice can also form on the exterior of the airplane and clog the air intake openings.

d. Loss of oil pressure.

1) Partial loss is normally a result of a malfunction in the oil pressure regulating system.

    a) Land at the nearest airport to investigate the cause and prevent engine damage.

2) Complete loss of oil pressure can indicate oil exhaustion or a faulty gauge.

    a) If this is accompanied by a rise in oil temperature, you should prepare yourself for an engine failure.

e. Fuel starvation.

1) Fuel starvation is normally indicated by a rough engine. It can be caused by an obstruction in the fuel line or by running a fuel tank empty.

    a) Check your fuel-flow gauge (if equipped) for an indication of fuel flowing to the engine.

    b) Mixture to full rich.

    c) Electric fuel pump on and check the fuel pressure gauge for normal pressure.

    d) Switch tanks.

    e) In some airplanes, if you run a fuel tank completely dry so the engine quits, it may take as long as 10 seconds before fuel is in the fuel lines to restart the engine.

2) Fuel starvation is normally due to poor fuel management/planning.

f. Engine compartment fire.

1) The presence of fire is noted through smoke, smell, and possibly heat in the cabin. It is essential that you check for the source first.

2) Engine fires are rare in flight.

    a) Perform the checklist in your *POH*.

    b) Since you will be turning off the fuel to starve the fire, you will be forced to execute an emergency landing.

    c) The use of a slip can help keep the smoke away from the cabin.

3) A fire in the cabin can become a hazardous situation. Know the procedure that is in your *POH*.

    a) With a fire you may want to close all vents, so as to prevent any drafts.

        i) If available, use an appropriately rated fire extinguisher.

            • During preflight, check the fire extinguisher for serviceability and the types of fires on which it can be used.

        ii) After discharging the extinguisher you need to ventilate the cabin.

4) If the smoke in the cabin indicates an electrical fire, you should immediately turn off the master switch.

    a) Then follow the checklist in your *POH*.
    b) Land as soon as possible.

5) If smoke is coming through your airplane's vents you need to turn off any environmental system, i.e., heat, air conditioner.

    a) Close all vents, and then check by opening to determine the source of the smoke.

    b) Land at the nearest airport to investigate the cause.

g. Electrical system malfunction.

1) Electrical system malfunction can be detected by monitoring your ammeter gauge.

2) A broken alternator belt is normally the cause of an alternator failure.

    a) Test your alternator by turning on your landing light. If there is no increase on your ammeter, you can assume an alternator failure.

    b) If a failure has occurred, reduce the electrical load by turning off all unnecessary electrical systems.

3) With only the battery supplying power, plan about 30 minutes of supply. Save as much power as possible, especially if your landing gear extension system uses an electric-driven pump.

4) An excess rate of charge can also have an adverse effect on your electrical equipment.

    a) Turn off all unnecessary equipment and land as soon as possible.

5) Follow the procedures in your *POH*.

h. Gear or flap malfunction.

1) Landing gear or flap malfunction can occur during retraction or extension or may be caused by another system malfunction, e.g., electrical failure.

2) Landing gear malfunction is normally shown by an indicator or lack of indication on the instrument panel.

    a) The gear lever may be down but there is no green-light indication that the gear is down and locked.

    b) You should check the indicators to ensure that a bulb is not blown.

    c) You can manually lower the landing gear in some airplanes, whereas in others you can release hydraulic pressure to allow the gear to fall.

    d) A thorough knowledge of the system will allow you to analyze the problem. Follow the procedures in your *POH*.

3) Wing flap malfunction is normally caused by an obstruction or a broken control.

    a) Understanding the effect of wing flaps on the airflow will help you through this situation.

    b) You can attempt to cycle the flaps by using the flap control to lower and raise the flaps.

    c) Leave the flap selector in the up position to relieve any mechanical pressure holding the flaps down. This will possibly allow the airflow to reduce the angle of flap.

    d) Operate below the maximum flap extension airspeed.

    e) Follow the checklist in your *POH* and land as soon as possible.

    i. **Door opening in flight.**

      1) Door opening during flight can be recognized by an increase in noise and/or a change in the cabin airflow.

        a) Check your *POH* for the proper procedures for closing a door in flight. If there are none, land as soon as possible to correct the situation.

    j. **Trim inoperative.**

      1) An inoperative trim will not allow you to reduce the control pressures.

        a) Plan for this during your descent and especially during your approach and landing.

        b) You may want to plan to land at a higher airspeed and a longer landing distance if you are unable to apply enough control pressure to keep the nose up.

      2) If using an electric-powered trim, disengage the electric connection, and determine if you can manually trim your airplane.

      3) Follow the recommended procedures in your *POH*.

    k. **Loss of pressurization.**

      1) A loss of pressurization (decompression) is the inability of the airplane's pressurization system to maintain its design pressure differential.

        a) This is caused by a malfunction in the pressurization system, or by structural damage to the airplane.

        b) Monitor your systems instruments for signs of problems.

      2) During decompression there may be a noise, and you may feel dazed. The cabin air will fill with fog, dust, or flying debris.

        a) The primary danger of decompression is hypoxia. You must use supplemental oxygen, especially if it is a rapid decompression.

      3) Follow the recommended procedures in your *POH*.

    l. **Other malfunctions.**

      1) Read your *POH* for all possible emergency procedures for systems and equipment malfunctions. You must know how all your airplane's systems operate, and the indications, causes, and your required action for the emergency procedure when a malfunction occurs.

C. Common errors during system and equipment malfunctions

  1. **Failure to understand the systems and equipment in your airplane.**

    a. You must know how the various systems and equipment operate in your airplane.

      1) Then you will be able to correctly analyze the malfunction and take the appropriate steps to correct the situation.

      2) You will also understand the effect(s) it will have on the operation of your airplane.

  2. **Failure to accomplish the emergency checklist.**

    a. Have your checklists readily available to you in the cockpit.

    b. Follow the checklist in order to take the appropriate steps to correct the malfunction and/or emergency.

END OF TASK -- END OF CHAPTER

CHAPTER XI
APPROACHES AND LANDINGS

XI.A. Normal and Crosswind Approaches and Landings 416
XI.B. Forward Slips to Landing 436
XI.C. Go-Around 441
XI.D. Short-Field Approach and Landing 446
XI.E. Soft-Field Approach and Landing 452

This chapter explains the five tasks (A-E) of Approaches and Landings. These tasks include elements of both knowledge and skill.

Each objective of a task lists, in sequence, the important elements that must be satisfactorily performed. The object includes:

1. Specifically what you should be able to do.
2. The conditions under which the task is to be performed.
3. The minimum acceptable standards of performance.

Be confident. You have prepared diligently and are better prepared and more skilled than the average private pilot applicant. Your examiner will base your ability to perform these tasks on the following.

1. Executing the task within your airplane's capabilities and limitations, including use of the airplane's systems.

2. Piloting your airplane with smoothness and accuracy.

3. Exercising good judgment.

4. Applying your aeronautical knowledge.

5. Showing mastery of your airplane within the standards outlined in this area of operation, with the successful outcome of a task never seriously in doubt.

This chapter discusses the factors that affect your airplane during the landing approach under normal and critical circumstances, and the techniques for positively controlling these factors. You must be able to make the transition from in-flight control with accuracy, smoothness, and positiveness.

Your examiner is required to test you on all five tasks. Each task is reproduced verbatim from the FAA Practical Test Standards in a shaded box. General discussion is presented under "A. General Information." This is followed by "B. Task Objectives," which is a detailed discussion of each element of the FAA's task.

NORMAL AND CROSSWIND APPROACHES AND LANDINGS

XI.A. TASK: NORMAL AND CROSSWIND APPROACHES AND LANDINGS

PILOT OPERATION - 5

REFERENCES: AC 61-21; Airplane Handbook and Flight Manual.

Objective. To determine that the applicant:

1. Exhibits knowledge by explaining the elements of normal and crosswind approaches and landings, including airspeeds, configurations, crosswind limitations, and related safety factors.

2. Maintains the proper ground track on final approach.

3. Establishes the approach and landing configuration and power required.

4. Maintains the recommended approach airspeed, ±5 kt.

5. Makes smooth, timely, and correct control application during the final approach and transition from approach to landing roundout.

6. Touches down smoothly at approximate stalling speed, at or within 500 ft. beyond a specified point, with no appreciable drift, and the airplane longitudinal axis aligned with the runway centerline.

7. Maintains directional control, increasing aileron deflection into the wind, as necessary, during the after-landing roll.

Note: If a crosswind condition does not exist, the applicant's knowledge of the TASK will be evaluated through oral testing.

A.   General Information

   1.   This is one of five tasks (A-E) in this area of operation. Your examiner is required to test you on this task.

   2.   *Pilot Operation - 5* refers to FAR 61.107(a)(5): Normal and crosswind takeoffs and landings.

   3.   FAA References

        AC 61-21: Flight Training Handbook
        Pilot's Operating Handbook (FAA-Approved Airplane Flight Manual)

   4.   The objective of this task is for you to demonstrate your ability to perform normal and crosswind approaches and landings.

        a.   If a crosswind condition does not exist, your knowledge of crosswind procedures will be orally tested.

B.   Task Objectives

   1.   **Exhibit your knowledge by explaining the elements of normal and crosswind approaches and landings, including airspeeds, configurations, crosswind limitations, and related safety factors.**

        a.   A normal approach and landing is one in which engine power is available, the wind is light or the final approach is made directly into the wind, the final approach path has no obstacles, and the landing surface is firm and of ample length to gradually bring your airplane to a stop.

1) A crosswind approach and landing involves the same basic principles as a normal approach and landing except the wind is blowing across rather than parallel to the final approach path.

   a) Crosswind landings are a little more difficult to perform than crosswind takeoffs, mainly due to different problems involved in maintaining accurate control of your airplane while its speed is decreasing rather than increasing as on takeoff.

   b) Virtually every landing will require at least some slight crosswind correction.

b. Normally, the initial power reduction is made on the downwind leg when you are abeam of your intended landing point.

   1) At this point you should begin a descent at the airspeed recommended in your *POH*. In the absence of a recommended speed, use 1.4 V_{S0}.

      a) EXAMPLE: If V_{S0} in your airplane is 60 kt., the airspeed on the base leg should be 84 kt. (1.4 x 60).

      b) In your airplane, initial approach speed (*POH*) _____, or 1.4 V_{S0} _____.

   2) On final approach you should use the airspeed in your *POH*. In the absence of the manufacturer's recommended airspeed, a speed equal to 1.3 V_{S0} should be used.

      a) EXAMPLE: If V_{S0} in your airplane is 60 kt., the airspeed on final approach should be 78 kt. (1.3 x 60).

      b) In your airplane, final approach speed (*POH*) _____, or 1.3 V_{S0} _____.

   3) The presence of strong, gusting winds or turbulent air may require you to increase your airspeed on final approach. This provides for more positive control of your airplane.

      a) The gust factor, the difference between the steady state wind and the maximum gust, should be factored into your final approach airspeed in some form.

         i) It should also be added to your various approach segment airspeeds for downwind, base, and final.

      b) One recommended technique is to use the normal approach speed plus one-half the gust factor.

         i) EXAMPLE: If the normal approach speed is 70 kt. and the wind gusts increase 20 kt., an airspeed of 80 kt. is appropriate.

         ii) Some pilots add all of the steady wind and one-half the gust, or all of the gust and no steady wind.

      c) Remember, your airspeed and whatever gust factor you select to add to your final approach speed should be flown only after all maneuvering has been completed and your airplane has been lined up on the final approach.

      d) When using a higher-than-normal approach speed, it may be expedient to use less than full flaps on landing.

      e) Follow the recommended procedures in your *POH*.

c.   Properly configuring your airplane throughout the various approach segments will assist you in flying a stabilized approach.

  1)   On the downwind leg, you should complete the Before Landing checklist in your *POH*, which includes gear extension (if retractable).

   a)   Before Landing checklist for the Piper Tomahawk.

PIPER TOMAHAWK PA-38-112
BEFORE LANDING CHECKLIST

1.   Fuel selector - PROPER TANK
2.   Seat backs - ERECT
3.   Belts/harness - FASTEN
4.   Electric fuel pump - ON
5.   Mixture - SET
6.   Flaps - SET - (89 KIAS max)
7.   Trim to 70 KIAS
8.   Final approach speed -
         Full flaps (Outboard Flow Strips Installed) - 62 KIAS
         Full flaps (Outboard and Inboard Flow Strips Installed) - 67 KIAS

For Academic Illustration/Training Purposes Only!
For Flight: Use your Pilot's Operating Handbook and FAA-Approved Airplane Flight Manual.

---

   b)   When abeam of your intended landing point, the power should be reduced and altitude held constant. As the airspeed slows below the maximum flap extended speed (V_{FE}) you should partially lower the flaps.

    i)   In your airplane, V_{FE} _____.

  2)   On the base leg, the flaps may be extended further, but full flaps are not recommended.

  3)   Once aligned with the runway centerline on the final approach, you should make the final flap selection. This is normally full flaps.

   a)   In turbulent air or strong gusty winds, you may elect not to use full flaps. This will allow you to maintain control more easily.

    i)   With less than full flaps, your airplane will be in a higher nose-up attitude.

d.   Each airplane, due to its design, has a crosswind limitation in which it can be safely landed. This is called the maximum crosswind component and it is found in your *POH*.

  1)   When the wind is neither a direct headwind nor a direct crosswind it can be divided into two components.

   a)   Headwind, and
   b)   Crosswind.

  2)   The diagram on the next page is a crosswind component chart that can be found in your *POH*.

   a)   EXAMPLE: You are landing on runway 4 and the wind is 070° at 40 kt. Enter the chart at the wind angle (angle between runway heading and wind direction), at Point A. Follow the line down to the windspeed of 40 kt., at Point B. Move horizontally to the left margin to determine a headwind component of 35 kt., Point C. From Point B move down vertically to determine a crosswind component of 20 kt., Point D. Check your *POH* to ensure this does not exceed the maximum crosswind component.

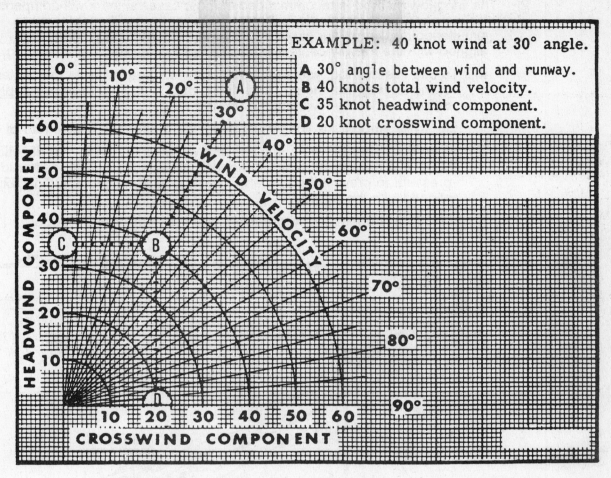

3) It is imperative that you avoid operations in wind conditions that exceed the capability (i.e., maximum crosswind component) of your airplane.

2. **Maintain the proper ground track on final approach.**

   a. Immediately after the base-to-final approach turn is completed, the longitudinal axis of your airplane should be aligned with the centerline of the runway so that drift (if any) will be recognized immediately.

   b. On a normal approach, with no wind drift, the longitudinal axis should be kept aligned with the runway centerline throughout the approach and landing.

      1) Any corrections should be made with coordinated aileron and rudder pressure.

   c. On a crosswind approach there are two usual methods of maintaining the proper ground track on final approach. These are the crab method and the wing-low method.

      1) The crab method is used first by establishing a heading (crab) toward the wind with the wings level so that your airplane's ground track remains aligned with the centerline of the runway.

         a) This is maintained until just prior to touchdown, when the longitudinal axis of the airplane must be quickly aligned with the runway.

            i) This requires a high degree of judgment and timing in removing the crab immediately prior to touchdown.

         b) This is best to use while on a long final approach until you are on a short final, when you should change to the wing-low method.

         c) Maintaining a crab as long as possible increases passenger comfort.

2) The wing-low method is recommended in most cases since it will compensate for a crosswind at any angle, but more importantly, it will enable you to simultaneously keep your airplane's ground track and longitudinal axis aligned with the runway centerline throughout the approach and landing.

    a) To use this method, you align your airplane's heading with the centerline of the runway, not the rate and direction of drift, then promptly apply drift correction by lowering the upwind wing.

        i) The amount the wing must be lowered depends on the rate of drift.

    b) When you lower the wing, the airplane will tend to turn in that direction. Thus, it is necessary to simultaneously apply sufficient opposite rudder pressure to prevent the turn and keep the airplane's longitudinal axis aligned with the runway.

        i) Drift is controlled with aileron, and the heading with rudder.

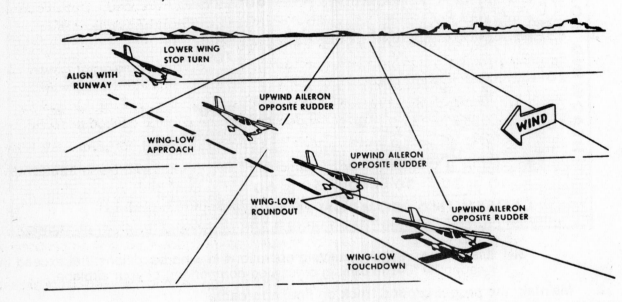

    c) Your airplane will now be slipping into the wind just enough that both the resultant flight path and the ground track are aligned with the runway.

    d) In a very strong crosswind, the required bank may be so steep that full opposite rudder will not prevent a turn. The wind is too strong to safely land on that particular runway with those wind conditions.

        i) Since the airplane's capabilities would be exceeded, it is imperative that the landing be made on a more favorable runway either at that airport or at an alternate airport.

3. **Establish the approach and landing configuration and power required.**

    a. The approach and landing configuration means that the gear is down (if retractable), wing flaps extended, and you are maintaining a reduced power setting.

    b. The lift/drag factors may be varied by you to adjust the descent through the use of the wing flaps.

        1) When the flaps are lowered, the airspeed will decrease unless the power is increased or the pitch attitude lowered.

2) After starting the final approach, you must then estimate where your airplane will land through discerning judgment of the descent angle.

    a) If it appears that the airplane is going to overshoot or land slightly beyond the desired spot, more flaps may be used if not fully extended or the power reduced further, and the pitch attitude lowered. This will result in a steeper approach.

    b) If the spot is being undershot and a shallower approach is needed, the power and the pitch attitude should be increased to readjust the descent angle and the airspeed.

        i) NEVER retract the flaps to correct for undershooting since that may suddenly decrease the lift and cause your airplane to sink even more rapidly.

c. During the approach to a landing, power is at a considerably lower than cruise setting and the airplane is flying at a relatively slower airspeed. Thus, you must trim your airplane to compensate for the change in aerodynamic forces.

4.   *Maintain the recommended approach airspeed, ±5 kt.*

a. Airspeed control is the most important factor in achieving landing precision. A well-executed landing begins in the traffic pattern with a stabilized approach.

    1) Once on final approach, slight adjustments in pitch and power may be necessary to maintain the descent attitude and the desired airspeed.

    2) Use the final approach speed in your *POH*. If one is not given, use 1.3 V_{so}.

        a) Make necessary adjustments to that speed if you are in turbulent air, or strong, gusty winds.

        b) Inform your examiner of your final approach airspeed.

b. The objective of a good final approach is to descend at an angle and airspeed that will permit your airplane to reach the desired touchdown point at an airspeed which will result in a minimum of floating just before touchdown.

    1) A fundamental key to flying a stabilized approach is the interrelationship of pitch and power.

        a) This interrelationship means that any changes to one element in the approach equation (e.g., airspeed, attitude) must be compensated for by adjustments in the other.

    2) Power should be adjusted as necessary to control the airspeed, and the pitch attitude adjusted SIMULTANEOUSLY to control the descent angle or to attain the desired altitudes along the approach path.

        a) By lowering the nose of your airplane and reducing power to keep your approach airspeed constant, a descent at a higher rate can be made to correct for being too high in the approach.

    3) The important point is: never let your airspeed drop below your approach speed and never let your airplane sink below the selected glide path.

5.   Make smooth, timely, and correct control application during the final approach and transition from approach to landing roundout.

a. During the approach you need to fly a stabilized approach, which means on glide path and on airspeed.

    1) Make adjustments in both pitch and power to maintain airspeed and glide path.

    2) Maintain the proper ground track while on final approach.

b. The roundout (flare) is a slow, smooth transition from a normal approach attitude to a landing attitude. When your airplane, in a normal descent, approaches what appears to be about 10 to 20 ft. above the ground, the roundout should be started, and once started should be a continuous process until the airplane touches down on the ground.

  1) Well before starting the roundout, it is imperative that you once again complete your Before Landing checklist.

  a) Recheck the landing gear for the down and locked indications, if so equipped.

  2) To start the roundout, power should be reduced to idle and back elevator pressure should be gradually applied to slowly increase the pitch attitude and angle of attack. This will cause your airplane's nose to gradually rise toward the desired landing attitude.

  a) The angle of attack should be increased at a rate that will allow your airplane to continue settling slowly as forward speed decreases.

  3) When the angle of attack is increased, the lift is momentarily increased, thereby decreasing the rate of descent.

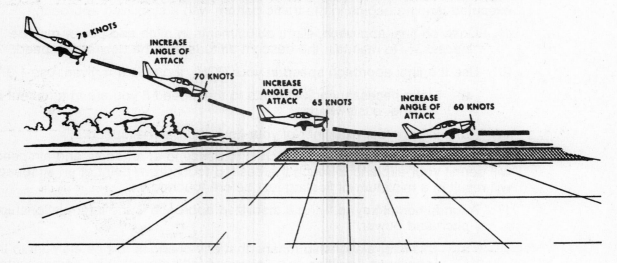

  a) Since power is normally reduced to idle during the roundout, the airspeed will gradually decrease. This, in turn, causes lift to decrease again and must be controlled by raising the nose and further increasing the angle of attack.

  b) During the roundout, the airspeed is being decreased to touchdown speed while the lift is being controlled so your airplane will settle gently onto the runway.

  4) The rate at which the roundout is executed depends on your height above the ground, rate of descent, and the pitch attitude.

  a) A roundout started excessively high must be executed more slowly than one from a lower height to allow your airplane to descend to the ground while the proper landing attitude is being established.

  b) The rate of rounding out must also be proportionate to the rate of closure with the ground. When your airplane appears to be descending slowly, the increase in pitch attitude must be made at a correspondingly slow rate.

5) The pitch attitude in a full-flap approach is considerably lower than in a no-flap approach. Thus, to attain the proper landing attitude before touching down, the nose must travel through a greater pitch change when flaps are fully extended.

6) Once the actual process of rounding out is started, the elevator control should not be pushed forward. If too much back pressure has been exerted, this pressure should be either slightly relaxed or held constant, depending on the degree of error.

   a) In some cases, you may find it necessary to add power slightly to prevent an excessive rate of sink, or a stall, all of which would result in a hard, drop-in landing.

7) You must be in the habit of keeping one hand on the throttle control throughout the approach and landing, should a sudden and unexpected hazardous situation require an immediate application of power.

c. In a crosswind approach, the roundout can be made as in a normal landing approach but the application of a crosswind correction must be continued as necessary to prevent drifting.

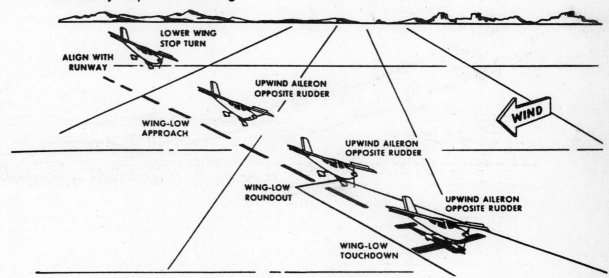

1) Since the airspeed decreases as the roundout progresses, the flight controls gradually become less effective. Thus, the crosswind correction being held would become inadequate.

   a) It is therefore necessary to gradually increase the deflection of the rudder and ailerons to maintain the proper amount of drift correction.

2) Do not level the wings. Keep the upwind wing down throughout the crosswind roundout.

   a) If the wings are leveled, your airplane will begin drifting and the touchdown will occur while drifting.

6. ***Touch down smoothly at approximate stalling speed, at or within 500 ft. beyond a specified point, with no appreciable drift, and your airplane's longitudinal axis aligned with the runway centerline.***

   a. The touchdown is the gentle settling of your airplane onto the runway. The touchdown should be made with the engine idling, and your airplane at minimum controllable airspeed, so that the airplane will touch down on the main gear at approximately stalling speed.

      1) As your airplane settles, the proper landing attitude must be attained by application of whatever back elevator pressure is necessary.

2) It seems contradictory that the way to make a good landing is to try to hold your airplane's wheels a few inches off the ground as long as possible with the elevators.

   a) Normally, when the wheels are about 2 or 3 ft. off the ground, the airplane will still be settling too fast for a gentle touchdown. Thus, this descent must be retarded by further back pressure on the elevators.

   b) Since your airplane is already close to its stalling speed and is settling, this added back pressure will only slow up the settling instead of stopping it. At the same time it will result in your airplane touching the ground in the proper landing attitude.

b. During a normal landing, a nosewheel-type airplane should contact the ground in a tail-low attitude, with the main wheels touching down first so that little or no weight is on the nose wheel.

1) After the main wheels make initial contact with the ground, back pressure on the elevator control should be held to maintain a positive angle of attack for aerodynamic braking and to hold the nosewheel off the ground until the airplane decelerates.

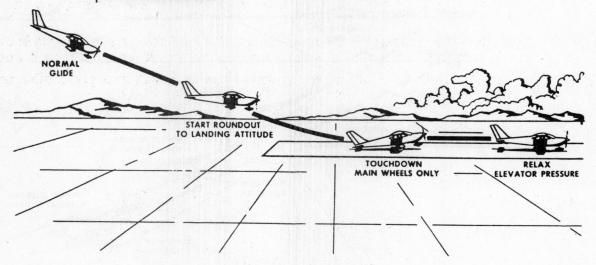

2) As the airplane's momentum decreases, back pressure may be gradually relaxed to allow the nosewheel to gently settle onto the runway.

   a) This will permit prompt steering with the nosewheel, if it is of the steerable type.

   b) At the same time it will cause a low angle of attack and negative lift on the wings to prevent floating or skipping, and will allow the full weight of the airplane to rest on the wheels for better braking action.

c. During a normal landing in a tailwheel-type airplane, the roundout and touchdown should be timed so that the wheels of the main landing gear and tailwheel touch down simultaneously (i.e., a 3-point landing). This requires fine timing, technique, and judgment of distance and altitude.

1) When the wheels make contact with the ground, the elevator control should be carefully held fully back to hold the tail down and the tailwheel on the ground.

   a) This provides more positive directional control of the airplane equipped with a steerable tailwheel, and prevents any tendency for the airplane to nose over.

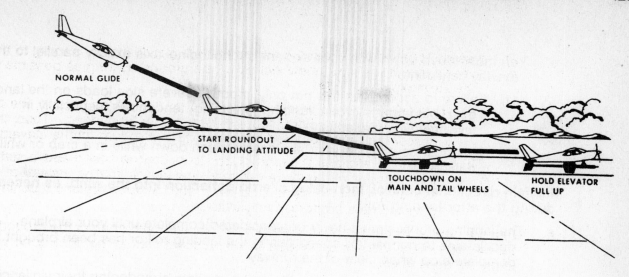

b) If the tailwheel is not on the ground, easing back on the elevator control may cause the airplane to become airborne again because the change in attitude will increase the angle of attack and produce enough lift for the airplane to fly.

d. During a crosswind touchdown, you must make prompt adjustments in the crosswind correction to assure that your airplane does not drift as it touches down.

1) The crosswind correction should be maintained throughout the roundout, and the touchdown made on the upwind main wheel.

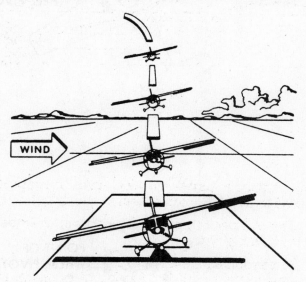

a) As the forward momentum decreases after initial contact the weight of the airplane will cause the downwind main wheel to gradually settle onto the runway.

2) In those airplanes having nosewheel steering interconnected with the rudder, the nosewheel may not be aligned with the runway as the wheels touch down because opposite rudder is being held in the crosswind correction.

a) This is the case in airplanes which have no centering cam built in the nose gear strut to keep the nosewheel straight until the strut is compressed.

b) To prevent swerving in the direction the nosewheel is offset, the corrective rudder pressure must be promptly relaxed just as the nosewheel touches down.

   e.   You must touch down with your airplane's longitudinal axis exactly parallel to the runway centerline.

      1)   Failure to accomplish this not only imposes severe side loads on the landing gear, but imparts groundlooping (swerving) tendencies, especially in tailwheel-type airplanes.

      2)   You must never allow your airplane to touch down while in a crab or while drifting.

7.   Maintain directional control, increasing aileron deflection into the wind, as necessary, during the after-landing roll.

   a.   The landing process must never be considered complete until your airplane decelerates to normal taxi speed during the landing roll or has been brought to a complete stop when clear of the runway.

      1)   Accidents have occurred as the result of pilots abandoning their vigilance and positive control after getting the airplane on the ground.

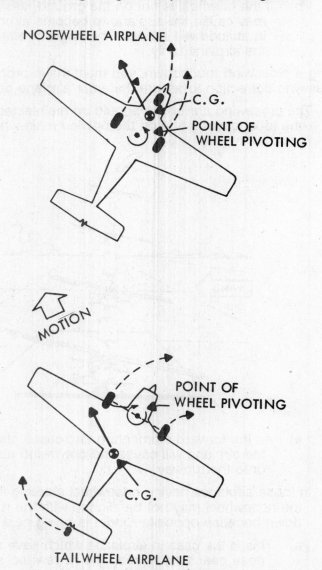

NOSEWHEEL AIRPLANE

C.G.

POINT OF WHEEL PIVOTING

MOTION

POINT OF WHEEL PIVOTING

C.G.

TAILWHEEL AIRPLANE

b.   After a nosewheel-type airplane is on the ground, back pressure on the elevator control may be gradually relaxed, placing normal weight on the nosewheel to aid in better steering.

   1)   With a tailwheel-type airplane, the elevator control should be held back as far as possible, until the airplane stops. This provides more positive control with tailwheel steering, tends to shorten the after-landing roll, and prevents bouncing and skipping.

c.   You must be alert for directional control problems immediately upon and after touchdown due to the ground friction on the wheels. The friction creates a pivot point on which a moment arm can act.

   1)   This is especially true in tailwheel-type airplanes because, unlike nosewheel-type airplanes, the CG is *behind* the main wheels.

      a)   Any difference between the direction in which the airplane is traveling and the direction in which it is headed will produce a moment about the pivot point of the wheels and the airplane will tend to swerve.

   2)   Nosewheel-type airplanes make the task of directional control easier because the CG, being *ahead* of the main landing wheels, presents a moment arm which tends to straighten the airplane's path during the touchdown and after-landing roll.

      a)   This should not lull you into a false sense of security.

d.   Another directional control problem in crosswind landings is due to the weathervaning tendency of your airplane. Characteristically, an airplane has a greater profile or side area behind the main landing gear than forward of it.

   1)   With the main landing wheels acting as a pivot point and the greater surface area exposed to a crosswind behind the pivot point, the airplane will tend to turn or weathervane into the wind.

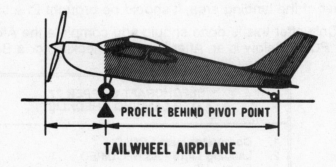

TAILWHEEL AIRPLANE

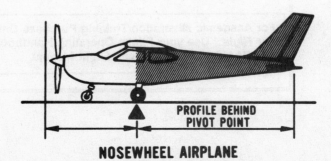

NOSEWHEEL AIRPLANE

   2)   This is characteristic of all airplanes but it is more prevalent in the tailwheel-type because the airplane's surface area behind the main landing gear is greater than in nosewheel-type airplanes.

e. Loss of directional control may lead to an aggravated, uncontrolled, tight turn on the ground (i.e., a ground loop).

   1) The combination of centrifugal force acting on the CG and ground friction on the main wheels resisting it during the ground loop may cause the airplane to tip, or lean, enough for the outside wingtip to contact the ground.

      a) This may impose a great enough sideward force to collapse the landing gear.

   2) Tailwheel-type airplanes are most susceptible to ground loops late in the after-landing roll because rudder effectiveness decreases with the decreasing airflow along the rudder surface as the airplane slows.

f. The ailerons serve the same purpose on the ground as they do in the air; they change the lift and drag components of the wings.

   1) While your airplane is decelerating during the after-landing roll, more and more aileron must be applied to keep the upwind wing from rising.

   2) Since your airplane is slowing down and there is less airflow around the ailerons, they become less effective. At the same time the relative wind is becoming more of a crosswind and exerting a greater lifting force on the upwind wing.

      a) Consequently, when the airplane is coming to a full stop the aileron control must be held FULLY toward the wind.

g. If available runway permits, the speed of the airplane should be allowed to dissipate in a normal manner by the friction and drag of the wheels on the ground.

   1) Brakes may be used if needed to slow the airplane. This is normally done near the end of the after-landing roll to ensure the airplane is moving slowly enough to exit the runway in a controlled manner.

h. After your airplane has been slowed sufficiently and has been turned onto a taxiway or clear of the landing area, it should be brought to a complete stop.

   1) Only after this is done should you complete the After-Landing checklist in the *POH*. Below is an After-Landing checklist for a Beech Skipper.

BEECHCRAFT SKIPPER 77
AFTER-LANDING CHECKLIST

1. **Carburetor Heat** - COLD
2. **Landing Light** - AS REQUIRED
3. **Flaps** - UP
4. **Elevator Trim Tab** - SET TO TAKE-OFF RANGE
5. **Rudder Trim** - SET TO 0

For Academic Illustration/Training Purposes Only!
For Flight: Use your Pilot's Operating Handbook and FAA-Approved Airplane Flight Manual.

C.   Common errors during normal and crosswind approaches and landings

1.   **Improper use of landing performance data and limitations.**

a.   Use your *POH* to determine the appropriate airspeeds for a normal and crosswind approach and landing.

b.   In gusty and/or strong crosswinds use the crosswind component chart to determine that you are not exceeding your airplane's crosswind limitations.

c.   Use your *POH* to determine data and limitations and do not attempt to do better than the data.

2.   **Failure to establish approach and landing configuration at appropriate time or in proper sequence.**

a.   Use the Before Landing checklist in your *POH* to ensure that you follow the proper sequence in establishing the correct approach and landing configuration for your airplane.

b.   You should initially start the checklist at midpoint on the downwind leg with the power reduction beginning once you are abeam of your intended point of landing.

1)   By the time you turn on final and align your airplane with the runway centerline you should be in the final landing configuration. Confirm this by completing your checklist once again.

3.   **Failure to establish and maintain a stabilized approach.**

a.   Once you are on final and aligned with the runway centerline you should make small adjustments to pitch and power to establish the correct descent angle (i.e., glide path) and airspeed.

1)   Remember, you must make simultaneous adjustments to both pitch and power.

2)   Large adjustments will result in a roller coaster ride.

b.   Lock in your airspeed and glide path as soon as possible.

1)   Never let your airspeed go below your approach speed, and

2)   Never let your airplane sink below your selected glide path, or the glide path of a visual approach slope indicator (i.e., VASI or PAPI).

4.   **Inappropriate removal of hand from throttle.**

a.   One hand should remain on the control yoke at all times.

b.   The other hand should remain on the throttle unless operating the microphone or making an adjustment, such as trim or flaps.

1)   Once you are on short final your hand should remain on the throttle, even if ATC gives you instruction (e.g., cleared to land).

a)   Your first priority is to fly your airplane and avoid doing tasks which may distract you from maintaining control.

b)   Fly first, talk later.

c.   You must be in the habit of keeping one hand on the throttle in case a sudden and unexpected hazardous situation should require an immediate application of power.

5. **Improper technique during roundout and touchdown.**

    a.   High roundout.

       1)   This occurs when you make the roundout too rapidly and your airplane is flying level too high above the runway.

          a)   If you continued the roundout, you would increase the wings' angle of attack to the critical angle while reducing the airspeed. Thus, you would stall your airplane and drop hard onto the runway.

       2)   To correct this, the pitch attitude should be held constant until the airplane decelerates enough to again start descending. Then the roundout can be continued to establish the proper landing attitude.

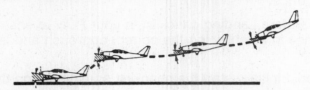

          a)   Use this technique only when you have an adequate amount of airspeed. It may be necessary to add a slight amount of power to prevent the airspeed from decreasing excessively and to avoid losing lift too rapidly.

       3)   Although back pressure on the elevator control may be relaxed slightly, the nose should not be lowered any perceptible amount to make the airplane descend when relatively close to the runway.

          a)   The momentary decrease in lift that would result from lowering the nose (i.e., decreasing angle of attack) may be so great that a nosewheel-type airplane might contact the ground with the nosewheel, which could then collapse.

          b)   Execute a go-around (see Task XI.C., Go-Around, on page 441) any time it appears that the nose should be lowered significantly.

    b.   Late or rapid roundout.

       1)   Starting the roundout too late or pulling the elevator control back too rapidly to prevent your airplane from touching down prematurely can impose a heavy load factor on the wing and cause an accelerated stall.

          a)   This is a dangerous situation because it may cause your airplane to land extremely hard on the main landing wheels, and then bounce back into the air.

             i)   As your airplane contacts the ground, the tail will be forced down very rapidly by the back pressure on the elevator and the inertia acting downward on the tail.

       2)   Recovery requires prompt and positive application of power prior to occurrence of the stall.

          a)   This may be followed by a normal landing, if sufficient runway is available, otherwise execute an immediate go-around.

    c.   Floating during roundout.

       1)   This is caused by using excessive speed on the final approach. Before touchdown can be made, your airplane may be well past the desired landing point and the available runway may be insufficient.

2)   If you dive your airplane excessively on final approach to land at the proper point, there will be an appreciable increase in airspeed. Consequently, the proper touchdown attitude cannot be established without producing an excessive angle of attack and lift. This will cause your airplane to gain altitude.

3)   Failure to anticipate ground effect may also result in floating.

4)   The recovery will depend on the amount of floating, the effect of a crosswind (if any), and the amount of runway remaining.

    a)   You must smoothly and gradually adjust the pitch attitude as your airplane decelerates to touchdown speed and starts to settle, so the proper landing attitude is attained at the moment of touchdown.

        i)   The slightest error in judgment will result in either ballooning or bouncing.

    b)   If a landing cannot be completed within 500 ft. of a specified point, you should immediately execute a go-around.

d.   Ballooning during roundout.

1)   If you misjudge the rate of sink during a landing and think your airplane is descending faster than it should, there is a tendency to increase the pitch attitude and angle of attack too rapidly.

    a)   This not only stops the descent, but actually starts your airplane climbing (i.e., ballooning).

    b)   Ballooning can be dangerous because the height above the ground is increasing and your airplane may be rapidly approaching a stalled condition.

2)   When ballooning is slight, a constant landing attitude may be held and the airplane allowed to settle onto the runway.

    a)   You must be extremely cautious of ballooning when there is a crosswind present because the crosswind correction may be inadvertently released or it may become inadequate.

    b)   Due to the lower airspeed after ballooning, the crosswind affects your airplane more. Consequently, the wing will have to be lowered even further to compensate for the increased drift.

        i)   You must ensure that the upwind wing is down and that directional control is maintained with opposite rudder.

3)   Depending on the severity of ballooning, the use of power may be helpful in cushioning the landing.

    a)   By adding power, thrust can be increased to keep the airspeed from decelerating too rapidly and the wings from suddenly losing lift, but the throttle must be closed immediately after touchdown.

   b)   Remember that torque will have been created as power is applied, thus it will be necessary to use rudder pressure to counteract this effect.

4)   When ballooning is excessive, or if you have any doubts, you should immediately execute a go-around.

e.   Bouncing during touchdown.

1)   When your airplane contacts the ground with a sharp impact as the result of an improper attitude or an excessive rate of sink, it tends to bounce back into the air.

   a)   Though your airplane's tires and shock struts provide some springing action, the airplane does not bounce as does a rubber ball.

   b)   Your airplane rebounds into the air because the wing's angle of attack was abruptly increased, producing a sudden addition of lift.

      i)   The change in angle of attack is the result of inertia instantly forcing the airplane's tail downward when the main wheels contact the ground sharply.

SMALL ANGLE OF ATTACK   DECREASING ANGLE OF ATTACK   RAPID INCREASE IN ANGLE OF ATTACK   NORMAL ANGLE OF ATTACK

   c)   The severity of the bounce depends on the airspeed at the moment of contact and the degree to which the angle of attack, or pitch attitude, was increased.

2)   The corrective action for a bounce is the same as for ballooning and similarly depends on its severity.

   a)   When it is very slight and there is not extreme change in your airplane's pitch attitude, a follow-up landing may be executed by applying sufficient power to cushion the subsequent touchdown, and smoothly adjusting the pitch to the proper touchdown attitude.

3)   Extreme caution and alertness must be exercised, especially when there is a crosswind. The crosswind correction will normally be released by inexperienced pilots when the airplane bounces.

   a)   When one main wheel of the airplane strikes the runway, the other wheel will touch down immediately afterwards, and the wings will become level.

   b)   Then, with no crosswind correction as the airplane bounces, the wind will cause the airplane to roll with the wind, thus exposing even more surface to the crosswind and drifting the airplane more rapidly.

   c)   Remember, the upwind wing will have to be lowered even further to compensate for the increased drift due to the slower airspeed.

f.   Hard landing.

1)   When your airplane contacts the ground during landings, its vertical speed is instantly reduced to zero. Unless provision is made to slow this vertical speed and cushion the impact of touchdown, the force of contact with the ground may be so great as to cause structural damage to the airplane.

2)   The purpose of pneumatic tires, rubber or oleo shock absorbers, and other such devices is, in part, to cushion the impact and to increase the time in which the airplane's vertical descent is stopped.

a) The importance of this cushion may be understood from the computation that a 6-in. free fall on landing is roughly equivalent to a 340-fpm descent.

b) Within a fraction of a second your airplane must be slowed from this rate of vertical descent to zero, without damage.

   i) During this time, the landing gear together with some aid from the lift of the wings must supply the necessary force to counteract the force of the airplane's inertia and weight.

3) The lift decreases rapidly as the airplane's forward speed is decreased, and the force on the landing gear increases as the shock struts and tires are compressed by the impact of touchdown.

a) When the descent stops, the lift will practically be zero, leaving the landing gear alone to carry both the airplane's weight and inertial forces.

b) The load imposed at the instant of touchdown may easily be three or four times the actual weight of the airplane depending on the severity of contact.

g. Touchdown in a drift or crab.

1) If the crosswind rollout and touchdown are made while your airplane is drifting or in a crab, it will contact the ground while moving sideways.

a) This will impose extreme side loads on the landing gear, and, if severe enough, may cause structural failure.

b) There are two factors that will cause the longitudinal axis and the direction of motion of your airplane to be misaligned during touchdown:

   i) Drifting,
   ii) Crabbing, or
   iii) A combination of both.

2) If you have not taken adequate corrective action to avoid drift during a crosswind landing, the main wheels' tire treads offer resistance to the airplane's sideward movement in respect to the ground. Consequently, any sideward velocity of the airplane is abruptly decelerated, as shown in the figure below.

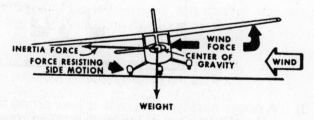

a) This creates a moment around the main wheel when it contacts the ground, tending to overturn or tip the airplane.

b) If the windward tip is raised by the action of this moment, all the weight and shock of landing will be borne by one main wheel. This may cause structural damage.

3) It is vital to prevent drift and keep the longitudinal axis of the airplane aligned with the runway during the roundout and touchdown.

6. **Poor directional control after touchdown.**

    a. Ground loop.

        1) A ground loop is an uncontrolled turn during ground operation that may occur while taxiing or taking off, but especially during the after-landing roll.

            a) It is not always caused by drift or weathervaning, although these may cause the initial swerve. Other reasons may include careless use of rudder, an uneven ground surface, or a soft spot that retards one main wheel of the airplane.

        2) Due to the characteristics of an airplane equipped with a tailwheel, the forces that cause a ground loop increase as the swerve increases.

            a) The initial swerve develops centrifugal force and this, acting at the CG (which is located behind the main wheels), swerves the airplane even more.

            b) If allowed to develop, the centrifugal force produced may become great enough to tip the airplane until one wing strikes the ground.

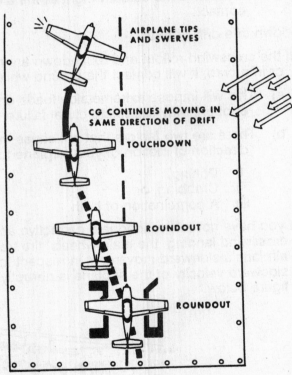

        3) A nosewheel-type airplane is less prone to ground loop. Since the CG is located forward of the main landing gear, any time a swerve develops, centrifugal force acting on the CG will tend to stop the swerving action.

        4) If your airplane touches down while drifting or in a crab, you should apply aileron toward the high wing and stop the swerve with the rudder.

        5) Brakes should be used to correct for turns or swerves only when the rudder is inadequate. You must exercise caution when applying corrective brake action because it is very easy to over-control and aggravate the situation.

            a) If brakes are used, sufficient brake should be applied on the low-wing (outside of the turn) to stop the swerve.

            b) When the wings are approximately level, the new direction must be maintained until the airplane has slowed to taxi speed or has stopped.

b.　Wing rising after touchdown.

　　1)　When landing in a crosswind there may be instances in which a wing will rise during the after-landing roll.

　　2)　Any time an airplane is rolling on the ground in a crosswind condition, the upwind wing is receiving a greater force from the wind than on the downwind wing. This causes a lift differential.

　　　　a)　Also, the wind striking the fuselage on the upwind side may further raise the wing by tending to tip or roll the fuselage.

　　3)　The corrective action is for you to immediately apply more aileron pressure toward the high wing and maintain directional control.

　　　　a)　The sooner the aileron is applied, the more effective it will be.

　　　　b)　The further a wing is allowed to rise before taking corrective action, the more airplane surface is exposed to the force of the crosswind. This reduces the effectiveness of the aileron.

7.　**Improper use of brakes.**

a.　Use the minimum amount of braking required, and let your airplane slow by the friction and drag of the wheels on the ground, if runway length permits.

b.　Never attempt to apply brakes until your airplane is firmly on the runway under complete control.

c.　Use equal pressure on both brakes to help prevent swerving and/or loss of directional control.

END OF TASK

FORWARD SLIPS TO LANDING

XI.B. TASK: FORWARD SLIPS TO LANDING

      PILOT OPERATION - 5

      REFERENCES: AC 61-21.

Objective. To determine that the applicant:

1. Exhibits knowledge by explaining the elements of a forward slip to a landing, including the purpose, technique, limitation, and the effect on airspeed indications.

2. Establishes a forward slip at a point from which a landing can be made in a desired area using the recommended airspeed and configuration.

3. Maintains a ground track aligned with the runway centerline.

4. Maintains an airspeed which results in minimum floating during the landing roundout.

5. Recovers smoothly from the slip.

6. Touches down smoothly at approximate stalling speed, at and within 500 ft. beyond a specified point, with no appreciable drift, and the airplane longitudinal axis aligned with the runway centerline.

7. Maintains directional control during the after-landing roll.

A. General Information

    1. This is one of five tasks (A-E) in this area of operation. Your examiner is required to test you on this task.

    2. *Pilot Operation - 5* refers to FAR 61.107(a)(5): Normal and crosswind takeoffs and landings.

    3. FAA References

        AC 61-21: Flight Training Handbook

    4. The objective of this task is for you to demonstrate your ability to perform a forward slip to a landing.

B.   Task Objectives

   1.   **Exhibit your knowledge by explaining the elements of a forward slip to a landing, including the purpose, technique, limitation, and the effect on airspeed indications.**

   a.   The primary purpose of a forward slip is to dissipate altitude without increasing your airplane's speed, particularly in airplanes not equipped with flaps.

   1)   There are many circumstances requiring the use of forward slips, such as in a landing approach over obstacles and in making forced landings, when it is always wise to allow an extra margin of altitude for safety in the original estimate of the approach.

   b.   The forward slip is a descent with one wing lowered and the airplane's longitudinal axis at an angle to the flight path. The flight path remains the same as before the slip was begun.

   1)   If there is any crosswind, the slip will be more effective and easier to recover if made toward the wind.

   2)   Slipping should be done with the engine idling. There is little logic in slipping to lose altitude if the power is still being used.

   3)   Altitude is lost in a slip by increasing drag caused by the air flow striking the wing-low side of the airplane. The L/D ratio decreases, which causes the rate of descent to increase.

   c.   The use of slips has definite limitations. Some pilots may try to lose altitude by violent slipping rather than by smoothly maneuvering and exercising good judgment and using only a slight or moderate slip.

   1)   In emergency landings, this erratic practice will invariably lead to trouble since enough excess speed may result to prevent touching down anywhere near the proper point, and very often will result in overshooting the entire field.

   d.   Because of the location of the pitot tube and static vents in some airplanes, the airspeed indicator may have considerable error when the airplane is in a slip.

   1)   If your airplane is subject to such errors, it is vital that you properly execute the slip to avoid airspeed excesses that may not register on the airspeed indicator.

   2)   You must recognize a properly performed slip by the attitude of your airplane, the sound of the airflow, and the feel of the flight controls.

   e.   Check your *POH* for any limitations on the use of a forward slip.

   1)   Some airplanes may be prohibited from performing a forward slip with the wing flaps extended.

   2)   Other airplanes may have a time limitation (i.e., slip can be used no more than 30 sec.).

2.   **Establish a forward slip at a point from which a landing can be made in a desired area using the recommended airspeed and configuration.**

   a.   Once you are assured that you can safely land in the desired area you should establish a forward slip.

   b.   Apply carburetor heat (if applicable) and reduce power to idle.

   1)   Extend the flaps, unless your *POH* prohibits slips with flaps extended.
   2)   Establish a pitch attitude that will maintain a normal final approach speed.

   c.   Assuming that your airplane is originally in straight flight, the wing on the side toward which the slip is to be made should be lowered by use of the ailerons.

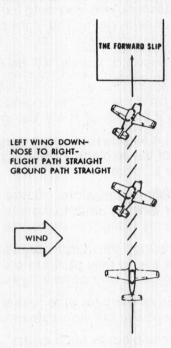

THE FORWARD SLIP

LEFT WING DOWN-
NOSE TO RIGHT-
FLIGHT PATH STRAIGHT
GROUND PATH STRAIGHT

WIND

   1)   Simultaneously, your airplane's nose must be yawed in the opposite direction with the rudder so that the airplane's longitudinal axis is at an angle to its flight path.

   a)   If rudder application is delayed, the airplane will turn in the direction of the lowered wing.

   2)   Use elevator control pressure to maintain the airplane's nose-down pitch attitude.

   a)   Do not allow the nose to rise.

   i)   This defeats the purpose of a slip, which is to achieve a greater rate of descent, and may lead to a stall.

   b)   Remember, if your airspeed indicator is subject to errors in slips, do not rely on it.

   i)   Maintain the proper pitch attitude by sight and feel.

3.   **Maintain a ground track aligned with the runway centerline.**

   a.   The degree to which the nose is yawed in the opposite direction from the bank should be such that your airplane maintains a ground track over the extended centerline of the runway.

4. **Maintain an airspeed which results in minimum floating during the landing roundout.**

    a.   You should maintain no more than the approach speed listing in your *POH*. If one is not recommended, use 1.3 V_{so}.

        1)   In your airplane, approach speed _____, or

        2)   1.3 V_{so} _____.

5. **Recover smoothly from the slip.**

    a.   Discontinuing the slip is accomplished by leveling the wings and simultaneously releasing the rudder pressure while maintaining the normal glide attitude.

    b.   If the pressure on the rudder is released abruptly the nose will swing too quickly into line and your airplane will tend to gain excess speed.

        1)   Also, momentum may swing the nose of your airplane past straight ahead. Recovery should be smooth.

6. ***Touch down smoothly at approximate stalling speed, at and within 500 ft. beyond a specified point, with no appreciable drift, and your airplane's longitudinal axis aligned with the runway centerline.***

    a.   If a slip is used during the last portion of a final approach, the longitudinal axis of your airplane must be realigned with the runway just prior to touchdown so that your airplane will touch down headed in the direction in which it is moving over the runway.

        1)   This requires timely action to discontinue the slip and realign your airplane's longitudinal axis with its direction of travel over the ground before touchdown.

        2)   Failure to accomplish this causes severe sideloads on the landing gear and violent ground looping tendencies.

    b.   If a crosswind condition is present, you should make the adjustment from a forward slip to a sideslip (i.e., the wing-low method) to counteract any drift.

    c.   Follow the same procedures for the touchdown as discussed in element 6 of Task XI.A., Normal and Crosswind Approaches and Landings, on page 416.

7. **Maintain directional control during the after-landing roll.**

    a.   Remember, the landing process must never be considered complete until your airplane decelerates to normal taxi speed during the landing roll or has been brought to a complete stop when clear of the runway.

    b.   After your airplane is clear of the runway and stopped, you should complete the after-landing checklist in the *POH*.

    c.   Follow the same procedures for the after-landing roll as discussed in element 7 of Task XI.A., Normal and Crosswind Approaches and Landings, on page 416.

C. Common errors during forward slips to a landing

    1. **Improper use of landing performance data and limitations.**

        a.   Use your *POH* to determine the appropriate airspeeds for a normal and crosswind approach and landing.

        b.   In gusty and/or strong crosswinds use the crosswind component chart to determine that you are not exceeding your airplane's crosswind limitations.

        c.   Use your *POH* to determine data and limitations and do not attempt to do better than the data.

2. **Failure to establish approach and landing configuration at appropriate time or in proper sequence.**

   a. Use the Before Landing checklist in your *POH* to ensure that you follow the proper sequence in establishing the correct approach and landing configuration for your airplane.

   b. You should be in your final landing configuration, if possible, before entering the slip.

3. **Failure to stabilize the slip.**

   a. Once you decide to use a slip, you must use the proper flight control application and power to establish the slip.

   b. Stabilize the slip as soon as possible. Avoid large corrections, as this will prevent you from maintaining a stabilized slip.

4. **Inappropriate removal of hand from throttle.**

   a. One hand should remain on the control yoke at all times.

   b. The other hand should remain on the throttle unless operating the microphone or making an adjustment, such as trim or flaps.

      1) Once you are on short final your hand should remain on the throttle, even if ATC gives you instruction (e.g., cleared to land).

         a) Your first priority is to fly your airplane and avoid doing tasks which may distract you from maintaining control.

         b) Fly first, talk later.

   c. You must be in the habit of keeping one hand on the throttle in case a sudden and unexpected hazardous situation should require an immediate application of power.

5. **Improper technique during transition from the slip to touchdown.**

   a. You should smoothly straighten the nose with the rudder, and use ailerons as necessary to correct for any crosswind.

   b. If you release the pressure on the rudder too abruptly, the nose will swing too quickly into line and your airplane's airspeed will increase.

      1) This may also cause the nose to swing past straight ahead.

   c. Failure to realign the airplane's longitudinal axis with the runway centerline will cause severe sideloads on the landing gear.

6. **Poor directional control after touchdown.**

   a. Use rudder to steer your airplane on the runway, and increase aileron deflection into the wind as airspeed increases.

   b. See Common Errors of Task XI.A., Normal and Crosswind Approaches and Landings, on page 416 for a discussion on ground loops and other directional control problems after touchdown.

7. **Improper use of brakes.**

   a. Use the minimum amount of braking required, and let your airplane slow by the friction and drag of the wheels on the ground, if runway length permits.

   b. Never attempt to apply brakes until your airplane is firmly on the runway under complete control.

   c. Use equal pressure on both brakes to help prevent swerving and/or loss of directional control.

END OF TASK

GO-AROUND

> **XI.C. TASK: GO-AROUND**
>
> *PILOT OPERATION - 5*
>
> REFERENCES: AC 61-21; Airplane Handbook and Flight Manual.
>
> **Objective.** To determine that the applicant:
>
> 1. Exhibits knowledge by explaining the elements of the go-around procedure, including proper decision, recommended airspeeds, drag effect of wing flaps and landing gear, and coping with undesirable pitch and yaw.
>
> 2. Makes a proper decision to go around.
>
> 3. Applies takeoff power and establishes the proper pitch attitude to attain the recommended airspeed.
>
> 4. Retracts the wing flaps, as recommended, and at a safe altitude.
>
> 5. Retracts the landing gear, if retractable, after a positive rate of climb has been established.
>
> 6. Trims the airplane and climbs at V_Y, ±5 kt., and tracks the appropriate traffic pattern.

A. General Information

    1. This is one of five tasks (A-E) in this area of operation. Your examiner is required to test you on this task.

    2. *Pilot Operation - 5* refers to FAR 61.107(a)(5): Normal and crosswind takeoffs and landings.

    3. FAA References

        AC 61-21: Flight Training Handbook
        Pilot's Operating Handbook (FAA-Approved Airplane Flight Manual)

    4. The objective of this task is for you to demonstrate your ability to make a proper decision to go around and then execute the go-around procedure.

    5. For safety reasons it may be necessary for you to discontinue your approach and attempt another approach under more favorable conditions.

        a. This is called a go-around from a rejected (balked) landing.

    6. Regardless of your height above the ground, a safe go-around can be accomplished if:

        a. An early decision is made,
        b. A sound plan is followed, and
        c. The procedure is performed properly.

    7. Consult your *POH* for the proper procedure to follow for your airplane.

        a. Below is the go-around (balked landing) checklist for a Cessna 152.

> **CESSNA MODEL 152**
> **BALKED LANDING CHECKLIST**
>
> 1. Throttle -- FULL OPEN
> 2. Carburetor Heat -- COLD
> 3. Wing Flaps -- RETRACT to 20°
> 4. Airspeed -- 55 KIAS
> 5. Wing Flaps -- RETRACT (slowly).
>
> **For Academic Illustration/Training Purposes Only!**
> *For Flight:* **Use your Pilot's Operating Handbook and FAA-Approved Airplane Flight Manual.**

    b.   This is an excellent example of a checklist that you will "do and then review." When you execute a go-around you will do it from memory and then review your checklist after you have initiated and stabilized your go-around.

    c.   You should constantly think about the possibility of having to perform a go-around during each approach and landing.

B.   **Task Objectives**

    1.   **Exhibit your knowledge by explaining the elements of the go-around procedure, including proper decision, recommended airspeeds, drag effect of wing flaps and landing gear, and coping with undesirable pitch and yaw.**

        a.   Occasionally it will be advisable, for safety reasons, to discontinue your approach and make another approach under more favorable conditions. These may include

           1)   Extremely low base-to-final turn.

           2)   Too high or too low final approach.

           3)   The unexpected appearance of hazards on the runway, e.g., another airplane failing to clear the runway on time.

           4)   Wake turbulence from a preceding aircraft.

           5)   Wind shear encounter.

           6)   Overtaking another aircraft on final approach.

           7)   ATC instructions to "go around."

        b.   Initially, you should establish a shallow climb pitch attitude and allow your airplane to accelerate to and maintain V_Y.

           1)   In your airplane, V_Y _____.

        c.   On most airplanes, full flaps produce more drag than the landing gear. Thus, it is generally recommended that flaps be retracted (at least partially) before retracting the landing gear, if so equipped.

        d.   When takeoff power is applied in the go-around you must cope with undesirable pitch and yaw.

           1)   Since you have trimmed your airplane for the approach (i.e., nose-up trim), the nose may rise sharply and veer to the left.

               a)   Proper elevator pressure must be applied to maintain a safe climbing pitch attitude.

               b)   Right rudder pressure must be increased to counteract torque, or P-factor, and to keep the nose straight.

    2.   **Make a proper decision to go around.**

        a.   The need to discontinue a landing may arise at any point in the landing process, but the most critical go-around is one started when very close to the ground. A timely decision must be made.

           1)   The earlier you recognize a dangerous situation, the sooner you can decide to reject the landing and start the go-around, and the safer this maneuver will be.

           2)   Never wait until the last possible moment to make a decision.

        b.   Official reports concerning go-around accidents frequently cite "pilot indecision" as a cause. This happens when a pilot fixates on trying to make a bad landing good, resulting in a late decision to go around.

           1)   This is natural, since the purpose of an approach is a landing.

           2)   Delays in deciding what to do cost valuable runway stopping distance. They also cause loss of valuable altitude as the approach continues.

    3)   If there is any question about making a safe touchdown and rollout, execute a go-around immediately.

  c. Once you decide to go around, stick to it! Too many airplanes have been lost because a pilot has changed his/her mind and tried to land after all.

3. Apply takeoff power and establish the proper pitch attitude to attain the recommended airspeed.

  a. Once you decide to go around, takeoff power should be applied immediately and your airplane's pitch attitude changes so as to slow or stop the descent.

    1) Power is the single most essential ingredient. Every precaution must be taken (i.e., completion of the Before Landing checklist) to assure that power is available when you need it.

      a) Adjust carburetor heat to OFF (cold) position, if appropriate.

      b) Check that mixture is full rich or appropriately leaned for high density altitude airport operations.

  b. As discussed earlier, you may have to cope with undesirable pitch and yaw due to the addition of full power in a nose-up trim configuration.

    1) You must use whatever control pressure is required to maintain the proper pitch attitude and to keep your airplane straight. This may require considerable pressure.

    2) While holding your airplane straight and in a safe climbing attitude, you should retrim your airplane to relieve any heavy control pressures.

      a) Since the airspeed will build up rapidly with the application of takeoff power and the controls will become more effective, this initial trim is to relieve the heavy pressures until a more precise trim can be made for the lighter pressures.

    3) If the pitch attitude is increased excessively in an effort to prevent your airplane from mushing onto the runway, it may cause the airplane to stall.

      a) This would be especially likely if no trim correction is made and the flaps remain fully extended.

  c. During the initial part of an extremely low go-around, your airplane may "mush" onto the runway and bounce. This situation is not particularly dangerous if the airplane is kept straight, and a constant, safe pitch attitude maintained.

    1) Your airplane will be approaching safe flying speed rapidly and the advanced power will cushion any secondary touchdown.

  d. Establish a shallow climb pitch attitude by use of outside visual references. You should have a knowledge of the visual clues to attain the attitude from your training.

4. Retract the wing flaps, as recommended, and at a safe altitude.

  a. Immediately after applying power and raising the nose, you should partially retract or place the wing flaps in the takeoff position, as stated in your *POH*. Use caution in retracting the flaps.

    1) It will probably be wise to retract the flaps intermittently in small increments to allow time for the airplane to accelerate progressively as the flaps are being raised.

    2) A sudden and complete retraction of the flaps at a very low airspeed could cause a loss of lift resulting in your airplane settling onto the ground.

  b. The final flap retraction should be made only after a positive rate of climb is established, the landing gear retracted (if retractable), and the airspeed is at V_Y.

5. **Retract the landing gear, if retractable, after a positive rate of climb has been established.**

    a.   Unless otherwise noted in your *POH*, the flaps are normally retracted (at least partially) before retracting the landing gear.

        1)   On most airplanes full flaps create more drag than the landing gear.

        2)   In case your airplane should inadvertently touch down as the go-around is initiated, it is desirable to have the landing gear in the down-and-locked position.

    b.   Never attempt to retract the landing gear until after a rough trim is accomplished and a positive rate of climb is established.

6. ***Trim your airplane and climb at V_Y, ±5 kt., and track the appropriate traffic pattern.***

    a.   After you have established a positive rate of climb and the landing gear is retracted (if retractable), adjust the pitch attitude to continue the climb at V_Y, ±5 kt.

        1)   Make the final flap retraction and trim your airplane.

    b.   Maintain a ground track parallel to the runway centerline and in a position where you can see the runway.

        1)   This is important if the go-around was made due to another airplane on the runway because you need to maintain visual contact to avoid another dangerous situation, especially if that airplane is taking off.

    c.   Now that you have your airplane under control, you can communicate with the tower or the appropriate ground station to advise that you are going around.

C. Common errors during a go-around

   1. **Failure to recognize a situation where a go-around is necessary.**

      a.   When there is any doubt of the safe outcome of a landing, the go-around should be initiated immediately.

      b.   Do not attempt to salvage a possible bad landing.

   2. **Hazards of delaying a decision to go around.**

      a.   This could lead to an accident because of insufficient runway to land or because it could prevent clearing obstacles on the departure end of the runway.

   3. **Improper power application.**

      a.   Power should be added smoothly and continuously.

      b.   Assure you have maximum power available at all times during the final approach by completing your Before Landing checklist.

   4. **Failure to control pitch attitude.**

      a.   You must be able to divide your attention to accomplish this procedure and maintain control of your airplane.

      b.   Learn the visual clues as to shallow climb and V_Y pitch attitudes, and then cross-check with the airspeed indicator.

   5. **Failure to compensate for torque effect.**

      a.   In a high-power, low airspeed configuration, right rudder pressure must be increased to counteract torque and to keep the airplane's nose straight.

6. **Improper trim technique.**

   a. Initial trim is important to relieve the heavy control pressures.

   b. Since your airplane may be in a nose-up trim configuration, the application of full power may cause the nose to rise sharply.

      1) This would require a considerable amount of forward elevator pressure to maintain the proper pitch attitude, and to prevent a stall/spin situation. The use of trim will decrease the pressure you will have to hold.

7. **Failure to maintain recommended airspeeds.**

   a. This will reduce the climb performance of your airplane and may create unsafe conditions due to obstructions or, if too slow, a stall/spin situation.

8. **Improper wing flap or landing gear retraction procedure.**

   a. Follow the procedures in your *POH*.

   b. On most airplanes, the flaps create more drag than the landing gear, thus you should raise (at least partially) the flaps before the landing gear, if retractable.

   c. Retract the landing gear only after a positive rate of climb is established, as indicated on the vertical speed indicator.

9. **Failure to maintain proper ground track during climbout.**

   a. Not maintaining the proper ground track may cause possible conflicts with other traffic and/or obstructions.

   b. You are expected by other traffic and/or ATC to maintain a ground track parallel to the runway centerline until at the proper position to turn crosswind.

10. **Failure to remain well clear of obstructions and other traffic.**

    a. Climb at V_x if necessary to clear any obstructions.

    b. Maintain visual contact with other traffic, especially if the go-around was due to departing traffic.

END OF TASK

SHORT-FIELD APPROACH AND LANDING

XI.D. TASK: SHORT-FIELD APPROACH AND LANDING

    PILOT OPERATION - 8

    REFERENCES: AC 61-21; Airplane Handbook and Flight Manual.

Objective. To determine that the applicant:

1. Exhibits knowledge by explaining the elements of a short-field approach and landing, including airspeed, configuration, and related safety factors.

2. Considers obstructions, landing surface, and wind conditions.

3. Selects a suitable touchdown point.

4. Establishes the short-field approach and landing configuration, airspeed, and descent angle.

5. Maintains control of the descent rate and the recommended airspeed, ±5 kt., along the extended runway centerline.

6. Touches down at or within 200 ft. beyond a specified point, with minimum float, no appreciable drift, and the airplane longitudinal axis aligned with the runway centerline.

7. Maintains directional control during the after-landing roll.

8. Applies braking and controls, as necessary, to stop in the shortest distance consistent with safety.

A. **General Information**

    1. This is one of five tasks (A-E) in this area of operation. Your examiner is required to test you on this task.

    2. *Pilot Operation - 8* refers to FAR 61.107(a)(8): Maximum performance takeoffs and landings.

    3. FAA References

        AC 61-21: Flight Training Handbook
        Pilot's Operating Handbook (FAA-Approved Airplane Flight Manual)

    4. The objective of this task is for you to demonstrate your ability to perform a short-field approach and landing.

B. **Task Objectives**

    1. **Exhibit your knowledge by explaining the elements of a short-field approach and landing, including airspeed, configuration, and related safety factors.**

        a. This maximum performance operation requires the use of procedures and techniques for the approach and landing at fields which have a relatively short landing area and/or where an approach must be made over obstacles which limit the available landing area.

            1) This is a critical maximum performance operation, as it requires you to fly your airplane at one of its critical performance capabilities while close to the ground in order to safely land in confined areas.

            2) This low-speed type of power-on approach is closely related to the performance of "flight at minimum controllable airspeeds."

        b. To land within a short field or a confined area, you must have precise, positive control of your airplane's rate of descent and airspeed to produce an approach that will clear any obstacles, result in little or no floating during the roundout, and permit your airplane to be stopped in the shortest possible distance.

        c. You must know, understand, and respect both your own and your airplane's limitations.

            1) Think ahead. Do not attempt to land on a short field from which a takeoff is beyond your capability or that of your airplane.

2.   **Consider obstructions, landing surface, and wind conditions.**

   a.   The height of obstructions will dictate how steep the approach will have to be. Know the type and height of the obstructions.

   b.   The landing surface will affect your airplane's braking/stopping distance. A headwind may shorten the distance, while a tailwind will significantly lengthen the landing distance.

   c.   Your *POH* has performance charts on landing distances required to clear a 50-ft. obstacle under the conditions specified on the chart. During your preflight preparation you need to ensure that you can land in a confined area, or short field, before attempting to do so.

3.   **Select a suitable touchdown point.**

   a.   Select a touchdown aim point that allows you to clear any obstacles and land with the greatest amount of runway available.

   b.   You should also select points along the approach path at which you will decide between continuing the approach or executing a go-around.

      1)   A go-around may be necessary if you are too low, too high, too slow, too fast, and/or not stabilized on the final approach.

4.   **Establish the short-field approach and landing configuration, airspeed, and descent angle.**

   a.   Follow the procedures in your *POH* to establish the proper short-field approach and landing checklist.

      1)   The following is a Short-Field Landing checklist for the Cessna 152.

CESSNA MODEL 152
SHORT-FIELD LANDING CHECKLIST

1.   Airspeed -- 60-70 KIAS (flaps UP).
2.   Wing Flaps -- 30° (below 85 KIAS).
3.   Airspeed -- MAINTAIN 54 KIAS.
4.   Power -- REDUCE to idle as obstacle is cleared.
5.   Touchdown -- MAIN WHEELS FIRST.
6.   Brakes -- APPLY HEAVILY.
7.   Wing Flaps -- RETRACT.

For Academic Illustration/Training Purposes Only!
For Flight: Use your Pilot's Operating Handbook and FAA-Approved Airplane Flight Manual.

---

   b.   In the absence of the manufacturer's recommended approach speed, a speed of not more than 1.3 V_{so} should be used.

      1)   EXAMPLE: If your airplane stalls at 60 kt. with power off, flaps extended, and gear extended, if retractable, (i.e., V_{so}), your approach speed should be no higher than 78 kt. (1.3 x 60).

         a)   In your airplane:

            Short-field approach speed _____, or

            V_{so} _____,

            1.3 V_{so} _____.

2)   In gusty air, no more than one-half the gust factor should be added.

3)   An excessive amount of airspeed may result in touchdown too far from the runway threshold or an after-landing roll that exceeds the available landing area.

c.   The final approach is normally started from an altitude of at least 500 ft. higher than the touchdown area.

   1)   Your descent angle may be steeper than the one used on a normal approach.

      a)   This steeper descent angle helps you pick a touchdown aim point closer to the base of any obstacle, which means a shorter landing distance.

      b)   The steeper descent angle means more altitude for a longer period of time, which can be converted to airspeed if needed by lowering the nose. This is good for safety because it prevents an approach that is simultaneously too low and too slow.

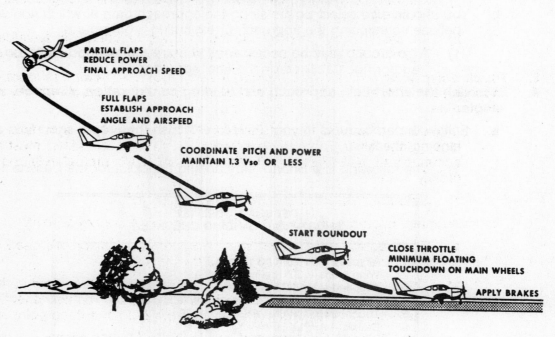

PARTIAL FLAPS
REDUCE POWER
FINAL APPROACH SPEED

FULL FLAPS
ESTABLISH APPROACH
ANGLE AND AIRSPEED

COORDINATE PITCH AND POWER
MAINTAIN 1.3 Vₛₒ OR LESS

START ROUNDOUT

CLOSE THROTTLE
MINIMUM FLOATING
TOUCHDOWN ON MAIN WHEELS

APPLY BRAKES

5.   *Maintain control of the descent rate and the recommended airspeed, ±5 kt., along the extended runway centerline.*

a.   After the landing gear (if retractable) and full flaps have been extended, you should simultaneously adjust the power and pitch attitude to establish and maintain the proper descent angle and airspeed.

   1)   Since short field approaches are power-on approaches, the pitch attitude is adjusted as necessary to establish and maintain the desired rate or angle of descent, and power is adjusted to maintain the desired airspeed.

      a)   However, a coordinated combination of both pitch and power adjustments is required.

      b)   When this is done properly, and the final approach is stabilized, very little change in your airplane's pitch attitude and power will be necessary to make corrections in the angle of descent and airspeed.

   2)   If it appears that the obstacle clearance is excessive and touchdown would occur well beyond the desired spot, leaving insufficient room to stop, power may be reduced while lowering the pitch attitude to increase the rate of descent while maintaining the proper airspeed.

3) If it appears that the descent angle will not ensure safe clearance of obstacles, power should be increased while simultaneously raising the pitch attitude to decrease the rate of descent and maintain the proper airspeed.

4) Care must be taken to avoid excessively low airspeed.

    a) If the speed is allowed to become too slow, an increase in pitch and application of full power may only result in a further rate of descent.

        i) This occurs when the angle of attack is so great and creates so much drag that the maximum available power is insufficient to overcome it.

    b) Only small power changes should be needed to maintain your desired airspeed, ±5 kt.

  b. Maintain a precise ground track along the extended runway centerline.

    1) Without a crosswind, you must align your airplane's longitudinal axis with the runway centerline.

    2) If a crosswind is present, use the crosswind techniques described in Task XI.A., Normal and Crosswind Approaches and Landings, on page 416.

6. Touch down at or within 200 ft. beyond a specified point, with minimum float, no appreciable drift, and your airplane's longitudinal axis aligned with the runway centerline.

  a. Since the final approach over obstacles is made at a steep approach angle and close to the stalling speed, the initiation of the roundout (flare) must be judged accurately to avoid flying into the ground, or stalling prematurely and sinking rapidly.

    1) Smoothly close the throttle during the roundout.

  b. You must touch down at or within 200 ft. beyond a specified point.

    1) Touchdown should occur at the minimum controllable airspeed at a pitch attitude which will produce a power-off stall.

    2) Upon touchdown, nosewheel-type airplanes should be held in this positive pitch attitude as long as the elevators/stabilator remains effective, and tailwheel-type airplanes should be firmly held in a three-point attitude.

        a) This will provide aerodynamic braking by the wings.

    3) A lack of floating during the roundout, with sufficient control to touch down properly, is one verification that the approach speed was correct.

    4) Do not attempt to hold the airplane off the ground as in a normal landing for a smoother touchdown.

  c. Use the proper crosswind technique to ensure your airplane's longitudinal axis is aligned with the runway centerline.

7. Maintain directional control during the after-landing roll.

  a. Remember, the landing process must never be considered complete until your airplane decelerates to normal taxi speed during the landing roll or has been brought to a complete stop when clear of the runway.

  b. After your airplane is clear of the runway and stopped, you should complete the after-landing checklist in the *POH*.

  c. Follow the same procedures for the after-landing roll as discussed in element 7 of Task XI.A., Normal and Crosswind Approaches and Landings, on page 416.

8. **Apply brakes and controls, as necessary, to stop in the shortest distance consistent with safety.**

    a. Braking can begin aerodynamically by maintaining the landing attitude after touchdown. Once you are sure that all wheels are solidly in ground contact, begin braking with the main wheel brakes while holding back elevator pressure.

    b. Airplanes with larger flap surfaces may benefit more from leaving the flaps down for drag braking, whereas smaller flaps may be retracted through the rollout to increase wheel contact with the ground and main wheel braking effectiveness.

    c. Follow the procedures in your *POH*.

C. Common errors during a short-field approach and landing

    1. **Improper use of landing performance data and limitations.**

        a. Use your *POH* to determine the appropriate airspeeds for a short-field approach and landing.

        b. In gusty and/or strong crosswinds, use the crosswind component chart to determine that you are not exceeding your airplane's crosswind limitations.

        c. Use your *POH* to determine minimum landing distances and do not attempt to do better than the data.

        d. The most common error, as well as the easiest to avoid, is to attempt a landing that is beyond the capabilities of your airplane and/or your flying skills. You need to remember that the distance needed for a safe landing is normally less than is needed for a safe takeoff. Plan ahead!

    2. **Failure to establish approach and landing configuration at appropriate time or in proper sequence.**

        a. Use the Before Landing checklist in your *POH* to ensure that you follow the proper sequence in establishing the correct approach and landing configuration for your airplane.

        b. You should initially start the checklist at midpoint on the downwind leg with the power reduction beginning once you are abeam of your intended point of landing.

            1) By the time you turn on final and align your airplane with the runway centerline you should be in the final landing configuration. Confirm this by completing your checklist once again.

    3. **Failure to establish and maintain a stabilized approach.**

        a. Once you are on final and aligned with the runway centerline you should make small adjustments to pitch and power to establish the correct descent angle (i.e., glide path) and airspeed.

            1) Remember, you must make simultaneous adjustments to both pitch and power.

            2) Large adjustments will result in a roller coaster ride.

        b. Lock in your airspeed and glide path as soon as possible.

            1) Never let your airspeed go below your approach speed, and

            2) Never let your airplane sink below your selected glide path, or the glide path of a visual approach slope indicator (i.e., VASI or PAPI).

4. **Improper technique in use of power, wing flaps, and trim.**

   a. Use power and pitch adjustments simultaneously to maintain the proper descent angle and airspeed.

   b. Wing flaps should be used in accordance with your *POH*.

   c. Trim to relieve control pressures to help in stabilizing the final approach.

5. **Inappropriate removal of hand from throttle.**

   a. One hand should remain on the control yoke at all times.

   b. The other hand should remain on the throttle unless operating the microphone or making an adjustment, such as trim or flaps.

      1) Once you are on short final your hand should remain on the throttle, even if ATC gives you instruction (e.g., cleared to land).

         a) Your first priority is to fly your airplane and avoid doing tasks which may distract you from maintaining control.

         b) Fly first, talk later.

   c. You must be in the habit of keeping one hand on the throttle in case a sudden and unexpected hazardous situation should require an immediate application of power.

6. **Improper technique during roundout and touchdown.**

   a. Do not attempt to hold the airplane off the ground.

   b. See Task XI.A, Normal and Crosswind Approaches and Landings, on page 416 for a detailed discussion of general landing errors.

   c. Remember, you have limited runway, so when in doubt, go around.

7. **Poor directional control after touchdown.**

   a. Use rudder to steer your airplane on the runway, and increase aileron deflection into the wind as airspeed increases.

   b. See Common Errors of Task XI.A., Normal and Crosswind Approaches and Landings, on page 416 for a discussion on ground loops and other directional control problems after touchdown.

8. **Improper use of brakes.**

   a. Never attempt to apply the brakes until your airplane is firmly on the runway under complete control.

   b. Use equal pressure on both brakes to prevent swerving and/or loss of directional control.

   c. Follow the braking procedures described in your *POH*.

END OF TASK

SOFT-FIELD APPROACH AND LANDING

XI.E. TASK: SOFT-FIELD APPROACH AND LANDING

   PILOT OPERATION - 8

   REFERENCES: AC 61-21; Airplane Handbook and Flight Manual.

Objective. To determine that the applicant:

1. Exhibits knowledge by explaining the elements of a soft-field approach and landing procedure, including airspeeds, configurations, operations on various surfaces, and related safety factors.

2. Evaluates obstructions, landing surface, and wind conditions.

3. Establishes the recommended soft-field approach and landing configuration and airspeed.

4. Maintains recommended airspeed, ±5 kt., along the extended runway centerline.

5. Touches down smoothly at minimum descent rate and groundspeed, with no appreciable drift, and the airplane longitudinal axis aligned with runway centerline.

6. Maintains directional control during the after-landing roll.

7. Maintains proper position of flight controls and sufficient speed to taxi on soft surface.

A. General Information

   1. This is one of five tasks (A-E) in this area of operation. Your examiner is required to test you on this task.

   2. *Pilot Operation - 8* refers to FAR 61.107(a)(8): Maximum performance takeoffs and landings.

   3. FAA References

      AC 61-21: Flight Training Handbook
      Pilot's Operating Handbook (FAA-Approved Airplane Flight Manual)

   4. The objective of this task is for you to demonstrate your ability to perform a soft-field approach and landing.

B. Task Objectives

   1. **Exhibit your knowledge by explaining the elements of a soft-field approach and landing procedure, including airspeeds, configurations, operations on various surfaces, and related safety factors.**

      a. The approach for the soft-field landing is similar to the normal approach used for operating into long, firm landing areas.

         1) The major difference between the two is that during the soft-field landing, the airplane is held 1 to 2 ft. off the surface as long as possible to dissipate the forward speed sufficiently to allow the wheels to touch down gently at minimum speed.

      b. Landing on fields that are rough or have soft surfaces (e.g. snow, mud, sand, or tall grass) requires special techniques.

         1) When landing on such surfaces, you must control your airplane in a manner such that the wings support the weight of the airplane as long as practical.

            a) This minimizes drag and stress put on the landing gear from the rough or soft surfaces.

      c. Follow the procedures prescribed in your *POH*.

2. **Evaluate obstructions, landing surface, and wind conditions.**

    a. During your approach you must look for any hazards or obstructions and then evaluate how they may effect your approach and landing.

        1) Be aware of traffic, both in the air and on the ground.

        2) Look out for vehicles and/or people on or near the runway.

        3) Check the approach area for any natural or man-made obstacles (e.g., trees, towers, or construction equipment).

        4) Your angle of descent on final approach may need to be steepened if obstacles are present.

    b. A soft field is any surface other than a paved one. You must take into account a hard-packed turf or a wet, high grass turf. Know the condition of the landing surface you will be operating into.

        1) If a surface is soft or wet, consider what effect that will have if your perform a crosswind landing, when one main wheel touches down before the other main wheel.

    c. You must know the wind conditions and how this will affect your airplane's landing performance. The effect of wind on the landing distance may be significant and deserves proper consideration.

        1) A headwind will decrease the landing distance, while a tailwind will greatly increase the landing distance.

        2) This is important if the landing area is short and/or in a confined area.

3. **Establish the recommended soft-field approach and landing configuration and airspeed.**

    a. Establish your airplane in the proper soft-field configuration as prescribed in your *POH*. This is usually similar to that used for a normal approach.

        1) The use of flaps during soft-field landings will aid in touching down at minimum speed and is recommended whenever practical.

            a) In low-wing airplanes, however, the flaps may suffer damage from mud, stones, or slush thrown up by the wheels. In such cases, it may be advisable not to use flaps.

    b. The final approach speed should be the same as for short-field final approach (not more than 1.3 V_{so}).

        1) EXAMPLE: If your airplane stalls at 60 kt. with power off, flaps extended, and gear extended (if retractable), your approach speed should be no higher than 78 kt. (1.3 x 60).

            a) In your airplane:

                Soft-field approach speed _____,

                V_{SO} _____,

                1.3 V_{SO} _____.

            b) In gusty air, no more than one-half the gust factor should be added.

    c. Trim your airplane as necessary throughout your approach. This will normally result in a nose-up trim configuration.

4. ***Maintain the recommended airspeed, ±5 kt., along the extended runway centerline.***

    a.   After the landing gear (if retractable) and full flaps have been extended, you should simultaneously adjust the power and pitch attitude to establish and maintain a stabilized approach at a constant descent angle and airspeed.

        1)   The pitch attitude is adjusted as necessary to establish and maintain the desired rate or angle of descent. Power is adjusted to maintain the recommended airspeed.

            a)   However, a coordinated combination of both pitch and power adjustments is required.

            b)   When this is done properly, very little change in your airplane's pitch attitude is necessary to make corrections in the angle of descent and only small power changes are needed to control the airspeed within 5 kt.

        2)   Care must be taken to avoid an excessively low airspeed.

            a)   If the speed is allowed to become too slow, an increase in pitch and application of full power may only result in a further rate of descent.

                i)   This occurs when the angle of attack is so great and creates so much drag that the maximum available power is insufficient to overcome it.

        3)   Only small power changes should be needed to maintain your desired airspeed, ±5 kt.

        4)   You should establish and maintain a minimum descent rate, given any obstructions in the approach path. This will assist you in setting up for a touchdown as softly as possible.

    b.   Maintain a precise ground track along the extended runway centerline.

        1)   Without a crosswind, you must align your airplane's longitudinal axis with the runway centerline.

        2)   If a crosswind is present, use the crosswind techniques described in Task XI.A., Normal and Crosswind Approaches and Landings, on page 416.

5. ***Touch down smoothly at minimum descent rate and groundspeed, with no appreciable drift, and your airplane's longitudinal axis aligned with the runway centerline.***

    a.   Maintain slight power throughout the roundout (flare) to assist in producing as soft a touchdown (i.e., minimum descent rate) as possible.

        1)   Attempt to hold your airplane about 1 to 2 ft. above the ground as long as possible to allow the touchdown to be made at the slowest possible airspeed with your airplane in a nose-high pitch attitude.

    b.   In a tailwheel-type airplane, the tailwheel should touch down simultaneously with or just before the main wheels, and then should be held down by maintaining firm back elevator pressure throughout the landing roll.

        1)   This will minimize any tendency for your airplane to nose over and will provide aerodynamic braking.

    c.   In nosewheel-type airplanes, after the main wheels touch the surface, you should hold sufficient back elevator pressure to keep the nosewheel off the ground until it can no longer aerodynamically be held off the surface.

        1)   At this time you should let the nosewheel come down to the ground on its own. Maintain full back elevator pressure at all times on a soft surface.

            a)   Maintaining slight power during and immediately after touchdown usually will aid in easing the nosewheel down.

    d.   Use the proper crosswind technique to ensure your airplane's longitudinal axis is aligned with the runway centerline.

6. Maintain directional control during the after-landing roll.

    a.   Hold and maintain full back elevator pressure during the after-landing roll. You must not let your airplane come to a stop on a soft surface, as it may become bogged down.

    b.   If flaps are used, it is generally inadvisable to retract them during the after-landing roll because they will increase lift on the wings and aid in keeping weight off the landing gear.

    c.   Follow the same procedures for the after-landing roll as discussed in element 7 of Task XI.A., Normal and Crosswind Approaches and Landings, on page 416.

7. Maintain proper position of flight controls and sufficient speed to taxi on the soft surface.

    a.   Maintain full back elevator pressure and the proper aileron deflection for a crosswind condition while on the ground.

        1)   The ailerons serve the same purpose on the ground as they do in the air; they change the lift and drag components of the wings.

            a)   While your airplane is decelerating during the after-landing roll, more and more aileron must be applied to keep the upwind wing from rising.

            b)   Since your airplane is slowing down and there is less airflow around the ailerons, they become less effective. At the same time the relative wind is becoming more of a crosswind and exerting a greater lifting force on the upwind wing.

                i)   Consequently, when you are taxiing the aileron control must be held FULLY into the wind.

    b.   Brakes are not needed on a soft surface. Avoid using the brakes because their use may impose a heavy load on the nosegear due to premature or hard contact with the landing surface, causing the nosewheel to dig in.

        1)   On a tailwheel-type airplane, the application of brakes may cause the main wheels to dig in, causing the airplane to nose over.

        2)   The soft or rough surface itself will normally provide sufficient friction to reduce your airplane's forward speed.

    c.   You must maintain enough speed while taxiing to prevent becoming bogged down on the soft surface.

        1)   You will often need to increase power after landing on a very soft surface to keep your airplane moving and prevent being stuck.

        2)   Care must be taken not to taxi excessively fast because if you taxi onto a very soft area, your airplane may bog down and bend the landing gear and/or nose over.

        3)   Keep your airplane moving at all times until you are at the point where you will be parking your airplane.

C.   Common errors during a soft-field approach and landing

    1.   Improper use of landing performance data and limitations.

        a.   Use your *POH* to determine the appropriate airspeeds for a soft-field approach and landing.

        b.   In gusty and/or strong crosswinds, use the crosswind component chart to determine that you are not exceeding your airplane's crosswind limitations.

        c.   Use your *POH* to determine data and limitations and do not attempt to do better than the data.

        d.   The most common error, as well as the easiest to avoid, is to attempt a landing that is beyond the capabilities of your airplane and/or your flying skills. Be sure that the surface of the field you plan to use is suitable for landing. Plan ahead!

    2.   Failure to establish approach and landing configuration at appropriate time or in proper sequence.

        a.   Use the Before Landing checklist in your *POH* to ensure that you follow the proper sequence in establishing the correct approach and landing configuration for your airplane.

        b.   You should initially start the checklist at midpoint on the downwind leg with the power reduction beginning once you are abeam of your intended point of landing.

            1)   By the time you turn on final and align your airplane with the runway centerline you should be in the proper configuration. Confirm this by completing your checklist, once again.

    3.   Failure to establish and maintain a stabilized approach.

        a.   Once you are on final and aligned with the runway centerline you should make small adjustments to pitch and power to establish the correct descent angle (i.e., glide path) and airspeed.

            1)   Remember, you must make simultaneous adjustments to both pitch and power.

            2)   Large adjustments will result in a roller coaster ride.

        b.   Lock in your airspeed and glide path as soon as possible.

            1)   Never let your airspeed go below your approach speed, and

            2)   Never let your airplane sink below your selected glide path, or the glide path of a visual approach slope indicator (i.e., VASI or PAPI).

    4.   Failure to consider the effect of wind and landing surface.

        a.   Proper planning will ensure knowledge of the landing surface condition, e.g., wet, dry, loose, hard packed.

        b.   Understand how the wind affects the landing distance required on a soft field.

    5.   Improper technique in use of power, wing flaps, and trim.

        a.   Use power and pitch adjustments simultaneously to maintain the proper descent angle and airspeed.

        b.   Wing flaps should be used in accordance with your *POH*.

        c.   Trim to relieve control pressures to help in stabilizing the final approach.

        d.   Remember to maintain slight power throughout the roundout, touchdown, and after-landing roll.

6.   **Inappropriate removal of hand from throttle.**

   a.   One hand should remain on the control yoke at all times.

   b.   The other hand should remain on the throttle unless operating the microphone or making an adjustment, such as trim or flaps.

   1)   Once you are on short final your hand should remain on the throttle, even if ATC gives you instruction (e.g., cleared to land).

   a)   Your first priority is to fly your airplane and avoid doing tasks which may distract you from maintaining control.

   b)   Fly first, talk later.

   c.   You must be in the habit of keeping one hand on the throttle in case a sudden and unexpected hazardous situation should require an immediate application of power.

7.   **Improper technique during roundout and touchdown.**

   a.   Maintain a little power, and hold the airplane off the ground as long as possible.

   b.   See Task XI.A., Normal and Crosswind Approaches and Landings, on page 416 for a detailed discussion of general landing errors.

   c.   Remember, if you have any doubts about the suitability of the field, go around.

8.   **Failure to hold back elevator pressure after touchdown.**

   a.   In a nosewheel-type airplane, this will keep weight off the nosewheel which could get bogged down causing the gear to bend and/or nose over the airplane.

   b.   In a tailwheel-type airplane, this keeps the tailwheel firmly on the surface to prevent the tendency to nose over.

9.   **Closing the throttle too soon after touchdown.**

   a.   On a soft field you must keep your airplane moving at all times.

10.   **Poor directional control after touchdown.**

   a.   Use rudder to steer your airplane on the runway, and increase aileron deflection into the wind as airspeed increases.

   b.   See Common Errors of Task XI.A., Normal and Crosswind Approaches and Landings, on page 416 for a discussion on ground loops and other directional control problems after touchdown.

11.   **Improper use of brakes.**

   a.   Brakes are not needed on a soft field and should be avoided.

   b.   On a very soft surface you may even need to increase power to avoid stopping and/or becoming bogged down on the runway.

END OF TASK -- END OF CHAPTER

APPENDIX A
FAA PRIVATE PILOT
PRACTICAL TEST STANDARDS
(FAA-S-8081-1A Reprinted)

The purpose of this appendix is to reproduce verbatim what you would get in PTS reprint books that are normally sold for $5.00 at FBOs.

All of these PTSs are reproduced (and explained, discussed, and illustrated!!) elsewhere throughout this book.

INTRODUCTION

The Aviation Standards National Field Office of the FAA has developed this practical test book as a standard to be used by FAA inspectors and designated pilot examiners when conducting airman practical tests (oral and flight tests). Flight instructors are expected to use this book when preparing applicants for practical tests.

This test book contains nine standards that set forth the practical test requirements for private pilot certification in all aircraft categories and associated classes.

For the purpose of private pilot certification practical testing, the following flight test guides were superseded September 1, 1985:

AC 61–54A	Private Pilot — Airplane (4–18–75)
AC 61–59A	Private and Commercial — Helicopter (3–3–77)
AC 61–60	Private and Commercial Pilot — Gyroplane (May 1973)
AC 61–61A	Private and Commercial Pilot — Glider (12–3–76)
AC 61–62A	Private and Commercial Pilot — Free Balloon (12–17–76)
AC 61–63	Private and Commercial Pilot — Lighter–Than– Air Airship (5–23–74)

This publication may be purchased from the Superintendent of Documents, U.S. Government Printing Office, Washington, DC 20402.

The FAA gratefully acknowledges the valuable assistance provided by organizations and individuals who have contributed their time and talent in development of the practical test standards.

Comments regarding this publication should be directed to:

U.S. Department of Transportation
Federal Aviation Administration
Aviation Standards National Field Office
Examinations Standards Branch, AVN–130
P.O. Box 25082
Oklahoma City, OK 73125

PRACTICAL TEST STANDARD CONCEPT

FAR's (Federal Aviation Regulations) specify the areas in which knowledge and skill must be demonstrated by the applicant before the issuance of a pilot certificate or rating. The FAR's provide the flexibility to permit the FAA to publish practical test standards containing specific TASKS (procedures and maneuvers) in which pilot competency must be demonstrated. The FAA will add, delete, or revise TASKS whenever it is determined that changes are needed in the interest of safety. Adherence to provisions of the regulations and the practical test standards is mandatory for the evaluation of pilot applicants.

FLIGHT INSTRUCTOR RESPONSIBILITY

An appropriately rated flight instructor is responsible for training the student to the acceptable standards as outlined in the objective of each TASK within the appropriate practical test standard. The flight instructor must certify that the applicant is able to perform safely as a private pilot and is competent to pass the required practical test for the certificate or rating sought.

EXAMINER[1] RESPONSIBILITY

The examiner who conducts the practical test is responsible for determining that the applicant meets standards outlined in the objective of each TASK within the appropriate practical test standard. The examiner shall meet this responsibility by accomplishing an ACTION that is appropriate for each TASK. For each TASK that involves "knowledge only" elements, the examiner will orally quiz the applicant on those elements. For each TASK that involves both "knowledge and skill" elements, the examiner will orally quiz the applicant regarding knowledge elements and ask the applicant to perform the skill elements. The examiner will determine that the applicant's knowledge and skill meets the objective in all required TASKS. Oral questioning may be used at any time during the practical test.

PRACTICAL TEST BOOK DESCRIPTION

This test book contains the following private pilot practical test standards:

Section 1	Airplane, Single–Engine Land
Section 2	Airplane, Multiengine Land
Section 3	Airplane, Single–Engine Sea
Section 4	Airplane, Multiengine Sea
Section 5	Rotorcraft, Helicopter
Section 6	Rotorcraft, Gyroplane
Section 7	Glider
Section 8	Lighter–Than–Air, Airship
Section 9	Lighter–Than–Air, Free–Balloon

The looseleaf feature of this test book enables the incorporation of changes which will be sold, as required. This will permit the dissemination of information concerning changes in regulations, pilot certification procedures, and other areas related to safety upon which emphasis should be placed.

[1] The word "examiner" is used to denote either the FAA inspector or FAA designated pilot examiner who conducts an official flight test.

PRACTICAL TEST STANDARD DESCRIPTION

The AREAS OF OPERATION are phases of flight arranged in a logical sequence within each standard. They begin with the preparation of the flight and end with the conclusion of the flight. The examiner, however, may conduct the practical test in any sequence that results in a complete and efficient test.

The TASKS are procedures and maneuvers appropriate to an AREA OF OPERATION. The AIRCRAFT CATEGORIES AND CLASSES appropriate to the TASKS are abbreviated in capital letters within parentheses immediately following each TASK. The meaning of each abbreviation follows:

ASEL	Airplane Single–Engine Land
AMEL	Airplane Multiengine Land
ASES	Airplane Single–Engine Sea
AMES	Airplane Multiengine Sea
RH	Rotorcraft Helicopter
RG	Rotorcraft Gyroplane
G	Glider (including powered glider)
LA	Lighter–Than–Air Airship
LB	Lighter–Than–Air Free Balloon

The number after the pilot operation relates that TASK to the regulatory requirement.

The REFERENCE identifies the publication(s) that describe(s) the TASK. Descriptions of TASKS are not included in the standards because this information can be found in the listed references. Publications other than those listed may be used for references if their content conveys substantially the same meaning as the referenced publications.

References upon which this practical test book is based include:

FAR Part 61	Certification: Pilots and Flight Instructors
FAR Part 91	General Operating and Flight Rules
AC 00–6	Aviation Weather
AC 00–45	Aviation Weather Services
AC 61–13	Basic Helicopter Handbook
AC 61–21	Flight Training Handbook
AC 61–23	Pilot's Handbook of Aeronautical Knowledge
AC 61–27	Instrument Flying Handbook
AC 61–84	Role of Preflight Preparation
AC 67–2	Medical Handbook for Pilots
AC 91–13	Cold Weather Operation of Aircraft
AC 91–55	Reduction of Electrical Systems Failure Following Engine Starting
AIM	Airman's Information Manual

NOTE: The latest revision of the references cited should be used.

The OBJECTIVE lists, in sequence, the important elements that must be satisfactorily performed to demonstrate competency in a TASK. The OBJECTIVE includes:

(1) specifically what the applicant should be able to do,
(2) the conditions under which the TASK is to be performed, and
(3) the minimum acceptable standards of performance.

USE OF THE PRACTICAL TEST BOOK

The FAA requires that each practical test be conducted in strict compliance with the appropriate practical test standards for the issuance of a pilot certificate or rating. When using the practical test book, the examiner must evaluate the applicant's knowledge and skill in sufficient depth to determine that the standards of performance listed for all TASKS are met.

When the examiner determines, during the performance of one TASK, that the knowledge and skill objective of another TASK is met, it may not be necessary to require the performance of the other TASK.

The examiner may, for any valid reason, elect to evaluate certain TASKS orally, such TASKS include those that do not conform to the manufacturer's recommendations or operating limitations or those that are impracticable, such as night flying, operations over congested areas, or unsuitable terrain, etc.

The examiner is not required to follow the precise order in which the AREAS OF OPERATION and TASKS appear in each section. The examiner may change the sequence or combine TASKS with similar objectives to conserve time. Examiners will develop a plan of action that includes the order and combination of TASKS to be demonstrated by the applicant in a manner that will result in an efficient and valid test. The examiner shall accurately evaluate the applicant's ability to perform safely as a pilot throughout the practical test.

Suggested examples of combining TASKS are:

(1) descending turns may be combined with high altitude emergencies;
(2) rectangular course may be combined with airport traffic pattern; and
(3) navigation during flight by reference to instruments may be combined with visual navigation.

Other TASKS with similar OBJECTIVES may be combined to conserve time. However, the OBJECTIVES of all TASKS must be demonstrated and evaluated at some time during the practical test.

Examiners will place special emphasis upon areas of aircraft operation which are most critical to flight safety. Among these areas are correct aircraft control and sound judgment in decision making. Although these areas may not be shown under each TASK, they are essential to flight safety and will receive careful evaluation throughout the practical test. If these areas are shown in the OBJECTIVE, additional emphasis will be placed on them. THE EXAMINER WILL ALSO EMPHASIZE STALL/SPIN AWARENESS, SPATIAL DISORIENTATION, COLLISION AVOIDANCE, WAKE TURBULENCE AVOIDANCE, LOW–LEVEL WIND SHEAR, USE OF THE CHECKLIST, AND OTHER AREAS AS DIRECTED BY FUTURE REVISIONS OF THIS STANDARD.

USE OF DISTRACTIONS DURING PRACTICAL TESTS

Numerous studies indicate that many accidents have occurred when the pilot's attention has been distracted during various phases of flight. Many accidents have resulted from engine failure during takeoffs and landings where safe flight was possible if the pilot had used correct control technique and divided attention properly.

Distractions that have been found to cause problems are:

(1) preoccupation with situations inside or outside the cockpit;
(2) maneuvering to avoid other traffic; or
(3) maneuvering to clear obstacles during takeoffs, climbs, approaches, or landings.

To strengthen this area of pilot training and evaluation, the examiner will provide realistic distractions throughout the practical test. Many distractions may be used to evaluate the applicant's ability to divide attention while maintaining safe flight. Some examples of distractions are:

(1) simulating engine failure;
(2) simulating radio tuning and communications;
(3) identifying a field suitable for emergency landings;
(4) identifying features or objects on the ground;
(5) reading the outside air temperature gauge;
(6) removing objects from the glove compartment or map case; and
(7) questioning by the examiner.

PRACTICAL TEST PREREQUISITES

An applicant for a private pilot practical test is required by FAR's to:

(1) pass the appropriate pilot written test since the beginning of the 24th month before the month in which the flight test is taken;

(2) obtain the applicable instruction and aeronautical experience prescribed for the pilot certificate or rating sought;

(3) possess a current medical certificate appropriate to the certificate or rating sought;

(4) meet the age requirement for the issuance of the certificate or rating sought; and

(5) obtain a written statement from an appropriately certificated flight instructor certifying that the applicant has been given flight instruction in preparation for the practical test within 60 days preceding the date of application. The statement shall also state that the instructor finds the applicant competent to pass the practical test, and that the applicant has satisfactory knowledge of the subject area(s) in which a deficiency was indicated by the airman written test report.

NOTE: AC 61-65, Certification: Pilots and Flight Instructors, states that the instructor may sign the instructor's recommendation on the reverse side of FAA Form 8710-1, Airman Certificate and/or Rating Application, in lieu of the previous statement provided, all appropriate FAR Part 61 requirements are substantiated by reliable records.

AIRCRAFT AND EQUIPMENT REQUIREMENTS FOR THE PRACTICAL TEST

The applicant is required to provide an appropriate and airworthy aircraft for the practical test. The aircraft must be equipped for, and its operating limitations must not prohibit the pilot operations required on the test.

SATISFACTORY PERFORMANCE

The ability of an applicant to perform the required TASKS is based on:

(1) executing TASKS within the aircraft's performance capabilities and limitations, including use of the aircraft's systems;

(2) executing emergency procedures and maneuvers appropriate to the aircraft;

(3) piloting the aircraft with smoothness and accuracy;

(4) exercising good judgment;

(5) applying aeronautical knowledge; and

(6) showing mastery of the aircraft within the standards outlined in this book, with the successful outcome of a TASK never seriously in doubt.

UNSATISFACTORY PERFORMANCE

If, in the judgment of the examiner, the applicant does not meet the standards of performance of any TASK performed, the associated PILOT OPERATION is failed and therefore, the practical test is failed.

The examiner or applicant may discontinue the test at any time after the failure of a PILOT OPERATION makes the applicant ineligible for the certificate or rating sought. The test will be continued ONLY with the consent of the applicant. If the test is discontinued, the applicant is entitled to credit for only those TASKS satisfactorily performed. However, during the retest and at the discretion of the examiner, any TASK may be re-evaluated, including those previously passed.

The tolerances stated in the OBJECTIVE represent the minimum performance expected in good flying conditions.

Consistently exceeding tolerances or failure to take prompt corrective action when tolerances are exceeded, is unsatisfactory performance.

Any action, or lack thereof, by the applicant which requires corrective intervention by the examiner to maintain safe flight will be disqualifying. The applicant shall use proper and effective scanning techniques to clear the area before performing maneuvers. Ineffective performance in these areas will be disqualifying.

RECORDING UNSATISFACTORY PERFORMANCE

The term PILOT OPERATION is used in regulations to denote areas (procedures and maneuvers) in which the applicant must demonstrate competency prior to being issued a pilot certificate. This practical test book uses terms AREA OF OPERATION and TASK to denote areas in which competency must be demonstrated. When a disapproval notice is issued, the examiner will record the applicant's unsatisfactory performance in terms of PILOT OPERATIONS appropriate to the practical test conducted.

I. AREA OF OPERATION:

PREFLIGHT PREPARATION

A. TASK: CERTIFICATES AND DOCUMENTS (ASEL)

PILOT OPERATION – 1

REFERENCES: FAR Parts 61 and 91; AC 61-21, AC 61-23; Pilot's Handbook and Flight Manual.

Objective.   To determine that the applicant:

1. Exhibits knowledge by explaining the appropriate –

   (a) pilot certificate, privileges and limitations.
   (b) medical certificate, class and duration.
   (c) personal pilot logbook or flight record.
   (d) FCC station license and operator's permit, as required.

2. Exhibits knowledge by locating and explaining the significance and importance of the –

   (a) airworthiness and registration certificates.
   (b) operating limitations, handbooks, or manuals.
   (c) equipment list.
   (d) weight and balance data.
   (e) maintenance requirements and appropriate records.

B. TASK: OBTAINING WEATHER INFORMATION (ASEL)

NOTE: This TASK is NOT required for the addition of a single–engine land class rating.

PILOT OPERATION – 1

REFERENCES: AC 00-6, AC 00-45, AC 61-21, AC 61-23, AC 61-84.

Objective.   To determine that the applicant:

1. Exhibits knowledge of aviation weather information by obtaining, reading, and analyzing –

   (a) weather reports and forecasts.
   (b) weather charts.
   (c) pilot weather reports.
   (d) SIGMET's and AIRMET's.
   (e) Notices to Airmen.
   (f) wind–shear reports.

2. Makes a competent go/no–go decision based on the available weather information.

C. TASK: DETERMINING PERFORMANCE AND LIMITATIONS (ASEL)

PILOT OPERATION – 1

REFERENCES: AC 61-21, AC 61-23, AC 61-84; Airplane Handbook and Flight Manual.

Objective.   To determine that the applicant:

1. Exhibits knowledge by explaining airplane weight and balance, performance, and limitations, including adverse aerodynamic effects of exceeding the limits.
2. Uses available and appropriate performance charts, tables, and data.
3. Computes weight and balance, and determines that weight and center of gravity will be within limits during all phases of the flight.
4. Calculates airplane performance, considering density altitude, wind, terrain, and other pertinent conditions.
5. Describes the effects of atmospheric conditions on airplane performance.
6. Makes a competent decision on whether the required performance is within the operating limitations of the airplane.

D. TASK: CROSS–COUNTRY FLIGHT PLANNING (ASEL)

NOTE: This TASK is NOT required for the addition of a single–engine land class rating.

PILOT OPERATION – 7

REFERENCES: AC 61-21, AC 61-23, AC 61-84.

Objective.   To determine that the applicant:

1. Exhibits knowledge by planning, within 30 minutes, a VFR cross–country flight of a duration near the range of the airplane, considering fuel and loading.
2. Selects and uses current and appropriate aeronautical charts.
3. Plots a course for the intended route of flight with fuel stops, if necessary.
4. Selects prominent en route check points.
5. Computes the flight time, headings, and fuel requirements.
6. Selects appropriate radio navigation aids and communication facilities.
7. Identifies airspace, obstructions, and alternate airports.
8. Extracts pertinent information from the Airport/Facility Directory and other flight publications, including NOTAM's.
9. Completes a navigation log.
10. Completes and files a VFR flight plan.

E. TASK: AIRPLANE SYSTEMS (ASEL)

PILOT OPERATION – 1

REFERENCES: AC 61-21; Airplane Handbook and Flight Manual.

Objective.   To determine that the applicant exhibits knowledge by explaining the airplane systems and operation including, as appropriate:

1. Primary flight controls and trim.
2. Wing flaps, leading edge devices, and spoilers.
3. Flight instruments.
4. Landing gear.
5. Engine.
6. Propeller.
7. Fuel system.
8. Hydraulic system.
9. Electrical system.
10. Environmental system.
11. Oil system.
12. Deice and anti–ice systems.
13. Avionics.
14. Vacuum system.

F. TASK: AEROMEDICAL FACTORS (ASEL)

PILOT OPERATION – 1

REFERENCES: AC 61-21, AC 67-2; AIM.

Objective.   To determine that the applicant:

1. Exhibits knowledge of the elements related to aeromedical factors, including the symptoms, effects, and corrective action of –

   (a) hypoxia.
   (b) hyperventilation.
   (c) middle ear and sinus problems.
   (d) spatial disorientation.
   (e) motion sickness.
   (f) carbon monoxide poisoning.

2. Exhibits knowledge of the effects of alcohol and drugs, and the relationship to flight safety.
3. Exhibits knowledge of nitrogen excesses during scuba dives, and how this affects a pilot or passenger during flight.

II. AREA OF OPERATION:
GROUND OPERATIONS

A. TASK: VISUAL INSPECTION (ASEL)

PILOT OPERATION – 1

REFERENCES: AC 61-21; Airplane Handbook and
Flight Manual.

Objective. To determine that the applicant:

1. Exhibits knowledge of airplane visual inspection by explaining the reasons for checking all items.
2. Inspects the airplane by following a checklist.
3. Determines that the airplane is in condition for safe flight emphasizing –

   (a) fuel quantity, grade, and type.
   (b) fuel contamination safeguards.
   (c) fuel venting.
   (d) oil quantity, grade, and type.
   (e) fuel, oil, and hydraulic leaks.
   (f) flight controls.
   (g) structural damage.
   (h) exhaust system.
   (i) tiedown, control lock, and wheel chock removal.
   (j) ice and frost removal.
   (k) security of baggage, cargo, and, equipment.

B. TASK: COCKPIT MANAGEMENT (ASEL)

PILOT OPERATION – 1

REFERENCE: AC 61-21.

Objective. To determine that the applicant:

1. Exhibits knowledge of cockpit management by explaining related safety and efficiency factors.
2. Organizes and arranges the material and equipment in an efficient manner.
3. Ensures that the safety belts and shoulder harnesses are fastened.
4. Adjusts and locks the rudder pedals and pilot's seat to a safe position and ensures full control movement.
5. Briefs occupants on the use of safety belts and emergency procedures.
6. Exhibits adequate crew coordination.

C. TASK: STARTING ENGINE (ASEL)

PILOT OPERATION – 1

REFERENCES: AC 61-21, AC 61-23, AC 91-13,
AC 91-55; Airplane Handbook and Flight Manual.

Objective. To determine that the applicant:

1. Exhibits knowledge by explaining engine starting procedures, including starting under various atmospheric conditions.
2. Performs all the items on the checklist.
3. Accomplishes correct starting procedures with emphasis on –

   (a) positioning the airplane to avoid creating hazards.
   (b) determining that the area is clear.
   (c) adjusting the engine controls.
   (d) setting the brakes.
   (e) preventing airplane movement after engine start.
   (f) avoiding excessive engine RPM and temperatures.
   (g) checking the engine instruments after engine start.

D. TASK: TAXIING (ASEL)

PILOT OPERATION – 2

REFERENCE: AC 61-21.

Objective. To determine that the applicant:

1. Exhibits knowledge by explaining safe taxi procedures.
2. Adheres to signals and clearances, and follows the proper taxi route.
3. Performs a brake check immediately after the airplane begins moving.
4. Controls taxi speed without excessive use of brakes.
5. Recognizes and avoids hazards.
6. Positions the controls for the existing wind conditions.
7. Avoids careless and reckless operations.

E. TASK: PRETAKEOFF CHECK (ASEL)

PILOT OPERATION – 1

REFERENCES: AC 61-21; Airplane Handbook and
Flight Manual.

Objective. To determine that the applicant:

1. Exhibits knowledge of the pretakeoff check by explaining the reasons for checking all items.
2. Positions the airplane to avoid creating hazards.
3. Divides attention inside and outside of the cockpit.
4. Accomplishes the checklist items.
5. Ensures that the airplane is in safe operating condition.
6. Reviews the critical takeoff performance airspeeds and distances.
7. Describes takeoff emergency procedures.
8. Obtains and interprets takeoff and departure clearances.

F. TASK: POSTFLIGHT PROCEDURES (ASEL)

PILOT OPERATION – 3

REFERENCES: AC 61-21; Airplane Handbook and
Flight Manual.

Objective. To determine that the applicant:

1. Exhibits knowledge by explaining the postflight procedures, including taxiing, parking, shutdown, securing, and postflight inspection.
2. Selects and taxies to the designated or suitable parking area, considering wind conditions and obstructions.
3. Parks the airplane properly.
4. Follows the recommended procedure for engine shutdown, cockpit securing, and deplaning passengers.
5. Secures the airplane properly.
6. Performs a satisfactory postflight inspection.

III. AREA OF OPERATION:
AIRPORT AND TRAFFIC PATTERN OPERATIONS

NOTE: This AREA OF OPERATION is NOT required for the addition of a single–engine land class rating.

A. TASK: RADIO COMMUNICATIONS AND ATC LIGHT SIGNALS (ASEL)

PILOT OPERATION – 2

REFERENCES: AC 61-21, AC 61-23; AIM.

Objective. To determine that the applicant:

1. Exhibits knowledge by explaining radio communication, ATC light signals, procedures at controlled and uncontrolled airports, and prescribed procedures for radio failure.
2. Selects the appropriate frequencies for the facilities to be used.
3. Transmits requests and reports using the recommended standard phraseology.
4. Receives, acknowledges, and complies with radio communications.

B. TASK: TRAFFIC PATTERN OPERATIONS (ASEL)

PILOT OPERATION – 2

REFERENCES: AC 61-21, AC 61-23; AIM.

Objective. To determine that the applicant:

1. Exhibits knowledge by explaining traffic pattern procedures at controlled and uncontrolled airports, including collision, wind shear, and wake turbulence avoidance.
2. Follows the established traffic pattern procedures according to instructions or rules.
3. Corrects for wind drift to follow the appropriate ground track.
4. Maintains proper spacing from other traffic.
5. Maintains the traffic pattern altitude, ±100 feet.
6. Maintains the desired airspeed, ±10 knots.
7. Completes the prelanding cockpit checklist.
8. Maintains orientation with the runway in use.

C. TASK: AIRPORT AND RUNWAY MARKING AND LIGHTING (ASEL)

PILOT OPERATION – 2

REFERENCES: AC 61-21; AIM.

Objective. To determine that the applicant:

1. Exhibits knowledge by explaining airport and runway markings and lighting aids.
2. Identifies and interprets airport, runway, taxiway marking, and lighting aids.

IV. AREA OF OPERATION:
TAKEOFFS AND CLIMBS

A. TASK: NORMAL AND CROSSWIND TAKEOFFS AND CLIMBS (ASEL)

PILOT OPERATION – 5

REFERENCES: AC 61-21; Airplane Handbook and Flight Manual.

Objective. To determine that the applicant:

1. Exhibits knowledge by explaining the elements of normal and crosswind takeoffs and climbs, including airspeeds, configurations, and emergency procedures.

2. Selects the recommended wing–flap setting.
3. Aligns the airplane on the runway centerline.
4. Applies aileron deflection properly.
5. Advances the throttle smoothly to maximum allowable power.
6. Checks engine instruments.
7. Maintains directional control on runway centerline.
8. Adjusts aileron deflection during acceleration.
9. Rotates at the recommended[1] airspeed and accelerates to V_Y, and establishes wind–drift correction.
10. Establishes the pitch attitude for V_Y and maintains V_Y, ±5 knots.
11. Retracts the wing flaps, as recommended, or at a safe altitude.
12. Retracts the landing gear, if retractable, after a positive rate of climb has been established and a safe landing can no longer be accomplished on the remaining runway.
13. Maintains takeoff power to a safe maneuvering altitude.
14. Maintains a straight track over the extended runway centerline until a turn is required.
15. Completes after–takeoff checklist.

NOTE: If a crosswind condition does not exist, the applicant's knowledge of the TASK will be evaluated through oral testing.

---

[1]The term "recommended" refers to the manufacturer's recommendation. If the manufacturer's recommendation is not available, the description in AC 61–21 will be used.

B. TASK: SHORT–FIELD TAKEOFF AND CLIMB (ASEL)

PILOT OPERATION – 8

REFERENCES: AC 61-21; Airplane Handbook and Flight Manual.

Objective. To determine that the applicant:

1. Exhibits knowledge by explaining the elements of a short–field takeoff and climb, including the significance of appropriate airspeeds and configurations, emergency procedures, and expected performance for existing operating conditions.
2. Selects the recommended wing–flap setting.
3. Positions the airplane at the beginning of the takeoff runway aligned on the runway centerline.
4. Advances the throttle smoothly to maximum allowable power.
5. Maintains directional control on the runway centerline.
6. Rotates at the recommended airspeed and accelerates to V_X.
7. Climbs at V_X or recommended airspeed, +5, –0 knots until obstacle is cleared, or until at least 50 feet above the surface, then accelerates to V_Y and maintains V_Y, ±5 knots.
8. Retracts the wing flaps, as recommended, or at a safe altitude.
9. Retracts the landing gear, if retractable, after a positive rate of climb has been established and a safe landing can no longer be accomplished on the remaining runway.
10. Maintains takeoff power to a safe maneuvering altitude.
11. Maintains a straight track over the extended runway centerline until a turn is required.
12. Completes after–takeoff checklist.

C.   TASK: SOFT–FIELD TAKEOFF AND CLIMB (ASEL)

PILOT OPERATION – 8

REFERENCES: AC 61-21; Airplane Handbook and Flight Manual.

Objective.   To determine that the applicant:

1. Exhibits knowledge by explaining the elements of a soft–field takeoff and climb, including the significance of appropriate airspeeds and configurations, emergency procedures, and hazards associated with climbing at an airspeed less than V_X.
2. Selects the recommended wing–flap setting.
3. Taxies onto the takeoff surface at a speed consistent with safety.
4. Aligns the airplane on takeoff path, without stopping, and advances the throttle smoothly to maximum allowable power.
5. Adjusts and maintains a pitch attitude which transfers the weight from the wheels to the wings as rapidly as possible.
6. Maintains directional control on the center of the takeoff path.
7. Lifts off at the lowest possible airspeed and remains in ground effect while accelerating.
8. Accelerates to and maintains V_X, +5, –0 knots, if obstructions must be cleared, otherwise to V_Y, ±5 knots.
9. Retracts the wing flaps, as recommended, and at a safe altitude.
10. Retracts the landing gear, if retractable, after a positive rate of climb has been establsihed and a landing can no longer be accomplished on the remaining runway.
11. Maintains takeoff power to a safe maneuvering altitude.
12. Maintains a straight track over the center of the extended takeoff path until a turn is required.
13. Completes after–takeoff checklist.

V. AREA OF OPERATION:
CROSS–COUNTRY FLYING

NOTE: This AREA OF OPERATION is NOT required for the addition of a single–engine land class rating.

A.   TASK: PILOTAGE AND DEAD RECKONING (ASEL)

PILOT OPERATION – 7

REFERENCES: AC 61-21, AC 61-23.

Objective.   To determine that the applicant:

1. Exhibits knowledge by explaining pilotage and dead reckoning techniques and procedures.
2. Follows the preplanned course solely by visual reference to landmarks.
3. Identifies landmarks by relating the surface features to chart symbols.
4. Navigates by means of precomputed headings, groundspeed, and elapsed time.
5. Combines pilotage and dead reckoning.
6. Verifies the airplane position within 3 nautical miles of the flight planned route at all times.
7. Arrives at the en route checkpoints and destination ±5 minutes of the initial or revised ETA.
8. Corrects for, and records, the differences between preflight fuel, groundspeed, and heading calculations and those determined en route.
9. Maintains the selected altitudes, within ±200 feet.
10. Maintains the desired heading, ±10°.
11. Follows the climb, cruise, and descent checklists.

B.   TASK: RADIO NAVIGATION (ASEL)

PILOT OPERATION – 7

REFERENCES: AC 61-21, AC 61-23.

Objective.   To determine that the applicant:

1. Exhibits knowledge by explaining radio navigation, equipment, procedures, and limitations.
2. Selects and identifies the desired radio facility.
3. Locates position relative to the radio navigation facility.
4. Intercepts and tracks a given radial or bearing.
5. Locates position using cross radials or bearings.
6. Recognizes or describes the indication of station passage.
7. Recognizes signal loss and takes appropriate action.
8. Maintains the appropriate altitude, ±200 feet.

C.   TASK: DIVERSION (ASEL)

PILOT OPERATION – 7

REFERENCES: AC 61-21, AC 61-23.

Objective.   To determine that the applicant:

1. Exhibits knowledge by explaining the procedures for diverting, including the recognition of adverse weather conditions.
2. Selects an appropriate alternate airport and route.
3. Diverts toward the alternate airport promptly.
4. Makes a reasonable estimate of heading, groundspeed, arrival time, and fuel consumption to the alternate airport.
5. Maintains the appropriate altitude, ±200 feet.

D.   TASK: LOST PROCEDURES (ASEL)

PILOT OPERATION – 7

REFERENCES: AC 61-21, AC 61-23.

Objective.   To determine that the applicant:

1. Exhibits knowledge by explaining lost procedures, including the reasons for –

    (a) maintaining the original or an appropriate heading, identifying landmarks, and climbing, if necessary.
    (b) proceeding to and identifying the nearest concentration of prominent landmarks.
    (c) using available radio navigation aids or contacting an appropriate facility for assistance.
    (d) planning a precautionary landing if deteriorating visibility and/or fuel exhaustion is imminent.

2. Selects the best course of action when given a lost situation.

VI. AREA OF OPERATION:
FLIGHT BY REFERENCE TO INSTRUMENTS

NOTE: This AREA OF OPERATION is NOT required for the addition of a single–engine land class rating.

A. TASK: STRAIGHT–AND–LEVEL FLIGHT (ASEL)

PILOT OPERATION – 6

REFERENCES: AC 61-21, AC 61-23, AC 61-27.

Objective.   To determine that the applicant:

1. Exhibits knowledge by explaining flight solely by reference to instruments as related to straight–and–level flight.
2. Makes smooth and coordinated control applications.
3. Maintains straight–and–level flight for at least 3 minutes.
4. Maintains the desired heading, ±10°.
5. Maintains the desired altitude, ±100 feet.
6. Maintains the desired airspeed, ±10 knots.

B. TASK: STRAIGHT, CONSTANT AIRSPEED CLIMBS (ASEL)

PILOT OPERATION – 6

REFERENCES: AC 61-21, AC 61-23, AC 61-27.

Objective.   To determine that the applicant:

1. Exhibits knowledge by explaining flight solely by reference to instruments as related to straight, constant airspeed climbs.
2. Establishes the climb pitch attitude and power setting on an assigned heading.
3. Makes smooth and coordinated control applications.
4. Maintains the desired heading, ±10°.
5. Maintains the desired airspeed, ±10 knots.
6. Levels off at the desired altitude, ±100 feet.

C. TASK: STRAIGHT, CONSTANT AIRSPEED DESCENTS (ASEL)

PILOT OPERATION – 6

REFERENCES: AC 61-21, AC 61-23, AC 61-27.

Objective.   To determine that the applicant:

1. Exhibits knowledge by explaining flight solely by reference to instruments as related to straight, constant airspeed descents.
2. Determines the minimum safe altitude at which the descent should be terminated.
3. Establishes the descent configuration, pitch, and power setting on the assigned heading.
4. Makes smooth and coordinated control applications.
5. Maintains the desired heading, ±10°.
6. Maintains the desired airspeed, ±10 knots.
7. Levels off at the desired altitude, ±100 feet.

D. TASK: TURNS TO HEADINGS (ASEL)

PILOT OPERATION – 6

REFERENCES: AC 61-21, AC 61-23, AC 61-27.

Objective.   To determine that the applicant:

1. Exhibits knowledge by explaining flight solely by reference to instruments as related to turns to headings.
2. Enters and maintains approximately a standard–rate turn with smooth and coordinated control applications.
3. Maintains the desired altitude, ±100 feet.
4. Maintains the desired airspeed, ±10 knots.
5. Maintains the desired bank angle.
6. Rolls out at the desired heading, ±10°.

E. TASK: UNUSUAL FLIGHT ATTITUDES (ASEL)

PILOT OPERATION – 6

REFERENCES: AC 61-21, AC 61-23, AC 61-27.

NOTE: Unusual flight attitudes, such as a start of a power–on spiral or an approach to a climbing stall, shall not exceed 45° bank or 10° pitch from level flight.

Objective.   To determine that the applicant:

1. Exhibits knowledge by explaining flight solely by reference to instruments as related to unusual flight attitudes.
2. Recognizes unusual flight attitudes promptly.
3. Properly interprets the instruments.
4. Recovers to a stabilized level flight attitude by prompt, smooth, coordinated control, applied in the proper sequence.
5. Avoids excessive load factor, airspeed, and stall.

F. TASK: RADIO AIDS AND RADAR SERVICES (ASEL)

PILOT OPERATION – 6

REFERENCES: AC 61-21, AC 61-23, AC 61-27.

Objective.   To determine that the applicant:

1. Exhibits knowledge by explaining radio aids and radar services available for use during flight solely by reference to instruments.
2. Selects, tunes, and identifies the appropriate facility.
3. Follows verbal instructions or radio navigation aids for guidance.
4. Determines the minimum safe altitude.
5. Maintains the desired altitude, ±100 feet.
6. Maintains the desired heading, ±10°.

VII. AREA OF OPERATION:
FLIGHT AT CRITICALLY SLOW AIRSPEEDS

A. TASK: FULL STALLS — POWER OFF (ASEL)

PILOT OPERATION – 4

REFERENCE: AC 61-21.

Objective. To determine that the applicant:

1. Exhibits knowledge by explaining the aerodynamic factors and flight situations that may result in full stalls — power off, including proper recovery procedures, and hazards of stalling during uncoordinated flight.
2. Selects an entry altitude that will allow the recoveries to be completed no lower than 1,500 feet AGL.
3. Establishes the normal approach or landing configuration and airspeed with the throttle closed or at a reduced power setting.
4. Establishes a straight glide or a gliding turn with a bank angle of 30°, ±10°, in coordinated flight.
5. Establishes and maintains a landing pitch attitude that will induce a full stall.
6. Recognizes the indications of a full stall and promptly recovers by decreasing the angle of attack, leveling the wings, and adjusting the power, as necessary, to regain normal flight attitude.
7. Retracts the wing flaps and landing gear (if retractable) and establishes straight–and–level flight or climb.
8. Avoids secondary stalls, excessive airspeed, excessive altitude loss, spins, and flight below 1,500 feet AGL.

B. TASK: FULL STALLS — POWER ON (ASEL)

PILOT OPERATION – 4

REFERENCE: AC 61-21.

Objective. To determine that the applicant:

1. Exhibits knowledge by explaining the aerodynamic factors and flight situations that may result in full stalls — power on, including proper recovery procedures, and hazards of stalling during uncoordinated flight.
2. Selects an entry altitude that will allow recoveries to be completed no lower than 1,500 feet AGL.
3. Establishes takeoff or normal climb configuration.
4. Establishes takeoff or climb airspeed before applying takeoff or climb power. (Reduced power may be used to avoid excessive pitch–up during entry only.)
5. Establishes and maintains a pitch attitude straight ahead or in a turn with a bank angle of 20°, ±10°, that will induce a full stall.
6. Applies proper control to maintain coordinated flight.
7. Recognizes the indications of a full stall and promptly recovers by decreasing the angle of attack, leveling the wings, and adjusting the power, as necessary, to regain normal flight attitude.
8. Retracts the wing flaps and landing gear (if retractable) and establishes straight–and–level flight or climb.
9. Avoids secondary stall, excessive airspeed, excessive altitude loss, spin, and flight below 1,500 feet AGL.

C. TASK: IMMINENT STALLS — POWER ON AND POWER OFF (ASEL)

PILOT OPERATION – 4

REFERENCE: AC 61-21.

Objective. To determine that the applicant:

1. Exhibits knowledge by explaining the aerodynamic factors associated with imminent stalls (power on and power off), an awareness of speed loss in different configurations, and the procedure for resuming normal flight attitude.
2. Selects an entry altitude that will allow recoveries to be completed no lower than 1,500 feet AGL.
3. Establishes either a takeoff, a climb, or an approach configuration with the appropriate power setting.
4. Establishes a pitch attitude on a constant heading, ±10°, or 20° bank turns, ±10°, that will induce an imminent stall.
5. Applies proper control to maintain coordinated flight.
6. Recognizes and recovers from imminent stalls at the first indication of buffeting or decay of control effectiveness by reducing angle of attack and adjusting power, as necessary, to regain normal flight attitude.
7. Avoids full stall, secondary stall, excessive airspeed, excessive altitude change, spin, and flight below 1,500 feet AGL.

D. TASK: MANEUVERING AT CRITICALLY SLOW AIRSPEED (ASEL)

PILOT OPERATION – 4

REFERENCE: AC 61-21.

Objective. To determine that the applicant:

1. Exhibits knowledge by explaining the flight characteristics and controllability associated with maneuvering at critically slow airspeeds.
2. Selects an entry altitude that will allow the maneuver to be performed no lower than 1,500 feet AGL.
3. Establishes and maintains a critically slow airspeed while –

   (a) in coordinated straight and turning flight in various configurations and bank angles, and
   (b) in coordinated departure climbs and landing approach descents in various configurations.

4. Maintains the desired altitude, ±100 feet, when a constant altitude is specified, and levels off from climbs and descents, ±100 feet.
5. Maintains the desired heading during straight flight, ±10°.
6. Maintains the specified bank angle, ±10°, in coordinated flight.
7. Maintains a critically slow airspeed, +5, –0 knots.

E. TASK: CONSTANT ALTITUDE TURNS (ASEL)

PILOT OPERATION – 10

REFERENCE: AC 61-21.

Objective. To determine that the applicant:

1. Exhibits knowledge by explaining the performance factors associated with constant altitude turns, including increased load factors, power required, and overbanking tendency.
2. Selects an altitude that will allow the maneuver to be performed no lower than 1,500 feet AGL.
3. Establishes an airspeed which does not exceed the airplane design maneuvering airspeed.
4. Enters a 360° turn maintaining a bank angle of 40° to 50° in coordinated flight.
5. Divides attention between airplane control and orientation.
6. Rolls out at the desired heading, ±10°.
7. Maintains the desired altitude, ±100 feet.

VIII. AREA OF OPERATION:
FLIGHT MANEUVERING BY REFERENCE TO GROUND OBJECTS

NOTE: This AREA OF OPERATION is NOT required for the addition of a single–engine land class rating.

A.   TASK: RECTANGULAR COURSE (ASEL)

   PILOT OPERATION – 3

   REFERENCE: AC 61-21.

Objective.   To determine that the applicant:

1.   Exhibits knowledge by explaining wind–drift correction in straight–and–turning flight, and the relationship of the rectangular course to airport traffic patterns.
2.   Selects a suitable reference area.
3.   Enters a left or right pattern at a desired distance from the selected reference area and at 600 to 1,000 feet AGL.
4.   Divides attention between airplane control and ground track, and maintains coordinated flight.
5.   Applies the necessary wind–drift corrections during straight–and–turning flight to maintain the desired ground track.
6.   Maintains the desired altitude, ±100 feet.
7.   Maintains the desired airspeed, ±10 knots.
8.   Avoids bank angles in excess of 45°.
9.   Reverses course, as directed by the examiner.

B.   TASK: S–TURNS ACROSS A ROAD (ASEL)

   PILOT OPERATION – 3

   REFERENCE: AC 61-21.

Objective.   To determine that the applicant:

1.   Exhibits adequate knowledge by explaining the procedures and wind–drift correction associated with S–turns.
2.   Selects a suitable ground reference line.
3.   Enters perpendicular to the selected reference line at 600 to 1,000 feet AGL.
4.   Divides attention between airplane control and ground track, and maintains coordinated flight.
5.   Applies the necessary wind–drift correction to track a constant radius turn on each side of the selected reference line.
6.   Reverses the direction of turn directly over the selected reference line.
7.   Maintains the desired altitude, ±100 feet.
8.   Maintains the desired airspeed, ±10 knots.

C.   TASK: TURNS AROUND A POINT (ASEL)

   PILOT OPERATION – 3

   REFERENCE: AC 61-21.

Objective.   To determine that the applicant:

1.   Exhibits knowledge by explaining the procedures and wind–drift correction associated with turns around a point.
2.   Selects suitable ground reference points.
3.   Enters a left or right turn at a desired distance from the selected reference point at 600 to 1,000 feet AGL.
4.   Divides attention between airplane control and ground track, and maintains coordinated flight.
5.   Applies the necessary wind–drift corrections to track a constant–radius turn around the selected reference point.
6.   Maintains the desired altitude, ±100 feet.
7.   Maintains the desired airspeed, ±10 knots.

IX. AREA OF OPERATION:
NIGHT FLIGHT OPERATIONS

NOTE: This AREA OF OPERATION is NOT required for the addition of a single–engine land class rating. However, if the applicant is to be evaluated on night flying operations, then the examiner must evaluate elements 1 through 3. Elements 4 through 8 may be evaluated at the option of the examiner.

Night flight operations will be evaluated ONLY if the applicant meets night flying regulatory requirements. If this AREA OF OPERATION is not evaluated, the applicant's certificate will bear the limitation, "Night Flying Prohibited."

A.   TASK: NIGHT FLIGHT (ASEL)

   PILOT OPERATION – 9

   REFERENCES: AC 61-21, AC 67-2.

Objective.   To determine that the applicant:

1.   Explains preparation, equipment, and factors essential to night flight.
2.   Determines airplane, airport, and navigation lighting.
3.   Exhibits knowledge by explaining night flying procedures, including safety precautions and emergency actions.
4.   Inspects the airplane by following the checklist which includes items essential for night flight operations.
5.   Starts, taxies, and performs pretakeoff check adhering to good operating practices.
6.   Performs takeoffs and climbs with emphasis on visual references.
7.   Navigates and maintains orientation under VFR conditions.
8.   Approaches and lands adhering to good operating practices for night flight operations.

X. AREA OF OPERATION:
EMERGENCY OPERATIONS

A. TASK: EMERGENCY APPROACH AND LANDING (SIMULATED)
(ASEL)

PILOT OPERATION – 10

REFERENCES: AC 61-21; Airplane Handbook and
Flight Manual.

Objective.   To determine that the applicant:

1. Exhibits knowledge by explaining approach and landing procedures to be used in various emergencies.
2. Establishes and maintains the recommended best–glide airspeed and configuration during simulated emergencies.
3. Selects a suitable landing area within gliding distance.
4. Plans and follows a flight pattern to the selected landing area, considering altitude, wind, terrain, obstructions, and other factors.
5. Follows an appropriate emergency checklist.
6. Attempts to determine the reason for the simulated malfunction.
7. Maintains positive control of the airplane.

NOTE: Examiner should terminate the emergency approach at or above minimum safe altitude.

B. TASK: SYSTEM AND EQUIPMENT MALFUNCTIONS (ASEL)

PILOT OPERATION – 10

REFERENCES: AC 61-21; Airplane Handbook and
Flight Manual.

Objective.   To determine that the applicant:

1. Exhibits knowledge by explaining causes of, indications of, and pilot actions for, malfunctions of various systems and equipment.
2. Analyzes the situation and takes appropriate action for simulated emergencies such as –

   (a) partial power loss.
   (b) rough running engine or overheat.
   (c) carburetor or induction icing.
   (d) loss of oil pressure.
   (e) fuel starvation.
   (f) engine compartment fire.
   (g) electrical system malfunction.
   (h) gear or flap malfunction.
   (i) door opening in flight.
   (j) trim inoperative.
   (k) loss of pressurization.
   (l) other malfunctions.

XI. AREA OF OPERATION:
APPROACHES AND LANDINGS

A. TASK: NORMAL AND CROSSWIND APPROACHES AND LANDINGS (ASEL)

PILOT OPERATION – 5

REFERENCES: AC 61-21; Airplane Handbook and Flight Manual.

Objective.   To determine that the applicant:

1. Exhibits knowledge by explaining the elements of normal and crosswind approaches and landings, including airspeeds, configurations, crosswind limitations, and related safety factors.
2. Maintains the proper ground track on final approach.
3. Establishes the approach and landing configuration and power required.
4. Maintains the recommended approach airspeed, ±5 knots.
5. Makes smooth, timely, and correct control application during the final approach and transition from approach to landing roundout.
6. Touches down smoothly at approximate stalling speed, at or within 500 feet beyond a specified point, with no appreciable drift, and the airplane longitudinal axis aligned with the runway centerline.
7. Maintains directional control, increasing aileron deflection into the wind, as necessary, during the after-landing roll.

NOTE: If a crosswind condition does not exist, the applicant's knowledge of the TASK will be evaluated through oral testing.

B. TASK: FORWARD SLIPS TO LANDING (ASEL)

PILOT OPERATION – 5

REFERENCE: AC 61-21.

Objective.   To determine that the applicant:

1. Exhibits knowledge by explaining the elements of a forward slip to a landing, including the purpose, technique, limitation, and the effect on airspeed indications.
2. Establishes a forward slip at a point from which a landing can be made in a desired area using the recommended airspeed and configuration.
3. Maintains a ground track aligned with the runway centerline.
4. Maintains an airspeed which results in minimum floating during the landing roundout.
5. Recovers smoothly from the slip.
6. Touches down smoothly at approximate stalling speed, at and within 500 feet beyond a specified point, with no appreciable drift, and the airplane longitudinal axis aligned with the runway centerline.
7. Maintains directional control during the after-landing roll.

C. TASK: GO-AROUND (ASEL)

PILOT OPERATION – 5

REFERENCES: AC 61-21; Airplane Handbook and Flight Manual.

Objective.   To determine that the applicant:

1. Exhibits knowledge by explaining the elements of the go-around procedure, including proper decision, recommended airspeeds, drag effect of wing flaps and landing gear, and coping with undesirable pitch and yaw.
2. Makes a proper decision to go around.
3. Applies takeoff power and establishes the proper pitch attitude to attain the recommended airspeed.
4. Retracts the wing flaps, as recommended, and at a safe altitude.
5. Retracts the landing gear, if retractable, after a positive rate of climb has been established.
6. Trims the airplane and climbs at V_Y ±5 knots, and tracks the appropriate traffic pattern.

D. TASK: SHORT-FIELD APPROACH AND LANDING (ASEL)

PILOT OPERATION – 8

REFERENCES: AC 61-21; Airplane Handbook and Flight Manual.

Objective.   To determine that the applicant:

1. Exhibits knowledge by explaining the elements of a short-field approach and landing, including airspeed, configuration, and related safety factors.
2. Considers obstructions, landing surface, and wind conditions.
3. Selects a suitable touchdown point.
4. Establishes the short-field approach and landing configuration, airspeed, and descent angle.
5. Maintains control of the descent rate and the recommended airspeed, ±5 knots, along the extended runway centerline.
6. Touches down at or within 200 feet beyond a specified point, with minimum float, no appreciable drift, and the airplane longitudinal axis aligned with the runway centerline.
7. Maintains directional control during the after-landing roll.
8. Applies braking and controls, as necessary, to stop in the shortest distance consistent with safety.

E. TASK: SOFT-FIELD APPROACH AND LANDING (ASEL)

PILOT OPERATION – 8

REFERENCES: AC 61-21; Airplane Handbook and Flight Manual.

Objective.   To determine that the applicant:

1. Exhibits knowledge by explaining the elements of a soft-field approach and landing procedure, including airspeeds, configurations, operations on various surfaces, and related safety factors.
2. Evaluates obstructions, landing surface, and wind conditions.
3. Establishes the recommended soft-field approach and landing configuration and airspeed.
4. Maintains recommended airspeed, ±5 knots, along the extended runway centerline.
5. Touches down smoothly at minimum descent rate and groundspeed, with no appreciable drift, and the airplane longitudinal axis aligned with runway centerline.
6. Maintains directional control during the after-landing roll.
7. Maintains proper position of flight controls and sufficient speed to taxi on soft surface.

APPENDIX B
FAR PART 141 -- PRIVATE PILOT
CERTIFICATION COURSE (AIRPLANES)

1. **APPLICABILITY.** This Appendix prescribes the minimum curriculum for a private pilot certification course (airplanes) required by §141.55.

2. **GROUND TRAINING.** The course must consist of at least 35 hr. of ground training in the following subjects:

   a. The Federal Aviation Regulations applicable to private pilot privileges, limitations, and flight operations; the rules of the National Transportation Safety Board pertaining to accident reporting; the use of the Airman's Information Manual; and the FAA Advisory Circular System.

   b. VFR navigation using pilotage, dead reckoning, and radio aids.

   c. The recognition of critical weather situations from the ground and in flight and the procurement and use of aeronautical weather reports and forecasts.

   d. The safe and efficient operation of airplanes, including high density airport operations, collision avoidance precautions, and radio communication procedures.

   e. Stall awareness, spin entry, spins, and spin recovery techniques.

3. **FLIGHT TRAINING.**

   a. The course must consist of at least 35 hr. of the flight training listed in this section and section 4 of this Appendix. Instruction in a pilot ground trainer that meets the requirements of §141.41(a)(1) may be credited for not more than 5 of the required 35 hr. of flight time. Instruction in a pilot ground trainer that meets the requirement of §141.41(a)(2) may be credited for not more than 2.5 hr. of the required 35 hr. of flight time.

   b. Each training flight must include a preflight briefing and a postflight critique of the student by the instructor assigned to that flight.

   c. Flight training must consist of at least 20 hr. of instruction in the following subjects:

      1) Preflight operations, including weight and balance determination, line inspection, starting and runups, and airplane servicing.

      2) Airport and traffic pattern operations, including operations at controlled airports, radio communications, and collision avoidance precautions.

      3) Flight maneuvering by reference to ground objects.

      4) Flight at slow airspeeds with realistic distractions, recognition of and recovery from stalls entered from straight flight and from turns.

      5) Normal and crosswind takeoffs and landings.

      6) Control and maneuvering an airplane solely by reference to instruments, including emergency descents and climbs using radio aids or radar directives.

      7) Cross-country flying using pilotage, dead reckoning, and radio aids, including a 2-hr. dual flight at least part of which must be on Federal airways.

      8) Maximum performance takeoffs and landings.

      9) Night flying, including 5 takeoffs and landings as sole manipulator of the controls, and VFR navigation.

      10) Emergency operations, including simulated aircraft and equipment malfunctions, lost procedures, and emergency go-arounds.

4. SOLO FLIGHTS. The course must provide at least 15 hr. of solo flights, including:

    a. Solo practice. Directed solo practice on all VFR flight operations for which flight instruction is required (except simulated emergencies) to develop proficiency, resourcefulness, and self-reliance; and

    b. Cross-country flights.

        1) 10 hr. of cross-country flights, each flight with a landing at a point more than 50 NM from the original departure point. One flight must be of at least 300 NM with landings at a minimum of three points, one of which is at least 100 NM from the original departure point; or

        2) If a pilot school or a provisional pilot school shows that it is located on an island from which cross-country flights cannot be accomplished without flying over water more than 10 NM from the nearest shoreline, it need not include cross-country flights under subparagraph (1) of this paragraph. However, if other airports that permit civil operations are available to which a flight may be made without flying over water more than 10 NM from the nearest shoreline, the school must include in its course, two round trip solo flights between those airports that are farthest apart, including a landing at each airport on both flights.

5. STAGE AND FINAL TESTS.

    a. Each student enrolled in a private pilot certification course must satisfactorily accomplish the stage and final test prescribed in this section. The written tests may not be credited for more than 3 hr. of the 35 hr. of required ground training, and the flight tests may not be credited for more than 4 hr. of the 35 hr. of required flight training.

    b. Each student must satisfactorily accomplish a written examination at the completion of each stage of training specified in the approved training syllabus for the private certification course and a final test at the conclusion of that course.

    c. Each student must satisfactorily accomplish a flight test at the completion of the first solo flight and at the completion of the first solo cross-country flight and at the conclusion of that course.

APPENDIX C
FAA SUGGESTED PART 61 FLIGHT SYLLABUS

This syllabus is not intended as a study guide for either flight instructors or student pilots. It contains an outline useful to instructors in assuring that students receive instruction in all of the fundamentals, procedures, and flight maneuvers necessary for proficient and safe flying. There is no time limit established to complete the lessons in this syllabus.

Federal Aviation Regulations, Part 61, establish the requirements for pilot and instructor certification. The following syllabus is reproduced from the FAA *Aviation Instructor's Handbook* (AC 60-14). This provides an example of a structured approach to flight training.

This syllabus is divided into lessons, each representing a unit of training important to a pilot course. A lesson is complete only when each item is learned or accomplished; not when a specified amount of time has been devoted to it. This is the completion standard. The instructor must be careful to see that the flight time devoted to this syllabus is sufficient to meet the requirements of FAR Part 61 for a private pilot certificate when the last lesson is completed.

Integrated flight instruction means instruction in which students are taught to perform each flight maneuver by both outside visual references (VR) and reference to instruments (IR) FROM THE FIRST TIME THE MANEUVER IS INTRODUCED.

LESSON NO. 1—DUAL

OBJECTIVE. To familiarize the student with the training airplane, its servicing, its operating characteristics, cabin controls, instruments, systems, preflight procedures, use of checklists, and safety precautions to be followed; to acquaint the student with the sensations of flight and the effect and use of controls; and to familiarize the student with the local flying area and airport.

CONTENT.
1. Preflight discussion.
2. Introduction.
   a. Airplane servicing.
   b. Purpose of preflight checks.
   c. Visual inspection.
   d. Importance of using a checklist.
   e. Engine starting procedure.
   f. Radio communications procedures.
   g. Taxiing.
   h. Pretakeoff checklist.
   i. Takeoff.
   j. Traffic pattern departure, climb-out, and level-off.
   k. Effect and use of controls (VR and IR).
   l. Straight-and-level flight (VR and IR).
   m. Medium bank turns (VR and IR).
   n. Local flying area familiarization.
   o. Collision avoidance.
   p. Wake turbulence avoidance.
   q. Traffic pattern entry, approach, landing, and parking.
   r. Ground safety.
3. Postflight critique and preview of next lesson.

COMPLETION STANDARDS. The lesson will have been successfully completed when the student understands how to service the airplane, the use of a checklist for the visual inspection, starting procedure, and engine run-up; displays a knowledge of the effect and use of controls; and has a reasonable familiarity with the local flying area and airport.

LESSON NO. 2—DUAL

OBJECTIVE. To develop the student's skill in the performance of the four basic flight maneuvers (climbs, descents, turns, and straight-and-level flight).

CONTENT.

1. Preflight discussion.
2. Review.
   a. Airplane servicing.
   b. Visual inspection.
   c. Engine starting procedure.
   d. Radio communications procedures.
   e. Taxiing.
   f. Pretakeoff checklist.
   g. Takeoff.
   h. Traffic pattern departure.
   i. Straight-and-level flight (VR and IR).
   j. Medium bank turns (VR and IR).
   k. Traffic pattern entry, approach, landing, and parking.
3. Introduction.
   a. Climbs and climbing turns (VR and IR).
   b. Glides and gliding turns (VR and IR).
   c. Torque effect.
   d. Level-off from climbs and glides (VR and IR).
4. Postflight critique and preview of next lesson.

COMPLETION STANDARDS. The lesson will have been successfully completed when the student can perform, with minimum assistance from the instructor, climbs, straight-and-level flight, turns, and glides. During straight-and-level flight the student should, with minimum instructor assistance, be able to maintain altitude within ±100 feet, airspeed within ±10 knots, and heading within ±10° of that assigned.

LESSON NO. 3—DUAL

OBJECTIVE. To review lessons One and Two; to develop the student's proficiency in the performance of the basic flight maneuvers; and to introduce maneuvering at minimum controllable airspeed and power-off stalls.

CONTENT.

1. Preflight discussion.
2. Review.
   a. Use of checklist.
   b. Engine starting procedure.
   c. Radio communications procedures.
   d. Takeoff.
   e. Traffic pattern departure.
   f. Climbs and climbing turns (VR and IR).
   g. Straight-and-level flight (VR and IR).
   h. Medium bank turns (VR and IR).
   i. Glides and gliding turns (VR and IR).
   j. Level-off procedures (VR and IR).
   k. Traffic pattern and landing.
3. Introduction.
   a. Maneuvering at minimum controllable airspeed (VR and IR).
   b. Power-off stalls (imminent and full) (VR and IR).
   c. Descents and descending turns, with power (VR and IR).
4. Postflight critique and preview of next lesson.

COMPLETION STANDARDS. The lesson will have been successfully completed when the student can display reasonable proficiency in the performance of the four basic flight maneuvers, and perform with minimum assistance, flight at minimum controllable airspeed. During this and subsequent flight lessons, the student should be able to perform the visual inspection, starting procedure, radio communications, taxiing, pretakeoff check, parking, and shut-down procedure without assistance. During climbs, level flight, turns, glides, and maneuvering at minimum controllable airspeed the student should, with minimum instructor assistance, be able to maintain assigned airspeed within ±10 knots. The student should also, with minimum instructor assistance, be able to maintain assigned altitude within ±100 feet and assigned heading within ±10°.

LESSON NO. 4—DUAL

OBJECTIVE. To review previous lessons, thereby increasing the student's competence in the performance of fundamental flight maneuvers; and to introduce power-on stalls, rectangular course, S-turns across a road, eights along a road, and elementary emergency landings.

CONTENT.

1. Preflight discussion.
2. Review.
   a. Takeoff.
   b. Traffic pattern departure.
   c. Climbs and climbing turns (VR and IR).
   d. Straight-and-level flight and medium bank turns (VR and IR).
   e. Maneuvering at minimum controllable airspeed (VR and IR).
   f. Power-off stalls (imminent and full) (VR and IR).
   g. Glides and gliding turns (VR and IR).
   h. Descents and descending turns, with power (VR and IR).
   i. Level-off procedures (VR and IR).
   j. Traffic pattern and landing.
3. Introduction.
   a. Power-on stalls (imminent and full) (VR and IR).
   b. Rectangular course.
   c. S-turns across a road.
   d. Eights along a road and eights across a road.
   e. Elementary emergency landings.
4. Postflight critique and preview of next lesson.

COMPLETION STANDARDS. The lesson will have been successfully completed when the student is competent to perform, with minimum instructor assistance, the procedures and maneuvers given during previous lessons. The student should achieve the ability to recognize stall indications and make safe prompt recoveries. The student should maintain assigned airspeed within ±10 knots, assigned altitude within ±100 feet, and assigned heading within ±10°, and display a basic knowledge of elementary emergency landings.

LESSON NO. 5—DUAL

OBJECTIVE. To review previous lessons, with emphasis on maneuvering by reference to ground objects. To develop the student's ability to perform climbs at best rate and best angle, crosswind takeoffs and landings; and to introduce emergency procedures, changes of airspeed and configuration, turns around a point, and eights around pylons.

CONTENT.

1. Preflight discussion.
2. Review.
   a. Takeoff.
   b. Climbs and climbing turns (VR and IR).
   c. Maneuvering at minimum controllable airspeed (VR and IR).
   d. Power-off and power-on stalls (imminent and full).
   e. Rectangular course.
   f. S-turns across a road.
   g. Eights along a road.
   h. Elementary emergency landings.
   i. Traffic pattern and landing.
3. Introduction.
   a. Crosswind takeoffs and landings.
   b. Climb at best rate (VR and IR).
   c. Climb at best angle (VR and IR).
   d. Emergency procedures.
   e. Change of airspeed and configuration (VR and IR).
   f. Turns around a point.
   g. Eights around pylons.
4. Postflight critique and preview of next lesson.

COMPLETION STANDARDS. The lesson will have been successfully completed when the student can recognize imminent and full stalls and make prompt effective recoveries, perform ground reference maneuvers with reasonably accurate wind drift corrections and good coordination, and has a proper concept of crosswind technique during takeoffs and landings. The student should have a working knowledge of emergency procedures, and be able to perform them with minimum assistance. During ground reference maneuvers, the student should maintain airspeed within ±10 knots, altitude within ±100 feet, and heading within ±10° of that desired.

LESSON NO. 6—DUAL

OBJECTIVE. To review previous lessons; to develop the student's ability to perform slips, accelerated stalls, cross-control stalls, and advanced emergency landings; to improve the student's proficiency in normal and crosswind takeoffs and landings; and to introduce balked takeoffs and go-arounds (rejected landings).

CONTENT.

1. Preflight discussion.
2. Review.
   a. Normal and crosswind takeoffs.
   b. Climbs at best rate and best angle (VR and IR).
   c. Power-off stalls (imminent and full) (VR and IR).
   d. Power-on stalls (imminent and full) (VR and IR).
   e. Change of airspeed and configuration (VR and IR).
   f. Turns around a point.
   g. Eights around pylons.
   h. Emergency procedures.
   i. Normal and crosswind landings.
3. Introduction.
   a. Balked takeoffs.
   b. Accelerated stalls.
   c. Cross-control stalls.
   d. 180° and 360° gliding approaches.
   e. Advanced emergency landings.
   f. Side slips and forward slips.
   g. Go-arounds (rejected landings).
4. Postflight critique and preview of next lesson.

COMPLETION STANDARDS. The lesson will have been successfully completed when the student can perform stall recoveries smoothly and promptly with a minimum loss of altitude, is able to make unassisted normal and crosswind takeoffs and landings, and can plan and fly emergency landing patterns with accuracy and consistency. The student should be able to execute balked takeoffs and go-arounds (rejected landings) without assistance, and should maintain assigned airspeed within ±10 knots, assigned altitude within ±100 feet, and assigned heading within ±10°.

LESSON NO. 7—DUAL

OBJECTIVE. To review previous lessons. To further develop the student's competence in takeoffs, traffic patterns, and landings through concentrated practice. To develop the student's ability to use slips during landing approaches and improve the ability to perform go-arounds (rejected landings).

CONTENT.

1. Preflight discussion.
2. Review.
   a. Normal and crosswind takeoffs.
   b. Normal and crosswind landings (touch-and-go and full-stop).
   c. Forward slips.
   d. Go-arounds (rejected landings).
   e. 180° and 360° gliding approaches.
   f. Advanced emergency landings.
   g. Emergency procedures.
3. Postflight critique and preview of next lesson.

COMPLETION STANDARDS. The lesson will have been successfully completed when the student can fly accurate traffic patterns and make unassisted normal and crosswind takeoffs and landings. The student should be competent in the go-around (rejected landing) procedure. During traffic patterns, the student should maintain desired airspeed within ±10 knots, desired altitude within ±100 feet, and desired heading within ±10°.

LESSON NO. 8—DUAL

OBJECTIVE. To review power-off stalls, maneuvering at minimum controllable airspeed, and advanced emergency landings. To continue to develop the student's competence in takeoffs, traffic patterns, and landings, and to improve the ability to recover from poor approaches and landings.

CONTENT

1. Preflight discussion.
2. Review.
   a. Normal and crosswind takeoffs.
   b. Power-off stalls (imminent and full) (VR and IR).
   c. Maneuvering at minimum controllable airspeed (VR and IR).
   d. Advanced emergency landings.
   e. Normal and crosswind landings (touch-and-go and full-stop).
   f. Go-arounds (rejected landings).
   g. Recovery from poor approaches and landings.
3. Postflight critique and preview of next lesson.

COMPLETION STANDARDS. The lesson will have been successfully completed when the student can demonstrate a degree of proficiency in normal and crosswind takeoffs and landings and traffic patterns, which is considered safe for solo. The student should display sound judgment and proper techniques in recoveries from poor approaches and landings. During traffic patterns, the student should maintain desired airspeed within ±10 knots, desired altitude within ±100 feet, and desired heading within ±10°.

LESSON NO. 9—DUAL AND SOLO

OBJECTIVE. To develop the student's competence to a level which will allow the safe accomplishment of the first supervised solo in the traffic pattern.

CONTENT

1. Preflight discussion.
2. Review.
   a. Normal and crosswind takeoffs.
   b. Normal and crosswind landings (full-stop).
   c. Go-arounds (rejected landings).
   d. Recovery from poor approaches and landings.
   e. Elementary emergency landings.
3. Introduction—first supervised solo in the traffic pattern. Three takeoffs and three full-stop landings should be performed.
4. Postflight critique and preview of next lesson.

COMPLETION STANDARDS. The lesson will have been successfully completed when the student safely accomplishes the first supervised solo in the traffic pattern.

LESSON NO. 10—DUAL AND SOLO

OBJECTIVE. To review previous lessons and to accomplish the student's second supervised solo in the traffic pattern.

CONTENT.

1. Preflight discussion.
2. Review.
   a. Takeoff and traffic departure.
   b. Climbs and climbing turns (VR and IR).
   c. Maneuvering at minimum controllable airspeed (VR and IR).
   d. Power-off stalls (imminent and full) (VR and IR).
   e. Advanced emergency landings.
   f. Traffic patterns, approaches and landings.
   g. Recovery from poor approaches and landings.
3. Introduction—second supervised solo in the traffic pattern. Three takeoffs, two touch-and-go, and one full-stop landing should be performed.
4. Postflight critique and preview of next lesson.

COMPLETION STANDARDS. The lesson will have been successfully completed when the student demonstrates solo competence in maneuvers performed and safely accomplishes the second supervised solo in the traffic pattern.

LESSON NO. 11—DUAL AND SOLO

OBJECTIVE. To review presolo maneuvers with higher levels of proficiency required. To introduce short and soft field takeoffs, and maximum climbs; and to accomplish the student's third supervised solo in the traffic pattern.

CONTENT.

1. Preflight discussion.
2. Review.
   a. Selected presolo maneuvers (VR and IR).
   b. Takeoffs, traffic patterns, and landings.
   c. Balked takeoff.
   d. Go-around (rejected landing).
   e. Recovery from poor approach and landing.
3. Introduction.
   a. Short field takeoffs and maximum climbs.
   b. Soft field takeoffs.
   c. Third supervised solo in the traffic pattern. At least three takeoffs and landings should be performed.
4. Postflight critique and preview of next lesson.

COMPLETION STANDARDS. The lesson will have been successfully completed when the student demonstrates solo competence in the selected presolo maneuvers performed and safely accomplishes the third supervised solo in the traffic pattern. The student should be able to perform short field takeoffs, soft field takeoffs, and maximum climbs without instructor assistance.

LESSON NO. 12—DUAL

OBJECTIVE. To refamiliarize the student with the local practice area and to improve proficiency in the presolo maneuvers in preparation for local area solo practice flights. To develop the student's ability to obtain radar and DF heading instructions and to become oriented in relation to a VOR, and to "home" to a nondirectional beacon using ADF. To introduce wheel landings (tail wheel airplanes).

CONTENT.

1. Preflight discussion.
2. Review.
   a. Practice area orientation.
   b. Power-off stalls (imminent and full) (VR and IR).
   c. Power-on stalls (imminent and full) (VR and IR).
   d. Maneuvering at minimum controllable airspeed (VR and IR).
   e. Turns around a point.
   f. Eights around pylons.
   g. Crosswind takeoffs and landings.
   h. 180° and 360° gliding approaches.
   i. Advanced emergency landings.
   j. Emergency procedures.
3. Introduction.
   a. Use of radar and DF heading instructions (VR and IR).
   b. VOR orientation (VR and IR).
   c. ADF "homing" (VR and IR).
   d. Wheel landings (tailwheel airplanes).
4. Postflight critique and preview of next lesson.

COMPLETION STANDARDS. The lesson will have been successfully completed when the student demonstrates an improved performance of the presolo maneuvers, is able to determine position in the local practice area by pilotage, VOR, or ADF; and can safely perform assigned maneuvers. The student should be competent in obtaining radar and DF heading instructions and in the performance of simulated emergency landings and emergency procedures.

LESSON NO. 13—SOLO

OBJECTIVE. To develop the student's confidence and proficiency through solo practice of assigned maneuvers.

CONTENT.

1. Preflight discussion.
2. Review.
   a. Normal and/or crosswind takeoffs and landings.
   b. Power-off stalls (imminent and full).
   c. Power-on stalls (imminent and full).
   d. Maneuvering at minimum controllable airspeed.
   e. Other maneuvers specified by the instructor during the preflight discussion.
3. Postflight critique and preview of next lesson.

COMPLETION STANDARDS. The lesson will have been successfully completed when the student has accomplished the solo review and practiced the basic and precision flight maneuvers, in addition to those specified by the instructor. The student should gain confidence and improve flying technique as a result of the solo practice period.

Now.

LESSON NO. 14—DUAL

OBJECTIVE. To improve the student's proficiency in previously covered procedures and maneuvers and to review advanced emergency landings, emergency procedures, and orientation by means of VOR and/or ADF.

CONTENT.
1. Preflight discussion.
2. Review.
   a. Normal and/or crosswind takeoffs and landings.
   b. Power-off stalls (imminent and full) (VR and IR).
   c. Power-on stalls (imminent and full) (VR and IR).
   d. Maneuvering at minimum controllable airspeed (VR and IR).
   e. Accelerated stalls.
   f. Eights around pylons.
   g. Short field and soft field takeoffs and landings.
   h. Advanced emergency landings.
   i. Emergency procedures.
   j. Orientation by means of VOR and/or ADF.
8. Postflight critique and preview of next lesson.

COMPLETION STANDARDS. The lesson will have been successfully completed when the student demonstrates an increased proficiency in previously covered procedures and maneuvers. The student should be able to maintain airspeed within ±10 knots, altitude within ±100 feet, and heading within ±10° of that desired.

LESSON NO. 15—SOLO

OBJECTIVE. To further develop the student's confidence and proficiency through solo practice of assigned maneuvers.

CONTENT.
1. Preflight discussion.
2. Review.
   a. Normal and/or crosswind takeoffs and landings.
   b. Turns around a point.
   c. Eights around pylons.
   d. Other maneuvers specified by the instructor during the preflight discussion.
3. Postflight critique and preview of next lesson.

COMPLETION STANDARDS. The lesson will have been successfully completed when the student has accomplished the solo review and thereby increased proficiency and confidence.

LESSON NO. 16—DUAL

OBJECTIVE. To develop the student's ability to plan, plot, and fly a 2-hour day cross-country flight with landings at two unfamiliar airports; to develop the student's proficiency in navigating by means of pilotage, dead reckoning, VOR, and/or ADF; and to develop the ability to take proper action in emergency situations.

CONTENT.

1. Preflight discussion.
   a. Planning flight, including weather check.
   b. Plotting course.
   c. Preparing log.
   d. Filing and closing VFR flight plan.
2. Introduction.
   a. Filing VFR flight plan.
   b. Pilotage.
   c. Dead reckoning.
   d. Tracking VOR radial and/or homing by ADF (VR and IR).
   e. Departure, en route, and arrival radio communications.
   f. Simulated diversion to an alternate airport.
   g. Unfamiliar airport procedures.
   h. Emergencies, including DF and radar heading instructions (VR and IR).
   i. Closing VFR flight plan.
3. Postflight critique and preview of next lesson.

COMPLETION STANDARDS. The lesson will have been successfully completed when, with instructor assistance, the student is able to perform the cross-country preflight planning, fly the planned course making necessary off-course corrections, and can make appropriate radio communications. The student should be competent in navigating by means of pilotage, dead reckoning, VOR, and/or ADF, and when so instructed, is able to accurately plan and fly a diversion to an alternate airport.

LESSON NO. 17—DUAL

OBJECTIVE. To improve the student's proficiency in cross-country operations through the planning, plotting, and flying of a second dual 2-hour day cross-country flight, with landings at two unfamiliar airports. To improve the student's competence in navigating by means of pilotage, dead reckoning, VOR, and ADF; and to further develop the ability to take proper action in emergency situations.

CONTENT.

1. Preflight discussion.
   a. Planning flight, including weather check.
   b. Plotting course.
   c. Preparing log.
   d. Filing and closing VFR flight plan.
2. Review.
   a. Filing VFR flight plan.
   b. Pilotage and dead reckoning.
   c. Radio navigation (VOR and/or ADF) (VR and IR).
   d. Departure, en route, and arrival radio communications.
   e. Simulated diversion to an alternate airport.
   f. Unfamiliar airport procedures.
   g. Emergencies, including DF and radar heading instructions (VR and IR).
   h. Closing VFR flight plan.
3. Postflight critique and preview of next lesson.

COMPLETION STANDARDS. The lesson will have been successfully completed when the student, with minimum instructor assistance, is able to plan, plot, and fly the planned course. Estimated times of arrival should be accurate with an apparent error of not more than 10 minutes. Any off-course corrections should be accomplished accurately and promptly. The student should be able to give the instructor an accurate position report at any time without hesitation. When given a "simulated lost" situation, the student should be able to initiate and follow an apppropriate "lost procedure."

LESSON NO. 18—SOLO

OBJECTIVE. To develop the student's ability to plan, plot, and fly a 3-hour solo day cross-country flight, with landings at two unfamiliar airports, thereby improving proficiency and confidence in the conduct of future solo cross-country flights. To improve the student's proficiency in navigating by means of pilotage, dead reckoning, VOR, and/or ADF; and to increase the ability to cope with new or unexpected flight situations.

CONTENT.

1. Preflight discussion.
   a. Planning flight, including weather check.
   b. Plotting course.
   c. Preparing log.
   d. Filing and closing VFR flight plan.
   e. Procedure at unfamiliar airports.
   f. Emergencies.
2. Review.
   a. Filing VFR flight plan.
   b. Pilotage.
   c. Dead reckoning.
   d. Radio navigation (VOR and/or ADF).
   e. Departure, en route, and arrival radio communications.
   f. Unfamiliar airport procedures.
   g. Closing VFR flight plan.
3. Postflight critique and preview of next lesson.

COMPLETION STANDARDS. The lesson will have been successfully completed when the student is able to plan, plot, and fly the 3-hour cross-country flight as assigned by the instructor. The instructor should determine how well the flight was conducted through oral questioning.

LESSON NO. 19—DUAL AND SOLO

OBJECTIVE. To develop the student's ability to make solo night flights in the local practice area and airport traffic pattern. To familiarize the student with such aspects of night operations as: night vision, night orientation, judgment of distance, use of cockpit lights, position lights, landing lights, and night emergency procedures.

CONTENT.

1. Preflight discussion.
   a. Night vision and vertigo.
   b. Orientation in local area.
   c. Judgment of distance.
   d. Aircraft lights.
   e. Airport lights.
   f. Taxi technique.
   g. Takeoff and landing technique.
   h. Collision avoidance.
   i. Unusual attitude recovery.
   j. Emergencies.
2. Introduction.
   a. Night visual inspection.
   b. Use of cockpit lights.
   c. Taxi techniques.
   d. Takeoff and traffic departure.
   e. Area orientation.
   f. Interpretation of aircraft and airport lights.
   g. Recovery from unusual attitudes (VR and IR).
   h. Radio communications.
   i. Traffic entry.
   j. Power approaches and full-stop landings.
   k. Use of landing lights.
   l. Simulated electrical failure to include at least one black-out landing.
3. Postflight critique and preview of next lesson.

COMPLETION STANDARDS. The lesson will have been successfully completed when the student displays the ability to maintain orientation in the local flying area and traffic pattern, can accurately interpret aircraft and runway lights, and can competently fly the traffic pattern and perform takeoffs and landings. The student should display, through oral quizzing and demonstrations, competence in performing night emergency procedures. At least five takeoffs and landings should be accomplished.

LESSON NO. 20—DUAL

OBJECTIVE. To develop the student's ability to plan, plot, and fly a 1½-hour night cross-country flight around a triangular course with at least one landing at an unfamiliar airport. To develop the student's competence in navigating at night by means of pilotage, dead reckoning, and VOR or ADF; and to develop the student's ability to take proper action in night emergency situations.

CONTENT.

1. Preflight discussion.
   a. Planning 1½-hour night cross-country flight, including weather check.
   b. Plotting course.
   c. Preparing log.
   d. Filing and closing VFR flight plan.

2. Introduction.
   a. Filing VFR flight plan.
   b. Proper use of cockpit lights and flashlight for chart reading.
   c. Pilotage—factors peculiar to night flying.
   d. Dead reckoning.
   e. Tracking VOR radial and/or homing by ADF.
   f. Departure, en route, and arrival radio communications.
   g. Simulated diversion to an alternate airport.
   h. Emergencies, including simulated failure of electrical system, also DF and radar heading instructions.
   i. Closing VFR flight plan.

3. Postflight critique and preview of next lesson.

COMPLETION STANDARDS. The lesson will have been successfully completed when, with minimum assistance from the instructor, the student is able to perform the night cross-country preflight planning, fly the planned course making necessary off-course corrections, and can make appropriate radio communications. The student should be competent in navigating by means of pilotage, dead reckoning, and VOR or ADF. The student should have a thorough knowledge of night emergency procedures.

LESSON NO. 21—SOLO

OBJECTIVE. To further develop the student's competence in cross-country operations through the planning, plotting, and flying of a second solo 3-hour day cross-country flight with landings at two unfamiliar airports. To improve the student's proficiency in navigating by means of pilotage, dead reckoning, VOR, and/or ADF; and to further increase the student's confidence and ability to properly handle unexpected flight situations.

CONTENT.

1. Preflight discussion.
   a. Planning flight, including weather check.
   b. Plotting course.
   c. Preparing log.
   d. Filing and closing VFR flight plan.
   e. Procedure at unfamiliar airports.
   f. Emergencies.

2. Review.
   a. Filing VFR flight plan.
   b. Pilotage and dead reckoning.
   c. Radio navigation (VOR and/or ADF).
   d. Departure, en route, and arrival radio procedures.
   e. Unfamiliar airport procedures.
   f. Closing VFR flight plan.

3. Postflight critique and preview of next lesson.

COMPLETION STANDARDS. The lesson will have been successfully completed when the student is able to plan, plot, and fly the second 3-hour day cross-country flight as assigned by the instructor. The instructor should determine how well the flight was conducted through oral questioning.

LESSON NO. 22—SOLO

OBJECTIVE. To further develop the student's competence in cross-country operations through the planning, plotting, and flying of a solo 4-hour day cross-country flight, with landings at three unfamiliar airports, each of which is more than 100 nautical miles from the other airports.

CONTENT.

1. Preflight discussion.
   a. Planning flight, including weather check.
   b. Plotting course.
   c. Preparing log.
   d. Filing and closing VFR flight plan.
   e. Procedure at unfamiliar airports.
   f. Emergencies.

2. Review.
   a. Filing VFR flight plan.
   b. Pilotage and dead reckoning.
   c. Radio navigation (VOR and/or ADF).
   d. Departure, en route, and arrival radio communications.
   e. Unfamiliar airport procedures.
   f. Closing VFR flight plan.

3. Postflight critique and preview of next lesson.

COMPLETION STANDARDS. The lesson will have been successfully completed when the student is able to plan, plot, and fly the 4-hour day cross-country flight as assigned by the instructor. The instructor should determine how well the flight was conducted through oral questioning.

LESSON NO. 23—DUAL

OBJECTIVE. To develop precision in the student's performance of procedures and maneuvers covered previously with emphasis directed to stalls.

CONTENT.

1. Preflight discussion.

2. Review.
   a. Power-off stalls (imminent and full) (VR and IR).
   b. Power-on stalls (imminent and full) (VR and IR).
   c. Maneuvering at minimum controllable airspeed (VR and IR).
   d. 180° and 360° gliding approaches.
   e. Advanced emergency landings.
   f. Slips.
   g. Crosswind takeoffs and landings.
   h. Short field and soft field takeoffs and landings.
   i. Emergency procedures.

3. Introduction of ASR approaches.

4. Postflight critique and preview of next lesson.

COMPLETION STANDARDS. The lesson will have been successfully completed when the student demonstrates improved performance in the various maneuvers given. The student should be able to make ASR approaches with minimum instructor assistance.

LESSON NO. 24—SOLO

OBJECTIVE. To further develop the student's competence through solo practice of assigned maneuvers. Emphasis will be directed to stalls.

CONTENT.

1. Preflight discussion.
2. Review.
   a. Power-on and power-off stalls (imminent and full).
   b. Maneuvering at minimum controllable airspeed.
   c. Short field and soft field takeoffs and landings.
   d. Other maneuvers assigned by the instructor during preflight discussion.
3. Postflight critique and preview of next lesson.

COMPLETION STANDARDS. The lesson will have been successfully completed when the student has accomplished the solo review and practiced the basic and precision flight maneuvers in addition to those specified by the instructor. The student should gain confidence and improve flying technique as a result of the solo practice period.

LESSON NO. 25—DUAL

OBJECTIVE. To develop improved performance and precision in the procedures and maneuvers covered previously with emphasis directed to ground track maneuvers.

CONTENT.

1. Preflight discussion.
2. Review.
   a. Maneuvering at minimum controllable airspeed.
   b. Turns around a point.
   c. Eights around pylons.
   d. 180° and 360° gliding approaches.
   e. Advanced emergency landings.
   f. Slips.
   g. Crosswind takeoffs and landings.
   h. Wheel landings (tail wheel airplane).
   i. ASR approach.
3. Postflight critique and preview of next lesson.

COMPLETION STANDARDS. The lesson will have been successfully completed when the student demonstrates improved performance in the maneuvers given.

LESSON NO. 26—SOLO

OBJECTIVE. To further develop the student's competence through solo practice of assigned maneuvers. Emphasis will be directed to ground track maneuvers.

CONTENT.

1. Preflight discussion.
2. Review.
   a. Turns around a point.
   b. Eights around pylons.
   c. Short and soft field takeoffs and landings.
   d. Wheel landings (tail wheel airplanes).
   e. Other maneuvers assigned by the instructor during the preflight discussion.
3. Postflight critique and preview of next lesson.

COMPLETION STANDARDS. The lesson will have been successfully completed when the student has accomplished the solo review. The student should gain proficiency in the ground track and other maneuvers assigned by the instructor.

LESSON NO. 27—SOLO

OBJECTIVE. To improve the student's proficiency in the pilot operations required on the private pilot (airplane) flight check.

CONTENT.

1. Preflight discussion.
2. Review.
   a. Ground track maneuvers.
   b. Power-on and power-off stalls (imminent and full).
   c. Maneuvering at minimum controllable airspeed.
   d. Crosswind takeoffs and landings.
   e. Other maneuvers assigned by the instructor during the preflight discussion.
3. Postflight critique and preview of next lesson.

COMPLETION STANDARDS. The lesson will have been successfully completed when the student has gained proficiency in the procedures and maneuvers assigned by the instructor.

LESSON NO. 28—DUAL

OBJECTIVE. To evaluate the student's performance of the procedures and maneuvers necessary to conduct flight operations as a private pilot.

CONTENT.

1. Preflight discussion.
2. Review.
   a. Power-on and power-off stalls (imminent and full).
   b. Maneuvering at minimum controllable airspeed.
   c. Ground track maneuvers.
   d. 180° and 360° gliding approaches.
   e. Advanced emergency landings.
   f. Short field and soft field takeoffs and landings.
   g. Crosswind takeoffs and landings.
   h. Straight-and-level flight, turns, climbs, descents, and recovery from unusual attitudes by reference to flight instruments.
   i. Tracking VOR radial and homing by ADF (VR and IR).
   j. Use of radar and DF heading instructions (VR and IR).
   k. ASR approach (VR and IR).
   l. Emergency operations.

COMPLETION STANDARDS. The lesson will have been successfully completed when the student satisfactorily performs the procedures and maneuvers selected to show competence in the pilot operations listed in the Private Pilot Practical Test Standards.

APPENDIX D
AVIATION WEATHER REPORTS AND FORECASTS

Surface Aviation Weather Report (SA) 487
Satellite Weather Pictures 493
Area Forecast (FA) 493
Terminal Forecast (FT) 496
Inflight Advisories (WST, WS, WA, CWA) 498
Pilot Weather Report (PIREP) 501
Radar Weather Report (RAREP) 502
Surface Analysis Chart 504
Weather Depiction Chart 508
Radar Summary Chart 510
Low-Level Prognostic Charts 512
Winds and Temperatures Aloft Forecast (FD) 514
Composite Moisture Stability Charts 516
Severe Weather Outlook Chart 518
Constant Pressure Analysis Charts 519

This appendix provides additional discussion and illustration to supplement the 9-page outline in Task I.B., Obtaining Weather Information, on page 89.

SURFACE AVIATION WEATHER REPORT (SA)

A. All Flight Service Stations (FSSs) make on-the-hour weather observations which are computerized and transmitted to all other FSSs.

B. A surface aviation weather report, also known as a sequence report, contains some or all of the following elements in the same sequence in every report:

1. Station designator.
2. Type and time of report.
3. Sky conditions and ceiling.
4. Visibility.
5. Weather and obstructions to vision.
6. Sea level pressure (mb).
7. Temperature and dewpoint.
8. Wind direction, speed, and character.
9. Altimeter setting (in. of Hg).
10. Remarks.

C.   An example of a Surface Aviation Weather Report is presented below. Its elements are numbered according to the list on the previous page. Then the interpretation for each numbered element is given.

SLC   SA 1251   M50 BKN   3   K   175   75/68   3010   003   VIRGA ALQDS
 1   2   3   4   5   6   7   8   9   10

1.   Salt Lake City.
2.   Record observation.
3.   Measured ceiling 5,000 ft. broken.
4.   Visibility 3 SM.
5.   Smoke.
6.   Pressure 1017.5 millibars.
7.   Temperature 75°F, dewpoint 68°F.
8.   Wind 300° at 10 kt.
9.   Altimeter setting 30.03.
10.   Remarks: Virga exists in all quadrants.

D.   Elements not occurring at the time of observation or not pertinent are omitted. When an element should be included but is unavailable, the letter "M" is transmitted in lieu of the missing element (remember, however, that M before the ceiling height indicates measured).

E.   Station designator (element 1). The station designator is a three-letter location identifier assigned to reporting stations located at airports.

F.   Type and time of report (element 2). There are two basic types of reports:

1.   Record observations (SA) are reports taken on the hour.

2.   Special reports (RS or SP) are observations taken when needed to report significant changes in weather.

a.   A record special (RS) reports a significant change in weather on the hour.

b.   A special (SP) is an observation taken other than on the hour to report a significant change in weather.

G.   Sky conditions and ceiling (element 3).

1.   A ceiling designator always precedes the height of the ceiling layer:

Coded	Meaning	Spoken
M	MEASURED. Heights determined by ceilometer, ceiling light, cloud detection radar, or by the unobscured portion of a landmark protruding into ceiling layer.	MEASURED CEILING
E	ESTIMATED. Heights determined from pilot reports, balloons, or other measurements not meeting criteria for measured ceiling.	ESTIMATED CEILING
W	INDEFINITE. Vertical visibility into a surface based obstruction. Regardless of method of determination, vertical visibility is classified as an indefinite ceiling.	INDEFINITE CEILING

2.   A layer is defined as clouds or obscuring phenomena with the base at approximately the same level.

3.   The height of the base of a layer precedes the sky cover designator. It is given in hundreds of ft. above ground level.

4. The sky condition is reported in SAs using the designators illustrated below.

	Meaning	Spoken
CLR	CLEAR. (Less than 0.1 sky cover.)	CLEAR
SCT	SCATTERED LAYER ALOFT. (0.1 through 0.5 sky cover.)	SCATTERED
BKN°	BROKEN LAYER ALOFT. (0.6 through 0.9 sky cover.)	BROKEN
OVC°	OVERCAST LAYER ALOFT. (More than 0.9, or 1.0 sky cover.)	OVERCAST
−SCT	THIN SCATTERED. } At least ½ of the sky cover aloft is transparent at and below the level of the layer aloft.	THIN SCATTERED
−BKN	THIN BROKEN.	THIN BROKEN
−OVC	THIN OVERCAST.	THIN OVERCAST
X°	SURFACE BASED OBSTRUCTION. (All of sky is hidden by surface based phenomena.)	SKY OBSCURED
−X	SURFACE BASED PARTIAL OBSCURATION. (0.1 or more, but not all, of sky is hidden by surface based phenomena.)	SKY PARTIALLY OBSCURED

* Sky condition represented by this designator may constitute a ceiling layer.

5. When more than one layer is reported, layers are given in ascending order according to height. For each layer above a lower layer or layers, the sky cover designator for that layer represents the total sky covered by that layer and all lower layers.

   a. EXAMPLE: 7 SCT 15 SCT E30 BKN, reports three layers:

   1) A scattered layer at 700 ft.

   2) Another scattered layer at 1,500 ft.

   3) A top layer estimated to be at 3,000 ft. In this case it is assumed that the total sky covered by all the layers exceeds 5/10. Therefore, the upper layer is reported as "estimated 3,000 ft. broken."

6. A scattered, broken, or overcast layer may be reported as "thin." To be classified as thin, a layer must be half or more transparent (remember that sky cover of a layer includes all sky cover below the layer).

   a. EXAMPLE: If the blue sky is observed at a station as being visible through half or more of the total sky cover reported by the higher layer, the sky report could appear as 8 SCT 350 -SCT which reads "800 ft. scattered, 35,000 ft. thin scattered."

7. Any phenomenon based at the surface and hiding all or part of the sky is reported as SKY OBSCURED (X) or SKY PARTIALLY OBSCURED (−X).

   a. An obscuration or partial obscuration may be precipitation, fog, dust, blowing snow, etc.

   b. No height value precedes the designator for partial obscuration if vertical visibility is not restricted overhead; e.g., −XM40 OVC reads as "sky partially obscured measured ceiling 4,000 ft. overcast."

   c. A height value precedes the designator for an obscuration and denotes the vertical visibility into the phenomena; e.g., W5 X reads as "indefinite ceiling 500 ft. sky obscured."

8. Ceiling is defined as either

   a. Vertical visibility into a surface-based obscuring phenomenon that hides all the sky, or

   b. Height of the lowest layer of clouds or obscuring phenomenon aloft that are reported as broken or overcast and not classified as thin.

9.   The letter "V" appended to the ceiling height indicates a variable ceiling; the range of the variability is shown in the remarks element of the report. Variable ceiling is reported only when it is critical to terminal operations.

   a.   EXAMPLE: M15V OVC and in the remarks CIG 15V18 means "measured ceiling 1,500 ft. variable overcast; ceiling variable between 1,500 and 1,800 ft."

H.   Visibility (element 4). Prevailing visibility is the greatest distance objects can be seen and identified through at least 180° of the horizon. Visibility is reported in statute miles (SM) and fractions. Prevailing visibility always follows the sky and ceiling element.

   1.   EXAMPLE: 1-1/2 means "visibility 1½ SM."

   2.   When visibility is critical at an airport with a weather observing station and a control tower, both facilities take visibility observations. When tower visibility is less than 4 SM, the lowest reported visibility of the two observations is the prevailing visibility. The other is reported in the remarks.

   a.   EXAMPLE: TWR VSBY 1/4 means "tower visibility ¼ SM."

   3.   The letter "V" suffixed to prevailing visibility denotes variable visibility; the range of visibility is shown in the remarks.

   a.   EXAMPLE: 3/4V and in the remarks, VSBY 1/2V1 means "visibility three quarters variable; visibility variable between ½ and 1 SM."

I.   Weather and obstructions to vision (element 5). When occurring at the station during the time of observation, weather and obstructions to vision are reported in the element immediately following visibility. If weather and obstructions to vision are observed at a distance from the station, they are reported in the remarks.

   1.   Weather symbols and meanings:

Coded	Spoken	Coded	Spoken
Tornado	TORNADO	ZL	FREEZING DRIZZLE
Funnel Cloud	FUNNEL CLOUD	A	HAIL
Waterspout	WATERSPOUT	IP	ICE PELLETS
T	THUNDERSTORM	IPW	ICE PELLET SHOWERS
T+	SEVERE THUNDERSTORM	S	SNOW
R	RAIN	SW	SNOW SHOWERS
RW	RAIN SHOWER	SP	SNOW PELLETS
L	DRIZZLE	SG	SNOW GRAINS
ZR	FREEZING RAIN	IC	ICE CRYSTALS

   a.   Precipitation is reported in one of three intensities. It follows the weather symbol.

   LIGHT   –
   MODERATE   (No sign)
   HEAVY   +

   b.   No intensity is reported for hail (A) or ice crystals (IC).
   c.   A thunderstorm is reported as "T" and a severe thunderstorm as "T+."

      1)   A *severe thunderstorm* is one in which surface wind is 50 kt. or greater and/or hail is 3/4 in. or more in diameter.

2. Obstructions to vision symbols and meanings:

Coded	Spoken
BD	BLOWING DUST
BN	BLOWING SAND
BS	BLOWING SNOW
BY	BLOWING SPRAY
D	DUST
F	FOG
GF	GROUND FOG
H	HAZE
IF	ICE FOG
K	SMOKE

    a. No intensities are reported for obstructions to vision.

3. EXAMPLE: 1-1/2 R+F means "visibility 1½ mi., heavy rain and fog."

4. When obscuring phenomena are surface based and partially obscure the sky, the remarks element reports tenths of sky hidden.

    a. D3 means 3/10 of the sky is hidden by dust.
    b. RF2 means 2/10 of the sky is hidden by rain and fog.

J. Sea level pressure (element 6). Sea level pressure reported in millibars (mb) follows the visibility or weather and obstruction to vision in the SA report. It is transmitted in three digits to the nearest tenth mb, with the decimal point omitted. Sea level pressure normally is greater than 960.0 mb and less than 1050.0 mb. The first 9 or 10 is omitted.

1. To decode, prefix a 9 or 10, whichever brings it closer to 1000.0 mb.

2. EXAMPLE:

As Reported	Decoded
980	998.0 mb
191	1019.1 mb
752	975.2 mb
456	1045.6 mb

K. Temperature and dewpoint (element 7). The next element in the SA report contains the temperature and dewpoint given in whole degrees Fahrenheit (°F).

1. A slash (/) separates the temperature element from the sea level pressure element. If the sea level pressure is not transmitted, a space separates the temperature from the preceding elements.

2. A slash also separates the temperature and the dewpoint.

3. A minus sign precedes the temperature or dewpoint when either of these temperatures is below 0°F.

4. EXAMPLE: /82/59 means "temperature 82°F, dewpoint 59°F."

L.   Wind (element 8). The surface wind element follows the dewpoint and is separated from it by a slash.

    1.   The wind is observed for 1 min. and the average direction and speed are reported in four digits.

        a.   The first two digits are the direction FROM which the wind is blowing. It is in tens of degrees referenced to true NORTH.

            1)   On the other hand, wind direction when verbally broadcast for the local station is referenced to magnetic. This is done so that you can more closely relate the wind direction to the landing runway.

            2)   When spoken, three digits are used. For instance, a wind from 10° is stated as 010°; 210° is stated as 210°.

            3)   To conserve space on the report the last digit (0) is omitted, i.e., 020° appears as 02, and 220° appears as 22.

        b.   The second two digits of the wind element are the wind speed in kt. A calm wind is reported as 0000.

        c.   EXAMPLE: 3010 means "wind is from 300° at 10 kt."

    2.   If the wind speed is 100 kt. or greater, 50 is added to the direction code and the hundreds digit of the speed is omitted.

        a.   EXAMPLE: 8315 can be recognized as a wind speed of 100 kt. or more because the first two digits are greater than 36 (36 represents a direction of 360° which is the largest number of degrees on the compass).

        b.   To decode, subtract 50 from 83 (83 − 50 = 33) and add 100 to the last two digits (15 + 100 = 115). The wind is from 330° at 115 kt.

    3.   A gust is a variation in wind speed of at least 10 kt. between peak winds and lulls. A squall is a sudden increase in speed of at least 15 kt. to a sustained speed of 20 kt. or more which lasts for at least 1 min. Gusts or squalls are reported by the letter "G" or "Q" respectively, following the average 1-min. wind speed. The peak speed of the gust or squall in kt. follows the letter.

        a.   EXAMPLE: 2123G38 means wind from 210° at 23 kt. gusting to peak speed of 38 kt.

    4.   When any part of the wind report is estimated, the letter "E" precedes the wind group.

        a.   EXAMPLE: E3122Q27 means wind from 310° estimated at 22 kt. with peak speed in squalls estimated at 27 kt.

M.   Altimeter setting (element 9). This element follows the wind group in an SA report and is separated by a slash. The normal range for altimeter settings is from 28.00 in. to 31.00 in. of Hg.

    1.   Only the last three digits are transmitted with the decimal point omitted.

    2.   To decode, prefix the coded value in the report with either a 2 or 3, whichever brings it closer to 30.00 in.

        a.   EXAMPLES:

            1)   998 means "altimeter setting 29.98 (in. of Hg)."
            2)   025 means "altimeter setting 30.25 (in. of Hg)."

N. Remarks (element 10). The remarks are the last element in an SA report. It too is separated from the altimeter setting by a slash. Remarks are added to cover unusual aspects of the weather. This element often contains information that is as important to you as that found in the main body of the report. Certain remarks are reported routinely, while others may be mentioned only when considered significant to aviation.

    1. The first part of the remarks element, when transmitted, is runway visibility or runway visual range.

        a. Runway visibility (VV) is the visibility from a particular location along an identified runway. It is reported in miles and fractions.

            1) EXAMPLE: R22VV1-1/2 means "runway 22, visibility 1½ mi."

        b. Runway visual range (VR) is the maximum horizontal distance down a specified runway at which a pilot can see and identify standard high intensity runway lights. It is reported in hundreds of ft.

            1) EXAMPLE: R30VR10V20 means "runway 30 visual range variable between 1,000 and 2,000 ft."

    2. The second part of the remarks element pertains to heights of bases and tops of sky cover layers, or obscuring phenomena. These remarks originate from pilots and are prefixed by "UA" which identifies the message as a pilot report. An additional "U" preceding the "UA" indicates an urgent report.

    3. The freezing level data, if applicable, are shown in the remarks of stations equipped with upper air observation equipment.

    4. Notices to Airmen (NOTAMs) may be added to the end of an SA report or transmitted as separate lines of information.

SATELLITE WEATHER PICTURES

A. Before weather satellites came into use, weather observations were limited to ground weather reports and PIREPs. At FSSs, weather satellites provide pictures of cloud cover every 30 min.

    1. These satellite photos are available in FSSs, on TV weather broadcasts, in newspapers, etc.

    2. They provide a photograph of weather (clouds) which may adversely affect your flight.

B. Infrared photos are also available to provide information about temperatures.

AREA FORECAST (FA)

A. An Area Forecast (FA) is a forecast of general weather conditions over an area consisting of several states or portions of states. You will use them for information about expected en route weather conditions and also to obtain an insight to weather conditions that might be expected at airports where weather reports or forecasts are not issued.

    1. Area Forecasts are issued every 8 hr. for a total validity period of 18 hr. This validity period includes expected weather for the following 12-hr. period with an additional 6-hr. categorical outlook.

        a. The time used in these forecasts is based on Coordinated Universal Time (UTC). It is stated in whole hr. with two digits and Z for Zulu time, e.g., 13Z.

        b. All distances except visibility are in NM. Visibility is in SM.

B.   Each FA is arranged using the same format (see Task I.B., Obtaining Weather Information, on page 89).

C.   EXAMPLE: The following is an excerpt from an FA.

    1.   MIAH FA 231945 AMD 1
       HAZARDS VALID UNTIL 240700

    2.   NC SC GA FL AND CSTL WTRS

    3.   FLT PRCTNS . . . IFR . . . NC SC GA AND CSTL WTRS
             . . . MTN OBSCN . . . NC SC GA
             . . . TURBC . . . NC SC GA
             . . . TSTMS . . . NC SC GA FL AND CSTL WTRS

    4.   TSTMS IMPLY SVR OR GTR TURBO SVR ICG LLWS AND IFR CONDS.

    5.   NON MSL HGTS NOTED BY AGL OR CIG.
       . . . .

    6.   MIAC FA 231845
       SYNOPSIS AND VFR CLDS/WX
       SYNOPSIS VALID UNTIL 241300
       CLDS/WX VALID UNTIL 240700 . . . OTLK VALID 240700-241300

    7.   SYNOPSIS . . . SFC LOW MOVG EWD ACRS TN THRU 06Z AND ACRS SRN VA
       06-13Z. A WMFNT E OF THE LOW MOVG NEWD ACRS NRN GA/CAROLINAS.
       DEEP MSTR N OF THE LOW/WMFNT MOVG SPRDG NWD. DRY STBL AMS SPRDG
       INTO WRN GA AT 19Z SPRDG EWD ACRS GA/SC AND NEWD INTO NC BY 13Z.

    8.   NC
       SEE AIRMET SIERRA FOR IFR AND MTN OBSCN.
       MTNS . . . 30 BKN-OVC 50 OVC LYRD 240. VSBY 3-5R-F. 22-00Z BCMG 30
        SCT-BKN 50 BKN LYRD 150. OCNL VSBY 3-5 IN SCT RW–. ISOLD TRW–.
        CB TOPS TO 350. OTLK . . . MVFR CIG RW F.
       RMNDR . . . 15-30 OVC. VSBY 3-5R-F. WDLY SCT EMBDD TRW PSBLY SVR. CB
        TOPS TO 450. 02-06Z BCMG 25 SCT-BKN 50 BKN LYRD 150. OCNL VSBY
        3-5 IN SCT RW–. ISOLD TRW–. OTLK . . . MVFR CIG RW F.

Interpretation:

    1.   The heading of the example states that this section of the FA deals with the Hazards/Flight Precautions section (H) and was issued on the 23rd day of the month at 1945 UTC for the Miami (MIA) forecast area. The hazards listed may be valid for the forecast period from 1945 UTC until 0700 UTC the next day.

       a.   Note that this is amendment 1 (AMD 1) to the FA for this section. This section was updated from the original forecast at 1900 UTC.

    2.   Forecast area (for all MIA FAs) includes NC, SC, GA, FL, and coastal waters (CSTL WTRS).

    3.   Flight Precaution statement. This states that IFR, mountain obscurations (MTN OBSCN), turbulence (TURBC), and thunderstorms (TSTMS) are forecast within the forecast period for the listed states within the designated FA boundaries.

4. "Thunderstorms imply severe or greater turbulence, severe icing, low-level wind shear, and IFR conditions." This statement is a reminder of the hazards existing in all thunderstorms and, thus, are not spelled out within the body of the FA.

5. All heights are MLS, unless noted by AGL or CIG.

    a. AGL means above ground level.

    b. CIG is a contraction for ceiling, which by definition is always expressed above ground.

6. Synopsis and VFR Clouds/Weather (C) heading also states the valid times of the synopsis, clouds and weather, and the outlook.

7. The synopsis briefly summarizes the location and movements of fronts, pressure systems, and circulation patterns for an 18-hr. period.

    a. In the example, a surface low is moving eastward across TN thru 0600Z (UTC) and across southern VA. From 0600Z-1300Z a warm front east of the low will be moving northeastward across northern GA and the Carolinas. Deep moisture north of the low/warm front moving and spreading northward. Dry stable air mass will be spreading into western GA at 1900Z, then spreading eastward across GA/SC and northeastward into NC by 1300Z.

8. VFR Clouds and Weather is a state-by-state summary of the forecast.

    a. Under each state it will refer you to any AIRMETs, which are listed at the end of the FA. (See the sideheading, Inflight Advisories, beginning on page 498).

    b. Obstructions to vision are included when forecast visibility is 6 SM or less. Expected precipitation or thunderstorms are always included.

    c. All heights are abbreviated by omitting the last two zeros. For example, 10,000 ft. is written as 100 and 1,500 ft. is written as 15.

    d. The following is a list of contractions and their definitions used to denote sky conditions in Area Forecasts (FA). These are listed along with the contractions or designators used in Terminal Forecasts (FT) so that a comparison can be made. Terminal Forecasts are discussed in the next sideheading.

FA Contraction	FT Designator	Definition
CLR	CLR	Sky Clear
SCT	SCT	Scattered
BKN	BKN	Broken
OVC	OVC	Overcast
OBSC	X	Obscured, obscure, or obscuring
PTLY OBSC	–X	Partially Obscured
THN	–	Thin
VRBL	V	Variable
CIG	C	Ceiling
INDEF	W	Indefinite

1) The following is a list of adjectives and their meanings as used to describe area coverage of showers and thunderstorms:

Adjectives	Coverage
Isolated	Extremely small number.
Few	15% or less of area or line.
Scattered	16% to 45% of area or line.
Numerous	More than 45% of area or line.

e.   The categorical outlook on the FA, identified by the contraction "OTLK," is found at the end of each paragraph in this section. It describes the outlook (valid for 6 hr.) for that particular area.

1)   Both Area Forecasts and Terminal Forecasts group ceiling and visibilities into categories which are used in the categorical outlook for these forecasts. The categorical outlook extends the Area Forecasts and the Terminal Forecasts for 6 hr. These outlooks are intended primarily for advanced flight planning.

LIFR (Low IFR)	Ceiling less than 500 ft. and/or visibility less than 1 SM.
IFR	Ceiling 500 to less than 1,000 ft. and/or visibility 1 to less than 3 SM.
MVFR (Marginal VFR)	Ceiling 1,000 to 3,000 ft. and/or visibility 3 to 5 SM inclusive.
VFR	Ceiling greater than 3,000 ft. and visibility greater than 5 SM; includes clear sky.

2)   In the example, the outlook (from 0700Z to 1300Z on the 24th) for NC (for both mountains and remainder) is marginal VFR due to ceilings in rain showers and fog.

TERMINAL FORECAST (FT)

A.   A Terminal Forecast (FT) differs from an FA in that the FT is a prediction of weather conditions to be expected for a specific airport rather than a larger area. The area covered in a Terminal Forecast is within a 5-NM radius of the center of the runway complex.

B.   Scheduled Terminal Forecasts are issued three times daily by Weather Service Forecast Offices (WSFOs) and are valid for a period of 24 hr. This validity period includes expected weather for the following 18 hr. with an additional 6-hr. categorical outlook.

C.   The format of the FT is essentially the same as that of the SA report, which was outlined on page 487 earlier in this appendix. If you can read and interpret the SAs, you should have no difficulty in reading FTs.

D.   Generally, the FT includes expected ceiling and clouds, visibility, weather and obstructions to vision, and surface wind conditions at each terminal. Also included are remarks that more completely describe expected weather. If a change is expected during the forecast period, this change and expected time of change are included. The last item included on each Terminal Forecast is the 6-hr. categorical outlook using the form as discussed for the FA.

E.   The following are examples of several Terminal Forecasts issued within the state of Texas on the 29th day of the month at 1440Z.

```
TX 291440
ABI 291515 100 SCT 250-BKN 1812. 18Z 50 SCT 100 SCT 250-BKN CHC C20X 1TRW+
   09Z VFR CHC TRW/RW..
ACT 291515 250 SCT 1910. 17Z 50 SCT 1910. 01Z 250 SCT. 09Z VFR..
ALI 291515  12 SCT SCT V BKN.  17Z 20 SCT ¦510 SCT OCNLY BKN. 20Z 35 SCT 1512
   OCNLY C35 BKN.  00Z CLR.  09Z VFR BCMG MVFR CIG 12Z..
AMA 291515 250 SCT 2310. 19Z 40 SCT 2312 SLGT CHC C20 BKN 2TRW G30. 02Z 250
   SCT 2010. 09Z VFR CLR..
```

1.   To aid in the interpretation and understanding, the FT for Abilene (ABI) has been divided into elements and lettered. This is followed by a plain language description or interpretation.

ABI   291515   100 SCT 250-BKN   _____ _____ 1812.
 a   b   c   d   e   f

_____ 18Z 50 SCT 100 SCT 250-BKN CHC C20X 1TRW+
    g   h

09Z VFR CHC TRW/RW..
  i   j

a.   **Station identifier.** ABI identifies the airport for which this FT applies as Abilene, Texas.

b.   **Date-Time group.** 291515 is the date and valid time for this forecast, beginning on the 29th day of the month at 1500Z (UTC) and ending at 1500Z the following day.

c.   **Sky and ceiling.** 100 SCT 250-BKN means 10,000 ft. scattered, 25,000 ft. thin broken. The broken clouds at 25,000 ft. may appear to be a ceiling, but the contraction BKN is preceded by a minus sign which means thin. Therefore, it does not constitute a ceiling. If the letter "C" precedes the numerical values (e.g., C 250 BKN), it would identify a forecast ceiling layer.

d.   **Visibility.** Absence of the visibility value implies that the visibility will be more than 6 SM. Abilene visibility is therefore forecast to be greater than 6 SM. When visibility is shown it is stated in whole and fractions of SM (e.g., 1 1/2 means visibility one and one-half SM).

e.   **Weather and obstructions to vision.** These elements are stated in symbols identical to those used in SA reports, and entered only when expected. An example is "S-BS" which means light snow and blowing snow. This element of FT is missing in the initial forecast period for Abilene, but is shown in the expected changes.

f.   **Wind.** 1812 means the expected wind for this forecast period is from 180° at 12 kt. Omission of the wind entry implies that the wind is forecast to be less than 6 kt.

g.   **Remarks.** The remarks are missing in the first portion of the forecast period because there was no significant weather that could be described more completely. An example of a remark, such as "OCNLY C 35 BKN" means occasional ceiling 3,500 ft. broken. Note that there is a remarks section in the expected changes.

h.   **Expected changes.** If weather conditions are expected to change during the forecast period, the earlier forecast conditions are followed by a period and the time by which conditions are expected to change. Expected changes follow the same format and sequence as previously described. For Abilene,

18Z 50 SCT 100 SCT 250-BKN CHC C20X 1TRW+

This means the expected change prior to 1800Z will be to 5,000-ft. scattered, 10,000-ft. scattered, 25,000-ft. thin broken with a chance of a ceiling, 2,000-ft. sky obscured, 1 SM visibility, thunderstorms and heavy rain showers.

i.   **6-hr. categorical outlook.** The categorical outlook covers the last 6 hr. of the forecast period. 09Z VFR CHC TRW/RW.. means that from 0900Z to 1500Z (the end of the forecast period), the weather is expected to be VFR (i.e., ceiling more than 3,000 ft. and visibility greater than 5 SM), except there is a chance of thunderstorms with rain showers or rain showers without thunderstorms.

j.   The ".." signals the end of the forecast for this specific terminal.

INFLIGHT ADVISORIES (WST, WS, WA, CWA)

A.   Inflight Advisories are unscheduled forecasts to advise aircraft in flight of the development of potentially hazardous weather. These advisories are available from weather service outlets. They are an excellent source of information for preflight planning and briefing.

    1.   All heights are stated MSL unless otherwise noted.
    2.   Ceilings are always AGL.

B.   There are four types of Inflight Advisories:

    1.   Convective SIGMET (WST).
    2.   SIGMET (WS).
    3.   AIRMET (WA).
    4.   Center Weather Advisories (CWA).

C.   The format of these advisories consists of a heading and text.

    1.   The heading identifies the

        a.   Issuing WSFO (Weather Service Forecast Office).
        b.   Type of advisory.
        c.   Valid period.

    2.   The text of the advisory contains

        a.   A message identifier, e.g., SIGMET ALPHA 2.

        b.   A flight precautions statement; e.g., statement about location, size, and movement of an area of thunderstorms.

D.   CONVECTIVE SIGMETs (WST). Three Convective SIGMET bulletins (EASTERN, CENTRAL, and WESTERN U.S.) are issued each hour at 55 min. past the hour (H + 55) and on an unscheduled basis as specials.

    1.   Each of the Convective SIGMET bulletins will be

        a.   Made up of one or more individually numbered Convective SIGMETs.
        b.   Valid for 2 hr.

    2.   On an hourly basis, an outlook is made for each of the three Convective SIGMET regions.

        a.   The outlook is a forecast for thunderstorm systems that are expected to require Convective SIGMET issuances during a time period 2 to 6 hr. into the future.

        b.   An outlook will always be made, even if there are no forecast systems that will require a Convective SIGMET issuance.

    3.   The Convective SIGMETs are taken from radar observations. They use the following criteria as a basis for issuance:

        a.   Severe thunderstorms due to

            1)   Surface winds greater than or equal to 50 kt.,
            2)   Hail greater than or equal to ¾ in. in diameter, or
            3)   Tornadoes.

        b.   Lines of thunderstorms.
        c.   Embedded thunderstorms.
        d.   Thunderstorms greater than or equal to LVL 4.

            1)   Thunderstorms are reported as level 1, 2, 3, 4, or 5 depending on their intensity. Level 1 is least intense and level 5 is most intense.

    4.   Convective SIGMETs are issued for the contiguous United States for any convective situation hazardous to all categories of aircraft.

        a.   In Alaska and Hawaii, these are issued as SIGMETs.

b. If there is no convective activity meeting the above criteria, the message "CONVECTIVE SIGMET . . . NONE" will be issued.

5. EXAMPLE:

```
MKCC WST 221655
CONVECTIVE SIGMET 17C
KS OK TX
VCNTY GLD-CDS LINE
NO SGFNT TSTMS RPRTD
FCST TO 1855Z
LINE TSTMS DVLPG BY 1755Z WILL MOV
EWD 30-35 KTS THRU 1855Z
HAIL TO 1 1/2 IN PSBL
```

Interpretation: Issued at 1655Z on the 22nd day of the month. It is the 17th CONVECTIVE SIGMET of the day in the Central U.S. Although no significant thunderstorm activity is noted at 1655Z, a line of thunderstorms is expected to develop by 1755Z near a Goodland-Childress line in the states of Kansas, Oklahoma, and Texas and move eastward 30-35 kt. possibly producing 1½ in. hail through 1855Z.

E. SIGMET (WS). A SIGMET is issued to advise pilots of weather considered potentially hazardous to all categories of aircraft other than convective activity. It is valid for the period stated in the advisory.

1. SIGMETs are based specifically on forecasts of

   a. Severe or extreme turbulence not associated with thunderstorms.
   b. Severe icing not associated with thunderstorms.
   c. Widespread sandstorms/duststorms, lowering visibility to less than 3 SM.

2. EXAMPLE:

```
DFWA UWS 051710
SIGMET NOVEMBER 1 VALID UNTIL 052110
AR LA MS
FROM MEM TO 30N MEI TO BTR TO MLU TO MEM
OCNL SVR ICING ABV FRZLVL EXPCD.
FRZLVL 080 E TO 120 W.
CONDS CONTG BYD 2100Z.
```

Interpretation: The SIGMET was issued for the DFW area at 1710Z on the 5th and is valid until 2110Z (Note maximum forecast period of 4 hr. for a SIGMET). The designator NOVEMBER identifies the phenomenon, in this case, severe icing. This is the first issuance of the SIGMET as indicated by UWS (Urgent Weather SIGMET) and NOVEMBER 1. The affected states within the DFW area are Arkansas, Louisiana, and Mississippi. VORs outline the entire area to be affected (irrespective of FA boundaries) by severe icing during the forecast period. Freezing level data and notation that conditions are expected to continue beyond 4 hr. are included.

F.   AIRMET (WA). An AIRMET is issued to advise pilots of weather that may be of operational interest to all aircraft and potentially hazardous to aircraft having limited capability because of lack of equipment, instrumentation, or pilot qualification. The AIRMET is valid for the period stated in the advisory. AIRMETs are at the end of an FA.

1.   AIRMETs are based specifically on forecasts of

   a.   Moderate icing.
   b.   Moderate turbulence.
   c.   Sustained winds of 30 kt. or more at the surface.
   d.   Widespread areas of visibility below 3 SM and/or ceilings less than 1,000 ft.
   e.   Extensive mountain obscurement.

2.   EXAMPLE:

   MIAZ WA 231945
   AIRMET ZULU FOR ICG AND FRZLVL VALID UNTIL 240200

   NO SGFNT ICG XPCD OUTSIDE CNVTV ACTVTY.

   FRZLVL . . . NC/SC/NRN-CNTRL GA . . . 95-115.
       SRN GA/NRN FL . . . 115-130. SRN FL . . . 130-150.

   Interpretation: Issued for the Miami (MIA) FA at 1945Z on the 23rd day of the month. AIRMET Zulu is for icing and freezing level and is valid until 0200Z on the 24th. No significant icing is expected outside convective activity. Freezing level for NC/SC/northern and central GA is 9,500 ft. to 11,500 ft.; southern GA/northern FL is 11,500 ft. to 13,000 ft.; and, southern FL is 13,000 ft. to 15,000 ft.

3.   AIRMET Sierra is for IFR and mountain obscuration and AIRMET Tango is for Turbulence.

G.   Center Weather Advisory (CWA)

1.   A Center Weather Advisory (CWA) is an unscheduled inflight flow control, air traffic and air crew *advisory* for use in anticipating and avoiding adverse weather conditions in the en route and terminal areas.

2.   The CWA is *not* a flight planning forecast but a *nowcast* for conditions beginning within the next 2 hr.

   a.   Maximum valid time of a CWA is 2 hr., i.e., no more than 2 hr. between issuance time and "valid until time."

3.   A CWA may be issued for the following three situations:

   a.   As a supplement to an *existing* inflight advisory or area forecast (FA) section for the purpose of improving or updating the definition of the phenomenon in terms of location, movement, extent, or intensity *relevant* to the ARTCC area of responsibility. This is important for the following reason. A SIGMET for severe turbulence issued by NAWAU may outline the entire ARTCC area for the total 4-hr. valid period but may only be covering a relatively small portion of the ARTCC area at any one time during the 4-hr. period.

   b.   When an inflight advisory has not yet been issued but conditions meet inflight advisory criteria based on current pilot reports and the information must be disseminated sooner than NAWAU can issue the inflight advisory. In this case of an impending SIGMET, the CWA will be issued as urgent "UCWA" to allow the fastest possible dissemination.

c. When inflight advisory criteria are not met but conditions are or will shortly be adversely affecting the safe flow of air traffic within the ARTCC area of responsibility.

4. Format of a CWA heading:

ARTCC Designator and Phenomenon number (numbers 1 through 6 used for replaceability)/"CWA"/issuance number (2 digits)/inflight advisory alphanumeric designator (if applicable)/date and time issued/"–"/valid until time.

5. Example of a CWA:

ZFW3 CWA 03 032140-2340
ISOLD SVR TSTM OVR MLU MOVG
SWWD 10 KTS. TOP 610. WND GUSTS TO
55 KTS. HAIL TO 1 INCH RPRTD AT MLU.
SVR TSTM CONTG BYND 2340.

Interpretation: CWA 03 was issued at 2140Z on the 3rd day of the month and is valid until 2340Z on the same day. Isolated severe thunderstorm over Monroe, LA (MLU) moving southwest at 10 kt. Cloud tops are at 61,000 ft. MSL. Monroe Regional Airport reported wind gusts to 55 kt. and hail to 1 in. in diameter. Severe thunderstorms will continue after 2340Z.

PILOT WEATHER REPORT (PIREP)

A. Pilot reports are reported in the "Remarks" section of hourly weather reports (SA). They consist of up to 12 sections:

1. **UA -- Routine PIREP, UUA -- Urgent PIREP**

2. **/OV -- Location**: Use 3-letter NAVAID idents only.

   a. **Fix**: /OV ABC, /OV ABC 090025.

   b. **Fix to fix**: /OV ABC-DEF, /OV ABC-DEF 120020, /OV ABC 045020-DEF 120005, /OV ABC-DEF-GHI.

3. **/TM -- Time**: 4 digits in UTC: /TM 0915.

4. **/FL -- Altitude/Flight Level**: 3 digits for hundreds of feet. If not known, use UNKN: /FL095, /FL310, /FL UNKN.

5. **/TP -- Type aircraft**: 4 digits maximum, if not known, use UNKN: /TP L329, /TP B727. /TP UNKN.

6. **/SK -- Cloud layers**: Describe as follows:

   a. Height of cloud base in hundreds of ft. MSL. If unknown, use UNKN.

   b. Cloud cover symbol.

   c. Height of cloud tops in hundreds of ft. MSL.

   d. Use slash (/) to separate layers.

   e. Use a space to separate each sub element.

   f. EXAMPLES: /SK 038 BKN, /SK 038 OVC 045, /SK 055 SCT 073/085 BKN 105, /SK UNKN OVC.

7. **/WX -- Weather**: Flight visibility reported first. Use standard weather symbols. Intensity is not reported: /WX FV02 R H, /WX FV01 TRW.

8. **/TA -- Air temperature in Celsius**: If below zero, prefix with a hyphen: /TA 15, /TA –06.

9. **/WV -- Wind**: Direction and speed in six digits. /WV 270045, /WV 280110.

10. **/TB -- Turbulence**: Use standard contractions for intensity and type (use CAT or CHOP when appropriate). Include altitude only if different from /FL. /TB EXTRM, /TB LGT-MDT BLO-090.

11. **/IC -- Icing**: Describe using standard intensity and type contractions. Include altitude only if different from /FL: /IC LGT-MDT RIME, /IC SVR CLR 028-045.

12. **/RM -- Remarks**: Use free form to clarify the report. Most hazardous element first: /RM LLWS –15KT SFC-003 DURGC RNWY 22 JFK.

B. **EXAMPLE: UA/OV CRP 180020 1629 FL050 /TP C182 /SK SCT V BKN 040-050**

1. This means that the pilot of a Cessna 182 reported scattered variable to broken clouds with bases 4,000 to 5,000 ft. MSL at a point on the 180° radial 20 NM from Corpus Christi, Texas.

2. Item-by-item translation of the PIREP:

> **UA** -- Pilot report • **OV CRP** -- Over Corpus Christi • **180020** -- 180°, 020 NM • **1629** -- 1629 UTC • **FL050** -- 5,000 ft. MSL • **TP** -- Type of airplane • **C182** -- Cessna 182 • **SK** -- Sky • **SCT V BKN** -- Scattered variable to broken • **040-050** -- 4,000 to 5,000 ft.

RADAR WEATHER REPORT (RAREP)

A. Thunderstorms and general areas of precipitation can be observed by radar. In addition to transmission as a separate report, some are included in scheduled weather broadcasts by Flight Service Stations.

1. Most radar stations issue RAREPs each hour at 35 min. after the hr. (H + 35).

B. Interpretation of RAREP.

1. Precipitation and Intensity Trend.

Intensity		Intensity Trend	
Symbol	Intensity	Symbol	Trend
–	Light	+	Increasing
(none)	Moderate		
+	Heavy	–	Decreasing
++	Very Heavy		
X	Intense	NC	No change
XX	Extreme		
U	Unknown	NEW	New echo

2.   **EXAMPLE:**   OKC 1934 LN 8TRW++/+ 86/40 164/60 199/115 15W L2425 MT570 AT
      159/65 2 INCH HAIL RPRTD THIS CELL MO1 NO2 ON3 PM34 QM3 RL2 SL9

   a.   Location identifier and time of radar observation (Oklahoma City RAREP at
         1934 UTC).

   b.   Echo pattern (LN). The radar echo pattern or configuration may be a

      1)   Line (LN) -- a line of precipitation echoes at least 30 NM long, at least five
            times as long as it is wide and at least 30% coverage within the line.

      2)   Fine Line (FINE LN) -- a unique clear air echo (usually precipitation-free and
            cloud-free) in the form of a thin or fine line on the radar scope. It represents
            a strong temperature/moisture boundary such as an advancing dry cold
            front.

      3)   Area (AREA) -- a group of echoes of similar type and not classified as a line.

      4)   Spiral Band Area (SPRL BAND AREA) -- an area of precipitation associated
            with a hurricane that takes on a spiral band configuration around the center.

      5)   Single Cell (CELL) -- a single isolated precipitation not reaching the ground.

      6)   Layer (LYR) -- an elevated layer of stratiform precipitation not reaching the
            ground.

   c.   Coverage in tenths (8/10 in the example).

   d.   Type, intensity, and intensity trend of weather. In the example, the radar depicted
         thunderstorms (T) and very heavy rainshowers (RW++) that are increasing in
         intensity (/+). Note that the intensity is separated from intensity trend by a slash.

   e.   Azimuth (reference true N) and range in NM of points defining the echo pattern
         (86/40 164/60 199/115 in the example).

   f.   Dimension of echo pattern (15W in the example). The dimension of an echo pattern
         is given when azimuth and range define only the center line of the pattern. In this
         example, 15W means the line has a total width of 15 NM, 7½ mi. either side of a
         center line drawn from the points given. D15 would mean a convective echo is
         15 NM in diameter around a given center point.

   g.   Pattern movement (the LINE is moving *from* 240° at 25 kt. in the example). This
         element may also show movement of individual storms or cells with a "C" or
         movement of an area with an "A."

   h.   Maximum top (MT) and location (57,000 ft. MSL on radial 159° at 65 NM in the
         example).

   i.   Remarks are self-explanatory using plain-language contractions.

   j.   The digital section is used for preparing the radar summary chart.

SURFACE ANALYSIS CHART

A. The Surface Analysis Chart (see page 505), often referred to as a surface weather chart, is the basic weather chart. The chart is prepared by the NWS from reports of existing weather conditions. Although it is computer prepared, it takes about 2 hr. to collect and transmit the information. The valid time of the map corresponds to the time of the plotted observations.

   1. A date and time (UTC) group gives the actual time of conditions portrayed on the map.

   2. The Surface Analysis Chart displays weather information (as of chart time) such as

      a. Surface wind direction and speed
      b. Temperature
      c. Dewpoint
      d. Position of fronts
      e. Areas of high or low pressure

   3. It gives a pictorial overview of the weather situation. You should keep in mind that weather systems move and conditions change.

B. Each reporting station is depicted on the chart by a small circle. Weather information pertaining to the station is placed in a standard pattern around this circle. This pattern is called a station model. The standard pattern of a station model follows with the explanation of the symbols.

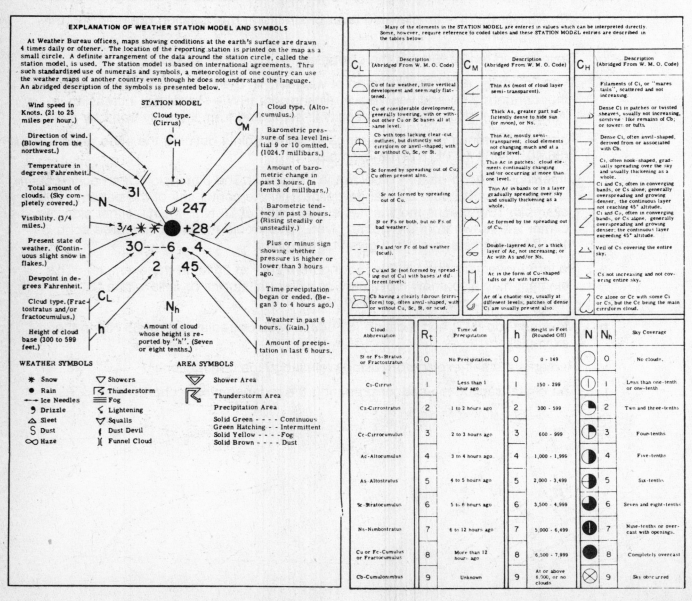

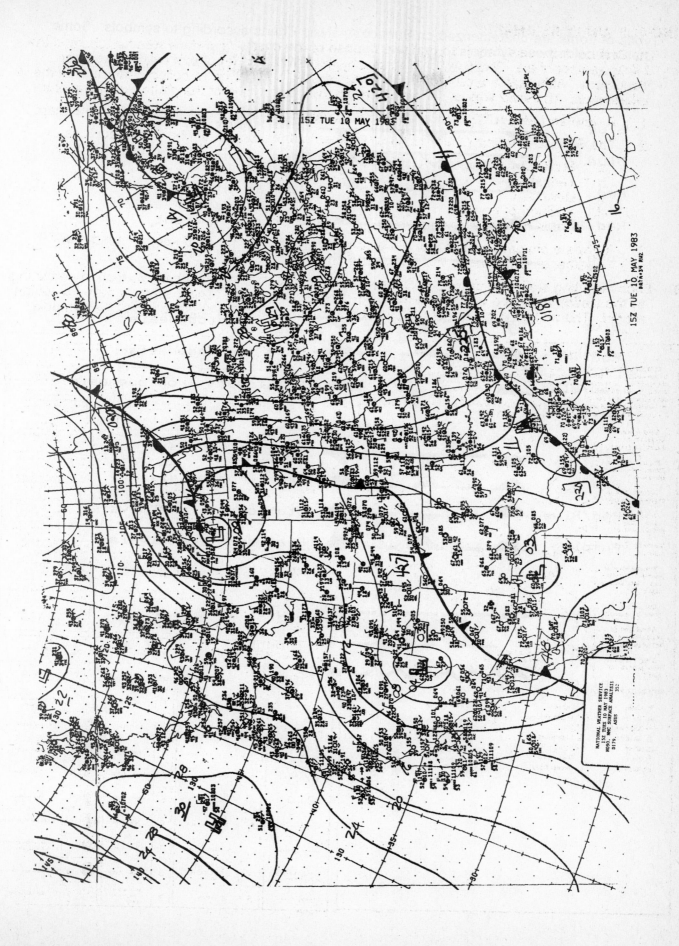

C. Types of fronts are characterized on Surface Analysis Charts according to symbols. Some stations color these symbols to facilitate the use of the chart.

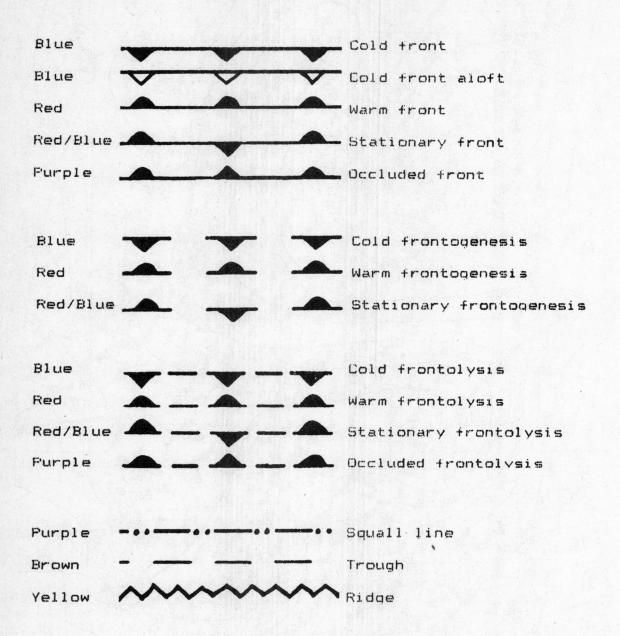

Blue	Cold front
Blue	Cold front aloft
Red	Warm front
Red/Blue	Stationary front
Purple	Occluded front
Blue	Cold frontogenesis
Red	Warm frontogenesis
Red/Blue	Stationary frontogenesis
Blue	Cold frontolysis
Red	Warm frontolysis
Red/Blue	Stationary frontolysis
Purple	Occluded frontolysis
Purple	Squall line
Brown	Trough
Yellow	Ridge

1. A three-digit number along the front indicates type, intensity, and character as shown below.

   a. Type of front

Code Figure	Description
0	Quasi-stationary at surface
1	Quasi-stationary above surface
2	Warm front at surface
3	Warm front above surface
4	Cold front at surface
5	Cold front above surface
6	Occlusion
7	Instability line
8	Intertropical front
9	Convergence line

   b. Intensity of front

Code Figure	Description
0	No specification
1	Weak, decreasing
2	Weak, little or no change
3	Weak, increasing
4	Moderate, decreasing
5	Moderate, little or no change
6	Moderate, increasing
7	Strong, decreasing
8	Strong, little or no change
9	Strong, increasing

   c. Character of front

Code Figure	Description
0	No specification
1	Frontal area activity, decreasing
2	Frontal area activity, little change
3	Frontal area activity, increasing
4	Intertropical
5	Forming or existence expected
6	Quasi-stationary
7	With waves
8	Diffuse
9	Position doubtful

D.   Solid lines depicting the pressure pattern are called isobars. They denote lines of equal pressure. Think of them as similar to terrain contour lines on geographic maps. Isobars usually encircle a high- or low-pressure area.

   1.   The two-digit numbers on the isobars denote the pressure in millibars (mb). To decode, simply add either a 9 or a 10 before the two digits, whichever brings it closer to 1000 mb (e.g., 04 means 1004 mb; 96 means 996 mb).

E.   The letter "H" on the chart marks the center of a high-pressure area. "L" marks the center of a low-pressure area. The actual pressure at each center is indicated by an underlined two-digit number which is decoded like the number along the isobars.

WEATHER DEPICTION CHART

A.   The Weather Depiction Chart is a national map (of the contiguous U.S.) giving a quick picture of the weather conditions as of the valid time stated on the chart. It is prepared from Surface Aviation Weather Reports (SAs), but it contains only a portion of the surface weather information.

   1.   Areas affected by clouds and weather can be seen at a glance.

   2.   The chart also shows major fronts and high- and low-pressure centers. It is considered a good place to begin a weather briefing for flight planning.

   3.   A weather depiction chart and the notations used on it are illustrated on the opposite page.

B.   An abbreviated station model is used to plot data consisting of total sky cover, cloud height or ceiling, weather and obstructions to vision, visibility, and an analysis.

   1.   Cloud height is the lowest ceiling shown in hundreds of feet. If there is no ceiling, it is the height of the lowest layer.

   2.   Weather and obstructions to vision are shown using the same symbol designators as the Surface Analysis Chart.

      a.   Visibility less than 7 mi. is entered in miles and fractions of miles.

   3.   The chart shows ceilings and visibilities at reporting stations and categorizes areas as:

      a.   IFR -- Ceiling less than 1,000 ft. and/or visibility less than 3 SM; outlined by a smooth line.

      b.   MVFR (Marginal VFR) -- Ceiling 1,000 ft. to 3,000 ft. inclusive and/or visibility 3 to 5 SM inclusive; outlined by a scalloped line.

      c.   VFR -- Ceiling greater than 3,000 ft. or unlimited and visibility greater than 5 SM; not outlined.

C.   The weather depiction chart is a choice place to begin your weather briefing and flight planning. It gives you a bird's-eye view at chart time of areas of favorable and adverse weather and frontal systems associated with the weather.

   1.   After you initially size up the general picture, your flight planning must consider all available weather reports and forecasts.

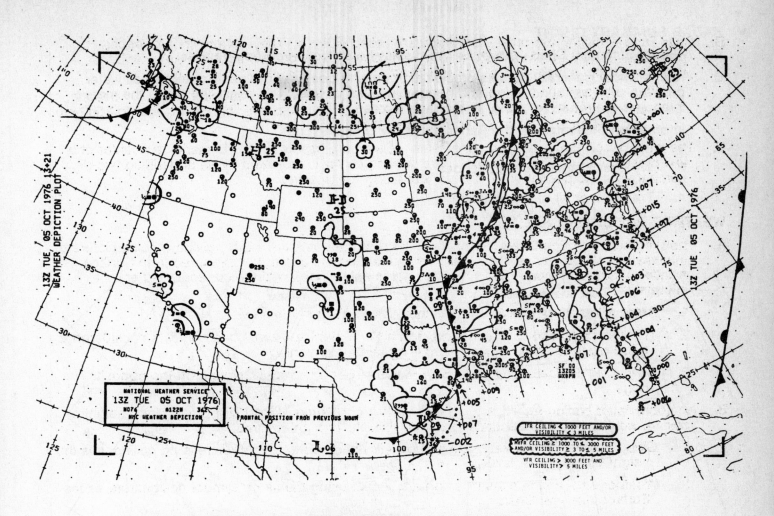

NOTATIONS USED ON WEATHER DEPICTION CHART

STATION MODEL

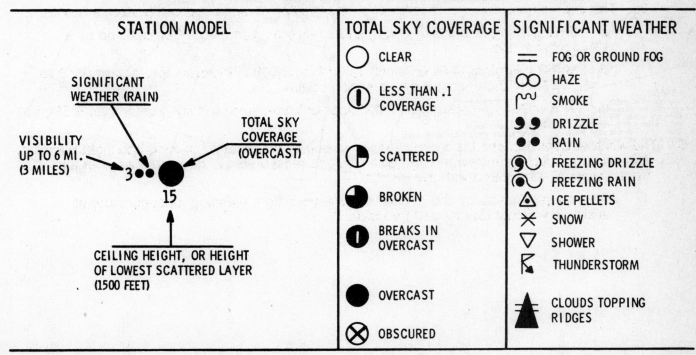

SIGNIFICANT WEATHER (RAIN)

TOTAL SKY COVERAGE (OVERCAST)

VISIBILITY UP TO 6 MI. (3 MILES)

3 ●● ●

15

CEILING HEIGHT, OR HEIGHT OF LOWEST SCATTERED LAYER (1500 FEET)

TOTAL SKY COVERAGE

○ CLEAR

◐ LESS THAN .1 COVERAGE

◕ SCATTERED

◕ BROKEN

◐ BREAKS IN OVERCAST

● OVERCAST

⊗ OBSCURED

SIGNIFICANT WEATHER

≡ FOG OR GROUND FOG

∞ HAZE

SMOKE

, , DRIZZLE

●● RAIN

FREEZING DRIZZLE

FREEZING RAIN

△ ICE PELLETS

✳ SNOW

▽ SHOWER

THUNDERSTORM

CLOUDS TOPPING RIDGES

RADAR SUMMARY CHART

A.   A Radar Summary Chart (shown below) displays a collection of radar reports.

B.   Weather radar generally detects precipitation only. It does not ordinarily detect small water droplets such as found in fog and nonprecipitating clouds. The larger the drops the more intense is the return (or echo) to the radar screen.

Information presented on the Radar Summary Chart includes

1.   Echo pattern and coverage
2.   Weather associated with echoes
3.   Intensity (contours)
4.   Trend (+ or −) of precipitation
5.   Height of echo bases and tops
6.   Movement of echoes

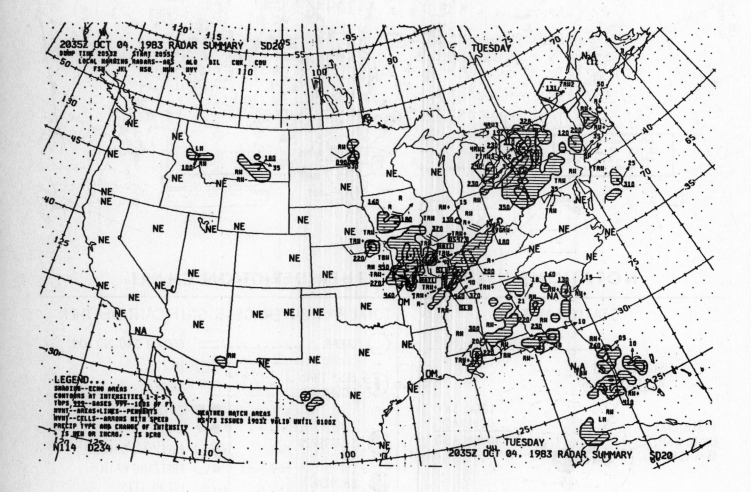

C. The arrangement of echoes as seen on the radarscope forms a certain pattern which is symbolized on the chart.

1. This pattern of echoes may be a line, an area, or an isolated cell. A cell is a concentrated mass of convection normally 20 NM or less in diameter. Echo coverage is the amount of space the echoes or cells occupy within an area or line.

2. The height of the tops and bases of echoes are shown on the chart in hundreds of ft. MSL.

   a. A horizontal line is used with the heights shown above and below the line denoting the top and base heights, respectively.

   b. No number below the line means the echo base was not reported.

   c. EXAMPLES:

   <u>450</u> Average tops 45,000 ft.

   <u>220</u> Bases 8,000 ft.; tops 22,000 ft.
   080

   <u>330</u> Top of an individual cell, 33,000 ft.

   <u>650/</u> Maximum tops, 65,000 ft.

   <u>A350</u> Tops 35,000 ft. reported by aircraft.

SYMBOL	MEANING	CALLED
(line symbol)	A line of echoes	Line
SLD	Over 9/10 coverage	Solid
WS999	Thunderstorm watch area	Thunderstorm watch area
WT999	Tornado watch area	Tornado watch area

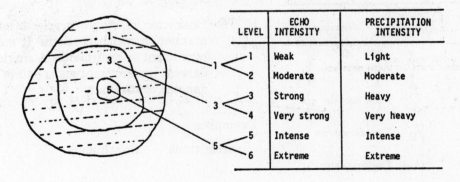

LEVEL	ECHO INTENSITY	PRECIPITATION INTENSITY
1	Weak	Light
2	Moderate	Moderate
3	Strong	Heavy
4	Very strong	Very heavy
5	Intense	Intense
6	Extreme	Extreme

NOTE: The numbers representing the intensity level do not appear on the chart. Beginning from the first contour line, bordering the area, the intensity level is 1 - 2; second contour is 3 - 4; and third contour is 5 - 6.

D.   The movements of individual storms, as well as a line or an area, are shown on Radar Summary
     Charts.

   1.   The movement of the individual storms within a line or area often differs from the
        movement of the overall storm pattern. These movements are depicted as shown:

        ³⁵ Individual echo movement to the northeast at 35 kt.

        Line or area movement to the east to 20 kt.
        (Note: A half flag represents 5 kt. Full flag is 10 kt.)

   2.   Areas which indicate a severe weather watch in effect are also included when appropriate.
        These areas are depicted by a dashed-line rectangle or square.

E.   If reports from a particular radar station do not appear on the chart, a symbol explains the
     reason for no echoes.

   1.   NE -- No echo (equipment operating but no echoes observed).
   2.   NA -- Observation not available.
   3.   OM -- Equipment out for maintenance.

LOW-LEVEL PROGNOSTIC CHARTS

A.   Low-level Prognostic Charts (called progs) forecast weather conditions expected to exist 12 and
     24 hr. in the future. They include two types of forecasts.

   1.   Significant weather (upper panels of the chart on the opposite page).

        a.   IFR areas (enclosed by smooth lines).
        b.   MVFR areas (enclosed by scalloped lines).
        c.   Moderate or greater turbulence areas.
        d.   Freezing levels.

   2.   Surface weather (lower panels of the chart on the opposite page).

        a.   Pressure centers and fronts.
        b.   Areas of forecast precipitation and/or thunderstorms.

B.   The following symbols are used on prog charts:

   1.   Standard weather symbols.

Symbol	Meaning	Symbol	Meaning
⌒	Moderate turbulence	▽	Rain shower
⋀	Severe turbulence	※	Snow shower
⊎	Moderate icing	⃧	Thunderstorms
⊎	Severe icing	∿	Freezing rain
•	Rain	ꓚ	Tropical storm
✳	Snow	⬤	Hurricane (typhoon)
୨	Drizzle		

NOTE: Character of stable precipitation is the
manner in which it occurs. It may be intermittent or continuous. A single symbol
denotes intermittent and a pair of symbols
denotes continuous.

Examples,

Intermittent	Continuous	
•	• •	Rain
୨	୨୨	Drizzle
✳	✳✳	Snow

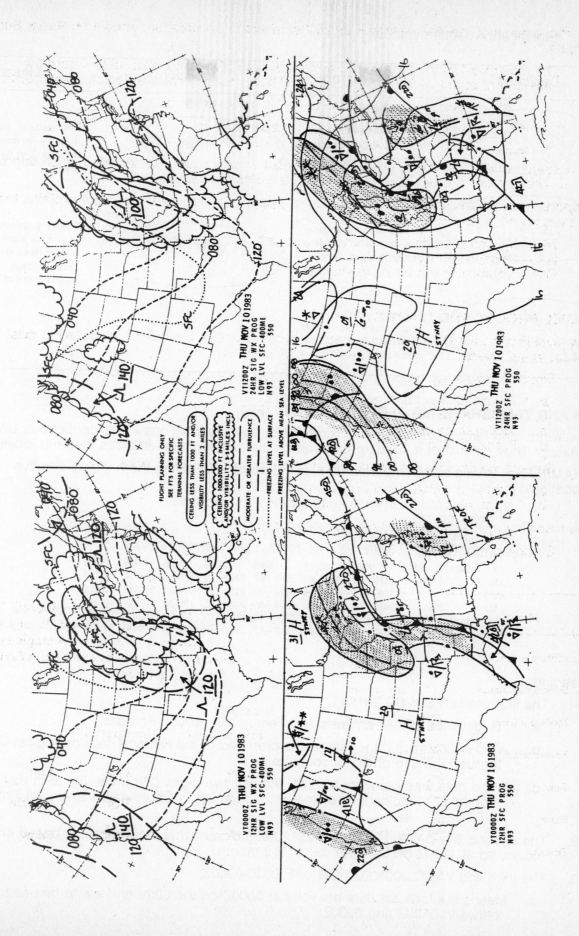

FLIGHT PLANNING ONLY
SEE FT5 FOR SPECIFIC
TERMINAL FORECASTS

CEILING LESS THAN 1000 FT AND/OR
VISIBILITY LESS THAN 3 MILES

CEILING 1000-3000 FT INCLUSIVE
AND/OR VISIBILITY 3-5 MILES INCL

MODERATE OR GREATER TURBULENCE

FREEZING LEVEL AT SURFACE

FREEZING LEVEL ABOVE MEAN SEA LEVEL

VT1200Z THU NOV 10 1983
24HR SIG WX PROG
LOW LVL SFC-400M£
N93   550

VT0000Z THU NOV 10 1983
12HR SIG WX PROG
LOW LVL SFC-400M£
N93   550

VT1200Z THU NOV 10 1983
24HR SFC PROG
N93   550

VT0000Z THU NOV 10 1983
12HR SFC PROG
N93   550

2.   Significant weather symbols.

Depiction	Meaning	Depiction	Meaning
	Showery precipitation (e.g. thunderstorms/rain showers covering half or more of the area		Intermittent precipitation (e.g. drizzle) covering less than half of the area
	Continuous precipitation (e.g. rain) covering half or more of the area		Showery precipitation (e.g. rain showers) embedded in an area of continuous rain covering half or more of the area
	Showery precipitation (e.g. snow showers) covering less than half of the area		

WINDS AND TEMPERATURES ALOFT FORECAST (FD)

A.   The winds and temperatures aloft are forecast for specific locations in the contiguous United States. They consist of a heading followed by forecasts at nine altitudes for each location.

B.   EXAMPLE: A Winds and Temperatures Aloft Forecast (FD) giving the heading and five locations:

```
FD WBC 291745
DATA BASED ON 291200Z
VALID 300600Z      FOR USE 0300-0900Z. TEMPS NEG ABV 24000
FT    3000    6000    9000   12000   18000   24000   30000   34000   39000
ABI           2213+19 2315+14 2313+08 2208-07 9900-19 990034 090644 101155
ABQ                   2605+17 9900+10 0710-05 0710-17 990033 990043 060655
AMA           2210    2409+16 2406+10 9900-06 9900-18 010534 350543 021055
ATL   2611    2611+17 2612+13 2612+08 2713-06 2712-18 281134 291143 300754
BNA   2414    2617+17 2617+12 2718+07 2819-07 2721-19 272434 272543 262554
```

C.   Heading.

1.   The first line is "FD WBC 291745."

   a.   FD identifies this as a Winds and Temperatures Aloft Forecast.

   b.   WBC indicates that the forecast is prepared at the National Meteorological Center through the use of digital computers.

   c.   In the date-time group of 291745, the first two digits (29) mean the 29th day of the month; 1745 indicates the time of the forecast in Coordinated Universal Time (UTC).

2.   The second line DATA BASED ON 291200Z indicates that the forecast is based on data collected at 1200Z on the 29th day of the month.

3.   The third line VALID 300600Z FOR USE 0300-0900Z,

   a.   Means the forecast data are valid at 0600Z on the 30th, and are to be used by pilots between 0300Z and 0900Z.

  b. The notation TEMPS NEG ABV 24,000 is always included. Since temperatures above 24,000 ft. are almost always negative, no sign preceding the temperature above this level is included unless it is positive.

  4. Forecast levels. The line labeled "FT" shows the nine standard levels in ft. for which the winds and temperatures apply. The levels through 12,000 ft. are based on true altitude, and the levels at 18,000 ft. and above are based on pressure altitude.

D. Body of the forecast.

  1. The station identifiers denoting the location for which the forecast applies are arranged in alphabetical order in a column down the left side of the data sheet.

  2. The coded wind and temperature information in digits for each station is found in columns under each level.

  3. Note that at some of the lower levels the wind and temperature information is omitted.

    a. Winds aloft are not forecast for levels within 1,500 ft. of the station elevation.

    b. No temperatures are forecast for the 3,000-ft. level or for a level within 2,500 ft. of the station elevation.

  4. A 4-digit group shows the wind direction in reference to true north and the wind speed in kt.

    a. EXAMPLE: In the Atlanta (ATL) forecast for the 3,000-ft. level, the group 2611 means the wind is forecast to be from 260° true at a speed of 11 kt.

    b. Note that to decode, you add a zero to the end of the first two digits giving the direction in increments of 10°. The second two digits give speed in kt.

  5. A 6-digit group includes the forecast temperature aloft in degrees Celsius.

    a. EXAMPLE: In the Abilene (ABI) forecast for the 6,000-ft. level, the group 2213+19 means the wind is forecast to be from 220° true at 13 kt. with a temperature of +19°C.

  6. If the wind speed is forecast to be 100 to 199 kt., the forecaster adds 50 to the direction and subtracts 100 from the speed. To decode, you must do the reverse: Subtract 50 from the direction and add 100 to the speed.

    a. EXAMPLE: If the forecast for the 39,000-ft. level appears as 731960, subtract 50 from 73 and add 100 to 19. The wind would be 230° true at 119 kt. with a temperature of −60°C.

    b. It is easy to know when the coded direction has been increased by 50. Coded direction (in tens of degrees) normally ranges from 01 (010°) to 36 (360°). Any coded direction with a numerical value greater than 36 indicates a wind of 100 kt. or greater. The coded direction for winds of 100 to 199 kt. thus ranges from 51 through 86.

  7. If the wind speed is forecast to be 199 kt. or more, the wind group is coded as 199 kt.; e.g., 7799 is decoded 270° at 199 kt. or more.

  8. When the forecast speed is less than 5 kt., the coded group is 9900 which means LIGHT AND VARIABLE.

  9. EXAMPLES: Decode these FD winds and temperatures:

Coded	Decoded
9900+00	Winds light and variable, temperature 0°C
2707	270° true at 7 kt.
850552	85 − 50 = 35; 05 + 100 = 105 350° true at 105 kt., temperature −52°C

COMPOSITE MOISTURE STABILITY CHARTS

A. The Composite Moisture Stability Chart is an analysis chart using observed upper air data and is issued twice daily.

  1. It has the following four panels:

     a. Stability
     b. Freezing level
     c. Precipitable water
     d. Average relative humidity

  2. Through analysis of this chart, you can determine the characteristics of a particular weather system in terms of stability, moisture, and possible aviation hazards.

B. The stability panel (upper left panel of chart on page 517) outlines areas of stable and unstable air.

  1. Two stability indices are computed for each upper air station: one is the lifted index and the other the K index.

     a. At each station, the lifted index is plotted above a short line and the K index below the line.

     b. An "M" indicates the value is missing.

  2. The lifted index is computed as if a parcel of air near the surface were lifted to 500 millibars (mb). As the air is lifted, it cools by expansion. The temperature the parcel would have at 500 mb is then subtracted from the environmental 500-mb temperature. The difference is the lifted index, which may be positive, zero, or negative.

     a. A positive index means that a parcel of air if lifted would be colder than existing air at 500 mb. The air is stable. Large positive values indicate very stable air.

     b. A zero index denotes that air if lifted to 500 mb would attain the same temperature as the existing 500-mb environmental temperature. The air is neutral (neither stable nor unstable).

     c. A negative index means that the low-level air if lifted to 500 mb would be warmer than the existing air at 500 mb. Such air is unstable and suggests the possibility of convection. Large negative values indicate very unstable air.

  3. The K index is primarily for the meteorologist.

C. The freezing level panel (lower left panel of chart on page 517) is an analysis of observed freezing-level data from upper air observations.

  1. Solid lines are contours of the lowest freezing level. They are drawn for 4,000-ft. intervals and labeled in hundreds of ft. MSL.

  2. When a station reports more than one crossing of the 0°C isotherm, the lowest crossing is used in the analysis.

  3. The contour analysis shows an overall view of the lowest observed freezing level. Always plan for possible icing in clouds or precipitation above the freezing level, especially between 0 and −10°C.

D. The precipitable water panel (upper right panel of chart on page 517) is an analysis of the water vapor content from the surface to the 500-mb level.

  1. The amount of water vapor observed is shown as precipitation water, which is the amount of liquid precipitation that would result if all water vapor were condensed.

  2. Stations with blackened-in circles indicate precipitable water values of 1.00 in. or more.

3. This panel is used to determine water vapor content in the air between surface and 500 mb. It is especially useful to meteorologists concerned with flash flood events.

4. By looking at the wind field upstream from your station, you can get an excellent indication of changes that will occur in moisture content, i.e., drying out or increasing moisture with time.

E. The average relative humidity panel (lower right panel on chart below) is an analysis of the average relative humidity from the surface to 500 mb, plotted as a percentage for each reporting station.

1. Station circles are blackened for humidities of 50% and higher.

2. Average relative humidities of 70% or greater are frequently associated with areas of clouds and possible precipitation.

3. This is because with such a high average relative humidity through approximately 18,000 ft., it is likely that a specific layer(s) will have 100% relative humidity with clouds and possibly precipitation.

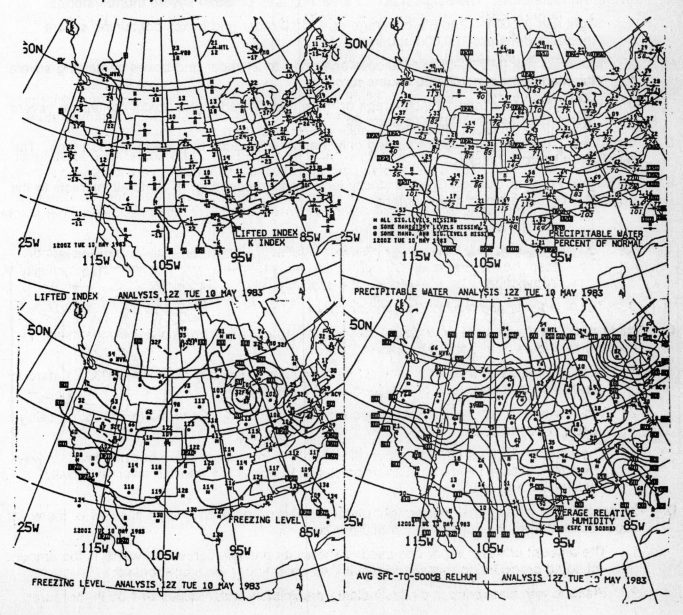

SEVERE WEATHER OUTLOOK CHART

A.   The Severe Weather Outlook Chart is a preliminary 24-hr. outlook for thunderstorm activity presented in two panels.

    1.   The left-hand panel covers the 12-hr. period 1200Z (UTC) - 0000Z.
    2.   The right-hand panel covers the remaining 12 hr., 0000Z - 1200Z.
    3.   The manually-prepared chart is issued once daily in the morning.

B.   General thunderstorms. A line with an arrowhead delineates an area of probable general thunderstorm activity.

    1.   When you face in the direction of the arrow, activity is expected to the right of the line.

    2.   An area labeled APCHG indicates probable general thunderstorm activity may approach severe intensity.

    3.   Approaching means winds greater than or equal to 35 kt. but less than 50 kt. and/or hail greater than or equal to ½ in. in diameter but less than ¾ in. (surface conditions).

C.   Severe thunderstorms. The single-hatched area indicates possible severe thunderstorms.

    1.   Slight risk (SLGT) -- 2 to 5% coverage or 4 to 10 radar grid boxes containing severe thunderstorms per 100,000 square mi.

    2.   Moderate risk (MDT) -- 6 to 10% coverage or 11 to 21 radar grid boxes containing severe thunderstorms per 100,000 square mi.

    3.   High risk -- More than 10% coverage or more than 21 radar grid boxes containing severe thunderstorms per 100,000 square mi.

D.   Tornadoes. Tornado watches are plotted only if a tornado watch is in effect at chart time. The watch area is cross-hatched.

E.   The Severe Weather Outlook Chart is strictly for advanced planning. It alerts all interests to the possibility of future storm development.

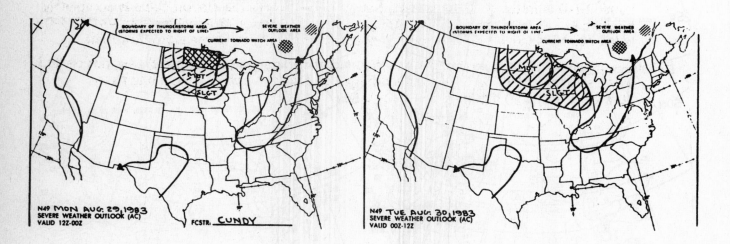

CONSTANT PRESSURE ANALYSIS CHARTS

A. Twice daily, five computer-prepared Constant Pressure Charts (850 mb, 700 mb, 500 mb, 300 mb, and 200 mb) are transmitted by facsimile, each valid at 1200Z (UR) and 0000Z.

    1. Plotted at each reporting station (at the level of the specified pressure) are the

        a. Observed temperature
        b. Temperature/dewpoint spread
        c. Wind
        d. Height of the pressure surface
        e. Height changes over the previous 12-hr. period

B.

    1. Wind -- wind direction (WD) and speed (WS) plotted to the nearest 10° and to the nearest 5 kt., respectively.

        a. 5 kt., 10 kt., 50 kt.
        b. If direction or speed is missing, "M" is plotted in H_C space.
        c. If speed is less than 3 kt., "LV" (light and variable) is plotted in H_C space.

    2. HGT -- height of constant pressure surface in meters.

    3. TT -- temperature to the nearest whole degree C; minus sign used if negative. Left blank if TT is missing. On the 850-mb chart, primarily in mountain regions where stations may be located above 850 mb of pressure, a bracketed temperature (and HGT) is a computed value. If two temperatures are plotted one above the other, the top temperature is used in the analysis.

    4. T-D -- temperature/dewpoint spread (or depression) to the nearest whole degree C. Left blank if T-D is missing. If T-D is less than or equal to 5°C, the station circle is completely blackened. IF T-D is greater than 29°C, an "X" is plotted. If TT is colder than −41°C, T-D is left blank because the air is too dry at those temperatures to measure dewpoint.

    5. H_C -- previous 12-hr. height change plotted in tens of meters (decameters). H_C not plotted when wind is "LV" or "M." +04 means height of pressure above station has risen 40 meters, 02 = 20 meters, 11 = 110 meters.

C.   Examples of radiosonde plotted data.

	(850 MB)	(700 MB)	(500 MB)	(300 MB)	(200 MB)
WIND	LIGHT AND VARIABLE	010° 20KTS	210° 60KTS	270° 25KTS	MISSING
TT	22°C	9°C	-19°C	-46°C	-60°C
T-D	4°C	17°C	> 29°C	not plotted	not plotted
DEW POINT	18°C	-8°C	DRY	DRY	DRY
HGT	1,479 meters	3,129 meters	5,580 meters	9,190 meters	11,910 meters
H_c	not plotted	MINUS 30 meters	PLUS 30 meters	+100 meters	not plotted

D.   From the charts you can approximate the observed temperature, wind, and temperature/dewpoint spread along your proposed route.

    1.   Usually you can select a Constant Pressure Chart close to your planned altitude. For altitudes about midway between two charted surfaces, interpolate between the two charts.

    2.   To readily delineate areas of high moisture content, station circles are shaded indicating temperature/dewpoint spreads of 5°C or less.

       a.   A small spread alerts you to possible cloudiness, precipitation, and icing.

    3.   Determine wind speed.

    4.   Wind direction parallels the contours.

    5.   Keep in mind that Constant Pressure Charts are observed weather.

AUTHOR'S RECOMMENDATION

The Experimental Aircraft Association, Inc. is a very successful and effective nonprofit organization that represents and serves those of us interested in flying, in general, and in sport aviation, in particular. I personally invite you to enjoy becoming a member:

$35 for a 1-year membership
$20 per year for individuals under 19 years old
Family membership available for $45 per year

Membership includes the monthly magazine *Sport Aviation*.

Write to: Experimental Aircraft Association, Inc.
P.O. Box 3086
Oshkosh, Wisconsin 54903-3086

Or call: (414) 426-4800
(800) 322-2412 (in Wisconsin: 1-800-236-4800)
(800) 843-3612

The annual EAA Oshkosh Fly-in is an unbelievable aviation spectacular with over 10,000 airplanes at one airport! Virtually everything aviation-oriented you can imagine! Plan to spend at least 1 day (not everything can be seen in a day) in Oshkosh (100 miles northwest of Milwaukee).

Convention dates: 1992 - July 31 through August 6
1993 - July 30 through August 5
1994 - July 29 through August 4

INSTRUCTOR CERTIFICATION FORM
PRIVATE PILOT WRITTEN TEST

Name: _____

      I certify that I have reviewed the above individual's completion of the *PRIVATE PILOT FAA WRITTEN EXAM* home-study course by Irvin N. Gleim for the FAA Private Pilot written test [covering the topics specified in FAR 61.105(a)(1) through (6)]. I find that (s)he has satisfactorily completed the course and find him/her competent to pass the written test.

_____	_____	_____	_____	_____
Signed	Date	Name	CFI Number	Expiration Date

* *

LOGBOOK ENDORSEMENT
FOR PRACTICAL TEST

      The following endorsement must be in your logbook and presented to your examiner at your practical test.

1. Endorsement for flight proficiency: FAR § 61.107(a)

      I certify that I have given Mr./Ms. _____ the flight instruction required by FAR § 61.107(a)(1) through (10) and find him/her competent to perform each pilot operation safely as a private pilot.

_____	_____	_____	_____	_____
Signed	Date	Name	CFI Number	Expiration Date

BOOKS AVAILABLE FROM GLEIM PUBLICATIONS, Inc.
WRITTEN EXAM BOOKS

Before pilots take their FAA written tests, they want to understand the answer to every FAA written test question. Gleim's written test books are widely used because they help pilots learn and understand exactly what they need to know to do well on their FAA written test.

Gleim's books contain all of the FAA's airplane questions (nonairplane questions are excluded). We have unscrambled the questions appearing in the FAA written test books and organized them into logical topics. Answer explanations are provided next to each question. Each of our chapters opens with a brief, user-friendly outline of exactly what you need to know to pass the written test. Information not directly tested is omitted to expedite your passing the written test. This additional information can be found in our flight maneuver and reference books and practical test prep books described below.

PRIVATE PILOT AND RECREATIONAL PILOT FAA WRITTEN EXAM ($12.95)

The FAA's written test for either certificate consists of 60 questions out of the 710 questions in our book.

INSTRUMENT PILOT FAA WRITTEN EXAM ($16.95)

The FAA's written test consists of 60 questions out of the 898 questions in our book. Also, those people who wish to become an instrument-rated flight instructor (CFII) or an instrument ground instructor (IGI) must take the FAA's written test of 50 questions from this book.

COMMERCIAL PILOT FAA WRITTEN EXAM ($14.95)

The FAA's written test will consist of 100 questions out of the 564 questions in our book.

FUNDAMENTALS OF INSTRUCTING FAA WRITTEN EXAM ($9.95)

The FAA's written test consists of 50 questions out of the 180 questions in our book. This is required of any person to become a flight instructor or ground instructor. The test only needs to be taken once. For example, if someone is already a flight instructor and wants to become a ground instructor, taking the FOI test a second time is not required.

FLIGHT/GROUND INSTRUCTOR FAA WRITTEN EXAM ($14.95)

The FAA's written test consists of 100 questions out of the 859 questions in our book. To be used for the Certificated Flight Instructor (CFI) written test and those who aspire to the Advanced Ground Instructor (AGI) rating for airplanes. Note that this book also covers what is known as the Basic Ground Instructor (BGI) rating. However, the BGI is **not** useful because it does not give the holder full authority to sign off private pilots to take their written test. In other words, this book should be used for the AGI rating.

AIRLINE TRANSPORT PILOT FAA WRITTEN EXAM ($23.95)

The FAA's written test consists of 80 questions each for the ATP Part 121, ATP Part 135, and the flight dispatcher certificate. This first edition contains a complete answer explanation to each of the 1,304 airplane ATP questions (111 helicopter questions are excluded). This difficult FAA written test is now made simple by Gleim. As with Gleim's other written test books, studying for the ATP will now be a learning and understanding experience rather than a memorization marathon -- at a lower cost and with higher test scores and less frustration!!

FAA PRACTICAL TEST PREP AND REFERENCE BOOKS

Our new Practical Test Prep books are designed to replace the FAA Practical Test Standards reprint booklets which are universally used by pilots preparing for the practical test. These new Practical Test Prep books will help prepare pilots for FAA practical tests as much as the Gleim written exam books prepare pilots for FAA written tests. Each task, objective, concept, requirement, etc., in the FAA's practical test standards is explained, analyzed, illustrated, and interpreted so pilots will be totally conversant with all aspects of their practical tests.

NOW AVAILABLE!

Private Pilot FAA Practical Test Prep	538 pages	($16.95)
Instrument Pilot FAA Practical Test Prep	514 pages	($17.95)
Commercial Pilot FAA Practical Test Prep	426 pages	($14.95)
Flight Instructor FAA Practical Test Prep	626 pages	($17.95)

PRIVATE PILOT HANDBOOK ($12.95)

A complete private pilot ground school text in outline format with many diagrams for ease in understanding. A complete, detailed index makes it more useful and saves time. It contains a special section on biennial flight reviews.

RECREATIONAL PILOT FLIGHT MANEUVERS ($11.95)

Contains, in outline format, pertinent information necessary to be a skilled recreational pilot. An excellent reference book to begin your flight training endeavors.

MAIL TO: **GLEIM PUBLICATIONS, Inc.**
P.O. Box 12848
University Station
Gainesville, FL 32604
OR CALL: **(800) 87-GLEIM, (904) 375-0772, FAX (904) 375-6940**

**THE BOOKS WITH
THE RED COVERS**

Our customer service staff is available to take your calls from 8:00 a.m. to 7:00 p.m.,
Monday through Friday, and 9:00 a.m. to 2:00 p.m., Saturday, Eastern Time.
Please have your VISA/MasterCard ready.

WRITTEN TEST BOOKS

Private/Recreational Pilot	Sixth (1992-1994) Edition	$12.95 ____
Instrument Pilot	Fourth (1992-1994) Edition	16.95 ____
Commercial Pilot	Fourth (1992-1994) Edition	14.95 ____
Fundamentals of Instructing	Fourth (1991-1993) Edition	9.95 ____
Flight/Ground Instructor	Fourth (1991-1993) Edition	14.95 ____
Airline Transport Pilot	First (1991-1993) Edition	23.95 ____

HANDBOOKS AND PRACTICAL TEST PREP BOOKS

Recreational Pilot Flight Maneuvers	(First Edition)	11.95 ____
Private Pilot Handbook	(Fourth Edition)	12.95 ____
Private Pilot FAA Practical Test Prep	(First Edition)	16.95 ____
Instrument Pilot FAA Practical Test Prep	(First Edition)	17.95 ____
Commercial Pilot FAA Practical Test Prep	(First Edition)	14.95 ____
Flight Instructor FAA Practical Test Prep	(First Edition)	17.95 ____

Shipping ____3.00

Add applicable sales tax for shipments within the State of Florida
Please call or write for additional charges for out-of-the-U.S. shipments
Printed 04/93. Prices subject to change without notice. We ship latest editions.

Sales Tax ____

TOTAL $____

---

1. *We process and ship orders within 1 day of receipt of your order. We generally ship via UPS for the Eastern U.S. and U.S. mail for the Western U.S.*

2. *Please PHOTOCOPY this order form for friends and others.*

3. *No CODs. All orders from individuals must be prepaid and are protected by our unequivocal refund policy.*

   Library and company orders may be on account. Shipping and handling charges will be added to the invoice, and to prepaid telephone orders.

Name _____
(please print)
Shipping Address _____
(street address required for UPS)

_____

City _____ State ____ Zip _____

☐ MasterCard/VISA   ☐ Check/Money Order   Telephone (___) _____

MasterCard/VISA No.

Expiration Date *(month/year)* ___ / ___

__ __ __ __ - __ __ __ __ - __ __ __ __ - __ __ __ __

Signature _____

009D

GLEIM PUBLICATIONS GUARANTEES
THE IMMEDIATE REFUND OF ALL RESALABLE TEXTS RETURNED IN 30 DAYS
SHIPPING AND HANDLING CHARGES ARE NONREFUNDABLE

P.S. We presume your local FBO or bookstore does not stock the books you are ordering from us directly. If you provide us with a name and address, we will invite them to do so.

BOOKS AVAILABLE FROM GLEIM PUBLICATIONS, Inc.
WRITTEN EXAM BOOKS

Before pilots take their FAA written tests, they want to understand the answer to every FAA written test question. Gleim's written test books are widely used because they help pilots learn and understand exactly what they need to know to do well on their FAA written test.

Gleim's books contain all of the FAA's airplane questions (nonairplane questions are excluded). We have unscrambled the questions appearing in the FAA written test books and organized them into logical topics. Answer explanations are provided next to each question. Each of our chapters opens with a brief, user-friendly outline of exactly what you need to know to pass the written test. Information not directly tested is omitted to expedite your passing the written test. This additional information can be found in our flight maneuver and reference books and practical test prep books described below.

PRIVATE PILOT AND RECREATIONAL PILOT FAA WRITTEN EXAM ($12.95)

The FAA's written test for either certificate consists of 60 questions out of the 710 questions in our book.

INSTRUMENT PILOT FAA WRITTEN EXAM ($16.95)

The FAA's written test consists of 60 questions out of the 898 questions in our book. Also, those people who wish to become an instrument-rated flight instructor (CFII) or an instrument ground instructor (IGI) must take the FAA's written test of 50 questions from this book.

COMMERCIAL PILOT FAA WRITTEN EXAM ($14.95)

The FAA's written test will consist of 100 questions out of the 564 questions in our book.

FUNDAMENTALS OF INSTRUCTING FAA WRITTEN EXAM ($9.95)

The FAA's written test consists of 50 questions out of the 180 questions in our book. This is required of any person to become a flight instructor or ground instructor. The test only needs to be taken once. For example, if someone is already a flight instructor and wants to become a ground instructor, taking the FOI test a second time is not required.

FLIGHT/GROUND INSTRUCTOR FAA WRITTEN EXAM ($14.95)

The FAA's written test consists of 100 questions out of the 859 questions in our book. To be used for the Certificated Flight Instructor (CFI) written test and those who aspire to the Advanced Ground Instructor (AGI) rating for airplanes. Note that this book also covers what is known as the Basic Ground Instructor (BGI) rating. However, the BGI is not useful because it does not give the holder full authority to sign off private pilots to take their written test. In other words, this book should be used for the AGI rating.

AIRLINE TRANSPORT PILOT FAA WRITTEN EXAM ($23.95)

The FAA's written test consists of 80 questions each for the ATP Part 121, ATP Part 135, and the flight dispatcher certificate. This first edition contains a complete answer explanation to each of the 1,304 airplane ATP questions (111 helicopter questions are excluded). This difficult FAA written test is now made simple by Gleim. As with Gleim's other written test books, studying for the ATP will now be a learning and understanding experience rather than a memorization marathon -- at a lower cost and with higher test scores and less frustration!!

FAA PRACTICAL TEST PREP AND REFERENCE BOOKS

Our new Practical Test Prep books are designed to replace the FAA Practical Test Standards reprint booklets which are universally used by pilots preparing for the practical test. These new Practical Test Prep books will help prepare pilots for FAA practical tests as much as the Gleim written exam books prepare pilots for FAA written tests. Each task, objective, concept, requirement, etc., in the FAA's practical test standards is explained, analyzed, illustrated, and interpreted so pilots will be totally conversant with all aspects of their practical tests.

NOW AVAILABLE!	Private Pilot FAA Practical Test Prep	538 pages	($16.95)
	Instrument Pilot FAA Practical Test Prep	514 pages	($17.95)
	Commercial Pilot FAA Practical Test Prep	426 pages	($14.95)
	Flight Instructor FAA Practical Test Prep	626 pages	($17.95)

PRIVATE PILOT HANDBOOK ($12.95)

A complete private pilot ground school text in outline format with many diagrams for ease in understanding. A complete, detailed index makes it more useful and saves time. It contains a special section on biennial flight reviews.

RECREATIONAL PILOT FLIGHT MANEUVERS ($11.95)

Contains, in outline format, pertinent information necessary to be a skilled recreational pilot. An excellent reference book to begin your flight training endeavors.

WRITTEN TEST BOOKS

Private/Recreational Pilot	Sixth (1992-1994) Edition	$12.95 ____
Instrument Pilot	Fourth (1992-1994) Edition	16.95 ____
Commercial Pilot	Fourth (1992-1994) Edition	14.95 ____
Fundamentals of Instructing	Fourth (1991-1993) Edition	9.95 ____
Flight/Ground Instructor	Fourth (1991-1993) Edition	14.95 ____
Airline Transport Pilot	First (1991-1993) Edition	23.95 ____

HANDBOOKS AND PRACTICAL TEST PREP BOOKS

Recreational Pilot Flight Maneuvers	(First Edition)	11.95 ____
Private Pilot Handbook	(Fourth Edition)	12.95 ____
Private Pilot FAA Practical Test Prep	(First Edition)	16.95 ____
Instrument Pilot FAA Practical Test Prep	(First Edition)	17.95 ____
Commercial Pilot FAA Practical Test Prep	(First Edition)	14.95 ____
Flight Instructor FAA Practical Test Prep	(First Edition)	17.95 ____

Shipping ____ 3.00

Add applicable sales tax for shipments within the State of Florida

Sales Tax ____

Please call or write for additional charges for out-of-the-U.S. shipments

Printed 04/93. Prices subject to change without notice. We ship latest editions.

TOTAL $____

1. We process and ship orders within 1 day of receipt of your order. We generally ship via UPS for the Eastern U.S. and U.S. mail for the Western U.S.

2. Please PHOTOCOPY this order form for friends and others.

3. No CODs. All orders from individuals must be prepaid and are protected by our unequivocal refund policy.

Library and company orders may be on account. Shipping and handling charges will be added to the invoice, and to prepaid telephone orders.

Name _____
(please print)

Shipping Address _____
(street address required for UPS)

_____

City _____ State ____ Zip _____

☐ MasterCard/VISA ☐ Check/Money Order Telephone (___) ____

MasterCard/VISA No. Expiration Date *(month/year)* ___/___

__ __ __ __ - __ __ __ __ - __ __ __ __ - __ __ __ __

Signature _____

009D

P.S. We presume your local FBO or bookstore does not stock the books you are ordering from us directly. If you provide us with a name and address, we will invite them to do so.

INDEX

A/FD 126
Abbreviated Briefing, Weather 91
Abbreviations 24
Absolute Altitude 144
Address Change 31
ADF
　Equipment 283
　Orientation 286
Administrator, Definition 24
Adverse Weather Conditions 295
Aerobatic Flight 52
Aeromedical Factors 171, 462
AI 148, 303
Ailerons 137
Air Density 12
Air Traffic Control, Definition 4
Aircraft
　Accidents 56
　Control, Instruments 304
　For Flight Test 28
　Inspection Programs, Changes to 54
　Lights 50
　Records Preservation 56
　Speed 43
Airframe Logbook 87
AIRMETs 90, 93, 95
Airplane
　Definition 24
　Parking 212
　Requirements, Practical Test 72
　Systems 132, 462
Airport
　Advisory Areas 124
　Data, Sectional Charts 116
　Definition 24
　In Vicinity of 44
　Lighting 387
　Marking and Lighting 239, 464
　Operations 215
　Radar Service Area 45, 122
　Traffic Areas 124
Airport/Facility Directory 126
Airspace 120
　Classifications 125
　Information, Sectional Charts 117
Airspeed 11
　Indicator 145, 303
　Normal 13
　Traffic Pattern 237
　Types of 145
Airworthiness
　Certificate 83, 86
　Civil Aircraft 39
Alcohol 40, 175
　And Drugs 40
　Offenses 26
　Tests 26
Alert Areas 124
Alphabet, Phonetic 225

ALS 241
ALT 143, 303
Alternate Air Source, Static Pressure ... 142
Alternate Airport 120, 295
Altimeter 143, 303
　Settings 43
Altitude
　Minimum Safe 43
　Reporting Equipment Use 52
　Types of 144
Analytical Skills 62
Angle of
　Attack 330
　Incidence 330
Annual Inspection 87
Anti-Ice Systems 168
Anti-Servo Tabs 139
Anticollision Light 387
Application Form, Practical Test 73
Application of Knowledge 62
Approach and Landing 415
　Checklist 237
　Emergency 399, 469
Approach Control 221
Approach Light Systems 247
Area Forecasts 89, 93, 493
ARROW 179
ARSAs 45, 122
ASI 145, 303
ATAs 124
ATC
　Clearances, Compliance 44
　Definition 4
　Light Signals 44, 216, 464
　Transponder
　　Tests 53
　　Use 52
Attitude Indicator 148, 303
Authority, Pilot in Command 39
Authorized Flight Examiners, Flight Test .. 29
Aviation Safety Reporting Program 40
Avionics 170
AWW 93

Balancing Tabs 139
Bank Instruments 302
Basic Empty Weight 10
Beacons, Rotating 246
Best Angle of Climb Airspeed 11
Best Rate of Climb Airspeed 11
Brake 154
　Checks 201
Budget, Private Pilot 8

Calibrated Airspeed 145
Carbon Monoxide 174

Carburetor
    Air Temperature Gauge 157, 411
    Heat 410
    Icing 409
    System 155
Careless Operation 40
CAS 145
Caution Range, ASI 146
Center of Gravity 332
    Moment Envelope 17
        Chart 102
Center Weather Advisory 93, 95
Centrifugal Force 151, 357
Centripetal Force 151
Certificate, Private Pilot 2
    Requirements 25
Certificates
    And Documents, Pilot 462
    Issued under Part 61 26
CG 332
    Position 99
Change of
    Address 31
    Name 27
Cheating, Written Test 28
Checklist 19
    Preflight 179
    Pretakeoff 205
Checkpoints, En Route 118
Chock, Wheel 183
CHT Gauge 157
Circuit Breakers 166
Civil Aircraft
    Airworthiness 39
    Certifications Required 49
Clearance 200
    ATC Compliance 44
    Delivery 222
Climbs 251
Closed Runway 242
Cockpit
    Familiarity 15
    Management 185, 463
Cognitive Ability 61
Collision Avoidance 230
Common Traffic Advisory Frequency 200
Communication
    Cockpit 186
    Facilities 120
Composite Moisture Stability Chart 516
Constant
    Altitude Turns 356, 467
    Pressure Analysis Chart 519
    Pressure Chart 94
Continental Control Area 120
Control
    Areas 121
    Lock 183
    Yoke 136
    Zones 122
Controlled
    Airports 219

Airspace 120
    Definition 24
Controls, Flight 182
Convective
    Outlook 93
    SIGMETs 93, 95
Cooling System, Airplane 157
Coordination, Crew 188
Cost, Private Pilot 8
Crew Coordination 188
Crewmember Interference 39
Crewmembers at Stations 42
Critically Slow Airspeed 354
Cross Radials and Bearings 291
Cross-Checking, Instruments 304
Cross-Country
    Flight Planning 462
    Flight Requirements, Student Pilots 32
    Flying 275, 465
Crosswind
    Approach and Landing 416, 470
    Component 110
    Limitation, Landing 418
    Performance 110
    Takeoffs and Climbs 252, 464
Cruise Performance 108
CTAF 200
Currency Requirements 84
CWA 93
Cylinder Head Temperature Gauge 157

Dead Reckoning 276, 465
DECIDE 398
Definitions 24
Deice Systems 168
Density Altitude 144
    Chart 103
Departure Control 221
Desired Ground Track 367
Destroyed Pilot Certificate 27
Dihedral 358
Displaced Threshold 242
Distance, Speed, and Time 120
Diversion 294, 465
Do and Read Checklist 19, 185
Door Opening in Flight 414
Dropping Objects 40
Drugs 175
    Drugs, Alcohol 40
    Offenses 26
Duration
    Flight Instructor Certificates 26
    Pilot Certificates 26

EGT Gauge 157
Electrical System
    Airplane 164
    Malfunction 413
Electronic Checklist 20
Elevators 136
ELTs 50, 87

Emergency 222
   Air Traffic Rules 47
   Approach and Landing 399, 469
   Locator Transmitter 50, 87
   Operations 469
   Procedures, Takeoff 209
En Route Checkpoints 118
Engine 155
   Failure 400
   Logbook 87
   Rough 409
   Shutdown 211
   Starting 189
Environmental System 166
Equipment
   List 87
      Airplane 83
   Malfunctions 408, 469
   Requirements, Practical Test 72
Evaluation 62
Exhaust
   Gas Temperature Gauge 157
   System 183
Experience, Pilot in Command 84
External Power Receptacle 189

FA 493
FAA
   Inspectors, Flight Test 29
   Practical Test 60, 70
   Written Test 60
FAA-Approved Flight Manual 9
Failure
   Engine 400
   Flight Test 79
      Retesting after 29
Falsification of Logbooks 30
FARs
   Part 61 25
      Training Programs 63
   Part 67 37
   Part 91 39
   Part 141 Training Programs 63
FAs 89, 93
FCC Station License 83
Federal Communication Commission Station License 83
Fire, Engine 412
Fixed
   Distance Markings, Runway 241
   Gear, Landing 153
   Pitch Propeller 159
   Slots 141
Flap
   Extension Airspeed 11
   Malfunction 413
   Operating Range, ASI 146
Flashlights 383
Flight
   Controls 182
   Crewmembers at Stations 42
   Examiners, Flight Test 29
   Experience, Private Pilot 6

Flight *(cont.)*
   Instruction 64
      Required 6
   Flight Portion, Practical Test 72
   Instructor Endorsement, Practical Test .. 74
   Limitations, Proximity of Space Flight Operations . 47
   Log 127, 129, 280
   Maneuver Analysis Sheets 65
   Manual Requirements 39
   Plan 130
   Planning 462
   Restrictions
      In Proximity of the President 47
      Temporary 46
   Review 30, 84
   Service Stations 90
   Syllabus, Part 61 473
   Test 69
      Areas 52
      Failure 79
      Prerequisites 28
      Private 7
      Procedures 28
   Time
      Computations 119
      Definition 24
   Training 59
      FAR Part 141 471
Float-Type Carburetor 155
FMAS 65
Form 8080-2 77
Form 8710-1 73
Format, PTS Tasks 71
Forward Slips, Landing 436, 470
Fowler Flap 140
Freezing Level Charts 94
Frost Removal 184
FSSs 90
FTs 93, 496
Fuel/Air Mixture 155
Fuel
   Contamination Safeguards 181
   Primers, Airplane 163
   Pump System, Airplane 162
   Quantity, Grade, Type 181
   Requirement Computations 119
   Requirements, VFR 47
   Starvation 412
   System
      Airplane 160
      Ice Protection 169
Full Stalls
   Power-Off 334, 467
   Power-On 340, 467
Fuses 166

Gear Malfunction 413
Generators 166
Geometric Pitch, Propeller 159
Glide Performance 109
Go/No-Go Decision 96
Go-Around, Landing 441, 470
Grade, Fuel 163

Ground
    Control 220
    Instruction 63
    Objects Maneuvering 363
    Operations 463
    Track Desired 367
    Training 59
        FAR Part 141 471
Gusting Winds, Landing 417
Gyroscopic Instruments 147

Hand Propping 190
Hand Signals, Ramp Personnel 200
Heading
    Computations 119
    Indicator 149, 303
HI 149, 303
Holding Position Markings 198, 241, 243
How Pilots Learn 60
Hurricane Advisory 93
Hydraulic System, Airplane 164
Hyperventilation 172
Hypoxia 172

I'm Safe Checklist 97, 171
IAS 145
Ice
    Carburetor 409
    Induction 409
    Removal 184
Ignition System, Airplane 158
Imminent Stalls 346, 467
Indicated Airspeed 145
Indicated Altitude 144
Induced Drag 353
Induction Icing 409
Inflight Advisories 93, 498
Inflight Briefing, Weather 92
Initial Climb 251
Inoperative Instruments and Equipment 51
Inspections 53
    Programs, Changes to 54
    Maintenance 53
Instruction Flight, Required 6
Instruments
    And Equipment
        Inoperative 51
        Requirements 49
    Definition 24
    Flight 301
    Interpretation 304
    Panel, Tomahawk 15
    Visual Scan 304
Interference with Crewmembers, Prohibition 39

Keel Effect 358
Kinesthesia 333
Knowledge and Skill Tasks, Practical Test 70
Knowledge Only Tasks, Practical Test 70

L/D MAX 353
Landings 415
    Checklist 237
    Emergency 399
    Landing Gear System 153
    Performance 111
    Weight 10
Landmarks, Visual Reference 277
Lateral Stability 358
Leading Edge Devices 141
Leaks, Fuel, Oil, Hydraulic 182
Learn, How Pilots 60
Learning Model 60
Learning Your Airplane 10
Levels of Cognitive Ability 61
Liftoff, Takeoff 251
Light Gun Signals 199
Light Signals, ATC 44, 217
Lights, Aircraft 50
Limitations
    Aircraft 462
    Pilot Certificates 27
    Pilots 83
LLWAS 96
Loading Graph 18
    CG 101
Logbooks 30
    Endorsement, Practical Test 74
    Pilot 29, 83, 85
Long-Term Memory 60
Lost
    Pilot Certificate 27
    Procedures 297, 465
Low-Level
    Prog Charts 512
    Significant Weather Prognostic 94
    Wind Shear Alert System 96

Magnetic Bearing 287
Magnetos, Airplane Engine 158
Main Landing Gear Assembly 153
Maintenance
    Operation after 53
    Pilot Performed 88
    Records 54
    Required 53, 83, 87
Malfunction
    Equipment 413, 469
    Flap 413
    Gear 413
Maneuvering
    Altitude, Safe 266
    At Slow Airspeed 351
    Ground Objects 363
    Speed 11
Master Switch, Electrical 165
Maximum
    Flaps Extended Speed 146
    Glide Speed 11
    Landing Weight 10
    Performance Takeoff and Climb 262

Maximum *(cont.)*
Ramp Weight 10
Rate of Climb Chart 107
Structural Cruising Speed 146
Takeoff Weight 10
Zero Fuel Weight 10
Medical
Certificate 83, 84
Definition 24
Duration 27
Special Issuance 38
Third Class 3
Deficiencies 30
Standards 37
MEL 14
Middle Ear Problems 173
Military
Operations Areas 124
Training Routes 124
Minimum
Drag 353
Equipment List 14
Safe Altitudes 43
Mixture Control 156
MOAs 124
Morse Code 225
Motion Sickness 174
MTRs 124
MULTICOM 218

Name Change 27
Narcotic Drugs 40
National Weather Service 89
Navigation Log 127
Navigational Lighting 387
NDB
Bearing Interception and Tracking 291
Stations 283
Tracking Inbound/Outbound 290
Never Exceed Speed 11, 146
Night
Experience 84
Flight Operations 381, 468
Vision 384
Normal
Approach and Landing 416, 470
Landing Differences 111
Operating Range, ASI 146
Takeoffs and Climbs 252, 464
NOS Charts 115
Nose Gear 154
NOTAMs 95, 126
Notice of Disapproval of Application 79
Notices to Airmen 95
NTSB Part 830 56
Numbers, Runway 240

OAT Gauge 157, 411
Obstructions 120
Lighting 247
Sectional Charts 117

Octane, Fuel 163
Oil
Pressure, Loss of 412
Quantity, Grade, Type 182
System 167
Operating
After Maintenance 53
Control Towers 44
In the Vicinity of an Airport 44
Limitations 87, 179
Near Other Aircraft 42
Operator, Definition 24
Optimizing Training 59
Oral Portion, Practical Test 72
Other Craft, Operating Near 42
Outlook Briefing, Weather 92
Outside Air Temperature Gauge 157, 411
Overbanking Tendency 358
Overdue Aircraft 56
Oxygen, Supplemental 50

PAPI 249
Parachutes and Parachuting 52
Parasite Drag 352
Parking, Airplane 212
Passing Grades, Written Test 27
Payload 10
PCA 121
Performance
Aircraft 98, 462
Data 13, 14
Phonetic Alphabet 225
PIC, Definition 24
Pilot
Certificate 83, 84
Duration 26
Temporary 78
Logbook 29, 83, 85
In Command 39
Definition 24
Experience 84
Weather Report 95, 498
Pilot's Operating Handbook 9, 72, 179
Pilotage 276, 465
PIREPs 95, 498
Pitch Instruments 302
Pitot-Static Ice Protection System . . . 142, 169
Placard Requirements 39
Plain Flap 140
POH 9, 72, 179
Positive Control Area 121
Postflight
Inspection 211
Procedures 211, 463
Power
Instruments 302
Settings, Normal 13
Power-Off
Full Stalls 334, 467
Stalling Speed 146
Power-On Full Stalls 340, 467

Practical Test 60, 69
   Private 7
   Standards 70, 459
Precision
   Gyroscopic 148
   Instrument Approach Runway Marking 241
Preflight 178, 463
   Action 42
   Checklist 129
   Preparation 82
Prelanding Cockpit Checklist 237
Prerequisites, Written Test 27
Preservation of Aircraft Wreckage 56
Pressure Altitude 144
Pressurization Loss 414
Pretakeoff Check 205, 463
Preventive Maintenance 53, 88
Primary Flight Controls 136
Private Pilot
   Certificate 2
   Certification Course, FAR Part 141 471
Privileges, Pilots 83
Problem Solving 62
Prohibited Areas 46, 123
Propeller 159
   Slip 159
Propping, Hand 190
PTSs 70, 459
Pulsating Visual Approach Slope Indicator 249

Qualification for Pilot Certificates 26

Radar
   Services 326, 466
   Summary Chart 94, 510
   Weather Report 92, 502
Radio
   Aids 326, 466
      Sectional Charts 117
   Communications 216, 464
   Failure Procedures 223
   Navigation 282, 465
   Aids 120
Ramp Weight 10
Range Performance 108
RAREP 92, 502
Rate of Climb Performance 107
Rating
   Definition 24
   Requirements 25
Read and Do Checklist 19, 185
Rebuilt Engine Maintenance Records 54
Recall Knowledge 61
Recent Flight Experience 30
Reckless Operation 40
Rectangular Course 364, 468
Registration Certificates 83, 86
Reports, NTSB 58
Required Flight Instruction 6
Requirements, Private Pilot 3
Responsibility, Pilot in Command 39

Restricted Areas 46, 123
Retesting after Failure 29
Retractable Gear, Landing 153
Right-of-Way Rules 43
Rigidity in Space, Gyroscopic 147
Rotating Beacons 246, 388
Rotation, Airplane 251
Rough Engine 409
Rudder 136
Runway
   Lights 245
   Marking and Lighting 239, 464
   Numbers 240

S-Turns across a Road 371, 468
SA 92, 487
Safe
   Altitudes 43
   Maneuvering Altitude 266
Safety Belts 42, 187
Sample Loading Problem 17
Satellite Weather Pictures 92, 493
Scanning for Other Traffic 229
Scuba Diving 175
Second in Command Qualifications 30
Secondary Stalls 339
Sectional Charts 115
Segmented Circles, Landing 244
Servo Tabs 139
Severe Weather
   Forecast Alerts 93
   Outlook Chart 94, 518
Short Takeoff and Landing Runway 242
Short-Field
   Approach and Landing 446, 470
   Takeoff and Climb 261, 464
Short-Term Memory 60
Shoulder Harnesses 187
SIGMETs 90, 93, 95
Sinus Problems 173
Situational Awareness, Cockpit 186
Slat 141
Slip, Propeller 159
Slotted Flap 140
Slow
   Airspeed Maneuvering 351
   Flight 329, 467
Soft-Field
   Approach and Landing 452, 470
   Takeoff and Climb 268, 465
Solo
   Flights, Private Pilots, FAR Part 141 472
   Requirements, Student Pilots 31
Space Flight Operations, Flight Limitations 47
Spatial Disorientation 173
Special
   Flight Forecast 93
   Use Airspace 123
   VFR Weather Minimums 49
Speed, Aircraft 43
Speed, Distance, and Time 120
Split Flap 140

Spoilers 141
Stability Charts 94
Stage and Final Test, Private Training,
 FAR Part 141 472
Stalls 330
   Speed 11, 331
   Warning Devices 333
Standard
   Briefing, Weather 90
   Empty Weight 10
Starting Engine 189, 463
Static Pressure System 142
Station
   License, FCC 85
   Passage 292
Steep Turns 467
STOL Runway 242
Stopway Areas 242
Straight, Constant Airspeed
   Climbs, Instrument 309, 466
   Descents, Instrument 313, 466
Straight-and-Level Flight, Instrument 306, 466
Structural Damage 183
Student Pilot
   Application 31
   Eligibility Requirements 31
   General Limitations 32
Supplemental Oxygen 50
Surface
   Analysis Chart 94, 504
   Aviation Weather Reports 92, 487
Sweepback 358
Synthesis 62
Systems, Airplane 132, 462

T&SI 150
Tailwheel Airplane, Taxi 197
Tailwheel-Type Airplanes 154
Takeoff 251
   Data 13, 105
   Performance 112
   Performance Chart 105
   Roll 251
   Weight 10
TAS 145
Task Format 71
Tasks, Practical Test 70
Taxiing 195, 463
   In Wind 203
Taxiway
   Lights 246
   Marking 198, 243
TC 152, 303
TCAs 33, 45, 122
Telling and Doing Technique 64
Temporary
   Flight Restrictions 46
   Pilot Certificates 26, 78
Terminal Control Areas 33, 45, 122
   Operations 32
Terminal Forecasts 93, 496

Third-Class Medical Certificate 3, 37
Threshold Marking 241
Tie Down 183
   Knots 213
Time, Distance, and Speed 120
Tomahawk Instrument Panel 15
Topographical Information, Sectional Charts 118
Touchdown Zone Marker 241
Tower Control 220
Tracking, Radials, Bearings 288
Traffic
   Pattern 235
      Altitude 237
      Definition 24
      Operations 215, 228, 464
   Surveillance 229
Transcribed Weather Broadcasts 93
Transfer of Maintenance Records 54
Transition Area 122
Transponder Tests 53
Trim
   Devices 138
   Flight Control 136
   Inoperative 414
   Tab 139
True
   Airspeed 145
   Altitude 144
Turbulence, Stalls 332
Turn
   And Slip Indicator 150
   Coordinator 152, 303
Turns
   Around a Point 376, 468
   To Headings, Instrument 317, 466
TWEB 93

Uncontrolled Airports 217
Understanding to Interpret 62
UNICOM 218
Unusual Flight Attitudes, Instrument 321, 466
Useful Load 10

V-Speeds 11
Vacuum System 170
VASI 247
Venting, Fuel 182
Vertical Speed Indicator 144, 303
Vertigo 173
VFR
   Cruising Altitudes 49, 119
   Flight Plan 47, 130
   Terminal Area Charts 115
   Weather Minimums 48
Vicinity of an Airport, Operating 44
Visual
   Approach Slope Indicator 247
   Inspection 178, 463
   Scan, Instruments 304

VOR
    Equipment   283
    Indications in Flight   285
    Tracking Figure   289
Vortices   232
VSI 144, 303
V$_X$ 265
V$_Y$ 255

WA   93
Wake Turbulence   232
Warning Areas   124
Weather
    Briefings   90
    Charts   94
    Depiction Chart 94, 508
    Information 89, 462
    Minimums for Special VFR   49
    Minimums, VFR   48
    Reports and Forecasts   487
Weight
    And Balance 16, 99
        Data 83, 87
        Record   16
    Change Formula   102
    Shift Formula   102
What to Take, Practical Test   73
Wind
    Correction Factors   364
    Drift
        And Ground Track   236
        Correction 255, 373
    Shear   231
        Reports   96
    Side of Flight Computer   120
    Socks   244
    Tees   244
    Tetrahedrons   244
    Winds and Temperatures Aloft Forecast 93, 514
Wing Flaps   139
    Setting, Takeoff   254
Working to be a Private Pilot   59
Written Test   60
    Passing Grades   27
    Prerequisites   27
    Private Pilot   4
WS   93
WST   93

Zero Fuel Weight   10

Please forward your suggestions, corrections, and comments to **Irvin N. Gleim • c/o Gleim Publications, Inc. • P.O. Box 12848 • University Station • Gainesville, Florida • 32604** for inclusion in the next edition of *Private Pilot FAA Practical Test Prep*. Please include your name and address so we can properly thank you for your interest.

1. _____

2. _____

3. _____

4. _____

5. _____

6. _____

7. _____

8. _____

9. _____

10. _____

11. _____

12. _____

13. _____

14. _____

15. _____

16. _____

17. _____

Name: _____

Address: _____

City/State/Zip: _____

Telephone: _____